The
Poetical Works
of
Oliver Wendell
Holmes

The

Poetical Works

of

Oliver Wendell

Holmes

Cambridge Edition

Revised and with a New Introduction
by Eleanor M. Tilton

Houghton Mifflin Company Boston

1975

First Printing   c

Library of Congress Cataloging in Publication Data

Holmes, Oliver Wendell, 1809–1894.
    The poetical works of Oliver Wendell Holmes.

    Includes bibliographical references and indexes.
    I. Tilton, Eleanor Marguerite, 1913–   ed.
II. Title.
PS1955.A1   1975   811'.3   74-30148
ISBN 0-395-18497-5

Printed in the United States of America

EDITOR'S NOTE

DR. OLIVER WENDELL HOLMES chose to collect scarcely two thirds of his poems. To this new edition of his poetry one hundred and forty-four poems have been added to those gathered in editions of 1891 and 1895. The Cambridge edition of 1895 was edited by Horace E. Scudder and Francis Garrison of the editorial staff of Houghton Mifflin Company. Based upon the Riverside Edition of Holmes's *Writings* (XI–XIII) of 1891, the text had had the benefit of Holmes's attention, and the headnotes not in square brackets are of his composition. To the Cambridge edition, seventeen poems not in the Riverside edition were added. The editors supplied a few notes and a chronology as well as additions (bracketed) to the headnotes.

A careful proofreader, well-known at 2 Park Street for his insistence on seeing revised proof, Holmes suffered intensely if any error escaped his eye, but he was eighty-two when the Riverside edition was published and had to admit: "the buckets of the Danaids are nothing to my memory in the way of leakage." There are a few errors of date and fact, and in this new edition, these have been corrected. In only one instance has the present editor taken the liberty of making a change that has no authority in either a manuscript or an earlier printing. In the poem "Rip Van Winkle, *M. D.*," written for Massachusetts Medical Society, the hero's name is twice followed by the initials "M. M. S. S., M. D." The first four initials make no sense even on the assumption of an in-joke. I believe Holmes intended to have his hero a member of the Massachusetts Medical Society and have therefore changed the initials to "M.M.M.S."

To this new edition have been added virtually all the extant poems Holmes chose not to collect and refused to add to the Riverside edition in spite of the entreaties of Scudder, a conscientious editor who strove with all his living authors to achieve completeness and accuracy. To the central text are added uncollected poems written between 1838 and 1894. These poems are printed in chronological order; ten poems for which no date has been determined or conjectured appear alphabetically at the end. Omitted are two-line verses, fragments, false starts, the mock poems parodying the work of tyros, and discarded stanzas (although a few of the last are included in the notes). One poem written in 1855 but broken up into separate poems when collected by Holmes is here treated as Scudder treated "Astræa." To Appendix II, we add the uncollected portions of "The Heart's Own Secret."

Making a small concession of respect to Holmes's memory, we here print all the hitherto uncollected early poems as additions to *Verses from the Oldest Portfolio*. And we let stand Holmes's deprecatory headnote as covering the case of these poems written between 1824–1833. The order here is also chronological except that "An Enigma I" and "Enigma II" are brought together because the second is the answer to the first. Brought together also are "Scenes from an Unpublished Play."

The new texts are drawn from manuscripts where these are available. Texts printed from Holmes's manuscripts are given as he wrote them. The punctuation of some text may be erratic; Holmes tended to put in his dramatic pointing as he wrote, but to leave out punctuation required by rule. Where there is no manuscript, the best printed text is used. In texts drawn from newspapers and magazines, manifest typographical errors are corrected as Holmes would wish them to be. One text presented problems. "An Unpublished Poem" (1838?) was first printed after Holmes's death; the full text is in a pamphlet in the same setting of type used for the printing of a cut version of the poem appearing in the *Boston Medical and Surgical Journal*. There is also a manuscript, not in Holmes's hand, differing from the printed version. Manifest errors in the manuscript suggest that the scribe was unfamiliar with medicine, but perhaps not unfamiliar with Holmes's handwriting. The punctuation in both texts is more confusing than helpful; there is no consistency in the accidentals of either. The text here is based on a collation of the manuscript and the printed texts, the editor tampering only with accidentals.

To the Cambridge edition of 1895, a few notes were added and these are retained except the last one which gives no information pertinent to the poems. In this new edition, additional notes have been supplied, for Holmes's many topical allusions tend to become obscure with time.

Finally, the chronology of 1895 has been replaced by an augmented and more nearly accurate chronology.

In the Acknowledgments following the new Introduction (replacing the original Biographical Sketch) are listed the sources for this new edition. The editor would like to single out here as a silent but invaluable partner the late Thomas Franklin Currier who once hoped to prepare a "complete" edition of the poems of Oliver Wendell Holmes.

E. M. T.

CONTENTS

CONTENTS

CONTENTS

CONTENTS

INTRODUCTION

LIKE FIREWORKS the day after or like the "banquet's dead bouquet" — with such similes Oliver Wendell Holmes describes the verses he provided his class-mates, his colleagues, his club, his university, and his city. From the day he was elected poet of the Class of '29 to the last year of his life, Holmes was in demand to celebrate an anniversary, welcome a celebrity, eulogize the dead, bid the traveler farewell, supply a hymn, reply to a toast, or "play Orpheus to the stones" of a monument. He had reason to complain that 'the mere touch of a warm adjective blisters my palm." His readiness of rhyme made him all too open to "men with argument and women with entreaty" when what was wanted was a poem.

With the popularity of *The Autocrat of the Breakfast-Table,* the requests in-creased until he became weary of his "corn-stalk fiddle" and spent his ingenuity devising ways to say "No." "You must call upon some other street musician," he crossly told a colleague. Among fellow-physicians he was "celebrated for ready wit, a good song, and a candid investigation," and the doctors claimed their share of songs. He begged for privacy, described the debilitating effects of composition upon the nervous system, and deployed his humor, rhetoric, and even rhyme to frame refusals, unless "struck full in the centre of volition." Out of the practice of refusal came "A Familiar Letter to Several Correspondents" of 1876, a con-fession disguised as admonition; the man bitten by "the rhyming tarantula" is beyond cure. In the same year, he gave the undergraduate editors of the *Harvard Advocate* "How the Old Horse Won the Bet" with its closing line: "A horse *can* trot, for all he's old." He was rather less confident than the line suggests.

He had long been exploring the puzzle of his own personality in essay and novel, playing off one alter ego against another, discovering how many there were, only one of them The Poet. Aware that his mind was "discursive, erratic, subject to electric attractions and repulsions," that to him life was "so vivid" that he was always "too eager to seize and exhaust its multitudinous impressions," he could in the persona of The Poet speak as if he supposed himself to be one. In another guise, that of The Master, he corrected himself: "I *have* some of the qualities that make a man a poet, and yet, I am not one."

In 1872, when he wrote these lines, he was inclined to retrospection. The younger Wendell Holmes was displaying an uncomfortably fierce concentration, even bringing his work to the dinner table, a spectacle that made the elder Holmes uneasy. At the same time the gambrel-roofed house in which he had been born was sold to the University. He had begun raking "cinders from the ashes" in 1869, and a succession of anniversaries in the 1870's would keep him at it. What he found was a life vivid to memory, but not laid out along any line of single-minded achievement.

On August 29, 1809, the Reverend Abiel Holmes, minister of the First Church of Cambridge, noted in his almanac the birth of the first boy in a household of daughters. The minister was a modified Calvinist, "liberal — for a Connecticut man," said a parishioner. Abiel Holmes had written a little poetry, published a history modestly called *Annals of America,* and contributed astronomical observations to the *Memoirs* of the American Academy of Arts and Sciences. He remained for a time undisturbed by the battle in the New England churches. In the struggle between the orthodox forces from his own college, Yale, and those of liberalism from Harvard, Abiel Holmes "maintained a . . . middle station" until a few months before his son's eighteenth birthday.

As a boy Wendell Holmes knew no unsettling crisis in a household slightly darkened by Calvinist teaching but brightened by a genial mother, a pair of lively sisters with Harvard beaux in attendance, a whimsical brother, ample space for play, and not very arduous schooling. There were disadvantages to being undersized, but he discovered that words and wit might be as effective in defense as fists. He had a rival with words, the overeducated daughter of Congressman Fuller. Margaret probably read more modern books than he, for the library in the gambrel-roofed house was deficient in light reading. It had a good supply of poetry, a little old-fashioned to be sure, but still poetry. He was entranced by the "sonorous resonance" of Pope's translation of Homer, and his ear caught the cadences of the heroic line of Dryden and Pope. He took to making up couplets in his head.

Abiel Holmes extracted admonitions from pear trees and bookworms for a son whose quickness of wit was not matched by industry, but he apparently did not consider a passion for fast horses and a precocious taste for cigars as signs of original sin. Holmes was taught that he was "conceived in sin, & born in inquity" but could say of his parents that in them "nature never allowed 'Grace' to lead them to inhuman conclusions." The strict observance of the sabbath was sometimes made more dreary by visiting ministers with the Yankee whine and dark allusions to damnation.

Holmes's first exposure to intense orthodoxy came during his year at Andover. In this "Dove's nest of Puritan faith," he encountered too many representatives of "rectilinear theology," a headmaster "bigoted, narrow-minded, and uncivilized," and a smiling teacher who turned out to be unjust and brutal. On his sixteenth birthday he appeared before the examiners of Harvard College, happy to exchange a "doctrinal boiler" for "a rational ice-chest."

When Holmes joined the Class of '29, he joined for life; only three classmates survived him, and of these the two that were able-bodied attended his funeral. Holmes had never agreed with the one, the abolitionist Samuel May, and had tried hard to convert the other, the Baptist Samuel Francis Smith, to a liberal religion. Such were loyalty and affection, however, that when politics or religion threatened to splinter the class, they chose a ground on which they could stand together, even to drink a toast during the Civil War to a southern classmate and "*his* constitution." Among the factions that divided the class as undergraduates, Holmes moved easily.

As a student, he maintained a respectable place on the rank lists, struck his teachers as "gifted" in languages, discovered the pleasure of chemistry, and acquired a reputation as a poet. In November 1828, the Reverend Andrews Norton solicited poems for a gift book *The Offering*. Here Holmes first appears in a book, bound in green silk as he boasted to his Andover friend Phinehas Barnes. He supplied his clubs with verses and at least one song.

In his senior year, the college commanded his muse for the Exhibition on April 28 and Commencement on August 26, 1829. The class elected him its poet. These commissions he executed to the satisfaction of the newspapers and the audiences. The class-day poem of his "hapless amour with too tall a maid" does not survive; the other two are here first collected. The Commencement program shows that Holmes had no enviable spot on the long program of orations and colloquia. The exercises were held in the First Church which was filled by nine o'clock in the morning; it was eight minutes of one before Holmes took the stage. Very small in stature and youthful in looks, he followed the tallest man in the class. He must have been even then an accomplished public performer, for annotated programs grade him as very good and "excellent," neither annotator otherwise lavish of praise. Emerson would later say of one of Holmes's occasional poems that he could not be sure how good it was, so skillfully had the poet delivered it. At not yet twenty Holmes could hold a hungry audience to attention; he was doing so still at seventy-four. During all the years he taught at the Harvard Medical School, he was assigned the one o'clock lecture hour because he could keep the hungry and the weary alert.

Equipped with a "fatal facility for rhyme," with "literary bantlings" in print, he had also a catholic curiosity. No subject of study was altogether repellent to him, although he was uncomfortable with mathematics and irritated by metaphysics. His classmate James Freeman Clarke reports Holmes as saying: "I'll tell you, James, what I think metaphysics is like. It is like a man splitting a log. When it is done, he has two more to split." Holmes was not among the young men excited by Coleridge's *Aids to Reflection*. For his future, he looked to law or medicine.

He had reason not to consider the ministry. In July 1827, the liberal parishioners of the First Church at Cambridge had addressed a memorial to their

minister. After two years of moves and countermoves, the struggle ended with
Abiel Holmes ousted from his pulpit two months before his son entered the
same church for his commencement day. In the opinion of the press and even
of the *ex parte* council that determined his removal, the minister was sacrificed
to both his liberal opponents and his orthodox supporters. Of what his son
thought at the time, there is no record. On his father's death in 1837, he had
occasion to speak. He saw the two parties as "pressing upon" his father "with
much care and policy for their own interests, and too little anxiety with regard
to him." Recollected indignation breaks into scorn of the "machinery of modern
Jesuitism" and "the Machiavellian contrivances" of deacons. In *Elsie Venner*
and *The Guardian Angel*, Holmes tells the story as he wished it had turned out.
Rankling more than the liberal party's behavior is that of the orthodox deacons
and the assistant these deacons hired for their minister after the split in the
church. The minister's son takes his revenge in the characters of Deacon Shearer
and the Reverend Bellamy Stoker.

Holmes tried first the law. How little the law attracted him is attested to by
the number of verses he contrived to write the moment he had encouragement.
A group of undergraduates founded a paper and invited Holmes to contribute.
By May of 1830 he was "writing poetry like a madman." He saw his poems in
print, not only in *The Collegian,* but in *The New-England Galaxy* and in *The
Amateur.* Anonymity did not conceal authorship, and he was asked to con-
tribute to two gift-books. To see his verses handsomely bound and accompanied
by an engraving was gratifying. He signed these poems with the distinctive
initials: O. W. H. Perhaps the editor of *The Token* knew that the "H." ap-
pended to three stanzas in the *Boston Daily Advertiser* of September 16, 1830
stood for Holmes. The poem was "Old Ironsides."

The poetic frenzy carried him through 1831 and inspired one of his best poems,
"The Last Leaf." Holmes said later that he invented the stanza pattern of the
poem to entrap an imitator. Whatever his motive, the melancholy cadence
effected by the short lines of the tail-rhyme suffuses the comic details of the
poem with a rueful tone. Pathos and comedy are held in delicate equilibrium.

The young writer had some reason for self-satisfaction but no illusions about
the "poet's lot," as he informed readers of *The New-England Magazine.* To it
he contributed two papers called "The Autocrat of the Breakfast-Table," trying
his hand at prose. One realization is sharp: "How much easier it is to be witty
on some old, hackneyed subjects, than to find out the ridiculous for one's self."
By 1832, Holmes was writing noticeably less. He had abandoned the law for
medicine and declared himself "in love with his starving delusion."

Fortunate in his teachers, Jacob Bigelow, John Collins Warren, and James
Jackson, Holmes gave the study of medicine concentration and devotion. He
became a skilled dissector. In the pharmacy of the Massachusetts General Hos-
pital, he used his love of chemistry. With Jackson, he went through the wards,

learning more of the cases than any of the other students. Other young men including Jackson's son had already gone to Paris to extend their study; Holmes resolved to follow them. Dr. Jackson wrote to his son: "Do not mind his apparent frivolity and you will soon find that he is intelligent and well-informed. *He has the true zeal.*"

Holmes sailed for Europe on March 29, 1833 and returned on December 15, 1835. In that interval he wrote no poetry, refused to write though asked, and referred rather grandly to "my own science." Philosophers, poets, and revolutionaries still frequented the Café Procope, but for the "medicals" from America the iniquities of Louis Phillipe mattered far less than the numerical method of Pierre Louis. Holmes sampled the theater and the Louvre, cultivated a passionate liking for painting, bought violets, books, and engravings, flirted with a grisette, but he went every morning to the wards of La Pitié. Before the regular sessions began, he would hear the admired Pierre Louis say to him: "Vous travaillez, monsieur, c'est bien ça." Affected by the "concentrated scientific atmosphere" of Paris, he wrote home earnestly of his new "passion for truth." From Louis he learned "not to take authority when I can have facts, not to guess when I can know." Elected to membership in the Société Médicale d'Observation and given access to Louis' wards, he learned to be "exact, methodical, and rigorous." Founded for work not for vanity, the society led by Louis made severe demands upon its members for attendance, papers, and self-criticism. Louis urged that young men engage in research before entering into practice, and he so advised the elder Jackson. In his memoir of his son, Dr. Jackson wrote sadly, regretting that he had not heeded Louis' advice, but in America "such a course would have been so singular, as in a measure to have separated him from other men."

The training itself made for separation, especially from admirers of Coleridge and Carlyle. On a Sunday evening in 1836 Holmes met an old acquaintance — Margaret Fuller. According to her, the conversation turned upon the question: "What view should the man of science take of his relation to eternal interests and his temporal pursuits?" The topic was surely hers; one cannot imagine a lapsed Calvinist fresh from a rigorous French medical training posing such a question. The diarist reports: "W. H. took the ground that there was no settling any-thing about God and the world, that if you went on zealously with any study, seeking truth alone, you would be led unconsciously to the proper ground." Complacently Miss Fuller concludes that she is Holmes's superior "in precision of thought and clearness of utterance." She is the more gratified because Holmes is her own age and one of those "who have really good minds." Behind Holmes's later satire of *The Dial* and its arrogant contributors lay the model of Pierre Louis' "modesty in the presence of nature." The principle "not to guess when you can know" underlay his lectures on the delusions of homeopathy, phrenology, hydropathy, and quack applications of mesmerism, all of which were resorted to by his fellow poets. He had come home with a mind sharpened to the difference between the aesthetic and the scientific modes of perceiving relationships; the difference was always present to him.

He came home to demands for poetry. In his absence his friends had kept his name alive by extravagant allusions to him in periodicals they edited. Park Benjamin asked for a poem for his *American Monthly Magazine,* was given among others "The Last Reader," and earned Holmes's wrath by amending a word. Although shaken by the editor's presumption and by a candid friend who thought the new poems not so good as the old, Holmes set himself to provide a song for the Harvard bicentennial dinner and a poem for Phi Beta Kappa. The song he had the audacity (the "brass," his brother said) to sing himself. The long poem for Phi Beta Kappa he learned by heart and delivered "with charming ease and propriety," according to the secretary of the Board of Overseers.

Welcomed by poets, editors, and his alma mater, Holmes claimed in the same year the attention of the doctors. He entered and won the competition for the Boylston Prize for Medicine. Not attempting an ambitious treatment of the set topic, he focused his essay, "Direct Exploration," upon a new instrument, the stethoscope, and its use. Mentioning his "zealous devotion" and "amiable disposition," his teachers got him the job of visiting physician at the Boston Dispensary.

Holmes wanted "a regular occupation," by which he could support himself and secure "a hold on the community." Being a poet would not satisfy this modest ambition; writing the preface to the volume of poems to appear in November, he renounced the rôle. He was rebuked for "literary suicide" and told by *The North American Review* that there was "no profession so engrossing as to leave no time for poetry." Ignoring this encouragement, he labored doggedly on the research for his essay on Intermittent Fever. The paper was historical rather than scientific, but the principles he had learned in Paris held. He was again competing for a prize; two were offered in 1837 and he won both. "It is almost useless to contend with him in an enterprise of this kind," said the local medical journal. *Poems* of November 1836 was followed by *Boylston Prize Dissertations* of January 1838 dedicated to P. Cha. A. Louis . . . "in the Recollection of His Invaluable Instructions and Unvarying Kindness."

In the twenty years between 1833 and 1853, Holmes wrote only as many poems as he had produced in the four years between 1829 and 1833. The poems were those his place in the community might require: occasional poems written to please his fellow physicians or his summer neighbors in Pittsfield, verses for Harvard and poems for Phi Beta Kappa at Dartmouth (1838) and Yale (1850). He resolved not to keep his reputation as a poet alive by "periodical gaspings." To this resolution, he made a few exceptions. He provided his classmate Clarke with verses for the *Western Messenger* and found himself in the unlikely company of Emerson and Margaret Fuller. He liked "An After-Dinner Poem" of 1843 well enough to offer it to *Graham's*. Originally called "Terpsichore," the poem dances over a wide field of contemporary follies; he probably knew that, clever as it was, its topicality required that it be published at once.

Earlier in 1843, he had written his most important medical essay, *The Contagiousness of Puerperal Fever*, a "candid investigation" in which he did not spare his colleagues grief. Written "in a great heat and with passionate indignation," the essay was the product of twenty-one days' intensive research in the literature of the disease and in the experiences of physicians he could cross-examine. That puerperal fever might be contagious had been suggested in 1842 by Dr. Francis Condie of Philadelphia, but the guess had been scouted by Dr. Charles D. Meigs, author of the standard American textbooks on obstetrics. In Boston Dr. Walter Channing had three times reported to the Boston Society for Medical Improvement on successive cases in his own practice; he too rejected the notion of contagion. The society had heard also of two deaths from dissection wounds incurred during autopsies on puerperal fever victims. On January 23, the pathologist John B. S. Jackson raised the question of the possibility of contagion. Within twenty-four hours, Holmes, done with "trivial discussion," was at work. On February 13 he presented his paper.

Asserting at the start that any doubter was ignorant of the evidence, he marshalled the facts to make good his thesis that doctors and nurses were culpable agents of infection. What had been suggested as early as 1773 and as recently as 1842 was made incontrovertible by Holmes's essay. It was printed in *The New England Journal of Medicine*; Holmes circulated an offprint, and an abstract was printed in *The American Journal of Medical Science*. It was the abstract that attracted attention in this country and in England, but with the evidence trimmed and without Holmes's eloquence, the argument did not convince all readers. Noticeably, obstetricians were least persuaded, including Channing, who had seen the full essay yet considered his "experience" sufficient rebuttal. Dr. Meigs attacked the concept of contagion, labelled Holmes's essay as among the "jejeune and fizzenless dreamings of sophomore writers," and loftily attributed deaths from puerperal fever to "Providence." To take arms against fatuity requires a compelling motive. Holmes reprinted his essay in 1855. Addressing his new introduction to medical students, he wrote: "I had rather rescue one mother from being poisoned by her attendant, than claim to have saved forty or fifty patients to whom I had carried the disease." He closed with his most splendid rhetoric:

> . . . Indifference will not do here; our Journals and Committees have no right to take up their pages with minute anatomy and tediously detailed cases, while it is a question whether the 'black death' of child-bed is to be scattered broadcast by the agency of the mother's friend and adviser. Let the men who mould

opinions look to it: if there is any voluntary blindness, any culpable negligence, even in such a matter, and the facts shall reach the public ear; the pestilence-carrier of the lying-in chamber must look to God for pardon, for man will never forgive him.

The motive behind the Boylston Prize Dissertations was ambition; that behind the puerperal fever essay of 1843 and 1855 was altruistic. But always the impetus to put his talents to work had to be immediate. Separated from colleagues who boasted of "cures," assumed that "experience" constituted evidence, and offered "Providence" as an explanation of what they were unwilling to face, he was separated also from his fellow poets who trusted to "intuition." With his eye on the immediate, Holmes struck his German-indoctrinated contemporaries as a man of "mere understanding," not a man of "imagination."

While Holmes taught the use of the microscope, the transcendentalists listened to papers on such modest subjects as "Man in the Ages." When they began to show themselves in their periodical *The Dial,* Holmes took notice of them. In "Terpsichore" he mocks their presumption. Addressing them as "Deluded infants," the doctor asks: "Will they ever know/ Some doubts must darken here below." A sane man might expect to answer the question: Is puerperal fever contagious? Only a "Bedlamite" would put conundrums to "Earth the tongueless" and "the deaf-mute Time!"

By 1843, Holmes had found his place in the community. In 1840 he married Amelia Lee Jackson, daughter of Judge Charles Jackson and niece of his loved teacher Dr. James Jackson. Holmes's first son and namesake, future Justice of the Supreme Court, was born March 9, 1841; his daughter Amelia on October 20, 1843; and his son Edward on October 17, 1846. The family lived at 8 Montgomery Place, not far from the Tremont Medical School where he now taught. By 1846, he had developed a respectable practice, had joined the staff of the Massachusetts General Hospital, had maintained his reputation as a poet, and had earned what he shrewdly called the "flattery of abuse." In April 1847, he received notice of his appointment as Parkman Professor of Anatomy and Physiology at the Massachusetts Medical College (i.e., Harvard). In May he attended the first meeting of the American Medical Association. He was made chairman of the Committee on Medical Literature; the devastating report presented the following year was entirely his work. He charged his colleagues with servility to England, the "habit of indolence," and poverty of mind, and documented the charges in a "scathing review" that took two hours to deliver.

Meanwhile his appointment as Parkman Professor entailed his making the Introductory Lecture. Such was his reputation that a number of gentlemen, transcendentalists among them, attended the lecture and even considered enrolling in his course. Holding the office of Dean, he supported the application of a woman; thereafter he consistently voted for the admission of women, more often than not their only advocate. Withdrawing from private practice in 1849, he began to appear with more regularity on the public lecture platform where he may be said to have been rehearsing for *The Autocrat*. Invited to give a series of lectures for the Lowell Institute of 1853, he chose the subject of "The English Poets of the Nineteenth Century." Romantic idealists, willing to hear him on anatomy or the "Races of Man," were astonished at his temerity in choosing to speak on Wordsworth and Coleridge.

Two letters written before he gave these lectures suggest his expectations as a reader. Writing Emerson to acknowledge the gift of *Poems* (1846), he admired the "genuineness" of Emerson's "descriptions of common scene and feelings" but admitted that much was to him "vague and mystical." What to Emerson was "a clear and simple image" seemed to him "to refract and distort" the idea. He wondered that Emerson could "undervalue" rhythm as a "means of expression." He is the more surprised because passages that have moved him most by the "beauty and strength of thought" have been "melodious" in spite of Emerson's "carelessness." Acknowledging that his mind is "different in tendencies and habits" from the minds of Emerson's intimates, he had found much to delight him.

To Hawthorne in 1851 he wrote without reservations:

> The imagination of our lean country men has always seemed to me as emaciated as their faces. I had been so morbidly set in this belief that but for your last two stories I should have . . . believed that all we were to look for in the way of such spontaneous growth were such languid, lifeless, sexless creations as in the view of certain people constitute the chief triumphs of a sister art as manifested among us.
>
> . . . The Yankee mind has for the most part . . . flowered in pots of English earth — but you have . . . raised yours . . . in the natural soil . . . the moment a fresh mind takes in the elements of common life about us and transfigures them I am contented to enjoy and admire . . .

The criteria he brought to his lectures on the English poets are revealed in these letters. He asked for melody and in the "prolix" Wordsworth found prose, or rhythms so elusive as to be undetectable to ears attuned to Pope; he found the "elements of common life," and the "homely truthfulness of the actual," but not yet for him their "transfiguration." In Byron and Moore he heard strong melodies, but both had too often found their matter elsewhere than in their "natural soil." The lectures were so well subscribed that the press wildly overestimated his profit from the size of the crowds. Even an unsympathetic reviewer observed: "His peculiar magnetism makes itself felt before his voice is heard." The "chime and emphasis of his voice" were as pleasing as his wit. The newspaper reports are less than coherent. Holmes's speech was distinct but rapid; the reporters had trouble keeping up with him. The chief victim of his wit was Carlyle whose judgment of Scott he satirically diagnosed. He is reported to have treated "tenderly" weaknesses he had been expected to mock. Some of his hearers regretted that he was not more reverential in his handling of Wordsworth, more censorious in his judgment of Byron, and more melodramatic in his account of the opium-eating Coleridge.

Originally the lecture room had been a place where serious listeners hoped to be instructed, but by the fifties it had become, as Holmes knew, a lion-trap, a place of amusement. The traveling was arduous for Holmes, liable to homesickness and asthma. Immaculate in his person, he suffered in ill-kept rural taverns. From the business of lecturing he was rescued by the founding of *The Atlantic Monthly*. The first editor, James Russell Lowell, made Holmes's promise to contribute a condition of his acceptance of the job; and thereafter each successive editor made sure of his contributions.

Holmes did not escape from the lecture room unscathed. In 1855, in his Address for the New England Society of New York, he had satirized the prohibitionists and abolitionists; reformers in the audience hissed. To the hisses he referred forgivingly in his poem the following evening, but the false reports of his lecture in the newspapers brought him letters. He did not answer the journalists, but the letters from Theodore Parker and Emerson, he had to answer. He told Parker: "I don't want to be bullied into Heaven by the pulpit — neither do I wish to be called hard names to make me better or more humane. But surely my attacks on this spirit, as shown in moral warfare, do not prove that I am a glutton, or a drunkard, or a defender of slavery." To Emerson he wrote: "If the law of conscience *carried out fully only by the ultra-abolitionists*, had been proclaimed in strict accordance with the law of love, I believe the question would be far more nearly solved than it is at present." He assures Emerson that he is not "undergoing any process of moral disintegration." Transcendentalists could be as dogmatic as Calvinists; between irresistible grace and the infallible conscience there was not much to choose.

The human race might require criticism, but Holmes thought it required charity even more, and the papers shortly to appear in the new magazine would try to show why. Lowell had wanted variety, and his first number guaranteed it. On page 48 appeared Emerson's "Brahma" followed by *The Autocrat of the Breakfast-Table*. All contributions were unsigned, but no reader was deceived. Holmes's provocative talk and Emerson's provoking poem drew attention to the first number. As successive numbers came out, the press repeatedly praised the Autocrat's talk. With the founding of *The Atlantic* and his admission to the Saturday Club in 1857, Holmes joined a second "community."

The format of the Breakfast-Table papers owes to the two papers written twenty-five years earlier only the title. The notion that every man might be his own Boswell had not then occurred to him, nor had he attempted to fill out the boarding-house table with refracting characters. The new format allowed his "discursive" mind free play. There was nothing in his life that could not evoke suggestive ideas. Cant, quackery, and fatuity were the objects of stringent comment in the breakfast-table books and in the novels. The religious press charged him with being a semi-infidel who poisoned the minds of his readers. The socially conscious, then as now, misapplied his definition of the "Brahmin." Chosen by Holmes for its association with learning and the priesthood, the word identified a physical and psychological type of which Edwards, Channing, and Emerson were representative as he makes plain in *Elsie Venner* of 1861 and in the poem "At the Saturday Club" of 1884.

Holmes delighted as many as he offended. Yet few of his contemporaries responded to that subject he thought "the noblest and most interesting"; namely, psychology. He asked for the study of "man, the individual, not the abstraction, the metaphysical or theological lay-figure." In *The Autocrat* he offers his image of the limited will as a drop of water imprisoned in a crystal. With the theme of human limitation, he made ready for "The Coming Era." In this poem of 1880 he foresees a day when the muse will yield to science, and "Physics will grasp imagination's wings," or so, in the fiction of the poem, he is being told by a new generation of "youthful sages."

He was prepared to psychologize even his addiction to verse. Whatever a poem cost him in nervous energy and however often he was moved to warn the tyro to beware of the rhymer's disease, he had still to write poetry. Late in life, asked to choose between *The Contagiousness of Puerperal Fever* and "The Chambered Nautilus," Holmes refused to answer. To have saved lives was reason for satisfaction, but he could not recall with any self-congratulation his savage frame of mind at the time of writing. The poem, on the other hand, had been written in a state of exhilaration he recalled with pleasure. In his lecture on Keats, the poet who had chosen poetry over medicine, Holmes had unequivocally expressed his approval of the choice. In the best account of the lecture (in Bryant's *New York Evening Post*), he is reported as saying: "it is a good thing to save a few lives, but it is better to have infused a new life into our language."

In *The Poet*, he suggests that he had not found a voice. He might more accurately have said that among many voices, he had not chosen one to be unmistakably his. The poems in *The Autocrat* alone illustrate his range from the romantic sublime of "The Chambered Nautilus" through the clever play of Latin and English in "Æstivation," to the colloquial "Deacon's Masterpiece"; rhythm, diction, tone are all radically different. "Contentment" and "Latter-Day Warnings" are less far apart, but the stance of the speaker in each is not the same. The gathering includes occasional poems in which good humor and appropriate sentiment are held together by the poet's sense of the occasion. Complementing them is the mock occasional poem "Ode for a Social Meeting" carefully revised to satisfy a teetotaler's taste. The voice of the professor in love with his subject is heard in the anatomist's hymn "The Living Temple." Only two poems are at all alike; "Parson Turrell's Legacy" matches "The Deacon's Masterpiece," to show that he could "do it twice."

So sure is Holmes's control of his tunes and his lyrics in whatever mode he chooses that he appears to speak in rhyme as easily as in prose. He can make the heroic couplet expressive of the harshest sarcasm, of genial humor, of solemn praise, of common talk. In some occasional poems he skates close to the cliché, but his diction is usually crisp; he tries to avoid the blurring word and the limp epithet. With a more sensitive ear than his contemporaries, he can make his cadences remarkably expressive.

Choosing the Professor to succeed the Autocrat, he carried on a running debate with the religious press. For the book he invented the alter ego of the crippled "Little Boston," provincial patriot and fierce defender of religious liberty. With this invention, he anticipated the admissions he would make seven years later in letters to Harriet Beecher Stowe. His necessary resistance to Calvinist training had, he thought, injured the "balance" of his intelligence: "I suppose all I write may show something of this, as the lame child limps at every step, as the crooked back shows through every garment."

The persistent misinterpretation of "The Deacon's Masterpiece" as an attack upon Calvinism is understandable in the light of Holmes's obsession. For this interpretation, first offered by Barrett Wendell, there is no evidence; Holmes's son testified to his father's never so describing it. In its context in *The Autocrat*, there is nothing to warrant such a reading. In a note of 1885, Holmes presents the poem in terms of its subtitle "A Logical Story" and its final line: "Logic is logic. That's all I say." In the first number of *The Autocrat*, the question is asked: "If a logical mind ever found out anything with its logic?" The answer promptly returned is: "I should say that its most frequent work was to build a *pons asinorum* over chasms which shrewd people can bestride without such a structure." The critic who reads the poem as a parable should apply it to all logical systems which, whatever their perfection of artificial structure, must collapse under pressure from nature.

Holmes's first novel, *Elsie Venner: A Romance of Destiny*, carried a warning in its subtitle. Not altogether fusing science and poetry, the novel is in part a "medicated" fantasy designed "to test the doctrine of 'original sin,'" and in part a documentary of New England village life. Fresh from exercising a license to be discursive, Holmes does not bring the varied matter of his novel into harmony. His psychological speculations are not suited to his heroine, for his image of the will as a moving drop of water enclosed in a crystal is not applicable to a child poisoned before birth. Minor figures in the novel are more suggestive than the ophidian heroine and her Gothic cousin Dick. The schoolteacher Helen Darley is a mild hysteric puzzled by her own aberrations and those of some of the children she teaches. She is moved to question the creed she had been taught. For this indictment of orthodox training Holmes was charged with "moral parricide" and accused of dissecting "before the world the character and memory of his father." A second figure in the novel, the vacillating preacher Fairweather, is represented as lost in his own spiritual needs and incapacitated for the care of other souls; he seeks refuge in the Catholic Church.

While the novel was running in *The Atlantic,* Holmes addressed his colleagues. "Currents and Counter-Currents in Medical Science" has as one topic the discoveries of the geologists who have "remodelled the beliefs of half the civilized world." The unsettling of traditional ideas has sent some men scurrying to the oldest dogma or the newest mystical fancy. Holmes recognizes here the comforts of Catholicism, which had drawn a number of recent converts from among the young, and the increasing attraction of spiritualism. Able to welcome the discoveries of the geologists, Holmes was able to welcome Darwinism and became at Boston dinner-tables the explicator of the new texts derived from nature not scripture.

In the following year, all questions went down before the one fact of the Civil War. The war, foreseen and feared by Unionists, evoked in Holmes the ardent patriot. In spirit he was deeply engaged, and that not solely because he had a son at the front. He had argued consistently for Union and the compromises undertaken to ensure it; now he threw his talent into the Union cause. With lecture, hymn, and exhortatory verse, he earned attack from the Copperheads.

Confident in public, in private he was anxious. Three times the alarming messages came to the house on Charles Street; it was the second that sent him on his "Hunt after the Captain." The psychologist found it curious that anxiety and weariness instead of blinding him to what he saw should have made him more alert and observant. He wrote out his worries to John Lothrop Motley. To this loved friend, he could write with freedom, shocked by the Jeremiahs he met in the street, by those prepared to abandon the Union, those prepared to submit to the South, and those whose chief concern was their pocketbooks. He met them all in the streets of Boston. He found more meanness than he supposed possible: "I believe our people are worked up to the *paying* point, which, I take it, is to the fighting point as boiling heat (212°) is to blood heat (98°)." He encountered young men whose temperatures were well below normal and old men who supposed that a little prudence might have prevented the "unlucky accident."

The correspondence with Motley prepared him for the Fourth of July oration of 1863. He had made fun of Fourth of July oratory in the past; now the motive for inventing his own was irresistible. Arguing for the inevitability of the conflict, he eloquently establishes what he calls (out of Spencer) the "law of simultaneous intellectual movement." He draws his illustrations from art, literature, science, and history, deploying the device of the wide-ranging catalogue to persuasive effect. To rebuke those who count the cost in dollars, he catalogues with manifest contempt the luxuries the northerner still enjoys: "If our property is taxed, it is only to teach us that liberty is worth paying for as well as fighting for." The rhetoric now shows tarnish but then comforted the speaker as well as the audience.

Holmes needed comfort; the letters from the battlefield were increasingly pessimistic. The view from Fredricksburg in 1862 was not the same as the view from Boston and Vienna; young Holmes charged his father and Motley with "ignorance." Not doubting the "right of our cause," he despaired of "success by arms." He concluded this "blowoff" by asking for six photographs of himself and had the envelope addressed by someone else "so that you may think it a bill." In the still harrowing days of 1864, Captain Holmes felt acutely the prolonged physical and emotional pressures of the war. He wrote ambiguously: "I have made up my mind to stay on the staff till the end of the campaign & then if I am alive, I shall resign — I have felt for some time that I didn't any longer believe in this being a duty . . ." By "this" he meant returning to service as a line officer after his three-year term ended, but only later letters explain the vague pronoun. Misunderstanding, the father replied at once; his letter, arriving the day after the young man had heroically carried a message through a nest of rebel raiders, provoked resentment. Conscious of virtue and exhausted by days of battle and nights of marching, the son wrote angrily of misunderstanding that impugned his honor. Five days later, with "a thousand loving thoughts," he acknowledged "delightful letters" from both parents and a box of cigars from his father.

When young Holmes supposed that he might die of the wounds received at Bull's Bluff, he recalled agreeing with his father, whose religious scepticism he shared, that there could be no deathbed recantation. Toward his father, he freely expressed respect, "sass," anger, and love. Between two vain, quick-witted, argumentative men, there was likely to be friction as well as love. The father admitted to being vain; the son, to being "disagreeable." Twenty years later in retrospective speeches about the war, the veteran echoes the sentiments of his father's address of July 4, 1863, and in "The Soldier's Faith" (1895) he remembers the "cynic force with which thoughts of common sense will assail the soldier in times of stress." The details of the speech suggest that he was rereading his own letters.

In 1865 with his hero at home, Dr. Holmes was meditating on heredity; he had a "case" before him — sceptic, poet (of the class of '61), patriot, and, the father hoped, potential judge. With heredity in mind, Holmes was glad to say: "Luckily my wife is one of the smartest and most capable women going." Heredity would be a theme in *The Guardian Angel* of 1867. James T. Fields had asked for "An American story," and Holmes took a hint from a medical friend for "a book on education with a physiological base." The novel fulfils these specifications, too explicitly the hostile reviewer in *The Nation* thought, lamenting the "atmosphere of carnality" he detected in the book. In his heroine Myrtle Hazard, Holmes created a more plausible case than Elsie Venner. Myrtle's difficulties in weathering the storms of adolescence, which so offended the sensibilities of *The Nation*, are worked out in terms of her conflicting inherited traits. To describe his sense that human beings have an unconscious knowledge of themselves that has only to be brought into consciousness for recognition to follow, Holmes uses the image of the undeveloped photographic plate from which the picture emerges as the photographer applies his wash. Shortly after he published the novel, Holmes had the satisfaction of finding similar conceptions in the writings of the Englishman Henry Maudsley (sometimes labeled the first psychiatrist).

With his usual sense of occasion, Holmes prepared his Phi Beta Kappa Address of 1870, *Mechanism in Thought and Morals*. In a sparkling performance, the professor and poet speak in one voice. Holmes uses his talent for selecting the bright image to show all that is known about the brain and the process of thinking in so far as thinking can be the subject of testing and measurement. With manifest delight he suggests the questions that can be asked and describes his own experiments, some devised to check the findings of others and some anticipatory of future experiments. He had traced the idea of unconscious thought to Leibnitz and then considered its variations in later theorists. His continuing attack on supposedly moribund theologies is prompted by his recognition of the subterranean life of old beliefs. He turns his address in this direction; it is not the scientist who can be charged with materialism, but the moralist:

> We hang men for our convenience and safety; sometimes shoot them for revenge. Thus we come to associate the infliction of punishment for offences as their satisfactory settlement, — a kind of neutralization of them, as of an acid with an alkali: so that we feel as if a jarring moral universe would be all right if only suffering enough were added to it.

The address was neatly timed. *The American Journal of Medical Psychology* was founded in 1870; in 1871, John E. Tyler, who had been a special lecturer in "Psychology and Medicine," became a full professor at the Medical School with his own department of neurology.

Among the visitors to the old house on Charles Street and the new house on Beacon Street, were the younger Holmes's brilliant friends: William James and his brother Henry; Charles Saunders Peirce, Henry Adams. In *The Poet at the Breakfast-Table* Holmes acknowledges that sons "do not walk in our ruts of thought or begin exactly where we left off, but they have a standpoint of their own." No scientist as his son's generation conceived of the scientist, Holmes took refuge in the fact that he was a poet and turned the breakfast table over to that alter ego. He might regret not having made himself a specialist, but as he confessed to S. Weir Mitchell, his "nature was to snatch at all the fruits of knowledge." The new book with his candid letters to Mitchell of the same year reveals that the fruits of psychological knowledge might be bitter, but nothing could put him to flight from the immediate world in which he was as interested as he was in his own "vicious and kicking brain." He could use the book to explain the new science to the old and to defend sentiment from the young. Through the Poet and the Master, the well-informed doctor speaks of Darwinism, the nebular hypothesis, the theories of Alexander Bain and Francis Galton, and the latest in bacteriology.

Moving easily into the post-Darwinian world, Holmes yet felt his years and the demands made upon him not only by a longer University term but by the responsibility of being a celebrity not shy in public. So much in love with "his native planet" that he hoped leaves of absence were permitted from heaven, even Holmes could find the "gilded age" too rich for absorption. He took in all he could and bore as well as he could a melancholy succession of losses: Agassiz, his sister Ann, his son-in-law, first Mary Motley and then Motley himself. His biography of Motley he wrote with love. He had never loved Sumner, but the senator's death and the disgraceful spectacle of drunken politicians at the funeral underscored "the ignoble aspect of the great republic." Was there any other way to treat the disorderly Tilden-Hayes campaign save by mocking it as he does in the poem "How Not to Settle It"?

With the loss of loved friends and relatives, he approached his seventieth birthday with "cheerful despair." Three years later on November 28, 1882 he entered his lecture room at the medical school for the last time and discovered more affection than he had bargained for. For once in his life he was speechless. Even the New York medical profession was prepared to subject the Boston celebrity to dinners and receptions. Expected to sing for his supper, Holmes resorted to the familiar "straight-backed measure with its stately stride." He is not sure that praise from the doctors is merited "For nature's servant far too often seen/ A loiterer by the wave of Hippocrene."

He was not done with his profession, for he had to perform at the dedication of the new Medical School Building. At that moment, Governor Ben Butler was investigating the Tewksbury Almshouse, exploiting the disposal of bodies to the medical school and the presumed horrors of the dissecting room — Holmes's domain. Butler made much of Holmes's having shown a piece of human skin to his classes. The dedication had been scheduled for May, but before evening on May 11, the building was gutted by fire. When the postponed day of dedication came in October, the building was to be opened for inspection, but someone locked the dissecting-room. At the end of his speech Holmes introduced the shocking topic of "the Anthropotomic Laboratory, known to plainer speech as the Dissecting-Room."

He let forth all his love for his subject and all his contempt for politicians whose "inflammatory representations" might provoke "midday mobs or midnight incendiarism." It is in the interest of intelligent citizens to "defend the anatomist and his place of labor." He went on to give examples of the relation between anatomical studies and surgery and concluded: "I cannot stop to moan over a scrap of human integument . . . for every lifeless body which served for these experiments a hundred or a thousand fellow-creatures have been saved from unutterable anguish, and many of them from premature death." Some member of the chastened medical faculty unlocked the doors of the dissecting room before the audience was released to make its tour of inspection.

Ostensibly retired, Holmes summoned in his final decade the spirit to write a second biography, a third novel, an account of one hundred days abroad, the tea-table coda to the breakfast-table series, and, of course, poems. Yet at Parker's of a Saturday he found "the company . . . more of ghosts than of flesh and blood." He put the feeling into a poem. "At the Saturday Club" is in the loved measure of the heroic couplet. Holmes steps lightly over the pavement of rhyme. He brings us naturally to the Parker House and into the empty dining room, the more empty for the detail of "the waiters lounging round the marble stairs." He gives his ghosts "robes of flesh," bringing Longfellow, Agassiz, Hawthorne, and Emerson before the eye and to the ear. He gives too the qualities of mind and work, and suggests his judgment so obliquely that it takes a moment to see that the effect of the epithets attached to Longfellow is that of unvarying softness; those attached to Agassiz give us the robust and vigorous. His admiration of Hawthorne's work is implicit in every line; the man is a mystery the poet is willing to leave unsolved. Still no lover of transcendentalism, Holmes exempts Emerson from censure. His simile descriptive of Emerson's slow searching for the right word is somewhat labored, but he finds the right images for this "wingéd Franklin."

When he wrote the poem, he was already at work on the biography of Emerson for the American Men of Letters series. The book brought him letters of praise. Lowell, a professor of literature inclined to snub the professor of anatomy, was grateful to be shown that Emerson, without "sensuous passion," had "spiritual passion enough and to spare." Perhaps more gratifying was a letter from Henry Adams, a contemporary of his son. Adams wished that the chapter on poetry had been longer, at the expense of the judgments of Emerson's admirers, for he preferred Holmes to "Mr. Emerson's echoes . . ." Holmes at close to seventy-five was surely pleased by Adams's comment on "the lightness of touch and the breadth of sympathy that makes your work so much superior to anything we other men, who call ourselves younger, succeed in doing." The work had tired Holmes; his brother John urged him to read novels "and have a blow-out at tea if you won't go anything stronger."

Instead of reading novels, he wrote one, beginning at once on *A Mortal Antipathy*. A novel by courtesy, the book does not control the author's discursive mind; on the contrary, the device of a literary society, which publishes its members' contributions, allows Holmes to disport himself on such subjects as interviewers, intellectual humility, and psychological relations to bodies of water. The book has two topics: the woman question and a case of childhood trauma. Satirizing the feminist and her opponent, he creates two bizarre maidens to expose the weakness of the intellectual arguments of the one and physiological arguments of the other. The "case" of the hero with his trauma-induced phobia was credible to Dr. S. Weir Mitchell but not to the ordinary reader. However casual a novel, the book shows that its author is still alert to his world.

Besieged by interviewers and flooded with letters, Holmes issued "A Cry From the Study" only to invite more letters, among them invitations to visit England. Leaving with his daughter in April, he arrived in time for the London "season." The round of breakfasts, luncheons, teas, and dinners persuaded Holmes that the "season" was suited to ruminants with several stomachs but not to an old man with only one. He went to the parties and took his three honorary degrees graciously, but he had his own desires. He was determined to see the Derby again. Traveling in state in the special train of the Prince of Wales, he was amused to compare his grandeur of 1886 with his lowly status of 1834. The poor student had seen Plenipotentiary in 1834; now the celebrity was to see Ormonde — two great horses, which the greater experts could not tell.

A compelling desire was to see his coevals. In intense excitement on June 7, Holmes heard Gladstone urge the passage of the Irish Home Rule bill, saw him go down to defeat, and heard him cheered even so. He walked home alone at two in the morning not displeased at the performance of this other gentleman of seventy-seven. Three days later he went to the Isle of Wight and wandered under the trees with Tennyson whose seclusion he respected too much to write of him. A sentimental traveler, Holmes looked for associations with his own past and with poets. He could not see the lark rising from Salisbury Plain, but at Windsor he heard the cuckoo's "wandering voice." In the same spirit he went to Paris, revisited remembered places, took coffee at the Café Procope, and made one visit to the modern world. In the rue Vauquelin, he presented his compliments to Louis Pasteur.

The return home was darkened by his wife's illness, but he wrote his book while his journey was fresh in his mind. Of his infirmities he made light; but griefs crowded one upon the other. His younger son had died in 1884, and now he would lose his wife. One number of *Over the Teacups* had appeared in *The Atlantic*; he abandoned the book. For a while his daughter's coming to live with him rejuvenated his bleak household and revived his waning spirits, but in 1889, his daughter too died. He met his griefs with fortitude, and in 1890, he picked up the abandoned book.

Candidly Holmes told his readers that he expected to repeat himself: "The area of consciousness is covered by layers of habitual thought . . . When we think we are thinking, we are . . . only listening to the sound of attrition between those inert elements of our intelligence." The Dictator presides over the tea-table along with a new alter ego "The Crank," on to whom Holmes shoves the responsibility for his firmest prejudices. He has new topics; though he has not the terms, he explores semantics and extrasensory perception. In 1858 he had delighted his readers with "The Deacon's Masterpiece"; in 1890 he matches his record with "The Broomstick Train." His readers rejoiced in this revivification of wit turned upon the new invention of the electric trolley car, but he himself called his last book the "wintry product of my freezing wits."

He was not idle in the last four years of his life and could meet demanding occasions with speech and rhyme. The work of preparing the Riverside Edition of his *Writings* could scarcely have been easy. He felt like Hamlet, "fat and short of breath," he told one of the editors at 2 Park Street. What appears to be his last poem, his translation from Sappho, is written in a very shaky hand. The poem is a love poem, but the stricken lover and the translator know too well the signs of impending death. On October 7, 1894, talking with his son, Holmes "simply ceased to breathe."

In 1872 in *The Poet at the Breakfast-Table*, Holmes had written: "Life is a fatal complaint and an eminently contagious one." Because life was an infection he was never tempted to avoid, Holmes had grown younger as he grew older, able to meet his son's generation more than halfway. Admiring his father's "fertile and suggestive intellect," Justice Holmes concluded that his father had "the most penetrating mind of all that lot."

Not bound to any literary fashion, Holmes's poetry cannot be confidently "placed." Poetry was for him "the science of the heart," and through every change of tune and topic, he consistently suggests that the human race is the better for candor and kindness, truth and laughter. Suffering and grief he acknowledges as realities, but not sin and evil. Against the moral earnestness that would rub the sheen from the many bright facets "in the crystalline order of things," he would all his life protest. It cannot be said that Holmes was no poet; it has to be said that he was so many other things as well.

Eleanor M. Tilton

Barnard College
April, 1974

ACKNOWLEDGMENTS

FOR PERMISSION to use Holmes's manuscripts, I am indebted to the Houghton Library, Harvard University; the Countway Library, Harvard Medical School; Harvard Law Library, Harvard University; the Harvard University Archives, The Henry E. Huntington Library, the Manuscript Division of the Library of Congress, Miss Miriam R. Small, and Mrs. Ward I. Gregg. The fragment from Margaret Fuller's diary is quoted with the permission of Houghton Library. For permission to use texts first printed in Currier's *Bibliography of Oliver Wendell Holmes,* I wish to thank New York University Press. The firm of Abelard-Schuman has allowed me to use poems first printed in my *Amiable Autocrat.* Harvard University Press has permitted the use of passages from *Touched With Fire.*

Of incalculable value were Thomas Franklin Currier's manuscript notes of variant readings. These notes (in my possession) were particularly useful in checking the 1895 texts. I have a special debt to Miss Carolyn Jakeman and Mr. Rodney G. Dennis of Houghton Library and Mr. Morris Cohen and Mrs. Erika S. Chadburn of the Harvard Law Library, all of whom were very helpful in the crisis of the "lost" manuscripts. I wish to thank also Mr. Richard J. Wolfe of the Countway Medical Library and his staff. The notes added to this edition are the fuller because of the labor of Margaret Notley Yackulic who also patiently typed and retyped revised manuscript.

The principal secondary works consulted are listed below with note of the abbreviations used in the notes. Titles marked with an asterisk are the sources of matter quoted in the Introduction.

E. M. T.

Currier, Thomas Franklin. *Bibliography of Oliver Wendell Holmes,* ed. Eleanor M. Tilton. New York: 1953. (C. & T.)

———. "Oliver Wendell Holmes, Poet Laureate of Harvard," *Proceedings of the Massachusetts Historical Society,* LXVII (1945), 436–451.

* Holmes, Oliver Wendell, Jr. *Speeches.* Boston: 1934.

*———. *Touched With Fire,* ed. Mark De Wolfe Howe. Cambridge, Massachusetts: 1946.

Ives, George B. *A Bibliography of Oliver Wendell Holmes.* Boston: 1907.

Lokensgard, Hjalmar. "Holmes Quizzes the Professors," *American Literature,* XIII (May 1941), 157–162.

* Morse, John T. *Life and Letters of Oliver Wendell Holmes.* Boston: 1897.

Small, Miriam R. "First and Last Surviving Poems of Dr. Oliver Wendell Holmes," *American Literature,* XV (January 1944), 416–420.

* Tilton, Eleanor M. *Amiable Autocrat.* New York: 1947. (A. A.)

————. " 'Literary Bantlings': Addenda to the Holmes Bibliography," *Papers of the Bibliographical Society of America,* LI (1957), 1–18.

————. "Dr. Holmes Answers the Question," *North Carolina Medical Journal,* VIII (1947), 12–14.

————. "Science and Sentiment," *Transactions of the Studies of the College of Physicians of Philadelphia,* 4th ser. XXVI (August, 1958), 89–98.

TO MY READERS

APRIL 8, 1862

NAY, blame me not; I might have spared
   Your patience many a trivial verse,
Yet these my earlier welcome shared,
   So, let the better shield the worse.

And some might say, " Those ruder songs
   Had freshness which the new have lost;
To spring the opening leaf belongs,
   The chestnut-burs await the frost."

When those I wrote, my locks were brown,
   When these I write — ah, well-a-day!
The autumn thistle's silvery down
   Is not the purple bloom of May!

Go, little book, whose pages hold
   Those garnered years in loving trust;
How long before your blue and gold
   Shall fade and whiten in the dust?

O sexton of the alcoved tomb,
   Where souls in leathern cerements lie,
Tell me each living poet's doom!
   How long before his book shall die?

It matters little, soon or late,
   A day, a month, a year, an age, —
I read oblivion in its date,
   And Finis on its title-page.

Before we sighed, our griefs were told;
   Before we smiled, our joys were sung;
And all our passions shaped of old
   In accents lost to mortal tongue.

In vain a fresher mould we seek, —
   Can all the varied phrases tell
That Babel's wandering children speak
   How thrushes sing or lilacs smell?

Caged in the poet's lonely heart,
  Love wastes unheard its tenderest tone ;
The soul that sings must dwell apart,
  Its inward melodies unknown.

Deal gently with us, ye who read !
  Our largest hope is unfulfilled, —
The promise still outruns the deed, —
  The tower, but not the spire, we build.

Our whitest pearl we never find ;
  Our ripest fruit we never reach ;
The flowering moments of the mind
  Drop half their petals in our speech.

These are my blossoms ; if they wear
  One streak of morn or evening's glow,
Accept them ; but to me more fair
  The buds of song that never blow.
    April 8, 1862.

EARLIER POEMS

[THE printing of *Poetry: a Metrical Essay* was made the occasion by the author for publishing the first collection of his poems in 1836. This contained the group afterward designated *Earlier Poems*, as well as most of those now grouped at the end of this volume under the heading *Verses from the Oldest Portfolio;* for when the volume of his verse had become considerable, Dr. Holmes thought best to winnow his first gathering, and to retain under the title *Earlier Poems* those which he regarded as constituent parts of his poetical product. The following passages are from the *Preface*, dated Boston, 1 November, 1836, which introduced the volume.

"The shorter pieces are arranged mainly with reference to the dignity of their subjects. A few remarks with regard to a species of writing in which the author has occasionally indulged, are offered to the consideration of those who are disposed to criticise rigorously; without the intention, however, of justifying all or any attempts at comic poetry, if they are bad specimens of their kind.

"The *extravagant* is often condemned as unnatural; as if a tendency of the mind, shown in all ages and forms, had not its foundation in nature. A series of hyperbolical images is considered beneath criticism by the same judges who would write treatises upon the sculptured satyrs and painted arabesques of antiquity, which are only hyperbole in stone and colors. As material objects in different lights repeat themselves in shadows variously elongated, contracted, or exaggerated, so our solid and sober thoughts caricature themselves in fantastic shapes inseparable from their originals, and having a unity in their extravagance, which proves them to have retained their proportions in certain respects, however differing in outline from their prototypes. To illustrate this by an example. Our idea of a certain great nation, an idea founded in substantial notions of its geography, its statistics, its history, in one aspect of the mind stretches into the sublime in the image of *Britannia*, and in another dilates into the sub-ridiculous in the person of *John Bull*. Both these personifications partially represent their object; both are useful and philosophical. And I am not afraid to say to the declaimers upon dignity of composition, that a metrical arabesque of a storm or a summer, if its images, though hyperbolical, are conceivable, and consistent with each other, is a perfectly healthy and natural exercise of the imagination, and not, as some might think, a voluntary degradation of its office. I argue, as I said before, for a principle, and not for my own attempt at its illustration.

"I had the intention of pointing out some accidental plagiarisms, or coincidences as they might be more mildly called, discovered principally by myself after the composition of the passages where they occur; but as they are, so far as I know, both innocent and insignificant, and as I have sometimes had literary pickpockets at my own skirts, I will leave them, like the apples of Atalanta, as an encouragement to sagacious critics, should any such follow my footsteps.

"I have come before the public like an actor who returns to fold his robes and make his bow to the audience. Already engaged in other duties, it has been with some effort that I have found time to adjust my own mantle; and I now willingly retire to more quiet labors, which, if less exciting, are more certain to be acknowledged as useful and received with gratitude; thankful that, not having staked all my hopes upon a single throw, I can sleep quietly after closing the last leaf of my little volume."]

OLD IRONSIDES

This was the popular name by which the frigate Constitution was known. The poem was first printed in the *Boston Daily Advertiser*, at the time when it was proposed to break up the old ship as unfit for service. I subjoin the paragraph which led to the writing of the poem. It is from the *Advertiser* of Tuesday, September 14, 1830: —

"*Old Ironsides.* — It has been affirmed upon good authority that the Secretary of the Navy has recommended to the Board of Navy Commissioners to dispose of the frigate Constitution. Since it has been understood that such a step was in contemplation we have heard but one opinion expressed, and that in decided disapprobation of the measure. Such a national object of interest, so endeared to our national pride as Old Ironsides is, should never by any act of our government cease to belong to the Navy, so long as our country is to be found upon the map of nations. In England it was lately determined by the Admiralty to cut the Victory, a one-hundred gun ship (which it will be recollected bore the flag of Lord Nelson at the battle of Trafalgar), down to a seventy-four, but so loud were the lamentations of the people upon the proposed measure that the intention was abandoned. We confidently anticipate that the Secretary of the Navy will in like manner consult the general wish in regard to the Constitution, and either let her remain in ordinary or rebuild her whenever the public service may require." — *New York Journal of Commerce.*

The poem was an impromptu outburst of feeling and was published on the next day but one after reading the above paragraph. [When *Poetry: a Metrical Essay* was published this poem was introduced as an interlude at the close of the second section.]

Ay, tear her tattered ensign down !
    Long has it waved on high,
And many an eye has danced to see
    That banner in the sky ;
Beneath it rung the battle shout,
    And burst the cannon's roar ; —
The meteor of the ocean air
    Shall sweep the clouds no more.

Her deck, once red with heroes' blood,
    Where knelt the vanquished foe,
When winds were hurrying o'er the flood,
    And waves were white below,
No more shall feel the victor's tread,
    Or know the conquered knee ; —
The harpies of the shore shall pluck
    The eagle of the sea !

Oh, better that her shattered hulk
    Should sink beneath the wave ;
Her thunders shook the mighty deep,
    And there should be her grave ;
Nail to the mast her holy flag,
    Set every threadbare sail,
And give her to the god of storms,
    The lightning and the gale !

THE LAST LEAF

The poem was suggested by the sight of a figure well known to Bostonians [in 1831 or 1832], that of Major Thomas Melville, "the last of the cocked hats," as he was sometimes called. The Major had been a personable young man, very evidently, and retained evidence of it in

    " The monumental pomp of age," —

which had something imposing and something odd about it for youthful eyes like mine. He was often pointed at as one of the "Indians" of the famous "Boston Tea-Party" of 1774. His aspect among the crowds of a later generation reminded me of a withered leaf which has held to its stem through the storms of autumn and winter, and finds itself still clinging to its bough while the new growths of spring are bursting their buds and spreading their foliage all around it. I make this explanation for the benefit of those who have been puzzled by the lines,

    " The last leaf upon the tree
        In the spring."

The way in which it came to be written in a somewhat singular measure was this. I had become a little known as a versifier, and I thought that one or two other young writers were following my efforts with imitations, not meant as parodies and hardly to be considered improvements on their models. I determined to write in a measure which would at once betray any copyist. So far as it was suggested by any previous poem, the echo must have come from Campbell's "Battle of the Baltic," with its short terminal lines, such as the last of these two,

    " By thy wild and stormy steep,
        Elsinore."

But I do not remember any poem in the same measure, except such as have been written since its publication.

The poem as first written had one of those false rhymes which produce a shudder in all educated persons, even in the poems of Keats and others who ought to have known better than to admit them.

The guilty verse ran thus : —

    " But now he walks the streets,
    And he looks at all he meets
        So forlorn,
    And he shakes his feeble head,
    That it seems as if he said,
        ' They are gone.' ! "

A little more experience, to say nothing of the sneer of an American critic in an English periodical, showed me that this would never do. Here was what is called a "cockney rhyme," — one in which the sound of the letter r is neglected — maltreated as the letter h is insulted by the average Briton by leaving it out everywhere except where it should be silent. Such an ill-mated pair as "forlorn" and "gone" could not possibly pass current in good rhyming society. But what to do about it was the question. I *must* keep

" They are gone ! "

and I could not think of any rhyme which I could work in satisfactorily. In this perplexity my friend, Mrs. Folsom, wife of that excellent scholar, Mr. Charles Folsom, then and for a long time the unsparing and infallible corrector of the press at Cambridge, suggested the line,

" Sad and wan,"

which I thankfully adopted and have always retained.

Good Abraham Lincoln had a great liking for the poem, and repeated it from memory to Governor Andrew, as the Governor himself told me. I have a copy of it made by the hand of Edgar Allan Poe.

[When this poem was issued with an accompaniment of illustration and decoration in 1894, Dr. Holmes wrote to his publishers : —

" I have read the proof you sent me and find nothing in it which I feel called upon to alter or explain.

" I have lasted long enough to serve as an illustration of my own poem. I am one of the very last of the leaves which still cling to the bough of life that budded in the spring of the nineteenth century. The days of my years are threescore and twenty, and I am almost half way up the steep incline which leads me toward the base of the new century so near to which I have already climbed.

" I am pleased to find that this poem, carrying with it the marks of having been written in the jocund morning of life, is still read and cared for. It was with a smile on my lips that I wrote it; I cannot read it without a sigh of tender remembrance. I hope it will not sadden my older readers, while it may amuse some of the younger ones to whom its experiences are as yet only floating fancies."]

I saw him once before,
As he passed by the door,
    And again
The pavement stones resound,
As he totters o'er the ground
    With his cane.

They say that in his prime,
Ere the pruning-knife of Time
    Cut him down,
Not a better man was found
By the Crier on his round
    Through the town.

But now he walks the streets,
And he looks at all he meets
    Sad and wan,
And he shakes his feeble head,
That it seems as if he said,
    " They are gone. "

The mossy marbles rest
On the lips that he has prest
    In their bloom,
And the names he loved to hear
Have been carved for many a year
    On the tomb.

My grandmamma has said —
Poor old lady, she is dead
    Long ago —
That he had a Roman nose,
And his cheek was like a rose
    In the snow;

But now his nose is thin,
And it rests upon his chin
    Like a staff,
And a crook is in his back,
And a melancholy crack
    In his laugh.

I know it is a sin
For me to sit and grin
    At him here ;
But the old three-cornered hat,
And the breeches, and all that,
    Are so queer !

And if I should live to be
The last leaf upon the tree
    In the spring,
Let them smile, as I do now,
At the old forsaken bough
    Where I cling.

THE CAMBRIDGE CHURCHYARD

[This poem was included as an interlude at the close of the first section in *Poetry : a Metrical Essay*, when that was published in book form.]

Our ancient church ! its lowly tower,
    Beneath the loftier spire,
Is shadowed when the sunset hour
    Clothes the tall shaft in fire ;
It sinks beyond the distant eye

Long ere the glittering vane,
High wheeling in the western sky,
   Has faded o'er the plain.

Like Sentinel and Nun, they keep
   Their vigil on the green ;
One seems to guard, and one to weep,
   The dead that lie between ;
And both roll out, so full and near,
   Their music's mingling waves,
They shake the grass, whose pennoned spear
   Leans on the narrow graves.

The stranger parts the flaunting weeds,
   Whose seeds the winds have strown
So thick, beneath the line he reads,
   They shade the sculptured stone;
The child unveils his clustered brow,
   And ponders for a while
The graven willow's pendent bough,
   Or rudest cherub's smile.

But what to them the dirge, the knell ?
   These were the mourner's share, —
The sullen clang, whose heavy swell
   Throbbed through the beating air ;
The rattling cord, the rolling stone,
   The shelving sand that slid,
And, far beneath, with hollow tone
   Rung on the coffin's lid.

The slumberer's mound grows fresh and
     green,
   Then slowly disappears ;
The mosses creep, the gray stones lean,
   Earth hides his date and years ;
But, long before the once-loved name
   Is sunk or worn away,
No lip the silent dust may claim,
   That pressed the breathing clay.

Go where the ancient pathway guides,
   See where our sires laid down
Their smiling babes, their cherished brides,
   The patriarchs of the town ;
Hast thou a tear for buried love ?
   A sigh for transient power ?
All that a century left above,
   Go, read it in an hour !

The Indian's shaft, the Briton's ball,
   The sabre's thirsting edge,
The hot shell, shattering in its fall,
   The bayonet's rending wedge, —
Here scattered death ; yet, seek the spot,

No trace thine eye can see,
No altar, — and they need it not
   Who leave their children free !

Look where the turbid rain-drops stand
   In many a chiselled square ;
The knightly crest, the shield, the brand
   Of honored names were there ; —
Alas ! for every tear is dried
   Those blazoned tablets knew,
Save when the icy marble's side
   Drips with the evening dew.

Or gaze upon yon pillared stone,
   The empty urn of pride ;
There stand the Goblet and the Sun, —
   What need of more beside ?
Where lives the memory of the dead,
   Who made their tomb a toy ?
Whose ashes press that nameless bed ?
   Go, ask the village boy !

Lean o'er the slender western wall,
   Ye ever-roaming girls ;
The breath that bids the blossom fall
   May lift your floating curls,
To sweep the simple lines that tell
   An exile's date and doom ;
And sigh, for where his daughters dwell,
   They wreathe the stranger's tomb.

And one amid these shades was born,
   Beneath this turf who lies,
Once beaming as the summer's morn,
   That closed her gentle eyes ;
If sinless angels love as we,
   Who stood thy grave beside,
Three seraph welcomes waited thee,
   The daughter, sister, bride !

I wandered to thy buried mound
   When earth was hid below
The level of the glaring ground,
   Choked to its gates with snow,
And when with summer's flowery waves
   The lake of verdure rolled,
As if a Sultan's white-robed slaves
   Had scattered pearls and gold.

Nay, the soft pinions of the air,
   That lift this trembling tone,
Its breath of love may almost bear
   To kiss thy funeral stone ;
And, now thy smiles have passed away,
   For all the joy they gave,

May sweetest dews and warmest ray
　　Lie on thine early grave !

When damps beneath and storms above
　　Have bowed these fragile towers,
Still o'er the graves yon locust grove
　　Shall swing its Orient flowers ;
And I would ask no mouldering bust,
　　If e'er this humble line,
Which breathed a sigh o'er others' dust,
　　Might call a tear on mine.

TO AN INSECT

The Katydid is "a species of grasshopper found in the United States, so called from the sound which it makes." WORCESTER.
I used to hear this insect in Providence, Rhode Island, but I do not remember hearing it in Cambridge, Massachusetts, where I passed my boyhood. It is well known in other towns in the neighborhood of Boston.

I LOVE to hear thine earnest voice,
　　Wherever thou art hid,
Thou testy little dogmatist,
　　Thou pretty Katydid !
Thou mindest me of gentlefolks, —
　　Old gentlefolks are they, —
Thou say'st an undisputed thing
　　In such a solemn way.

Thou art a female, Katydid !
　　I know it by the trill
That quivers through thy piercing notes,
　　So petulant and shrill ;
I think there is a knot of you
　　Beneath the hollow tree, —
A knot of spinster Katydids, —
　　Do Katydids drink tea ?

Oh, tell me where did Katy live,
　　And what did Katy do ?
And was she very fair and young,
　　And yet so wicked, too ?
Did Katy love a naughty man,
　　Or kiss more cheeks than one ?
I warrant Katy did no more
　　Than many a Kate has done.

Dear me ! I 'll tell you all about
　　My fuss with little Jane,
And Ann, with whom I used to walk
　　So often down the lane,
And all that tore their locks of black,

Or wet their eyes of blue, —
Pray tell me, sweetest Katydid,
　　What did poor Katy do ?

Ah no ! the living oak shall crash,
　　That stood for ages still,
The rock shall rend its mossy base
　　And thunder down the hill,
Before the little Katydid
　　Shall add one word, to tell
The mystic story of the maid
　　Whose name she knows so well.

Peace to the ever-murmuring race !
　　And when the latest one
Shall fold in death her feeble wings
　　Beneath the autumn sun,
Then shall she raise her fainting voice,
　　And lift her drooping lid,
And then the child of future years
　　Shall hear what Katy did.

THE DILEMMA

Now, by the blessed Paphian queen,
Who heaves the breast of sweet sixteen ;
By every name I cut on bark
Before my morning star grew dark ;
By Hymen's torch, by Cupid's dart,
By all that thrills the beating heart ;
The bright black eye, the melting blue, —
I cannot choose between the two.

I had a vision in my dreams ; —
I saw a row of twenty beams ;
From every beam a rope was hung,
In every rope a lover swung ;
I asked the hue of every eye
That bade each luckless lover die ;
Ten shadowy lips said, heavenly blue,
And ten accused the darker hue.

I asked a matron which she deemed
With fairest light of beauty beamed ;
She answered, some thought both were
　　fair, —
Give her blue eyes and golden hair.
I might have liked her judgment well,
But, as she spoke, she rung the bell,
And all her girls, nor small nor few,
Came marching in, — their eyes were blue.

I asked a maiden ; back she flung
The locks that round her forehead hung,

And turned her eye, a glorious one,
Bright as a diamond in the sun,
On me, until beneath its rays
I felt as if my hair would blaze ;
She liked all eyes but eyes of green ;
She looked at me ; what could she mean ?

Ah ! many lids Love lurks between,
Nor heeds the coloring of his screen ;
And when his random arrows fly,
The victim falls, but knows not why.
Gaze not upon his shield of jet,
The shaft upon the string is set ;
Look not beneath his azure veil,
Though every limb were cased in mail.

Well, both might make a martyr break
The chain that bound him to the stake ;
And both, with but a single ray,
Can melt our very hearts away ;
And both, when balanced, hardly seem
To stir the scales, or rock the beam ;
But that is dearest, all the while,
That wears for us the sweetest smile.

MY AUNT

My aunt ! my dear unmarried aunt !
    Long years have o'er her flown ;
Yet still she strains the aching clasp
    That binds her virgin zone ;
I know it hurts her, — though she looks
    As cheerful as she can ;
Her waist is ampler than her life,
    For life is but a span.

My aunt ! my poor deluded aunt !
    Her hair is almost gray ;
Why will she train that winter curl
    In such a spring-like way ?
How can she lay her glasses down,
    And say she reads as well,
When through a double convex lens
    She just makes out to spell ?

Her father — grandpapa ! forgive
    This erring lip its smiles —
Vowed she should make the finest girl
    Within a hundred miles ;
He sent her to a stylish school ;
    'T was in her thirteenth June ;
And with her, as the rules required,
    "Two towels and a spoon."

They braced my aunt against a board,
    To make her straight and tall ;
They laced her up, they starved her down,
    To make her light and small ;
They pinched her feet, they singed her
        hair,
    They screwed it up with pins ; —
Oh, never mortal suffered more
    In penance for her sins.

So, when my precious aunt was done,
    My grandsire brought her back ;
(By daylight, lest some rabid youth
    Might follow on the track ;)
"Ah !" said my grandsire, as he shook
    Some powder in his pan,
"What could this lovely creature do
    Against a desperate man !"

Alas ! nor chariot, nor barouche,
    Nor bandit cavalcade,
Tore from the trembling father's arms
    His all-accomplished maid.
For her how happy had it been !
    And Heaven had spared to me
To see one sad, ungathered rose
    On my ancestral tree.

REFLECTIONS OF A PROUD
PEDESTRIAN

I saw the curl of his waving lash,
    And the glance of his knowing eye,
And I knew that he thought he was cutting
        a dash,
    As his steed went thundering by.

And he may ride in the rattling gig,
    Or flourish the Stanhope gay,
And dream that he looks exceeding big
    To the people that walk in the way ;

But he shall think, when the night is still,
    On the stable-boy's gathering numbers,
And the ghost of many a veteran bill
    Shall hover around his slumbers ;

The ghastly dun shall worry his sleep,
    And constables cluster around him,
And he shall creep from the wood-hole
        deep
    Where their spectre eyes have found
        him !

Ay! gather your reins, and crack your
    thong,
  And bid your steed go faster;
He does not know, as he scrambles along,
  That he has a fool for his master;

And hurry away on your lonely ride,
  Nor deign from the mire to save me;
I will paddle it stoutly at your side
  With the tandem that nature gave me!

DAILY TRIALS

BY A SENSITIVE MAN

    OH, there are times
When all this fret and tumult that we hear
Do seem more stale than to the sexton's
    ear
    His own dull chimes.

    Ding dong! ding dong!
The world is in a simmer like a sea
Over a pent volcano, — woe is me
    All the day long!

    From crib to shroud!
Nurse o'er our cradles screameth lullaby,
And friends in boots tramp round us as we
    die,
    Snuffling aloud.

    At morning's call
The small-voiced pug-dog welcomes in the
    sun,
And flea-bit mongrels, wakening one by
    one,
    Give answer all.

    When evening dim
Draws round us, then the lonely cater-
    waul,
Tart solo, sour duet, and general squall, —
    These are our hymn.

    Women, with tongues
Like polar needles, ever on the jar;
Men, plugless word-spouts, whose deep
    fountains are
    Within their lungs.

    Children, with drums
Strapped round them by the fond paternal
    ass;

Peripatetics with a blade of grass
    Between their thumbs.

    Vagrants, whose arts
Have caged some devil in their mad
    machine,
Which grinding, squeaks, with husky
    groans between,
    Come out by starts.

    Cockneys that kill
Thin horses of a Sunday, — men, with
    clams,
Hoarse as young bisons roaring for their
    dams
    From hill to hill.

    Soldiers, with guns,
Making a nuisance of the blessed air,
Child-crying bellman, children in despair,
    Screeching for buns.

    Storms, thunders, waves!
Howl, crash, and bellow till ye get your
    fill;
Ye sometimes rest; men never can be still
    But in their graves.

EVENING

BY A TAILOR

    DAY hath put on his jacket, and around
His burning bosom buttoned it with stars.
Here will I lay me on the velvet grass,
That is like padding to earth's meagre ribs,
And hold communion with the things about
    me.
Ah me! how lovely is the golden braid
That binds the skirt of night's descending
    robe!
The thin leaves, quivering on their silken
    threads,
Do make a music like to rustling satin,
As the light breezes smooth their downy
    nap.

    Ha! what is this that rises to my touch,
So like a cushion?   Can it be a cabbage?
It is, it is that deeply injured flower,
Which boys do flout us with; — but yet I
    love thee,
Thou giant rose, wrapped in a green sur-
    tout.

Doubtless in Eden thou didst blush as
    bright
As these, thy puny brethren; and thy
    breath
Sweetened the fragrance of her spicy air;
But now thou seemest like a bankrupt beau,
Stripped of his gaudy hues and essences,
And growing portly in his sober garments.

Is that a swan that rides upon the water?
Oh no, it is that other gentle bird,
Which is the patron of our noble calling.
I well remember, in my early years,
When these young hands first closed upon
    a goose;
I have a scar upon my thimble finger,
Which chronicles the hour of young ambi-
    tion.
My father was a tailor, and his father,
And my sire's grandsire, all of them were
    tailors;
They had an ancient goose, — it was an
    heirloom
From some remoter tailor of our race.
It happened I did see it on a time
When none was near, and I did deal with it,
And it did burn me, — oh, most fearfully!

It is a joy to straighten out one's limbs,
And leap elastic from the level counter,
Leaving the petty grievances of earth,
The breaking thread, the din of clashing
    shears,
And all the needles that do wound the
    spirit,
For such a pensive hour of soothing silence.
Kind Nature, shuffling in her loose undress,
Lays bare her shady bosom; — I can feel
With all around me; — I can hail the
    flowers
That sprig earth's mantle, — and yon quiet
    bird,
That rides the stream, is to me as a brother.
The vulgar know not all the hidden pockets,
Where Nature stows away her loveliness.
But this unnatural posture of the legs
Cramps my extended calves, and I must go
Where I can coil them in their wonted fash-
    ion.

THE DORCHESTER GIANT

The "pudding-stone" is a remarkable con-
glomerate found very abundantly in the towns
mentioned, all of which are in the neighbor-
hood of Boston. We used in those primitive
days to ask friends to *ride* with us when we
meant to take them to *drive* with us.
[It is interesting to see how the same sub-
ject presented itself to the poet in different
moods. There is a passage in *The Professor at
the Breakfast-Table* which begins, "I wonder
whether the boys who live in Roxbury and
Dorchester are ever moved to tears or filled
with silent awe as they look upon the rocks and
fragments of 'pudding-stone' abounding in
those localities." Then follows a half page of
eloquent speculation on the pudding-stone.]

THERE was a giant in time of old,
    A mighty one was he;
He had a wife, but she was a scold,
So he kept her shut in his mammoth fold;
    And he had children three.

It happened to be an election day,
    And the giants were choosing a king;
The people were not democrats then,
They did not talk of the rights of men,
    And all that sort of thing.

Then the giant took his children three,
    And fastened them in the pen;
The children roared; quoth the giant, "Be
    still!"
And Dorchester Heights and Milton Hill
    Rolled back the sound again.

Then he brought them a pudding stuffed
    with plums,
    As big as the State-House dome;
Quoth he, "There's something for you to
    eat;
So stop your mouths with your 'lection
    treat,
    And wait till your dad comes home."

So the giant pulled him a chestnut stout,
    And whittled the boughs away;
The boys and their mother set up a shout,
Said he, "You're in, and you can't get out,
    Bellow as loud as you may."

Off he went, and he growled a tune
    As he strode the fields along;
'T is said a buffalo fainted away,
And fell as cold as a lump of clay,
    When he heard the giant's song.

But whether the story's true or not,
    It is n't for me to show;

There 's many a thing that 's twice as queer
In somebody's lectures that we hear,
　　And those are true, you know.

.　　.　　.　　.　　.　　.　　.　　.

What are those lone ones doing now,
　　The wife and the children sad ?
Oh, they are in a terrible rout,
Screaming, and throwing their pudding
　　　　about,
　　Acting as they were mad.

They flung it over to Roxbury hills,
　　They flung it over the plain,
And all over Milton and Dorchester too
Great lumps of pudding the giants threw ;
　　They tumbled as thick as rain.

.　　.　　.　　.　　.　　.　　.　　.

Giant and mammoth have passed away,
　　For ages have floated by ;
The suet is hard as a marrow-bone,
And every plum is turned to a stone,
　　But there the puddings lie.

And if, some pleasant afternoon,
　　You 'll ask me out to ride,
The whole of the story I will tell,
And you shall see where the puddings fell,
　　And pay for the punch beside.

TO THE PORTRAIT OF "A LADY"

IN THE ATHENÆUM GALLERY

WELL, Miss, I wonder where you live,
　　I wonder what 's your name,
I wonder how you came to be
　　In such a stylish frame ;
Perhaps you were a favorite child,
　　Perhaps an only one ;
Perhaps your friends were not aware
　　You had your portrait done !

Yet you must be a harmless soul ;
　　I cannot think that Sin

Would care to throw his loaded dice,
　　With such a stake to win ;
I cannot think you would provoke
　　The poet's wicked pen,
Or make young women bite their lips,
　　Or ruin fine young men.

Pray, did you ever hear, my love,
　　Of boys that go about,
Who, for a very trifling sum,
　　Will snip one's picture out ?
I 'm not averse to red and white,
　　But all things have their place,
I think a profile cut in black
　　Would suit your style of face !

I love sweet features ; I will own
　　That I should like myself
To see my portrait on a wall,
　　Or bust upon a shelf ;
But nature sometimes makes one up
　　Of such sad odds and ends,
It really might be quite as well
　　Hushed up among one's friends !

THE COMET

THE Comet !　He is on his way,
　　And singing as he flies ;
The whizzing planets shrink before
　　The spectre of the skies ;
Ah ! well may regal orbs burn blue,
　　And satellites turn pale,
Ten million cubic miles of head,
　　Ten billion leagues of tail !

On, on by whistling spheres of light
　　He flashes and he flames ;
He turns not to the left nor right,
　　He asks them not their names ;
One spurn from his demoniac heel, —
　　Away, away they fly,
Where darkness might be bottled up
　　And sold for " Tyrian dye."

And what would happen to the land,
　　And how would look the sea,
If in the bearded devil's path
　　Our earth should chance to be ?
Full hot and high the sea would boil,
　　Full red the forests gleam ;
Methought I saw and heard it all
　　In a dyspeptic dream !

I saw a tutor take his tube
    The Comet's course to spy ;
I heard a scream, — the gathered rays
    Had stewed the tutor's eye ;
I saw a fort, — the soldiers all
    Were armed with goggles green ;
Pop cracked the guns ! whiz flew the
    balls !
    Bang went the magazine !

I saw a poet dip a scroll
    Each moment in a tub,
I read upon the warping back,
    "The Dream of Beelzebub ;"
He could not see his verses burn,
    Although his brain was fried,
And ever and anon he bent
    To wet them as they dried.

I saw the scalding pitch roll down
    The crackling, sweating pines,
And streams of smoke, like water-spouts,
    Burst through the rumbling mines ;
I asked the firemen why they made
    Such noise about the town ;
They answered not, — but all the while
    The brakes went up and down.

I saw a roasting pullet sit
    Upon a baking egg ;
I saw a cripple scorch his hand
    Extinguishing his leg ;
I saw nine geese upon the wing
    Towards the frozen pole,
And every mother's gosling fell
    Crisped to a crackling coal.

I saw the ox that browsed the grass
    Writhe in the blistering rays,
The herbage in his shrinking jaws
    Was all a fiery blaze ;
I saw huge fishes, boiled to rags,
    Bob through the bubbling brine ;
And thoughts of supper crossed my soul ;
    I had been rash at mine.

Strange sights ! strange sounds ! O fearful
    dream !
    Its memory haunts me still,
The steaming sea, the crimson glare,
    That wreathed each wooded hill ;
Stranger ! if through thy reeling brain
    Such midnight visions sweep,
Spare, spare, oh,.spare thine evening meal,
    And sweet shall be thy sleep !

THE MUSIC-GRINDERS

THERE are three ways in which men take
    One's money from his purse,
And very hard it is to tell
    Which of the three is worse ;
But all of them are bad enough
    To make a body curse.

You 're riding out some pleasant day,
    And counting up your gains ;
A fellow jumps from out a bush,
    And takes your horse's reins,
Another hints some words about
    A bullet in your brains.

It 's hard to meet such pressing friends
    In such a lonely spot ;
It 's very hard to lose your cash,
    But harder to be shot ;
And so you take your wallet out,
    Though you would rather not.

Perhaps you 're going out to dine, —
    Some odious creature begs
You 'll hear about the cannon-ball
    That carried off his pegs,
And says it is a dreadful thing
    For men to lose their legs.

He tells you of his starving wife,
    His children to be fed,
Poor little, lovely innocents,
    All clamorous for bread, —
And so you kindly help to put
    A bachelor to bed.

You 're sitting on your window-seat,
    Beneath a cloudless moon ;
You hear a sound, that seems to wear
    The semblance of a tune,
As if a broken fife should strive
    To drown a cracked bassoon.

And nearer, nearer still, the tide
    Of music seems to come,
There 's something like a human voice,
    And something like a drum ;
You sit in speechless agony,
    Until your ear is numb.

Poor " home, sweet home " should seem to
    be
    A very dismal place ;

Your "auld acquaintance" all at once
  Is altered in the face ;
Their discords sting through Burns and
    Moore,
  Like hedgehogs dressed in lace.

You think they are crusaders, sent
  From some infernal clime,
To pluck the eyes of Sentiment,
  And dock the tail of Rhyme,
To crack the voice of Melody,
  And break the legs of Time.

But hark ! the air again is still,
  The music all is ground,
And silence, like a poultice, comes
  To heal the blows of sound ;
It cannot be, — it is, — it is, —
  A hat is going round !

No ! Pay the dentist when he leaves
  A fracture in your jaw,
And pay the owner of the bear
  That stunned you with his paw,
And buy the lobster that has had
  Your knuckles in his claw ;

But if you are a portly man,
  Put on your fiercest frown,
And talk about a constable
  To turn them out of town ;
Then close your sentence with an oath,
  And shut the window down !

And if you are a slender man,
  Not big enough for that,
Or, if you cannot make a speech,
  Because you are a flat,
Go very quietly and drop
  A button in the hat !

THE TREADMILL SONG

THE stars are rolling in the sky,
  The earth rolls on below,
And we can feel the rattling wheel
  Revolving as we go.
Then tread away, my gallant boys,
  And make the axle fly ;
Why should not wheels go round about,
  Like planets in the sky ?

Wake up, wake up, my duck-legged man,
  And stir your solid pegs !

Arouse, arouse, my gawky friend,
  And shake your spider legs ;
What though you 're awkward at the
    trade,
  There 's time enough to learn, —
So lean upon the rail, my lad,
  And take another turn.

They 've built us up a noble wall,
  To keep the vulgar out ;
We 've nothing in the world to do
  But just to walk about ;
So faster, now, you middle men,
  And try to beat the ends, —
It 's pleasant work to ramble round
  Among one's honest friends.

Here, tread upon the long man's toes,
  He sha'n't be lazy here, —
And punch the little fellow's ribs,
  And tweak that lubber's ear, —
He 's lost them both, — don't pull his
    hair,
  Because he wears a scratch,
But poke him in the further eye,
  That is n't in the patch.

Hark ! fellows, there 's the supper-bell,
  And so our work is done ;
It 's pretty sport, — suppose we take
  A round or two for fun !
If ever they should turn me out,
  When I have better grown,
Now hang me, but I mean to have
  A treadmill of my own !

THE SEPTEMBER GALE

This tremendous hurricane occurred on the
23d of September, 1815. I remember it well,
being then seven years old. A full account of
it was published, I think, in the records of the
American Academy of Arts and Sciences.
Some of my recollections are given in *The
Seasons*, an article to be found in a book of
mine entitled *Pages from an Old Volume of
Life.*

I 'M not a chicken ; I have seen
  Full many a chill September,
And though I was a youngster then,
  That gale I well remember ;
The day before, my kite-string snapped,
  And I, my kite pursuing,
The wind whisked off my palm-leaf hat ;
  For me two storms were brewing !

It came as quarrels sometimes do,
  When married folks get clashing ;
There was a heavy sigh or two,
  Before the fire was flashing, —
A little stir among the clouds,
  Before they rent asunder, —
A little rocking of the trees,
  And then came on the thunder.

Lord ! how the ponds and rivers boiled !
  They seemed like bursting craters !
And oaks lay scattered on the ground
  As if they were p'taters ;
And all above was in a howl,
  And all below a clatter, —
The earth was like a frying-pan,
  Or some such hissing matter.

It chanced to be our washing-day,
  And all our things were drying ;
The storm came roaring through the
    lines,
  And set them all a flying ;
I saw the shirts and petticoats
  Go riding off like witches ;
I lost, ah ! bitterly I wept, —
  I lost my Sunday breeches !

I saw them straddling through the air,
  Alas ! too late to win them ;
I saw them chase the clouds, as if
  The devil had been in them ;
They were my darlings and my pride,
  My boyhood's only riches, —
"Farewell, farewell," I faintly cried, —
  "My breeches ! O my breeches ! "

That night I saw them in my dreams,
  How changed from what I knew
    them !
The dews had steeped their faded threads,
  The winds had whistled through them !
I saw the wide and ghastly rents
  Where demon claws had torn them ;
A hole was in their amplest part,
  As if an imp had worn them.

I have had many happy years,
  And tailors kind and clever,
But those young pantaloons have gone
  Forever and forever !
And not till fate has cut the last
  Of all my earthly stitches,
This aching heart shall cease to mourn
  My loved, my long-lost breeches !

THE HEIGHT OF THE RIDICU-LOUS

I WROTE some lines once on a time
  In wondrous merry mood,
And thought, as usual, men would say
  They were exceeding good.

They were so queer, so very queer,
  I laughed as I would die ;
Albeit, in the general way,
  A sober man am I.

I called my servant, and he came ;
  How kind it was of him
To mind a slender man like me,
  He of the mighty limb.

" These to the printer," I exclaimed,
  And, in my humorous way,
I added, (as a trifling jest,)
  " There 'll be the devil to pay."

He took the paper, and I watched,
  And saw him peep within ;
At the first line he read, his face
  Was all upon the grin.

He read the next ; the grin grew broad,
  And shot from ear to ear ;
He read the third ; a chuckling noise
  I now began to hear.

The fourth ; he broke into a roar ;
  The fifth ; his waistband split ;
The sixth ; he burst five buttons off,
  And tumbled in a fit.

Ten days and nights, with sleepless eye,
  I watched that wretched man,
And since, I never dare to write
  As funny as I can.

THE LAST READER

I SOMETIMES sit beneath a tree
  And read my own sweet songs ;
Though naught they may to others be,
  Each humble line prolongs
A tone that might have passed away,
But for that scarce remembered lay.

I keep them like a lock or leaf
  That some dear girl has given ;
Frail record of an hour, as brief
  As sunset clouds in heaven.

But spreading purple twilight still
High over memory's shadowed hill.

They lie upon my pathway bleak,
    Those flowers that once ran wild,
As on a father's careworn cheek
    The ringlets of his child ;
The golden mingling with the gray,
And stealing half its snows away.

What care I though the dust is spread
    Around these yellow leaves,
Or o'er them his sarcastic thread
    Oblivion's insect weaves ?
Though weeds are tangled on the stream,
It still reflects my morning's beam.

And therefore love I such as smile
    On these neglected songs,
Nor deem that flattery's needless wile
    My opening bosom wrongs ;
For who would trample, at my side,
A few pale buds, my garden's pride ?

It may be that my scanty ore
    Long years have washed away,
And where were golden sands before
    Is naught but common clay ;
Still something sparkles in the sun
For memory to look back upon.

And when my name no more is heard,
    My lyre no more is known,
Still let me, like a winter's bird,
    In silence and alone,
Fold over them the weary wing
Once flashing through the dews of spring.

Yes, let my fancy fondly wrap
    My youth in its decline,
And riot in the rosy lap
    Of thoughts that once were mine,
And give the worm my little store
When the last reader reads no more !

POETRY

A METRICAL ESSAY, READ BEFORE THE
PHI BETA KAPPA SOCIETY, HARVARD
UNIVERSITY, AUGUST, 1836

TO CHARLES WENTWORTH UPHAM, THE FOL-
LOWING METRICAL ESSAY IS AFFECTIONATELY
INSCRIBED.

This Academic Poem presents the simple
and partial views of a young person trained
after the schools of classical English verse as
represented by Pope, Goldsmith, and Camp-
bell, with whose lines his memory was early
stocked. It will be observed that it deals
chiefly with the constructive side of the poet's
function. That which makes him a poet is
not the power of writing melodious rhymes, it
is not the possession of ordinary human sensi-
bilities nor even of both these qualities in con-
nection with each other. I should rather say,
if I were now called upon to define it, it is the
power of transfiguring the experiences and
shows of life into an aspect which comes from
his imagination and kindles that of others.
Emotion is its stimulus and language furnishes
its expression ; but these are not all, as some
might infer was the doctrine of the poem
before the reader.

A common mistake made by young persons
who suppose themselves to have the poetical
gift is that their own spiritual exaltation finds
a true expression in the conventional phrases
which are borrowed from the voices of the
singers whose inspiration they think they
share.

Looking at this poem as an expression of
some aspects of the *ars poetica*, with some
passages which I can read even at this mature
period of life without blushing for them, it
may stand as the most serious representation
of my early efforts. Intended as it was for
public delivery, many of its paragraphs may
betray the fact by their somewhat rhetorical
and sonorous character.

SCENES of my youth ! awake its slumber-
    ing fire !
Ye winds of Memory, sweep the silent lyre !
Ray of the past, if yet thou canst appear,
Break through the clouds of Fancy's wan-
    ing year ;
Chase from her breast the thin autumnal
    snow,
If leaf or blossom still is fresh below !

Long have I wandered ; the returning
    tide
Brought back an exile to his cradle's side ;
And as my bark her time-worn flag un-
    rolled,
To greet the land-breeze with its faded
    fold,
So, in remembrance of my boyhood's time,
I lift these ensigns of neglected rhyme ;
Oh, more than blest, that, all my wander-
    ings through,
My anchor falls where first my pennons
    flew !

The morning light, which rains its
    quivering beams
Wide o'er the plains, the summits, and the
    streams,
In one broad blaze expands its golden glow
On all that answers to its glance below ;
Yet, changed on earth, each far reflected
    ray
Braids with fresh hues the shining brow of
    day ;
Now, clothed in blushes by the painted
    flowers,
Tracks on their cheeks the rosy-fingered
    hours ;
Now, lost in shades, whose dark entangled
    leaves
Drip at the noontide from their pendent
    eaves,
Fades into gloom, or gleams in light again
From every dew-drop on the jewelled plain.

We, like the leaf, the summit, or the
    wave,
Reflect the light our common nature gave,
But every sunbeam, falling from her throne,
Wears on our hearts some coloring of our
    own :
Chilled in the slave, and burning in the free,
Like the sealed cavern by the sparkling
    sea ;
Lost, like the lightning in the sullen clod,
Or shedding radiance, like the smiles of
    God ;
Pure, pale in Virtue, as the star above,
Or quivering roseate on the leaves of Love ;
Glaring like noontide, where it glows upon
Ambition's sands, — the desert in the
    sun, —
Or soft suffusing o'er the varied scene
Life's common coloring, — intellectual
    green.

Thus Heaven, repeating its material
    plan,
Arched over all the rainbow mind of man ;
But he who, blind to universal laws,
Sees but effects, unconscious of their
    cause, —
Believes each image in itself is bright,
Not robed in drapery of reflected light, —
Is like the rustic who, amidst his toil,
Has found some crystal in his meagre soil,
And, lost in rapture, thinks for him alone
Earth worked her wonders on the spark-
    ling stone,

Nor dreams that Nature, with as nice a line,
Carved countless angles through the bound-
    less mine.

Thus err the many, who, entranced to find
Unwonted lustre in some clearer mind,
Believe that Genius sets the laws at naught
Which chain the pinions of our wildest
    thought ;
Untaught to measure, with the eye of art,
The wandering fancy or the wayward heart ;
Who match the little only with the less,
And gaze in rapture at its slight excess,
Proud of a pebble, as the brightest gem
Whose light might crown an emperor's
    diadem.

And, most of all, the pure ethereal fire
Which seems to radiate from the poet's lyre
Is to the world a mystery and a charm,
An Ægis wielded on a mortal's arm,
While Reason turns her dazzled eye away,
And bows her sceptre to her subject's sway ;
And thus the poet, clothed with godlike
    state,
Usurped his Maker's title — to create ;
He, whose thoughts differing not in shape,
    but dress,
What others feel more fitly can express,
Sits like the maniac on his fancied throne,
Peeps through the bars, and calls the world
    his own.

There breathes no being but has some
    pretence
To that fine instinct called poetic sense :
The rudest savage, roaming through the
    wild ;
The simplest rustic, bending o'er his child ;
The infant, listening to the warbling bird ;
The mother, smiling at its half-formed
    word ;
The boy uncaged, who tracks the fields
    at large ;
The girl, turned matron to her babe-like
    charge ;
The freeman, casting with unpurchased
    hand
The vote that shakes the turret of the land ;
The slave, who, slumbering on his rusted
    chain,
Dreams of the palm-trees on his burning
    plain ;
The hot-cheeked reveller, tossing down the
    wine,

To join the chorus pealing "Auld lang
   syne;"
The gentle maid, whose azure eye grows
   dim,
While Heaven is listening to her evening
   hymn;
The jewelled beauty, when her steps draw
   near
The circling dance and dazzling chande-
   lier;
E'en trembling age, when Spring's renew-
   ing air
Waves the thin ringlets of his silvered
   hair;—
All, all are glowing with the inward flame,
Whose wider halo wreathes the poet's
   name,
While, unembalmed, the silent dreamer
   dies,
His memory passing with his smiles and
   sighs!

If glorious visions, born for all mankind,
The bright auroras of our twilight mind;
If fancies, varying as the shapes that lie
Stained on the windows of the sunset sky;
If hopes, that beckon with delusive gleams,
Till the eye dances in the void of dreams;
If passions, following with the winds that
   urge
Earth's wildest wanderer to her farthest
   verge;—
If these on all some transient hours bestow
Of rapture tingling with its hectic glow,
Then all are poets; and if earth had rolled
Her myriad centuries, and her doom were
   told,
Each moaning billow of her shoreless wave
Would wail its requiem o'er a poet's grave!

If to embody in a breathing word
Tones that the spirit trembled when it
   heard;
To fix the image all unveiled and warm,
And carve in language its ethereal form,
So pure, so perfect, that the lines express
No meagre shrinking, no unlaced excess;
To feel that art, in living truth, has taught
Ourselves, reflected in the sculptured
   thought;—
If this alone bestow the right to claim
The deathless garland and the sacred name,
Then none are poets save the saints on high,
Whose harps can murmur all that words
   deny!

But though to none is granted to reveal
In perfect semblance all that each may feel,
As withered flowers recall forgotten love,
So, warmed to life, our faded passions move
In every line, where kindling fancy throws
The gleam of pleasures or the shade of
   woes.

When, schooled by time, the stately queen
   of art
Had smoothed the pathways leading to the
   heart,
Assumed her measured tread, her solemn
   tone,
And round her courts the clouds of fable
   thrown,
The wreaths of heaven descended on her
   shrine,
And wondering earth proclaimed the Muse
   divine.
Yet if her votaries had but dared profane
The mystic symbols of her sacred reign,
How had they smiled beneath the veil to
   find
What slender threads can chain the mighty
   mind!

Poets, like painters, their machinery
   claim,
And verse bestows the varnish and the
   frame;
Our grating English, whose Teutonic jar
Shakes the racked axle of Art's rattling
   car,
Fits like mosaic in the lines that gird
Fast in its place each many-angled word;
From Saxon lips Anacreon's numbers
   glide,
As once they melted on the Teian tide,
And, fresh transfused, the Iliad thrills
   again
From Albion's cliffs as o'er Achaia's plain!
The proud heroic, with its pulse-like beat,
Rings like the cymbals clashing as they
   meet;
The sweet Spenserian, gathering as it
   flows,
Sweeps gently onward to its dying close,
Where waves on waves in long succession
   pour,
Till the ninth billow melts along the shore;
The lonely spirit of the mournful lay,
Which lives immortal as the verse of Gray,
In sable plumage slowly drifts along,
On eagle pinion, through the air of song;

The glittering lyric bounds elastic by,
With flashing ringlets and exulting eye,
While every image, in her airy whirl,
Gleams like a diamond on a dancing girl!

Born with mankind, with man's ex-
    panded range
And varying fates the poet's numbers
    change;
Thus in his history may we hope to find
Some clearer epochs of the poet's mind,
As from the cradle of its birth we trace,
Slow wandering forth, the patriarchal
    race.

I

When the green earth, beneath the
    zephyr's wing,
Wears on her breast the varnished buds of
    Spring;
When the loosed current, as its folds
    uncoil,
Slides in the channels of the mellowed soil;
When the young hyacinth returns to seek
The air and sunshine with her emerald
    beak;
When the light snowdrops, starting from
    their cells,
Hang each pagoda with its silver bells;
When the frail willow twines her trailing
    bow
With pallid leaves that sweep the soil
    below;
When the broad elm, sole empress of the
    plain,
Whose circling shadow speaks a century's
    reign,
Wreathes in the clouds her regal dia-
    dem, —
A forest waving on a single stem; —
Then mark the poet; though to him un-
    known
The quaint-mouthed titles, such as scholars
    own,
See how his eye in ecstasy pursues
The steps of Nature tracked in radiant
    hues;
Nay, in thyself, whate'er may be thy fate,
Pallid with toil or surfeited with state,
Mark how thy fancies, with the vernal
    rose,
Awake, all sweetness, from their long re-
    pose;
Then turn to ponder o'er the classic page,
Traced with the idyls of a greener age,

And learn the instinct which arose to
    warm
Art's earliest essay and her simplest form.

To themes like these her narrow path
    confined
The first-born impulse moving in the
    mind;
In vales unshaken by the trumpet's sound,
Where peaceful Labor tills his fertile
    ground,
The silent changes of the rolling years,
Marked on the soil or dialled on the
    spheres,
The crested forests and the colored
    flowers,
The dewy grottos and the blushing
    bowers, —
These, and their guardians, who, with
    liquid names,
Strephons and Chloes, melt in mutual
    flames,
Woo the young Muses from their mountain
    shade,
To make Arcadias in the lonely glade.

Nor think they visit only with their
    smiles
The fabled valleys and Elysian isles;
He who is wearied of his village plain
May roam the Edens of the world in vain.
'T is not the star-crowned cliff, the cata-
    ract's flow,
The softer foliage or the greener glow,
The lake of sapphire or the spar-hung
    cave,
The brighter sunset or the broader wave,
Can warm his heart whom every wind has
    blown
To every shore, forgetful of his own.

Home of our childhood! how affection
    clings
And hovers round thee with her seraph
    wings!
Dearer thy hills, though clad in autumn
    brown,
Than fairest summits which the cedars
    crown!
Sweeter the fragrance of thy summer
    breeze
Than all Arabia breathes along the seas!
The stranger's gale wafts home the exile's
    sigh,
For the heart's temple is its own blue sky!

Oh happiest they, whose early love un-
changed,
Hopes undissolved, and friendship unes-
tranged,
Tired of their wanderings, still can deign
to see
Love, hopes, and friendship, centring all in
thee!

And thou, my village! as again I tread
Amidst thy living and above thy dead;
Though some fair playmates guard with
chaster fears
Their cheeks, grown holy with the lapse of
years;
Though with the dust some reverend locks
may blend,
Where life's last mile-stone marks the
journey's end;
On every bud the changing year recalls,
The brightening glance of morning mem-
ory falls,
Still following onward as the months un-
close
The balmy lilac or the bridal rose;
And still shall follow, till they sink once
more
Beneath the snow-drifts of the frozen
shore,
As when my bark, long tossing in the gale,
Furled in her port her tempest-rended sail!

What shall I give thee? Can a simple
lay,
Flung on thy bosom like a girl's bouquet,
Do more than deck thee for an idle hour,
Then fall unheeded, fading like the flower?
Yet, when I trod, with footsteps wild and
free,
The crackling leaves beneath yon linden-
tree,
Panting from play or dripping from the
stream,
How bright the visions of my boyish
dream!
Or, modest Charles, along thy broken
edge,
Black with soft ooze and fringed with
arrowy sedge,
As once I wandered in the morning sun,
With reeking sandal and superfluous gun,
How oft, as Fancy whispered in the gale,
Thou wast the Avon of her flattering tale!
Ye hills, whose foliage, fretted on the
skies,

Prints shadowy arches on their evening dyes,
How should my song with holiest charm in-
vest
Each dark ravine and forest-lifting crest!
How clothe in beauty each familiar scene,
Till all was classic on my native green!

As the drained fountain, filled with au-
tumn leaves,
The field swept naked of its garnered
sheaves,
So wastes at noon the promise of our dawn,
The springs all choking, and the harvest
gone.

Yet hear the lay of one whose natal star
Still seemed the brightest when it shone
afar;
Whose cheek, grown pallid with ungracious
toil,
Glows in the welcome of his parent soil;
And ask no garlands sought beyond the tide,
But take the leaflets gathered at your side.

II

But times were changed; the torch of
terror came,
To light the summits with the beacon's
flame;
The streams ran crimson, the tall mountain
pines
Rose a new forest o'er embattled lines;
The bloodless sickle lent the warrior's steel,
The harvest bowed beneath his chariot
wheel;
Where late the wood-dove sheltered her
repose
The raven waited for the conflict's close;
The cuirassed sentry walked his sleepless
round
Where Daphne smiled or Amaryllis
frowned;
Where timid minstrels sung their blushing
charms,
Some wild Tyrtæus called aloud, "To
arms!"

When Glory wakes, when fiery spirits
leap,
Roused by her accents from their tranquil
sleep,
The ray that flashes from the soldier's crest
Lights, as it glances, in the poet's breast;—
Not in pale dreamers, whose fantastic lay

Toys with smooth trifles like a child at play,
But men, who act the passions they inspire,
Who wave the sabre as they sweep the lyre!

Ye mild enthusiasts, whose pacific frowns
Are lost like dew-drops caught in burning
    towns,
Pluck as ye will the radiant plumes of fame,
Break Cæsar's bust to make yourselves a
    name;
But if your country bares the avenger's
    blade
For wrongs unpunished or for debts unpaid,
When the roused nation bids her armies
    form,
And screams her eagle through the gather-
    ing storm,
When from your ports the bannered frigate
    rides,
Her black bows scowling to the crested tides,
Your hour has past; in vain your feeble
    cry
As the babe's wailing to the thundering sky!

Scourge of mankind! with all the dread
    array
That wraps in wrath thy desolating way,
As the wild tempest wakes the slumbering
    sea,
Thou only teachest all that man can be.
Alike thy tocsin has the power to charm
The toil-knit sinews of the rustic's arm,
Or swell the pulses in the poet's veins,
And bid the nations tremble at his strains.

The city slept beneath the moonbeam's
    glance,
Her white walls gleaming through the vines
    of France,
And all was hushed, save where the foot-
    steps fell,
On some high tower, of midnight sentinel.
But one still watched; no self-encircled
    woes
Chased from his lids the angel of repose;
He watched, he wept, for thoughts of bitter
    years
Bowed his dark lashes, wet with burning
    tears:
His country's sufferings and her children's
    shame
Streamed o'er his memory like a forest's
    flame;
Each treasured insult, each remembered
    wrong,

Rolled through his heart and kindled into
    song.
His taper faded; and the morning gales
Swept through the world the war-song of
    Marseilles!

Now, while around the smiles of Peace
    expand,
And Plenty's wreaths festoon the laughing
    land;
While France ships outward her reluctant
    ore,
And half our navy basks upon the shore;
From ruder themes our meek-eyed Muses
    turn
To crown with roses their enamelled urn.

If e'er again return those awful days
Whose clouds were crimsoned with the
    beacon's blaze,
Whose grass was trampled by the soldier's
    heel,
Whose tides were reddened round the rush-
    ing keel,
God grant some lyre may wake a nobler
    strain
To rend the silence of our tented plain!
When Gallia's flag its triple fold displays,
Her marshalled legions peal the Marseil-
    laise;
When round the German close the war-
    clouds dim,
Far through their shadows floats his battle-
    hymn;
When, crowned with joy, the camps of Eng-
    land ring,
A thousand voices shout, "God save the
    King!"
When victory follows with our eagle's
    glance,
Our nation's anthem pipes a country dance!

Some prouder Muse, when comes the
    hour at last,
May shake our hillsides with her bugle-
    blast;
Not ours the task; but since the lyric dress
Relieves the statelier with its sprightliness,
Hear an old song, which some, perchance,
    have seen
In stale gazette or cobwebbed magazine.
There was an hour when patriots dared pro-
    fane
The mast that Britain strove to bow in vain;
And one, who listened to the tale of shame,

Whose heart still answered to that sacred
    name,
Whose eye still followed o'er his country's
    tides
Thy glorious flag, our brave Old Ironsides!
From yon lone attic, on a smiling morn,
Thus mocked the spoilers with his school-
    boy scorn.

III

When florid Peace resumed her golden
    reign,
And arts revived, and valleys bloomed
    again,
While War still panted on his broken
    blade,
Once more the Muse her heavenly wing
    essayed.
Rude was the song : some ballad, stern and
    wild,
Lulled the light slumbers of the soldier's
    child;
Or young romancer, with his threatening
    glance
And fearful fables of his bloodless lance,
Scared the soft fancy of the clinging girls,
Whose snowy fingers smoothed his raven
    curls.
But when long years the stately form had
    bent,
And faithless Memory her illusions lent,
So vast the outlines of Tradition grew
That History wondered at the shapes she
    drew,
And veiled at length their too ambitious
    hues
Beneath the pinions of the Epic Muse.

Far swept her wing; for stormier days
    had brought
With darker passions deeper tides of
    thought.
The camp's harsh tumult and the conflict's
    glow,
The thrill of triumph and the gasp of woe,
The tender parting and the glad return,
The festal banquet and the funeral urn,
And all the drama which at once uprears
Its spectral shadows through the clash of
    spears,
From camp and field to echoing verse
    transferred,
Swelled the proud song that listening
    nations heard.

Why floats the amaranth in eternal
    bloom
O'er Ilium's turrets and Achilles' tomb?
Why lingers fancy where the sunbeams
    smile
On Circe's gardens and Calypso's isle?
Why follows memory to the gate of Troy
Her plumed defender and his trembling
    boy ?
Lo! the blind dreamer, kneeling on the
    sand
To trace these records with his doubtful
    hand;
In fabled tones his own emotion flows,
And other lips repeat his silent woes;
In Hector's infant see the babes that shun
Those deathlike eyes, unconscious of the
    sun,
Or in his hero hear himself implore,
"Give me to see, and Ajax asks no more!"

Thus live undying through the lapse of
    time
The solemn legends of the warrior's clime;
Like Egypt's pyramid or Pæstum's fane,
They stand the heralds of the voiceless
    plain.
Yet not like them, for Time, by slow de-
    grees,
Saps the gray stone and wears the em-
    broidered frieze,
And Isis sleeps beneath her subject Nile,
And crumbled Neptune strews his Dorian
    pile;
But Art's fair fabric, strengthening as it
    rears
Its laurelled columns through the mist of
    years,
As the blue arches of the bending skies
Still gird the torrent, following as it flies,
Spreads, with the surges bearing on man-
    kind,
Its starred pavilion o'er the tides of mind!

In vain the patriot asks some lofty lay
To dress in state our wars of yesterday.
The classic days, those mothers of ro-
    mance,
That roused a nation for a woman's glance;
The age of mystery, with its hoarded
    power,
That girt the tyrant in his storied tower,
Have passed and faded like a dream of
    youth,
And riper eras ask for history's truth.

On other shores, above their mouldering
  towns,
In sullen pomp the tall cathedral frowns,
Pride in its aisles and paupers at the door,
Which feeds the beggars whom it fleeced
  of yore.
Simple and frail, our lowly temples throw
Their slender shadows on the paths below;
Scarce steal the winds, that sweep his
  woodland tracks,
The larch's perfume from the settler's axe,
Ere, like a vision of the morning air,
His slight-framed steeple marks the house
  of prayer;
Its planks all reeking and its paint un-
  dried,
Its rafters sprouting on the shady side,
It sheds the raindrops from its shingled
  eaves
Ere its green brothers once have changed
  their leaves.

Yet Faith's pure hymn, beneath its
  shelter rude,
Breathes out as sweetly to the tangled
  wood
As where the rays through pictured glories
  pour
On marble shaft and tessellated floor; —
Heaven asks no surplice round the heart
  that feels,
And all is holy where devotion kneels.

Thus on the soil the patriot's knee
  should bend
Which holds the dust once living to de-
  fend;
Where'er the hireling shrinks before the
  free,
Each pass becomes " a new Thermopylæ! "
Where'er the battles of the brave are won,
There every mountain "looks on Mara-
  thon! "

Our fathers live; they guard in glory
  still
The grass-grown bastions of the fortressed
  hill;
Still ring the echoes of the trampled
  gorge,
With *God and Freedom! England and
  Saint George!*
The royal cipher on the captured gun
Mocks the sharp night-dews and the blis-
  tering sun;

The red-cross banner shades its captor's
  bust,
Its folds still loaded with the conflict's
  dust;
The drum, suspended by its tattered
  marge,
Once rolled and rattled to the Hessian's
  charge;
The stars have floated from Britannia's
  mast,
The redcoat's trumpets blown the rebel's
  blast.

Point to the summits where the brave
  have bled,
Where every village claims its glorious
  dead;
Say, when their bosoms met the bayonet's
  shock,
Their only corselet was the rustic frock;
Say, when they mustered to the gathering
  horn,
The titled chieftain curled his lip in scorn,
Yet, when their leader bade his lines ad-
  vance,
No musket wavered in the lion's glance;
Say, when they fainted in the forced
  retreat,
They tracked the snowdrifts with their
  bleeding feet,
Yet still their banners, tossing in the blast,
Bore *Ever Ready*, faithful to the last,
Through storm and battle, till they waved
  again
On Yorktown's hills and Saratoga's plain !

Then, if so fierce the insatiate patriot's
  flame,
Truth looks too pale and history seems too
  tame,
Bid him await some new Columbiad's page,
To gild the tablets of an iron age,
And save his tears, which yet may fall upon
Some fabled field, some fancied Washington!

IV

But once again, from their Æolian cave,
The winds of Genius wandered on the wave.
Tired of the scenes the timid pencil drew,
Sick of the notes the sounding clarion blew,
Sated with heroes who had worn so long
The shadowy plumage of historic song,
The new-born poet left the beaten course,
To track the passions to their living source.

Then rose the Drama; — and the world
    admired
Her varied page with deeper thought in-
    spired:
Bound to no clime, for Passion's throb is
    one
In Greenland's twilight or in India's sun;
Born for no age, for all the thoughts that
    roll
In the dark vortex of the stormy soul,
Unchained in song, no freezing years can
    tame;
God gave them birth, and man is still the
    same.

So full on life her magic mirror shone,
Her sister Arts paid tribute to her throne;
One reared her temple, one her canvas
    warmed,
And Music thrilled, while Eloquence in-
    formed.
The weary rustic left his stinted task
For smiles and tears, the dagger and the
    mask;
The sage, turned scholar, half forgot his lore,
To be the woman he despised before.
O'er sense and thought she threw her golden·
    chain,
And Time, the anarch, spares her deathless
    reign.

Thus lives Medea, in our tamer age,
As when her buskin pressed the Grecian
    stage ;
Not in the cells where frigid learning delves
In Aldine folios mouldering on their shelves,
But breathing, burning in the glittering
    throng,
Whose thousand bravos roll untired along,
Circling and spreading through the gilded
    halls,
From London's galleries to San Carlo's
    walls!

Thus shall he live whose more than mor-
    tal name
Mocks with its ray the pallid torch of
    Fame;
So proudly lifted that it seems afar
No earthly Pharos, but a heavenly star,
Who, unconfined to Art's diurnal bound,
Girds her whole zodiac in his flaming round,
And leads the passions, like the orb that
    guides,
From pole to pole, the palpitating tides!

V

Though round the Muse the robe of song
    is thrown,
Think not the poet lives in verse alone.
Long ere the chisel of the sculptor taught
The lifeless stone to mock the living thought;
Long ere the painter bade the canvas glow
With every line the forms of beauty know;
Long ere the iris of the Muses threw
On every leaf its own celestial hue,
In fable's dress the breath of genius poured,
And warmed the shapes that later times
    adored.

Untaught by Science how to forge the
    keys
That loose the gates of Nature's mysteries;
Unschooled by Faith, who, with her angel
    tread,
Leads through the labyrinth with a single
    thread,
His fancy, hovering round her guarded
    tower,
Rained through its bars like Danae's golden
    shower.

He spoke; the sea-nymph answered from
    her cave;
He called; the naiad left her mountain
    wave:
He dreamed of beauty; lo, amidst his dream,
Narcissus, mirrored in the breathless stream,
And night's chaste empress, in her bridal
    play,
Laughed through the foliage where Endy-
    mion lay;
And ocean dimpled, as the languid swell
Kissed the red lip of Cytherea's shell:
Of power, — Bellona swept the crimson
    field,
And blue-eyed Pallas shook her Gorgon
    shield;
O'er the hushed waves their mightier mon-
    arch drove,
And Ida trembled to the tread of Jove!

So every grace that plastic language
    knows
To nameless poets its perfection owes.
The rough-hewn words to simplest thoughts
    confined
Were cut and polished in their nicer mind;
Caught on their edge, imagination's ray
Splits into rainbows, shooting far away; —

From sense to soul, from soul to sense, it
flies,
And through all nature links analogies;
He who reads right will rarely look upon
A better poet than his lexicon!

There is a race which cold, ungenial skies
Breed from decay, as fungous growths
arise ;
Though dying fast, yet springing fast again,
Which still usurps an unsubstantial reign,
With frames too languid for the charms of
sense,
And minds worn down with action too in-
tense;
Tired of a world whose joys they never
knew,
Themselves deceived, yet thinking all un-
true;
Scarce men without, and less than girls
within,
Sick of their life before its cares begin; —
The dull disease, which drains their feeble
hearts,
To life's decay some hectic thrills imparts,
And lends a force which, like the maniac's
power,
Pays with blank years the frenzy of an hour.

And this is Genius! Say, does Heaven
degrade
The manly frame, for health, for action
made?
Break down the sinews, rack the brow
with pains,
Blanch the bright cheek and drain the pur-
ple veins,
To clothe the mind with more extended
sway,
Thus faintly struggling in degenerate clay ?

No! gentle maid, too ready to admire,
Though false its notes, the pale enthu-
siast's lyre;
If this be genius, though its bitter springs
Glowed like the morn beneath Aurora's
wings,
Seek not the source whose sullen bosom
feeds
But fruitless flowers and dark, envenomed
weeds.

But, if so bright the dear illusion seems,
Thou wouldst be partner of thy poet's
dreams,

And hang in rapture on his bloodless
charms,
Or die, like Raphael, in his angel arms,
Go and enjoy thy blessed lot, — to share
In Cowper's gloom or Chatterton's despair!

Not such were they whom, wandering
o'er the waves,
I looked to meet, but only found their
graves;
If friendship's smile, the better part of
fame,
Should lend my song the only wreath I
claim,
Whose voice would greet me with a
sweeter tone,
Whose living hand more kindly press my
own,
Than theirs, — could Memory, as her
silent tread
Prints the pale flowers that blossom o'er
the dead,
Those breathless lips, now closed in peace,
restore,
Or wake those pulses hushed to beat no
more?

Thou calm, chaste scholar ! I can see
thee now,
The first young laurels on thy pallid brow,
O'er thy slight figure floating lightly down
In graceful folds the academic gown,
On thy curled lip the classic lines that
taught
How nice the mind that sculptured them
with thought,
And triumph glistening in the clear blue
eye,
Too bright to live, — but oh, too fair to
die!

And thou, dear friend, whom Science
still deplores,
And Love still mourns, on ocean-severed
shores,
Though the bleak forest twice has bowed
with snow
Since thou wast laid its budding leaves
below,
Thine image mingles with my closing
strain,
As when we wandered by the turbid Seine,
Both blessed with hopes, which revelled,
bright and free,
On all we longed or all we dreamed to be;

To thee the amaranth and the cypress
fell, —
And I was spared to breathe this last fare-
well!

But lived there one in unremembered
days,
Or lives there still, who spurns the poet's
bays,
Whose fingers, dewy from Castalia's
springs,
Rest on the lyre, yet scorn to touch the
strings?
Who shakes the senate with the silver tone
The groves of Pindus might have sighed to
own?
Have such e'er been? Remember Can-
ning's name!
Do such still live? Let "Alaric's Dirge"
proclaim!

Immortal Art! where'er the rounded
sky
Bends o'er the cradle where thy children
lie,
Their home is earth, their herald every
tongue

Whose accents echo to the voice that sung.
One leap of Ocean scatters on the sand
The quarried bulwarks of the loosening
land;
One thrill of earth dissolves a century's
toil
Strewed like the leaves that vanish in the
soil;
One hill o'erflows, and cities sink below,
Their marbles splintering in the lava's
glow;
But one sweet tone, scarce whispered to
the air,
From shore to shore the blasts of ages
bear;
One humble name, which oft, perchance,
has borne
The tyrant's mockery and the courtier's
scorn,
Towers o'er the dust of earth's forgotten
graves,
As once, emerging through the waste of
waves,
The rocky Titan, round whose shattered
spear
Coiled the last whirlpool of the drowning
sphere!

POEMS PUBLISHED BETWEEN 1837 AND 1848

[An English and enlarged edition of Dr. Holmes's *Poems* followed the American edition of 1836, and was furnished with a biographical sketch of the poet, but the second American edition was copyrighted in 1848, and published nominally in 1849. It contained the poems already published and a further group, as here presented. The preface to the earlier volume was omitted, and the new edition was introduced by a note headed "From a letter of the Author to the Publishers," from which the following passages are taken.

"As these productions are to be given to the public again at your particular request, I must trust that you will make all proper explanations. I need hardly remind you that a part of them appeared in a volume published about a dozen years ago; that when this volume had been some time out of print, another edition was printed, at your suggestion, in London, but I suppose sold principally to this country; and that the present edition is published to please you rather than to gratify myself. You will, therefore, take the entire responsibility of the second and third appearances, except so far as my consent involved me in the transactions.

"Let me remark, also, that it was only to suit your wishes that several copies of verses, which sound very much like school exercises, were allowed to remain unexpunged. If anybody takes the trouble to attack them, you may say that they belong to the department of 'Early' or 'Juvenile' Poems, and should be so ticketed. But stand up for the new verses, especially those added in this edition. Say that those two names, 'Terpsichore' and 'Urania,' may perhaps sound a little fantastic, but were merely intended as suggestive titles, and fall back upon Herodotus. Say that many of the lesser poems were written for meetings more or less convivial, and must of course show something like the fire-work frames on the morning of July 5th. If any objection is made to that bacchanalian song, say that the author entirely recedes from several of the sentiments contained in it, especially that about strong drink being a natural want. But ask, if a few classical reminiscences at a banquet may not be quite as like to keep out something worse, as to stand in the way of something better.

"If anything pleasant should be said about 'the new edition,' you may snip it out of the paper and save it for me. If contrary opinions are expressed, be so good as *not* to mark with brackets, carefully envelop, and send to me, as is the custom with many friends."]

THE PILGRIM'S VISION

In the hour of twilight shadows
  The Pilgrim sire looked out;
He thought of the "bloudy Salvages"
  That lurked all round about,
Of Wituwamet's pictured knife
  And Pecksuot's whooping shout;
For the baby's limbs were feeble,
  Though his father's arms were stout.

His home was a freezing cabin,
  Too bare for the hungry rat;
Its roof was thatched with ragged grass,
  And bald enough of that;
The hole that served for casement
  Was glazed with an ancient hat,

And the ice was gently thawing
  From the log whereon he sat.

Along the dreary landscape
  His eyes went to and fro,
The trees all clad in icicles,
  The streams that did not flow;
A sudden thought flashed o'er him, —
  A dream of long ago, —
He smote his leathern jerkin,
  And murmured, "Even so!"

"Come hither, God-be-Glorified,
  And sit upon my knee;
Behold the dream unfolding,
  Whereof I spake to thee
By the winter's hearth in Leyden
  And on the stormy sea.

True is the dream's beginning, —
  So may its ending be !

"I saw in the naked forest
  Our scattered remnant cast,
A screen of shivering branches
  Between them and the blast;
The snow was falling round them,
  The dying fell as fast;
I looked to see them perish,
  When lo, the vision passed.

"Again mine eyes were opened; —
  The feeble had waxed strong,
The babes had grown to sturdy men,
  The remnant was a throng;
By shadowed lake and winding stream,
  And all the shores along,
The howling demons quaked to hear
  The Christian's godly song.

"They slept, the village fathers,
  By river, lake, and shore
When far adown the steep of Time
  The vision rose once more :
I saw along the winter snow
  A spectral column pour,
And high above their broken ranks
  A tattered flag they bore.

"Their Leader rode before them,
  Of bearing calm and high,
The light of Heaven's own kindling
  Throned in his awful eye;
These were a Nation's champions
  Her dread appeal to try.
God for the right ! I faltered,
  And lo, the train passed by.

"Once more ; — the strife is ended,
  The solemn issue tried,
The Lord of Hosts, his mighty arm
  Has helped our Israel's side;
Gray stone and grassy hillock
  Tell where our martyrs died,
But peaceful smiles the harvest,
  And stainless flows the tide.

"A crash, as when some swollen cloud
  Cracks o'er the tangled trees !
With side to side, and spar to spar,
  Whose smoking decks are these ?
I know Saint George's blood-red cross,
  Thou Mistress of the Seas,

But what is she whose streaming bars
  Roll out before the breeze ?

" Ah, well her iron ribs are knit,
  Whose thunders strive to quell
The bellowing throats, the blazing lips,
  That pealed the Armada's knell !
The mist was cleared, — a wreath of stars
  Rose o'er the crimsoned swell,
And, wavering from its haughty peak,
  The cross of England fell !

"O trembling Faith ! though dark the
    morn,
  A heavenly torch is thine ;
While feebler races melt away,
  And paler orbs decline,
Still shall the fiery pillar's ray
  Along thy pathway shine,
To light the chosen tribe that sought
  This Western Palestine !

"I see the living tide roll on;
  It crowns with flaming towers
The icy capes of Labrador,
  The Spaniard's 'land of flowers' !
It streams beyond the splintered ridge
  That parts the northern showers;
From eastern rock to sunset wave
  The Continent is ours !"

He ceased, the grim old soldier-saint,
  Then softly bent to cheer
The Pilgrim-child, whose wasting face
  Was meekly turned to hear;
And drew his toil-worn sleeve across
  To brush the manly tear
From cheeks that never changed in woe,
  And never blanched in fear.

The weary Pilgrim slumbers,
  His resting-place unknown ;
His hands were crossed, his lids were
    closed,
  The dust was o'er him strown ;
The drifting soil, the mouldering leaf,
  Along the sod were blown ;
His mound has melted into earth,
  His memory lives alone.

So let it live unfading,
  The memory of the dead,
Long as the pale anemone
  Springs where their tears were shed,

Or, raining in the summer's wind
  In flakes of burning red,
The wild rose sprinkles with its leaves
  The turf where once they bled!

Yea, when the frowning bulwarks
  That guard this holy strand
Have sunk beneath the trampling surge
  In beds of sparkling sand,
While in the waste of ocean
  One hoary rock shall stand,
Be this its latest legend,—
  HERE WAS THE PILGRIM'S LAND!

THE STEAMBOAT

SEE how yon flaming herald treads
  The ridged and rolling waves,
As, crashing o'er their crested heads,
  She bows her surly slaves!
With foam before and fire behind,
  She rends the clinging sea,
That flies before the roaring wind,
  Beneath her hissing lee.

The morning spray, like sea-born flowers,
  With heaped and glistening bells,
Falls round her fast, in ringing showers,
  With every wave that swells;
And, burning o'er the midnight deep,
  In lurid fringes thrown,
The living gems of ocean sweep
  Along her flashing zone.

With clashing wheel and lifting keel,
  And smoking torch on high,
When winds are loud and billows reel,
  She thunders foaming by;
When seas are silent and serene,
  With even beam she glides,
The sunshine glimmering through the green
  That skirts her gleaming sides.

Now, like a wild nymph, far apart
  She veils her shadowy form,
The beating of her restless heart
  Still sounding through the storm;
Now answers, like a courtly dame,
  The reddening surges o'er,
With flying scarf of spangled flame,
  The Pharos of the shore.

To-night yon pilot shall not sleep,
  Who trims his narrowed sail;

To-night yon frigate scarce shall keep
  Her broad breast to the gale;
And many a foresail, scooped and strained,
  Shall break from yard and stay,
Before this smoky wreath has stained
  The rising mist of day.

Hark! hark! I hear yon whistling shroud,
  I see yon quivering mast;
The black throat of the hunted cloud
  Is panting forth the blast!
An hour, and, whirled like winnowing chaff,
  The giant surge shall fling
His tresses o'er yon pennon staff,
  White as the sea-bird's wing!

Yet rest, ye wanderers of the deep;
  Nor wind nor wave shall tire
Those fleshless arms, whose pulses leap
  With floods of living fire;
Sleep on, and, when the morning light
  Streams o'er the shining bay,
Oh think of those for whom the night
  Shall never wake in day!

LEXINGTON

SLOWLY the mist o'er the meadow was
    creeping,
  Bright on the dewy buds glistened the
    sun,
When from his couch, while his children
    were sleeping,
  Rose the bold rebel and shouldered his
    gun.
    Waving her golden veil
    Over the silent dale,
Blithe looked the morning on cottage and
    spire;
    Hushed was his parting sigh,
    While from his noble eye
Flashed the last sparkle of liberty's fire.

On the smooth green where the fresh leaf
    is springing
  Calmly the first-born of glory have met;
Hark! the death-volley around them is
    ringing!
  Look! with their life-blood the young
    grass is wet!
    Faint is the feeble breath,
    Murmuring low in death,
"Tell to our sons how their fathers have
    died;"

Nerveless the iron hand,
Raised for its native land,
Lies by the weapon that gleams at its side.

Over the hillsides the wild knell is tolling,
    From their far hamlets the yeomanry
        come;
As through the storm-clouds the thunder-
        burst rolling,
    Circles the beat of the mustering drum.
        Fast on the soldier's path
        Darken the waves of wrath, —
Long have they gathered and loud shall
        they fall;
        Red glares the musket's flash,
        Sharp rings the rifle's crash,
Blazing and clanging from thicket and
    wall.

Gayly the plume of the horseman was dan-
        cing,
    Never to shadow his cold brow again;
Proudly at morning the war-steed was
        prancing,
    Reeking and panting he droops on the
        rein;
        Pale is the lip of scorn,
        Voiceless the trumpet horn,
Torn is the silken-fringed red cross on
    high;
        Many a belted breast
        Low on the turf shall rest
Ere the dark hunters the herd have passed
    by.

Snow-girdled crags where the hoarse wind
        is raving,
    Rocks where the weary floods murmur
        and wail,
Wilds where the fern by the furrow is
        waving,
    Reeled with the echoes that rode on the
        gale;
        Far as the tempest thrills
        Over the darkened hills,
Far as the sunshine streams over the plain,
        Roused by the tyrant band,
        Woke all the mighty land,
Girded for battle, from mountain to main.

Green be the graves where her martyrs are
        lying!
    Shroudless and tombless they sunk to
        their rest,
While o'er their ashes the starry fold flying

Wraps the proud eagle they roused
        from his nest.
        Borne on her Northern pine,
        Long o'er the foaming brine
Spread her broad banner to storm and to
        sun;
        Heaven keep her ever free,
        Wide as o'er land and sea
Floats the fair emblem her heroes have
    won!

ON LENDING A PUNCH-BOWL

This "punch-bowl" was, according to old
family tradition, a *caudle-cup*. It is a massive
piece of silver, its cherubs and other orna-
ments of coarse repoussé work, and has two
handles like a loving-cup, by which it was
held, or passed from guest to guest.

THIS ancient silver bowl of mine, it tells of
        good old times,
Of joyous days and jolly nights, and merry
        Christmas chimes;
They were a free and jovial race, but
        honest, brave, and true,
Who dipped their ladle in the punch when
        this old bowl was new.

A Spanish galleon brought the bar, — so
        runs the ancient tale;
'T was hammered by an Antwerp smith,
        whose arm was like a flail;
And now and then between the strokes, for
        fear his strength should fail,
He wiped his brow and quaffed a cup of
        good old Flemish ale.

'T was purchased by an English squire to
        please his loving dame,
Who saw the cherubs, and conceived a
        longing for the same;
And oft as on the ancient stock another
        twig was found,
'T was filled with caudle spiced and hot,
        and handed smoking round.

But, changing hands, it reached at length a
        Puritan divine,
Who used to follow Timothy, and take a
        little wine,
But hated punch and prelacy; and so it
        was, perhaps,
He went to Leyden, where he found con-
        venticles and schnapps.

And then, of course, you know what's
    next: it left the Dutchman's shore
With those that in the Mayflower came, —
    a hundred souls and more, —
Along with all the furniture, to fill their
    new abodes, —
To judge by what is still on hand, at least
    a hundred loads.

'T was on a dreary winter's eve, the night
    was closing dim,
When brave Miles Standish took the bowl,
    and filled it to the brim;
The little Captain stood and stirred the
    posset with his sword,
And all his sturdy men-at-arms were
    ranged about the board.

He poured the fiery Hollands in, — the
    man that never feared, —
He took a long and solemn draught, and
    wiped his yellow beard;
And one by one the musketeers — the men
    that fought and prayed —
All drank as 't were their mother's milk,
    and not a man afraid.

That night, affrighted from his nest, the
    screaming eagle flew,
He heard the Pequot's ringing whoop, the
    soldier's wild halloo;
And there the sachem learned the rule he
    taught to kith and kin :
" Run from the white man when you find
    he smells of Hollands gin ! "

A hundred years, and fifty more, had
    spread their leaves and snows,
A thousand rubs had flattened down each
    little cherub's nose,
When once again the bowl was filled, but
    not in mirth or joy, —
'T was mingled by a mother's hand to
    cheer her parting boy.

Drink, John, she said, 't will do you good,
    — poor child, you 'll never bear
This working in the dismal trench, out in
    the midnight air;
And if — God bless me ! — you were hurt,
    't would keep away the chill.
So John *did* drink, — and well he wrought
    that night at Bunker's Hill !

I tell you, there was generous warmth in
    good old English cheer;
I tell you, 't was a pleasant thought to
    bring its symbol here.
'T is but the fool that loves excess; hast
    thou a drunken soul ?
Thy bane is in thy shallow skull, not in my
    silver bowl !

I love the memory of the past, — its
    pressed yet fragrant flowers, —
The moss that clothes its broken walls, the
    ivy on its towers;
Nay, this poor bauble it bequeathed, — my
    eyes grow moist and dim,
To think of all the vanished joys that
    danced around its brim.

Then fill a fair and honest cup, and bear it
    straight to me;
The goblet hallows all it holds, whate'er
    the liquid be;
And may the cherubs on its face protect
    me from the sin
That dooms one to those dreadful words,
    — " My dear, where *have* you
    been ? "

A SONG

FOR THE CENTENNIAL CELEBRATION OF HARVARD COLLEGE, 1836

This song, which I had the temerity to
sing myself (*felix audacia*, Mr. Franklin Dexter had the goodness to call it), was sent in
a little too late to be printed with the official
account of the celebration. It was written
at the suggestion of Dr. Jacob Bigelow, who
thought the popular tune " The Poacher's
Song " would be a good model for a lively
ballad or ditty. He himself wrote the admirable Latin song to be found in the record of
the meeting.

When the Puritans came over
    Our hills and swamps to clear,
The woods were full of catamounts,
    And Indians red as deer,
With tomahawks and scalping-knives,
    That make folks' heads look queer;
Oh the ship from England used to bring
    A hundred wigs a year !

The crows came cawing through the air
  To pluck the Pilgrims' corn,
The bears came snuffing round the door
  Whene'er a babe was born,
The rattlesnakes were bigger round
  Than the butt of the old ram's horn
The deacon blew at meeting time
  On every " Sabbath " morn.

But soon they knocked the wigwams
    down,
  And pine-tree trunk and limb
Began to sprout among the leaves
  In shape of steeples slim;
And out the little wharves were stretched
  Along the ocean's rim,
And up the little school-house shot
  To keep the boys in trim.

And when at length the College rose,
  The sachem cocked his eye
At every tutor's meagre ribs
  Whose coat-tails whistled by:
But when the Greek and Hebrew words
  Came tumbling from his jaws,
The copper-colored children all
  Ran screaming to the squaws.

And who was on the Catalogue
  When college was begun ?
Two nephews of the President,
  And the Professor's son ;
(They turned a little Indian by,
  As brown as any bun;)
Lord ! how the seniors knocked about
  The freshman class of one !

They had not then the dainty things
  That commons now afford,
But succotash and hominy
  Were smoking on the board ;
They did not rattle round in gigs,
  Or dash in long-tailed blues,
But always on Commencement days
  The tutors blacked their shoes.

God bless the ancient Puritans !
  Their lot was hard enough;
But honest hearts make iron arms,
  And tender maids are tough ;
So love and faith have formed and fed
  Our true-born Yankee stuff,
And keep the kernel in the shell
  The British found so rough !

THE ISLAND HUNTING-SONG

The island referred to is a domain of
princely proportions, which has long been the
seat of a generous hospitality. Naushon is its
old Indian name. William Swain, Esq., com-
monly known as " the Governor," was the pro-
prietor of it at the time when this song was
written. Mr. John M. Forbes is his worthy
successor in territorial rights and as a hospit-
able entertainer. The Island Book has been
the recipient of many poems from visitors and
friends of the owners of the old mansion. [In
The Autocrat, section ii., is an animated account
of Naushon, followed by a poem, Sun and
Shadow, written there.]

No more the summer floweret charms,
  The leaves will soon be sere,
And Autumn folds his jewelled arms
  Around the dying year ;
So, ere the waning seasons claim
  Our leafless groves awhile,
With golden wine and glowing flame
  We 'll crown our lonely isle.

Once more the merry voices sound
  Within the antlered hall,
And long and loud the baying hounds
  Return the hunter's call ;
And through the woods, and o'er the hill,
  And far along the bay,
The driver's horn is sounding shrill, —
  Up, sportsmen, and away !

No bars of steel or walls of stone
  Our little empire bound,
But, circling with his azure zone,
  The sea runs foaming round ;
The whitening wave, the purpled skies,
  The blue and lifted shore,
Braid with their dim and blending dyes
  Our wide horizon o'er.

And who will leave the grave debate
  That shakes the smoky town,
To rule amid our island-state,
  And wear our oak-leaf crown ?
And who will be awhile content
  To hunt our woodland game,
And leave the vulgar pack that scent
  The reeking track of fame ?

Ah, who that shares in toils like these
  Will sigh not to prolong

Our days beneath the broad-leaved trees,
 Our nights of mirth and song ?
Then leave the dust of noisy streets,
 Ye outlaws of the wood,
And follow through his green retreats
 Your noble Robin Hood.

DEPARTED DAYS

YES, dear departed, cherished days,
 Could Memory's hand restore
Your morning light, your evening rays,
 From Time's gray urn once more,
Then might this restless heart be still,
 This straining eye might close,
And Hope her fainting pinions fold,
 While the fair phantoms rose.

But, like a child in ocean's arms,
 We strive against the stream,
Each moment farther from the shore
 Where life's young fountains gleam ;
Each moment fainter wave the fields,
 And wider rolls the sea;
The mist grows dark, — the sun goes
 down, —
 Day breaks, — and where are we ?

THE ONLY DAUGHTER

ILLUSTRATION OF A PICTURE

THEY bid me strike the idle strings,
 As if my summer days
Had shaken sunbeams from their wings
 To warm my autumn lays ;
They bring to me their painted urn,
 As if it were not time
To lift my gauntlet and to spurn
 The lists of boyish rhyme;
And were it not that I have still
 Some weakness in my heart
That clings around my stronger will
 And pleads for gentler art,
Perchance I had not turned away
 The thoughts grown tame with toil,
To cheat this lone and pallid ray,
 That wastes the midnight oil.

Alas ! with every year I feel
 Some roses leave my brow ;
Too young for wisdom's tardy seal,
 Too old for garlands now.

Yet, while the dewy breath of spring
 Steals o'er the tingling air,
And spreads and fans each emerald wing
 The forest soon shall wear,
How bright the opening year would seem,
 Had I one look like thine
To meet me when the morning beam
 Unseals these lids of mine !
Too long I bear this lonely lot,
 That bids my heart run wild
To press the lips that love me not,
 To clasp the stranger's child.

How oft beyond the dashing seas,
 Amidst those royal bowers,
Where danced the lilacs in the breeze,
 And swung the chestnut-flowers,
I wandered like a wearied slave
 Whose morning task is done,
To watch the little hands that gave
 Their whiteness to the sun;
To revel in the bright young eyes,
 Whose lustre sparkled through
The sable fringe of Southern skies
 Or gleamed in Saxon blue !
How oft I heard another's name
 Called in some truant's tone ;
Sweet accents ! which I longed to claim,
 To learn and lisp my own !

Too soon the gentle hands, that pressed
 The ringlets of the child,
Are folded on the faithful breast
 Where first he breathed and smiled;
Too oft the clinging arms untwine,
 The melting lips forget,
And darkness veils the bridal shrine
 Where wreaths and torches met ;
If Heaven but leaves a single thread
 Of Hope's dissolving chain,
Even when her parting plumes are spread
 It bids them fold again;
The cradle rocks beside the tomb;
 The cheek now changed and chill
Smiles on us in the morning bloom
 Of one that loves us still.

Sweet image ! I have done thee wrong
 To claim this destined lay ;
The leaf that asked an idle song
 Must bear my tears away.
Yet in thy memory shouldst thou keep
 This else forgotten strain,
Till years have taught thine eyes to weep,
 And flattery's voice is vain;

Oh then, thou fledgling of the nest,
  Like the long-wandering dove,
Thy weary heart may faint for rest,
  As mine, on changeless love;
And while these sculptured lines retrace
  The hours now dancing by,
This vision of thy girlish grace
  May cost thee, too, a sigh.

SONG

WRITTEN FOR THE DINNER GIVEN TO
CHARLES DICKENS BY THE YOUNG
MEN OF BOSTON, FEBRUARY 1, 1842

THE stars their early vigils keep,
  The silent hours are near,
When drooping eyes forget to weep, —
  Yet still we linger here ;
And what — the passing churl may ask —
  Can claim such wondrous power,
That Toil forgets his wonted task,
  And Love his promised hour ?

The Irish harp no longer thrills,
  Or breathes a fainter tone ;
The clarion blast from Scotland's hills,
  Alas ! no more is blown ;
And Passion's burning lip bewails
  Her Harold's wasted fire,
Still lingering o'er the dust that veils
  The Lord of England's lyre.

But grieve not o'er its broken strings,
  Nor think its soul hath died,
While yet the lark at heaven's gate
    sings,
  As once o'er Avon's side ;
While gentle summer sheds her bloom,
  And dewy blossoms wave,
Alike o'er Juliet's storied tomb
  And Nelly's nameless grave.

Thou glorious island of the sea !
  Though wide the wasting flood
That parts our distant land from thee,
  We claim thy generous blood;
Nor o'er thy far horizon springs
  One hallowed star of fame,
But kindles, like an angel's wings,
  Our western skies in flame !

LINES

RECITED AT THE BERKSHIRE JUBILEE,
  PITTSFIELD, MASS., AUGUST 23, 1844

[Before reading these *Lines*, the poet spoke
as follows :

"One of my earliest recollections is of an
annual pilgrimage made by my parents to the
west. The young horse was brought up, fatted
by a week's rest and high feeding, prancing and
caracoling to the door. It came to the corner
and was soon over the western hills. He was
gone a fortnight ; and one afternoon — it al-
ways seems to me it was a sunny afternoon —
we saw an equipage crawling from the west
toward the old homestead ; the young horse,
who set out fat and prancing, worn thin and
reduced by a long journey — the chaise cov-
ered with dust, and all speaking of a terrible
crusade, a formidable pilgrimage. Winter-
evening stories told me where — to Berkshire,
to the borders of New York, to the old domain,
owned so long that there seemed a kind of he-
reditary love for it. Many years passed away,
and I travelled down the beautiful Rhine. I
wished to see the equally beautiful Hudson. I
found myself at Albany ; a few hours' ride
brought me to Pittsfield, and I went to the
little spot, the scene of this pilgrimage — a
mansion — and found it surrounded by a beau-
tiful meadow, through which the winding river
made its course in a thousand fantastic curves ;
the mountains reared their heads around it,
the blue air which makes our city-pale cheeks
again to deepen with the hue of health, cours-
ing about it pure and free. I recognized it as
the scene of the annual pilgrimage. Since then
I have made an annual visit to it.

"In 1735, Hon. Jacob Wendell, my grand-
father in the maternal line, bought a township
not then laid out — the township of Poontoo-
suck — and that little spot which we still hold
is the relic of twenty-four thousand acres of
baronial territory. When I say this, no feel-
ing which can be the subject of ridicule ani-
mates my bosom. I know too well that the
hills and rocks outlast our families. I know
we fall upon the places we claim, as the leaves
of the forest fall, and as passed the soil from
the hands of the original occupants into the
hands of my immediate ancestors, I know it
must pass from me and mine ; and yet with
pleasure and pride I feel I can take every in-
habitant by the hand and say, If I am not a
son or a grandson, or even a nephew of this
fair county, I am at least allied to it by hered-
itary relation."]

COME back to your mother, ye children, for shame,
Who have wandered like truants for riches or fame !
With a smile on her face, and a sprig in her cap,
She calls you to feast from her bountiful lap.

Come out from your alleys, your courts, and your lanes,
And breathe, like young eagles, the air of our plains ;
Take a whiff from our fields, and your excellent wives
Will declare it 's all nonsense insuring your lives.

Come you of the law, who can talk, if you please,
Till the man in the moon will allow it 's a cheese,
And leave "the old lady, that never tells lies,"
To sleep with her handkerchief over her eyes.

Ye healers of men, for a moment decline
Your feats in the rhubarb and ipecac line;
While you shut up your turnpike, your neighbors can go
The old roundabout road to the regions below.

You clerk, on whose ears are a couple of pens,
And whose head is an ant-hill of units and tens,
Though Plato denies you, we welcome you still
As a featherless biped, in spite of your quill.

Poor drudge of the city ! how happy he feels,
With the burs on his legs and the grass at his heels !
No *dodger* behind, his bandannas to share,
No constable grumbling, " You must n't walk there ! "

In yonder green meadow, to memory dear,
He slaps a mosquito and brushes a tear;

The dew-drops hang round him on blossoms and shoots,
He breathes but one sigh for his youth and his boots.

There stands the old school-house, hard by the old church;
That tree at its side had the flavor of birch;
Oh, sweet were the days of his juvenile tricks,
Though the prairie of youth had so many " big licks."

By the side of yon river he weeps and he slumps,
The boots fill with water, as if they were pumps,
Till, sated with rapture, he steals to his bed,
With a glow in his heart and a cold in his head.

'T is past, — he is dreaming, — I see him again ;
The ledger returns as by legerdemain;
His neckcloth is damp with an easterly flaw,
And he holds in his fingers an omnibus straw.

He dreams the chill gust is a blossomy gale,
That the straw is a rose from his dear native vale ;
And murmurs, unconscious of space and of time,
" A 1. Extra super. Ah, is n't it PRIME ! "

Oh, what are the prizes we perish to win
To the first little "shiner " we caught with a pin !
No soil upon earth is so dear to our eyes
As the soil we first stirred in terrestrial pies !

Then come from all parties and parts to our feast ;
Though not at the " Astor," we'll give you at least
A bite at an apple, a seat on the grass,
And the best of cold — water — at nothing a glass.

NUX POSTCŒNATICA

I was sitting with my microscope, upon my
    parlor rug,
With a very heavy quarto and a very lively
    bug ;
The true bug had been organized with only
    two antennæ,
But the humbug in the copperplate would
    have them twice as many.

And I thought, like Dr. Faustus, of the
    emptiness of art,
How we take a fragment for the whole,
    and call the whole a part,
When I heard a heavy footstep that was
    loud enough for two,
And a man of forty entered, exclaiming,
    " How d' ye do ? "

He was not a ghost, my visitor, but solid
    flesh and bone ;
He wore a Palo Alto hat, his weight was
    twenty stone;
(It 's odd how hats expand their brims as
    riper years invade,
As if when life had reached its noon it
    wanted them for shade !)

I lost my focus, — dropped my book, —
    the bug, who was a flea,
At once exploded, and commenced experi-
    ments on me.
They have a certain heartiness that fre-
    quently appalls,—
Those mediæval gentlemen in semilunar
    smalls !

" My boy," he said, (colloquial ways, — the
    vast, broad-hatted man,)
" Come dine with us on Thursday next, —
    you must, you know you can;
We 're going to have a roaring time, with
    lots of fun and noise,
Distinguished guests, et cetera, the JUDGE,
    and all the boys."

Not so, — I said, — my temporal bones are
    showing pretty clear.
It 's time to stop, — just look and see that
    hair above this ear;
My golden days are more than spent, —
    and, what is very strange,
If these are real silver hairs, I 'm getting
    lots of change.

Besides — my prospects — don't you know
    that people won't employ
A man that wrongs his manliness by laugh-
    ing like a boy ?
And suspect the azure blossom that unfolds
    upon a shoot,
As if wisdom's old potato could not flourish
    at its root ?

It 's a very fine reflection, when you 're
    etching out a smile
On a copperplate of faces that would
    stretch at least a mile,
That, what with sneers from enemies and
    cheapening shrugs of friends,
It will cost you all the earnings that a
    month of labor lends !

It 's a vastly pleasing prospect, when you 're
    screwing out a laugh,
That your very next year's income is dimin-
    ished by a half,
And a little boy trips barefoot that Pegasus
    may go,
And the baby's milk is watered that your
    Helicon may flow !

No ; — the joke has been a good one, — but
    I 'm getting fond of quiet,
And I don't like deviations from my cus-
    tomary diet ;
So I think I will not go with you to hear
    the toasts and speeches,
But stick to old Montgomery Place, and
    have some pig and peaches.

The fat man answered : Shut your mouth,
    and hear the genuine creed ;
The true essentials of a feast are only fun
    and feed ;
The force that wheels the planets round
    delights in spinning tops,
And that young earthquake t' other day
    was great at shaking props.

I tell you what, philosopher, if all the lon-
    gest heads
That ever knocked their sinciputs in stretch-
    ing on their beds
Were round one great mahogany, I 'd beat
    those fine old folks
With twenty dishes, twenty fools, and
    twenty clever jokes !

Why, if Columbus should be there, the
    company would beg
He 'd show that little trick of his of bal-
    ancing the egg !
Milton to Stilton would give in, and Solo-
    mon to Salmon,
And Roger Bacon be a bore, and Francis
    Bacon gammon !

And as for all the "patronage" of all the
    clowns and boors
That squint their little narrow eyes at any
    freak of yours,
Do leave them to your prosier friends, —
    such fellows ought to die
When rhubarb is so very scarce and ipecac
    so high !

And so I come, — like Lochinvar, to tread
    a single measure, —
To purchase with a loaf of bread a sugar-
    plum of pleasure,
To enter for the cup of glass that 's run
    for after dinner,
Which yields a single sparkling draught,
    then breaks and cuts the winner.

Ah, that 's the way delusion comes, — a
    glass of old Madeira,
A pair of visual diaphragms revolved by
    Jane or Sarah,
And down go vows and promises without
    the slightest question
If eating words won't compromise the or-
    gans of digestion!

And yet, among my native shades, beside
    my nursing mother,
Where every stranger seems a friend, and
    every friend a brother,
I feel the old convivial glow (unaided) o'er
    me stealing, —
The warm, champagny, old-particular,
    brandy-punchy feeling.

We 're all alike; — Vesuvius flings the sco-
    riæ from his fountain,
But down they come in volleying rain back
    to the burning mountain;
We leave, like those volcanic stones, our
    precious Alma Mater,
But will keep dropping in again to see the
    dear old crater.

VERSES FOR AFTER-DINNER

PHI BETA KAPPA SOCIETY, 1844

I was thinking last night, as I sat in the
    cars,
With the charmingest prospect of cinders
    and stars,
Next Thursday is — bless me! — how hard
    it will be,
If that cannibal president calls upon me !

There is nothing on earth that he will not
    devour,
From a tutor in seed to a freshman in
    flower ;
No sage is too gray, and no youth is too
    green,
And you can't be too plump, though you 're
    never too lean.

While others enlarge on the boiled and the
    roast,
He serves a raw clergyman up with a toast,
Or catches some doctor, quite tender and
    young,
And basely insists on a bit of his tongue.

Poor victim, prepared for his classical
    spit,
With a stuffing of praise and a basting of
    wit,
You may twitch at your collar and wrinkle
    your brow,
But you 're up on your legs, and you 're in
    for it now.

Oh, think of your friends, — they are wait-
    to hear
Those jokes that are thought so remark-
    ably queer ;
And all the Jack Horners of metrical buns
Are prying and fingering to pick out the
    puns.

Those thoughts which, like chickens, will
    always thrive best
When reared by the heat of the natural
    nest,
Will perish if hatched from their embryo
    dream
In the mist and the glow of convivial steam.

Oh pardon me, then, if I meekly retire,
With a very small flash of ethereal fire;
No rubbing will kindle your Lucifer
    match,
If the *fiz* does not follow the primitive
    scratch.

Dear friends, who are listening so sweetly
    the while,
With your lips double-reefed in a snug
    little smile,
I leave you two fables, both drawn from
    the deep, —
The shells you can drop, but the pearls you
    may keep.

.   .   .   .

The fish called the FLOUNDER, perhaps
    you may know,
Has one side for use and another for
    show;
One side for the public, a delicate brown,
And one that is white, which he always
    keeps down.

A very young flounder, the flattest of
    flats,
(And they're none of them thicker than
    opera hats,)
Was speaking more freely than charity
    taught
Of a friend and relation that just had been
    caught.

"My! what an exposure! just see what a
    sight!
I blush for my race, — he is showing his
    white!
Such spinning and wriggling, — why, what
    does he wish?
How painfully small to respectable fish!"

Then said an old SCULPIN, — "My free-
    dom excuse,
You're playing the cobbler with holes in
    your shoes;
Your brown side is up, — but just wait till
    you're tried
And you'll find that all flounders are
    white on one side."

.   .   .   .

There's a slice near the PICKEREL'S pecto-
    ral fins,
Where the *thorax* leaves off and the *venter*
    begins,

Which his brother, survivor of fish-hooks
    and lines,
Though fond of his family, never declines.

He loves his relations; he feels they'll be
    missed;
But that one little tidbit he cannot resist;
So your bait may be swallowed, no matter
    how fast,
For you catch your next fish with a piece
    of the last.

And thus, O survivor, whose merciless
    fate
Is to take the next hook with the presi-
    dent's bait,
You are lost while you snatch from the
    end of his line
The morsel he rent from this bosom of
    mine!

A MODEST REQUEST

COMPLIED WITH AFTER THE DINNER AT
PRESIDENT EVERETT'S INAUGURATION

SCENE, — a back parlor in a certain square,
Or court, or lane, — in short, no matter
    where;
Time, — early morning, dear to simple
    souls
Who love its sunshine and its fresh-baked
    rolls;
Persons, — take pity on this telltale blush,
That, like the Æthiop, whispers, "Hush,
    oh hush!"

Delightful scene! where smiling comfort
    broods,
Nor business frets, nor anxious care in-
    trudes;
O si sic omnia! were it ever so!
But what is stable in this world below?
Medio e fonte, — Virtue has her faults, —
The clearest fountains taste of Epsom
    salts;
We snatch the cup and lift to drain it
    dry,
Its central dimple holds a drowning fly!
Strong is the pine by Maine's ambrosial
    streams,
But stronger augers pierce its thickest
    beams;

No iron gate, no spiked and panelled door,
Can keep out death, the postman, or the
    bore.
Oh for a world where peace and silence
    reign,
And blunted dulness terebrates in vain!
— The door-bell jingles, — enter Richard
    Fox,
And takes this letter from his leathern box.

" Dear Sir, —
            In writing on a former day,
One little matter I forgot to say;
I now inform you in a single line,
On Thursday next our purpose is to *dine.*
The act of feeding, as you understand,
Is but a fraction of the work in hand;
Its nobler half is that ethereal meat
The papers call 'the intellectual treat;'
Songs, speeches, toasts, around the festive
    board
Drowned in the juice the College pumps
    afford;
For only water flanks our knives and
    forks,
So, sink or float, we swim without the
    corks.
Yours is the art, by native genius taught,
To clothe in eloquence the naked thought;
Yours is the skill its music to prolong
Through the sweet effluence of mellifluous
    song;
Yours the quaint trick to cram the pithy line
That cracks so crisply over bubbling wine ;
And since success your various gifts at-
    tends,
We — that is, I and all your numerous
    friends —
Expect from you — your single self a
    host —
A speech, a song, excuse me, *and* a toast;
Nay, not to haggle on so small a claim,
A few of each, or several of the same. "
    (Signed),   Yours, *most truly,* —— "

            No! my sight must fail, —
If that ain't Judas on the largest scale !
Well, this *is* modest; — nothing else than
    that ?
My coat ? my boots ? my pantaloons ? my
    hat ?
My stick ? my gloves ? as well as all my
    wits,
Learning and linen, — everything that
    fits !

Jack, said my lady, is it grog you 'll try,
Or punch, or toddy, if perhaps you 're
    dry ?
Ah, said the sailor, though I can't refuse,
You know, my lady, 't ain't for me to
    choose ;
I 'll take the grog to finish off my lunch,
And drink the toddy while you mix the
    punch.

* * *

THE SPEECH.   (The speaker, rising to be
    seen,
Looks very red, because so very green.)
I rise — I rise — with unaffected fear,
(Louder ! — speak louder ! — who the
    deuce can hear ?)
I rise — I said — with undisguised dis-
    may —
— Such are my feelings as I rise, I say !
Quite unprepared to face this learned
    throng,
Already gorged with eloquence and song ;
Around my view are ranged on either
    hand
The genius, wisdom, virtue of the land ;
" Hands that the rod of empire might have
    swayed "
Close at my elbow stir their lemonade;
Would you like Homer learn to write and
    speak,
That bench is groaning with its weight of
    Greek;
Behold the naturalist who in his teens
Found six new species in a dish of greens;
And lo, the master in a statelier walk,
Whose annual ciphering takes a ton of
    chalk;
And there the linguist, who by common
    roots
Thro' all their nurseries tracks old Noah's
    shoots, —
How Shem's proud children reared the
    Assyrian piles,
While Ham's were scattered through the
    Sandwich Isles !
— Fired at the thought of all the present
    shows,
My kindling fancy down the future flows :
I see the glory of the coming days
O'er Time's horizon shoot its streaming
    rays ;
Near and more near the radiant morning
    draws
In living lustre (rapturous applause);

From east to west the blazing heralds run,
Loosed from the chariot of the ascending
sun,
Through the long vista of uncounted years
In cloudless splendor (three tremendous
cheers).
My eye prophetic, as the depths unfold,
Sees a new advent of the age of gold;
While o'er the scene new generations press,
New heroes rise the coming time to bless, —
Not such as Homer's, who, we read in Pope,
Dined without forks and never heard of
soap, —
Not such as May to Marlborough Chapel
brings,
Lean, hungry, savage, anti-everythings,
Copies of Luther in the pasteboard style, —
But genuine articles, the true Carlyle ;
While far on high the blazing orb shall
shed
Its central light on Harvard's holy head,
And learning's ensigns ever float unfurled
Here in the focus of the new-born world !
The speaker stops, and, trampling down
the pause,
Roars through the hall the thunder of ap-
plause,
One stormy gust of long-suspended Ahs !
One whirlwind chaos of insane Hurrahs !

THE SONG. But this demands a briefer
line, —
A shorter muse, and not the old long Nine;
Long metre answers for a common song,
Though common metre does not answer
long.

She came beneath the forest dome
  To seek its peaceful shade,
An exile from her ancient home,
  A poor, forsaken maid;
No banner, flaunting high above,
  No blazoned cross, she bore ;
One holy book of light and love
  Was all her worldly store.

The dark brown shadows passed away,
  And wider spread the green,
And where the savage used to stray
  The rising mart was seen;
So, when the laden winds had brought
  Their showers of golden rain,
Her lap some precious gleanings caught,
  Like Ruth's amid the grain.

But wrath soon gathered uncontrolled
  Among the baser churls,
To see her ankles red with gold,
  Her forehead white with pearls.
" Who gave to thee the glittering bands
  That lace thine azure veins ?
Who bade thee lift those snow-white
  hands
  We bound in gilded chains ? "

" These are the gems my children gave,"
  The stately dame replied;
" The wise, the gentle, and the brave,
  I nurtured at my side.
If envy still your bosom stings,
  Take back their rims of gold;
My sons will melt their wedding-rings,
  And give a hundred-fold ! "

THE TOAST. Oh tell me, ye who thought-
less ask
Exhausted nature for a threefold task,
In wit or pathos if one share remains,
A safe investment for an ounce of brains !
Hard is the job to launch the desperate
pun,
A pun-job dangerous as the Indian one.
Turned by the current of some stronger
wit
Back from the object that you mean to
hit,
Like the strange missile which the Austra-
lian throws,
Your verbal *boomerang* slaps you on the
nose.
One vague inflection spoils the whole with
doubt,
One trivial letter ruins all, left out;
A knot can choke a felon into clay,
A not will save him, spelt without the *k ;*
The smallest word has some unguarded
spot,
And danger lurks in *i* without a dot.

Thus great Achilles, who had shown his
zeal
In healing wounds, died of a wounded heel;
Unhappy chief, who, when in childhood
doused,
Had saved his bacon had his feet been
soused !
Accursed heel that killed a hero stout !
Oh, had your mother known that you were
out,

Death had not entered at the trifling part
That still defies the small chirurgeon's art
With corns and bunions, — not the glo-
rious John,
Who wrote the book we all have pondered
on,
But other bunions, bound in fleecy hose,
To " Pilgrim's Progress " unrelenting foes !

A HEALTH, unmingled with the reveller's
wine,
To him whose title is indeed divine;
Truth's sleepless watchman on her mid-
night tower,
Whose lamp burns brightest when the
tempests lower.
On, who can tell with what a leaden flight
Drag the long watches of his weary night,
While at his feet the hoarse and blinding
gale
Strews the torn wreck and bursts the
fragile sail,
When stars have faded, when the wave is
dark,
When rocks and sands embrace the foun-
dering bark !
But still he pleads with unavailing cry,
Behold the light, O wanderer, look or die !

A health, fair Themis ! Would the en-
chanted vire
Wreathed its green tendrils round this cup
of thine !
If Learning's radiance fill thy modern
court,
Its glorious sunshine streams through
Blackstone's port !
Lawyers are thirsty, and their clients
too, —
Witness at least, if memory serve me true,
Those old tribunals, famed for dusty suits,
Where men sought justice ere they brushed
their boots;
And what can match, to solve a learned
doubt,
The warmth within that comes from " cold
without " ?

Health to the art whose glory is to give
The crowning boon that makes it life to
live.
Ask not her home; — the rock where
nature flings
Her arctic lichen, last of living things;

The gardens, fragrant with the orient's
balm,
From the low jasmine to the star-like
palm,
Hail her as mistress o'er the distant waves,
And yield their tribute to her wandering
slaves.
Wherever, moistening the ungrateful soil,
The tear of suffering tracks the path of
toil,
There, in the anguish of his fevered hours,
Her gracious finger points to healing
flowers;
Where the lost felon steals away to die,
Her soft hand waves before his closing
eye;
Where hunted misery finds his darkest
lair,
The midnight taper shows her kneeling
there!
VIRTUE, — the guide that men and nations
own;
And LAW, — the bulwark that protects her
throne;
And HEALTH, — to all its happiest charm
that lends;
These and their servants, man's untiring
friends:
Pour the bright lymph that Heaven itself
lets fall,
In one fair bumper let us toast them all!

THE PARTING WORD

I MUST leave thee, lady sweet!
Months shall waste before we meet;
Winds are fair and sails are spread,
Anchors leave their ocean bed;
Ere this shining day grow dark,
Skies shall gird my shoreless bark.
Through thy tears, O lady mine,
Read thy lover's parting line.

When the first sad sun shall set,
Thou shalt tear thy locks of jet;
When the morning star shall rise,
Thou shalt wake with weeping eyes;
When the second sun goes down,
Thou more tranquil shalt be grown,
Taught too well that wild despair
Dims thine eyes and spoils thy hair.

All the first unquiet week
Thou shalt wear a smileless cheek;

In the first month's second half
Thou shalt once attempt to laugh;
Then in Pickwick thou shalt dip,
Slightly puckering round the lip,
Till at last, in sorrow's spite,
Samuel makes thee laugh outright.

While the first seven mornings last,
Round thy chamber bolted fast
Many a youth shall fume and pout,
" Hang the girl, she 's always out!"
While the second week goes round,
Vainly shall they ring and pound ;
When the third week shall begin,
" Martha, let the creature in."

Now once more the flattering throng
Round thee flock with smile and song,
But thy lips, unweaned as yet,
Lisp, " Oh, how can I forget!"
Men and devils both contrive
Traps for catching girls alive;
Eve was duped, and Helen kissed, —
How, oh how, can you resist ?

First be careful of your fan,
Trust it not to youth or man;
Love has filled a pirate's sail
Often with its perfumed gale.
Mind your kerchief most of all,
Fingers touch when kerchiefs fall;
Shorter ell than mercers clip
Is the space from hand to lip.

Trust not such as talk in tropes,
Full of pistols, daggers, ropes;
All the hemp that Russia bears
Scarce would answer lovers' prayers;
Never thread was spun so fine,
Never spider stretched the line,
Would not hold the lovers true
That would really swing for you.

Fiercely some shall storm and swear,
Beating breasts in black despair;
Others murmur with a sigh,
You must melt, or they will die:
Painted words on empty lies,
Grubs with wings like butterflies;
Let them die, and welcome, too;
Pray what better could they do ?

Fare thee well: if years efface
From thy heart love's burning trace,

Keep, oh keep that hallowed seat
From the tread of vulgar feet;
If the blue lips of the sea
Wait with icy kiss for me,
Let not thine forget the vow,
Sealed how often, Love, as now.

A SONG OF OTHER DAYS

As o'er the glacier's frozen sheet
  Breathes soft the Alpine rose,
So through life's desert springing sweet
  The flower of friendship grows;
And as where'er the roses grow
  Some rain or dew descends,
'T is nature's law that wine should flow
  To wet the lips of friends.
    Then once again, before we part,
      My empty glass shall ring;
    And he that has the warmest heart
      Shall loudest laugh and sing.

They say we were not born to eat;
  But gray-haired sages think
It means, Be moderate in your meat,
  And partly live to drink.
For baser tribes the rivers flow
  That know not wine or song ;
Man wants but little drink below,
  But wants that little strong.
    Then once again, etc.

If one bright drop is like the gem
  That decks a monarch's crown,
One goblet holds a diadem
  Of rubies melted down !
A fig for Cæsar's blazing brow,
  But, like the Egyptian queen,
Bid each dissolving jewel glow
  My thirsty lips between.
    Then once again, etc.

The Grecian's mound, the Roman's urn,
  Are silent when we call,
Yet still the purple grapes return
  To cluster on the wall ;
It was a bright Immortal's head
  They circled with the vine,
And o'er their best and bravest dead
  They poured the dark-red wine.
    Then once again, etc.

Methinks o'er every sparkling glass
  Young Eros waves his wings,

And echoes o'er its dimples pass
  From dead Anacreon's strings ;
And, tossing round its beaded brim
  Their locks of floating gold,
With bacchant dance and choral hymn
  Return the nymphs of old.
    Then once again, etc.

A welcome then to joy and mirth,
  From hearts as fresh as ours,
To scatter o'er the dust of earth
  Their sweetly mingled flowers;
'T is Wisdom's self the cup that fills
  In spite of Folly's frown,
And Nature, from her vine-clad hills,
  That rains her life-blood down !
    Then once again, before we part,
      My empty glass shall ring;
    And he that has the warmest heart
      Shall loudest laugh and sing.

SONG

FOR A TEMPERANCE DINNER TO WHICH
LADIES WERE INVITED (NEW YORK
MERCANTILE LIBRARY ASSOCIATION,
NOVEMBER, 1842)

[In the *Professor* Dr. Holmes makes the following reference to this song : —
"I once wrote a song about wine, in which I spoke so warmly of it, that I was afraid some would think it was written *inter pocula ;* whereas it was composed in the bosom of my family, under the most tranquillizing domestic influences.
" — The divinity student turned towards me, looking mischievous. — Can you tell me, — he said, — who wrote a song for a temperance celebration once, of which the following is a verse ? —

" Alas for the loved one, too gentle and fair
  The joys of the banquet to chasten and share !
  Her eye lost its light that his goblet might shine,
  And the rose of her cheek was dissolved in his wine !

I did, — I answered. — What are you going to do about it ? — I will tell you another line I wrote long ago : —

  " Don't be ' consistent,'— but be simply *true.*"]

A HEALTH to dear woman ! She bids us
    untwine,
From the cup it encircles, the fast-clinging
    vine;

But her cheek in its crystal with pleasure
    will glow,
And mirror its bloom in the bright wave
    below.

A health to sweet woman ! The days are
    no more
When she watched for her lord till the
    revel was o'er,
And smoothed the white pillow, and
    blushed when he came,
As she pressed her cold lips on his forehead
    of flame.

Alas for the loved one ! too spotless and fair
The joys of his banquet to chasten and
    share;
Her eye lost its light that his goblet might
    shine,
And the rose of her cheek was dissolved in
    his wine.

Joy smiles in the fountain, health flows in
    the rills,
As their ribbons of silver unwind from the
    hills;
They breathe not the mist of the bacchanal's dream,
But the lilies of innocence float on their
    stream.

Then a health and a welcome to woman
    once more !
She brings us a passport that laughs at our
    door ;
It is written on crimson, — its letters are
    pearls, —
It is countersigned *Nature.* — So, room for
    the Girls !

A SENTIMENT

THE pledge of Friendship ! it is still divine,
Though watery floods have quenched its
    burning wine ;
Whatever vase the sacred drops may hold,
The gourd, the shell, the cup of beaten
    gold,
Around its brim the hand of Nature
    throws
A garland sweeter than the banquet's rose.
Bright are the blushes of the vine-wreathed
    bowl,

Warm with the sunshine of Anacreon's
    soul,
But dearer memories gild the tasteless
    wave
That fainting Sidney perished as he gave.
'T is the heart's current lends the cup its
    glow,
Whate'er the fountain whence the draught
    may flow, —
The diamond dew-drops sparkling through
    the sand,
Scooped by the Arab in his sunburnt hand,
Or the dark streamlet oozing from the
    snow,
Where creep and crouch the shuddering
    Esquimaux;
Ay, in the stream that, ere again we meet,
Shall burst the pavement, glistening at our
    feet,
And, stealing silent from its leafy hills,
Thread all our alleys with its thousand
    rills,—
In each pale draught if generous feeling
    blend,
And o'er the goblet friend shall smile on
    friend,
Even cold Cochituate every heart shall
    warm,
And genial Nature still defy reform !

A RHYMED LESSON

(URANIA)

This poem was delivered before the Boston
Mercantile Library Association, October 14,
1846.

YES, dear Enchantress, — wandering far
    and long,
In realms unperfumed by the breath of
    song,
Where flowers ill-flavored shed their sweets
    around,
And bitterest roots invade the ungenial
    ground,
Whose gems are crystals from the Epsom
    mine,
Whose vineyards flow with antimonial wine,
Whose gates admit no mirthful feature in,
Save one gaunt mocker, the Sardonic grin,
Whose pangs are real, not the woes of
    rhyme
That blue-eyed misses warble out of time; —

Truant, not recreant to thy sacred claim,
Older by reckoning, but in heart the same,
Freed for a moment from the chains of
    toil,
I tread once more thy consecrated soil;
Here at thy feet my old allegiance own,
Thy subject still, and loyal to thy throne !

My dazzled glance explores the crowded
    hall;
Alas, how vain to hope the smiles of all !
I know my audience. All the gay and
    young
Love the light antics of a playful tongue;
And these, remembering some expansive
    line
My lips let loose among the nuts and wine,
Are all impatience till the opening pun
Proclaims the witty shamfight is begun.
Two fifths at least, if not the total half,
Have come infuriate for an earthquake
    laugh;
I know full well what alderman has tied
His red bandanna tight about his side;
I see the mother, who, aware that boys
Perform their laughter with superfluous
    noise,
Beside her kerchief brought an extra one
To stop the explosions of her bursting son;
I know a tailor, once a friend of mine,
Expects great doings in the button line, —
For mirth's concussions rip the outward
    case,
And plant the stitches in a tenderer place.
I know my audience, — these shall have
    their due;
A smile awaits them ere my song is through!

I know myself. Not servile for applause,
My Muse permits no deprecating clause;
Modest or vain, she will not be denied
One bold confession due to honest pride;
And well she knows the drooping veil of song
Shall save her boldness from the caviller's
    wrong.
Her sweeter voice the Heavenly Maid im-
    parts
To tell the secrets of our aching hearts:
For this, a suppliant, captive, prostrate,
    bound,
She kneels imploring at the feet of sound;
For this, convulsed in thought's maternal
    pains,
She loads her arms with rhyme's resound-
    ing chains;

Faint though the music of her fetters be,
It lends one charm,— her lips are ever
free !

Think not I come, in manhood's fiery
noon,
To steal his laurels from the stage buffoon;
His sword of lath the harlequin may wield;
Behold the star upon my lifted shield !
Though the just critic pass my humble
name,
And sweeter lips have drained the cup of
fame,
While my gay stanza pleased the banquet's
lords,
The soul within was tuned to deeper chords!
Say, shall my arms, in other conflicts taught
To swing aloft the ponderous mace of
thought,
Lift, in obedience to a school-girl's law,
Mirth's tinsel wand or laughter's tickling
straw ?
Say, shall I wound with satire's rankling
spear
The pure, warm hearts that bid me wel-
come here ?
No! while I wander through the land of
dreams,
To strive with great and play with trifling
themes,
Let some kind meaning fill the varied line.
You have your judgment; will you trust to
mine ?

———

Between two breaths what crowded mys-
teries lie,—
The first short gasp, the last and long-
drawn sigh!
Like phantoms painted on the magic slide,
Forth from the darkness of the past we
glide,
As living shadows for a moment seen
In airy pageant on the eternal screen,
Traced by a ray from one unchanging
flame,
Then seek the dust and stillness whence
we came.

But whence and why, our trembling
souls inquire,
Caught these dim visions their awakening
fire ?
Oh, who forgets when first the piercing
thought

Through childhood's musings found its
way unsought ?
I AM;— I LIVE. The mystery and the
fear
When the dread question, WHAT HAS
BROUGHT ME HERE ?
Burst through life's twilight, as before the
sun
Roll the deep thunders of the morning gun!
Are angel faces, silent and serene,
Bent on the conflicts of this little scene,
Whose dream-like efforts, whose unreal
strife,
Are but the preludes to a larger life ?

Or does life's summer see the end of all,
These leaves of being mouldering as they
fall,
As the old poet vaguely used to deem,
As WESLEY questioned in his youthful
dream ?
Oh, could such mockery reach our souls
indeed,
Give back the Pharaohs' or the Athenian's
creed;
Better than this a Heaven of man's de-
vice, —
The Indian's sports, the Moslem's para-
dise !

Or is our being's only end and aim
To add new glories to our Maker's name,
As the poor insect, shrivelling in the blaze,
Lends a faint sparkle to its streaming
rays ?
Does earth send upward to the Eternal's
ear
The mingled discords of her jarring sphere
To swell his anthem, while creation rings
With notes of anguish from its shattered
strings ?
Is it for this the immortal Artist means
These conscious, throbbing, agonized ma-
chines ?

Dark is the soul whose sullen creed can
bind
In chains like these the all-embracing
Mind;
No! two-faced bigot, thou dost ill reprove
The sensual, selfish, yet benignant Jove,
And praise a tyrant throned in lonely
pride,
Who loves himself, and cares for naught
beside;

Who gave thee, summoned from primeval
    night,
A thousand laws, and not a single right, —
A heart to feel, and quivering nerves to
    thrill,
The sense of wrong, the death - defying
    will;
Who girt thy senses with this goodly
    frame,
Its earthly glories and its orbs of flame,
Not for thyself, unworthy of a thought,
Poor helpless victim of a life unsought,
But all for him, unchanging and supreme,
The heartless centre of thy frozen scheme!

Trust not the teacher with his lying
    scroll,
Who tears the charter of thy shuddering
    soul;
The God of love, who gave the breath that
    warms
All living dust in all its varied forms,
Asks not the tribute of a world like this
To fill the measure of his perfect bliss.
Though winged with life through all its
    radiant shores,
Creation flowed with unexhausted stores
Cherub and seraph had not yet enjoyed;
For this he called thee from the quicken-
    ing void!
Nor this alone ; a larger gift was thine,
A mightier purpose swelled his vast de-
    sign:
Thought, — conscience, — will, — to make
    them all thine own,
He rent a pillar from the eternal throne!

Made in his image, thou must nobly
    dare
The thorny crown of sovereignty to share.
With eye uplifted, it is thine to view,
From thine own centre, Heaven's o'erarch-
    ing blue;
So round thy heart a beaming circle lies
No fiend can blot, no hypocrite disguise;
From all its orbs one cheering voice is
    heard,
Full to thine ear it bears the Father's
    word,
Now, as in Eden where his first-born trod:
"Seek thine own welfare, true to man and
    God!"
Think not too meanly of thy low estate;
Thou hast a choice; to choose is to cre-
    ate!

Remember whose the sacred lips that tell,
Angels approve thee when thy choice is
    well;
Remember, One, a judge of righteous men,
Swore to spare Sodom if she held but ten!
Use well the freedom which thy Master
    gave,
(Think'st thou that Heaven can tolerate a
    slave ?)
And He who made thee to be just and true
Will bless thee, love thee, — ay, respect
    thee too!

Nature has placed thee on a changeful
    tide,
To breast its waves, but not without a
    guide;
Yet, as the needle will forget its aim,
Jarred by the fury of the electric flame,
As the true current it will falsely feel,
Warped from its axis by a freight of steel;
So will thy CONSCIENCE lose its balanced
    truth
If passion's lightning fall upon thy youth,
So the pure effluence quit its sacred hold
Girt round too deeply with magnetic gold.
Go to yon tower, where busy science
    plies
Her vast antennæ, feeling through the
    skies:
That little vernier on whose slender lines
The midnight taper trembles as it shines,
A silent index, tracks the planets' march
In all their wanderings through the
    ethereal arch;
Tells through the mist where dazzled
    Mercury burns,
And marks the spot where Uranus returns.
So, till by wrong or negligence effaced,
The living index which thy Maker traced
Repeats the line each starry Virtue draws
Through the wide circuit of creation's
    laws;
Still tracks unchanged the everlasting ray
Where the dark shadows of temptation
    stray,
But, once defaced, forgets the orbs of
    light,
And leaves thee wandering o'er the ex-
    panse of night.

"What is thy creed ?" a hundred lips
    inquire;
"Thou seekest God beneath what Christian
    spire ?"

Nor ask they idly, for uncounted lies
Float upward on the smoke of sacrifice;
When man's first incense rose above the plain,
Of earth's two altars one was built by Cain !
  Uncursed by doubt, our earliest creed we take;
We love the precepts for the teacher's sake;
The simple lessons which the nursery taught
Fell soft and stainless on the buds of thought,
And the full blossom owes its fairest hue
To those sweet tear-drops of affection's dew.
  Too oft the light that led our earlier hours
Fades with the perfume of our cradle flowers;
The clear, cold question chills to frozen doubt,
Tired of beliefs, we dread to live without:
Oh then, if Reason waver at thy side,
Let humbler Memory be thy gentle guide;
Go to thy birthplace, and, if faith was there,
Repeat thy father's creed, thy mother's prayer!
  Faith loves to lean on Time's destroying arm,
And age, like distance, lends a double charm;
In dim cathedrals, dark with vaulted gloom,
What holy awe invests the saintly tomb !
There pride will bow, and anxious care expand,
And creeping avarice come with open hand;
The gay can weep, the impious can adore,
From morn's first glimmerings on the chancel floor
Till dying sunset sheds his crimson stains
Through the faint halos of the irised panes.
  Yet there are graves, whose rudely-shapen sod
Bears the fresh footprints where the sexton trod;
Graves where the verdure has not dared to shoot,
Where the chance wild-flower has not fixed its root,
Whose slumbering tenants, dead without a name,
The eternal record shall at length proclaim

Pure as the holiest in the long array
Of hooded, mitred, or tiaraed clay!

  Come, seek the air; some pictures we may gain
Whose passing shadows shall not be in vain;
Not from the scenes that crowd the stranger's soil,
Not from our own amidst the stir of toil,
But when the Sabbath brings its kind release,
And Care lies slumbering on the lap of Peace.

  The air is hushed, the street is holy ground;
Hark! The sweet bells renew their welcome sound:
As one by one awakes each silent tongue,
It tells the turret whence its voice is flung.

  The Chapel, last of sublunary things
That stirs our echoes with the name of Kings,
Whose bell, just glistening from the font and forge,
Rolled its proud requiem for the second George,
Solemn and swelling, as of old it rang,
Flings to the wind its deep, sonorous clang;
The simpler pile, that, mindful of the hour
When Howe's artillery shook its half-built tower,
Wears on its bosom, as a bride might do,
The iron breastpin which the "Rebels" threw,
Wakes the sharp echoes with the quivering thrill
Of keen vibrations, tremulous and shrill;
Aloft, suspended in the morning's fire,
Crash the vast cymbals from the Southern spire;
The Giant, standing by the elm-clad green,
His white lance lifted o'er the silent scene,
Whirling in air his brazen goblet round,
Swings from its brim the swollen floods of sound;
While, sad with memories of the olden time,
Throbs from his tower the Northern Minstrel's chime, —
Faint, single tones, that spell their ancient song,
But tears still follow as they breathe along.

Child of the soil, whom fortune sends to
range
Where man and nature, faith and customs
change,
Borne in thy memory, each familiar tone
Mourns on the winds that sigh in every
zone.
When Ceylon sweeps thee with her per-
fumed breeze
Through the warm billows of the Indian
seas;
When — ship and shadow blended both in
one —
Flames o'er thy mast the equatorial sun,
From sparkling midnight to refulgent
noon
Thy canvas swelling with the still monsoon;
When through thy shrouds the wild tor-
nado sings,
And thy poor sea-bird folds her tattered
wings, —
Oft will delusion o'er thy senses steal,
And airy echoes ring the Sabbath peal !
Then, dim with grateful tears, in long array
Rise the fair town, the island-studded bay,
Home, with its smiling board, its cheering
fire,
The half-choked welcome of the expecting
sire,
The mother's kiss, and, still if aught re-
main,
Our whispering hearts shall aid the silent
strain.
Ah, let the dreamer o'er the taffrail lean
To muse unheeded, and to weep unseen;
Fear not the tropic's dews, the evening's
chills,
His heart lies warm among his triple hills !

Turned from her path by this deceitful
gleam,
My wayward fancy half forgets her theme.
See through the streets that slumbered in
repose
The living current of devotion flows,
Its varied forms in one harmonious band:
Age leading childhood by its dimpled hand;
Want, in the robe whose faded edges fall
To tell of rags beneath the tartan shawl;
And wealth, in silks that, fluttering to ap-
pear,
Lift the deep borders of the proud cash-
mere.
See, but glance briefly, sorrow-worn and
pale,

Those sunken cheeks beneath the widow's
veil;
Alone she wanders where with *him* she trod,
No arm to stay her, but she leans on God.
While other doublets deviate here and
there,
What secret handcuff binds that pretty
pair ?
Compactest couple ! pressing side to side, —
Ah, the white bonnet that reveals the bride !
By the white neckcloth, with its strait-
ened tie,
The sober hat, the Sabbath-speaking eye,
Severe and smileless, he that runs may read
The stern disciple of Geneva's creed:
Decent and slow, behold his solemn march;
Silent he enters through yon crowded arch.
A livelier bearing of the outward man,
The light-hued gloves, the undevout rattan,
Now smartly raised or half profanely
twirled, —
A bright, fresh twinkle from the week-day
world, —
Tell their plain story; yes, thine eyes be-
hold
A cheerful Christian from the liberal fold.
Down the chill street that curves in
gloomiest shade
What marks betray yon solitary maid ?
The cheek's red rose that speaks of balm-
ier air,
The Celtic hue that shades her braided hair,
The gilded missal in her kerchief tied, —
Poor Nora, exile from Killarney's side !
Sister in toil, though blanched by colder
skies,
That left their azure in her downcast eyes,
See pallid Margaret, Labor's patient child,
Scarce weaned from home, the nursling of
the wild,
Where white Katahdin o'er the horizon
shines,
And broad Penobscot dashes through the
pines.
Still, as she hastes, her careful fingers hold
The unfailing hymn-book in its cambric
fold.
Six days at drudgery's heavy wheel she
stands,
The seventh sweet morning folds her
weary hands.
Yes, child of suffering, thou mayst well
be sure
He who ordained the Sabbath loves the
poor!

This weekly picture faithful Memory
    draws,
Nor claims the noisy tribute of applause;
Faint is the glow such barren hopes can
    lend,
And frail the line that asks no loftier end.
    Trust me, kind listener, I will yet be-
        guile
Thy saddened features of the promised
    smile.
This magic mantle thou must well divide,
It has its sable and its ermine side;
Yet, ere the lining of the robe appears,
Take thou in silence what I give in tears.

Dear listening soul, this transitory scene
Of murmuring stillness, busily serene, —
This solemn pause, the breathing-space of
    man,
The halt of toil's exhausted caravan, —
Comes sweet with music to thy wearied
    ear;
Rise with its anthems to a holier sphere !

Deal meekly, gently, with the hopes
    that guide
The lowliest brother straying from thy
    side:
If right, they bid thee tremble for thine
    own;
If wrong, the verdict is for God alone !

What though the champions of thy faith
    esteem
The sprinkled fountain or baptismal
    stream;
Shall jealous passions in unseemly strife
Cross their dark weapons o'er the waves of
    life ?

Let my free soul, expanding as it can,
Leave to his scheme the thoughtful Puri-
    tan;
But Calvin's dogma shall my lips deride ?
In that stern faith my angel Mary died;
Or ask if mercy's milder creed can save,
Sweet sister, risen from thy new-made
    grave ?

True, the harsh founders of thy church
    reviled
That ancient faith, the trust of Erin's
    child;
Must thou be raking in the crumbled past
For racks and fagots in her teeth to cast ?

See from the ashes of Helvetia's pile
The whitened skull of old Servetus smile !
Round her young heart thy "Romish
    Upas" threw
Its firm, deep fibres, strengthening as she
    grew;
Thy sneering voice may call them "Popish
    tricks,"
Her Latin prayers, her dangling crucifix,
But *De Profundis* blessed her father's
    grave,
That "idol" cross her dying mother gave!
    What if some angel looks with equal eyes
On her and thee, the simple and the wise,
Writes each dark fault against thy brighter
    creed,
And drops a tear with every foolish bead!
    Grieve, as thou must, o'er history's reek-
        ing page;
Blush for the wrongs that stain thy happier
    age;
Strive with the wanderer from the better
    path,
Bearing thy message meekly, not in wrath;
Weep for the frail that err, the weak that
    fall,
Have thine own faith, — but hope and
    pray for all !

Faith; Conscience; Love. A meaner
    task remains,
And humbler thoughts must creep in
    lowlier strains.
Shalt thou be honest ? Ask the worldly
    schools,
And all will tell thee knaves are busier
    fools;
Prudent ? Industrious ? Let not modern
    pens
Instruct "Poor Richard's " fellow-citizens.

Be firm! One constant element in luck
Is genuine solid old Teutonic pluck.
See yon tall shaft; it felt the earthquake's
    thrill,
Clung to its base, and greets the sunrise
    still.

Stick to your aim: the mongrel's hold
    will slip,
But only crowbars loose the bulldog's grip;
Small as he looks, the jaw that never
    yields
Drags down the bellowing monarch of the
    fields !

Yet in opinions look not always back, —
Your wake is nothing, mind the coming
track;
Leave what you 've done for what you have
to do;
Don't be "consistent," but be simply true.

Don't catch the fidgets; you have found
your place
Just in the focus of a nervous race,
Fretful to change and rabid to discuss,
Full of excitements, always in a fuss.
Think of the patriarchs; then compare as
men
These lean-cheeked maniacs of the tongue
and pen!
Run, if you like, but try to keep your
breath;
Work like a man, but don't be worked to
death;
And with new notions, — let me change
the rule, —
Don't strike the iron till it 's slightly cool.

Choose well your *set*; our feeble nature
seeks
The aid of clubs, the countenance of
cliques;
And with this object settle first of all
Your weight of metal and your size of
ball.
Track not the steps of such as hold you
cheap,
Too mean to prize, though good enough to
keep;
The "real, genuine, no-mistake Tom
Thumbs"
Are little people fed on great men's
crumbs.
Yet keep no followers of that hateful
brood
That basely mingles with its wholesome
food
The tumid reptile, which, the poet said,
Doth wear a precious jewel in his head.

If the wild filly, "Progress," thou
wouldst ride,
Have young companions ever at thy side;
But wouldst thou stride the stanch old
mare, "Success,"
Go with thine elders, though they please
thee less.
Shun such as lounge through afternoons
and eves,

And on thy dial write, "Beware of
thieves!"
Felon, of minutes, never taught to feel
The worth of treasures which thy fingers
steal,
Pick my left pocket of its silver dime,
But spare the right, — it holds my golden
time!

Does praise delight thee? Choose some
ultra side, —
A sure old recipe, and often tried;
Be its apostle, congressman, or bard,
Spokesman or jokesman, only drive it hard;
But know the forfeit which thy choice
abides,
For on two wheels the poor reformer
rides, —
One black with epithets the *anti* throws,
One white with flattery painted by the *pros.*

Though books on MANNERS are not out
of print,
An honest tongue may drop a harmless
hint.
Stop not, unthinking, every friend you
meet,
To spin your wordy fabric in the street;
While you are emptying your colloquial
pack,
The fiend *Lumbago* jumps upon his back.
Nor cloud his features with the unwel-
come tale
Of how he looks, if haply thin and pale;
Health is a subject for his child, his wife,
And the rude office that insures his life.
Look in his face, to meet thy neighbor's
soul,
Not on his garments, to detect a hole;
"How to observe" is what thy pages show,
Pride of thy sex, Miss Harriet Martineau!
Oh, what a precious book the one would be
That taught observers what they 're *not* to
see!

I tell in verse — 't were better done in
prose —
One curious trick that everybody knows;
Once form this habit, and it 's very strange
How long it sticks, how hard it is to
change.
Two friendly people, both disposed to
smile,
Who meet, like others, every little while,
Instead of passing with a pleasant bow,

And "How d' ye do?" or "How's your
    uncle now?"
Impelled by feelings in their nature kind,
But slightly weak and somewhat undefined,
Rush at each other, make a sudden stand,
Begin to talk, expatiate, and expand;
Each looks quite radiant, seems extremely
    struck,
Their meeting so was such a piece of luck;
Each thinks the other thinks he's greatly
    pleased
To screw the vice in which they both are
    squeezed ;
So there they talk, in dust, or mud, or
    snow,
Both bored to death, and both afraid to
    go !
  Your hat once lifted, do not hang your
    fire,
Nor, like slow Ajax, fighting still, retire;
When your old castor on your crown you
    clap,
Go off; you 've mounted your percussion
    cap.

  Some words on LANGUAGE may be well
    applied,
And take them kindly, though they touch
    your pride.
Words lead to things; a scale is more pre-
    cise, —
Coarse speech, bad grammar, swearing,
    drinking, vice.
Our cold Northeaster's icy fetter clips
The native freedom of the Saxon lips;
See the brown peasant of the plastic South,
How all his passions play about his mouth!
With us, the feature that transmits the
    soul,
A frozen, passive, palsied breathing-hole.
The crampy shackles of the ploughboy's
    walk
Tie the small muscles when he strives to
    talk;
Not all the pumice of the polished town
Can smooth this roughness of the barnyard
    down;
Rich, honored, titled, he betrays his race
By this one mark, — he's awkward in the
    face ; —
Nature's rude impress, long before he
    knew
The sunny street that holds the sifted few.
  It can't be helped, though, if we 're taken
    young,

We gain some freedom of the lips and
    tongue;
But school and college often try in vain
To break the padlock of our boyhood's
    chain:
One stubborn word will prove this axiom
    true, —
No quondam rustic can enunciate *view*.

  A few brief stanzas may be well em-
    ployed
To speak of errors we can all avoid.
  Learning condemns beyond the reach of
    hope
The careless lips that speak of sŏap for
    sōap;
Her edict exiles from her fair abode
The clownish voice that utters rŏad for
    rōad:
Less stern to him who calls his cōat a cŏat,
And steers his bōat, believing it a bŏat,
She pardoned one, our classic city's boast,
Who said at Cambridge mŏst instead of
    mōst,
But knit her brows and stamped her angry
    foot
To hear a Teacher call a rōot a rŏŏt.

  Once more: speak clearly, if you speak
    at all ;
Carve every word before you let it fall ;
Don't, like a lecturer or dramatic star,
Try over-hard to roll the British R ;
Do put your accents in the proper spot ;
Don't, — let me beg you, — don't say
    "How?" for "What?"
And when you stick on conversation's burs,
Don't strew your pathway with those
    dreadful *urs*.

  From little matters let us pass to less,
And lightly touch the mysteries of DRESS ;
The outward forms the inner man reveal, —
We guess the pulp before we cut the peel.

  I leave the broadcloth, — coats and all
    the rest, —
The dangerous waistcoat, called by cock-
    neys "vest,"
The things named "pants" in certain
    documents,
A word not made for gentlemen, but
    "gents ;"
One single precept might the whole con-
    dense:

Be sure your tailor is a man of sense;
But add a little care, a decent pride,
And always err upon the sober side.

Three pairs of boots one pair of feet de-
mands,
If polished daily by the owner's hands;
If the dark menial's visit save from this,
Have twice the number, — for he 'll some-
times miss.
One pair for critics of the nicer sex,
Close in the instep's clinging circumflex,
Long, narrow, light; the Gallic boot of love,
A kind of cross between a boot and glove.
Compact, but easy, strong, substantial,
square,
Let native art compile the medium pair.
The third remains, and let your tasteful
skill
Here show some relics of affection still;
Let no stiff cowhide, reeking from the tan,
No rough caoutchouc, no deformed brogan,
Disgrace the tapering outline of your feet,
Though yellow torrents gurgle through the
street.

Wear seemly gloves; not black, nor yet
too light,
And least of all the pair that once was
white;
Let the dead party where you told your
loves
Bury in peace its dead bouquets and gloves;
Shave like the goat, if so your fancy bids,
But be a parent, — don't neglect your kids.

Have a good hat; the secret of your looks
Lives with the beaver in Canadian brooks;
Virtue may flourish in an old cravat,
But man and nature scorn the shocking hat.
Does beauty slight you from her gay
abodes ?
Like bright Apollo, you must take to
Rhoades, —
Mount the new castor, — ice itself will melt;
Boots, gloves, may fail; the hat is always
felt!

Be shy of breastpins; plain, well-ironed
white,
With small pearl buttons, — two of them
in sight, —
Is always genuine, while your gems may
pass,
Though real diamonds, for ignoble glass.

But spurn those paltry Cisatlantic lies
That round his breast the shabby rustic ties;
Breathe not the name profaned to hallow
things
The indignant laundress blushes when she
brings!

Our freeborn race, averse to every check,
Has tossed the yoke of Europe from its
neck;
From the green prairie to the sea-girt town,
The whole wide nation turns its collars
down.
The stately neck is manhood's manliest
part;
It takes the life-blood freshest from the
heart.
With short, curled ringlets close around it
spread,
How light and strong it lifts the Grecian
head!
Thine, fair Erechtheus of Minerva's wall;
Or thine, young athlete of the Louvre's
hall,
Smooth as the pillar flashing in the sun
That filled the arena where thy wreaths
were won,
Firm as the band that clasps the antlered
spoil
Strained in the winding anaconda's coil!
I spare the contrast; it were only kind
To be a little, nay, intensely blind.
Choose for yourself: I know it cuts your
ear;
I know the points will sometimes interfere;
I know that often, like the filial John,
Whom sleep surprised with half his drapery
on,
You show your features to the astonished
town
With one side standing and the other
down; —
But oh, my friend! my favorite fellow-
man!
If Nature made you on her modern plan,
Sooner than wander with your windpipe
bare, —
The fruit of Eden ripening in the air, —
With that lean head-stalk, that protruding
chin,
Wear standing collars, were they made of
tin!
And have a neckcloth — by the throat of
Jove! —
Cut from the funnel of a rusty stove!

The long-drawn lesson narrows to its
  close,
Chill, slender, slow, the dwindled current
  flows;
Tired of the ripples on its feeble springs,
Once more the Muse unfolds her upward
  wings.

Land of my birth, with this unhallowed
  tongue,
Thy hopes, thy dangers, I perchance had
  sung;
But who shall sing, in brutal disregard
Of all the essentials of the " native bard " ?
  Lake, sea, shore, prairie, forest, moun-
    tain, fall,
His eye omnivorous must devour them all;
The tallest summits and the broadest tides
His foot must compass with its giant strides,
Where Ocean thunders, where Missouri
  rolls,
And tread at once the tropics and the
  poles;
His food all forms of earth, fire, water, air,
His home all space, his birthplace every-
  where.

Some grave compatriot, having seen per-
  haps
The pictured page that goes in Worcester's
  Maps,
And read in earnest what was said in jest,
" Who drives fat oxen " — please to add
  the rest, —
Sprung the odd notion that the poet's
  dreams
Grow in the ratio of his hills and streams;
And hence insisted that the aforesaid
  " bard,"
Pink of the future, fancy's pattern-card,
The babe of nature in the " giant West,"
Must be of course her biggest and her
  best.

Oh! when at length the expected bard
  shall come,
Land of our pride, to strike thine echoes
  dumb,
(And many a voice exclaims in prose and
  rhyme,
It 's getting late, and he 's behind his time,)
When all thy mountains clap their hands
  in joy,
And all thy cataracts thunder, " That 's
  the boy," —

Say if with him the reign of song shall end,
And Heaven declare its final dividend !

Be calm, dear brother! whose impas-
  sioned strain
Comes from an alley watered by a drain;
The little Mincio, dribbling to the Po,
Beats all the epics of the Hoang Ho;
If loved in earnest by the tuneful maid,
Don't mind their nonsense, — never be
  afraid !

The nurse of poets feeds her wingèd
  brood
By common firesides, on familiar food;
In a low hamlet, by a narrow stream,
Where bovine rustics used to doze and
  dream,
She filled young William's fiery fancy full,
While old John Shakespeare talked of
  beeves and wool !

No Alpine needle, with its climbing spire,
Brings down for mortals the Promethean
  fire,
If careless nature have forgot to frame
An altar worthy of the sacred flame.
  Unblest by any save the goatherd's lines,
Mont Blanc rose soaring through his " sea
  of pines; "
In vain the rivers from their ice-caves flash;
No hymn salutes them but the Ranz des
  Vaches,
Till lazy Coleridge, by the morning's light,
Gazed for a moment on the fields of white,
And lo! the glaciers found at length a
  tongue,
Mont Blanc was vocal, and Chamouni sung !

Children of wealth or want, to each is
  given
One spot of green, and all the blue of
  heaven !
Enough if these their outward shows im-
  part;
The rest is thine, — the scenery of the heart.
  If passion's hectic in thy stanzas glow,
Thy heart's best life-blood ebbing as they
  flow;
If with thy verse thy strength and bloom
  distil,
Drained by the pulses of the fevered
  thrill;
If sound's sweet effluence polarize thy
  brain,

And thoughts turn crystals in thy fluid
strain, —
Nor rolling ocean, nor the prairie's bloom,
Nor streaming cliffs, nor rayless cavern's
gloom,
Need'st thou, young poet, to inform thy
line;
Thy own broad signet stamps thy song
divine !
    Let others gaze where silvery streams
are rolled,
And chase the rainbow for its cup of gold;
To thee all landscapes wear a heavenly dye,
Changed in the glance of thy prismatic eye;
Nature evoked thee in sublimer throes,
For thee her inmost Arethusa flows, —
The mighty mother's living depths are
stirred, —
Thou art the starred Osiris of the herd!

    A few brief lines; they touch on solemn
chords,
And hearts may leap to hear their honest
words;
Yet, ere the jarring bugle-blast is blown,
The softer lyre shall breathe its soothing
tone.

    New England! proudly may thy children
claim
Their honored birthright by its humblest
name!
Cold are thy skies, but, ever fresh and
clear,
No rank malaria stains thine atmosphere;
No fungous weeds invade thy scanty soil,
Scarred by the ploughshares of unslumber-
ing toil.
Long may the doctrines by thy sages
taught,
Raised from the quarries where their sires
have wrought,
Be like the granite of thy rock-ribbed
land, —
As slow to rear, as obdurate to stand;
And as the ice that leaves thy crystal mine
Chills the fierce alcohol in the Creole's
wine,
So may the doctrines of thy sober school
Keep the hot theories of thy neighbors
cool!

    If ever, trampling on her ancient path,
Cankered by treachery or inflamed by
wrath,

With smooth "Resolves" or with dis-
cordant cries,
The mad Briareus of disunion rise,
Chiefs of New England! by your sires'
renown,
Dash the red torches of the rebel down !
Flood his black hearthstone till its flames
expire,
Though your old Sachem fanned his coun-
cil-fire !

    But if at last, her fading cycle run,
The tongue must forfeit what the arm has
won,
Then rise, wild Ocean ! roll thy surging
shock
Full on old Plymouth's desecrated rock !
Scale the proud shaft degenerate hands
have hewn,
Where bleeding Valor stained the flowers
of June!
Sweep in one tide her spires and turrets
down,
And howl her dirge above Monadnock's
crown !

    List not the tale; the Pilgrim's hallowed
shore,
Though strewn with weeds, is granite at
the core;
Oh, rather trust that He who made her
free
Will keep her true as long as faith shall be!
    Farewell ! yet lingering through the
destined hour,
Leave, sweet Enchantress, one memorial
flower !

    An Angel, floating o'er the waste of
snow
That clad our Western desert, long ago,
(The same fair spirit who, unseen by day,
Shone as a star along the Mayflower's
way,) —
Sent, the first herald of the Heavenly plan,
To choose on earth a resting-place for
man, —
Tired with his flight along the unvaried
field,
Turned to soar upwards, when his glance
revealed
A calm, bright bay enclosed in rocky
bounds,
And at its entrance stood three sister
mounds.

The Angel spake: "This threefold hill
    shall be
The home of Arts, the nurse of Liberty !
One stately summit from its shaft shall
    pour
Its deep-red blaze along the darkened
    shore;
Emblem of thoughts that, kindling far and
    wide,
In danger's night shall be a nation's guide.
One swelling crest the citadel shall crown,
Its slanted bastions black with battle's
    frown,
And bid the sons that tread its scowling
    heights
Bare their strong arms for man and all his
    rights!
One silent steep along the northern wave
Shall hold the patriarch's and the hero's
    grave;
When fades the torch, when o'er the peace-
    ful scene
The embattled fortress smiles in living
    green,
The cross of Faith, the anchor staff of
    Hope,
Shall stand eternal on its grassy slope;
There through all time shall faithful
    Memory tell,
' Here Virtue toiled, and Patriot Valor
    fell;
Thy free, proud fathers slumber at thy
    side;
Live as they lived, or perish as they
    died ! ' "

AN AFTER-DINNER POEM

(TERPSICHORE)

Read at the Annual Dinner of the Phi Beta
Kappa Society, at Cambridge, August 24,
1843.

IN narrowest girdle, O reluctant Muse,
In closest frock and Cinderella shoes,
Bound to the foot-lights for thy brief dis-
    play,
One zephyr step, and then dissolve away!

Short is the space that gods and men can
    spare
To Song's twin brother when she is not
    there.

Let others water every lusty line,
As Homer's heroes did their purple wine;
Pierian revellers ! Know in strains like
    these
The native juice, the real honest squeeze, —
Strains that, diluted to the twentieth
    power,
In yon grave temple might have filled an
    hour.
Small room for Fancy's many-chorded
    lyre,
For Wit's bright rockets with their trains
    of fire,
For Pathos, struggling vainly to surprise
The iron tutor's tear-denying eyes,
For Mirth, whose finger with delusive
    wile
Turns the grim key of many a rusty smile,
For Satire, emptying his corrosive flood
On hissing Folly's gas-exhaling brood,
The pun, the fun, the moral, and the joke,
The hit, the thrust, the pugilistic poke, —
Small space for these, so pressed by nig-
    gard Time,
Like that false matron, known to nursery
    rhyme, —
Insidious Morey, — scarce her tale begun,
Ere listening infants weep the story done.

Oh, had we room to rip the mighty bags
That Time, the harlequin, has stuffed with
    rags!
Grant us one moment to unloose the
    strings,
While the old graybeard shuts his leather
    wings.
But what a heap of motley trash appears
Crammed in the bundles of successive
    years!
As the lost rustic on some festal day
Stares through the concourse in its vast
    array, —
Where in one cake a throng of faces runs,
All stuck together like a sheet of buns, —
And throws the bait of some unheeded
    name,
Or shoots a wink with most uncertain aim,
So roams my vision, wandering over all,
And strives to choose, but knows not where
    to fall.

Skins of flayed authors, husks of dead re-
    views,
The turn-coat's clothes, the office-seeker's
    shoes,

Scraps from cold feasts, where conversation runs
Through mouldy toasts to oxidated puns,
And grating songs a listening crowd endures,
Rasped from the throats of bellowing amateurs;
Sermons, whose writers played such dangerous tricks
Their own heresiarchs called them heretics,
(Strange that one term such distant poles should link,
The Priestleyan's copper and the Puseyan's zinc);
Poems that shuffle with superfluous legs
A blindfold minuet over addled eggs,
Where all the syllables that end in èd,
Like old dragoons, have cuts across the head;
Essays so dark Champollion might despair
To guess what mummy of a thought was there,
Where our poor English, striped with foreign phrase,
Looks like a zebra in a parson's chaise;
Lectures that cut our dinners down to roots,
Or prove (by monkeys) men should stick to fruits, —
Delusive error, as at trifling charge
Professor Gripes will certify at large;
Mesmeric pamphlets, which to facts appeal,
Each fact as slippery as a fresh-caught eel;
And figured heads, whose hieroglyphs invite
To wandering knaves that discount fools at sight:
Such things as these, with heaps of unpaid bills,
And candy puffs and homœopathic pills,
And ancient bell-crowns with contracted rim,
And bonnets hideous with expanded brim,
And coats whose memory turns the sartor pale,
Their sequels tapering like a lizard's tail, —
How might we spread them to the smiling day,
And toss them, fluttering like the new-mown hay,
To laughter's light or sorrow's pitying shower,
Were these brief minutes lengthened to an hour.

The narrow moments fit like Sunday shoes, —
How vast the heap, how quickly must we choose!
A few small scraps from out his mountain mass
We snatch in haste, and let the vagrant pass.
This shrunken CRUST that Cerberus could not bite,
Stamped (in one corner) "Pickwick copyright,"
Kneaded by youngsters, raised by flattery's yeast,
Was once a loaf, and helped to make a feast.
He for whose sake the glittering show appears
Has sown the world with laughter and with tears,
And they whose welcome wets the bumper's brim
Have wit and wisdom, — for they all quote him.
So, many a tongue the evening hour prolongs
With spangled speeches, — let alone the songs;
Statesmen grow merry, lean attorneys laugh,
And weak teetotals warm to half and half,
And beardless Tullys, new to festive scenes,
Cut their first crop of youth's precocious greens,
And wits stand ready for impromptu claps,
With loaded barrels and percussion caps,
And Pathos, cantering through the minor keys,
Waves all her onions to the trembling breeze;
While the great Feasted views with silent glee
His scattered limbs in Yankee fricassee.

Sweet is the scene where genial friendship plays
The pleasing game of interchanging praise.
Self-love, grimalkin of the human heart,
Is ever pliant to the master's art;
Soothed with a word, she peacefully withdraws
And sheathes in velvet her obnoxious claws,
And thrills the hand that smooths her glossy fur
With the light tremor of her grateful purr.

But what sad music fills the quiet hall,
If on her back a feline rival fall !
And oh, what noises shake the tranquil house
If old Self-interest cheats her of a mouse !

Thou, O my country, hast thy foolish ways,
Too apt to purr at every stranger's praise;
But if the stranger touch thy modes or laws,
Off goes the velvet and out come the claws !
And thou, Illustrious ! but too poorly paid
In toasts from Pickwick for thy great crusade,
Though, while the echoes labored with thy name,
The public trap denied thy little game,
Let other lips our jealous laws revile, —
The marble Talfourd or the rude Carlyle, —
But on thy lids, which Heaven forbids to close
Where'er the light of kindly nature glows,
Let not the dollars that a churl denies
Weigh like the shillings on a dead man's eyes !
Or, if thou wilt, be more discreetly blind,
Nor ask to see all wide extremes combined.
Not in our wastes the dainty blossoms smile
That crowd the gardens of thy scanty isle.
There white-cheeked Luxury weaves a thousand charms;
Here sun-browned Labor swings his naked arms.
Long are the furrows he must trace between
The ocean's azure and the prairie's green ;
Full many a blank his destined realm displays,
Yet sees the promise of his riper days:
Far through yon depths the panting engine moves,
His chariots ringing in their steel-shod grooves;
And Erie's naiad flings her diamond wave
O'er the wild sea-nymph in her distant cave!
While tasks like these employ his anxious hours,
What if his cornfields are not edged with flowers ?
Though bright as silver the meridian beams

Shine through the crystal of thine English streams,
Turbid and dark the mighty wave is whirled
That drains our Andes and divides a world !

But lo ! a PARCHMENT ! Surely it would seem
The sculptured impress speaks of power supreme ;
Some grave design the solemn page must claim
That shows so broadly an emblazoned name.
A sovereign's promise ! Look, the lines afford
All Honor gives when Caution asks his word :
There sacred Faith has laid her snow-white hands,
And awful Justice knit her iron bands ;
Yet every leaf is stained with treachery's dye,
And every letter crusted with a lie.
Alas ! no treason has degraded yet
The Arab's salt, the Indian's calumet ;
A simple rite, that bears the wanderer's pledge,
Blunts the keen shaft and turns the dagger's edge;
While jockeying senates stop to sign and seal,
And freeborn statesmen legislate to steal.
Rise, Europe, tottering with thine Atlas load,
Turn thy proud eye to Freedom's blest abode,
And round her forehead, wreathed with heavenly flame,
Bind the dark garland of her daughter's shame !
Ye ocean clouds, that wrap the angry blast,
Coil her stained ensign round its haughty mast,
Or tear the fold that wears so foul a scar,
And drive a bolt through every blackened star !
Once more, — once only, — we must stop so soon :
What have we here ? A GERMAN-SILVER SPOON ;
A cheap utensil, which we often see
Used by the dabblers in æsthetic tea,
Of slender fabric, somewhat light and thin,
Made of mixed metal, chiefly lead and tin ;
The bowl is shallow, and the handle small,
Marked in large letters with the name JEAN PAUL.

Small as it is, its powers are passing
  strange,
For all who use it show a wondrous change ;
And first, a fact to make the barbers stare,
It beats Macassar for the growth of hair.
See those small youngsters whose expansive
  ears
Maternal kindness grazed with frequent
  shears ;
Each bristling crop a dangling mass be-
  comes,
And all the spoonies turn to Absaloms !
Nor this alone its magic power displays,
It alters strangely all their works and
  ways ;
With uncouth words they tire their tender
  lungs,
The same bald phrases on their hundred
  tongues :
" Ever " " The Ages " in their page ap-
  pear,
" Alway " the bedlamite is called a
  " Seer ; "
On every leaf the " earnest " sage may
  scan,
Portentous bore ! their " many-sided "
  man, —
A weak eclectic, groping vague and dim,
Whose every angle is a half-starved whim,
Blind as a mole and curious as a lynx,
Who rides a beetle, which he calls a
  " Sphinx."
And oh, what questions asked in clubfoot
  rhyme
Of Earth the tongueless and the deaf-mute
  Time !
Here babbling " Insight " shouts in Nature's
  ears
His last conundrum on the orbs and spheres ;
There Self-inspection sucks its little thumb,
With " Whence am I ? " and " Wherefore
  did I come ? "
Deluded infants ! will they ever know
Some doubts must darken o'er the world
  below,
Though all the Platos of the nursery trail
Their " clouds of glory " at the go-cart's
  tail ?
Oh might these couplets their attention
  claim

That gain their author the Philistine's
  name !
(A stubborn race, that, spurning foreign
  law,
Was much belabored with an ass's jaw.)

Melodious Laura ! From the sad retreats
That hold thee, smothered with excess of
  sweets,
Shade of a shadow, spectre of a dream,
Glance thy wan eye across the Stygian
  stream !
The slipshod dreamer treads thy fragrant
  halls,
The sophist's cobwebs hang thy roseate
  walls,
And o'er the crotchets of thy jingling tunes
The bard of mystery scrawls his crooked
  " runes."
Yes, thou art gone, with all the tuneful
  hordes
That candied thoughts in amber-colored
  words,
And in the precincts of thy late abodes
The clattering verse-wright hammers Or-
  phic odes.
Thou, soft as zephyr, wast content to fly
On the gilt pinions of a balmy sigh ;
He, vast as Phœbus on his burning wheels,
Would stride through ether at Orion's heels.
Thy emblem, Laura, was a perfume-jar,
And thine, young Orpheus, is a pewter star.
The balance trembles, — be its verdict told
When the new jargon slumbers with the
  old !

———

Cease, playful goddess ! From thine airy
  bound
Drop like a feather softly to the ground ;
This light bolero grows a ticklish dance,
And there is mischief in thy kindling
  glance.
To-morrow bids thee, with rebuking frown,
Change thy gauze tunic for a home-made
  gown,
Too blest by fortune if the passing day
Adorn thy bosom with its frail bouquet,
But oh, still happier if the next forgets
Thy daring steps and dangerous pirouettes !

MEDICAL POEMS

[THIS division was made when the River-side Edition was arranged, but by accident the last number in the division was at that time omitted.]

THE MORNING VISIT

A SICK man's chamber, though it often boast
The grateful presence of a literal toast,
Can hardly claim, amidst its various wealth,
The right unchallenged to propose a health;
Yet though its tenant is denied the feast,
Friendship must launch his sentiment at least,
As prisoned damsels, locked from lovers' lips,
Toss them a kiss from off their fingers' tips.

The morning visit, — not till sickness falls
In the charmed circles of your own safe walls;
Till fever's throb and pain's relentless rack
Stretch you all helpless on your aching back;
Not till you play the patient in your turn,
The morning visit's mystery shall you learn.

'T is a small matter in your neighbor's case,
To charge your fee for showing him your face;
You skip up-stairs, inquire, inspect, and touch,
Prescribe, take leave, and off to twenty such.

But when at length, by fate's transferred decree,
The visitor becomes the visitee,
Oh, then, indeed, it pulls another string ;
Your ox is gored, and that's a different thing !

Your friend is sick : phlegmatic as a Turk,
You write your recipe and let it work;
Not yours to stand the shiver and the frown,
And sometimes worse, with which your draught goes down.
Calm as a clock your knowing hand directs,
Rhei, jalapæ ana grana sex,
Or traces on some tender missive's back,
Scrupulos duos pulveris ipecac;
And leaves your patient to his qualms and gripes,
Cool as a sportsman banging at his snipes.
But change the time, the person, and the place,
And be yourself "the interesting case,"
You'll gain some knowledge which it's well to learn ;
In future practice it may serve your turn.
Leeches, for instance, — pleasing creatures quite;
Try them, — and bless you, — don't you find they bite ?
You raise a blister for the smallest cause,
But be yourself the sitter whom it draws,
And trust my statement, you will not deny
The worst of draughtsmen is your Spanish fly !
It's mighty easy ordering when you please,
Infusi sennæ capiat uncias tres ;
It's mighty different when you quackle down
Your own three ounces of the liquid brown.
Pilula, pulvis, — pleasant words enough,
When other throats receive the shocking stuff;
But oh, what flattery can disguise the groan
That meets the gulp which sends it through your own !

Be gentle, then, though Art's unsparing
    rules
Give you the handling of her sharpest
    tools;
Use them not rashly, — sickness is enough;
Be always "ready," but be never "rough."

Of all the ills that suffering man endures,
The largest fraction liberal Nature cures;
Of those remaining, 't is the smallest part
Yields to the efforts of judicious Art;
But simple *Kindness*, kneeling by the bed
To shift the pillow for the sick man's head,
Give the fresh draught to cool the lips that
    burn,
Fan the hot brow, the weary frame to
    turn, —
Kindness, untutored by our grave M. D.'s,
But Nature's graduate, when she schools to
    please,
Wins back more sufferers with her voice
    and smile
Than all the trumpery in the druggist's
    pile.

Once more, be *quiet :* coming up the stair,
Don't be a plantigrade, a human bear,
But, stealing softly on the silent toe,
Reach the sick chamber ere you 're heard
    below.
Whatever changes there may greet your
    eyes,
Let not your looks proclaim the least sur-
    prise;
It 's not your business by your face to show
All that your patient does not want to
    know;
Nay, use your optics with considerate care,
And don't abuse your privilege to stare.
But if your eyes may probe him overmuch,
Beware still further how you rudely touch;
Don't clutch his carpus in your icy fist,
But warm your fingers ere you take the
    wrist.
If the poor victim needs must be percussed,
Don't make an anvil of his aching bust;
(Doctors exist within a hundred miles
Who thump a thorax as they 'd hammer
    piles;)
If you must listen to his doubtful chest,
Catch the essentials, and ignore the rest.
Spare him; the sufferer wants of you and
    art
A track to steer by, not a finished chart.
So of your questions : don't in mercy try

To pump your patient absolutely dry ;
He 's not a mollusk squirming in a dish,
You 're not Agassiz, and he 's not a fish.

And last, not least, in each perplexing case,
Learn the sweet magic of a *cheerful face;*
Not always smiling, but at least serene,
When grief and anguish cloud the anxious
    scene.
Each look, each movement, every word and
    tone,
Should tell your patient you are all his
    own;
Not the mere artist, purchased to attend,
But the warm, ready, self-forgetting friend,
Whose genial visit in itself combines
The best of cordials, tonics, anodynes.

Such is the *visit* that from day to day
Sheds o'er my chamber its benignant ray.
I give his health, who never cared to claim
Her babbling homage from the tongue of
    Fame;
Unmoved by praise, he stands by all con
    fest,
The truest, noblest, wisest, kindest, best.

THE TWO ARMIES

[Written for and read at a meeting of the
Massachusetts Medical Society in 1858.
In printing these verses in the *Autocrat*,
where they are referred to the " Professor," the
poet says: " He introduced them with a few
remarks, he told me, of which the only one he
remembered was this : that he had rather
write a single line which one among them
should think worth remembering than set them
all laughing with a string of epigrams."]

As Life's unending column pours,
    Two marshalled hosts are seen, —
Two armies on the trampled shores
    That Death flows black between.

One marches to the drum-beat's roll,
    The wide-mouthed clarion's bray,
And bears upon a crimson scroll,
    " Our glory is to slay."

One moves in silence by the stream,
    With sad, yet watchful eyes.
Calm as the patient planet's gleam
    That walks the clouded skies.

Along its front no sabres shine,
  No blood-red pennons wave ;
Its banner bears the single line,
  "Our duty is to save."

For those no death-bed's lingering shade;
  At Honor's trumpet-call,
With knitted brow and lifted blade
  In Glory's arms they fall.

For these no clashing falchions bright,
  No stirring battle-cry ;
The bloodless stabber calls by night, —
  Each answers, "Here am I ! "

For those the sculptor's laurelled bust,
  The builder's marble piles,
The anthems pealing o'er their dust
  Through long cathedral aisles.

For these the blossom-sprinkled turf
  That floods the lonely graves
When Spring rolls in her sea-green surf
  In flowery-foaming waves.

Two paths lead upward from below,
  And angels wait above,
Who count each burning life-drop's flow,
  Each falling tear of Love.

Though from the Hero's bleeding breast
  Her pulses Freedom drew,
Though the white lilies in her crest
  Sprang from that scarlet dew, —

While Valor's haughty champions wait
  Till all their scars are shown,
Love walks unchallenged through the gate,
  To sit beside the Throne !

THE STETHOSCOPE SONG

A PROFESSIONAL BALLAD

THERE was a young man in Boston town,
  He bought him a stethoscope nice and
    new,
All mounted and finished and polished
    down,
  With an ivory cap and a stopper too.

It happened a spider within did crawl,
  And spun him a web of ample size,
Wherein there chanced one day to fall
  A couple of very imprudent flies.

The first was a bottle-fly, big and blue,
  The second was smaller, and thin and
    long ;
So there was a concert between the two,
  Like an octave flute and a tavern gong.

Now being from Paris but recently,
  This fine young man would show his skill ,
And so they gave him, his hand to try,
  A hospital patient extremely ill.

Some said that his *liver* was short of *bile,*
  And some that his *heart* was over size,
While some kept arguing, all the while,
  He was crammed with *tubercles* up to his
    eyes.

This fine young man then up stepped he,
  And all the doctors made a pause ;
Said he, The man must die, you see,
  By the fifty-seventh of Louis's laws.

But since the case is a desperate one,
  To explore his chest it may be well ;
For if he should die and it were not done,
  You know the *autopsy* would not tell.

Then out his stethoscope he took,
  And on it placed his curious ear ;
Mon Dieu ! said he, with a knowing look,
  Why, here is a sound that 's mighty
    queer !

The *bourraonnement* is very clear, —
  Amphoric buzzing, as I 'm alive !
Five doctors took their turn to hear ;
  Amphoric buzzing, said all the five.

There 's *empyema* beyond a doubt ;
  We 'll plunge a *trocar* in his side.
The diagnosis was made out, —
  They tapped the patient ; so he died.

Now such as hate new-fashioned toys
  Began to look extremely glum ;
They said that *rattles* were made for boys,
  And vowed that his *buzzing* was all a
    hum.

There was an old lady had long been sick,
  And what was the matter none did
    know :
Her pulse was slow, though her tongue was
    quick ;
  To her this knowing youth must go.

So there the nice old lady sat,
With phials and boxes all in a row ;
She asked the young doctor what he was
at,
To thump her and tumble her ruffles
so.

Now, when the stethoscope came out,
The flies began to buzz and whiz :
Oh, ho ! the matter is clear, no doubt ;
An *aneurism* there plainly is.

The *bruit de râpe* and the *bruit de scie*
And the *bruit de diable* are all combined ;
How happy Bouillaud would be,
If he a case like this could find !

Now, when the neighboring doctors found
A case so rare had been descried,
They every day her ribs did pound
In squads of twenty ; so she died.

Then six young damsels, slight and frail,
Received this kind young doctor's cares ;
They all were getting slim and pale,
And short of breath on mounting stairs.

They all made rhymes with " sighs " and
" skies,"
And loathed their puddings and buttered
rolls,
And dieted, much to their friends' surprise,
On pickles and pencils and chalk and
coals.

So fast their little hearts did bound,
The frightened insects buzzed the more ;
So over all their chests he found
The *râle sifflant* and the *râle sonore.*

He shook his head. There's grave dis-
ease, —
I greatly fear you all must die ;
A slight *post-mortem,* if you please,
Surviving friends would gratify.

The six young damsels wept aloud,
Which so prevailed on six young men
That each his honest love avowed,
Whereat they all got well again.

This poor young man was all aghast ;
The price of stethoscopes came down ;
And so he was reduced at last
To practise in a country town.

The doctors being very sore,
A stethoscope they did devise
That had a rammer to clear the bore,
With a knob at the end to kill the flies.

Now use your ears, all you that can,
But don't forget to mind your eyes,
Or you may be cheated, like this young
man,
By a couple of silly, abnormal flies.

EXTRACTS FROM A MEDICAL POEM

THE STABILITY OF SCIENCE

THE feeble sea-birds, blinded in the
storms,
On some tall lighthouse dash their little
forms,
And the rude granite scatters for their
pains
Those small deposits that were meant for
brains.
Yet the proud fabric in the morning's sun
Stands all unconscious of the mischief done ;
Still the red beacon pours its evening rays
For the lost pilot with as full a blaze, —
Nay, shines, all radiance, o'er the scattered
fleet
Of gulls and boobies brainless at its feet.
I tell their fate, though courtesy disclaims
To call our kind by such ungentle names ;
Yet, if your rashness bid you vainly dare,
Think of their doom, ye simple, and be-
ware !
See where aloft its hoary forehead rears
The towering pride of twice a thousand
years !
Far, far below the vast incumbent pile
Sleeps the gray rock from art's Ægean isle ;
Its massive courses, circling as they rise,
Swell from the waves to mingle with the
skies ;
There every quarry lends its marble spoil,
And clustering ages blend their common
toil ;
The Greek, the Roman, reared its ancient
walls,
The silent Arab arched its mystic halls ;
In that fair niche, by countless billows
laved,
Trace the deep lines that Sydenham en-
graved ;

On yon broad front that breasts the chang-
ing swell,
Mark where the ponderous sledge of Hun-
ter fell;
By that square buttress look where Louis
stands,
The stone yet warm from his uplifted
hands;
And say, O Science, shall thy life-blood
freeze,
When fluttering folly flaps on walls like
these?

A PORTRAIT

Thoughtful in youth, but not austere in
age;
Calm, but not cold, and cheerful though a
sage;
Too true to flatter and too kind to sneer,
And only just when seemingly severe;
So gently blending courtesy and art
That wisdom's lips seemed borrowing
friendship's heart.
Taught by the sorrows that his age had
known
In others' trials to forget his own,
As hour by hour his lengthened day de-
clined,
A sweeter radiance lingered o'er his mind.
Cold were the lips that spoke his early
praise,
And hushed the voices of his morning days,
Yet the same accents dwelt on every
tongue,
And love renewing kept him ever young.

A SENTIMENT

Ὁ βίος βραχύς, — life is but a song;
Ἡ τέχνη μακρή, — art is wondrous long;
Yet to the wise her paths are ever fair,
And Patience smiles, though Genius may
despair.
Give us but knowledge, though by slow
degrees,
And blend our toil with moments bright as
these;
Let Friendship's accents cheer our doubt-
ful way,
And Love's pure planet lend its guiding
ray, —
Our tardy Art shall wear an angel's wings,
And life shall lengthen with the joy it
brings!

A POEM

FOR THE MEETING OF THE AMERICAN
MEDICAL ASSOCIATION AT NEW YORK,
MAY 5, 1853

I HOLD a letter in my hand, —
A flattering letter, more 's the pity, —
By some contriving junto planned,
And signed *per order of Committee*.
It touches every tenderest spot, —
My patriotic predilections,
My well-known — something — don't ask
what, —
My poor old songs, my kind affections.

They make a feast on Thursday next,
And hope to make the feasters merry;
They own they 're something more per-
plexed
For poets than for port and sherry.
They want the men of — (word torn out);
Our friends will come with anxious faces,
(To see our blankets off, no doubt,
And trot us out and show our paces.)

They hint that papers by the score
Are rather musty kind of rations, —
They don't exactly mean a bore,
But only trying to the patience;
That such as — you know who I mean —
Distinguished for their — what d' ye
call 'em —
Should bring the dews of Hippocrene
To sprinkle on the faces solemn.

— The same old story: that 's the chaff
To catch the birds that sing the ditties;
Upon my soul, it makes me laugh
To read these letters from Committees!
They 're all *so* loving and *so* fair, —
All for *your* sake such kind compunction;
'T would save your carriage half its wear
To touch its wheels with such an unc-
tion!

Why, who am I, to lift me here
And beg such learned folk to listen,
To ask a smile, or coax a tear
Beneath these stoic lids to glisten?
As well might some arterial thread
Ask the whole frame to feel it gushing,
While throbbing fierce from heel to head
The vast aortic tide was rushing.

As well some hair-like nerve might strain
   To set its special streamlet going,
While through the myriad-channelled
      brain
The burning flood of thought was flowing;
Or trembling fibre strive to keep
   The springing haunches gathered shorter,
While the scourged racer, leap on leap,
   Was stretching through the last hot
      quarter !

Ah me ! you take the bud that came
   Self-sown in your poor garden's borders,
And hand it to the stately dame
   That florists breed for, all she orders.
She thanks you, — it was kindly meant —
   (A pale affair, not worth the keeping,) —
Good morning; and your bud is sent
   To join the tea-leaves used for sweeping.

Not always so, kind hearts and true, —
   For such I know are round me beating;
Is not the bud I offer you,
   Fresh gathered for the hour of meeting,
Pale though its outer leaves may be,
   Rose-red in all its inner petals ? —
Where the warm life we cannot see —
   The life of love that gave it — settles.

We meet from regions far away,
   Like rills from distant mountains stream-
      ing;
The sun is on Francisco's bay,
   O'er Chesapeake the lighthouse gleaming;
While summer girds the still bayou
   In chains of bloom, her bridal token,
Monadnock sees the sky grow blue,
   His crystal bracelet yet unbroken.

Yet Nature bears the selfsame heart
   Beneath her russet-mantled bosom
As where, with burning lips apart,
   She breathes and white magnolias blos-
      som;
The selfsame founts her chalice fill
   With showery sunlight running over,
On fiery plain and frozen hill,
   On myrtle-beds and fields of clover.

I give you *Home !* its crossing lines
   United in one golden suture,
And showing every day that shines
   The present growing to the future, —
A flag that bears a hundred stars
   In one bright ring, with love for centre,

Fenced round with white and crimson bars
   No prowling treason dares to enter !

O brothers, home may be a word
   To make affection's living treasure,
The wave an angel might have stirred,
   A stagnant pool of selfish pleasure ;
HOME ! It is where the day-star springs
And where the evening sun reposes,
Where'er the eagle spreads his wings,
   From northern pines to southern roses !

A SENTIMENT

[Distributed among the members gathered
at the meeting of the American Medical As-
sociation, in Philadelphia, May 1, 1855.]

   A TRIPLE health to Friendship, Science,
      Art,
From heads and hands that own a common
      heart !
Each in its turn the others' willing slave,
Each in its season strong to heal and save.

   Friendship's blind service, in the hour of
      need,
Wipes the pale face, and lets the victim
      bleed.
Science must stop to reason and explain;
ART claps his finger on the streaming vein.

   But Art's brief memory fails the hand at
      last ;
Then SCIENCE lifts the flambeau of the past.
When both their equal impotence deplore,
When Learning sighs, and Skill can do no
      more,
The tear of FRIENDSHIP pours its heavenly
      balm,
And soothes the pang no anodyne may
      calm !

RIP VAN WINKLE, M. D.

AN AFTER-DINNER PRESCRIPTION TAKEN
BY THE MASSACHUSETTS MEDICAL SO-
CIETY, AT THEIR MEETING HELD MAY
25, 1870

CANTO FIRST

OLD Rip Van Winkle had a grandson
      Rip,
Of the paternal block a genuine chip, —

A lazy, sleepy, curious kind of chap;
He, like his grandsire, took a mighty nap,
Whereof the story I propose to tell
In two brief cantos, if you listen well.

The times were hard when Rip to man-
    hood grew;
They always will be when there's work to
    do.
He tried at farming, — found it rather
    slow, —
And then at teaching — what he did n't
    know;
Then took to hanging round the tavern
    bars,
To frequent toddies and long-nine cigars,
Till Dame Van Winkle, out of patience,
    vexed
With preaching homilies, having for their
    text
A mop, a broomstick, aught that might
    avail
To point a moral or adorn a tale,
Exclaimed, "I have it! Now, then, Mr.
    V. !
He's good for *something*, — make him an
    M. D. ! "

The die was cast; the youngster was
    content ;
They packed his shirts and stockings, and
    he went.
How hard he studied it were vain to tell ;
He drowsed through Wistar, nodded over
    Bell,
Slept sound with Cooper, snored aloud on
    Good;
Heard heaps of lectures, — doubtless under-
    stood, —
A constant listener, for he did not fail
To carve his name on every bench and rail.

Months grew to years ; at last he counted
    three,
And Rip Van Winkle found himself M. D.
Illustrious title ! in a gilded frame
He set the sheepskin with his Latin name,
RIPUM VAN WINKLUM, QUEM we — SCIMUS
    — know
IDONEUM ESSE — to do so and so.
He hired an office ; soon its walls displayed
His new diploma and his stock in trade,
A mighty arsenal to subdue disease,
Of various names, whereof I mention these :
Lancets and bougies, great and little squirt,

Rhubarb and Senna, Snakeroot, Thorough-
    wort,
Ant. Tart., Vin. Colch., Pil. Cochiæ, and
    Black Drop,
Tinctures of Opium, Gentian, Henbane,
    Hop,
Pulv. Ipecacuanhæ, which for lack
Of breath to utter men call Ipecac,
Camphor and Kino, Turpentine, Tolu,
Cubebs, "Copeevy," Vitriol, — white and
    blue, —
Fennel and Flaxseed, Slippery Elm and
    Squill,
And roots of Sassafras, and "Sassaf'rill,"
Brandy, — for colics, — Pinkroot, death on
    worms, —
Valerian, calmer of hysteric squirms,
Musk, Assafœtida, the resinous gum
Named from its odor, — well, it does smell
    some, —
Jalap, that works not wisely, but too well,
Ten pounds of Bark and six of Calomel.

For outward griefs he had an ample store,
Some twenty jars and gallipots, or more:
Ceratum simplex — housewives oft compile
The same at home, and call it "wax and
    ile;"
Unguentum resinosum — change its name,
The "drawing salve" of many an ancient
    dame;
Argenti Nitras, also Spanish flies,
Whose virtue makes the water-bladders
    rise —
(Some say that spread upon a toper's skin
They draw no water, only rum or gin) ;
Leeches, sweet vermin ! don't they charm
    the sick ?
And Sticking-plaster — how it hates to
    stick !
Emplastrum Ferri — ditto *Picis*, Pitch;
Washes and Powders, Brimstone for the —
    which,
Scabies or *Psora*, is thy chosen name
Since Hahnemann's goose-quill scratched
    thee into fame,
Proved thee the source of every nameless
    ill,
Whose sole specific is a moonshine pill,
Till saucy Science, with a quiet grin,
Held up the Acarus, crawling on a pin ?
— Mountains have labored and have
    brought forth mice :
The Dutchman's theory hatched a brood of
    — twice

I 've wellnigh said them — words unfitting
    quite
For these fair precincts and for ears polite.

The surest foot may chance at last to
    slip,
And so at length it proved with Doctor
    Rip.
One full-sized bottle stood upon the shelf,
Which held the medicine that he took him-
    self ;
Whate'er the reason, it must be confessed
He filled that bottle oftener than the rest;
What drug it held I don't presume to
    know —
The gilded label said " Elixir Pro."

One day the Doctor found the bottle
    full,
And, being thirsty, took a vigorous pull,
Put back the " Elixir " where 't was al-
    ways found,
And had old Dobbin saddled and brought
    round.
— You know those old-time rhubarb-colored
    nags
That carried Doctors and their saddle-
    bags ;
Sagacious beasts ! they stopped at every
    place
Where blinds were shut — knew every
    patient's case —
Looked up and thought — The baby 's in a
    fit —
That won't last long — he 'll soon be
    through with it;
But shook their heads before the knockered
    door
Where some old lady told the story o'er
Whose endless stream of tribulation flows
For gastric griefs and peristaltic woes.

What jack-o'-lantern led him from his
    way,
And where it led him, it were hard to
    say;
Enough that wandering many a weary mile
Through paths the mountain sheep trod
    single file,
O'ercome by feelings such as patients
    know
Who dose too freely with " Elixir Pro.,"
He tumbl — dismounted, slightly in a heap,
And lay, promiscuous, lapped in balmy
    sleep.

Night followed night, and day succeeded
    day,
But snoring still the slumbering Doctor
    lay.
Poor Dobbin, starving, thought upon his
    stall,
And straggled homeward, saddle-bags and
    all.
The village people hunted all around,
But Rip was missing, — never could be
    found.
" Drownded," they guessed; — for more
    than half a year
The pouts and eels *did* taste uncommon
    queer;
Some said of apple-brandy — other some
Found a strong flavor of New England rum.

Why can't a fellow hear the fine things
    said
About a fellow when a fellow 's dead ?
The best of doctors — so the press de-
    clared —
A public blessing while his life was spared,
True to his country, bounteous to the poor,
In all things temperate, sober, just, and
    pure ;
The best of husbands ! echoed Mrs. Van,
And set her cap to catch another man.

So ends this Canto — if it 's *quantum suff.*,
We 'll just stop here and say we 've had
    enough,
And leave poor Rip to sleep for thirty
    years ;
I grind the organ — if you lend your ears
To hear my second Canto, after that
We 'll send around the monkey with the
    hat.

CANTO SECOND

So thirty years had passed — but not a
    word
In all that time of Rip was ever heard;
The world wagged on — it never does go
    back —
The widow Van was now the widow Mac —
France was an Empire — Andrew J. was
    dead,
And Abraham L. was reigning in his stead.
Four murderous years had passed in savage
    strife,
Yet still the rebel held his bloody knife.
— At last one morning — who forgets the
    day

When the black cloud of war dissolved
     away ? —
The joyous tidings spread o'er land and
     sea,
Rebellion done for ! Grant has captured
     Lee !
Up every flagstaff sprang the Stars and
     Stripes —
Out rushed the Extras wild with mammoth
     types —
Down went the laborer's hod, the school-
     boy's book —
"Hooraw !" he cried, " the rebel army 's
     took ! "
Ah ! what a time ! the folks all mad with
     joy:
Each fond, pale mother thinking of her
     boy;
Old gray-haired fathers meeting — " Have
     — you — heard ? "
And then a choke — and not another word ;
Sisters all smiling — maidens, not less dear,
In trembling poise between a smile and
     tear;
Poor Bridget thinking how she 'll stuff the
     plums
In that big cake for Johnny when he comes;
Cripples afoot ; rheumatics on the jump;
Old girls so loving they could hug the
     pump ;
Guns going bang ! from every fort and
     ship ;
They banged so loud at last they wakened
     Rip.

I spare the picture, how a man appears
Who 's been asleep a score or two of years ;
You all have seen it to perfection done
By Joe Van Wink — I mean Rip Jefferson.
Well, so it was ; old Rip at last came back,
Claimed his old wife — the present widow
     Mac —
Had his old sign regilded, and began
To practise physic on the same old plan.

Some weeks went by — it was not long
     to wait —
And " please to call " grew frequent on the
     slate.
He had, in fact, an ancient, mildewed air,
A long gray beard, a plenteous lack of
     hair, —
The musty look that always recommends
Your good old Doctor to his ailing friends.
— Talk of your science ! after all is said

There 's nothing like a bare and shiny head;
Age lends the graces that are sure to please ;
Folks want their Doctors mouldy, like their
     cheese.

So Rip began to look at people's tongues
And thump their briskets (called it "sound
     their lungs "),
Brushed up his knowledge smartly as he
     could,
Read in old Cullen and in Doctor Good.
The town was healthy ; for a month or two
He gave the sexton little work to do.

About the time when dog-day heats be-
     gin,
The summer's usual maladies set in ;
With autumn evenings dysentery came,
And dusky typhoid lit his smouldering
     flame;
The blacksmith ailed, the carpenter was
     down,
And half the children sickened in the town.
The sexton's face grew shorter than be-
     fore —
The sexton's wife a brand-new bonnet
     wore —
Things looked quite serious — Death had
     got a grip
On old and young, in spite of Doctor Rip.

And now the Squire was taken with a
     chill —
Wife gave " hot-drops " — at night an In-
     dian pill;
Next morning, feverish — bedtime, getting
     worse —
Out of his head — began to rave and curse;
The Doctor sent for — double quick he
     came :
Ant. Tart. gran. duo, and repeat the same
If no et cetera.   Third day — nothing new;
Percussed his thorax till 't was black and
     blue —
Lung-fever threatening — something of the
     sort —
Out with the lancet — let him bleed — a
     quart —
Ten leeches next — then blisters to his side;
Ten grains of calomel ; just then he died.

The Deacon next required the Doctor's
     care —
Took cold by sitting in a draught of air —
Pains in the back, but what the matter is

Not quite so clear, — wife calls it "rheu-
matiz."
Rubs back with flannel — gives him some-
thing hot —
" Ah ! " says the Deacon, " that goes *nigh*
the spot."
Next day a *rigor* — " Run, my little man,
And say the Deacon sends for Doctor Van."
The Doctor came — percussion as before,
Thumping and banging till his ribs were
sore —
" Right side the flattest " — then more vig-
orous raps —
" Fever — that 's certain — pleurisy, per-
haps.
A quart of blood will ease the pain, no
doubt,
Ten leeches next will help to suck it out,
Then clap a blister on the painful part —
But first two grains of *Antimonium Tart*.
Last with a dose of cleansing calomel
Unload the portal system — (that sounds
well !) "

But when the selfsame remedies were
tried,
As all the village knew, the Squire had
died;
The neighbors hinted: " This will never do;
He 's killed the Squire — he 'll kill the
Deacon too."

Now when a doctor's patients are per-
plexed,
A *consultation* comes in order next —
You know what that is ? In a certain place
Meet certain doctors to discuss a case
And other matters, such as weather, crops,
Potatoes, pumpkins, lager-beer, and hops.
For what 's the use ! — there 's little to be
said,
Nine times in ten your man 's as good as
dead;
At best a talk (the secret to disclose)
Where three men guess and *sometimes* one
man knows.

The counsel summoned came without de-
lay —
Young Doctor Green and shrewd old Doc-
tor Gray —
They heard the story — " Bleed ! " says
Doctor Green,
" That 's downright murder ! cut his throat,
you mean !

Leeches ! the reptiles ! Why, for pity's
sake,
Not try an adder or a rattlesnake ?
Blisters ! Why bless you, they 're against
the law —
It 's rank assault and battery if they draw !
Tartrate of Antimony ! shade of Luke,
Stomachs turn pale at thought of such re-
buke !
The portal system ! What 's the man
about ?
Unload your nonsense ! Calomel 's played
out !
You 've been asleep — you 'd better sleep
away
Till some one calls you."

" Stop ! " says Doctor Gray —
" The story is you slept for thirty years;
With brother Green, I own that it appears
You must have slumbered most amazing
sound;
But sleep once more till thirty years come
round,
You 'll find the lancet in its honored place,
Leeches and blisters rescued from disgrace,
Your drugs redeemed from fashion's pass-
ing scorn,
And counted safe to give to babes unborn."

Poor sleepy Rip, M. M. M. S., M. D.,
A puzzled, serious, saddened man was he ;
Home from the Deacon's house he
plodded slow
And filled one bumper of " Elixir Pro."
" Good-by," he faltered, " Mrs. Van, my
dear !
I'm going to sleep, but wake me once a
year ;
I don't like bleaching in the frost and dew,
I'll take the barn, if all the same to you.
Just once a year — remember ! no mistake!
Cry, ' Rip Van Winkle ! time for you to
wake ! '
Watch for the week in May when laylocks
blow,
For then the Doctors meet, and I must
go."

Just once a year the Doctor's worthy
dame
Goes to the barn and shouts her husband's
name;
" Come, Rip Van Winkle ! " (giving him
a shake)

"Rip! Rip Van Winkle! time for you to
    wake!
Laylocks in blossom! 't is the month of
    May —
The Doctors' meeting is this blessed day,
And come what will, you know I heard you
    swear
You 'd never miss it, but be always there!"

And so it is, as every year comes round
Old Rip Van Winkle here is always found.
You 'll quickly know him by his mildewed
    air,
The hayseed sprinkled through his scanty
    hair,
The lichens growing on his rusty suit —
I 've seen a toadstool sprouting on his
    boot —
— Who says I lie? Does any man pre-
    sume? —
Toadstool! No matter — call it a mush-
    room.
Where is his seat? He moves it every
    year;
But look, you 'll find him, — he is always
    here, —
Perhaps you 'll track him by a whiff you
    know —
A certain flavor of " Elixir Pro."

Now, then, I give you — as you seem to
    think
We can give toasts without a drop to
    drink —
Health to the mighty sleeper, — long live
    he!
Our brother Rip, M. M. M. S., M. D. !

POEM

READ AT THE DINNER GIVEN TO THE
AUTHOR BY THE MEDICAL PROFES-
SION OF THE CITY OF NEW YORK,
APRIL 12, 1883.

HAVE I deserved your kindness? Nay,
    my friends,
While the fair banquet its illusion lends
Let me believe it, though the blood may
    rush
And to my cheek recall the maiden blush
That o'er it flamed with momentary blaze
When first I heard the honeyed words of
    praise;

Let me believe it while the roses wear
Their bloom unwithering in the heated
    air;
Too soon, too soon, their glowing leaves
    must fall,
The laughing echoes leave the silent hall,
Joy drop his garland, turn his empty cup,
And weary Labor take his burden up, —
How weighs that burden they can tell
    alone
Whose dial marks no moment as their own.

Am I your creditor? Too well I know
How Friendship pays the debt it does not
    owe,
Shapes a poor semblance fondly to its
    mind,
Adds all the virtues that it fails to find,
Adorns with graces to its heart's content,
Borrows from love what nature never
    lent,
Till what with halo, jewels, gilding, paint,
The veriest sinner deems himself a saint.
Thus while you pay these honors as my
    due
I owe my value's larger part to you,
And in the tribute of the hour I see
Not what I am, but what I ought to be.

Friends of the Muse, to you of right belong
The first staid footsteps of my square-toed
    song;
Full well I know the strong heroic line
Has lost its fashion since I made it mine;
But there are tricks old singers will not
    learn,
And this grave measure still must serve
    my turn.
So the old bird resumes the selfsame note
His first young summer wakened in his
    throat;
The selfsame tune the old canary sings,
And all unchanged the bobolink's carol
    rings;
When the tired songsters of the day are
    still
The thrush repeats his long-remembered
    trill;
Age alters not the crow's persistent caw,
The Yankee's "Haow," the stammering
    Briton's " Haw;"
And so the hand that takes the lyre for
    you
Plays the old tune on strings that once
    were new.

Nor let the rhymester of the hour deride
The straight - backed measure with its
 stately stride;
It gave the mighty voice of Dryden scope;
It sheathed the steel-bright epigrams of
 Pope;
In Goldsmith's verse it learned a sweeter
 strain;
Byron and Campbell wore its clanking
 chain;
I smile to listen while the critic's scorn
Flouts the proud purple kings have nobly
 worn;
Bid each new rhymer try his dainty skill
And mould his frozen phrases as he will;
We thank the artist for his neat device;
The shape is pleasing, though the stuff is
 ice.

Fashions will change — the new costume
 allures,
Unfading still the better type endures;
While the slashed doublet of the cavalier
Gave the old knight the pomp of chanticleer,
Our last-hatched dandy with his glass and
 stick
Recalls the semblance of a new-born
 chick;
(To match the model he is aiming at
He ought to wear an eggshell for a
 hat;) —
Which of these objects would a painter
 choose,
And which Velasquez or Van Dyck re-
 fuse?

When your kind summons reached my
 calm retreat,
Who are the friends, I questioned, I shall
 meet?
Some in young manhood, shivering with
 desire
To feel the genial warmth of fortune's
 fire, —
Each with his bellows ready in his hand
To puff the flame just waiting to be
 fanned;
Some heads half-silvered, some with snow-
 white hair, —
A crown ungarnished glistening here and
 there,
The mimic moonlight gleaming on the
 scalps
As evening's empress lights the shining
 Alps;

But count the crowds that throng your
 festal scenes,
How few that knew the century in its
 teens!

Save for the lingering handful fate be-
 friends,
Life's busy day the Sabbath decade ends;
When that is over, how with what remains
Of nature's outfit, muscle, nerve, and
 brains?
Were this a pulpit I should doubtless
 preach,
Were this a platform I should gravely
 teach,
But to no solemn duties I pretend
In my vocation at the table's end;
So as my answer let me tell instead
What Landlord Porter — rest his soul! —
 once said.

A feast it was that none might scorn to
 share;
Cambridge and Concord's demigods were
 there, —
"And who were they?" You know as
 well as I
The stars long glittering in our Eastern
 sky, —
The names that blazon our provincial
 scroll
Ring round the world with Britain's drum-
 beat roll!

Good was the dinner, better was the talk;
Some whispered, devious was the home-
 ward walk;
The story came from some reporting spy, —
They lie, those fellows, — oh, how they *do*
 lie!
Not ours those foot-tracks in the new-fallen
 snow, —
Poets and sages never zigzagged so!

Now Landlord Porter, grave, concise, se-
 vere,
Master, nay, monarch in his proper sphere,
Though to belles-lettres he pretended not,
Lived close to Harvard, so knew what was
 what;
And having bards, philosophers, and such,
To eat his dinner, put the finest touch
His art could teach, those learned mouths
 to fill
With the best proofs of gustatory skill;

And finding wisdom plenty at his board,
Wit, science, learning, all his guests had
　　stored,
By way of contrast, ventured to produce,
To please their palates, an inviting goose.
Better it were the company should starve
Than hands unskilled that goose attempt to
　　carve;
None but the master-artist shall assail
The bird that turns the mightiest surgeon
　　pale.

One voice arises from the banquet-hall.
The landlord answers to the pleading call;
Of stature tall, sublime of port he stands,
His blade and bident gleaming in his hands;
Beneath his glance the strong-knit joints
　　relax
As the weak knees before the headsman's
　　axe.

And Landlord Porter lifts his glittering
　　knife
As some stout warrior armed for bloody
　　strife;
All eyes are on him; some in whispers ask,
What man is he who dares this dangerous
　　task?
When lo! the triumph of consummate art,
With scarce a touch the creature drops
　　apart!
As when the baby in his nurse's lap
Spills on the carpet a dissected snap.

Then the calm sage, the monarch of the
　　lyre,
Critics and men of science all admire,
And one whose wisdom I will not impeach,
Lively, not churlish, somewhat free of
　　speech,
Speaks thus: "Say, master, what of worth
　　is left
In birds like this, of breast and legs be-
　　reft?"
And Landlord Porter, with uplifted eyes,
Smiles on the simple querist, and replies:
"When from a goose you 've taken legs
　　and breast,
Wipe lips, thank God, and leave the poor
　　the rest!"

Kind friends, sweet friends, I hold it hardly
　　fair
With that same bird your minstrel to com-
　　pare,

Yet in a certain likeness we agree,
No wrong to him and no offence to me;
I take him for the moral he has lent,
My partner, — to a limited extent.

When the stern Landlord whom we all
　　obey
Has carved from life its seventh great
　　slice away,
Is the poor fragment left in blank collapse
A pauper remnant of unvalued scraps?

I care not much what Solomon has said,
Before his time to nobler pleasures dead;
Poor man! he needed half a hundred lives
With such a babbling wilderness of wives!
But is there nothing that may well employ
Life's winter months, — no sunny hour of
　　joy?

While o'er the fields the howling tempests
　　rage,
The prisoned linnet warbles in its cage;
When chill November through the forest
　　blows,
The greenhouse shelters the untroubled
　　rose;
Round the high trellis creeping tendrils
　　twine,
And the ripe clusters fill with blameless
　　wine;
We make the vine forget the winter's cold,
But how shall age forget its growing old?

Though doing right is better than deceit,
Time is a trickster it is fair to cheat;
The honest watches ticking in your fobs
Tell every minute how the rascal robs.
To clip his forelock and his scythe to hide,
To lay his hour-glass gently on its side,
To slip the cards he marked upon the
　　shelf
And deal him others you have marked
　　yourself,
If not a virtue cannot be a sin,
For the old rogue is sure at last to win.
What does he leave when life is well-nigh
　　spent
To lap its evening in a calm content?
Art, letters, science, these at least befriend
Our day's brief remnant to its peaceful
　　end, —
Peaceful for him who shows the setting
　　sun
A record worthy of his Lord's Well done!

When he, the master whom I will not
name,
Known to our calling, not unknown to
fame,
At life's extremest verge, half conscious
lay,
Helpless and sightless, dying day by day,
His brain, so long with varied wisdom
fraught,
Filled with the broken enginery of thought,
A flitting vision often would illume
His darkened world, and cheer its deepen-
ing gloom, —
A sunbeam struggling through the long
eclipse, —
And smiles of pleasure play around his lips.
He loved the art that shapes the dome and
spire;
The Roman's page, the ring of Byron's
lyre,
And oft when fitful memory would return
To find some fragment in her broken urn,
Would wake to life some long-forgotten
hour,
And lead his thought to Pisa's terraced
tower,
Or trace in light before his rayless eye
The dome-crowned Pantheon printed on
the sky;
Then while the view his ravished soul ab-
sorbs
And lends a glitter to the sightless orbs,
The patient watcher feels the stillness
stirred
By the faint murmur of some classic word,
Or the long roll of Harold's lofty rhyme,
"Simple, erect, severe, austere, sub-
lime," —
Such were the dreams that soothed his
couch of pain,
The sweet nepenthe of the worn-out brain.

Brothers in art, who live for others' needs
In duty's bondage, mercy's gracious deeds,
Of all who toil beneath the circling sun
Whose evening rest than yours more fairly
won ?
Though many a cloud your struggling
morn obscures,
What sunset brings a brighter sky than
yours ?

I, who your labors for a while have shared,
New tasks have sought, with new com-
panions fared,
For nature's servant far too often seen
A loiterer by the waves of Hippocrene;
Yet round the earlier friendship twines the
new,
My footsteps wander, but my heart is
true,
Nor e'er forgets the living or the dead
Who trod with me the paths where science
led.

How can I tell you, O my loving friends !
What light, what warmth, your joyous
welcome lends
To life's late hour ? Alas ! my song is
sung,
Its fading accents falter on my tongue.
Sweet friends, if, shrinking in the banquet's
blaze,
Your blushing guest must face the breath
of praise,
Speak not too well of one who scarce will
know
Himself transfigured in its roseate glow;
Say kindly of him what is, chiefly, true,
Remembering always he belongs to you;
Deal with him as a truant, if you will,
But claim him, keep him, call him brother
still !

SONGS IN MANY KEYS

1849–1861

PROLOGUE

THE piping of our slender, peaceful reeds
Whispers uncared for while the trumpets
    bray ;
Song is thin air ; our hearts' exulting play
Beats time but to the tread of marching
    deeds,
Following the mighty van that Freedom
    leads,
Her glorious standard flaming to the day !
The crimsoned pavement where a hero
    bleeds
Breathes nobler lessons than the poet's lay.
Strong arms, broad breasts, brave hearts,
    are better worth
Than strains that sing the ravished echoes
    dumb.
Hark ! 't is the loud reverberating drum
Rolls o'er the prairied West, the rock-
    bound North:
The myriad-handed Future stretches forth
Its shadowy palms. Behold, we come, —
    we come !

Turn o'er these idle leaves. Such toys as
    these
Were not unsought for, as, in languid
    dreams,
We lay beside our lotus-feeding streams,
And nursed our fancies in forgetful ease.
It matters little if they pall or please,
Dropping untimely, while the sudden
    gleams
Glare from the mustering clouds whose
    blackness seems
Too swollen to hold its lightning from the
    trees.
Yet, in some lull of passion, when at last
These calm revolving moons that come and
    go —
Turning our months to years, they creep so
    slow —

Have brought us rest, the not unwelcome
    past
May flutter to thee through these leaflets,
    cast
On the wild winds that all around us blow.
    May 1, 1861.

AGNES

The story of Sir Harry Frankland and Agnes Surriage is told in the ballad with a very strict adhesion to the facts. These were obtained from information afforded me by the Rev. Mr. Webster, of Hopkinton, in company with whom I visited the Frankland Mansion in that town, then standing ; from a very interesting Memoir, by the Rev. Elias Nason, of Medford ; and from the manuscript diary of Sir Harry, or more properly Sir Charles Henry Frankland, now in the library of the Massachusetts Historical Society.

At the time of the visit referred to, old Julia was living, and on our return we called at the house where she resided.[1] Her account is little more than paraphrased in the poem. If the incidents are treated with a certain liberality at the close of the fifth part, the essential fact that Agnes rescued Sir Harry from the ruins after the earthquake, and their subsequent marriage as related, may be accepted as literal truth. So with regard to most of the trifling details which are given ; they are taken from the record.

It is greatly to be regretted that the Frankland Mansion no longer exists. It was accidentally burned on the 23d of January, 1858, a year or two after the first sketch of this ballad was written. A visit to it was like stepping out of the century into the years before the Revolution. A new house, similar in plan and arrangements to the old one, has been built upon its site, and the terraces, the clump of box, and the lilacs doubtless remain to bear witness to the truth of this story.

[1] She was living June 10, 1861.

The story, which I have told literally in rhyme, has been made the subject of a carefully studied and interesting romance by Mr. E. L. Bynner.

PART I. THE KNIGHT

THE tale I tell is gospel true,
　As all the bookmen know,
And pilgrims who have strayed to view
　The wrecks still left to show.

The old, old story, — fair, and young,
　And fond, — and not too wise, —
That matrons tell, with sharpened tongue,
　To maids with downcast eyes.

Ah ! maidens err and matrons warn
　Beneath the coldest sky;
Love lurks amid the tasselled corn
　As in the bearded rye !

But who would dream our sober sires
　Had learned the old world's ways,
And warmed their hearths with lawless fires
　In Shirley's homespun days ?

'T is like some poet's pictured trance
　His idle rhymes recite, —
This old New England-born romance
　Of Agnes and the Knight;

Yet, known to all the country round,
　Their home is standing still,
Between Wachusett's lonely mound
　And Shawmut's threefold hill.

One hour we rumble on the rail,
　One half-hour guide the rein,
We reach at last, o'er hill and dale,
　The village on the plain.

With blackening wall and mossy roof,
　With stained and warping floor,
A stately mansion stands aloof
　And bars its haughty door.

This lowlier portal may be tried,
　That breaks the gable wall;
And lo ! with arches opening wide,
　Sir Harry Frankland's hall !

'T was in the second George's day
　They sought the forest shade,

The knotted trunks they cleared away,
　The massive beams they laid,

They piled the rock-hewn chimney tall,
　They smoothed the terraced ground,
They reared the marble-pillared wall
　That fenced the mansion round.

Far stretched beyond the village bound
　The Master's broad domain;
With page and valet, horse and hound,
　He kept a goodly train.

And, all the midland county through,
　The ploughman stopped to gaze
Whene'er his chariot swept in view
　Behind the shining bays,

With mute obeisance, grave and slow,
　Repaid by nod polite, —
For such the way with high and low
　Till after Concord fight.

Nor less to courtly circles known
　That graced the three-hilled town
With far-off splendors of the Throne,
　And glimmerings from the Crown;

Wise Phipps, who held the seals of state
　For Shirley over sea;
Brave Knowles, whose press-gang moved of late
　The King Street mob's decree;

And judges grave, and colonels grand,
　Fair dames and stately men,
The mighty people of the land,
　The " World " of there and then.

'T was strange no Chloe's " beauteous Form,"
　And " Eyes' cœlestial Blew,"
This Strephon of the West could warm,
　No Nymph his Heart subdue !

Perchance he wooed as gallants use,
　Whom fleeting loves enchain,
But still unfettered, free to choose,
　Would brook no bridle-rein.

He saw the fairest of the fair,
　But smiled alike on all;
No band his roving foot might snare,
　No ring his hand enthrall.

PART II. THE MAIDEN

Why seeks the knight that rocky cape
  Beyond the Bay of Lynn?
What chance his wayward course may shape
  To reach its village inn?

No story tells; whate'er we guess,
  The past lies deaf and still,
But Fate, who rules to blight or bless,
  Can lead us where she will.

Make way! Sir Harry's coach and four,
  And liveried grooms that ride!
They cross the ferry, touch the shore
  On Winnisimmet's side.

They hear the wash on Chelsea Beach, —
  The level marsh they pass,
Where miles on miles the desert reach
  Is rough with bitter grass.

The shining horses foam and pant,
  And now the smells begin
Of fishy Swampscott, salt Nahant,
  And leather-scented Lynn.

Next, on their left, the slender spires
  And glittering vanes that crown
The home of Salem's frugal sires,
  The old, witch-haunted town.

So onward, o'er the rugged way
  That runs through rocks and sand,
Showered by the tempest-driven spray,
  From bays on either hand,

That shut between their outstretched arms
  The crews of Marblehead,
The lords of ocean's watery farms,
  Who plough the waves for bread.

At last the ancient inn appears,
  The spreading elm below,
Whose flapping sign these fifty years
  Has seesawed to and fro.

How fair the azure fields in sight
  Before the low-browed inn!
The tumbling billows fringe with light
  The crescent shore of Lynn;

Nahant thrusts outward through the waves
  Her arm of yellow sand,

And breaks the roaring surge that braves
  The gauntlet on her hand;

With eddying whirl the waters lock
  Yon treeless mound forlorn,
The sharp-winged sea-fowl's breeding-rock,
  That fronts the Spouting Horn;

Then free the white-sailed shallops glide,
  And wide the ocean smiles,
Till, shoreward bent, his streams divide
  The two bare Misery Isles.

The master's silent signal stays
  The wearied cavalcade;
The coachman reins his smoking bays
  Beneath the elm-tree's shade.

A gathering on the village green!
  The cocked-hats crowd to see,
On legs in ancient velveteen,
  With buckles at the knee.

A clustering round the tavern-door
  Of square-toed village boys,
Still wearing, as their grandsires wore,
  The old-world corduroys!

A scampering at the "Fountain" inn, —
  A rush of great and small, —
With hurrying servants' mingled din
  And screaming matron's call!

Poor Agnes! with her work half done
  They caught her unaware;
As, humbly, like a praying nun,
  She knelt upon the stair;

Bent o'er the steps, with lowliest mien
  She knelt, but not to pray, —
Her little hands must keep them clean,
  And wash their stains away.

A foot, an ankle, bare and white,
  Her girlish shapes betrayed, —
"Ha! Nymphs and Graces!" spoke the
    Knight;
  "Look up, my beauteous Maid!"

She turned, — a reddening rose in bud,
  Its calyx half withdrawn, —
Her cheek on fire with damasked blood
  Of girlhood's glowing dawn!

He searched her features through and
    through,
  As royal lovers look
On lowly maidens, when they woo
  Without the ring and book.

"Come hither, Fair one! Here, my Sweet!
  Nay, prithee, look not down!
Take this to shoe those little feet,"—
  He tossed a silver crown.

A sudden paleness struck her brow,—
  A swifter blush succeeds;
It burns her cheek; it kindles now
  Beneath her golden beads.

She flitted, but the glittering eye
  Still sought the lovely face.
Who was she? What, and whence? and
    why
  Doomed to such menial place?

A skipper's daughter,— so they said,—
  Left orphan by the gale
That cost the fleet of Marblehead
  And Gloucester thirty sail.

Ah! many a lonely home is found
  Along the Essex shore,
That cheered its goodman outward bound,
  And sees his face no more!

"Not so," the matron whispered,— "sure
  No orphan girl is she,—
The Surriage folk are deadly poor
  Since Edward left the sea,

"And Mary, with her growing brood,
  Has work enough to do
To find the children clothes and food
  With Thomas, John, and Hugh.

"This girl of Mary's, growing tall,—
  (Just turned her sixteenth year,)—
To earn her bread and help them all,
  Would work as housemaid here."

So Agnes, with her golden beads,
  And naught beside as dower,
Grew at the wayside with the weeds,
  Herself a garden-flower.

'T was strange, 't was sad,— so fresh, so
    fair!
  Thus Pity's voice began.

Such grace! an angel's shape and air!
  The half-heard whisper ran.

For eyes could see in George's time,
  As now in later days,
And lips could shape, in prose and rhyme,
  The honeyed breath of praise.

No time to woo! The train must go
  Long ere the sun is down,
To reach, before the night-winds blow,
  The many-steepled town.

'T is midnight,— street and square are
    still;
  Dark roll the whispering waves
That lap the piers beneath the hill
  Ridged thick with ancient graves.

Ah, gentle sleep! thy hand will smooth
  The weary couch of pain,
When all thy poppies fail to soothe
  The lover's throbbing brain!

'T is morn,— the orange-mantled sun
  Breaks through the fading gray,
And long and loud the Castle gun
  Peals o'er the glistening bay.

"Thank God 't is day!" With eager eye
  He hails the morning shine:—
"If art can win, or gold can buy,
  The maiden shall be mine!"

PART III. THE CONQUEST

"Who saw this hussy when she came?
  What is the wench, and who?"
They whisper. Agnes— is her name?
  Pray what has she to do?

The housemaids parley at the gate,
  The scullions on the stair,
And in the footmen's grave debate
  The butler deigns to share.

Black Dinah, stolen when a child,
  And sold on Boston pier,
Grown up in service, petted, spoiled,
  Speaks in the coachman's ear:

"What, all this household at his will?
  And all are yet too few?
More servants, and more servants still,—
  This pert young madam too!"

" *Servant!* fine servant ! " laughed aloud
　　The man of coach and steeds;
" She looks too fair, she steps too proud,
　　This girl with golden beads !

" I tell you, you may fret and frown,
　　And call her what you choose,
You 'll find my Lady in her gown,
　　Your Mistress in her shoes ! "

Ah, gentle maidens, free from blame,
　　God grant you never know
The little whisper, loud with shame,
　　That makes the world your foe !

Why tell the lordly flatterer's art,
　　That won the maiden's ear, —
The fluttering of the frightened heart,
　　The blush, the smile, the tear ?

Alas ! it were the saddening tale
　　That every language knows, —
The wooing wind, the yielding sail,
　　The sunbeam and the rose.

And now the gown of sober stuff
　　Has changed to fair brocade,
With broidered hem, and hanging cuff,
　　And flower of silken braid ;

And clasped around her blanching wrist
　　A jewelled bracelet shines,
Her flowing tresses' massive twist
　　A glittering net confines ;

And mingling with their truant wave
　　A fretted chain is hung;
But ah ! the gift her mother gave, —
　　Its beads are all unstrung !

Her place is at the master's board,
　　Where none disputes her claim;
She walks beside the mansion's lord,
　　His bride in all but name.

The busy tongues have ceased to talk,
　　Or speak in softened tone,
So gracious in her daily walk
　　The angel light has shown.

No want that kindness may relieve
　　Assails her heart in vain,
The lifting of a ragged sleeve
　　Will check her palfrey's rein.

A thoughtful calm, a quiet grace
　　In every movement shown,
Reveal her moulded for the place
　　She may not call her own.

And, save that on her youthful brow
　　There broods a shadowy care,
No matron sealed with holy vow
　　In all the land so fair !

PART IV. THE RESCUE

A ship comes foaming up the bay,
　　Along the pier she glides;
Before her furrow melts away,
　　A courier mounts and rides.

"Haste, Haste, post Haste ! " the letters
　　　bear ;
　"Sir Harry Frankland, These."
Sad news to tell the loving pair !
　　The knight must cross the seas.

" Alas ! we part ! " — the lips that spoke
　　Lost all their rosy red,
As when a crystal cup is broke,
　　And all its wine is shed.

"Nay, droop not thus, — where'er," he
　　　cried,
　" I go by land or sea,
My love, my life, my joy, my pride,
　　Thy place is still by me ! "

Through town and city, far and wide,
　　Their wandering feet have strayed,
From Alpine lake to ocean tide,
　　And cold Sierra's shade.

At length they see the waters gleam
　　Amid the fragrant bowers
Where Lisbon mirrors in the stream
　　Her belt of ancient towers.

Red is the orange on its bough,
　　To-morrow's sun shall fling
O'er Cintra's hazel-shaded brow
　　The flush of April's wing.

The streets are loud with noisy mirth,
　　They dance on every green;
The morning's dial marks the birth
　　Of proud Braganza's queen.

At eve beneath their pictured dome
　The gilded courtiers throng;
The broad moidores have cheated Rome
　Of all her lords of song.

Ah ! Lisbon dreams not of the day —
　Pleased with her painted scenes —
When all her towers shall slide away
　As now these canvas screens !

The spring has passed, the summer fled,
　And yet they linger still,
Though autumn's rustling leaves have
　　spread
　The flank of Cintra's hill.

The town has learned their Saxon name,
　And touched their English gold,
Nor tale of doubt nor hint of blame
　From over sea is told.

Three hours the first November dawn
　Has climbed with feeble ray
Through mists like heavy curtains drawn
　Before the darkened day.

How still the muffled echoes sleep !
　Hark ! hark ! a hollow sound, —
A noise like chariots rumbling deep
　Beneath the solid ground.

The channel lifts, the water slides
　And bares its bar of sand,
Anon a mountain billow strides
　And crashes o'er the land.

The turrets lean, the steeples reel
　Like masts on ocean's swell,
And clash a long discordant peal,
　The death-doomed city's knell.

The pavement bursts, the earth upheaves
　Beneath the staggering town !
The turrets crack — the castle cleaves —
　The spires come rushing down.

Around, the lurid mountains glow
　With strange unearthly gleams;
While black abysses gape below,
　Then close in jagged seams.

The earth has folded like a wave,
　And thrice a thousand score,
Clasped, shroudless, in their closing grave,
　The sun shall see no more !

And all is over.　Street and square
　In ruined heaps are piled;
Ah ! where is she, so frail, so fair,
　Amid the tumult wild ?

Unscathed, she treads the wreck - piled
　　street,
　Whose narrow gaps afford
A pathway for her bleeding feet,
　To seek her absent lord.

A temple's broken walls arrest
　Her wild and wandering eyes;
Beneath its shattered portal pressed,
　Her lord unconscious lies.

The power that living hearts obey
　Shall lifeless blocks withstand ?
Love led her footsteps where he lay, —
　Love nerves her woman's hand:

One cry, — the marble shaft she grasps, —
　Up heaves the ponderous stone : —
He breathes, — her fainting form he
　　clasps, —
　Her life has bought his own !

PART V.　THE REWARD

How like the starless night of death
　Our being's brief eclipse,
When faltering heart and failing breath
　Have bleached the fading lips !

She lives !　What guerdon shall repay
　His debt of ransomed life ?
One word can charm all wrongs away, —
　The sacred name of WIFE !

The love that won her girlish charms
　Must shield her matron fame,
And write beneath the Frankland arms
　The village beauty's name.

Go, call the priest ! no vain delay
　Shall dim the sacred ring !
Who knows what change the　passing
　　day,
　The fleeting hour, may bring ?

Before the holy altar bent,
　There kneels a goodly pair;
A stately man, of high descent,
　A woman, passing fair.

No jewels lend the blinding sheen
  That meaner beauty needs,
But on her bosom heaves unseen
  A string of golden beads.

The vow is spoke, — the prayer is said, —
  And with a gentle pride
The Lady Agnes lifts her head,
  Sir Harry Frankland's bride.

No more her faithful heart shall bear
  Those griefs so meekly borne, —
The passing sneer, the freezing stare,
  The icy look of scorn;

No more the blue-eyed English dames
  Their haughty lips shall curl,
Whene'er a hissing whisper names
  The poor New England girl.

But stay ! — his mother's haughty brow, —
  The pride of ancient race, —
Will plighted faith, and holy vow,
  Win back her fond embrace ?

Too well she knew the saddening tale
  Of love no vow had blest,
That turned his blushing honors pale
  And stained his knightly crest.

They seek his Northern home, — alas :
  He goes alone before; —
His own dear Agnes may not pass
  The proud, ancestral door.

He stood before the stately dame;
  He spoke; she calmly heard,
But not to pity, nor to blame;
  She breathed no single word.

He told his love, — her faith betrayed;
  She heard with tearless eyes;
Could she forgive the erring maid ?
  She stared in cold surprise.

How fond her heart, he told, — how
    true;
  The haughty eyelids fell; —
The kindly deeds she loved to do;
  She murmured, " It is well."

But when he told that fearful day,
  And how her feet were led
To where entombed in life he lay,
  The breathing with the dead,

And how she bruised her tender breasts
  Against the crushing stone,
That still the strong-armed clown protests
  No man can lift alone, —

Oh ! then the frozen spring was broke;
  By turns she wept and smiled; —
" Sweet Agnes ! " so the mother spoke,
  " God bless my angel child !

" She saved thee from the jaws of death, —
  'T is thine to right her wrongs;
I tell thee, — I, who gave thee breath, —
  To her thy life belongs ! "

Thus Agnes won her noble name,
  Her lawless lover's hand;
The lowly maiden so became
  A lady in the land !

PART VI. CONCLUSION

The tale is done ; it little needs
  To track their after ways,
And string again the golden beads
  Of love's uncounted days.

They leave the fair ancestral isle
  For bleak New England's shore;
How gracious is the courtly smile
  Of all who frowned before !

Again through Lisbon's orange bowers
  They watch the river's gleam,
And shudder as her shadowy towers
  Shake in the trembling stream.

Fate parts at length the fondest pair;
  His cheek, alas ! grows pale;
The breast that trampling death could
    spare
  His noiseless shafts assail.

He longs to change the heaven of blue
  For England's clouded sky, —
To breathe the air his boyhood knew;
  He seeks them but to die.

Hard by the terraced hillside town,
  Where healing streamlets run,
Still sparkling with their old renown, —
  The " Waters of the Sun," —

The Lady Agnes raised the stone
  That marks his honored grave,

And there Sir Harry sleeps alone
  By Wiltshire Avon's wave.

The home of early love was dear;
  She sought its peaceful shade,
And kept her state for many a year,
  With none to make afraid.

At last the evil days were come
  That saw the red cross fall;
She hears the rebels' rattling drum, —
  Farewell to Frankland Hall !

I tell you, as my tale began,
  The hall is standing still;
And you, kind listener, maid or man,
  May see it if you will.

The box is glistening huge and green,
  Like trees the lilacs grow,
Three elms high-arching still are seen,
  And one lies stretched below.

The hangings, rough with velvet flowers,
  Flap on the latticed wall;
And o'er the mossy ridgepole towers
  The rock-hewn chimney tall.

The doors on mighty hinges clash
  With massive bolt and bar,
The heavy English-moulded sash
  Scarce can the night-winds jar.

Behold the chosen room he sought
  Alone, to fast and pray,
Each year, as chill November brought
  The dismal earthquake day.

There hung the rapier blade he wore,
  Bent in its flattened sheath;
The coat the shrieking woman tore
  Caught in her clenching teeth; —

The coat with tarnished silver lace
  She snapped at as she slid,
And down upon her death-white face
  Crashed the huge coffin's lid.

A graded terrace yet remains;
  If on its turf you stand
And look along the wooded plains
  That stretch on either hand,

The broken forest walls define
  A dim, receding view,

Where, on the far horizon's line,
  He cut his vista through.

If further story you shall crave,
  Or ask for living proof,
Go see old Julia, born a slave
  Beneath Sir Harry's roof.

She told me half that I have told,
  And she remembers well
The mansion as it looked of old
  Before its glories fell; —

The box, when round the terraced square
  Its glossy wall was drawn;
The climbing vines, the snow-balls fair,
  The roses on the lawn.

And Julia says, with truthful look
  Stamped on her wrinkled face,
That in her own black hands she took
  The coat with silver lace.

And you may hold the story light,
  Or, if you like, believe;
But there it was, the woman's bite, —
  A mouthful from the sleeve.

Now go your ways; — I need not tell
  The moral of my rhyme;
But, youths and maidens, ponder well
  This tale of olden time !

THE PLOUGHMAN

ANNIVERSARY OF THE BERKSHIRE AGRI-
CULTURAL SOCIETY, OCTOBER 4, 1849

[At this anniversary, Dr. Holmes not only
read the following poem, but was chairman of
the committee on the ploughing match, and
read the report which will be found in the notes
at the end of this volume.]

CLEAR the brown path, to meet his coulter's
    gleam !
Lo ! on he comes, behind his smoking
    team,
With toil's bright dew-drops on his sun-
    burnt brow,
The lord of earth, the hero of the plough !

First in the field before the reddening
    sun,
Last in the shadows when the day is done,

Line after line, along the bursting sod,
Marks the broad acres where his feet have
    trod;
Still, where he treads, the stubborn clods
    divide,
The smooth, fresh furrow opens deep and
    wide;
Matted and dense the tangled turf up-
    heaves,
Mellow and dark the ridgy cornfield
    cleaves;
Up the steep hillside, where the laboring
    train
Slants the long track that scores the level
    plain;
Through the moist valley, clogged with
    oozing clay,
The patient convoy breaks its destined way ;
At every turn the loosening chains resound,
The swinging ploughshare circles glisten-
    ing round,
Till the wide field one billowy waste ap-
    pears,
And wearied hands unbind the panting
    steers.

These are the hands whose sturdy labor
    brings
The peasant's food, the golden pomp of
    kings;
This is the page, whose letters shall be seen
Changed by the sun to words of living
    green;
This is the scholar, whose immortal pen
Spells the first lesson hunger taught to
    men;
These are the lines which heaven-com-
    manded Toil
Shows on his deed, — the charter of the
    soil !

O gracious Mother, whose benignant
    breast
Wakes us to life, and lulls us all to rest,
How thy sweet features, kind to every
    clime,
Mock with their smile the wrinkled front
    of time !
We stain thy flowers, — they blossom o'er
    the dead;
We rend thy bosom, and it gives us bread ;
O'er the red field that trampling strife has
    torn,
Waves the green plumage of thy tasselled
    corn;

Our maddening conflicts scar thy fairest
    plain,
Still thy soft answer is the growing grain.
Yet, O our Mother, while uncounted
    charms
Steal round our hearts in thine embracing
    arms,
Let not our virtues in thy love decay,
And thy fond sweetness waste our strength
    away.

No ! by these hills, whose banners now dis-
    played
In blazing cohorts Autumn has arrayed;
By yon twin summits, on whose splintery
    crests
The tossing hemlocks hold the eagles'
    nests;
By these fair plains the mountain circle
    screens,
And feeds with streamlets from its dark
    ravines, —
True to their home, these faithful arms
    shall toil
To crown with peace their own untainted
    soil;
And, true to God, to freedom, to mankind,
If her chained bandogs Faction shall un-
    bind,
These stately forms, that bending even now
Bowed their strong manhood to the humble
    plough,
Shall rise erect, the guardians of the land,
The same stern iron in the same right hand,
Till o'er their hills the shouts of triumph run,
The sword has rescued what the plough-
    share won !

SPRING

WINTER is past ; the heart of Nature
    warms
Beneath the wrecks of unresisted storms;
Doubtful at first, suspected more than seen,
The southern slopes are fringed with ten-
    der green;
On sheltered banks, beneath the dripping
    eaves,
Spring's earliest nurslings spread their
    glowing leaves,
Bright with the hues from wider pictures
    won,
White, azure, golden, — drift, or sky, or
    sun, —

The snowdrop, bearing on her patient
    breast
The frozen trophy torn from Winter's
    crest;
The violet, gazing on the arch of blue
Till her own iris wears its deepened hue;
The spendthrift crocus, bursting through
    the mould
Naked and shivering with his cup of gold.
Swelled with new life, the darkening elm
    on high
Prints her thick buds against the spotted
    sky;
On all her boughs the stately chestnut
    cleaves
The gummy shroud that wraps her embryo
    leaves;
The house-fly, stealing from his narrow
    grave,
Drugged with the opiate that November
    gave,
Beats with faint wing against the sunny
    pane,
Or crawls, tenacious, o'er its lucid plain;
From shaded chinks of lichen - crusted
    walls,
In languid curves, the gliding serpent
    crawls;
The bog's green harper, thawing from his
    sleep,
Twangs a hoarse note and tries a shortened
    leap;
On floating rails that face the softening
    noons
The still shy turtles range their dark pla-
    toons,
Or, toiling aimless o'er the mellowing
    fields,
Trail through the grass their tessellated
    shields.

At last young April, ever frail and fair,
Wooed by her playmate with the golden
    hair,
Chased to the margin of receding floods
O'er the soft meadows starred with open-
    ing buds,
In tears and blushes sighs herself away,
And hides her cheek beneath the flowers of
    May.

Then the proud tulip lights her beacon
    blaze,
Her clustering curls the hyacinth displays;

O'er her tall blades the crested fleur-de-
    lis,
Like blue-eyed Pallas, towers erect and
    free;
With yellower flames the lengthened sun-
    shine glows,
And love lays bare the passion-breathing
    rose;
Queen of the lake, along its reedy verge
The rival lily hastens to emerge,
Her snowy shoulders glistening as she
    strips,
Till morn is sultan of her parted lips.

Then bursts the song from every leafy
    glade,
The yielding season's bridal serenade;
Then flash the wings returning Summer
    calls
Through the deep arches of her forest
    halls, —
The bluebird, breathing from his azure
    plumes
The fragrance borrowed where the myrtle
    blooms;
The thrush, poor wanderer, dropping
    meekly down,
Clad in his remnant of autumnal brown;
The oriole, drifting like a flake of fire
Rent by a whirlwind from a blazing spire.
The robin, jerking his spasmodic throat,
Repeats, imperious, his *staccato* note;
The crack-brained bobolink courts his
    crazy mate,
Poised on a bulrush tipsy with his weight;
Nay, in his cage the lone canary sings,
Feels the soft air, and spreads his idle wings.

Why dream I here within these caging
    walls,
Deaf to her voice, while blooming Nature
    calls;
Peering and gazing with insatiate looks
Through blinding lenses, or in wearying
    books ?
Off, gloomy spectres of the shrivelled past !
Fly with the leaves that fill the autumn
    blast !
Ye imps of Science, whose relentless chains
Lock the warm tides within these living
    veins,
Close your dim cavern, while its captive
    strays
Dazzled and giddy in the morning's blaze !

THE STUDY

YET in the darksome crypt I left so late,
Whose only altar is its rusted grate, —
Sepulchral, rayless, joyless as it seems,
Shamed by the glare of May's refulgent
    beams, —
While the dim seasons dragged their
    shrouded train,
Its paler splendors were not quite in vain.
From these dull bars the cheerful firelight's
    glow
Streamed through the casement o'er the
    spectral snow;
Here, while the night-wind wreaked its
    frantic will
On the loose ocean and the rock-bound hill,
Rent the cracked topsail from its quiver-
    ing yard,
And rived the oak a thousand storms had
    scarred,
Fenced by these walls the peaceful taper
    shone,
Nor felt a breath to slant its trembling
    cone.

Not all unblest the mild interior scene
When the red curtain spread its falling
    screen;
O'er some light task the lonely hours were
    past,
And the long evening only flew too fast;
Or the wide chair its leathern arms would
    lend
In genial welcome to some easy friend,
Stretched on its bosom with relaxing nerves,
Slow moulding, plastic, to its hollow curves;
Perchance indulging, if of generous creed,
In brave Sir Walter's dream-compelling
    weed.
Or, happier still, the evening hour would
    bring
To the round table its expected ring,
And while the punch-bowl's sounding depths
    were stirred, —
Its silver cherubs smiling as they heard, —
Our hearts would open, as at evening's hour
The close-sealed primrose frees its hidden
    flower.

Such the warm life this dim retreat has
    known,
Not quite deserted when its guests were
    flown;

Nay, filled with friends, an unobtrusive set,
Guiltless of calls and cards and etiquette,
Ready to answer, never known to ask,
Claiming no service, prompt for every task.

On those dark shelves no housewife hand
    profanes,
O'er his mute files the monarch folio reigns;
A mingled race, the wreck of chance and
    time,
That talk all tongues and breathe of every
    clime,
Each knows his place, and each may claim
    his part
In some quaint corner of his master's
    heart.
This old Decretal, won from Kloss's hoards,
Thick-leaved, brass-cornered, ribbed with
    oaken boards,
Stands the gray patriarch of the graver
    rows,
Its fourth ripe century narrowing to its
    close;
Not daily conned, but glorious still to view,
With glistening letters wrought in red and
    blue.
There towers Stagira's all-embracing sage,
The Aldine anchor on his opening page;
There sleep the births of Plato's heavenly
    mind,
In yon dark tomb by jealous clasps con-
    fined,
"Olim e libris" (dare I call it mine?)
Of Yale's grave Head and Killingworth's
    divine!
In those square sheets the songs of Maro
    fill
The silvery types of smooth-leaved Basker-
    ville;
High over all, in close, compact array,
Their classic wealth the Elzevirs display.
In lower regions of the sacred space
Range the dense volumes of a humbler
    race;
There grim chirurgeons all their mysteries
    teach,
In spectral pictures, or in crabbed speech;
Harvey and Haller, fresh from Nature's
    page,
Shoulder the dreamers of an earlier age,
Lully and Geber, and the learned crew
That loved to talk of all they could not do.
Why count the rest, — those names of later
    days
That many love, and all agree to praise, —

Or point the titles, where a glance may
   read
The dangerous lines of party or of creed ?
Too well, perchance, the chosen list would
   show
What few may care and none can claim to
   know.
Each has his features, whose exterior seal
A brush may copy, or a sunbeam steal ;
Go to his study, — on the nearest shelf
Stands the mosaic portrait of himself.

   What though for months the tranquil
      dust descends,
Whitening the heads of these mine ancient
   friends,
While the damp offspring of the modern
   press
Flaunts on my table with its pictured dress;
Not less I love each dull familiar face,
Nor less should miss it from the appointed
   place;
I snatch the book, along whose burning
   leaves
His scarlet web our wild romancer weaves,
Yet, while proud Hester's fiery pangs I
   share,
My old MAGNALIA must be standing *there!*

THE BELLS

WHEN o'er the street the morning peal is
   flung
From yon tall belfry with the brazen
   tongue,
Its wide vibrations, wafted by the gale,
To each far listener tell a different tale.
   The sexton, stooping to the quivering
      floor
Till the great caldron spills its brassy roar,
Whirls the hot axle, counting, one by one,
Each dull concussion, till his task is done.
   Toil's patient daughter, when the wel-
      come note
Clangs through the silence from the
   steeple's throat,
Streams, a white unit, to the checkered
   street,
Demure, but guessing whom she soon shall
   meet;
The bell, responsive to her secret flame,
With every note repeats her lover's name.
   The lover, tenant of the neighboring
      lane,

Sighing, and fearing lest he sigh in vain,
Hears the stern accents, as they come and
   go,
Their only burden one despairing No !
   Ocean's rough child, whom many a
      shore has known
Ere homeward breezes swept him to his
   own,
Starts at the echo as it circles round,
A thousand memories kindling with the
   sound;
The early favorite's unforgotten charms,
Whose blue initials stain his tawny arms;
His first farewell, the flapping canvas
   spread,
The seaward streamers crackling overhead,
His kind, pale mother, not ashamed to
   weep
Her first-born's bridal with the haggard
   deep,
While the brave father stood with tearless
   eye,
Smiling and choking with his last good-by.

   'T is but a wave, whose spreading circle
      beats,
With the same impulse, every nerve it
   meets,
Yet who shall count the varied shapes that
   ride
On the round surge of that aerial tide !

   O child of earth ! If floating sounds like
      these
Steal from thyself their power to wound or
   please,
If here or there thy changing will inclines,
As the bright zodiac shifts its rolling signs,
Look at thy heart, and when its depths are
   known,
Then try thy brother's, judging by thine own,
But keep thy wisdom to the narrower
   range,
While its own standards are the sport of
   change,
Nor count us rebels when we disobey
The passing breath that holds thy passion's
   sway.

NON–RESISTANCE

PERHAPS too far in these considerate
   days
Has patience carried her submissive ways;

Wisdom has taught us to be calm and
   meek,
To take one blow, and turn the other
   cheek;
It is not written what a man shall do
If the rude caitiff smite the other too !

   Land of our fathers, in thine hour of
     need
God help thee, guarded by the passive
   creed !
As the lone pilgrim trusts to beads and
   cowl,
When through the forest rings the gray
   wolf's howl;
As the deep galleon trusts her gilded
   prow
When the black corsair slants athwart her
   bow;
As the poor pheasant, with his peaceful
   mien,
Trusts to his feathers, shining golden-green,
When the dark plumage with the crimson
   beak
Has rustled shadowy from its splintered
   peak, —
So trust thy friends, whose babbling
   tongues would charm
The lifted sabre from thy foeman's arm,
Thy torches ready for the answering peal
From bellowing fort and thunder-freighted
   keel !

THE MORAL BULLY

YON whey-faced brother, who delights to
   wear
A weedy flux of ill-conditioned hair,
Seems of the sort that in a crowded place
One elbows freely into smallest space;
A timid creature, lax of knee and hip,
Whom small disturbance whitens round
   the lip;
One of those harmless spectacled machines,
The Holy-Week of Protestants convenes;
Whom school-boys question if their walk
   transcends
The last advices of maternal friends;
Whom John, obedient to his master's sign,
Conducts, laborious, up to *ninety-nine*,
While Peter, glistening with luxurious
   scorn,
Husks his white ivories like an ear of
   corn;

Dark in the brow and bilious in the cheek,
Whose yellowish linen flowers but once a
   week,
Conspicuous, annual, in their threadbare
   suits,
And the laced high-lows which they call
   their boots,
Well mayst thou *shun* that dingy front
   severe,
But him, O stranger, him thou canst not
   fear !
   Be slow to judge, and slower to despise,
Man of broad shoulders and heroic size !
The tiger, writhing from the boa's rings,
Drops at the fountain where the cobra
   stings.
In that lean phantom, whose extended
   glove
Points to the text of universal love,
Behold the master that can tame thee
   down
To crouch, the vassal of his Sunday frown;
His velvet throat against thy corded wrist,
His loosened tongue against thy doubled
   fist !

   The MORAL BULLY, though he never
     swears,
Nor kicks intruders down his entry stairs,
Though meekness plants his backward-
   sloping hat,
And non-resistance ties his white cravat,
Though his black broadcloth glories to be
   seen
In the same plight with Shylock's gaber-
   dine,
Hugs the same passion to his narrow
   breast
That heaves the cuirass on the trooper's
   chest,
Hears the same hell-hounds yelling in his
   rear
That chase from port the maddened buc-
   caneer,
Feels the same comfort while his acrid
   words
Turn the sweet milk of kindness into
   curds,
Or with grim logic prove, beyond debate,
That all we love is worthiest of our hate,
As the scarred ruffian of the pirate's
   deck,
When his long swivel rakes the staggering
   wreck !

Heaven keep us all ! Is every rascal
    clown
Whose arm is stronger free to knock us
    down ?
Has every scarecrow, whose cachectic soul
Seems fresh from Bedlam, airing on pa-
    role,
Who, though he carries but a doubtful
    trace
Of angel visits on his hungry face,
From lack of marrow or the coins to pay,
Has dogged some vices in a shabby way,
The right to stick us with his cutthroat
    terms, .
And bait his homilies with his brother
    worms ?

THE MIND'S DIET

No life worth naming ever comes to
    good
If always nourished on the selfsame food;
The creeping mite may live so if he please,
And feed on Stilton till he turns to cheese,
But cool Magendie proves beyond a doubt,
If mammals try it, that their eyes drop
    out.

No reasoning natures find it safe to feed,
For their sole diet, on a single creed ;
It spoils their eyeballs while it spares their
    tongues,
And starves the heart to feed the noisy
    lungs.

When the first larvæ on the elm are
    seen,
The crawling wretches, like its leaves, are
    green;
Ere chill October shakes the latest down,
They, like the foliage, change their tint to
    brown;
On the blue flower a bluer flower you
    spy,
You stretch to pluck it — 't is a butterfly ;
The flattened tree-toads so resemble bark,
They 're hard to find as Ethiops in the
    dark;
The woodcock, stiffening to fictitious mud,
Cheats the young sportsman thirsting for
    his blood ;
So by long living on a single lie,
Nay, on one truth, will creatures get its
    dye ;

Red, yellow, green, they take their sub-
    ject's hue, —
Except when squabbling turns them black
    and blue !

OUR LIMITATIONS

WE trust and fear, we question and
    believe,
From life's dark threads a trembling faith
    to weave,
Frail as the web that misty night has spun,
Whose dew-gemmed awnings glitter in the
    sun.
While the calm centuries spell their lessons
    out,
Each truth we conquer spreads the realm
    of doubt;
When Sinai's summit was Jehovah's
    throne,
The chosen Prophet knew his voice alone;
When Pilate's hall that awful question
    heard,
The Heavenly Captive answered not a
    word.

Eternal Truth ! beyond our hopes and
    fears
Sweep the vast orbits of thy myriad
    spheres !
From age to age, while History carves
    sublime
On her waste rock the flaming curves of
    time,
How the wild swayings of our planet show
That worlds unseen surround the world we
    know.

THE OLD PLAYER

THE curtain rose; in thunders long and
    loud
The galleries rung; the veteran actor
    bowed.
In flaming line the telltales of the stage
Showed on his brow the autograph of age;
Pale, hueless waves amid his clustered hair,
And umbered shadows, prints of toil and
    care ;
Round the wide circle glanced his vacant
    eye, —
He strove to speak, — his voice was but a
    sigh.

Year after year had seen its short-lived
　　race
Flit past the scenes and others take their
　　place;
Yet the old prompter watched his accents
　　still,
His name still flaunted on the evening's
　　bill.
Heroes, the monarchs of the scenic floor,
Had died in earnest and were heard no
　　more;
Beauties, whose cheeks such roseate bloom
　　o'erspread
They faced the footlights in unborrowed
　　red,
Had faded slowly through successive
　　shades
To gray duennas, foils of younger maids;
Sweet voices lost the melting tones that
　　start
With Southern throbs the sturdy Saxon
　　heart,
While fresh sopranos shook the painted sky
With their long, breathless, quivering
　　locust-cry.
Yet there he stood, — the man of other
　　days,
In the clear present's full, unsparing blaze,
As on the oak a faded leaf that clings
While a new April spreads its burnished
　　wings.

How bright yon rows that soared in
　　triple tier,
Their central sun the flashing chandelier!
How dim the eye that sought with doubtful
　　aim
Some friendly smile it still might dare to
　　claim!
How fresh these hearts! his own how worn
　　and cold!
Such the sad thoughts that long-drawn
　　sigh had told.
　No word yet faltered on his trembling
　　tongue;
Again, again, the crashing galleries rung.
As the old guardsman at the bugle's blast
Hears in its strain the echoes of the past,
So, as the plaudits rolled and thundered
　　round,
A life of memories startled at the sound.
　He lived again, — the page of earliest
　　days, —
Days of small fee and parsimonious
　　praise;

Then lithe young Romeo — hark that sil-
　　vered tone,
From those smooth lips — alas! they were
　　his own.
Then the bronzed Moor, with all his love
　　and woe,
Told his strange tale of midnight melting
　　snow;
And dark-plumed Hamlet, with his cloak
　　and blade,
Looked on the royal ghost, himself a
　　shade.
All in one flash, his youthful memories
　　came,
Traced in bright hues of evanescent flame,
As the spent swimmer's in the lifelong
　　dream,
While the last bubble rises through the
　　stream.

　Call him not old, whose visionary brain
Holds o'er the past its undivided reign.
For him in vain the envious seasons roll
Who bears eternal summer in his soul.
If yet the minstrel's song, the poet's lay,
Spring with her birds, or children at their
　　play,
Or maiden's smile, or heavenly dream of
　　art,
Stir the few life-drops creeping round his
　　heart,
Turn to the record where his years are
　　told, —
Count his gray hairs, — they cannot make
　　him old!
　What magic power has changed the
　　faded mime?
One breath of memory on the dust of time.
As the last window in the buttressed wall
Of some gray minster tottering to its fall,
Though to the passing crowd its hues are
　　spread,
A dull mosaic, yellow, green, and red,
Viewed from within, a radiant glory shows
When through its pictured screen the sun-
　　light flows,
And kneeling pilgrims on its storied pane
See angels glow in every shapeless stain;
So streamed the vision through his sunken-
　　eye,
Clad in the splendors of his morning sky.
　All the wild hopes his eager boyhood
　　knew,
All the young fancies riper years proved
　　true.

The sweet, low-whispered words, the win-
    ning glance
From queens of song, from Houris of the
    dance,
Wealth's lavish gift, and Flattery's soothing
    phrase,
And Beauty's silence when her blush was
    praise,
And melting Pride, her lashes wet with
    tears,
Triumphs and banquets, wreaths and crowns
    and cheers,
Pangs of wild joy that perish on the
    tongue,
And all that poets dream, but leave un-
    sung !

In every heart some viewless founts are
    fed
From far-off hillsides where the dews were
    shed:
On the worn features of the weariest face
Some youthful memory leaves its hidden
    trace,
As in old gardens left by exiled kings
The marble basins tell of hidden springs,
But, gray with dust, and overgrown with
    weeds,
Their choking jets the passer little heeds,
Till time's revenges break their seals away,
And, clad in rainbow light, the waters
    play.

Good night, fond dreamer ! let the cur-
    tain fall:
The world 's a stage, and we are players all.
A strange rehearsal ! Kings without their
    crowns,
And threadbare lords, and jewel-wearing
    clowns,
Speak the vain words that mock their
    throbbing hearts,
As Want, stern prompter ! spells them out
    their parts.
The tinselled hero whom we praise and pay
Is twice an actor in a twofold play.
We smile at children when a painted screen
Seems to their simple eyes a real scene;
Ask the poor hireling, who has left his
    throne
To seek the cheerless home he calls his own,
Which of his double lives most real seems,
The world of solid fact or scenic dreams ?
Canvas, or clouds, — the footlights, or the
    spheres, —

The play of two short hours, or seventy
    years ?
    Dream on ! Though Heaven may woo
    our open eyes,
Through their closed lids we look on fairer
    skies;
Truth is for other worlds, and hope for this;
The cheating future lends the present's
    bliss;
Life is a running shade, with fettered
    hands,
That chases phantoms over shifting sands,
Death a still spectre on a marble seat,
With ever clutching palms and shackled
    feet;
The airy shapes that mock life's slender
    chain,
The flying joys he strives to clasp in vain,
Death only grasps; to live is to pursue, —
Dream on ! there 's nothing but illusion
    true !

A POEM

DEDICATION OF THE PITTSFIELD CEME-
TERY, SEPTEMBER 9, 1850

ANGEL of Death ! extend thy silent
    reign !
Stretch thy dark sceptre o'er this new do-
    main !
No sable car along the winding road
Has borne to earth its unresisting load;
No sudden mound has risen yet to show
Where the pale slumberer folds his arms
    below;
No marble gleams to bid his memory live
In the brief lines that hurrying Time can
    give;
Yet, O Destroyer ! from thy shrouded
    throne
Look on our gift; this realm is all thine
    own !

Fair is the scene; its sweetness oft be-
    guiled
From their dim paths the children of the
    wild;
The dark-haired maiden loved its grassy
    dells,
The feathered warrior claimed its wooded
    swells,
Still on its slopes the ploughman's ridges
    show

The pointed flints that left his fatal bow,
Chipped with rough art and slow barbarian
  toil, —
Last of his wrecks that strews the alien
  soil !
  Here spread the fields that heaped their
  ripened store
Till the brown arms of Labor held no more;
The scythe's broad meadow with its dusky
  blush;
The sickle's harvest with its velvet flush;
The green-haired maize, her silken tresses
  laid,
In soft luxuriance, on her harsh brocade;
The gourd that swells beneath her tossing
  plume;
The coarser wheat that rolls in lakes of
  bloom, —
Its coral stems and milk-white flowers alive
With the wide murmurs of the scattered
  hive;
Here glowed the apple with the pencilled
  streak
Of morning painted on its southern cheek;
The pear's long necklace strung with golden
  drops,
Arched, like the banian, o'er its pillared
  props;
Here crept the growths that paid the la-
  borer's care
With the cheap luxuries wealth consents to
  spare;
Here sprang the healing herbs which could
  not save
The hand that reared them from the neigh-
  boring grave.

Yet all its varied charms, forever free
From task and tribute, Labor yields to thee:
No more, when April sheds her fitful rain,
The sower's hand shall cast its flying grain;
No more, when Autumn strews the flaming
  leaves,
The reaper's band shall gird its yellow
  sheaves ;
For thee alike the circling seasons flow
Till the first blossoms heave the latest
  snow.
In the stiff clod below the whirling drifts,
In the loose soil the springing herbage lifts,
In the hot dust beneath the parching weeds,
Life's withering flower shall drop its
  shrivelled seeds;
Its germ entranced in thy unbreathing sleep
Till what thou sowest mightier angels reap !

Spirit of Beauty ! let thy graces blend
With loveliest Nature all that Art can lend.
Come from the bowers where Summer's
  life-blood flows
Through the red lips of June's half-open
  rose,
Dressed in bright hues, the loving sun-
  shine's dower;
For tranquil Nature owns no mourning
  flower.
  Come from the forest where the beech's
  screen
Bars the fierce noonbeam with its flakes of
  green;
Stay the rude axe that bares the shadowy
  plains,
Stanch the deep wound that dries the
  maple's veins.
  Come with the stream whose silver-
  braided rills
Fling their unclasping bracelets from the
  hills,
Till in one gleam, beneath the forest's
  wings,
Melts the white glitter of a hundred
  springs.
  Come from the steeps where look majes-
  tic forth
From their twin thrones the Giants of the
  North
On the huge shapes, that, crouching at their
  knees,
Stretch their broad shoulders, rough with
  shaggy trees.
Through the wide waste of ether, not in
  vain,
Their softened gaze shall reach our distant
  plain;
There, while the mourner turns his aching
  eyes
On the blue mounds that print the bluer
  skies,
Nature shall whisper that the fading view
Of mightiest grief may wear a heavenly
  hue.
Cherub of Wisdom ! let thy marble page
Leave its sad lesson, new to every age;
Teach us to live, not grudging every breath
To the chill winds that waft us on to death,
But ruling calmly every pulse it warms,
And tempering gently every word it forms.
Seraph of Love ! in heaven's adoring zone,
Nearest of all around the central throne,
While with soft hands the pillowed turf we
  spread

That soon shall hold us in its dreamless bed,
With the low whisper, — Who shall first be laid
In the dark chamber's yet unbroken shade ? —
Let thy sweet radiance shine rekindled here,
And all we cherish grow more truly dear.
Here in the gates of Death's o'erhanging vault,
Oh, teach us kindness for our brother's fault:
Lay all our wrongs beneath this peaceful sod,
And lead our hearts to Mercy and its God.

FATHER of all ! in Death's relentless claim
We read thy mercy by its sterner name;
In the bright flower that decks the solemn bier,
We see thy glory in its narrowed sphere;
In the deep lessons that affliction draws,
We trace the curves of thy encircling laws;
In the long sigh that sets our spirits free,
We own the love that calls us back to Thee !

Through the hushed street, along the silent plain,
The spectral future leads its mourning train,
Dark with the shadows of uncounted bands,
Where man's white lips and woman's wringing hands
Track the still burden, rolling slow before,
That love and kindness can protect no more;
The smiling babe that, called to mortal strife,
Shuts its meek eyes and drops its little life;
The drooping child who prays in vain to live,
And pleads for help its parent cannot give;
The pride of beauty stricken in its flower;
The strength of manhood broken in an hour;
Age in its weakness, bowed by toil and care,
Traced in sad lines beneath its silvered hair.

The sun shall set, and heaven's resplendent spheres
Gild the smooth turf unhallowed yet by tears,

But ah ! how soon the evening stars will shed
Their sleepless light around the slumbering dead !

Take them, O Father, in immortal trust !
Ashes to ashes, dust to kindred dust,
Till the last angel rolls the stone away,
And a new morning brings eternal day !

TO GOVERNOR SWAIN

[Mr. William W. Swain was a New Bedford merchant, who became the owner of the island of Naushon, where he exercised a generous hospitality, and was given the title of Governor in playful affection. He had a passionate love for every tree and stone on the island, and was buried in a beautiful open glade in the woods there. The island passed into the possession of Mr. John M. Forbes, who married Governor Swain's niece. Dr. Holmes speaks of his own entertainment at Naushon in the *Autocrat*, pp. 39–41. This poem was written at Pittsfield in 1851.]

DEAR GOVERNOR, if my skiff might brave
The winds that lift the ocean wave,
The mountain stream that loops and swerves
Through my broad meadow's channelled curves
Should waft me on from bound to bound
To where the River weds the Sound,
The Sound should give me to the Sea,
That to the Bay, the Bay to thee.

It may not be ; too long the track
To follow down or struggle back.
The sun has set on fair Naushon
Long ere my western blaze is gone;
The ocean disk is rolling dark
In shadows round your swinging bark,
While yet the yellow sunset fills
The stream that scarfs my spruce-clad hills;
The day-star wakes your island deer
Long ere my barnyard chanticleer;
Your mists are soaring in the blue
While mine are sparks of glittering dew.

It may not be; oh, would it might,
Could I live o'er that glowing night !
What golden hours would come to life,
What goodly feats of peaceful strife, —
Such jests, that, drained of every joke,

The very bank of language broke, —
Such deeds, that Laughter nearly died
With stitches in his belted side;
While Time, caught fast in pleasure's
    chain,
His double goblet snapped in twain,
And stood with half in either hand, —
Both brimming full, — but not of sand !

It may not be; I strive in vain
To break my slender household chain, —
Three pairs of little clasping hands,
One voice, that whispers, not commands.
Even while my spirit flies away,
My gentle jailers murmur nay;
All shapes of elemental wrath
They raise along my threatened path;
The storm grows black, the waters rise,
The mountains mingle with the skies,
The mad tornado scoops the ground,
The midnight robber prowls around, —
Thus, kissing every limb they tie,
They draw a knot and heave a sigh,
Till, fairly netted in the toil,
My feet are rooted to the soil.
Only the soaring wish is free ! —
And that, dear Governor, flies to thee !

TO AN ENGLISH FRIEND

THE seed that wasteful autumn cast
To waver on its stormy blast,
Long o'er the wintry desert tost,
Its living germ has never lost.
Dropped by the weary tempest's wing,
It feels the kindling ray of spring,
And, starting from its dream of death,
Pours on the air its perfumed breath.

So, parted by the rolling flood,
The love that springs from common blood
Needs but a single sunlit hour
Of mingling smiles to bud and flower;
Unharmed its slumbering life has flown,
From shore to shore, from zone to zone,
Where summer's falling roses stain
The tepid waves of Pontchartrain,
Or where the lichen creeps below
Katahdin's wreaths of whirling snow.

Though fiery sun and stiffening cold
May change the fair ancestral mould,
No winter chills, no summer drains
The life-blood drawn from English veins,

Still bearing whereso'er it flows
The love that with its fountain rose,
Unchanged by space, unwronged by time,
From age to age, from clime to clime !

AFTER A LECTURE ON WORDS-
WORTH

[In 1853 Dr. Holmes gave a course of lectures before the Lowell Institute in Boston on English Poetry of the Nineteenth Century, and this and the following five poems were postludes to the lectures.]

COME, spread your wings, as I spread mine,
    And leave the crowded hall
For where the eyes of twilight shine
    O'er evening's western wall.

These are the pleasant Berkshire hills,
    Each with its leafy crown;
Hark ! from their sides a thousand rills
    Come singing sweetly down.

A thousand rills; they leap and shine,
    Strained through the shadowy nooks,
Till, clasped in many a gathering twine,
    They swell a hundred brooks.

A hundred brooks, and still they run
    With ripple, shade, and gleam,
Till, clustering all their braids in one,
    They flow a single stream.

A bracelet spun from mountain mist,
    A silvery sash unwound,
With ox-bow curve and sinuous twist
    It writhes to reach the Sound.

This is my bark, — a pygmy's ship:
    Beneath a child it rolls;
Fear not, — one body makes it dip,
    But not a thousand souls.

Float we the grassy banks between;
    Without an oar we glide;
The meadows, drest in living green,
    Unroll on either side.

Come, take the book we love so well,
    And let us read and dream
We see whate'er its pages tell,
    And sail an English stream.

Up to the clouds the lark has sprung,
    Still trilling as he flies;

The linnet sings as there he sung;
  The unseen cuckoo cries,

And daisies strew the banks along,
  And yellow kingcups shine,
With cowslips, and a primrose throng,
  And humble celandine.

Ah foolish dream ! when Nature nursed
  Her daughter in the West,
The fount was drained that opened first ;
  She bared her other breast.

On the young planet's orient shore
  Her morning hand she tried;
Then turned the broad medallion o'er
  And stamped the sunset side.

Take what she gives, her pine's tall stem,
  Her elm with hanging spray;
She wears her mountain diadem
  Still in her own proud way.

Look on the forests' ancient kings,
  The hemlock's towering pride:
Yon trunk had thrice a hundred rings,
  And fell before it died.

Nor think that Nature saves her bloom
  And slights our grassy plain;
For us she wears her court costume, —
  Look on its broidered train;

The lily with the sprinkled dots,
  Brands of the noontide beam;
The cardinal, and the blood-red spots,
  Its double in the stream,

As if some wounded eagle's breast,
  Slow throbbing o'er the plain,
Had left its airy path impressed
  In drops of scarlet rain.

And hark ! and hark ! the woodland rings;
  There thrilled the thrush's soul;
And look ! that flash of flamy wings, —
  The fire-plumed oriole !

Above, the hen-hawk swims and swoops,
  Flung from the bright, blue sky;
Below, the robin hops, and whoops
  His piercing Indian cry.

Beauty runs virgin in the woods
  Robed in her rustic green,

And oft a longing thought intrudes,
  As if we might have seen

Her every finger's every joint
  Ringed with some golden line,
Poet whom Nature did anoint !
  Had our wild home been thine.

Yet think not so ; Old England's blood
  Runs warm in English veins;
But wafted o'er the icy flood
  Its better life remains:

Our children know each wildwood smell,
  The bayberry and the fern,
The man who does not know them well
  Is all too old to learn.

Be patient ! On the breathing page
  Still pants our hurried past;
Pilgrim and soldier, saint and sage, —
  The poet comes the last !

Though still the lark-voiced matins ring
  The world has known so long;
The wood-thrush of the West shall sing
  Earth's last sweet even-song !

AFTER A LECTURE ON MOORE

SHINE soft, ye trembling tears of light
  That strew the mourning skies;
Hushed in the silent dews of night
  The harp of Erin lies.

What though her thousand years have past
  Of poets, saints, and kings, —
Her echoes only hear the last
  That swept those golden strings.

Fling o'er his mound, ye star-lit bowers,
  The balmiest wreaths ye wear,
Whose breath has lent your earth-born
    flowers
  Heaven's own ambrosial air.

Breathe, bird of night, thy softest tone,
  By shadowy grove and rill;
Thy song will soothe us while we own
  That his was sweeter still.

Stay, pitying Time, thy foot for him
  Who gave thee swifter wings,
Nor let thine envious shadow dim
  The light his glory flings.

If in his cheek unholy blood
  Burned for one youthful hour,
'Twas but the flushing of the bud
  That blooms a milk-white flower.

Take him, kind mother, to thy breast,
  Who loved thy smiles so well,
And spread thy mantle o'er his rest
  Of rose and asphodel.

The bark has sailed the midnight sea,
  The sea without a shore,
That waved its parting sign to thee, —
  "A health to thee, Tom Moore!"

And thine long lingering on the strand,
  Its bright-hued streamers furled,
Was loosed by age, with trembling hand,
  To seek the silent world.

Not silent! no, the radiant stars
  Still singing as they shine,
Unheard through earth's imprisoning bars,
  Have voices sweet as thine.

Wake, then, in happier realms above,
  The songs of bygone years,
Till angels learn those airs of love
  That ravished mortal ears!

AFTER A LECTURE ON KEATS

" Purpureos spargam flores."

THE wreath that star-crowned Shelley gave
Is lying on thy Roman grave,
Yet on its turf young April sets
Her store of slender violets;
Though all the Gods their garlands shower,
I too may bring one purple flower.
Alas! what blossom shall I bring,
That opens in my Northern spring?
The garden beds have all run wild,
So trim when I was yet a child;
Flat plantains and unseemly stalks
Have crept across the gravel walks;
The vines are dead, long, long ago,
The almond buds no longer blow.
No more upon its mound I see
The azure, plume-bound fleur-de-lis;
Where once the tulips used to show,
In straggling tufts the pansies grow;
The grass has quenched my white-rayed
    gem,

The flowering " Star of Bethlehem,"
Though its long blade of glossy green
And pallid stripe may still be seen.
Nature, who treads her nobles down,
And gives their birthright to the clown,
Has sown her base-born weedy things
Above the garden's queens and kings.
Yet one sweet flower of ancient race
Springs in the old familiar place.
When snows were melting down the vale,
And Earth unlaced her icy mail,
And March his stormy trumpet blew,
And tender green came peeping through,
I loved the earliest one to seek
That broke the soil with emerald beak,
And watch the trembling bells so blue
Spread on the column as it grew.
Meek child of earth! thou wilt not shame
The sweet, dead poet's holy name;
The God of music gave thee birth,
Called from the crimson-spotted earth,
Where, sobbing his young life away,
His own fair Hyacinthus lay.
The hyacinth my garden gave
Shall lie upon that Roman grave!

AFTER A LECTURE ON SHELLEY

ONE broad, white sail in Spezzia's treacher-
    ous bay;
  On comes the blast; too daring bark, be-
    ware!
The cloud has clasped her; lo! it melts
    away;
  The wide, waste waters, but no sail is
    there.

Morning: a woman looking on the sea;
  Midnight: with lamps the long veranda
    burns;
Come, wandering sail, they watch, they
    burn for thee!
  Suns come and go, alas! no bark returns.

And feet are thronging on the pebbly
    sands,
  And torches flaring in the weedy caves,
Where'er the waters lay with icy hands
  The shapes uplifted from their coral
    graves.

Vainly they seek; the idle quest is o'er;
  The coarse, dark women, with their hang-
    ing locks,

And lean, wild children gather from the
  shore
To the black hovels bedded in the rocks.

But Love still prayed, with agonizing wail,
  "One, one last look, ye heaving waters,
    yield!"
Till Ocean, clashing in his jointed mail,
  Raised the pale burden on his level
    shield.

Slow from the shore the sullen waves retire;
  His form a nobler element shall claim;
Nature baptized him in ethereal fire,
  And Death shall crown him with a wreath
    of flame.

Fade, mortal semblance, never to return;
  Swift is the change within thy crimson
    shroud;
Seal the white ashes in the peaceful urn;
  All else has risen in yon silvery cloud.

Sleep where thy gentle Adonais lies,
  Whose open page lay on thy dying heart,
Both in the smile of those blue-vaulted
    skies,
  Earth's fairest dome of all divinest art.

Breathe for his wandering soul one passing
    sigh,
  O happier Christian, while thine eye
    grows dim, —
In all the mansions of the house on high,
  Say not that Mercy has not one for him!

AT THE CLOSE OF A COURSE OF LECTURES

As the voice of the watch to the mariner's
  dream,
As the footstep of Spring on the ice-girdled
  stream,
There comes a soft footstep, a whisper, to
  me, —
The vision is over, — the rivulet free!

We have trod from the threshold of turbu-
  lent March,
Till the green scarf of April is hung on the
  larch,
And down the bright hillside that welcomes
  the day,
We hear the warm panting of beautiful
  May.

We will part before Summer has opened
  her wing,
And the bosom of June swells the bodice of
  Spring,
While the hope of the season lies fresh in
  the bud,
And the young life of Nature runs warm in
  our blood.

It is but a word, and the chain is unbound,
The bracelet of steel drops unclasped to the
  ground;
No hand shall replace it, — it rests where
  it fell, —
It is but one word that we all know too well.

Yet the hawk with the wildness untamed
  in his eye,
If you free him, stares round ere he springs
  to the sky;
The slave whom no longer his fetters re-
  strain
Will turn for a moment and look at his
  chain.

Our parting is not as the friendship of
  years,
That chokes with the blessing it speaks
  through its tears;
We have walked in a garden, and, looking
  around,
Have plucked a few leaves from the myrtles
  we found.

But now at the gate of the garden we stand,
And the moment has come for unclasping
  the hand;
Will you drop it like lead, and in silence
  retreat
Like the twenty crushed forms from an
  omnibus seat?

Nay! hold it one moment, — the last we
  may share, —
I stretch it in kindness, and not for my
  fare;
You may pass through the doorway in rank
  or in file,
If your ticket from Nature is stamped with
  a smile.

For the sweetest of smiles is the smile as
  we part,
When the light round the lips is a ray from
  the heart;

And lest a stray tear from its fountain might swell,
We will seal the bright spring with a quiet farewell.

THE HUDSON

AFTER A LECTURE AT ALBANY

[Given in December, 1854.]

'T WAS a vision of childhood that came with its dawn,
Ere the curtain that covered life's day-star was drawn;
The nurse told the tale when the shadows grew long,
And the mother's soft lullaby breathed it in song.

" There flows a fair stream by the hills of the West," —
She sang to her boy as he lay on her breast;
"Along its smooth margin thy fathers have played;
Beside its deep waters their ashes are laid."

I wandered afar from the land of my birth,
I saw the old rivers, renowned upon earth,
But fancy still painted that wide-flowing stream
With the many-hued pencil of infancy's dream.

I saw the green banks of the castle-crowned Rhine,
Where the grapes drink the moonlight and change it to wine;
I stood by the Avon, whose waves as they glide
Still whisper his glory who sleeps at their side.

But my heart would still yearn for the sound of the waves
That sing as they flow by my forefathers' graves;
If manhood yet honors my cheek with a tear,
I care not who sees it, — nor blush for it here !

Farewell to the deep-bosomed stream of the West !
I fling this loose blossom to float on its breast;
Nor let the dear love of its children grow cold,
Till the channel is dry where its waters have rolled !

THE NEW EDEN

MEETING OF THE BERKSHIRE HORTICULTURAL SOCIETY, AT STOCKBRIDGE, SEPTEMBER 13, 1854

[Mr. J. E. A. Smith, in his *The Poet among the Hills*, says that the theme of this poem was suggested by the severe drought in Berkshire County in the summer of 1854, and that after delivering the poem Dr. Holmes acceded to the request of a local editor who wished to print it, on condition that he should have as many proofs and make as many alterations as he chose, and in the end a hundred copies of the poem printed by itself. He had sixteen proofs and doubled the length of the poem; besides giving it a more serious tone.]

SCARCE could the parting ocean close,
  Seamed by the Mayflower's cleaving bow,
When o'er the rugged desert rose
  The waves that tracked the Pilgrim's plough.

Then sprang from many a rock-strewn field
  The rippling grass, the nodding grain,
Such growths as English meadows yield
  To scanty sun and frequent rain.

But when the fiery days were done,
  And Autumn brought his purple haze,
Then, kindling in the slanted sun,
  The hillsides gleamed with golden maize.

The food was scant, the fruits were few:
  A red-streak glistening here and there;
Perchance in statelier precincts grew
  Some stern old Puritanic pear.

Austere in taste, and tough at core,
  Its unrelenting bulk was shed,
To ripen in the Pilgrim's store
  When all the summer sweets were fled.

Such was his lot, to front the storm
  With iron heart and marble brow,
Nor ripen till his earthly form
  Was cast from life's autumnal bough.

But ever on the bleakest rock
  We bid the brightest beacon glow,
And still upon the thorniest stock
  The sweetest roses love to blow.

So on our rude and wintry soil
  We feed the kindling flame of art,
And steal the tropic's blushing spoil
  To bloom on Nature's ice-clad heart.

See how the softening Mother's breast
  Warms to her children's patient wiles, —
Her lips by loving Labor pressed
  Break in a thousand dimpling smiles,

From when the flushing bud of June
  Dawns with its first auroral hue,
Till shines the rounded harvest-moon,
  And velvet dahlias drink the dew.

Nor these the only gifts she brings;
  Look where the laboring orchard groans,
And yields its beryl-threaded strings
  For chestnut burs and hemlock cones.

Dear though the shadowy maple be,
  And dearer still the whispering pine,
Dearest yon russet-laden tree
  Browned by the heavy rubbing kine !

There childhood flung its rustling stone,
  There venturous boyhood learned to
    climb, —
How well the early graft was known
  Whose fruit was ripe ere harvest-time !

Nor be the Fleming's pride forgot,
  With swinging drops and drooping bells,
Freckled and splashed with streak and
    spot,
  On the warm-breasted, sloping swells;

Nor Persia's painted garden-queen, —
  Frail Houri of the trellised wall, —
Her deep-cleft bosom scarfed with
    green, —
  Fairest to see, and first to fall.

———

When man provoked his mortal doom,
  And Eden trembled as he fell,
When blossoms sighed their last perfume,
  And branches waved their long farewell,

One sucker crept beneath the gate,
  One seed was wafted o'er the wall,
One bough sustained his trembling weight;
  These left the garden, — these were all.

And far o'er many a distant zone
  These wrecks of Eden still are flung:
The fruits that Paradise hath known
  Are still in earthly gardens hung.

Yes, by our own unstoried stream
  The pink-white apple-blossoms burst
That saw the young Euphrates gleam, —
  That Gihon's circling waters nursed.

For us the ambrosial pear displays
  The wealth its arching branches hold,
Bathed by a hundred summery days
  In floods of mingling fire and gold.

And here, where beauty's cheek of flame
  With morning's earliest beam is fed,
The sunset-painted peach may claim
  To rival its celestial red.

———

What though in some unmoistened vale
  The summer leaf grow brown and sere,
Say, shall our star of promise fail
  That circles half the rolling sphere,

From beaches salt with bitter spray,
  O'er prairies green with softest rain,
And ridges bright with evening's ray,
  To rocks that shade the stormless main ?

If by our slender-threaded streams
  The blade and leaf and blossom die,
If, drained by noontide's parching beams,
  The milky veins of Nature dry,

See, with her swelling bosom bare,
  Yon wild-eyed Sister in the West, —
The ring of Empire round her hair,
  The Indian's wampum on her breast !

We saw the August sun descend,
  Day after day, with blood-red stain,
And the blue mountains dimly blend
  With smoke-wreaths from the burning
    plain;

Beneath the hot Sirocco's wings
  We sat and told the withering hours,
Till Heaven unsealed its hoarded springs,
  And bade them leap in flashing showers.

Yet in our Ishmael's thirst we knew
  The mercy of the Sovereign hand
Would pour the fountain's quickening dew
  To feed some harvest of the land.

No flaming swords of wrath surround
  Our second Garden of the Blest;
It spreads beyond its rocky bound,
  It climbs Nevada's glittering crest.

God keep the tempter from its gate !
  God shield the children, lest they fall
From their stern fathers' free estate, —
  Till Ocean is its only wall !

SEMI – CENTENNIAL CELEBRA-TION OF THE NEW ENGLAND SOCIETY

NEW YORK, DECEMBER 22, 1855

NEW ENGLAND, we love thee; no time can
  erase
From the hearts of thy children the smile
  on thy face.
'T is the mother's fond look of affection and
  pride,
As she gives her fair son to the arms of his
  bride.

His bride may be fresher in beauty's young
  flower;
She may blaze in the jewels she brings with
  her dower.
But passion must chill in Time's pitiless
  blast;
The one that first loved us will love to the
  last.

You have left the dear land of the lake and
  the hill,
But its winds and its waters will talk with
  you still.
"Forget not," they whisper, "your love is
  our debt,"
And echo breathes softly, "We never for-get."

The banquet's gay splendors are gleaming
  around,
But your hearts have flown back o'er the
  waves of the Sound;
They have found the brown home where
  their pulses were born;
They are throbbing their way through the
  trees and the corn.

There are roofs you remember, — their
  glory is fled;
There are mounds in the churchyard, — one
  sigh for the dead.
There are wrecks, there are ruins, all scat-tered around;
But Earth has no spot like that corner of
  ground.

Come, let us be cheerful, — remember last
  night,
How they cheered us, and — never mind —
  meant it all right;
To-night, we harm nothing, — we love in the
  lump;
Here's a bumper to Maine, in the juice of
  the pump !

Here's to all the good people, wherever
  they be,
Who have grown in the shade of the liberty-tree;
We all love its leaves, and its blossoms and
  fruit,
But pray have a care of the fence round its
  root.

We should like to talk big; it 's a kind of a
  right,
When the tongue has got loose and the
  waistband grown tight;
But, as pretty Miss Prudence remarked to
  her beau,
On its own heap of compost no biddy should
  crow.

Enough ! There are gentlemen waiting to
  talk,
Whose words are to mine as the flower to
  the stalk.
Stand by your old mother whatever be-fall;
God bless all her children ! Good night to
  you all !

FAREWELL

TO J. R. LOWELL

[On the occasion of Lowell's going abroad in the spring of 1855.]

FAREWELL, for the bark has her breast to
    the tide,
And the rough arms of Ocean are stretched
    for his bride;
The winds from the mountain stream over
    the bay;
One clasp of the hand, then away and
    away!

I see the tall mast as it rocks by the
    shore;
The sun is declining, I see it once more;
To-day like the blade in a thick-waving
    field,
To-morrow the spike on a Highlander's
    shield.

Alone, while the cloud pours its treacherous
    breath,
With the blue lips all round her whose
    kisses are death;
Ah, think not the breeze that is urging her
    sail
Has left her unaided to strive with the
    gale.

There are hopes that play round her, like
    fires on the mast,
That will light the dark hour till its dan-
    ger has past;
There are prayers that will plead with the
    storm when it raves,
And whisper "Be still!" to the turbulent
    waves.

Nay, think not that Friendship has called
    us in vain
To join the fair ring ere we break it again;
There is strength in its circle, — you lose
    the bright star,
But its sisters still chain it, though shining
    afar.

I give you one health in the juice of the
    vine,
The blood of the vineyard shall mingle
    with mine;

Thus, thus let us drain the last dew-drops
    of gold,
As we empty our hearts of the blessings
    they hold.

FOR THE MEETING OF THE BURNS CLUB

1856

THE mountains glitter in the snow
  A thousand leagues asunder;
Yet here, amid the banquet's glow,
  I hear their voice of thunder;
Each giant's ice-bound goblet clinks;
  A flowing stream is summoned;
Wachusett to Ben Nevis drinks;
  Monadnock to Ben Lomond!

Though years have clipped the eagle's
    plume
  That crowned the chieftain's bonnet,
The sun still sees the heather bloom,
  The silver mists lie on it;
With tartan kilt and philibeg,
  What stride was ever bolder
Than his who showed the naked leg
  Beneath the plaided shoulder?

The echoes sleep on Cheviot's hills,
  That heard the bugles blowing
When down their sides the crimson rills
  With mingled blood were flowing;
The hunts where gallant hearts were game,
  The slashing on the border,
The raid that swooped with sword and
    flame,
  Give place to "law and order."

Not while the rocking steeples reel
  With midnight tocsins ringing,
Not while the crashing war-notes peal,
  God sets his poets singing;
The bird is silent in the night,
  Or shrieks a cry of warning
While fluttering round the beacon-light, —
  But hear him greet the morning!

The lark of Scotia's morning sky!
  Whose voice may sing his praises?
With Heaven's own sunlight in his eye,
  He walked among the daisies,
Till through the cloud of fortune's wrong
  He soared to fields of glory;

But left his land her sweetest song
  And earth her saddest story.

'T is not the forts the builder piles
  That chain the earth together;
The wedded crowns, the sister isles,
  Would laugh at such a tether;
The kindling thought, the throbbing words,
  That set the pulses beating,
Are stronger than the myriad swords
  Of mighty armies meeting.

Thus while within the banquet glows,
  Without, the wild winds whistle,
We drink a triple health, — the Rose,
  The Shamrock, and the Thistle !
Their blended hues shall never fade
  Till War has hushed his cannon, —
Close-twined as ocean-currents braid
  The Thames, the Clyde, the Shannon !

ODE FOR WASHINGTON'S BIRTHDAY

CELEBRATION OF THE MERCANTILE LIBRARY ASSOCIATION, FEBRUARY 22, 1856

WELCOME to the day returning,
  Dearer still as ages flow,
While the torch of Faith is burning,
  Long as Freedom's altars glow !
See the hero whom it gave us
  Slumbering on a mother's breast;
For the arm he stretched to save us,
  Be its morn forever blest !

Hear the tale of youthful glory,
  While of Britain's rescued band
Friend and foe repeat the story,
  Spread his fame o'er sea and land,
Where the red cross, proudly streaming,
  Flaps above the frigate's deck,
Where the golden lilies, gleaming,
  Star the watch-towers of Quebec.

Look ! The shadow on the dial
  Marks the hour of deadlier strife;
Days of terror, years of trial,
  Scourge a nation into life.
Lo, the youth, become her leader !
  All her baffled tyrants yield;
Through his arm the Lord hath freed her;
  Crown him on the tented field !

Vain is Empire's mad temptation !
  Not for him an earthly crown !
He whose sword hath freed a nation
  Strikes the offered sceptre down.
See the throneless Conqueror seated,
  Ruler by a people's choice;
See the Patriot's task completed;
  Hear the Father's dying voice !

" By the name that you inherit,
  By the sufferings you recall,
Cherish the fraternal spirit;
  Love your country first of all !
Listen not to idle questions
  If its bands may be untied;
Doubt the patriot whose suggestions
  Strive a nation to divide ! "

Father ! We, whose ears have tingled
  With the discord-notes of shame, —
We, whose sires their blood have mingled
  In the battle's thunder-flame, —
Gathering, while this holy morning
  Lights the land from sea to sea,
Hear thy counsel, heed thy warning;
  Trust us, while we honor thee !

BIRTHDAY OF DANIEL WEBSTER

JANUARY 18, 1856

WHEN life hath run its largest round
  Of toil and triumph, joy and woe,
How brief a storied page is found
  To compass all its outward show !

The world-tried sailor tires and droops;
  His flag is rent, his keel forgot;
His farthest voyages seem but loops
  That float from life's entangled knot.

But when within the narrow space
  Some larger soul hath lived and wrought,
Whose sight was open to embrace
  The boundless realms of deed and
    thought, —

When, stricken by the freezing blast,
  A nation's living pillars fall,
How rich the storied page, how vast,
  A word, a whisper, can recall !

No medal lifts its fretted face,
  Nor speaking marble cheats your eye,

Yet, while these pictured lines I trace,
 A living image passes by:

A roof beneath the mountain pines;
 The cloisters of a hill-girt plain;
The front of life's embattled lines;
 A mound beside the heaving main.

These are the scenes: a boy appears;
 Set life's round dial in the sun,
Count the swift arc of seventy years,
 His frame is dust; his task is done.

Yet pause upon the noontide hour,
 Ere the declining sun has laid
His bleaching rays on manhood's power,
 And look upon the mighty shade.

No gloom that stately shape can hide,
 No change uncrown its brow; behold!
Dark, calm, large-fronted, lightning-eyed,
 Earth has no double from its mould!

Ere from the fields by valor won
 The battle-smoke had rolled away,
And bared the blood-red setting sun,
 His eyes were opened on the day.

His land was but a shelving strip
 Black with the strife that made it free;
He lived to see its banners dip
 Their fringes in the Western sea.

The boundless prairies learned his name,
 His words the mountain echoes knew.
The Northern breezes swept his fame
 From icy lake to warm bayou.

In toil he lived; in peace he died;
 When life's full cycle was complete,
Put off his robes of power and pride,
 And laid them at his Master's feet.

His rest is by the storm-swept waves
 Whom life's wild tempests roughly tried,
Whose heart was like the streaming caves
 Of ocean, throbbing at his side.

Death's cold white hand is like the snow
 Laid softly on the furrowed hill,
It hides the broken seams below,
 And leaves the summit brighter still.

In vain the envious tongue upbraids;
 His name a nation's heart shall keep

Till morning's latest sunlight fades
 On the blue tablet of the deep!

THE VOICELESS

["Read what the singing-women — one to
ten thousand of the suffering women — tell us,
and think of the griefs that die unspoken!
Nature is in earnest when she makes a woman;
and there are women enough lying in the next
churchyard with very commonplace blue slate
stones at their head and feet, for whom it was
just as true that 'all sounds of life assumed one
tone of love,' as for Letitia Landon, of whom
Elizabeth Browning said it; but she could give
words to her grief, and they could not. — Will
you hear a few stanzas of mine?" *The Auto-
crat of the Breakfast Table*, p. 306.]

WE count the broken lyres that rest
 Where the sweet wailing singers slumber,
But o'er their silent sister's breast
 The wild-flowers who will stoop to number?
A few can touch the magic string,
 And noisy Fame is proud to win them: —
Alas for those that never sing,
 But die with all their music in them!

Nay, grieve not for the dead alone
 Whose song has told their hearts' sad story, —
Weep for the voiceless, who have known
 The cross without the crown of glory!
Not where Leucadian breezes sweep
 O'er Sappho's memory-haunted billow,
But where the glistening night-dews weep
 On nameless sorrow's churchyard pillow.

O hearts that break and give no sign
 Save whitening lip and fading tresses,
Till Death pours out his longed-for wine
 Slow-dropped from Misery's crushing presses, —
If singing breath or echoing chord
 To every hidden pang were given,
What endless melodies were poured,
 As sad as earth, as sweet as heaven!

THE TWO STREAMS

[In his paper, *My Hunt after the Captain*, Dr.
Holmes has a paragraph upon an alleged pla-

giarism in this poem. It will be found in the
Notes at the end of this volume.]

BEHOLD the rocky wall
  That down its sloping sides
Pours the swift rain-drops, blending, as
    they fall,
  In rushing river-tides !

Yon stream, whose sources run
  Turned by a pebble's edge,
Is Athabasca, rolling toward the sun
  Through the cleft mountain-ledge.

The slender rill had strayed,
  But for the slanting stone,
To evening's ocean, with the tangled braid
  Of foam-flecked Oregon.

So from the heights of Will
  Life's parting stream descends,
And, as a moment turns its slender rill,
  Each widening torrent bends, —

From the same cradle's side,
  From the same mother's knee, —
One to long darkness and the frozen tide,
  One to the Peaceful Sea !

THE PROMISE

NOT charity we ask,
  Nor yet thy gift refuse;
Please thy light fancy with the easy task
  Only to look and choose.

The little-heeded toy
  That wins thy treasured gold
May be the dearest memory, holiest joy,
  Of coming years untold.

Heaven rains on every heart,
  But there its showers divide,
The drops of mercy choosing, as they part,
  The dark or glowing side.

One kindly deed may turn
  The fountain of thy soul
To love's sweet day-star, that shall o'er thee
    burn
  Long as its currents roll !

The pleasures thou hast planned, —
  Where shall their memory be

When the white angel with the freezing
    hand
  Shall sit and watch by thee ?

Living, thou dost not live,
  If mercy's spring run dry ;
What Heaven has lent thee wilt thou freely
    give,
  Dying, thou shalt not die !

HE promised even so !
  To thee his lips repeat, —
Behold, the tears that soothed thy sister's
    woe
  Have washed thy Master's feet.

AVIS

This is a true story. Avis, Avise, or Avice
(they pronounce it *Avvis*) is a real breathing
person. Her home is not more than an hour
and a half's space from the palaces of the great
ladies who might like to look at her. They
may see her and the little black girl she gave
herself to, body and soul, when nobody else
could bear the sight of her infirmity, — leaving
home at noon, or even after breakfast, and
coming back in season to undress for the even-
ing's party.

I MAY not rightly call thy name, —
  Alas ! thy forehead never knew
The kiss that happier children claim,
  Nor glistened with baptismal dew.

Daughter of want and wrong and woe,
  I saw thee with thy sister-band,
Snatched from the whirlpool's narrowing
    flow
  By Mercy's strong yet trembling hand.

"Avis !" — With Saxon eye and cheek,
  At once a woman and a child,
The saint uncrowned I came to seek
  Drew near to greet us, — spoke, and
    smiled.

God gave that sweet sad smile she wore
  All wrong to shame, all souls to win, —
A heavenly sunbeam sent before
  Her footsteps through a world of sin.

"And who is Avis ?" — Hear the tale
  The calm-voiced matrons gravely tell, —
The story known through all the vale
  Where Avis and her sisters dwell.

With the lost children running wild,
  Strayed from the hand of human care,
They find one little refuse child
  Left helpless in its poisoned lair.

The primal mark is on her face, —
  The chattel-stamp, — the pariah-stain
That follows still her hunted race, —
  The curse without the crime of Cain.

How shall our smooth-turned phrase relate
  The little suffering outcast's ail ?
Not Lazarus at the rich man's gate
  So turned the rose-wreathed revellers
    pale.

Ah, veil the living death from sight
  That wounds our beauty-loving eye !
The children turn in selfish fright,
  The white-lipped nurses hurry by.

Take her, dread Angel ! Break in love
  This bruisèd reed and make it thine ! —
No voice descended from above,
  But Avis answered, " She is mine."

The task that dainty menials spurn
  The fair young girl has made her own;
Her heart shall teach, her hand shall learn
  The toils, the duties yet unknown.

So Love and Death in lingering strife
  Stand face to face from day to day,
Still battling for the spoil of Life
  While the slow seasons creep away.

Love conquers Death; the prize is won;
  See to her joyous bosom pressed
The dusky daughter of the sun, —
  The bronze against the marble breast !

Her task is done ; no voice divine
  Has crowned her deeds with saintly fame.
No eye can see the aureole shine
  That rings her brow with heavenly flame.

Yet what has holy page more sweet,
  Or what had woman's love more fair,
When Mary clasped her Saviour's feet
  With flowing eyes and streaming hair ?

Meek child of sorrow, walk unknown,
  The Angel of that earthly throng,
And let thine image live alone
  To hallow this unstudied song !

THE LIVING TEMPLE

[The Professor, who is credited with this verse, was supposed to call it *The Anatomist's Hymn.*]

Not in the world of light alone,
Where God has built his blazing throne,
Nor yet alone in earth below,
With belted seas that come and go,
And endless isles of sunlit green,
Is all thy Maker's glory seen:
Look in upon thy wondrous frame, —
Eternal wisdom still the same !

The smooth, soft air with pulse-like waves
Flows murmuring through its hidden caves,
Whose streams of brightening purple rush,
Fired with a new and livelier blush,
While all their burden of decay
The ebbing current steals away,
And red with Nature's flame they start
From the warm fountains of the heart.

No rest that throbbing slave may ask,
Forever quivering o'er his task,
While far and wide a crimson jet
Leaps forth to fill the woven net
Which in unnumbered crossing tides
The flood of burning life divides,
Then, kindling each decaying part,
Creeps back to find the throbbing heart.

But warmed with that unchanging flame
Behold the outward moving frame,
Its living marbles jointed strong
With glistening band and silvery thong,
And linked to reason's guiding reins
By myriad rings in trembling chains,
Each graven with the threaded zone
Which claims it as the master's own.

See how yon beam of seeming white
Is braided out of seven-hued light,
Yet in those lucid globes no ray
By any chance shall break astray.
Hark how the rolling surge of sound,
Arches and spirals circling round,
Wakes the hushed spirit through thine ear
With music it is heaven to hear.

Then mark the cloven sphere that holds
All thought in its mysterious folds;
That feels sensation's faintest thrill,
And flashes forth the sovereign will;
Think on the stormy world that dwells

Locked in its dim and clustering cells !
The lightning gleams of power it sheds
Along its hollow glassy threads !

O Father ! grant thy love divine
To make these mystic temples thine !
When wasting age and wearying strife
Have sapped the leaning walls of life,
When darkness gathers over all,
And the last tottering pillars fall,
Take the poor dust thy mercy warms,
And mould it into heavenly forms !

AT A BIRTHDAY FESTIVAL

TO J. R. LOWELL

FEBRUARY 22, 1859

WE will not speak of years to-night, —
  For what have years to bring
But larger floods of love and light,
  And sweeter songs to sing ?

We will not drown in wordy praise
  The kindly thoughts that rise;
If Friendship own one tender phrase,
  He reads it in our eyes.

We need not waste our school-boy art
  To gild this notch of Time; —
Forgive me if my wayward heart
  Has throbbed in artless rhyme.

Enough for him the silent grasp
  That knits us hand in hand,
And he the bracelet's radiant clasp
  That locks our circling band.

Strength to his hours of manly toil !
  Peace to his starlit dreams !
Who loves alike the furrowed soil,
  The music-haunted streams !

Sweet smiles to keep forever bright
  The sunshine on his lips,
And faith that sees the ring of light
  Round nature's last eclipse !

A BIRTHDAY TRIBUTE

TO J. F. CLARKE. APRIL 4, 1860

WHO is the shepherd sent to lead,
  Through pastures green, the Master's
    sheep ?

What guileless " Israelite indeed "
  The folded flock may watch and keep ?

He who with manliest spirit joins
  The heart of gentlest human mould,
With burning light and girded loins,
  To guide the flock, or watch the fold;

True to all Truth the world denies,
  Not tongue-tied for its gilded sin;
Not always right in all men's eyes,
  But faithful to the light within;

Who asks no meed of earthly fame,
  Who knows no earthly master's call,
Who hopes for man, through guilt and
    shame,
  Still answering, "God is over all;"

Who makes another's grief his own,
  Whose smile lends joy a double cheer;
Where lives the saint, if such be known ?—
  Speak softly, — such an one is here !

O faithful shepherd ! thou hast borne
  The heat and burden of the day;
Yet, o'er thee, bright with beams un-
    shorn,
  The sun still shows thine onward way.

To thee our fragrant love we bring,
  In buds that April half displays,
Sweet first-born angels of the spring,
  Caught in their opening hymn of praise.

What though our faltering accents fail,
  Our captives know their message well,
Our words unbreathed their lips exhale,
  And sigh more love than ours can tell.

THE GRAY CHIEF

FOR THE MEETING OF THE MASSACHU-SETTS MEDICAL SOCIETY, 1859

[In honor of Dr. James Jackson.]

'T IS sweet fo fight our battles o'er,
  And crown with honest praise
The gray old chief, who strikes no more
  The blow of better days.

Before the true and trusted sage
  With willing hearts we bend,

When years have touched with hallowing age
  Our Master, Guide, and Friend.

For all his manhood's labor past,
  For love and faith long tried,
His age is honored to the last,
  Though strength and will have died.

But when, untamed by toil and strife,
  Full in our front he stands,
The torch of light, the shield of life,
  Still lifted in his hands,

No temple, though its walls resound
  With bursts of ringing cheers,
Can hold the honors that surround
  His manhood's twice-told years !

THE LAST LOOK

W. W. SWAIN

[Written at Naushon, September 22, 1858.
W. W. Swain was an only son of Governor
Swain, mentioned before, p. 89, and lies by the
side of his father and mother in the island
grave.]

BEHOLD — not him we knew !
This was the prison which his soul looked
    through,
  Tender, and brave, and true.

His voice no more is heard;
And his dead name — that dear familiar
    word —
  Lies on our lips unstirred.

He spake with poet's tongue;
Living, for him the minstrel's lyre was
    strung :
  He shall not die unsung !

Grief tried his love, and pain;
And the long bondage of his martyr-chain
  Vexed his sweet soul, — in vain !

It felt life's surges break,
As, girt with stormy seas, his island lake,
  Smiling while tempests wake.

How can we sorrow more ?
Grieve not for him whose heart had gone
    before
  To that untrodden shore !

Lo, through its leafy screen,
A gleam of sunlight on a ring of green,
  Untrodden, half unseen !

Here let his body rest,
Where the calm shadows that his soul
    loved best
  May slide above his breast.

Smooth his uncurtained bed;
And if some natural tears are softly shed,
  It is not for the dead.

Fold the green turf aright
For the long hours before the morning's
    light,
  And say the last Good Night !

And plant a clear white stone
Close by those mounds which hold his
    loved, his own, —
  Lonely, but not alone.

Here let him sleeping lie,
Till Heaven's bright watchers slumber in
    the sky
  And Death himself shall die !

IN MEMORY OF CHARLES WENTWORTH UPHAM, JR.

APRIL 15, 1860

HE was all sunshine; in his face
  The very soul of sweetness shone;
Fairest and gentlest of his race;
  None like him we can call our own.

Something there was of one that died
  In her fresh spring-time long ago,
Our first dear Mary, angel-eyed,
  Whose smile it was a bliss to know.

Something of her whose love imparts
  Such radiance to her day's decline,
We feel its twilight in our hearts
  Bright as the earliest morning-shine.

Yet richer strains our eye could trace
  That made our plainer mould more
    fair,
That curved the lip with happier grace,
  That waved the soft and silken hair.

Dust unto dust ! the lips are still
  That only spoke to cheer and bless;
The folded hands lie white and chill
  Unclasped from sorrow's last caress.

Leave him in peace ; he will not heed
  These idle tears we vainly pour,
Give back to earth the fading weed
  Of mortal shape his spirit wore.

"Shall I not weep my heartstrings torn,
  My flower of love that falls half blown,
My youth uncrowned, my life forlorn,
  A thorny path to walk alone ? "

O Mary ! one who bore thy name,
  Whose Friend and Master was divine,
Sat waiting silent till He came,
  Bowed down in speechless grief like
    thine.

"Where have ye laid him ? " "Come,"
  they say,
  Pointing to where the loved one slept;
Weeping, the sister led the way, —
  And, seeing Mary, "Jesus wept."

He weeps with thee, with all that mourn,
  And He shall wipe thy streaming eyes
Who knew all sorrows, woman-born, —
  Trust in his word ; thy dead shall rise !

MARTHA

DIED JANUARY 7, 1861

[Written on the death of an old family servant.]

SEXTON ! Martha's dead and gone;
  Toll the bell ! toll the bell !
Her weary hands their labor cease;
Good night, poor Martha, — sleep in
  peace !
    Toll the bell !

Sexton ! Martha's dead and gone;
  Toll the bell ! toll the bell !
For many a year has Martha said,
"I'm old and poor, — would I were
  dead ! "
    Toll the bell !

Sexton ! Martha's dead and gone;
  Toll the bell ! toll the bell !

She 'll bring no more, by day or night,
Her basket full of linen white.
    Toll the bell !

Sexton ! Martha's dead and gone;
  Toll the bell ! toll the bell !
'T is fitting she should lie below
A pure white sheet of drifted snow.
    Toll the bell !

Sexton ! Martha's dead and gone;
  Toll the bell ! toll the bell !
Sleep, Martha, sleep, to wake in light,
Where all the robes are stainless white.
    Toll the bell !

MEETING OF THE ALUMNI OF HARVARD COLLEGE

1857

I THANK you, MR. PRESIDENT, you 've
  kindly broke the ice;
Virtue should always be the first, — I 'm
  only SECOND VICE —
(A vice is something with a screw that 's
  made to hold its jaw
Till some old file has played away upon an
  ancient saw).

Sweet brothers by the Mother's side, the
  babes of days gone by,
All nurslings of her Juno breasts whose
  milk is never dry,
We come again, like half-grown boys, and
  gather at her beck
About her knees, and on her lap, and cling-
  ing round her neck.

We find her at her stately door, and in her
  ancient chair,
Dressed in the robes of red and green she
  always loved to wear.
Her eye has all its radiant youth, her cheek
  its morning flame;
We drop our roses as we go, hers flourish
  still the same.

We have been playing many an hour, and
  far away we 've strayed,
Some laughing in the cheerful sun, some
  lingering in the shade;

And some have tired, and laid them down
    where darker shadows fall, —
Dear as her loving voice may be, they can-
    not hear its call.

What miles we 've travelled since we shook
    the dew-drops from our shoes
We gathered on this classic green, so famed
    for heavy dues !
How many boys have joined the game, how
    many slipped away,
Since we 've been running up and down,
    and having out our play !

One boy at work with book and brief, and
    one with gown and band,
One sailing vessels on the pool, one digging
    in the sand,
One flying paper kites on change, one plant-
    ing little pills, —
The seeds of certain annual flowers well
    known as little bills.

What maidens met us on our way, and
    clasped us hand in hand !
What cherubs, — not the legless kind, that
    fly, but never stand !
How many a youthful head we 've seen put
    on its silver crown !
What sudden changes back again to youth's
    empurpled brown !

But fairer sights have met our eyes, and
    broader lights have shone,
Since others lit their midnight lamps where
    once we trimmed our own
A thousand trains that flap the sky with
    flags of rushing fire,
And, throbbing in the Thunderer's hand,
    Thought's million-chorded lyre.

We 've seen the sparks of Empire fly be-
    yond the mountain bars,
Till, glittering o'er the Western wave, they
    joined the setting stars;
And ocean trodden into paths that tram-
    pling giants ford,
To find the planet's vertebræ and sink its
    spinal cord.

We 've tried reform, — and chloroform, —
    and both have turned our brain;
When France called up the photograph, we
    roused the foe to pain;

Just so those earlier sages shared the chap-
    let of renown, —
Hers sent a bladder to the clouds, ours
    brought their lightning down.

We 've seen the little tricks of life, its var-
    nish and veneer,
Its stucco-fronts of character flake off and
    disappear,
We 've learned that oft the brownest hands
    will heap the biggest pile,
And met with many a " perfect brick " be-
    neath a rimless " tile."

What dreams we 've had of deathless name,
    as scholars, statesmen, bards,
While Fame, the lady with the trump, held
    up her picture cards !
Till, having nearly played our game, she
    gayly whispered, " Ah !
I said you should be something grand, —
    you 'll soon be grandpapa."

Well, well, the old have had their day, the
    young must take their turn;
There 's something always to forget, and
    something still to learn;
But how to tell what 's old or young, the
    tap-root from the sprigs,
Since Florida revealed her fount to Ponce
    de Leon Twiggs ?

The wisest was a Freshman once, just
    freed from bar and bolt,
As noisy as a kettle-drum, as leggy as a
    colt;
Don't be too savage with the boys, — the
    Primer does not say
The kitten ought to go to church because
    the cat doth prey.

The law of merit and of age is not the rule
    of three;
Non constat that A. M. must prove as busy
    as A. B.
When Wise the father tracked the son,
    ballooning through the skies,
He taught a lesson to the old, — go thou
    and do like Wise !

Now then, old boys, and reverend youth, of
    high or low degree,
Remember how we only get one annual out
    of three,

And such as dare to simmer down three
    dinners into one
Must cut their salads mighty short, and
    pepper well with fun.

I've passed my zenith long ago, it's time
    for me to set;
A dozen planets wait to shine, and I am
    lingering yet,
As sometimes in the blaze of day a milk-
    and-watery moon
Stains with its dim and fading ray the lus-
    trous blue of noon.

Farewell! yet let one echo rise to shake our
    ancient hall;
God save the Queen, — whose throne is
    here, — the Mother of us all!
Till dawns the great commencement-day on
    every shore and sea,
And "Expectantur" all mankind, to take
    their last Degree!

THE PARTING SONG

FESTIVAL OF THE ALUMNI, 1857

The noon of summer sheds its ray
    On Harvard's holy ground;
The Matron calls, the sons obey,
    And gather smiling round.

CHORUS

Then old and young together stand,
    The sunshine and the snow,
As heart to heart, and hand in hand,
    We sing before we go!

Her hundred opening doors have swung;
    Through every storied hall
The pealing echoes loud have rung,
    "Thrice welcome one and all!"
      Then old and young, etc.

We floated through her peaceful bay,
    To sail life's stormy seas;
But left our anchor where it lay
    Beneath her green old trees.
      Then old and young, etc.

As now we lift its lengthening chain,
    That held us fast of old,
The rusted rings grow bright again, —
    Their iron turns to gold.
      Then old and young, etc.

Though scattered ere the setting sun,
    As leaves when wild winds blow,
Our home is here, our hearts are one,
    Till Charles forgets to flow.
      Then old and young, etc.

FOR THE MEETING OF THE NATIONAL SANITARY ASSOCIATION

1860

What makes the Healing Art divine?
    The bitter drug we buy and sell,
The brands that scorch, the blades that
    shine,
    The scars we leave, the "cures" we
    tell?

Are these thy glories, holiest Art, —
    The trophies that adorn thee best, —
Or but thy triumph's meanest part, —
    Where mortal weakness stands con-
    fessed?

We take the arms that Heaven supplies
    For Life's long battle with Disease,
Taught by our various need to prize
    Our frailest weapons, even these.

But ah! when Science drops her shield —
    Its peaceful shelter proved in vain —
And bares her snow-white arm to wield
    The sad, stern ministry of pain;

When shuddering o'er the fount of life,
    She folds her heaven-anointed wings,
To lift unmoved the glittering knife
    That searches all its crimson springs;

When, faithful to her ancient lore,
    She thrusts aside her fragrant balm
For blistering juice, or cankering ore,
    And tames them till they cure or calm;

When in her gracious hand are seen
    The dregs and scum of earth and seas,
Her kindness counting all things clean
    That lend the sighing sufferer ease;

Though on the field that Death has won,
    She save some stragglers in retreat; —
These single acts of mercy done
    Are but confessions of defeat.

What though our tempered poisons save
  Some wrecks of life from aches and ails;
Those grand specifics Nature gave
  Were never poised by weights or scales !

God lent his creatures light and air,
  And waters open to the skies;
Man locks him in a stifling lair,
  And wonders why his brother dies !

In vain our pitying tears are shed,
  In vain we rear the sheltering pile
Where Art weeds out from bed to bed
  The plagues we planted by the mile !

Be that the glory of the past;
  With these our sacred toils begin:
So flies in tatters from its mast
  The yellow flag of sloth and sin,

And lo ! the starry folds reveal
  The blazoned truth we hold so dear:
To guard is better than to heal, —
  The shield is nobler than the spear !

FOR THE BURNS CENTENNIAL CELEBRATION

JANUARY 25, 1859

[In a passage at the close of *Mechanism in Thought and Morals*, Dr. Holmes applies the ninth, tenth and twelfth stanzas of this poem to Dickens.]

HIS birthday. — Nay, we need not speak
  The name each heart is beating, —
Each glistening eye and flushing cheek
  In light and flame repeating !

We come in one tumultuous tide, —
  One surge of wild emotion, —
As crowding through the Frith of Clyde
  Rolls in the Western Ocean ;

As when yon cloudless, quartered moon
  Hangs o'er each storied river,
The swelling breasts of Ayr and Doon
  With sea-green wavelets quiver.

The century shrivels like a scroll, —
  The past becomes the present, —

And face to face, and soul to soul,
  We greet the monarch-peasant.

While Shenstone strained in feeble flights
  With Corydon and Phillis, —
While Wolfe was climbing Abraham's heights
  To snatch the Bourbon lilies, —

Who heard the wailing infant's cry,
  The babe beneath the sheeling,
Whose song to-night in every sky
  Will shake earth's starry ceiling, —

Whose passion-breathing voice ascends
  And floats like incense o'er us,
Whose ringing lay of friendship blends
  With labor's anvil chorus ?

We love him, not for sweetest song,
  Though never tone so tender;
We love him, even in his wrong, —
  His wasteful self-surrender.

We praise him, not for gifts divine, —
  His Muse was born of woman, —
His manhood breathes in every line, —
  Was ever heart more human ?

We love him, praise him, just for this :
  In every form and feature,
Through wealth and want, through woe and bliss,
  He saw his fellow-creature !

No soul could sink beneath his love, —
  Not even angel blasted;
No mortal power could soar above
  The pride that all outlasted !

Ay ! Heaven had set one living man
  Beyond the pedant's tether, —
His virtues, frailties, HE may scan,
  Who weighs them all together !

I fling my pebble on the cairn
  Of him, though dead, undying;
Sweet Nature's nursling, bonniest bairn
  Beneath her daisies lying.

The waning suns, the wasting globe,
  Shall spare the minstrel's story, —
The centuries weave his purple robe,
  The mountain-mist of glory !

AT A MEETING OF FRIENDS

AUGUST 29, 1859

[The occasion was the fiftieth birthday of
Dr. Holmes.]

I REMEMBER — why, yes ! God bless me !
    and was it so long ago ?
I fear I 'm growing forgetful, as old folks
    do, you know;
It must have been in 'forty — I would say
    'thirty-nine —
We talked this matter over, I and a friend
    of mine.

He said, "Well now, old fellow, I 'm
    thinking that you and I,
If we act like other people, shall be older
    by and by;
What though the bright blue ocean is
    smooth as a pond can be,
There is always a line of breakers to fringe
    the broadest sea.

" We 're taking it mighty easy, but that is
    nothing strange,
For up to the age of thirty we spend our
    years like change;
But creeping up towards the forties, as
    fast as the old years fill,
And Time steps in for payment, we seem
    to change a bill."

" I know it," I said, " old fellow ; you
    speak the solemn truth;
A man can't live to a hundred and likewise
    keep his youth;
But what if the ten years coming shall
    silver-streak my hair,
You know I shall then be forty; of course
    I shall not care.

" At forty a man grows heavy and tired of
    fun and noise;
Leaves dress to the five-and-twenties and
    love to the silly boys;
No foppish tricks at forty, no pinching of
    waists and toes,
But high-low shoes and flannels and good
    thick worsted hose."

But one fine August morning I found my-
    self awake:
My birthday: — By Jove, I 'm forty ! Yes,
    forty and no mistake !
Why, this is the very milestone, I think I
    used to hold,
That when a fellow had come to, a fellow
    would then be old !

But that is the young folks' nonsense;
    they 're full of their foolish stuff;
A man 's in his prime at forty, — I see *that*
    plain enough;
At *fifty* a man *is* wrinkled, and *may be* bald
    or gray;
I call men old at fifty, in spite of all they
    say.

At last comes another August with mist
    and rain and shine;
Its mornings are slowly counted and creep
    to twenty-nine,
And when on the western summits the fad-
    ing light appears,
It touches with rosy fingers the last of my
    fifty years.

There have been both men and women
    whose hearts were firm and bold,
But there never was one of fifty that loved
    to say " I 'm old;"
So any elderly person that strives to shirk
    his years,
Make him stand up at a table and try him
    by his peers.

Now here I stand at fifty, my jury gathered
    round;
Sprinkled with dust of silver, but not yet
    silver-crowned,
Ready to meet your verdict, waiting to
    hear it told;
Guilty of fifty summers; speak ! Is the
    verdict *old?*

No ! say that his hearing fails him; say
    that his sight grows dim;
Say that he 's getting wrinkled and weak in
    back and limb,
Losing his wits and temper, but pleading,
    to make amends,
The youth of his fifty summers he finds in
    his twenty friends.

BOSTON COMMON; THREE PIC-TURES

FOR THE FAIR IN AID OF THE FUND TO PROCURE BALL'S STATUE OF WASH-INGTON

NOVEMBER 14, 1859

1630

ALL overgrown with bush and fern,
And straggling clumps of tangled trees,
With trunks that lean and boughs that turn,
Bent eastward by the mastering breeze, —
With spongy bogs that drip and fill
A yellow pond with muddy rain, ·
Beneath the shaggy southern hill
Lies wet and low the Shawmut plain.
And hark ! the trodden branches crack;
A crow flaps off with startled scream;
A straying woodchuck canters back;
A bittern rises from the stream;
Leaps from his lair a frightened deer;
An otter plunges in the pool; —
Here comes old Shawmut's pioneer,
The parson on his brindled bull !

1774

The streets are thronged with trampling feet,
The northern hill is ridged with graves,
But night and morn the drum is beat
To frighten down the "rebel knaves."
The stones of King Street still are red,
And yet the bloody red-coats come:
I hear their pacing sentry's tread,
The click of steel, the tap of drum,
And over all the open green,
Where grazed of late the harmless kine,
The cannon's deepening ruts are seen,
The war-horse stamps, the bayonets shine.
The clouds are dark with crimson rain
Above the murderous hirelings' den,
And soon their whistling showers shall stain
The pipe-clayed belts of Gage's men.

186-

Around the green, in morning light,
The spired and palaced summits blaze,
And, sunlike, from her Beacon-height
The dome-crowned city spreads her rays;
They span the waves, they belt the plains,
They skirt the roads with bands of white,
Till with a flash of gilded panes
Yon farthest hillside bounds the sight.
Peace, Freedom, Wealth ! no fairer view,
Though with the wild-bird's restless wings
We sailed beneath the noontide's blue
Or chased the moonlight's endless rings !
Here, fitly raised by grateful hands
His holiest memory to recall,
The Hero's, Patriot's image stands;
He led our sires who won them all !

THE OLD MAN OF THE SEA

A NIGHTMARE DREAM BY DAYLIGHT

Do you know the Old Man of the Sea, of the Sea ?
Have you met with that dreadful old man ?
If you have n't been caught, you will be, you will be;
For catch you he must and he can.

He does n't hold on by your throat, by your throat,
As of old in the terrible tale;
But he grapples you tight by the coat, by the coat,
Till its buttons and button-holes fail.

There 's the charm of a snake in his eye, in his eye,
And a polypus-grip in his hands;
You cannot go back, nor get by, nor get by,
If you look at the spot where he stands.

Oh, you 're grabbed ! See his claw on your sleeve, on your sleeve !
It is Sindbad's Old Man of the Sea !
You 're a Christian, no doubt you believe, you believe :
You 're a martyr, whatever you be !

Is the breakfast-hour past ? They must wait, they must wait,
While the coffee boils sullenly down,
While the Johnny-cake burns on the grate, on the grate,
And the toast is done frightfully brown

Yes, your dinner will keep; let it cool, let
    it cool,
  And Madam may worry and fret,
And children half-starved go to school, go
    to school;
  He can't think of sparing you yet.

Hark! the bell for the train! "Come
    along! Come along!
  For there is n't a second to lose."
"ALL ABOARD!" (He holds on.) "Fsht!
    ding-dong! Fsht! ding-dong!" —
  You can follow on foot, if you choose.

There 's a maid with a cheek like a peach,
    like a peach,
  That is waiting for you in the church; —
But he clings to your side like a leech, like
    a leech,
  And you leave your lost bride in the
    lurch.

There 's a babe in a fit, — hurry quick!
    hurry quick!
  To the doctor's as fast as you can!
The baby is off, while you stick, while you
    stick,
  In the grip of the dreadful Old Man!

I have looked on the face of the Bore, of
    the Bore;
  The voice of the Simple I know;
I have welcomed the Flat at my door, at
    my door;
  I have sat by the side of the Slow;

I have walked like a lamb by the friend, by
    the friend,
  That stuck to my skirts like a bur;
I have borne the stale talk without end,
    without end,
  Of the sitter whom nothing could stir:

But my hamstrings grow loose, and I shake,
    and I shake,
  At the sight of the dreadful Old Man;
Yea, I quiver and quake, and I take, and I
    take,
  To my legs with what vigor I can!

Oh the dreadful Old Man of the Sea, of the
    Sea!
  He 's come back like the Wandering
    Jew!

He has had his cold claw upon me, upon
    me, —
  And be sure that he 'll have it on you!

INTERNATIONAL ODE

OUR FATHERS' LAND

This ode was sung in unison by twelve hun-
dred children of the public schools to the air
of "God save the Queen" at the visit of the
Prince of Wales to Boston, October 18, 1860.

GOD bless our Fathers' Land!
Keep her in heart and hand
    One with our own!
From all her foes defend,
Be her brave People's Friend,
On all her realms descend,
    Protect her Throne!

Father, with loving care
Guard Thou her kingdom's Heir,
    Guide all his ways:
Thine arm his shelter be,
From him by land and sea
Bid storm and danger flee,
    Prolong his days!

Lord, let War's tempest cease,
Fold the whole Earth in peace
    Under thy wings!
Make all thy nations one,
All hearts beneath the sun,
Till Thou shalt reign alone,
    Great King of kings!

VIVE LA FRANCE

A SENTIMENT OFFERED AT THE DINNER
TO H. I. H. THE PRINCE NAPOLEON,
AT THE REVERE HOUSE, SEPTEMBER
25, 1861

THE land of sunshine and of song!
  Her name your hearts divine;
To her the banquet's vows belong
  Whose breasts have poured its wine;
Our trusty friend, our true ally
  Through varied change and chance:
So, fill your flashing goblets high, —
  I give you, VIVE LA FRANCE!

Above our hosts in triple folds
   The selfsame colors spread,
Where Valor's faithful arm upholds
   The blue, the white, the red;
Alike each nation's glittering crest
   Reflects the morning's glance, —
Twin eagles, soaring east and west:
   Once more, then, VIVE LA FRANCE !

Sister in trial ! who shall count
   Thy generous friendship's claim,
Whose blood ran mingling in the fount
   That gave our land its name,
Till Yorktown saw in blended line
   Our conquering arms advance,
And victory's double garlands twine
   Our banners ?   VIVE LA FRANCE !

O land of heroes ! in our need
   One gift from Heaven we crave
To stanch these wounds that vainly bleed, —
   The wise to lead the brave !
Call back one Captain of thy past
   From glory's marble trance,
Whose name shall be a bugle-blast
   To rouse us ! VIVE LA FRANCE !

Pluck Condé's baton from the trench,
   Wake up stout Charles Martel,
Or find some woman's hand to clench
   The sword of La Pucelle !
Give us one hour of old Turenne, —
   One lift of Bayard's lance, —
Nay, call Marengo's Chief again
   To lead us ! VIVE LA FRANCE !

Ah, hush ! our welcome Guest shall hear
   But sounds of peace and joy;
No angry echo vex thine ear,
   Fair Daughter of Savoy !
Once more ! the land of arms and arts,
   Of glory, grace, romance;
Her love lies warm in all our hearts:
   God bless her ! VIVE LA FRANCE !

BROTHER JONATHAN'S LAMENT FOR SISTER CAROLINE

MARCH 25, 1861

SHE has gone, — she has left us in passion
   and pride, —
Our stormy-browed sister, so long at our
   side !

She has torn her own star from our firma-
   ment's glow,
And turned on her brother the face of a
   foe !

Oh, Caroline, Caroline, child of the sun,
We can never forget that our hearts have
   been one, —
Our foreheads both sprinkled in Liberty's
   name,
From the fountain of blood with the finger
   of flame !

You were always too ready to fire at a
   touch;
But we said, "She is hasty, — she does not
   mean much."
We have scowled, when you uttered some
   turbulent threat;
But Friendship still whispered, "Forgive
   and forget !"

Has our love all died out ?   Have its altars
   grown cold ?
Has the curse come at last which the fathers
   foretold ?
Then Nature must teach us the strength of
   the chain
That her petulant children would sever in
   vain.

They may fight till the buzzards are gorged
   with their spoil,
Till the harvest grows black as it rots in
   the soil,
Till the wolves and the catamounts troop
   from their caves,
And the shark tracks the pirate, the lord of
   the waves:

In vain is the strife !   When its fury is past,
Their fortunes must flow in one channel at
   last,
As the torrents that rush from the moun-
   tains of snow
Roll mingled in peace through the valleys
   below.

Our Union is river, lake, ocean, and sky:
Man breaks not the medal, when God cuts
   the die !
Though darkened with sulphur, though
   cloven with steel,
The blue arch will brighten, the waters will
   heal !

Oh, Caroline, Caroline, child of the sun,
There are battles with Fate that can never
   be won!
The star-flowering banner must never be
   furled,
For its blossoms of light are the hope of
   the world!

Go, then, our rash sister! afar and aloof,
Run wild in the sunshine away from our
   roof;
But when your heart aches and your feet
   have grown sore,
Remember the pathway that leads to our
   door!

POEMS OF THE CLASS OF '29

1851–1889

[" THE class of 1829 at Harvard College, of which I am a member, graduated, according to the triennial, fifty-nine in number. It is sixty years, then, since that time; and as they were, on an average, about twenty years old, those who survive must have reached fourscore years. Of the fifty-nine graduates ten only are living, or were at the last accounts; one in six, very nearly. In the first ten years after graduation, our third decade, when we were between twenty and thirty years old, we lost three members, — about one in twenty; between the ages of thirty and forty, eight died, — one in seven of those the decade began with; from forty to fifty, only two, — or one in twenty-four; from fifty to sixty, eight, — or one in six; from sixty to seventy, fifteen, — or two out of every five; from seventy to eighty, twelve, — or one in two. The greatly increased mortality which began with our seventh decade went on steadily increasing. At sixty we come ' within range of the rifle-pits,' to borrow an expression from my friend Weir Mitchell." *Over The Teacups*, p. 28. A list of the members of the class is given in the Notes at the end of this volume, and will serve to identify the initials which stand at the head of one and another poem.]

BILL AND JOE

COME, dear old comrade, you and I
Will steal an hour from days gone by,
The shining days when life was new,
And all was bright with morning dew,
The lusty days of long ago,
When you were Bill and I was Joe.

Your name may flaunt a titled trail
Proud as a cockerel's rainbow tail,
And mine as brief appendix wear
As Tam O'Shanter's luckless mare;
To-day, old friend, remember still
That I am Joe and you are Bill.

You 've won the great world's envied prize,
And grand you look in people's eyes,
With H O N. and L L. D.
In big brave letters, fair to see, —
Your fist, old fellow! off they go! —
How are you, Bill? How are you, Joe?

You 've worn the judge's ermined robe;
You 've taught your name to half the globe;
You 've sung mankind a deathless strain;
You 've made the dead past live again:
The world may call you what it will,
But you and I are Joe and Bill.

The chaffing young folks stare and say
" See those old buffers, bent and gray, —
They talk like fellows in their teens!
Mad, poor old boys! That 's what it
        means," —
And shake their heads; they little know
The throbbing hearts of Bill and Joe! —

How Bill forgets his hour of pride,
While Joe sits smiling at his side;
How Joe, in spite of time's disguise,
Finds the old schoolmate in his eyes, —
Those calm, stern eyes that melt and fill
As Joe looks fondly up at Bill.

Ah, pensive scholar, what is fame?
A fitful tongue of leaping flame;
A giddy whirlwind's fickle gust,
That lifts a pinch of mortal dust;
A few swift years, and who can show
Which dust was Bill and which was Joe?

The weary idol takes his stand,
Holds out his bruised and aching hand,
While gaping thousands come and go, —
How vain it seems, this empty show!
Till all at once his pulses thrill; —
'T is poor old Joe's " God bless you,
        Bill! "

And shall we breathe in happier spheres
The names that pleased our mortal ears;
In some sweet lull of harp and song
For earth-born spirits none too long,
Just whispering of the world below
Where this was Bill and that was Joe?

No matter; while our home is here
No sounding name is half so dear;
When fades at length our lingering day,
Who cares what pompous tombstones say?
Read on the hearts that love us still,
Hic jacet Joe.   *Hic jacet* Bill.

A SONG OF "TWENTY-NINE"

1851

THE summer dawn is breaking
    On Auburn's tangled bowers,
The golden light is waking
    On Harvard's ancient towers;
        The sun is in the sky
        That must see us do or die,
    Ere it shine on the line
        Of the CLASS OF '29.

At last the day is ended,
    The tutor screws no more,
By doubt and fear attended
    Each hovers round the door,
        Till the good old Præses cries,
        While the tears stand in his eyes,
    "You have passed, and are classed
        With the BOYS OF '29."

Not long are they in making
    The college halls their own,
Instead of standing shaking,
    Too bashful to be known;
        But they kick the Seniors' shins
        Ere the second week begins,
    When they stray in the way
        Of the BOYS OF '29.

If a jolly set is trolling
    The last *Der Freischutz* airs,
Or a "cannon bullet" rolling
    Comes bouncing down the stairs,
        The tutors, looking out,
        Sigh, "Alas! there is no doubt,

'T is the noise of the Boys
    Of the CLASS OF '29."

Four happy years together,
    By storm and sunshine tried,
In changing wind and weather,
    They rough it side by side,
        Till they hear their Mother cry,
        "You are fledged, and you must fly,"
    And the bell tolls the knell
        Of the days of '29.

Since then, in peace or trouble,
    Full many a year has rolled,
And life has counted double
    The days that then we told;
        Yet we'll end as we've begun,
        For though scattered, we are one,
    While each year sees us here,
        Round the board of '29.

Though fate may throw between us
    The mountains or the sea,
No time shall ever wean us,
    No distance set us free;
        But around the yearly board,
        When the flaming pledge is poured,
    It shall claim every name
        On the roll of '29.

To yonder peaceful ocean
    That glows with sunset fires,
Shall reach the warm emotion
    This welcome day inspires,
        Beyond the ridges cold
        Where a brother toils for gold,
    Till it shine through the mine
        Round the BOY OF '29.

If one whom fate has broken
    Shall lift a moistened eye,
We'll say, before he's spoken —
    "Old Classmate, don't you cry!
        Here, take the purse I hold,
        There's a tear upon the gold —
    It was mine — it is thine —
        A'n't we BOYS OF '29?"

As nearer still and nearer
    The fatal stars appear,
The living shall be dearer
    With each encircling year,
        Till a few old men shall say,
        "We remember 't is the day —

Let it pass with a glass
For the CLASS OF '29."

As one by one is falling
  Beneath the leaves or snows,
Each memory still recalling,
  The broken ring shall close,
    Till the nightwinds softly pass
    O'er the green and growing grass,
  Where it waves on the graves
    Of the BOYS OF '29 !

QUESTIONS AND ANSWERS

1841

WHERE, oh where are the visions of morn-
    ing,
  Fresh as the dews of our prime ?
Gone, like tenants that quit without warn-
    ing,
  Down the back entry of time.

Where, oh where are life's lilies and roses,
  Nursed in the golden dawn's smile ?
Dead as the bulrushes round little Moses,
  On the old banks of the Nile.

Where are the Marys, and Anns, and
    Elizas,
  Loving and lovely of yore ?
Look in the columns of old Advertisers, —
  Married and dead by the score.

Where the gray colts and the ten-year-old
    fillies,
  Saturday's triumph and joy ?
Gone, like our friend πόδας ὠκὺς Achilles,
  Homer's ferocious old boy.

Die-away dreams of ecstatic emotion,
  Hopes like young eagles at play,
Vows of unheard-of and endless devotion,
  How ye have faded away !

Yet, though the ebbing of Time's mighty
    river
  Leave our young blossoms to die,
Let him roll smooth in his current for-
    ever,
  Till the last pebble is dry.

AN IMPROMPTU

NOT PREMEDITATED

1853

THE clock has struck noon; ere it thrice
    tell the hours
We shall meet round the table that blushes
    with flowers,
And I shall blush deeper with shame-
    driven blood
That I came to the banquet and brought
    not a bud.

Who cares that his verse is a beggar in art
If you see through its rags the full throb
    of his heart ?
Who asks if his comrade is battered and
    tanned
When he feels his warm soul in the clasp
    of his hand ?

No ! be it an epic, or be it a line,
The Boys will all love it because it is mine;
I sung their last song on the morn of the
    day
That tore from their lives the last blossom
    of May.

It is not the sunset that glows in the wine,
But the smile that beams over it, makes it
    divine;
I scatter these drops, and behold, as they
    fall,
The day-star of memory shines through
    them all !

And these are the last; they are drops that
    I stole
From a wine-press that crushes the life
    from the soul,
But they ran through my heart and they
    sprang to my brain
Till our twentieth sweet summer was smil-
    ing again !

THE OLD MAN DREAMS

1854

OH for one hour of youthful joy !
  Give back my twentieth spring !

I 'd rather laugh, a bright-haired boy,
   Than reign, a gray-beard king.

Off with the spoils of wrinkled age !
   Away with Learning's crown !
Tear out life's Wisdom-written page,
   And dash its trophies down !

One moment let my life-blood stream
   From boyhood's fount of flame !
Give me one giddy, reeling dream
   Of life all love and fame !

My listening angel heard the prayer,
   And, calmly smiling, said,
"If I but touch thy silvered hair
   Thy hasty wish hath sped.

"But is there nothing in thy track,
   To bid thee fondly stay,
While the swift seasons hurry back
   To find the wished-for day ?"

"Ah, truest soul of womankind !
   Without thee what were life ?
One bliss I cannot leave behind:
   I 'll take — my — precious — wife !"

The angel took a sapphire pen
   And wrote in rainbow dew,
The man would be a boy again,
   And be a husband too !

"And is there nothing yet unsaid,
   Before the change appears ?
Remember, all their gifts have fled
   With those dissolving years."

"Why, yes;" for memory would recall
   My fond paternal joys;
"I could not bear to leave them all —
   I 'll take — my — girl — and — boys."

The smiling angel dropped his pen, —
   "Why, this will never do;
The man would be a boy again,
   And be a father too !"

And so I laughed, — my laughter woke
   The household with its noise, —
And wrote my dream, when morning broke,
   To please the gray-haired boys.

REMEMBER — FORGET

1855

AND what shall be the song to-night,
   If song there needs must be ?
If every year that brings us here
   Must steal an hour from me ?
Say, shall it ring a merry peal,
   Or heave a mourning sigh
O'er shadows cast, by years long past,
   On moments flitting by ?

Nay, take the first unbidden line
   The idle hour may send,
No studied grace can mend the face
   That smiles as friend on friend;
The balsam oozes from the pine,
   The sweetness from the rose,
And so, unsought, a kindly thought
   Finds language as it flows.

The years rush by in sounding flight,
   I hear their ceaseless wings;
Their songs I hear, some far, some near,
   And thus the burden rings:
"The morn has fled, the noon has past,
   The sun will soon be set,
The twilight fade to midnight shade;
   Remember — and Forget !"

Remember all that time has brought —
   The starry hope on high,
The strength attained, the courage gained,
   The love that cannot die.
Forget the bitter, brooding thought, —
   The word too harshly said,
The living blame love hates to name,
   The frailties of the dead !

We have been younger, so they say,
   But let the seasons roll,
He doth not lack an almanac
   Whose youth is in his soul.
The snows may clog life's iron track,
   But does the axle tire,
While bearing swift through bank and drift
   The engine's heart of fire ?

I lift a goblet in my hand;
   If good old wine it hold,
An ancient skin to keep it in
   Is just the thing, we 're told.

We 're grayer than the dusty flask, —
  We 're older than our wine;
Our corks reveal the " white top " seal,
  The stamp of '29.

Ah, Boys ! we clustered in the dawn,
  To sever in the dark;
A merry crew, with loud halloo,
  We climbed our painted bark;
We sailed her through the four years'
    cruise,
  We 'll sail her to the last,
Our dear old flag, though but a rag,
  Still flying on her mast.

So gliding on, each winter's gale
  Shall pipe us all on deck,
Till, faint and few, the gathering crew
  Creep o'er the parting wreck,
Her sails and streamers spread aloft
  To fortune's rain or shine,
Till storm or sun shall all be one,
  And down goes TWENTY-NINE !

OUR INDIAN SUMMER

1856

YOU 'll believe me, dear boys, 't is a pleas-
  ure to rise,
With a welcome like this in your darling
  old eyes;
To meet the same smiles and to hear the
  same tone
Which have greeted me oft in the years
  that have flown.

Were I gray as the grayest old rat in the
  wall,
My locks would turn brown at the sight of
  you all;
If my heart were as dry as the shell on the
  sand,
It would fill like the goblet I hold in my
  hand.

There are noontides of autumn when sum-
  mer returns,
Though the leaves are all garnered and
  sealed in their urns,
And the bird on his perch, that was silent
  so long,
Believes the sweet sunshine and breaks into
  song.

We have caged the young birds of our
  beautiful June;
Their plumes are still bright and their
  voices in tune;
One moment of sunshine from faces like
  these
And they sing as they sung in the green-
  growing trees.

The voices of morning ! how sweet is their
  thrill
When the shadows have turned, and the
  evening grows still !
The text of our lives may get wiser with
  age,
But the print was so fair on its twentieth
  page !

Look off from your goblet and up from
  your plate,
Come, take the last journal, and glance at
  its date:
Then think what we fellows should say and
  should do,
If the 6 were a 9 and the 5 were a 2.

Ah, no ! for the shapes that would meet
  with us here,
From the far land of shadows, are ever too
  dear !
Though youth flung around us its pride and
  its charms,
We should see but the comrades we clasped
  in our arms.

A health to our future — a sigh for our
  past,
We love, we remember, we hope to the
  last;
And for all the base lies that the almanacs
  hold,
While we 've youth in our hearts we can
  never grow old !

MARE RUBRUM

1858

FLASH out a stream of blood-red wine,
  For I would drink to other days,
And brighter shall their memory shine,
  Seen flaming through its crimson blaze !
The roses die, the summers fade,
  But every ghost of boyhood's dream

By nature's magic power is laid
 To sleep beneath this blood-red stream !

It filled the purple grapes that lay,
 And drank the splendors of the sun,
Where the long summer's cloudless day
 Is mirrored in the broad Garonne;
It pictures still the bacchant shapes
 That saw their hoarded sunlight shed, —
The maidens dancing on the grapes, —
 Their milk-white ankles splashed with
  red.

Beneath these waves of crimson lie,
 In rosy fetters prisoned fast,
Those flitting shapes that never die, —
 The swift-winged visions of the past.
Kiss but the crystal's mystic rim,
 Each shadow rends its flowery chain,
Springs in a bubble from its brim,
 And walks the chambers of the brain.

Poor beauty ! Time and fortune's wrong
 No shape nor feature may withstand;
Thy wrecks are scattered all along,
 Like emptied sea-shells on the sand;
Yet, sprinkled with this blushing rain,
 The dust restores each blooming girl,
As if the sea-shells moved again
 Their glistening lips of pink and pearl.

Here lies the home of school-boy life,
 With creaking stair and wind-swept hall,
And, scarred by many a truant knife,
 Our old initials on the wall;
Here rest, their keen vibrations mute,
 The shout of voices known so well,
The ringing laugh, the wailing flute,
 The chiding of the sharp-tongued bell.

Here, clad in burning robes, are laid
 Life's blossomed joys, untimely shed,
And here those cherished forms have
  strayed
We miss awhile, and call them dead.
 What wizard fills the wondrous glass ?
What soil the enchanted clusters grew ?
 That buried passions wake and pass
In beaded drops of fiery dew ?

Nay, take the cup of blood-red wine, —
 Our hearts can boast a warmer glow,
Filled from a vintage more divine,

Calmed, but not chilled, by winter's
  snow !
To-night the palest wave we sip
 Rich as the priceless draught shall be
That wet the bride of Cana's lip, —
 The wedding wine of Galilee !

THE BOYS

1859

HAS there any old fellow got mixed with
 the boys ?
If there has, take him out, without making
 a noise.
Hang the Almanac's cheat and the Cata-
 logue's spite !
Old Time is a liar ! We 're twenty to-
 night !

We 're twenty ! We 're twenty ! Who
 says we are more ?
He 's tipsy, — young jackanapes ! — show
 him the door !
"Gray temples at twenty ?" — Yes ! *white*
 if we please;
Where the snow-flakes fall thickest there 's
 nothing can freeze !

Was it snowing I spoke of ? Excuse the
 mistake !
Look close, — you will see not a sign of a
 flake !
We want some new garlands for those we
 have shed, —
And these are white roses in place of the red.

We 've a trick, we young fellows, you may
 have been told,
Of talking (in public) as if we were old: —
That boy we call "Doctor," and this we
 call "Judge;"
It 's a neat little fiction, — of course it 's all
 fudge.

That fellow 's the "Speaker," — the one on
 the right;
"Mr. Mayor," my young one, how are you
 to-night ?
That 's our "Member of Congress," we say
 when we chaff;
There 's the "Reverend" What 's his
 name ? — don't make me laugh.

That boy with the grave mathematical
look
Made believe he had written a wonderful
book,
And the ROYAL SOCIETY thought it was
true!
So they chose him right in; a good joke it
was, too!

There's a boy, we pretend, with a three-
decker brain,
That could harness a team with a logical
chain;
When he spoke for our manhood in syl-
labled fire,
We called him "The Justice," but now
he's "The Squire."

And there's a nice youngster of excellent
pith, —
Fate tried to conceal him by naming him
Smith;
But he shouted a song for the brave and
the free, —
Just read on his medal, "My country,"
"of thee!"

You hear that boy laughing? — You think
he's all fun;
But the angels laugh, too, at the good he
has done;
The children laugh loud as they troop to
his call,
And the poor man that knows him laughs
loudest of all!

Yes, we're boys, — always playing with
tongue or with pen, —
And I sometimes have asked, — Shall we
ever be men?
Shall we always be youthful, and laughing,
and gay,
Till the last dear companion drops smiling
away?

Then here's to our boyhood, its gold and
its gray!
The stars of its winter, the dews of its
May!
And when we have done with our life-last-
ing toys,
Dear Father, take care of thy children,
THE BOYS!

LINES

1860

I'M ashamed, — that's the fact, — it's a
pitiful case, —
Won't any kind classmate get up in my
place?
Just remember how often I've risen be-
fore, —
I blush as I straighten my legs on the floor!

There are stories, once pleasing, too many
times told, —
There are beauties once charming, too
fearfully old, —
There are voices we've heard till we know
them so well,
Though they talked for an hour they'd
have nothing to tell.

Yet, Classmates! Friends! Brothers! Dear
blessed old boys!
Made one by a lifetime of sorrows and joys,
What lips have such sounds as the poorest
of these,
Though honeyed, like Plato's, by musical
bees?

What voice is so sweet and what greeting
so dear
As the simple, warm welcome that waits
for us here?
The love of our boyhood still breathes in
its tone,
And our hearts throb the answer, "He's
one of our own!"

Nay! count not our numbers; some sixty
we know,
But these are above, and those under the
snow;
And thoughts are still mingled wherever
we meet
For those we remember with those that we
greet.

We have rolled on life's journey, — how
fast and how far!
One round of humanity's many-wheeled car,
But up-hill and down-hill, through rattle
and rub,
Old, true Twenty-niners! we've stuck to
our hub!

While a brain lives to think, or a bosom to
  feel,
We will cling to it still like the spokes of
  a wheel !
And age, as it chills us, shall fasten the
  tire
That youth fitted round in his circle of
  fire !

A VOICE OF THE LOYAL NORTH

1861

(JANUARY THIRD)

WE sing "Our Country's" song to-night
  With saddened voice and eye;
Her banner droops in clouded light
  Beneath the wintry sky.
We 'll pledge her once in golden wine
  Before her stars have set:
Though dim one reddening orb may shine,
  We have a Country yet.

'T were vain to sigh o'er errors past,
  The fault of sires or sons;
Our soldier heard the threatening blast,
  And spiked his useless guns;
He saw the star-wreathed ensign fall,
  By mad invaders torn;
But saw it from the bastioned wall
  That laughed their rage to scorn !

What though their angry cry is flung
  Across the howling wave, —
They smite the air with idle tongue
  The gathering storm who brave;
Enough of speech ! the trumpet rings;
  Be silent, patient, calm, —
God help them if the tempest swings
  The pine against the palm !

Our toilsome years have made us tame;
  Our strength has slept unfelt;
The furnace-fire is slow to flame
  That bids our ploughshares melt;
'T is hard to lose the bread they win
  In spite of Nature's frowns, —
To drop the iron threads we spin
  That weave our web of towns,

To see the rusting turbines stand
  Before the emptied flumes,
To fold the arms that flood the land
  With rivers from their looms, —

But harder still for those who learn
  The truth forgot so long;
When once their slumbering passions burn,
  The peaceful are the strong !

The Lord have mercy on the weak,
  And calm their frenzied ire,
And save our brothers ere they shriek,
  "We played with Northern fire !"
The eagle hold his mountain height, —
  The tiger pace his den !
Give all their country, each his right !
  God keep us all ! Amen !

J. D. R.

1862

THE friends that are, and friends that
  were,
  What shallow waves divide !
I miss the form for many a year
  Still seated at my side.

I miss him, yet I feel him still
  Amidst our faithful band,
As if not death itself could chill
  The warmth of friendship's hand.

His story other lips may tell, —
  For me the veil is drawn;
I only knew he loved me well,
  He loved me — and is gone !

VOYAGE OF THE GOOD SHIP UNION

1862

'T IS midnight: through my troubled
  dream
  Loud wails the tempest's cry;
Before the gale, with tattered sail,
  A ship goes plunging by.
What name ? Where bound ? — The
  rocks around
  Repeat the loud halloo.
— The good ship Union, Southward bound:
  God help her and her crew !

And is the old flag flying still
  That o'er your fathers flew,
With bands of white and rosy light,
  And field of starry blue ?

— Ay ! look aloft ! its folds full oft
  Have braved the roaring blast,
And still shall fly when from the sky
  This black typhoon has past !

Speak, pilot of the storm-tost bark !
  May I thy peril share ?
— O landsman, there are fearful seas
  The brave alone may dare !
— Nay, ruler of the rebel deep,
  What matters wind or wave ?
The rocks that wreck your reeling deck
  Will leave me naught to save !

O landsman, art thou false or true ?
  What sign hast thou to show ?
— The crimson stains from loyal veins
  That hold my heart-blood's flow !
— Enough ! what more shall honor claim ?
  I know the sacred sign;
Above thy head our flag shall spread,
  Our ocean path be thine !

The bark sails on; the Pilgrim's Cape
  Lies low along her lee,
Whose headland crooks its anchor-flukes
  To lock the shore and sea.
No treason here ! it cost too dear
  To win this barren realm !
And true and free the hands must be
  That hold the whaler's helm !

Still on ! Manhattan's narrowing bay
  No rebel cruiser scars;
Her waters feel no pirate's keel
  That flaunts the fallen stars !
— But watch the light on yonder height, —
  Ay, pilot, have a care !
Some lingering cloud in mist may shroud
  The capes of Delaware !

Say, pilot, what this fort may be,
  Whose sentinels look down
From moated walls that show the sea
  Their deep embrasures' frown ?
The Rebel host claims all the coast,
  But these are friends, we know,
Whose footprints spoil the "sacred soil,"
  And this is ? — Fort Monroe !

The breakers roar, — how bears the
    shore ?
  — The traitorous wreckers' hands
Have quenched the blaze that poured its rays
  Along the Hatteras sands.

— Ha ! say not so ! I see its glow !
  Again the shoals display
The beacon light that shines by night,
  The Union Stars by day !

The good ship flies to milder skies,
  The wave more gently flows,
The softening breeze wafts o'er the seas
  The breath of Beaufort's rose.
What fold is this the sweet winds kiss,
  Fair-striped and many-starred,
Whose shadow palls these orphaned walls,
  The twins of Beauregard ?

What ! heard you not Port Royal's doom ?
  How the black war-ships came
And turned the Beaufort roses' bloom
  To redder wreaths of flame ?
How from Rebellion's broken reed
  We saw his emblem fall,
As soon his cursèd poison-weed
  Shall drop from Sumter's wall ?

On ! on ! Pulaski's iron hail
  Falls harmless on Tybee !
The good ship feels the freshening gales,
  She strikes the open sea;
She rounds the point, she threads the keys
  That guard the Land of Flowers,
And rides at last where firm and fast
  Her own Gibraltar towers !

The good ship Union's voyage is o'er,
  At anchor safe she swings,
And loud and clear with cheer on cheer
  Her joyous welcome rings:
Hurrah ! Hurrah ! it shakes the wave,
  It thunders on the shore, —
One flag, one land, one heart, one hand,
  One Nation, evermore !

"CHOOSE YOU THIS DAY WHOM YE WILL SERVE"

1863

YES, tyrants, you hate us, and fear while
    you hate
The self-ruling, chain-breaking, throne-
    shaking State !
The night-birds dread morning, — your
    instinct is true, —
The day-star of Freedom brings midnight
    for you !

Why plead with the deaf for the cause of
    mankind ?
The owl hoots at noon that the eagle is
    blind !
We ask not your reasons, — 't were wast-
    ing our time, —
Our life is a menace, our welfare a crime !

We have battles to fight, we have foes to
    subdue, —
Time waits not for us, and we wait not for
    you !
The mower mows on, though the adder
    may writhe
And the copper-head coil round the blade
    of his scythe !

" No sides in this quarrel," your statesmen
    may urge,
Of school-house and wages with slave-pen
    and scourge ! —
No sides in the quarrel ! proclaim it as
    well
To the angels that fight with the legions of
    hell !

They kneel in God's temple, the North and
    the South,
With blood on each weapon and prayers in
    each mouth.
Whose cry shall be answered ?   Ye Heav-
    ens, attend
The lords of the lash as their voices
    ascend !

" O Lord, we are shaped in the image of
    Thee, —
Smite down the base millions that claim to
    be free,
And lend thy strong arm to the soft-handed
    race
Who eat *not* their bread in the sweat of
    their face ! "

So pleads the proud planter.   What echoes
    are these ?
The bay of his bloodhound is borne on the
    breeze,
And, lost in the shriek of his victim's
    despair,
His voice dies unheard. — Hear the Puri-
    tan's prayer !

" O Lord, that didst smother mankind in
    thy flood,

The sun is as sackcloth, the moon is as
    blood,
The stars fall to earth as untimely are
    cast
The figs from the fig-tree that shakes in
    the blast !

" All nations, all tribes in whose nostrils is
    breath
Stand gazing at Sin as she travails with
    Death !
Lord, strangle the monster that struggles
    to birth,
Or mock us no more with thy 'Kingdom
    on Earth ' !

" If Ammon and Moab must reign in the
    land
Thou gavest thine Israel, fresh from thy
    hand,
Call Baäl and Ashtaroth out of their graves
To be the new gods for the empire of
    slaves ! "

Whose God will ye serve, O ye rulers of
    men ?
Will ye build you new shrines in the slave-
    breeder's den ?
Or bow with the children of light, as they
    call
On the Judge of the Earth and the Father
    of All ?

Choose wisely, choose quickly, for time
    moves apace, —
Each day is an age in the life of our
    race !
Lord, lead them in love, ere they hasten in
    fear
From the fast-rising flood that shall girdle
    the sphere !

F. W. C.

1864

FAST as the rolling seasons bring
    The hour of fate to those we love,
Each pearl that leaves the broken string
    Is set in Friendship's crown above.
As narrower grows the earthly chain,
    The circle widens in the sky ;
These are our treasures that remain,
    But those are stars that beam on high.

We miss — oh, how we miss ! — *his* face, —
  With trembling accents speak his name.
Earth cannot fill his shadowed place
  From all her rolls of pride and fame.
Our song has lost the silvery thread
  That carolled through his jocund lips;
Our laugh is mute, our smile is fled,
  And all our sunshine in eclipse.

And what and whence the wondrous charm
  That kept his manhood boylike still, —
That life's hard censors could disarm
  And lead them captive at his will ?
His heart was shaped of rosier clay, —
  His veins were filled with ruddier fire, —
Time could not chill him, fortune sway,
  Nor toil with all its burdens tire.

His speech burst throbbing from its fount
  And set our colder thoughts aglow,
As the hot leaping geysers mount
  And falling melt the Iceland snow.
Some word, perchance, we counted rash, —
  Some phrase our calmness might disclaim,
Yet 't was the sunset's lightning's flash,
  No angry bolt, but harmless flame.

Man judges all, God knoweth each;
  We read the rule, He sees the law;
How oft his laughing children teach
  The truths his prophets never saw !
O friend, whose wisdom flowered in mirth,
  Our hearts are sad, our eyes are dim;
He gave thy smiles to brighten earth, —
  We trust thy joyous soul to Him !

Alas ! — our weakness Heaven forgive !
  We murmur, even while we trust,
" How long earth's breathing burdens live,
  Whose hearts, before they die, are dust ! "
But thou ! — through grief's untimely tears
  We ask with half-reproachful sigh —
" Couldst thou not watch a few brief years
  Till Friendship faltered, 'Thou mayst
  die ' ? "

Who loved our boyish years so well ?
  Who knew so well their pleasant tales,
And all those livelier freaks could tell
  Whose oft-told story never fails ?
In vain we turn our aching eyes, —
  In vain we stretch our eager hands, —
Cold in his wintry shroud he lies
  Beneath the dreary drifting sands !

Ah, speak not thus ! *He* lies not there !
  We see him, hear him as of old !
He comes ! He claims his wonted chair ;
  His beaming face we still behold !
His voice rings clear in all our songs,
  And loud his mirthful accents rise;
To us our brother's life belongs, —
  Dear friends, a classmate never dies !

THE LAST CHARGE

1864

Now, men of the North ! will you join in
  the strife
For country, for freedom, for honor, for
  life ?
The giant grows blind in his fury and
  spite, —
One blow on his forehead will settle the
  fight !

Flash full in his eyes the blue lightning of
  steel,
And stun him with cannon-bolts, peal upon
  peal !
Mount, troopers, and follow your game to
  its lair,
As the hound tracks the wolf and the
  beagle the hare !

Blow, trumpets, your summons, till slug-
  gards awake !
Beat, drums, till the roofs of the faint-
  hearted shake !
Yet, yet, ere the signet is stamped on the
  scroll,
Their names may be traced on the blood-
  sprinkled roll !

Trust not the false herald that painted your
  shield:
True honor *to-day* must be sought on the
  field !
Her scutcheon shows white with a blazon of
  red, —
The life-drops of crimson for liberty shed !

The hour is at hand, and the moment draws
  nigh;
The dog-star of treason grows dim in the
  sky;

Shine forth from the battle-cloud, light of
   the morn,
Call back the bright hour when the Nation
   was born !

The rivers of peace through our valleys
   shall run,
As the glaciers of tyranny melt in the sun;
Smite, smite the proud parricide down
   from his throne, —
His sceptre once broken, the world is our
   own !

OUR OLDEST FRIEND

1865

I GIVE you the health of the oldest friend
That, short of eternity, earth can lend, —
A friend so faithful and tried and true
That nothing can wean him from me and
   you.

When first we screeched in the sudden
   blaze
Of the daylight's blinding and blasting rays,
And gulped at the gaseous, groggy air,
This old, old friend stood waiting there.

And when, with a kind of mortal strife,
We had gasped and choked into breathing
   life,
He watched by the cradle, day and night,
And held our hands till we stood upright.

From gristle and pulp our frames have
   grown
To stringy muscle and solid bone;
While we were changing, he altered not;
We might forget, but he never forgot.

He came with us to the college class, —
Little cared he for the steward's pass !
All the rest must pay their fee,
But the grim old dead-head entered free.

He stayed with us while we counted o'er
Four times each of the seasons four;
And with every season, from year to year,
The dear name Classmate he made more
   dear.

He never leaves us, — he never will,
Till our hands are cold and our hearts are
   still;

On birthdays, and Christmas, and New-
   Year's too,
He always remembers both me and you.

Every year this faithful friend
His little present is sure to send;
Every year, wheresoe'er we be,
He wants a keepsake from you and me.

How he loves us ! he pats our heads,
And, lo ! they are gleaming with silver
   threads;
And he's always begging one lock of hair,
Till our shining crowns have nothing to
   wear.

At length he will tell us, one by one,
" My child, your labor on earth is done;
And now you must journey afar to see
My elder brother, — Eternity ! "

And so, when long, long years have passed,
Some dear old fellow will be the last, —
Never a boy alive but he
Of all our goodly company !

When he lies down, but not till then,
Our kind Class-Angel will drop the pen
That writes in the day-book kept above
Our lifelong record of faith and love.

So here's a health in homely rhyme
To our oldest classmate, Father Time !
May our last survivor live to be
As bald and as wise and as tough as he !

SHERMAN'S IN SAVANNAH

A HALF-RHYMED IMPROMPTU

1865

LIKE the tribes of Israel,
   Fed on quails and manna,
Sherman and his glorious band
Journeyed through the rebel land,
Fed from Heaven's all-bounteous hand,
   Marching on Savannah !

As the moving pillar shone,
   Streamed the starry banner
All day long in rosy light,
Flaming splendor all the night,
Till it swooped in eagle flight
   Down on doomed Savannah !

Glory be to God on high !
Shout the loud Hosanna !
Treason's wilderness is past,
Canaan's shore is won at last,
Peal a nation's trumpet-blast, —
Sherman 's in Savannah !

Soon shall Richmond's tough old hide
Find a tough old tanner !
Soon from every rebel wall
Shall the rag of treason fall,
Till our banner flaps o'er all
As it crowns Savannah !

MY ANNUAL

1866

How long will this harp which you once
    loved to hear
Cheat your lips of a smile or your eyes of
    a tear ?
How long stir the echoes it wakened of old,
While its strings were unbroken, untar-
    nished its gold ?

Dear friends of my boyhood, my words do
    you wrong;
The heart, the heart only, shall throb in
    my song;
It reads the kind answer that looks from
    your eyes, —
" We will bid our old harper play on till
    he dies."

Though Youth, the fair angel that looked
    o'er the strings,
Has lost the bright glory that gleamed on
    his wings,
Though the freshness of morning has
    passed from its tone,
It is still the old harp that was always
    your own.

I claim not its music, — each note it affords
I strike from your heart-strings, that lend
    me its chords;
I know you will listen and love to the last,
For it trembles and thrills with the voice
    of your past.

Ah, brothers ! dear brothers ! the harp
    that I hold
No craftsman could string and no artisan
    mould;

He shaped it, He strung it, who fashioned
    the lyres
That ring with the hymns of the seraphim
    choirs.

Not mine are the visions of beauty it brings,
Not mine the faint fragrance around it that
    clings;
Those shapes are the phantoms of years
    that are fled,
Those sweets breathe from roses your sum-
    mers have shed.

Each hour of the past lends its tribute to
    this,
Till it blooms like a bower in the Garden
    of Bliss;
The thorn and the thistle may grow as
    they will,
Where Friendship unfolds there is Paradise
    still.

The bird wanders careless while summer
    is green,
The leaf-hidden cradle that rocked him
    unseen;
When Autumn's rude fingers the woods
    have undressed,
The boughs may look bare, but they show
    him his nest.

Too precious these moments ! the lustre
    they fling
Is the light of our year, is the gem of its
    ring,
So brimming with sunshine, we almost for-
    get
The rays it has lost, and its border of jet.

While round us the many-hued halo is shed,
How dear are the living, how near are the
    dead !
One circle, scarce broken, these waiting be-
    low,
Those walking the shores where the aspho-
    dels blow !

Not life shall enlarge it nor death shall
    divide, —
No brother new-born finds his place at my
    side;
No titles shall freeze us, no grandeurs in-
    fest,
His Honor, His Worship, are boys like the
    rest.

Some won the world's homage, their names
we hold dear, —
But Friendship, not Fame, is the counter-
sign here;
Make room by the conqueror crowned in
the strife
For the comrade that limps from the battle
of life !

What tongue talks of battle ? Too long
we have heard
In sorrow, in anguish, that terrible word;
It reddened the sunshine, it crimsoned the
wave,
It sprinkled our doors with the blood of our
brave.

Peace, Peace come at last, with her garland
of white;
Peace broods in all hearts as we gather to-
night;
The blazon of Union spreads full in the
sun;
We echo its words, — We are one ! We
are one !

ALL HERE

1867

IT is not what we say or sing,
That keeps our charm so long unbroken,
Though every lightest leaf we bring
May touch the heart as friendship's
token;
Not what we sing or what we say
Can make us dearer to each other;
We love the singer and his lay,
But love as well the silent brother.

Yet bring whate'er your garden grows,
Thrice welcome to our smiles and
praises;
Thanks for the myrtle and the rose,
Thanks for the marigolds and daisies;
One flower erelong we all shall claim,
Alas ! unloved of Amaryllis —
Nature's last blossom — need I name
The wreath of threescore's silver lilies ?

How many, brothers, meet to-night
Around our boyhood's covered embers ?
Go read the treasured names aright
The old triennial list remembers;

Though twenty wear the starry sign
That tells a life has broke its tether,
The fifty-eight of 'twenty-nine —
God bless THE BOYS ! — are all together !

These come with joyous look and word,
With friendly grasp and cheerful greet-
ing, —
Those smile unseen, and move unheard,
The angel guests of every meeting;
They cast no shadow in the flame
That flushes from the gilded lustre,
But count us — we are still the same;
One earthly band, one heavenly cluster !

Love dies not when he bows his head
To pass beyond the narrow portals, —
The light these glowing moments shed
Wakes from their sleep our lost immor-
tals;
They come as in their joyous prime,
Before their morning days were num-
bered, —
Death stays the envious hand of Time, —
The eyes have not grown dim that slum-
bered !

The paths that loving souls have trod
Arch o'er the dust where worldlings
grovel
High as the zenith o'er the sod, —
The cross above the sexton's shovel !
We rise beyond the realms of day:
They seem to stoop from spheres of glory
With us one happy hour to stray,
While youth comes back in song and
story.

Ah ! ours is friendship true as steel
That war has tried in edge and temper;
It writes upon its sacred seal
The priest's *ubique — omnes — semper !*
It lends the sky a fairer sun
That cheers our lives with rays as steady
As if our footsteps had begun
To print the golden streets already !

The tangling years have clinched its knot
Too fast for mortal strength to sunder;
The lightning bolts of noon are shot;
No fear of evening's idle thunder !
Too late ! too late ! — no graceless hand
Shall stretch its cords in vain endeavor
To rive the close encircling band
That made and keeps us one forever !

So when upon the fated scroll
  The falling stars have all descended,
And, blotted from the breathing roll,
  Our little page of life is ended,
We ask but one memorial line
  Traced on thy tablet, Gracious Mother:
"My children. Boys of '29.
  In pace. How they loved each other !"

ONCE MORE

1868

Will I come ? That *is* pleasant ! I beg to
    inquire
If the gun that I carry has ever missed
    fire ?
And which was the muster-roll — mention
    but one —
That missed your old comrade who carries
    the gun ?

You see me as always, my hand on the
    lock,
The cap on the nipple, the hammer full
    cock;
It is rusty, some tell me; I heed not the
    scoff;
It is battered and bruised, but it always
    goes off !

"Is it loaded ?" I 'll bet you ! What
    does n't it hold ?
Rammed full to the muzzle with memories
    untold;
Why, it scares me to fire, lest the pieces
    should fly
Like the cannons that burst on the Fourth
    of July !

One charge is a remnant of College-day
    dreams
(Its wadding is made of forensics and
    themes);
Ah, visions of fame ! what a flash in the
    pan
As the trigger was pulled by each clever
    young man !

And love ! Bless my stars, what a cart-
    ridge is there !
With a wadding of rose-leaves and ribbons
    and hair, —

All crammed in one verse to go off at a
    shot !
"Were there ever such sweethearts ?" Of
    course there were not !

And next, — what a load ! it will split the
    old gun, —
Three fingers, — four fingers, — five fingers
    of fun !
Come tell me, gray sages, for mischief and
    noise
Was there ever a lot like us fellows, "The
    Boys" ?

Bump ! bump ! down the staircase the can-
    non-ball goes, —
Aha, old Professor ! Look out for your
    toes !
Don't think, my poor Tutor, to *sleep* in your
    bed, —
Two "Boys"— 'twenty-niners — room over
    your head !

Remember the nights when the tar-barrel
    blazed !
From red "Massachusetts" the war-cry
    was raised;
And "Hollis" and "Stoughton" reëchoed
    the call;
Till P—— poked his head out of Holworthy
    Hall !

Old P——, as we called him, — at fifty or
    so, —
Not exactly a bud, but not quite in full
    blow;
In ripening manhood, suppose we should
    say,
Just nearing his prime, as we boys are to-
    day !

Oh say, can you look through the vista of
    age
To the time when old Morse drove the reg-
    ular stage ?
When Lyon told tales of the long-vanished
    years,
And Lenox crept round with the rings in
    his ears ?

And dost thou, my brother, remember in-
    deed
The days of our dealings with Willard and
    Read ?

When "Dolly" was kicking and running
    away,
And punch came up smoking on Fille-
    brown's tray?

But where are the Tutors, my brother, oh
    tell! —
And where the Professors, remembered so
    well?
The sturdy old Grecian of Holworthy
    Hall,
And Latin, and Logic, and Hebrew, and
    all?

"They are dead, the old fellows" (we
    called them so then,
Though we since have found out they were
    lusty young men).
They are *dead*, do you tell me? — but how
    do you know?
You 've filled once too often. I doubt if
    it 's so.

I 'm thinking. I 'm thinking. Is this
    'sixty-eight?
It 's not quite so clear. It admits of de-
    bate.
I *may* have been dreaming. I rather in-
    cline
To think — yes, I 'm certain — it is 'twenty-
    nine!

"By Zhorzhe!" — as friend Sales is accus-
    tomed to cry, —
You tell me they 're dead, but I know it 's
    a lie!
Is Jackson not President? — What was 't
    you said?
It can't be; you 're joking; what, — all of
    'em dead?

Jim, — Harry, — Fred, — Isaac, — all gone
    from our side?
They could n't have left us, — no, not if
    they tried.
Look, — there 's our old Præses, — he
    can't find his text;
See, — P—— rubs his leg, as he growls out
    "*The next!*"

I told you 't was nonsense. Joe, give us a
    song!
Go harness up "Dolly," and fetch her
    along! —

Dead! Dead! You false graybeard, I
    swear they are not!
Hurrah for Old Hickory! — Oh, I forgot!

Well, *one* we have with us (how could he
    contrive
To deal with us youngsters and still to
    survive?)
Who wore for our guidance authority's
    robe, —
No wonder he took to the study of Job!

And now, as my load was uncommonly
    large,
Let me taper it off with a classical charge;
When that has gone off, I shall drop my
    old gun —
And then stand at ease, for my service is
    done.

Bibamus ad Classem vocatam " The Boys "
Et eorum Tutorem cui nomen est " Noyes; "
Et floreant, valeant, vigeant tam,
Non Peircius ipse enumeret quam!

THE OLD CRUISER

1869

HERE 's the old cruiser, 'Twenty-nine,
Forty times she 's crossed the line;
Same old masts and sails and crew,
Tight and tough and as good as new.

Into the harbor she bravely steers
Just as she 's done for these forty years, —
Over her anchor goes, splash and clang!
Down her sails drop, rattle and bang!

Comes a vessel out of the dock
Fresh and spry as a fighting-cock,
Feathered with sails and spurred with
    steam,
Heading out of the classic stream.

Crew of a hundred all aboard,
Every man as fine as a lord.
Gay they look and proud they feel,
Bowling along on even keel.

On they float with wind and tide,
Gain at last the old ship's side;
Every man looks down in turn, —
Reads the name that 's on her stern.

"Twenty-nine ! — *Diable* you say !
That was in Skipper Kirkland's day !
What was the Flying Dutchman's name ?
This old rover must be the same.

"Ho ! you Boatswain that walks the deck,
How does it happen you 're not a wreck ?
One and another have come to grief,
How have you dodged by rock and reef ? "

Boatswain, lifting one knowing lid,
Hitches his breeches and shifts his quid :
"Hey ? What is it ? Who 's come to
   grief ?
Louder, young swab, I 'm a little deaf."

"I say, old fellow, what keeps your boat
With all you jolly old boys afloat,
When scores of vessels as good as she
Have swallowed the salt of the bitter sea ?

"Many a crew from many a craft
Goes drifting by on a broken raft
Pieced from a vessel that clove the brine
Taller and prouder than 'Twenty-nine.

"Some capsized in an angry breeze,
Some were lost in the narrow seas,
Some on snags and some on sands
Struck and perished and lost their hands.

"Tell us young ones, you gray old man,
What is your secret, if you can.
We have a ship as good as you,
Show us how to keep our crew."

So in his ear the youngster cries ;
Then the gray Boatswain straight re-
   plies : —
"All your crew be sure you know, —
Never let one of your shipmates go.

"If he leaves you, change your tack,
Follow him close and fetch him back ;
When you 've hauled him in at last,
Grapple his flipper and hold him fast.

"If you 've wronged him, speak him fair,
Say you 're sorry and make it square ;
If he 's wronged you, wink so tight
None of you see what 's plain in sight.

"When the world goes hard and wrong,
Lend a hand to help him along ;

When his stockings have holes to darn,
Don't you grudge him your ball of yarn.

"Once in a twelvemonth, come what may,
Anchor your ship in a quiet bay,
Call all hands and read the log,
And give 'em a taste of grub and grog.

"Stick to each other through thick and
   thin ;
All the closer as age leaks in ;
Squalls will blow and clouds will frown,
But stay by your ship till you all go
   down ! "

ADDED FOR THE ALUMNI MEETING,
JUNE 29, 1869.

So the gray Boatswain of 'Twenty-nine
Piped to "The Boys" as they crossed the
   line ;
Round the cabin sat thirty guests,
Babes of the nurse with a thousand breasts.

There were the judges, grave and grand,
Flanked by the priests on either hand ;
There was the lord of wealth untold,
And the dear good fellow in broadcloth old.

Thirty men, from twenty towns,
Sires and grandsires with silvered
   crowns, —
Thirty school-boys all in a row, —
Bens and Georges and Bill and Joe.

In thirty goblets the wine was poured,
But threescore gathered around the
   board, —
For lo ! at the side of every chair
A shadow hovered — we all were there !

HYMN FOR THE CLASS–MEET- ING

1869

THOU Gracious Power, whose mercy lends
The light of home, the smile of friends,
Our gathered flock thine arms infold
As in the peaceful days of old.

Wilt thou not hear us while we raise,
In sweet accord of solemn praise,

The voices that have mingled long
In joyous flow of mirth and song?

For all the blessings life has brought,
For all its sorrowing hours have taught,
For all we mourn, for all we keep,
The hands we clasp, the loved that sleep;

The noontide sunshine of the past,
These brief, bright moments fading fast,
The stars that gild our darkening years,
The twilight ray from holier spheres;

We thank thee, Father! let thy grace
Our narrowing circle still embrace,
Thy mercy shed its heavenly store,
Thy peace be with us evermore!

EVEN-SONG

1870

It may be, yes, it must be, Time that
        brings
    An end to mortal things,
That sends the beggar Winter in the train
    Of Autumn's burdened wain, —
Time, that is heir of all our earthly state,
    And knoweth well to wait
Till sea hath turned to shore and shore to
        sea,
    If so it need must be,
Ere he make good his claim and call his
        own
    Old empires overthrown, —
Time, who can find no heavenly orb too
        large
    To hold its fee in charge,
Nor any motes that fill its beam so small,
    But he shall care for all, —
It may be, must be, — yes, he soon shall
        tire
    This hand that holds the lyre.

Then ye who listened in that earlier day
    When to my careless lay
I matched its chords and stole their first-
        born thrill,
    With untaught rudest skill
Vexing a treble from the slender strings
    Thin as the locust sings
When the shrill-crying child of summer's
        heat
    Pipes from its leafy seat,

The dim pavilion of embowering green
    Beneath whose shadowy screen
The small sopranist tries his single note
    Against the song-bird's throat,
And all the echoes listen, but in vain;
    They hear no answering strain, —
Then ye who listened in that earlier day
    Shall sadly turn away,

Saying, "The fire burns low, the hearth is
        cold
    That warmed our blood of old;
Cover its embers and its half-burnt brands,
    And let us stretch our hands
Over a brighter and fresh-kindled flame;
    Lo, this is not the same,
The joyous singer of our morning time,
    Flushed high with lusty rhyme!
Speak kindly, for he bears a human heart,
    But whisper him apart, —
Tell him the woods their autumn robes
        have shed
    And all their birds have fled,
And shouting winds unbuild the naked
        nests
    They warmed with patient breasts;
Tell him the sky is dark, the summer
        o'er,
    And bid him sing no more!"

Ah, welladay! if words so cruel-kind
    A listening ear might find!
But who that hears the music in his soul
    Of rhythmic waves that roll
Crested with gleams of fire, and as they
        flow
    Stir all the deeps below
Till the great pearls no calm might ever
        reach
    Leap glistening on the beach, —
Who that has known the passion and the
        pain,
    The rush through heart and brain,
The joy so like a pang his hand is pressed
    Hard on his throbbing breast,
When thou, whose smile is life and bliss
        and fame
    Hast set his pulse aflame,
Muse of the lyre! can say farewell to thee?
    Alas! and must it be?

In many a clime, in many a stately tongue,
    The mighty bards have sung;
To these the immemorial thrones belong
    And purple robes of song;

Yet the slight minstrel loves the slender
    tone
His lips may call his own,
And finds the measure of the verse more
    sweet,
    Timed by his pulse's beat,
Than all the hymnings of the laurelled
    throng.
    Say not I do him wrong,
For Nature spoils her warblers, — them she
    feeds
    In lotus-growing meads
And pours them subtle draughts from
    haunted streams
    That fill their souls with dreams.

Full well I know the gracious mother's
    wiles
    And dear delusive smiles !
No callow fledgling of her singing brood
    But tastes that witching food,
And hearing overhead the eagle's wing,
    And how the thrushes sing,
Vents his exiguous chirp, and from his nest
    Flaps forth — we know the rest.
I own the weakness of the tuneful kind, —
    Are not all harpers blind ?
I sang too early, must I sing too late ?
    The lengthening shadows wait
The first pale stars of twilight, — yet how
    sweet
    The flattering whisper's cheat, —
"Thou hast the fire no evening chill can
    tame,
    Whose coals outlast its flame !"

Farewell, ye carols of the laughing morn,
    Of earliest sunshine born !
The sower flings the seed and looks not back
    Along his furrowed track;
The reaper leaves the stalks for other
    hands
    To gird with circling bands;
The wind, earth's careless servant, truant-
    born,
    Blows clean the beaten corn
And quits the thresher's floor, and goes his
    way
    To sport with ocean's spray;
The headlong-stumbling rivulet scrambling
    down
    To wash the sea-girt town,
Still babbling of the green and billowy
    waste
    Whose salt he longs to taste,

Ere his warm wave its chilling clasp may
    feel
    Has twirled the miller's wheel.

The song has done its task that makes us
    bold
    With secrets else untold, —
And mine has run its errand; through the
    dews
    I tracked the flying Muse;
The daughter of the morning touched my
    lips
    With roseate finger-tips;
Whether I would or would not, I must
    sing
    With the new choirs of spring;
Now, as I watch the fading autumn day
    And trill my softened lay,
I think of all that listened, and of one
    For whom a brighter sun
Dawned at high summer's noon. Ah, com-
    rades dear,
    Are not all gathered here ?
Our hearts have answered. — Yes ! they
    hear our call :
    All gathered here ! all ! all !

THE SMILING LISTENER

1871

PRECISELY. I see it. You all want to say
That a tear is too sad and a laugh is too gay;
You could stand a faint smile, you could
    manage a sigh,
But you value your ribs, and you don't
    want to cry.

And why at our feast of the clasping of
    hands
Need we turn on the stream of our lachry-
    mal glands ?
Though we see the white breakers of age
    on our bow,
Let us take a good pull in the jolly-boat
    now !

It 's hard if a fellow cannot feel content
When a banquet like this does n't cost him
    a cent,
When his goblet and plate he may empty
    at will,
And our kind Class Committee will settle
    the bill.

And here 's your old friend, the identical
bard
Who has rhymed and recited you verse by
the yard
Since the days of the empire of Andrew
the First
Till you 're full to the brim and feel ready
to burst.

It 's awful to think of, — how year after
year
With his piece in his pocket he waits for
you here;
No matter who 's missing, there always is
one
To lug out his manuscript, sure as a gun.

" Why won't he stop writing ? " Humanity
cries:
The answer is briefly, " He can't if he
tries;
He has played with his foolish old feather
so long,
That the goose-quill in spite of him cackles
in song."

You have watched him with patience from
morning to dusk
Since the tassel was bright o'er the green
of the husk,
And now — it 's too bad — it 's a pitiful
job —
He has shelled the ripe ear till he 's come
to the cob.

I see one face beaming — it listens so well
There must be some music yet left in my
shell —
The wine of my soul is not thick on the
lees;
One string is unbroken, one friend I can
please !

Dear comrade, the sunshine of seasons gone
by
Looks out from your tender and tear-
moistened eye,
A pharos of love on an ice-girdled coast, —
Kind soul ! — Don't you hear me ? — He 's
deaf as a post !

Can it be one of Nature's benevolent tricks
That you grow hard of hearing as I grow
prolix ?

And that look of delight which would an-
gels beguile
Is the deaf man's prolonged unintelligent
smile ?

Ah! the ear may grow dull, and the eye
may wax dim,
But they still know a classmate — they
can't mistake him;
There is something to tell us, " That 's one
of our band,"
Though we groped in the dark for a touch
of his hand.

Well, Time with his snuffers is prowling
about
And his shaky old fingers will soon snuff
us out ;
There 's a hint for us all in each pendulum
tick,
For we 're low in the tallow and long in the
wick.

You remember Rossini — you 've been at
the play ?
How his overture-endings keep crashing
away
Till you think, " It 's all over — it can't but
stop now —
That 's the screech and the bang of the
final bow-wow."

And you find you 're mistaken ; there 's
lots more to come,
More banging, more screeching of fiddle
and drum,
Till when the last ending is finished and
done,
You feel like a horse when the winning-
post 's won.

So I, who have sung to you, merry, or sad,
Since the days when they called me a
promising lad,
Though I 've made you more rhymes than
a tutor could scan,
Have a few more still left, like the razor-
strop man.

Now pray don't be frightened — I 'm ready
to stop
My galloping anapests' clatter and pop —
In fact, if you say so, retire from to-day
To the garret I left, on a poet's half-pay.

And yet — I can't help it — perhaps — who
    can tell ?
You might miss the poor singer you treated
    so well,
And confess you could stand him five min-
    utes or so,
" It was so like old times we remember, you
    know."

'T is not that the music can signify much,
But then there are chords that awake with
    a touch, —
And our hearts can find echoes of sorrow
    and joy
To the winch of the minstrel who hails
    from Savoy.

So this hand-organ tune that I cheerfully
    grind
May bring the old places and faces to
    mind,
And seen in the light of the past we recall
The flowers that have faded bloom fairest
    of all !

OUR SWEET SINGER

J. A.

1872

ONE memory trembles on our lips;
    It throbs in every breast;
In tear-dimmed eyes, in mirth's eclipse,
    The shadow stands confessed.

O silent voice, that cheered so long
    Our manhood's marching day,
Without thy breath of heavenly song,
    How weary seems the way !

Vain every pictured phrase to tell
    Our sorrowing heart's desire, —
The shattered harp, the broken shell,
    The silent unstrung lyre;

For youth was round us while he sang;
    It glowed in every tone;
With bridal chimes the echoes rang,
    And made the past our own.

Oh blissful dream ! Our nursery joys
    We know must have an end,
But love and friendship's broken toys
    May God's good angels mend !

The cheering smile, the voice of mirth
    And laughter's gay surprise
That please the children born of earth,
    Why deem that Heaven denies ?

Methinks in that refulgent sphere
    That knows not sun or moon,
An earth-born saint might long to hear
    One verse of " Bonny Doon; "

Or walking through the streets of gold
    In heaven's unclouded light,
His lips recall the song of old
    And hum " The sky is bright."

And can we smile when thou art dead ?
    Ah, brothers, even so !
The rose of summer will be red,
    In spite of winter's snow.

Thou wouldst not leave us all in gloom
    Because thy song is still,
Nor blight the banquet-garland's bloom
    With grief's untimely chill.

The sighing wintry winds complain, —
    The singing bird has flown, —
Hark ! heard I not that ringing strain,
    That clear celestial tone ?

How poor these pallid phrases seem,
    How weak this tinkling line,
As warbles through my waking dream
    That angel voice of thine !

Thy requiem asks a sweeter lay;
    It falters on my tongue;
For all we vainly strive to say,
    Thou shouldst thyself have sung !

H. C. M. H. S. J. K. W.

1873

THE dirge is played, the throbbing death-
    peal rung,
    The sad-voiced requiem sung ;
On each white urn where memory
    dwells
The wreath of rustling immortelles
    Our loving hands have hung,
And balmiest leaves have strown and ten
    derest blossoms flung.

The birds that filled the air with songs
have flown,
   The wintry blasts have blown,
And these for whom the voice of spring
Bade the sweet choirs their carols sing
   Sleep in those chambers lone
Where snows untrodden lie, unheard the
   nightwinds moan.

We clasp them all in memory, as the vine
   Whose running stems untwine
The marble shaft, and steal around
The lowly stone, the nameless mound;
   With sorrowing hearts resign
Our brothers true and tried, and close our
   broken line.

How fast the lamps of life grow dim and die
   Beneath our sunset sky !
Still fading, as along our track
We cast our saddened glances back,
   And while we vainly sigh
The shadowy day recedes, the starry night
   draws nigh.

As when from pier to pier across the tide
   With even keel we glide,
The lights we left along the shore
Grow less and less, while more, yet more
   New vistas open wide
Of fair illumined streets and casements
   golden-eyed.

Each closing circle of our sunlit sphere
   Seems to bring heaven more near:
Can we not dream that those we love
Are listening in the world above
   And smiling as they hear
The voices known so well of friends that
   still are dear ?

Does all that made us human fade away
   With this dissolving clay ?
Nay, rather deem the blessed isles
Are bright and gay with joyous smiles,
   That angels have their play,
And saints that tire of song may claim
   their holiday.

All else of earth may perish; love alone
   Not heaven shall find outgrown !
Are they not here, our spirit guests,
With love still throbbing in their breasts ?
   Once more let flowers be strown.
Welcome, ye shadowy forms, we count you
   still our own !

WHAT I HAVE COME FOR

1873

I HAVE come with my verses — I think I
   may claim
It is not the first time I have tried on the
   same.
They were puckered in rhyme, they were
   wrinkled in wit;
But your hearts were so large that they
   made them a fit.

I have come — not to tease you with more
   of my rhyme,
But to feel as I did in the blessed old time;
I want to hear him with the Brobdingnag
   laugh —
We count him at least as three men and a
   half.

I have come to meet judges so wise and so
   grand
That I shake in my shoes while they're
   shaking my hand;
And the prince among merchants who put
   back the crown
When they tried to enthrone him the King
   of the Town.

I have come to see George — Yes, I think
   there are four,
If they all were like these I could wish
   there were more.
I have come to see one whom we used to
   call "Jim,"
I want to see — oh, don't I want to see
   him ?

I have come to grow young — on my word
   I declare
I have thought I detected a change in my
   hair !
One hour with "The Boys" will restore it
   to brown —
And a wrinkle or two I expect to rub down.

Yes, that's what I've come for, as all of
   us come;
When I meet the dear Boys I could wish I
   were dumb.
You asked me, you know, but it's spoiling
   the fun;
I have told what I came for; my ditty is
   done.

OUR BANKER

1874

OLD TIME, in whose bank we deposit our
    notes,
Is a miser who always wants guineas for
    groats;
He keeps all his customers still in arrears
By lending them minutes and charging
    them years.

The twelvemonth rolls round and we never
    forget
On the counter before us to pay him our
    debt.
We reckon the marks he has chalked on
    the door,
Pay up and shake hands and begin a new
    score.

How long he will lend us, how much we
    may owe,
No angel will tell us, no mortal may
    know.
At fivescore, at fourscore, at threescore
    and ten,
He may close the account with a stroke of
    his pen.

This only we know, — amid sorrows and
    joys
Old Time has been easy and kind with
    "The Boys."
Though he must have and will have and
    does have his pay,
We have found him good-natured enough
    in his way.

He never forgets us, as others will do, —
I am sure he knows me, and I think he
    knows you,
For I see on your foreheads a mark that
    he lends
As a sign he remembers to visit his friends.

In the shape of a classmate (a wig on his
    crown, —
His day-book and ledger laid carefully
    down)
He has welcomed us yearly, a glass in his
    hand,
And pledged the good health of our bro-
    therly band.

He 's a thief, we must own, but how many
    there be
That rob us less gently and fairly than he:
He has stripped the green leaves that were
    over us all,
But they let in the sunshine as fast as they
    fall.

Young beauties may ravish the world with
    a glance
As they languish in song, as they float in
    the dance, —
They are grandmothers now we remember
    as girls,
And the comely white cap takes the place
    of the curls.

But the sighing and moaning and groaning
    are o'er,
We are pining and moping and sleepless
    no more,
And the hearts that were thumping like
    ships on the rocks
Beat as quiet and steady as meeting-house
    clocks.

The trump of ambition, loud sounding and
    shrill,
May blow its long blast, but the echoes are
    still,
The spring-tides are past, but no billow
    may reach
The spoils they have landed far up on the
    beach.

We see that Time robs us, we know that
    he cheats,
But we still find a charm in his pleasant
    deceits,
While he leaves the remembrance of all
    that was best,
Love, friendship, and hope, and the promise
    of rest.

Sweet shadows of twilight! how calm their
    repose,
While the dewdrops fall soft in the breast
    of the rose!
How blest to the toiler his hour of release
When the vesper is heard with its whisper
    of peace!

Then here 's to the wrinkled old miser,
    our friend;
May he send us his bills to the century's end,

And lend us the moments no sorrow alloys,
Till he squares his account with the last of
"The Boys."

FOR CLASS MEETING

1875

IT is a pity and a shame — alas ! alas ! I
know it is,
To tread the trodden grapes again, but so
it has been, so it is;
The purple vintage long is past, with
ripened clusters bursting so
They filled the wine-vats to the brim, —
't is strange you will be thirsting so !

Too well our faithful memory tells what
might be rhymed or sung about,
For all have sighed and some have wept
since last year's snows were flung
about;
The beacon flame that fired the sky, the
modest ray that gladdened us,
A little breath has quenched their light, and
deepening shades have saddened us.

No more our brother's life is ours for cheer-
ing or for grieving us,
One only sadness they bequeathed, the sor-
row of their leaving us;
Farewell ! Farewell ! — I turn the leaf I
read my chiming measure in;
Who knows but something still is there a
friend may find a pleasure in ?

For who can tell by what he likes what other
people's fancies are ?
How all men think the best of wives their
own particular Nancies are ?
If what I sing you brings a smile, you will
not stop to catechise,
Nor read Bœotia's lumbering line with
nicely scanning Attic eyes.

Perhaps the alabaster box that Mary broke
so lovingly,
While Judas looked so sternly on, the Mas-
ter so approvingly,
Was not so fairly wrought as those that
Pilate's wife and daughters had,
Or many a dame of Judah's line that drank
of Jordan's waters had.

Perhaps the balm that cost so dear, as some
remarked officiously,
The precious nard that filled the room with
fragrance so deliciously,
So oft recalled in storied page and sung in
verse melodious,
The dancing girl had thought too cheap, —
that daughter of Herodias.

Where now are all the mighty deeds that
Herod boasted loudest of ?
Where now the flashing jewelry the te-
trarch's wife was proudest of ?
Yet still to hear how Mary loved, all tribes
of men are listening,
And still the sinful woman's tears like stars
in heaven are glistening.

'T is not the gift our hands have brought,
the love it is we bring with it, —
The minstrel's lips may shape the song, his
heart in tune must sing with it;
And so we love the simple lays, and wish
we might have more of them,
Our poet brothers sing for us, — there must
be half a score of them.

It may be that of fame and name our voices
once were emulous, —
With deeper thoughts, with tenderer throbs
their softening tones are tremu-
lous;
The dead seem listening as of old, ere
friendship was bereft of them;
The living wear a kinder smile, the remnant
that is left of them.

Though on the once unfurrowed brows the
harrow-teeth of Time may show,
Though all the strain of crippling years the
halting feet of rhyme may show,
We look and hear with melting hearts, for
what we all remember is
The morn of Spring, nor heed how chill the
sky of gray November is.

Thanks to the gracious powers above from
all mankind that singled us,
And dropped the pearl of friendship in the
cup they kindly mingled us,
And bound us in a wreath of flowers with
hoops of steel knit under it;—
Nor time, nor space, nor chance, nor change,
nor death himself shall sunder it !

"AD AMICOS"

1876

"Dumque virent genua
Et decet, obducta solvatur fonte senectus."

THE muse of boyhood's fervid hour
  Grows tame as skies get chill and hazy;
Where once she sought a passion-flower,
  She only hopes to find a daisy.
Well, who the changing world bewails?
  Who asks to have it stay unaltered?
Shall grown-up kittens chase their tails?
  Shall colts be never shod or haltered?

Are we "The Boys" that used to make
  The tables ring with noisy follies?
Whose deep-lunged laughter oft would
    shake
  The ceiling with its thunder-volleys?
Are we the youths with lips unshorn,
  At beauty's feet unwrinkled suitors,
Whose memories reach tradition's morn, —
  The days of prehistoric tutors?

"The Boys" we knew, — but who are these
  Whose heads might serve for Plutarch's
    sages,
Or Fox's martyrs, if you please,
  Or hermits of the dismal ages?
"The Boys" we knew — can these be
    those?
  Their cheeks with morning's blush were
    painted; —
Where are the Harrys, Jims, and Joes
  With whom we once were well ac-
    quainted?

If we are they, we 're not the same;
  If they are we, why then they 're mask-
    ing;
Do tell us, neighbor What 's-your-name,
  Who are you? — What 's the use of
    asking?
You once were George, or Bill, or Ben;
  There 's you, yourself — there 's you,
    that other —
I know you now — I knew you then —
  You used to be your younger brother!

You both are all our own to-day, —
  But ah! I hear a warning whisper;
Yon roseate hour that flits away
  Repeats the Roman's sad *paulisper*.

Come back! come back! we 've need of
    you
  To pay you for your word of warning;
We 'll bathe your wings in brighter dew
  Than ever wet the lids of morning!

Behold this cup; its mystic wine
  No alien's lip has ever tasted;
The blood of friendship's clinging vine,
  Still flowing, flowing, yet unwasted:
Old Time forgot his running sand
  And laid his hour-glass down to fill it,
And Death himself with gentle hand
  Has touched the chalice, not to spill it.

Each bubble rounding at the brim
  Is rainbowed with its magic story;
The shining days with age grown dim
  Are dressed again in robes of glory;
In all its freshness spring returns
  With song of birds and blossoms tender;
Once more the torch of passion burns,
  And youth is here in all its splendor!

Hope swings her anchor like a toy,
  Love laughs and shows the silver arrow
We knew so well as man and boy, —
  The shaft that stings through bone and
    marrow;
Again our kindling pulses beat,
  With tangled curls our fingers dally,
And bygone beauties smile as sweet
  As fresh-blown lilies of the valley.

O blessed hour! we may forget
  Its wreaths, its rhymes, its songs, its
    laughter,
But not the loving eyes we met,
  Whose light shall gild the dim hereafter.
How every heart to each grows warm!
  Is one in sunshine's ray? We share it.
Is one in sorrow's blinding storm?
  A look, a word, shall help him bear it.

"The Boys" we were, "The Boys" we 'll
    be
  As long as three, as two, are creeping;
Then here 's to him — ah! which is he? —
  Who lives till all the rest are sleeping;
A life with tranquil comfort blest,
  The young man's health, the rich man's
    plenty,
All earth can give that earth has best,
  And heaven at fourscore years and
    twenty.

HOW NOT TO SETTLE IT

1877

I LIKE, at times, to hear the steeples'
chimes
  With sober thoughts impressively that
    mingle;
But sometimes, too, I rather like — don't
    you ? —
  To hear the music of the sleigh bells'
    jingle.

I like full well the deep resounding swell
  Of mighty symphonies with chords in-
    woven;
But sometimes, too, a song of Burns —
    don't you ?
  After a solemn storm-blast of Beetho-
    ven.

Good to the heels the well-worn slipper
    feels
  When the tired player shuffles off the
    buskin;
A page of Hood may do a fellow good
  After a scolding from Carlyle or Ruskin.

Some works I find, — say Watts upon the
    Mind, —
  No matter though at first they seemed
    amusing,
Not quite the same, but just a little tame
  After some five or six times' reperusing.

So, too, at times when melancholy rhymes
  Or solemn speeches sober down a dinner,
I 've seen it 's true, quite often, — have n't
    you ? —
  The best-fed guests perceptibly grow
    thinner.

Better some jest (in proper terms ex-
    pressed)
  Or story (strictly moral) even if musty,
Or song we sung when these old throats
    were young, —
  Something to keep our souls from get-
    ting rusty.

The poorest scrap from memory's ragged
    lap
  Comes like an heirloom from a dear
    dead mother —

Hush ! there 's a tear that has no business
    here,
  A half-formed sigh that ere its birth we
    smother.

We cry, we laugh; ah, life is half and half,
  Now bright and joyous as a song of
    Herrick's,
Then chill and bare as funeral-minded
    Blair;
  As fickle as a female in hysterics.

If I could make you cry I would n't try;
  If you have hidden smiles I 'd like to
    find them,
And that although, as well I ought to
    know,
  The lips of laughter have a skull behind
    them.

Yet when I think we may be on the brink
  Of having Freedom's banner to dispose
    of,
All crimson - hued, because the Nation
    would
  Insist on cutting its own precious nose
    off,

I feel indeed as if we rather need
  A sermon such as preachers tie a text
    on.
If Freedom dies because a ballot lies,
  She earns her grave; 't is time to call the
    sexton !

But if a fight can make the matter right,
  Here are we, classmates, thirty men of
    mettle;
We 're strong and tough, we 've lived nigh
    long enough, —
  What if the Nation gave it us to settle ?

The tale would read like that illustrious
    deed
  When Curtius took the leap the gap
    that filled in,
Thus: " Fivescore years, good friends, as
    it appears,
  At last this people split on Hayes and
    Tilden.

" One half cried, 'See ! the choice is S. J.
    T. !'
  And one half swore as stoutly it was t'
    other;

Both drew the knife to save the Nation's
life
By wholesale vivisection of each other.

"Then rose in mass that monumental
Class, —
'Hold! hold!' they cried, 'give us,
give us the daggers!'
'Content! content!' exclaimed with one
consent
The gaunt ex-rebels and the carpet-bag-
gers.

"Fifteen each side, the combatants divide,
So nicely balanced are their predilections;
And first of all a tear-drop each lets fall,
A tribute to their obsolete affections.

"Man facing man, the sanguine strife be-
gan,
Jack, Jim and Joe against Tom, Dick
and Harry,
Each several pair its own account to
square,
Till both were down or one stood soli-
tary.

"And the great fight raged furious all the
night
Till every integer was made a fraction;
Reader, wouldst know what history has to
show
As net result of the above transaction?

"Whole coat-tails, four; stray fragments,
several score;
A heap of spectacles; a deaf man's trum-
pet;
Six lawyers' briefs; seven pocket-handker-
chiefs;
Twelve canes wherewith the owners used
to stump it;

"Odd rubber-shoes; old gloves of different
hues;
Tax-bills, — unpaid, — and several empty
purses;
And, saved from harm by some protecting
charm,
A printed page with Smith's immortal
verses;

"Trifles that claim no very special name, —
Some useful, others chiefly ornamental;

Pins, buttons, rings, and other trivial things,
With various wrecks, capillary and dental.

"Also, one flag, — 't was nothing but a rag,
And what device it bore it little matters;
Red, white, and blue, but rent all through
and through,
'Union forever' torn to shreds and tat-
ters.

"They fought so well not one was left to
tell
Which got the largest share of cuts and
slashes;
When heroes meet, both sides are bound to
beat;
They telescoped like cars in railroad
smashes.

"So the great split that baffled human wit
And might have cost the lives of twenty
millions,
As all may see that know the rule of three,
Was settled just as well by these civilians.

"As well. Just so. Not worse, not better.
No,
Next morning found the Nation still
divided;
Since all were slain, the inference is plain
They left the point they fought for un-
decided."

If not quite true, as I have told it you, —
This tale of mutual extermination,
To minds perplexed with threats of what
comes next,
Perhaps may furnish food for contem-
plation.

To cut men's throats to help them count
their votes
Is asinine — nay, worse — ascidian folly;
Blindness like that would scare the mole
and bat,
And make the liveliest monkey melan-
choly.

I say once more, as I have said before,
If voting for our Tildens and our Hayeses
Means only fight, then, Liberty, good night!
Pack up your ballot-box and go to blazes!

Unfurl your blood-red flags, you murderous
    hags,
  You *pétroleuses* of Paris, fierce and foamy;
We 'll sell our stock in Plymouth's blasted
    rock,
    Pull up our stakes and migrate to Daho-
    mey !

THE LAST SURVIVOR

1878

YES ! the vacant chairs tell sadly we are
    going, going fast,
And the thought comes strangely o'er me,
    who will live to be the last ?
When the twentieth century's sunbeams
    climb the far-off eastern hill,
With his ninety winters burdened, will he
    greet the morning still ?

Will he stand with Harvard's nurslings
    when they hear their mother's call
And the old and young are gathered in the
    many alcoved hall ?
Will he answer to the summons when they
    range themselves in line
And the young mustachioed marshal calls
    out "Class of '29" ?

Methinks I see the column as its lengthened
    ranks appear
In the sunshine of the morrow of the nine-
    teen hundredth year ;
Through the yard 't is creeping, winding,
    by the walls of dusky red, —
What shape is that which totters at the long
    procession's head ?

Who knows this ancient graduate of four-
    score years and ten, —
What place he held, what name he bore
    among the sons of men ?
So speeds the curious question; its answer
    travels slow;
"'T is the last of sixty classmates of
    seventy years ago."

His figure shows but dimly, his face I
    scarce can see, —
There 's something that reminds me, — it
    looks like — is it he ?

He ? *Who ?* No voice may whisper what
    wrinkled brow shall claim
The wreath of stars that circles our last
    survivor's name.

Will he be some veteran minstrel, left to
    pipe in feeble rhyme
All the stories and the glories of our gay
    and golden time ?
Or some quiet, voiceless brother in whose
    lonely, loving breast
Fond memory broods in silence, like a dove
    upon her nest ?

Will it be some old *Emeritus*, who taught
    so long ago
The boys that heard him lecture have
    heads as white as snow ?
Or a pious, painful preacher, holding forth
    from year to year
Till his colleague got a colleague whom the
    young folks flocked to hear ?

Will it be a rich old merchant in a square-
    tied white cravat,
Or selectman of a village in a pre-historic
    hat ?
Will his dwelling be a mansion in a marble-
    fronted row,
Or a homestead by a hillside where the
    huckleberries grow ?

I can see our one survivor, sitting lonely by
    himself, —
All his college text-books round him,
    ranged in order on their shelf;
There are classic "interliners" filled with
    learning's choicest pith,
Each *cum notis variorum, quas recensuit doctus*
    Smith;

Physics, metaphysics, logic, mathematics —
    all the lot
Every wisdom-crammed octavo he has
    mastered and forgot,
With the ghosts of dead professors stand-
    ing guard beside them all;
And the room is full of shadows which
    their lettered backs recall.

How the past spreads out in vision with its
    far receding train,
Like a long embroidered arras in the cham-
    bers of the brain,

From opening manhood's morning when
first we learned to grieve
To the fond regretful moments of our sor-
row-saddened eve !

What early shadows darkened our idle
summer's joy
When death snatched roughly from us that
lovely bright-eyed boy !
The years move swiftly onwards ; the
deadly shafts fall fast, —
Till all have dropped around him — lo,
there he stands, — the last !

Their faces flit before him, some rosy-hued
and fair,
Some strong in iron manhood, some worn
with toil and care;
Their smiles no more shall greet him on
cheeks with pleasure flushed !
The friendly hands are folded, the pleasant
voices hushed !

. . . .
My picture sets me dreaming; alas ! and
can it be
Those two familiar faces we never more
may see ?
In every entering footfall I think them
drawing near,
With every door that opens I say, " At
last they 're here ! "

The willow bends unbroken when angry
tempests blow,
The stately oak is levelled and all its
strength laid low ;
So fell that tower of manhood, undaunted,
patient, strong,
White with the gathering snowflakes, who
faced the storm so long.

And he, — what subtle phrases their vary-
ing light must blend
To paint as each remembers our many-
featured friend !
His wit a flash auroral that laughed in
every look,
His talk a sunbeam broken on the ripples
of a brook,

Or, fed from thousand sources, a fountain's
glittering jet,
Or careless handfuls scattered of diamond
sparks unset;

Ah, sketch him, paint him, mould him in
every shape you will,
He was *himself* — the only — the one un-
pictured still !

Farewell ! our skies are darkened and yet
the stars will shine,
We 'll close our ranks together and still
fall into line
Till one is left, one only, to mourn for all
the rest;
And Heaven bequeath their memories to
him who loves us best !

THE ARCHBISHOP AND GIL
BLAS

A MODERNIZED VERSION

1879

I DON'T think I feel much older; I 'm
aware I 'm rather gray,
But so are many young folks; I meet 'em
every day.
I confess I 'm more particular in what I
eat and drink,
But one's taste improves with culture;
that is all it means, I think.

Can you read as once you used to? Well,
the printing is so bad,
No young folks' eyes can read it like the
books that once we had.
Are you quite as quick of hearing? Please
to say that once again.
Don't I use plain words, your Reverence?
Yes, I often use a cane,

But it 's not because I need it, — no, I al-
ways liked a stick;
And as one might lean upon it, 't is as well
it should be thick.
Oh, I 'm smart, I 'm spry, I 'm lively, —
I can walk, yes, that I can,
On the days I feel like walking, just as
well as you, young man !

*Don't you get a little sleepy after dinner every
day?*
Well, I doze a little, sometimes, but that
always was my way.

Don't you cry a little easier than some twenty
  years ago ?
Well, my heart is very tender, but I think
  't was always so.

Don't you find it sometimes happens that you
  can't recall a name ?
Yes, I know such lots of people, — but my
  memory 's not to blame.
What ! You think my memory 's fail-
  ing ! Why, it 's just as bright and
  clear, —
I remember my great-grandma ! She 's
  been dead these sixty year !

Is your voice a little trembly ? Well, it may
  be, now and then,
But I write as well as ever with a good old-
  fashioned pen ;
It 's the Gillotts make the trouble, — not
  at all my finger-ends, —
That is why my hand looks shaky when I
  sign for dividends.

Don't you stoop a little, walking ? It 's a
  way I 've always had,
I have always been round-shouldered, ever
  since I was a lad.
Don't you hate to tie your shoe-strings ? Yes,
  I own it — that is true.
Don't you tell old stories over ? I am not
  aware I do.

Don't you stay at home of evenings ? Don't
  you love a cushioned seat
In a corner, by the fireside, with your slippers
  on your feet ?
Don't you wear warm fleecy flannels ? Don't
  you muffle up your throat ?
Don't you like to have one help you when
  you 're putting on your coat ?

Don't you like old books you 've dogs-eared,
  you can't remember when ?
Don't you call it late at nine o'clock and go to
  bed at ten ?
How many cronies can you count of all you
  used to know
Who called you by your Christian name some
  fifty years ago ?

How look the prizes to you that used to fire
  your brain ?
You 've reared your mound — how high is it
  above the level plain ?

You 've drained the brimming golden cup that
  made your fancy reel,
You 've slept the giddy potion off, — now tell
  us how you feel !

You 've watched the harvest ripening till every
  stem was cropped,
You 've seen the rose of beauty fade till every
  petal dropped,
You 've told your thought, you 've done your
  task, you 've tracked your dial round,
— I backing down ! Thank Heaven, not
  yet ! I 'm hale and brisk and sound,

And good for many a tussle, as you shall
  live to see;
My shoes are not quite ready yet, — don't
  think you 're rid of me !
Old Parr was in his lusty prime when he
  was older far,
And where will you be if I live to beat old
  Thomas Parr ?

Ah well, — I know, — at every age life has a
  certain charm, —
You 're going ? Come, permit me, please, I
  beg you 'll take my arm.
I take your arm ! Why take your arm ?
  I 'd thank you to be told
I 'm old enough to walk alone, but not so
  very old !

THE SHADOWS

1880

" How many have gone ? " was the ques-
  tion of old
  Ere Time our bright ring of its jewels
    bereft;
Alas ! for too often the death-bell has
  tolled,
  And the question we ask is, " How many
    are left ? "

Bright sparkled the wine; there were *fifty*
  that quaffed;
  For a decade had slipped and had taken
    but three.
How they frolicked and sung, how they
  shouted and laughed,
  Like a school full of boys from their
    benches set free !

There were speeches and toasts, there were
    stories and rhymes,
  The hall shook its sides with their mer-
    riment's noise;
As they talked and lived over the college-
    day times, —
  No wonder they kept their old name of
    " The Boys " !

The seasons moved on in their rhythmical
    flow
  With mornings like maidens that pouted
    or smiled,
With the bud and the leaf and the fruit
    and the snow,
  And the year-books of Time in his al-
    coves were piled.

There were *forty* that gathered where fifty
    had met;
  Some locks had got silvered, some lives
    had grown sere,
But the laugh of the laughers was lusty as
    yet,
  And the song of the singers rose ringing
    and clear.

Still flitted the years; there were *thirty*
    that came;
  " The Boys " they were still, and they
    answered their call;
There were foreheads of care, but the
    smiles were the same,
  And the chorus rang loud through the
    garlanded hall.

The hour - hand moved on, and they
    gathered again;
  There were *twenty* that joined in the
    hymn that was sung;
But ah ! for our song-bird we listened in
    vain, —
  The crystalline tones like a seraph's that
    rung !

How narrow the circle that holds us to-
    night !
  How many the loved ones that greet us
    no more,
As we meet like the stragglers that come
    from the fight,
  Like the mariners flung from a wreck on
    the shore !

We look through the twilight for those we
    have lost;
  The stream rolls between us, and yet
    they seem near;
Already outnumbered by those who have
    crossed,
  Our band is transplanted, its home is not
    here !

They smile on us still — is it only a
    dream ? —
  While fondly or proudly their names we
    recall;
They beckon — they come — they are
    crossing the stream —
  Lo ! the Shadows ! the Shadows ! room
    — room for them all !

BENJAMIN PEIRCE

ASTRONOMER, MATHEMATICIAN
1809–1880

1881

For him the Architect of all
Unroofed our planet's starlit hall;
Through voids unknown to worlds unseen
His clearer vision rose serene.

With us on earth he walked by day,
His midnight path how far away !
We knew him not so well who knew
The patient eyes his soul looked through;

For who his untrod realm could share
Of us that breathe this mortal air,
Or camp in that celestial tent
Whose fringes gild our firmament ?

How vast the workroom where he brought
The viewless implements of thought !
The wit how subtle, how profound,
That Nature's tangled webs unwound;

That through the clouded matrix saw
The crystal planes of shaping law,
Through these the sovereign skill that
    planned, —
The Father's care, the Master's hand !

To him the wandering stars revealed
The secrets in their cradle sealed:

The far-off, frozen sphere that swings
Through ether, zoned with lucid rings;

The orb that rolls in dim eclipse
Wide wheeling round its long ellipse, —
His name Urania writes with these
And stamps it on her Pleiades.

We knew him not ?   Ah, well we knew
The manly soul, so brave, so true,
The cheerful heart that conquered age,
The childlike silver-bearded sage.

No more his tireless thought explores
The azure sea with golden shores;
Rest, wearied frame ! the stars shall keep
A loving watch where thou shalt sleep.

Farewell ! the spirit needs must rise,
So long a tenant of the skies, —
Rise to that home all worlds above
Whose sun is God, whose light is love.

IN THE TWILIGHT

1882

Not bed-time yet ! The night-winds blow,
The stars are out, — full well we know
    The nurse is on the stair,
With hand of ice and cheek of snow,
And frozen lips that whisper low,
"Come, children, it is time to go
    My peaceful couch to share."

No years a wakeful heart can tire;
Not bed-time yet ! Come, stir the fire
    And warm your dear old hands;
Kind Mother Earth we love so well
Has pleasant stories yet to tell
Before we hear the curfew bell;
    Still glow the burning brands.

Not bed-time yet ! We long to know
What wonders time has yet to show,
    What unborn years shall bring;
What ship the Arctic pole shall reach,
What lessons Science waits to teach,
What sermons there are left to preach,
    What poems yet to sing.

What next ? we ask; and is it true
The sunshine falls on nothing new,
    As Israel's king declared ?

Was ocean ploughed with harnessed fire ?
Were nations coupled with a wire ?
Did Tarshish telegraph to Tyre ?
    How Hiram would have stared !

And what if Sheba's curious queen,
Who came to see, — and to be seen, —
    Or something new to seek,
And swooned, as ladies sometimes do,
At sights that thrilled her through and
    through,
Had heard, as she was "coming to,"
    A locomotive's shriek,

And seen a rushing railway train
As she looked out along the plain
    From David's lofty tower, —
A mile of smoke that blots the sky
And blinds the eagles as they fly
Behind the cars that thunder by
    A score of leagues an hour !

See to my *fiat lux* respond
This little slumbering fire-tipped wand, —
    One touch, — it bursts in flame !
Steal me a portrait from the sun, —
One look, — and lo ! the picture done !
Are these old tricks, King Solomon,
    We lying moderns claim ?

Could you have spectroscoped a star ?
If both those mothers at your bar,
    The cruel and the mild,
The young and tender, old and tough,
Had said, "Divide, — you 're right, though
    rough," —
Did old Judea know enough
    To etherize the child ?

These births of time our eyes have seen,
With but a few brief years between;
    What wonder if the text,
For other ages doubtless true,
For coming years will never do, —
Whereof we all should like a few,
    If but to see what next.

If such things have been, such may be;
Who would not like to live and see —
    If Heaven may so ordain —
What waifs undreamed of, yet in store,
The waves that roll forevermore
On life's long beach may cast ashore
    From out the mist-clad main ?

Will Earth to pagan dreams return
To find from misery's painted urn
  That all save hope has flown, —
Of Book and Church and Priest bereft,
The Rock of Ages vainly cleft,
Life's compass gone, its anchor left,
  Left, — lost, — in depths unknown?

Shall Faith the trodden path pursue
The *crux ansata* wearers knew
  Who sleep with folded hands,
Where, like a naked, lidless eye,
The staring Nile rolls wandering by
Those mountain slopes that climb the sky
  Above the drifting sands?

Or shall a nobler Faith return,
Its fanes a purer gospel learn,
  With holier anthems ring,
And teach us that our transient creeds
Were but the perishable seeds
Of harvests sown for larger needs,
  That ripening years shall bring?

Well, let the present do its best,
We trust our Maker for the rest,
  As on our way we plod;
Our souls, full dressed in fleshly suits,
Love air and sunshine, flowers and fruits,
The daisies better than their roots
  Beneath the grassy sod.

Not bed-time yet! The full-blown flower
Of all the year — this evening hour —
  With friendship's flame is bright;
Life still is sweet, the heavens are fair,
Though fields are brown and woods are
    bare,
And many a joy is left to share
  Before we say Good-night!

And when, our cheerful evening past,
The nurse, long waiting, comes at last,
  Ere on her lap we lie
In wearied nature's sweet repose,
At peace with all her waking foes,
Our lips shall murmur, ere they close,
  Good-night! and not Good-by!

A LOVING-CUP SONG

1883

COME, heap the fagots! Ere we go
Again the cheerful hearth shall glow;

We 'll have another blaze, my boys!
When clouds are black and snows are
    white,
Then Christmas logs lend ruddy light
  They stole from summer days, my boys,
  They stole from summer days.

And let the Loving-Cup go round,
The Cup with blessed memories crowned,
  That flows whene'er we meet, my boys;
No draught will hold a drop of sin
If love is only well stirred in
  To keep it sound and sweet, my boys,
  To keep it sound and sweet.

Give me, to pin upon my breast,
The blossoms twain I love the best,
  A rosebud and a pink, my boys;
Their leaves shall nestle next my heart,
Their perfumed breath shall own its part
  In every health we drink, my boys,
  In every health we drink.

The breathing blossoms stir my blood,
Methinks I see the lilacs bud
  And hear the bluebirds sing, my boys;
Why not? Yon lusty oak has seen
Full tenscore years, yet leaflets green
  Peep out with every spring, my boys,
  Peep out with every spring.

Old Time his rusty scythe may whet,
The unmowed grass is glowing yet
  Beneath the sheltering snow, my boys;
And if the crazy dotard ask,
Is love worn out? Is life a task?
  We 'll bravely answer No! my boys,
  We 'll bravely answer No!

For life's bright taper is the same
Love tipped of old with rosy flame
  That heaven's own altar lent, my boys,
To glow in every cup we fill
Till lips are mute and hearts are still,
  Till life and love are spent, my boys,
  Till life and love are spent.

THE GIRDLE OF FRIENDSHIP

1884

SHE gathered at her slender waist
  The beauteous robe she wore;
Its folds a golden belt embraced,
  One rose-hued gem it bore.

The girdle shrank; its lessening round
　Still kept the shining gem,
But now her flowing locks it bound,
　A lustrous diadem.

And narrower still the circlet grew;
　Behold ! a glittering band,
Its roseate diamond set anew,
　Her neck's white column spanned.

Suns rise and set; the straining clasp
　The shortened links resist,
Yet flashes in a bracelet's grasp
　The diamond, on her wrist.

At length, the round of changes past
　The thieving years could bring,
The jewel, glittering to the last,
　Still sparkles in a ring.

So, link by link, our friendships part,
　So loosen, break, and fall,
A narrowing zone; the loving heart
　Lives changeless through them all.

THE LYRE OF ANACREON

1885

THE minstrel of the classic lay
　Of love and wine who sings
Still found the fingers run astray
　That touched the rebel strings.

Of Cadmus he would fain have sung,
　Of Atreus and his line;
But all the jocund echoes rung
　With songs of love and wine.

'Ah, brothers ! I would fain have caught
　Some fresher fancy's gleam;
My truant accents find, unsought,
　The old familiar theme.

Love, Love ! but not the sportive child
　With shaft and twanging bow,
Whose random arrows drove us wild
　Some threescore years ago;

Not Eros, with his joyous laugh,
　The urchin blind and bare,
But Love, with spectacles and staff,
　And scanty, silvered hair.

Our heads with frosted locks are white,
　Our roofs are thatched with snow,
But red, in chilling winter's spite,
　Our hearts and hearthstones glow.

Our old acquaintance, Time, drops in,
　And while the running sands
Their golden thread unheeded spin,
　He warms his frozen hands.

Stay, wingèd hours, too swift, too sweet,
　And waft this message o'er
To all we miss, from all we meet
　On life's fast-crumbling shore:

Say that, to old affection true,
　We hug the narrowing chain
That binds our hearts, — alas, how few
　The links that yet remain !

The fatal touch awaits them all
　That turns the rocks to dust;
From year to year they break and fall, —
　They break, but never rust.

Say if one note of happier strain
　This worn-out harp afford, —
One throb that trembles, not in vain, —
　Their memory lent its chord.

Say that when Fancy closed her wings
　And Passion quenched his fire,
Love, Love, still echoed from the strings
　As from Anacreon's lyre !

THE OLD TUNE

THIRTY-SIXTH VARIATION

1886

THIS shred of song you bid me bring
　Is snatched from fancy's embers;
Ah, when the lips forget to sing,
　The faithful heart remembers !

Too swift the wings of envious Time
　To wait for dallying phrases,
Or woven strands of labored rhyme
　To thread their cunning mazes.

A word, a sigh, and lo, how plain
　Its magic breath discloses
Our life's long vista through a lane
　Of threescore summers' roses !

One language years alone can teach:
  Its roots are young affections
That feel their way to simplest speech
  Through silent recollections.

That tongue is ours.   How few the words
  We need to know a brother !
As simple are the notes of birds,
  Yet well they know each other.

This freezing month of ice and snow
  That brings our lives together
Lends to our year a living glow
  That warms its wintry weather.

So let us meet as eve draws nigh,
  And life matures and mellows,
Till Nature whispers with a sigh,
  "Good-night, my dear old fellows ! "

THE BROKEN CIRCLE

1887

[What is half a century to a place like
Stonehenge ? Nothing dwarfs an individual
life like one of these massive, almost unchang-
ing monuments of an antiquity which refuses
to be measured. . . . The broken circle of
stones, some in their original position, some
bending over like old men, some lying pros-
trate, suggested the thoughts which took form
in the following verses. *Our Hundred Days
in Europe*, pp. 110, 111.]

I STOOD on Sarum's treeless plain,
  The waste that careless Nature owns;
Lone tenants of her bleak domain,
  Loomed huge and gray the Druid stones.

Upheaved in many a billowy mound
  The sea-like, naked turf arose,
Where wandering flocks went nibbling
      round
  The mingled graves of friends and foes.

The Briton, Roman, Saxon, Dane,
  This windy desert roamed in turn;
Unmoved these mighty blocks remain
  Whose story none that lives may learn.

Erect, half buried, slant or prone,
  These awful listeners, blind and dumb,
Hear the strange tongues of tribes unknown,
  As wave on wave they go and come.

"Who are you, giants, whence and why ? "
  I stand and ask in blank amaze;
My soul accepts their mute reply:
  "A mystery, as are you that gaze.

"A silent Orpheus wrought the charm
  From riven rocks their spoils to bring;
A nameless Titan lent his arm
  To range us in our magic ring.

"But Time with still and stealthy stride,
  That climbs and treads and levels all,
That bids the loosening keystone slide,
  And topples down the crumbling wall, —

"Time, that unbuilds the quarried past,
  Leans on these wrecks that press the
      sod;
They slant, they stoop, they fall at last,
  And strew the turf their priests have
      trod.

"No more our altar's wreath of smoke
  Floats up with morning's fragrant dew;
The fires are dead, the ring is broke,
  Where stood the many stand the few."

My thoughts had wandered far away,
  Borne off on Memory's outspread wing,
To where in deepening twilight lay
  The wrecks of friendship's broken ring.

Ah me ! of all our goodly train
  How few will find our banquet hall !
Yet why with coward lips complain
  That this must lean, and that must fall ?

Cold is the Druid's altar-stone,
  Its vanished flame no more returns;
But ours no chilling damp has known, —
  Unchanged, unchanging, still it burns.

So let our broken circle stand
  A wreck, a remnant, yet the same,
While one last, loving, faithful hand
  Still lives to feed its altar-flame!

THE ANGEL-THIEF

1888

TIME is a thief who leaves his tools behind
      him;
  He comes by night, he vanishes at dawn;

We track his footsteps, but we never find
  him:
  Strong locks are broken, massive bolts
    are drawn,

And all around are left the bars and borers,
  The splitting wedges and the prying
    keys,
Such aids as serve the soft-shod vault-ex-
    plorers
  To crack, wrench open, rifle as they
    please.

Ah, these are tools which Heaven in mercy
    lends us !
  When gathering rust has clenched our
    shackles fast,
Time is the angel-thief that Nature sends us
  To break the cramping fetters of our
    past.

Mourn as we may for treasures he has
    taken,
  Poor as we feel of hoarded wealth bereft,
More precious are those implements for-
    saken,
  Found in the wreck his ruthless hands
    have left.

Some lever that a casket's hinge has
    broken
  Pries off a bolt, and lo! our souls are
    free;
Each year some Open Sesame is spoken,
  And every decade drops its master-key.

So as from year to year we count our treas-
    ure,
  Our loss seems less, and larger look our
    gains;
Time's wrongs repaid in more than even
    measure, —
  We lose our jewels, but we break our
    chains.

AFTER THE CURFEW

1889

[The only remaining meeting of the class at
Parker's was in 1890, three present. There
was no poem.]

THE Play is over. While the light
  Yet lingers in the darkening hall,

I come to say a last Good-night
  Before the final *Exeunt all.*

We gathered once, a joyous throng:
  The jovial toasts went gayly round;
With jest, and laugh, and shout, and song,
  We made the floors and walls resound.

We come with feeble steps and slow,
  A little band of four or five,
Left from the wrecks of long ago,
  Still pleased to find ourselves alive.

Alive ! How living, too, are they
  Whose memories it is ours to share!
Spread the long table's full array, —
  There sits a ghost in every chair!

One breathing form no more, alas !
  Amid our slender group we see;
With him we still remained " The Class," —
  Without his presence what are we ?

The hand we ever loved to clasp, —
  That tireless hand which knew no rest, —
Loosed from affection's clinging grasp,
  Lies nerveless on the peaceful breast.

The beaming eye, the cheering voice,
  That lent to life a generous glow,
Whose every meaning said " Rejoice,"
  We see, we hear, no more below.

The air seems darkened by his loss,
  Earth's shadowed features look less fair,
And heavier weighs the daily cross
  His willing shoulders helped us bear.

Why mourn that we, the favored few
  Whom grasping Time so long has spared
Life's sweet illusions to pursue,
  The common lot of age have shared?

In every pulse of Friendship's heart
  There breeds unfelt a throb of pain, —
One hour must rend its links apart,
  Though years on years have forged the
    chain.

So ends " The Boys," — a lifelong play.
  We too must hear the Prompter's call
To fairer scenes and brighter day:
  Farewell ! I let the curtain fall.

POEMS FROM THE AUTOCRAT OF THE BREAKFAST-TABLE

1857–1858

[THE collection under this heading is not complete, since a few of the poems had been placed by the author in other divisions. Inasmuch as the poems when first printed were in many cases introduced by a prose passage, these introductions are here reproduced, without the editorial brackets. The same method has been followed with the two succeeding groups.]

THE CHAMBERED NAUTILUS

We need not trouble ourselves about the distinction between this [the Pearly Nautilus] and the Paper Nautilus, the *Argonauta* of the ancients. The name applied to both shows that each has long been compared to a ship, as you may see more fully in *Webster's Dictionary* or the *Encyclopedia*, to which he refers. If you will look into Roget's *Bridgewater Treatise* you will find a figure of one of these shells and a section of it. The last will show you the series of enlarging compartments successively dwelt in by the animal that inhabits the shell, which is built in a widening spiral. [This poem seemed to share with Dorothy Q. Dr. Holmes's interest, if one may judge by the frequency with which he chose it for reading or for autograph albums. He says on receipt of an album from the Princess of Wales, " I copied into it the last verse of a poem of mine called *The Chambered Nautilus*, as I have often done for plain republican albums."]

THIS is the ship of pearl, which, poets feign,
    Sails the unshadowed main, —
    The venturous bark that flings
On the sweet summer wind its purpled wings
In gulfs enchanted, where the Siren sings,
    And coral reefs lie bare,
Where the cold sea-maids rise to sun their streaming hair.

Its webs of living gauze no more unfurl;
    Wrecked is the ship of pearl !
    And every chambered cell,
Where its dim dreaming life was wont to dwell,
As the frail tenant shaped his growing shell,
    Before thee lies revealed, —
Its irised ceiling rent, its sunless crypt unsealed !

Year after year beheld the silent toil
    That spread his lustrous coil;
    Still, as the spiral grew,
He left the past year's dwelling for the new,
Stole with soft step its shining archway through,
    Built up its idle door,
Stretched in his last-found home, and knew the old no more.

Thanks for the heavenly message brought by thee,
    Child of the wandering sea,
    Cast from her lap, forlorn !
From thy dead lips a clearer note is born
Than ever Triton blew from wreathèd horn !
    While on mine ear it rings,
Through the deep caves of thought I hear a voice that sings : —

Build thee more stately mansions, O my soul,
    As the swift seasons roll !
    Leave thy low-vaulted past !
Let each new temple, nobler than the last,
Shut thee from heaven with a dome more vast,

Till thou at length art free,
Leaving thine outgrown shell by life's un-
    resting sea !

SUN AND SHADOW

[The isle where this poem was written was
Naushon, already celebrated in the poems *To
Governor Swain* and *The Island Hunting-Song*.]
How can a man help writing poetry in such a
place ?   When the sun is in the west, vessels
sailing in an easterly direction look bright or
dark to one who observes them from the north
or south, according to the tack they are sailing
upon. Watching them from one of the windows
of the great mansion, I saw these perpetual
changes, and moralized thus : —

As I look from the isle, o'er its billows of
    green,
  To the billows of foam-crested blue,
Yon bark, that afar in the distance is
    seen,
Half dreaming, my eyes will pursue:
Now dark in the shadow, she scatters the
    spray
  As the chaff in the stroke of the flail;
Now white as the sea-gull, she flies on her
    way,
  The sun gleaming bright on her sail.

Yet her pilot is thinking of dangers to
    shun, —
  Of breakers that whiten and roar;
How little he cares, if in shadow or sun
  They see him who gaze from the shore !
He looks to the beacon that looms from the
    reef,
  To the rock that is under his lee,
As he drifts on the blast, like a wind-
    wafted leaf,
  O'er the gulfs of the desolate sea.

Thus drifting afar to the dim-vaulted caves
  Where life and its ventures are laid,
The dreamers who gaze while we battle
    the waves
  May see us in sunshine or shade;
Yet true to our course, though the shadows
    grow dark,
  We 'll trim our broad sail as before,
And stand by the rudder that governs the
    bark,
  Nor ask how we look from the shore !

MUSA

The throbbing flushes of the poetical inter-
mittent have been coming over me from time
to time of late. Did you ever see that elec-
trical experiment which consists in passing a
flash through letters of goldleaf in a darkened
room, whereupon some name or legend springs
out of the darkness in characters of fire ?
There are songs all written out in my soul,
which I could read, if the flash might pass
through them, — but the fire must come down
from heaven. Ah ! but what if the stormy
nimbus of youthful passion has blown by, and
one asks for lightning from the ragged *cirrus*
of dissolving aspirations, or the silvered cumu-
lus of sluggish satiety ? I will call on her
whom the dead poets believed in, whom living
ones no longer worship, — the immortal maid,
who, name her what you will, — Goddess,
Muse, Spirit of Beauty, — sits by the pillow
of every youthful poet and bends over his pale
forehead until her tresses lie upon his cheek
and rain their gold into his dream.

O MY lost beauty ! — hast thou folded
    quite
  Thy wings of morning light
  Beyond those iron gates
Where Life crowds hurrying to the hag-
    gard Fates,
And Age upon his mound of ashes waits
  To chill our fiery dreams,
Hot from the heart of youth plunged in his
    icy streams ?

Leave me not fading in these weeds of
    care,
  Whose flowers are silvered hair !
  Have I not loved thee long,
Though my young lips have often done
    thee wrong,
And vexed thy heaven-tuned ear with care-
    less song ?
  Ah, wilt thou yet return,
Bearing thy rose-hued torch, and bid thine
    altar burn ?

Come to me ! — I will flood thy silent
    shrine
  With my soul's sacred wine,
  And heap thy marble floors
As the wild spice-trees waste their **fragrant**
    stores,
In leafy islands walled with madrepores

And lapped in Orient seas,
When all their feathery palms toss, plume-
    like, in the breeze.

Come to me!—thou shalt feed on honeyed
    words,
    Sweeter than song of birds;—
    No wailing bulbul's throat,
No melting dulcimer's melodious note
When o'er the midnight wave its murmurs
    float,
    Thy ravished sense might soothe
With flow so liquid-soft, with strain so vel-
    vet smooth.

Thou shalt be decked with jewels, like a
    queen,
    Sought in those bowers of green
    Where loop the clustered vines
And the close-clinging dulcamara twines, —
Pure pearls of Maydew where the moon-
    light shines,
    And Summer's fruited gems,
And coral pendants shorn from Autumn's
    berried stems.

Sit by me drifting on the sleepy waves, —
    Or stretched by grass-grown graves,
    Whose gray, high-shouldered stones,
Carved with old names Life's time-worn
    roll disowns,
Lean, lichen-spotted, o'er the crumbled
    bones
    Still slumbering where they lay
While the sad Pilgrim watched to scare
    the wolf away.

Spread o'er my couch thy visionary wing !
    Still let me dream and sing, —
    Dream of that winding shore
Where scarlet cardinals bloom — for me
    no more, —
The stream with heaven beneath its liquid
    floor,
    And clustering nenuphars
Sprinkling its mirrored blue like golden-
    chaliced stars !

Come while their balms the linden-blos-
    soms shed ! —
    Come while the rose is red, —
    While blue-eyed Summer smiles
On the green ripples round yon sunken
    piles

Washed by the moon-wave warm from In-
    dian isles,
    And on the sultry air
The chestnuts spread their palms like holy
    men in prayer !

Oh for thy burning lips to fire my brain
    With thrills of wild, sweet pain ! —
    On life's autumnal blast,
Like shrivelled leaves, youth's passion-
    flowers are cast, —
Once loving thee, we love thee to the
    last ! —
    Behold thy new-decked shrine,
And hear once more the voice that breathed
    " Forever thine ! "

A PARTING HEALTH

TO J. L. MOTLEY

[Upon his return to England after the publi-
cation of the *History of the Dutch Republic* in
1857.]

YES, we knew we must lose him, — though
    friendship may claim
To blend her green leaves with the laurels
    of fame;
Though fondly, at parting, we call him our
    own,
'T is the whisper of love when the bugle has
    blown.

As the rider that rests with the spur on his
    heel,
As the guardsman that sleeps in his corse-
    let of steel,
As the archer that stands with his shaft on
    the string,
He stoops from his toil to the garland we
    bring.

What pictures yet slumber unborn in his
    loom,
Till their warriors shall breathe and their
    beauties shall bloom,
While the tapestry lengthens the life-glow-
    ing dyes
That caught from our sunsets the stain of
    their skies !

In the alcoves of death, in the charnels of
    time,

Where flit the gaunt spectres of passion and
crime,
There are triumphs untold, there are mar-
tyrs unsung,
There are heroes yet silent to speak with
his tongue !

Let us hear the proud story which time has
bequeathed
From lips that are warm with the freedom
they breathed !
Let him summon its tyrants, and tell us
their doom,
Though he sweep the black past like Van
Tromp with his broom !

. . . .

The dream flashes by, for the west-winds
awake
On pampas, on prairie, o'er mountain and
lake,
To bathe the swift bark, like a sea-girdled
shrine,
With incense they stole from the rose and
the pine.

So fill a bright cup with the sunlight that
gushed
When the dead summer's jewels were tram-
pled and crushed:
THE TRUE KNIGHT OF LEARNING, — the
world holds him dear, —
Love bless him, Joy crown him, God speed
his career !

WHAT WE ALL THINK

I think few persons have a greater disgust
for plagiarism than myself. If I had even sus-
pected that the idea in question was borrowed,
I should have disclaimed originality, or men-
tioned the coincidence, as I once did in a case
where I had happened to hit on an idea of
Swift's. — But what shall I do with these verses
I was going to read you ? I am afraid that
half mankind would accuse me of stealing their
thoughts, if I printed them. I am convinced
that several of you, especially if you are getting
a little on in life, will recognize some of these
sentiments as having passed through your con-
sciousness at some time. I can't help it, — it
is too late now. The verses are written, and
you must have them.

THAT age was older once than now,
In spite of locks untimely shed,

Or silvered on the youthful brow;
That babes make love and children wed.

That sunshine had a heavenly glow,
Which faded with those " good old days"
When winters came with deeper snow,
And autumns with a softer haze.

That — mother, sister, wife, or child —
The "best of women" each has known.
Were school-boys ever half so wild ?
How young the grandpapas have grown !

That but for this our souls were free,
And but for that our lives were blest;
That in some season yet to be
Our cares will leave us time to rest.

Whene'er we groan with ache or pain, —
Some common ailment of the race, —
Though doctors think the matter plain, —
That ours is " a peculiar case."

That when like babes with fingers burned
We count one bitter maxim more,
Our lesson all the world has learned,
And men are wiser than before.

That when we sob o'er fancied woes,
The angels hovering overhead
Count every pitying drop that flows,
And love us for the tears we shed.

That when we stand with tearless eye
And turn the beggar from our door
They still approve us when we sigh,
" Ah, had I but one thousand more ! "

Though temples crowd the crumbled brink
O'erhanging truth's eternal flow,
Their tablets bold with what we think,
Their echoes dumb to what we know;

That one unquestioned text we read,
All doubt beyond, all fear above,
Nor crackling pile nor cursing creed
Can burn or blot it: GOD IS LOVE !

SPRING HAS COME

INTRA MUROS

THE sunbeams, lost for half a year,
Slant through my pane their morning
rays;

For dry northwesters cold and clear,
  The east blows in its thin blue haze.

And first the snowdrop's bells are seen,
  Then close against the sheltering wall
The tulip's horn of dusky green,
  The peony's dark unfolding ball.

The golden-chaliced crocus burns;
  The long narcissus-blades appear;
The cone-beaked hyacinth returns
  To light her blue-flamed chandelier.

The willow's whistling lashes, wrung
  By the wild winds of gusty March,
With sallow leaflets lightly strung,
  Are swaying by the tufted larch.

The elms have robed their slender spray
  With full-blown flower and embryo leaf;
Wide o'er the clasping arch of day
  Soars like a cloud their hoary chief.

See the proud tulip's flaunting cup,
  That flames in glory for an hour, —
Behold it withering, — then look up, —
  How meek the forest monarch's flower !

When wake the violets, Winter dies;
  When sprout the elm-buds, Spring is
    near;
When lilacs blossom, Summer cries,
  " Bud, little roses !   Spring is here ! "

The windows blush with fresh bouquets,
  Cut with their Maydew on the lips;
The radish all its bloom displays,
  Pink as Aurora's finger-tips.

Nor less the flood of light that showers
  On beauty's changed corolla-shades, —
The walks are gay as bridal bowers
  With rows of many-petalled maids.

The scarlet shell-fish click and clash
  In the blue barrow where they slide;
The horseman, proud of streak and splash,
  Creeps homeward from his morning ride.

Here comes the dealer's awkward string,
  With neck in rope and tail in knot, —
Rough colts, with careless country-swing,
  In lazy walk or slouching trot.

Wild filly from the mountain-side,
  Doomed to the close and chafing thills,
Lend me thy long, untiring stride
  To seek with thee thy western hills !

I hear the whispering voice of Spring,
  The thrush's trill, the robin's cry,
Like some poor bird with prisoned wing
  That sits and sings, but longs to fly.

Oh for one spot of living green, —
  One little spot where leaves can grow, —
To love unblamed, to walk unseen,
  To dream above, to sleep below !

PROLOGUE

Of course I wrote the prologue I was asked
to write. I did not see the play, though. I
knew there was a young lady in it, and that
somebody was in love with her, and she was in
love with him, and somebody (an old tutor, I
believe) wanted to interfere, and, very natur-
ally, the young lady was too sharp for him.
The play of course ends charmingly; there is
a general reconciliation, and all concerned form
a line and take each other's hands, as people
always do after they have made up their quar-
rels, — and then the curtain falls, — if it does
not stick, as it commonly does at private theat-
rical exhibitions, in which case a boy is detailed
to pull it down, which he does, blushing vio-
lently.

Now, then, for my prologue. I am not going
to change my cæsuras and cadences for any-
body ; so if you do not like the heroic, or iam-
bic trimeter brachycatalectic, you had better
not wait to hear it.

A PROLOGUE ?   Well, of course the ladies
    know, —
I have my doubts.   No matter, — here we
    go !
What is a Prologue ?   Let our Tutor
    teach:
Pro means beforehand; logos stands for
    speech.
'T is like the harper's prelude on the
    strings,
The prima donna's courtesy ere she sings;
Prologues in metre are to other pros
As worsted stockings are to engine-hose.
" The world 's a stage," — as Shakespeare
    said, one day;
The stage a world — was what he meant
    to say.

The outside world's a blunder, that is
    clear;
The real world that Nature meant is here.
Here every foundling finds its lost mamma;
Each rogue, repentant, melts his stern papa;
Misers relent, the spendthrift's debts are
    paid,
The cheats are taken in the traps they laid;
One after one the troubles all are past
Till the fifth act comes right side up at
    last,
When the young couple, old folks, rogues,
    and all,
Join hands, *so* happy at the curtain's fall.
Here suffering virtue ever finds relief,
And black-browed ruffians always come to
    grief.
When the lorn damsel, with a frantic
    screech,
And cheeks as hueless as a brandy-peach,
Cries, "Help, kyind Heaven!" and drops
    upon her knees
On the green — baize, — beneath the (can-
    vas) trees, —
See to her side avenging Valor fly: —
"Ha! Villain! Draw! Now, Terraitorr,
    yield or die!"
When the poor hero flounders in despair,
Some dear lost uncle turns up millionnaire,
Clasps the young scapegrace with paternal
    joy,
Sobs on his neck, "*My boy!* My boy!!
    MY BOY!!!"

Ours, then, sweet friends, the real world
    to-night,
Of love that conquers in disaster's spite.
Ladies, attend! While woeful cares and
    doubt
Wrong the soft passion in the world with-
    out,
Though fortune scowl, though prudence
    interfere,
One thing is certain: Love will triumph
    here!
Lords of creation, whom your ladies rule, —
The world's great masters, when you're
    out of school, —
Learn the brief moral of our evening's play:
Man has his will, — but woman has her
    way!
While man's dull spirit toils in smoke and
    fire,
Woman's swift instinct threads the electric
    wire, —

The magic bracelet stretched beneath the
    waves
Beats the black giant with his score of
    slaves.
All earthly powers confess your sovereign
    art
But that one rebel, — woman's wilful heart.
All foes you master, but a woman's wit
Lets daylight through you ere you know
    you're hit.
So, just to picture what her art can do,
Hear an old story, made as good as new.

Rudolph, professor of the headsman's trade,
Alike was famous for his arm and blade.
One day a prisoner Justice had to kill
Knelt at the block to test the artist's skill.
Bare-armed, swart-visaged, gaunt, and
    shaggy-browed,
Rudolph the headsman rose above the
    crowd.
His falchion lighted with a sudden gleam,
As the pike's armor flashes in the stream.
He sheathed his blade; he turned as if to
    go;
The victim knelt, still waiting for the blow.
"Why strikest not? Perform thy mur-
    derous act,"
The prisoner said. (His voice was slightly
    cracked.)
"Friend, I *have* struck," the artist straight
    replied;
"Wait but one moment, and yourself de-
    cide."
He held his snuff-box, — "Now then, if
    you please!"
The prisoner sniffed, and, with a crashing
    sneeze,
Off his head tumbled, — bowled along the
    floor, —
Bounced down the steps; — the prisoner
    said no more!
Woman! thy falchion is a glittering eye;
If death lurk in it, oh how sweet to die!
Thou takest hearts as Rudolph took the
    head;
We die with love, and never dream we're
    dead!

LATTER-DAY WARNINGS

I should have felt more nervous about the
late comet, if I had thought the world was
ripe. But it is very green yet, if I am not
mistaken; and besides, there is a great deal

of coal to use up, which I cannot bring myself
to think was made for nothing. If certain
things, which seem to me essential to a millen-
nium, had come to pass, I should have been
frightened; but they have n't.

WHEN legislators keep the law,
  When banks dispense with bolts and
    locks,
When berries — whortle, rasp, and straw —
  Grow bigger *downwards* through the
    box, —

When he that selleth house or land
  Shows leak in roof or flaw in right, —
When haberdashers choose the stand
  Whose window hath the broadest light, —

When preachers tell us all they think,
  And party leaders all they mean, —
When what we pay for, that we drink,
  From real grape and coffee-bean, —

When lawyers take what they would give,
  And doctors give what they would take, —
When city fathers eat to live,
  Save when they fast for conscience'
    sake, —

When one that hath a horse on sale
  Shall bring his merit to the proof,
Without a lie for every nail
  That holds the iron on the hoof, —

When in the usual place for rips
  Our gloves are stitched with special care,
And guarded well the whalebone tips
  Where first umbrellas need repair, —

When Cuba's weeds have quite forgot
  The power of suction to resist,
And claret-bottles harbor not
  Such dimples as would hold your fist, —

When publishers no longer steal,
  And pay for what they stole before, —
When the first locomotive's wheel
  Rolls through the Hoosac Tunnel's
    bore; —

Till then let Cumming blaze away,
  And Miller's saints blow up the globe;
But when you see that blessed day,
  Then order your ascension robe!

ALBUM VERSES

WHEN Eve had led her lord away,
  And Cain had killed his brother,
The stars and flowers, the poets say,
  Agreed with one another

To cheat the cunning tempter's art,
  And teach the race its duty,
By keeping on its wicked heart
  Their eyes of light and beauty.

A million sleepless lids, they say,
  Will be at least a warning;
And so the flowers would watch by day,
  The stars from eve to morning.

On hill and prairie, field and lawn,
  Their dewy eyes upturning,
The flowers still watch from reddening
    dawn
  Till western skies are burning.

Alas! each hour of daylight tells
  A tale of shame so crushing,
That some turn white as sea-bleached
    shells,
  And some are always blushing.

But when the patient stars look down
  On all their light discovers,
The traitor's smile, the murderer's frown,
  The lips of lying lovers,

They try to shut their saddening eyes,
  And in the vain endeavor
We see them twinkling in the skies,
  And so they wink forever.

A GOOD TIME GOING!

[A farewell poem to Charles Mackay.]

BRAVE singer of the coming time,
  Sweet minstrel of the joyous present,
Crowned with the noblest wreath of rhyme,
  The holly-leaf of Ayrshire's peasant,
Good by! Good by! — Our hearts and
    hands,
  Our lips in honest Saxon phrases,
Cry, God be with him, till he stands
  His feet among the English daisies!

'T is here we part; — for other eyes
  The busy deck, the fluttering streamer,
The dripping arms that plunge and rise,
  The waves in foam, the ship in tremor,
The kerchiefs waving from the pier,
  The cloudy pillar gliding o'er him,
The deep blue desert, lone and drear,
  With heaven above and home before
    him !

His home ! — the Western giant smiles,
  And twirls the spotty globe to find it; —
This little speck the British Isles ?
  'T is but a freckle, — never mind it !
He laughs, and all his prairies roll,
  Each gurgling cataract roars and chuck-
    les,
And ridges stretched from pole to pole
  Heave till they crack their iron knuckles !

But Memory blushes at the sneer,
  And Honor turns with frown defiant,
And Freedom, leaning on her spear,
  Laughs louder than the laughing giant:
" An islet is a world," she said,
  " When glory with its dust has blended,
And Britain keeps her noble dead
  Till earth and seas and skies are rended ! "

Beneath each swinging forest-bough
  Some arm as stout in death reposes, —
From wave-washed foot to heaven-kissed
    brow
  Her valor's life-blood runs in roses;
Nay, let our brothers of the West
  Write smiling in their florid pages,
One half her soil has walked the rest
  In poets, heroes, martyrs, sages !

Hugged in the clinging billow's clasp,
  From sea - weed fringe to mountain
    heather,
The British oak with rooted grasp
  Her slender handful holds together; —
With cliffs of white and bowers of green,
  And Ocean narrowing to caress her,
And hills and threaded streams between,—
  Our little mother isle, God bless her !

In earth's broad temple where we stand,
  Fanned by the eastern gales that brought
    us,
We hold the missal in our hand,
  Bright with the lines our Mother taught
    us.

Where'er its blazoned page betrays
  The glistening links of gilded fetters,
Behold, the half-turned leaf displays
  Her rubric stained in crimson letters !

Enough ! To speed a parting friend
  'T is vain alike to speak and listen; —
Yet stay, — these feeble accents blend
  With rays of light from eyes that glis-
    ten.
Good by! once more, — and kindly tell
  In words of peace the young world's
    story, —
And say, besides, we love too well
  Our mothers' soil, our fathers' glory !

THE LAST BLOSSOM

THOUGH young no more, we still would
    dream
  Of beauty's dear deluding wiles;
The leagues of life to graybeards seem
  Shorter than boyhood's lingering miles.

Who knows a woman's wild caprice ?
  It played with Goethe's silvered hair,
And many a Holy Father's " niece "
  Has softly smoothed the papal chair.

When sixty bids us sigh in vain
  To melt the heart of sweet sixteen,
We think upon those ladies twain
  Who loved so well the tough old Dean.

We see the Patriarch's wintry face,
  The maid of Egypt's dusky glow,
And dream that Youth and Age embrace,
  As April violets fill with snow.

Tranced in her lord's Olympian smile
  His lotus-loving Memphian lies, —
The musky daughter of the Nile,
  With plaited hair and almond eyes.

Might we but share one wild caress
  Ere life's autumnal blossoms fall,
And Earth's brown, clinging lips impress
  The long cold kiss that waits us all !

My bosom heaves, remembering yet
  The morning of that blissful day,
When Rose, the flower of spring, I met,
  And gave my raptured soul away.

Flung from her eyes of purest blue,
   A lasso, with its leaping chain,
Light as a loop of larkspurs, flew
   O'er sense and spirit, heart and brain.

Thou com'st to cheer my waning age,
   Sweet vision, waited for so long !
Dove that would seek the poet's cage
   Lured by the magic breath of song !

She blushes ! Ah, reluctant maid,
   Love's *drapeau rouge* the truth has told !
O'er girlhood's yielding barricade
   Floats the great Leveller's crimson fold !

Come to my arms ! — love heeds not years;
   No frost the bud of passion knows.
Ha ! what is this my frenzy hears ?
   A voice behind me uttered, — Rose !

Sweet was her smile, — but not for me;
   Alas! when woman looks *too* kind,
Just turn your foolish head and see, —
   Some youth is walking close behind !

CONTENTMENT

" Man wants but little here below "

Should you like to hear what moderate wishes
life brings one to at last ? I used to be very
ambitious, — wasteful, extravagant, and lux-
urious in all my fancies. Read too much in
the *Arabian Nights*. Must have the lamp, —
could n't do without the ring. Exercise every
morning on the brazen horse. Plump down
into castles as full of little milk-white prin-
cesses as a nest is of young sparrows. All
love me dearly at once. — Charming idea of
life, but too high-colored for the reality. I
have outgrown all this; my tastes have be-
come exceedingly primitive, — almost, perhaps,
ascetic. We carry happiness into our condi-
tion, but must not hope to find it there. I
think you will be willing to hear some lines
which embody the subdued and limited desires
of my maturity.

LITTLE I ask; my wants are few;
   I only wish a hut of stone,
(A *very plain* brown stone will do,)
   That I may call my own; —
And close at hand is such a one,
In yonder street that fronts the sun.

Plain food is quite enough for me;
   Three courses are as good as ten; —
If Nature can subsist on three,
   Thank Heaven for three. Amen !
I always thought cold victual nice; —
My *choice* would be vanilla-ice.

I care not much for gold or land; —
   Give me a mortgage here and there, —
Some good bank-stock, some note of
     hand,
   Or trifling railroad share, —
I only ask that Fortune send
A *little* more than I shall spend.

Honors are silly toys, I know,
   And titles are but empty names;
I would, *perhaps*, be Plenipo, —
   But only near St. James ;
I 'm very sure I should not care
To fill our Gubernator's chair.

Jewels are baubles; 't is a sin
   To care for such unfruitful things; —
One good-sized diamond in a pin, —
   Some, *not so large*, in rings, —
A ruby, and a pearl, or so,
Will do for me; — I laugh at show.

My dame should dress in cheap attire;
   (Good, heavy silks are never dear;) —
I own perhaps I *might* desire
   Some shawls of true Cashmere, —
Some marrowy crapes of China silk,
Like wrinkled skins on scalded milk.

I would not have the horse I drive
   So fast that folks must stop and stare;
An easy gait — two forty-five —
   Suits me; I do not care; —
Perhaps, for just a *single spurt*,
Some seconds less would do no hurt.

Of pictures, I should like to own
   Titians and Raphaels three or four, —
I love so much their style and tone,
   One Turner, and no more,
(A landscape, — foreground golden dirt, —
The sunshine painted with a squirt.)

Of books but few, — some fifty score
   For daily use, and bound for wear;
The rest upon an upper floor; —
   Some *little* luxury *there*
Of red morocco's gilded gleam
And vellum rich as country cream.

Busts, cameos, gems, — such things as
  these,
  Which others often show for pride,
I value for their power to please,
  And selfish churls deride; —
One Stradivarius, I confess,
Two Meerschaums, I would fain possess.

Wealth's wasteful tricks I will not learn,
  Nor ape the glittering upstart fool; —
Shall not carved tables serve my turn,
  But *all* must be of buhl?
Give grasping pomp its double share, —
  I ask but *one* recumbent chair.

Thus humble let me live and die,
  Nor long for Midas' golden touch;
If Heaven more generous gifts deny,
  I shall not miss them *much*, —
Too grateful for the blessing lent
Of simple tastes and mind content!

ÆSTIVATION

AN UNPUBLISHED POEM, BY MY LATE LATIN TUTOR

Your talking Latin — said I — reminds me
of an odd trick of one of my old tutors. He
read so much of that language, that his Eng-
lish half turned into it. He got caught in
town, one hot summer, in pretty close quarters,
and wrote, or began to write, a series of city
pastorals. Eclogues he called them, and meant
to have published them by subscription. I re-
member some of his verses, if you want to hear
them. — You, Sir (addressing myself to the
divinity-student), and all such as have been
through college, or what is the same thing,
received an honorary degree, will understand
them without a dictionary. The old man had
a great deal to say about "æstivation," as he
called it, in opposition, as one might say, to
hibernation. Intramural æstivation, or town-
life in summer, he would say, is a peculiar
form of suspended existence, or semi-asphyxia.
One wakes up from it about the beginning of
the last week in September. This is what I
remember of his poem: —

IN candent ire the solar splendor flames;
The foles, languescent, pend from arid
  rames;
His humid front the cive, anheling, wipes,
And dreams of erring on ventiferous ripes.

How dulce to vive occult to mortal eyes,
Dorm on the herb with none to supervise,
Carp the suave berries from the crescent
  vine,
And bibe the flow from longicaudate kine!

To me, alas! no verdurous visions come,
Save yon exiguous pool's conferva-scum, —
No concave vast repeats the tender hue
That laves my milk-jug with celestial blue!

Me wretched! Let me curr to quercine
  shades!
Effund your albid hausts, lactiferous maids!
Oh, might I vole to some umbrageous
  clump, —
Depart, — be off, — excede, — evade, —
  erump!

THE DEACON'S MASTERPIECE

OR, THE WONDERFUL "ONE-HOSS SHAY"

A LOGICAL STORY

[The following note was prefaced to the
poem when it appeared in an illustrated edi-
tion.]
  "The Wonderful One-Hoss Shay" is a per-
fectly intelligible conception, whatever ma-
terial difficulties it presents. It is conceivable
that a being of an order superior to human-
ity should so understand the conditions of
matter that he could construct a machine
which should go to pieces, if not into its con-
stituent atoms, at a given moment of the
future. The mind may take a certain pleasure
in this picture of the impossible. The event
follows as a logical consequence of the presup-
posed condition of things.
  There is a practical lesson to be got out of
the story. Observation shows us in what point
any particular mechanism is most likely to
give way. In a wagon, for instance, the weak
point is where the axle enters the hub or nave.
When the wagon breaks down, three times out
of four, I think, it is at this point that the
accident occurs. The workman should see to
it that this part should never give way; then
find the next vulnerable place, and so on, until
he arrives logically at the perfect result at-
tained by the deacon.

HAVE you heard of the wonderful one-hoss
  shay,
That was built in such a logical way
It ran a hundred years to a day,

And then, of a sudden, it — ah, but stay,
I 'll tell you what happened without delay,
Scaring the parson into fits,
Frightening people out of their wits, —
Have you ever heard of that, I say ?

Seventeen hundred and fifty-five.
Georgius Secundus was then alive, —
Snuffy old drone from the German hive.
That was the year when Lisbon-town
Saw the earth open and gulp her down,
And Braddock's army was done so brown,
Left without a scalp to its crown.
It was on the terrible Earthquake-day
That the Deacon finished the one-hoss shay.

Now in building of chaises, I tell you what,
There is always *somewhere* a weakest spot, —
In hub, tire, felloe, in spring or thill,
In panel, or crossbar, or floor, or sill,
In screw, bolt, thoroughbrace, — lurking
    still,
Find it somewhere you must and will, —
Above or below, or within or without, —
And that 's the reason, beyond a doubt,
That a chaise *breaks down*, but does n't
    wear out.

But the Deacon swore (as Deacons do,
With an " I dew vum," or an " I tell *yeou* ")
He would build one shay to beat the taown
'N' the keounty 'n' all the kentry raoun';
It should be so built that it *could n'* break
    daown:
" Fur," said the Deacon, " 't 's mighty plain
Thut the weakes' place mus' stan' the'
    strain;
'N' the way t' fix it, uz I maintain,
        Is only jest
T' make that place uz strong uz the rest."

So the Deacon inquired of the village folk
Where he could find the strongest oak,
That could n't be split nor bent nor broke, —
That was for spokes and floor and sills;
He sent for lancewood to make the thills;
The crossbars were ash, from the
    straightest trees,
The panels of white-wood, that cuts like
    cheese,
But lasts like iron for things like these;
The hubs of logs from the " Settler's
    ellum," —
Last of its timber, — they could n't sell
    'em,

Never an axe had seen their chips,
And the wedges flew from between their
    lips,
Their blunt ends frizzled like celery-tips;
Step and prop-iron, bolt and screw,
Spring, tire, axle, and linchpin too,
Steel of the finest, bright and blue;
Thoroughbrace bison-skin, thick and wide;
Boot, top, dasher, from tough old hide
Found in the pit when the tanner died.
That was the way he " put her through."
" There ! " said the Deacon, " naow she 'll
    dew ! "

Do ! I tell you, I rather guess
She was a wonder, and nothing less !
Colts grew horses, beards turned gray,
Deacon and deaconess dropped away,
Children and grandchildren — where were
    they ?
But there stood the stout old one-hoss shay
As fresh as on Lisbon-earthquake-day !

EIGHTEEN HUNDRED; — it came and found
The Deacon's masterpiece strong and
    sound.
Eighteen hundred increased by ten; —
" Hahnsum kerridge " they called it then.
Eighteen hundred and twenty came; —
Running as usual; much the same.
Thirty and forty at last arrive,
And then come fifty, and FIFTY-FIVE.

Little of all we value here
Wakes on the morn of its hundredth year
Without both feeling and looking queer.
In fact, there 's nothing that keeps its
    youth,
So far as I know, but a tree and truth.
(This is a moral that runs at large;
Take it. — You 're welcome. — No **extra**
    charge.)

FIRST OF NOVEMBER, — the Earthquake-
    day, —
There are traces of age in the one-hoss
    shay,
A general flavor of mild decay,
But nothing local, as one may say.
There could n't be, — for the Deacon's art
Had made it so like in every part
That there was n't a chance for one to
    start.
For the wheels were just as strong as the
    thills,

And the floor was just as strong as the sills,
And the panels just as strong as the floor,
And the whipple-tree neither less nor
    more,
And the back crossbar as strong as the fore,
And spring and axle and hub *encore.*
And yet, *as a whole,* it is past a doubt
In another hour it will be *worn out!*

First of November, 'Fifty-five!
This morning the parson takes a drive.
Now, small boys, get out of the way!
Here comes the wonderful one-hoss shay,
Drawn by a rat-tailed, ewe-necked bay.
"Huddup!" said the parson. — Off went
    they.
The parson was working his Sunday's
    text, —
Had got to *fifthly,* and stopped perplexed
At what the — Moses — was coming next.
All at once the horse stood still,
Close by the meet'n'-house on the hill.
First a shiver, and then a thrill,
Then something decidedly like a spill, —
And the parson was sitting upon a rock,
At half past nine by the meet'n'-house
    clock, —
Just the hour of the Earthquake shock!
What do you think the parson found,
When he got up and stared around?
The poor old chaise in a heap or mound,
As if it had been to the mill and ground!
You see, of course, if you 're not a dunce,
How it went to pieces all at once, —
All at once, and nothing first, —
Just as bubbles do when they burst.

End of the wonderful one-hoss shay.
Logic is logic. That 's all I say.

PRELUDE

[In introducing *Parson Turell's Legacy,* the Autocrat amused his readers with an account of his friend the Professor's experiments in chloroform. The Professor was about to read the poem, but upon delivering the *Prelude,* his MS. was taken from him by the Autocrat, who finished the reading.]

I 'M the fellah that tole one day
The tale of the won'erful one-hoss-shay.
Wan' to hear another? Say.
— Funny, was n' it? Made *me* laugh, —
I 'm too modest, I am, by half, —

Made me laugh 's though I sh'd split, —
Cahn' a fellah like fellah's own wit?
— Fellahs keep sayin', — "Well, now that 's
    nice:
Did it once, but cahn' do it twice." —
Dōn' you b'lieve the' 'z no more fat;
Lots in the kitch'n 'z good 'z that.
Fus'-rate throw, 'n' no mistake, —
Han' us the props for another shake; —
Know I 'll try, 'n' guess I 'll win;
Here sh' goes for hit 'm ag'in!

PARSON TURELL'S LEGACY

OR, THE PRESIDENT'S OLD ARM-CHAIR

A MATHEMATICAL STORY

FACTS respecting an old arm-chair.
At Cambridge. Is kept in the College
    there.
Seems but little the worse for wear.
That 's remarkable when I say
It was old in President Holyoke's day.
(One of his boys, perhaps you know,
Died, *at one hundred,* years ago.)
He took lodgings for rain or shine
Under green bed-clothes in '69.

Know old Cambridge? Hope you do. —
Born there? Don't say so! I was, too.
(Born in a house with a gambrel-roof, —
Standing still, if you must have proof. —
"Gambrel? — Gambrel?" — Let me beg
You 'll look at a horse's hinder leg, —
First great angle above the hoof, —
That 's the gambrel; hence gambrel-roof.)
Nicest place that ever was seen, —
Colleges red and Common green,
Sidewalks brownish with trees between.
Sweetest spot beneath the skies
When the canker-worms don't rise, —
When the dust, that sometimes flies
Into your mouth and ears and eyes,
In a quiet slumber lies,
Not in the shape of unbaked pies
Such as barefoot children prize.

A kind of harbor it seems to be,
Facing the flow of a boundless sea.
Rows of gray old Tutors stand
Ranged like rocks above the sand;
Rolling beneath them, soft and green,
Breaks the tide of bright sixteen, —
One wave, two waves, three waves, four, —
Sliding up the sparkling floor:

Then it ebbs to flow no more,
Wandering off from shore to shore
With its freight of golden ore !
Pleasant place for boys to play; —
Better keep your girls away;
Hearts get rolled as pebbles do
Which countless fingering waves pursue,
And every classic beach is strown
With heart-shaped pebbles of blood-red
    stone.

But this is neither here nor there;
I 'm talking about an old arm-chair.
You 've heard, no doubt, of PARSON TU-
    RELL ?
Over at Medford he used to dwell;
Married one of the Mathers' folk;
Got with his wife a chair of oak, —
Funny old chair with seat like wedge,
Sharp behind and broad front edge, —
One of the oddest of human things,
Turned all over with knobs and rings, —
But heavy, and wide, and deep, and
    grand, —
Fit for the worthies of the land, —
Chief Justice Sewall a cause to try in,
Or Cotton Mather to sit — and lie — in.
Parson Turell bequeathed the same
To a certain student, — SMITH by name;
These were the terms, as we are told:
" Saide Smith saide Chaire to have and
    holde;
When he doth graduate, then to passe
To y° oldest Youth in y° Senior Classe.
On payment of " — (naming a certain
    sum) —
" By him to whom y° Chaire shall come;
He to y° oldest Senior next,
And soe forever," — (thus runs the text,) —
" But one Crown lesse than he gave to
    claime,
That being his Debte for use of same."

Smith transferred it to one of the BROWNS,
And took his money, — five silver crowns.
Brown delivered it up to MOORE,
Who paid, it is plain, not five, but four.
Moore made over the chair to LEE,
Who gave him crowns of silver three.
Lee conveyed it unto DREW,
And now the payment, of course, was two.
Drew gave up the chair to DUNN, —
All he got, as you see, was one.
Dunn released the chair to HALL,
And got by the bargain no crown at all.

And now it passed to a second BROWN,
Who took it and likewise *claimed a crown*.
When *Brown* conveyed it unto WARE,
Having had one crown, to make it fair,
He paid him two crowns to take the chair;
And *Ware*, being honest, (as all Wares be,)
He paid one POTTER, who took it, three.
Four got ROBINSON; five got DIX;
JOHNSON *primus* demanded six;
And so the sum kept gathering still
Till after the battle of Bunker's Hill.

When paper money became so cheap,
Folks would n't count it, but said " a heap,"
A certain RICHARDS, — the books de-
    clare, —
(A. M. in '90 ? I 've looked with care
Through the Triennial, — *name not there*,) —
This person, Richards, was offered then
Eightscore pounds, but would have ten;
Nine, I think, was the sum he took, —
Not quite certain, — but see the book.
By and by the wars were still,
But nothing had altered the Parson's will.
The old arm-chair was solid yet,
But saddled with such a monstrous debt !
Things grew quite too bad to bear,
Paying such sums to get rid of the chair !
But dead men's fingers hold awful tight,
And there was the will in black and white,
Plain enough for a child to spell.
What should be done no man could tell,
For the chair was a kind of nightmare
    curse,
And every season but made it worse.

As a last resort, to clear the doubt,
They got old GOVERNOR HANCOCK out.
The Governor came with his Lighthorse
    Troop
And his mounted truckmen, all cock-a-
    hoop;
Halberds glittered and colors flew,
French horns whinnied and trumpets blew,
The yellow fifes whistled between their
    teeth,
And the bumble-bee bass-drums boomed
    beneath;
So he rode with all his band,
Till the President met him, cap in hand.
The Governor " hefted " the crowns, and
    said, —
" A will is a will, and the Parson 's dead."
The Governor hefted the crowns. Said
    he, —

"There is your p'int.   And here's my fee.
These are the terms you must fulfil, —
On such conditions I BREAK THE WILL!"
The Governor mentioned what these should
be.
(Just wait a minute and then you'll see.)
The President prayed.   Then all was still,
And the Governor rose and BROKE THE
WILL!
"About those conditions?" Well, now you
go
And do as I tell you, and then you'll know.
Once a year, on Commencement day,
If you'll only take the pains to stay,
You'll see the President in the CHAIR,
Likewise the Governor sitting there.
The President rises; both old and young
May hear his speech in a foreign tongue,
The meaning whereof, as lawyers swear,
Is this: Can I keep this old arm-chair?
And then his Excellency bows,
As much as to say that he allows.
The Vice-Gub. next is called by name;
He bows like t' other, which means the same.
And all the officers round 'em bow,
As much as to say that *they* allow.
And a lot of parchments about the chair
Are handed to witnesses then and there,
And then the lawyers hold it clear
That the chair is safe for another year.

God bless you, Gentlemen! Learn to give
Money to colleges while you live.
Don't be silly and think you'll try
To bother the colleges, when you die,
With codicil this, and codicil that,
That Knowledge may starve while Law
grows fat;
For there never was pitcher that would n't
spill,
And there's always a flaw in a donkey's
will!

ODE FOR A SOCIAL MEETING

WITH SLIGHT ALTERATIONS BY A TEE-TOTALER

Here is a little poem I sent a short time
since to a committee for a certain celebration.

I understood that it was to be a festive and
convivial occasion, and ordered myself accordingly. It seems the president of the day was
what is called a "teetotaler." I received a
note from him in the following words, containing the copy subjoined, with the emendations
annexed to it.

"DEAR SIR, — Your poem gives good satisfaction to the committee.   The sentiments
expressed with reference to liquor are not, however, those generally entertained by this community.   I have therefore consulted the clergyman of this place, who has made some slight
changes, which he thinks will remove all objections, and keep the valuable portions of the
poem.   Please to inform me of your charge
for said poem.   Our means are limited, etc.,
etc., etc.

"Yours with respect."
Here it is with the slight alterations.

COME! fill a fresh bumper, for why should
we go
While the ~~nectar~~ [logwood] still reddens our cups as
they flow?
Pour out the ~~rich juices~~ [decoction] still bright with the
sun,
Till o'er the brimmed crystal the ~~rubies~~ [dye-stuff]
shall run.

The ~~purple-globed clusters~~ [half-ripened apples] their life-dews
have bled;
How sweet is the ~~breath~~ [taste] of the ~~fragrance~~ [sugar of lead.]
~~they shed!~~
For summer's ~~last roses~~ [rank poisons] lie hid in the ~~wines~~ [wines!!!]
That were garnered by ~~maidens who~~ [stable-boys smoking]
~~laughed thro' the vines~~ [long-nines].

Then a ~~smile~~ [scowl], and a ~~glass~~ [howl], and a ~~toast~~ [scoff], and
a ~~cheer~~ [sneer],
For all ~~the good wine, and we've some of it~~ [strychnine and whiskey, and ratsbane and]
~~here!~~ [beer!]
In cellar, in pantry, in attic, in hall,
~~Long live the gay servant that laughs for~~ [Down, down with the tyrant that masters us all!]
~~us all!~~

POEMS FROM THE PROFESSOR AT THE BREAKFAST-TABLE

1858–1859

UNDER THE VIOLETS

HER hands are cold; her face is white;
  No more her pulses come and go;
Her eyes are shut to life and light; —
  Fold the white vesture, snow on snow,
  And lay her where the violets blow.

But not beneath a graven stone,
  To plead for tears with alien eyes;
A slender cross of wood alone
  Shall say, that here a maiden lies
  In peace beneath the peaceful skies.

And gray old trees of hugest limb
  Shall wheel their circling shadows round
To make the scorching sunlight dim
  That drinks the greenness from the
    ground,
  And drop their dead leaves on her mound.

When o'er their boughs the squirrels run,
  And through their leaves the robins call,
And, ripening in the autumn sun,
  The acorns and the chestnuts fall,
  Doubt not that she will heed them all.

For her the morning choir shall sing
  Its matins from the branches high,
And every minstrel-voice of Spring,
  That trills beneath the April sky,
  Shall greet her with its earliest cry.

When, turning round their dial-track,
  Eastward the lengthening shadows pass,
Her little mourners, clad in black,
  The crickets, sliding through the grass,
  Shall pipe for her an evening mass.

At last the rootlets of the trees
  Shall find the prison where she lies,
And bear the buried dust they seize
  In leaves and blossoms to the skies.
  So may the soul that warmed it rise !

If any, born of kindlier blood,
  Should ask, What maiden lies below ?
Say only this : A tender bud,
  That tried to blossom in the snow,
  Lies withered where the violets blow.

HYMN OF TRUST

O LOVE Divine, that stooped to share
  Our sharpest pang, our bitterest tear,
On Thee we cast each earth-born care,
  We smile at pain while Thou art near !

Though long the weary way we tread,
  And sorrow crown each lingering year,
No path we shun, no darkness dread,
  Our hearts still whispering, Thou art
    near !

When drooping pleasure turns to grief,
  And trembling faith is changed to fear,
The murmuring wind, the quivering leaf,
  Shall softly tell us, Thou art near !

On Thee we fling our burdening woe,
  O Love Divine, forever dear,
Content to suffer while we know,
  Living and dying, Thou art near !

A SUN–DAY HYMN

LORD of all being ! throned afar,
Thy glory flames from sun and star ;
Centre and soul of every sphere,
Yet to each loving heart how near !

Sun of our life, thy quickening ray
Sheds on our path the glow of day;
Star of our hope, thy softened light
Cheers the long watches of the night.

Our midnight is thy smile withdrawn;
Our noontide is thy gracious dawn;
Our rainbow arch thy mercy's sign;
All, save the clouds of sin, are thine!

Lord of all life, below, above,
Whose light is truth, whose warmth is love,
Before thy ever-blazing throne
We ask no lustre of our own.

Grant us thy truth to make us free,
And kindling hearts that burn for thee,
Till all thy living altars claim
One holy light, one heavenly flame!

THE CROOKED FOOTPATH

AH, here it is! the sliding rail
  That marks the old remembered spot, —
The gap that struck our school-boy trail, —
  The crooked path across the lot.

It left the road by school and church,
  A pencilled shadow, nothing more,
That parted from the silver-birch
  And ended at the farm-house door.

No line or compass traced its plan;
  With frequent bends to left or right,
In aimless, wayward curves it ran,
  But always kept the door in sight.

The gabled porch, with woodbine green, —
  The broken millstone at the sill, —
Though many a rood might stretch between,
  The truant child could see them still.

No rocks across the pathway lie, —
  No fallen trunk is o'er it thrown, —
And yet it winds, we know not why,
  And turns as if for tree or stone.

Perhaps some lover trod the way
  With shaking knees and leaping heart, —
And so it often runs astray
  With sinuous sweep or sudden start.

Or one, perchance, with clouded brain
  From some unholy banquet reeled, —

And since, our devious steps maintain
  His track across the trodden field.

Nay, deem not thus, — no earthborn will
  Could ever trace a faultless line;
Our truest steps are human still, —
  To walk unswerving were divine!

Truants from love, we dream of wrath; —
  Oh, rather let us trust the more!
Through all the wanderings of the path
  We still can see our Father's door!

IRIS, HER BOOK

I PRAY thee by the soul of her that bore
    thee,
By thine own sister's spirit I implore
    thee,
Deal gently with the leaves that lie before
    thee!

For Iris had no mother to infold her,
Nor ever leaned upon a sister's shoulder,
Telling the twilight thoughts that Nature
    told her.

She had not learned the mystery of awak-
    ing
Those chorded keys that soothe a sorrow's
    aching,
Giving the dumb heart voice, that else
    were breaking.

Yet lived, wrought, suffered. Lo, the pic-
    tured token!
Why should her fleeting day-dreams fade
    unspoken,
Like daffodils that die with sheaths un-
    broken?

She knew not love, yet lived in maiden
    fancies, —
Walked simply clad, a queen of high ro-
    mances,
And talked strange tongues with angels in
    her trances.

Twin-souled she seemed, a twofold nature
    wearing:
Sometimes a flashing falcon in her dar-
    ing,
Then a poor mateless dove that droops de-
    spairing.

Questioning all things: Why her Lord had
  sent her?
What were these torturing gifts, and where-
  fore lent her?
Scornful as spirit fallen, its own tormentor.

And then all tears and anguish: Queen of
  Heaven,
Sweet Saints, and Thou by mortal sorrows
  riven,
Save me! Oh, save me! Shall I die for-
  given?

And then — Ah, God! But nay, it little
  matters:
Look at the wasted seeds that autumn
  scatters,
The myriad germs that Nature shapes and
  shatters!

If she had — Well! She longed, and knew
  not wherefore.
Had the world nothing she might live to
  care for?
No second self to say her evening prayer
  for?

She knew the marble shapes that set men
  dreaming,
Yet with her shoulders bare and tresses
  streaming
Showed not unlovely to her simple seem-
  ing.

Vain? Let it be so! Nature was her
  teacher.
What if a lonely and unsistered creature
Loved her own harmless gift of pleasing
  feature,

Saying, unsaddened, — This shall soon be
  faded,
And double-hued the shining tresses
  braided,
And all the sunlight of the morning shaded?

This her poor book is full of saddest fol-
  lies,
Of tearful smiles and laughing melancholies,
With summer roses twined and wintry
  hollies.

In the strange crossing of uncertain chances,
Somewhere, beneath some maiden's tear-
  dimmed glances

May fall her little book of dreams and
  fancies.

Sweet sister! Iris, who shall never name
  thee,
Trembling for fear her open heart may
  shame thee,
Speaks from this vision-haunted page to
  claim thee.

Spare her, I pray thee! If the maid is
  sleeping,
Peace with her! she has had her hour of
  weeping.
No more! She leaves her memory in thy
  keeping.

ROBINSON OF LEYDEN

HE sleeps not here; in hope and prayer
  His wandering flock had gone before,
But he, the shepherd, might not share
  Their sorrows on the wintry shore.

Before the Speedwell's anchor swung,
  Ere yet the Mayflower's sail was spread,
While round his feet the Pilgrims clung,
  The pastor spake, and thus he said: —

"Men, brethren, sisters, children dear!
  God calls you hence from over sea;
Ye may not build by Haerlem Meer,
  Nor yet along the Zuyder-Zee.

" Ye go to bear the saving word
  To tribes unnamed and shores untrod;
Heed well the lessons ye have heard
  From those old teachers taught of God.

" Yet think not unto them was lent
  All light for all the coming days,
And Heaven's eternal wisdom spent
  In making straight the ancient ways;

" The living fountain overflows
  For every flock, for every lamb,
Nor heeds, though angry creeds oppose
  With Luther's dike or Calvin's dam."

He spake; with lingering, long embrace,
  With tears of love and partings fond,
They floated down the creeping Maas,
  Along the isle of Ysselmond.

They passed the frowning towers of Briel,
  The "Hook of Holland's" shelf of sand,
And grated soon with lifting keel
  The sullen shores of Fatherland.

No home for these! — too well they knew
  The mitred king behind the throne; —
The sails were set, the pennons flew,
  And westward ho! for worlds unknown.

And these were they who gave us birth,
  The Pilgrims of the sunset wave,
Who won for us this virgin earth,
  And freedom with the soil they gave.

The pastor slumbers by the Rhine, —
  In alien earth the exiles lie, —
Their nameless graves our holiest shrine,
  His words our noblest battle-cry!

Still cry them, and the world shall hear,
  Ye dwellers by the storm-swept sea!
Ye *have* not built by Haerlem Meer,
  Nor on the land-locked Zuyder-Zee!

ST. ANTHONY THE REFORMER

HIS TEMPTATION

The Reformers have good heads, generally.
Their faces are commonly serene enough, and
they are lambs in private intercourse, even
though their voices may be like

"The wolf's long howl from Oonalaska's shore,"

when heard from the platform. Their greatest
spiritual danger is from the perpetual *flattery
of abuse* to which they are exposed. These
lines are meant to caution them.

No fear lest praise should make us proud!
  We know how cheaply that is won;
The idle homage of the crowd
  Is proof of tasks as idly done.

A surface-smile may pay the toil
  That follows still the conquering Right,
With soft, white hands to dress the spoil
  That sun-browned valor clutched in fight.

Sing the sweet song of other days,
  Serenely placid, safely true,
And o'er the present's parching ways
  The verse distils like evening dew.

But speak in words of living power, —
  They fall like drops of scalding rain
That plashed before the burning shower
  Swept o'er the cities of the plain!

Then scowling Hate turns deadly pale, —
  Then Passion's half-coiled adders spring,
And, smitten through their leprous mail,
  Strike right and left in hope to sting.

If thou, unmoved by poisoning wrath,
  Thy feet on earth, thy heart above,
Canst walk in peace thy kingly path,
  Unchanged in trust, unchilled in love, —

Too kind for bitter words to grieve,
  Too firm for clamor to dismay,
When Faith forbids thee to believe,
  And Meekness calls to disobey, —

Ah, then beware of mortal pride!
  The smiling pride that calmly scorns
Those foolish fingers, crimson dyed
  In laboring on thy crown of thorns!

THE OPENING OF THE PIANO

In the little southern parlor of the house
    you may have seen
With the gambrel-roof, and the gable look-
    ing westward to the green,
At the side toward the sunset, with the
    window on its right,
Stood the London-made piano I am dream-
    ing of to-night!

Ah me! how I remember the evening when
    it came!
What a cry of eager voices, what a group
    of cheeks in flame,
When the wondrous box was opened that
    had come from over seas,
With its smell of mastic-varnish and its
    flash of ivory keys!

Then the children all grew fretful in the
    restlessness of joy,
For the boy would push his sister, and the
    sister crowd the boy,
Till the father asked for quiet in his grave
    paternal way,
But the mother hushed the tumult with
    the words, "Now, Mary, play."

For the dear soul knew that music was a
 very sovereign balm;
She had sprinkled it over Sorrow and seen
 its brow grow calm,
In the days of slender harpsichords with
 tapping tinkling quills,
Or carolling to her spinet with its thin me-
 tallic thrills.

So Mary, the household minstrel, who
 always loved to please,
Sat down to the new "Clementi," and
 struck the glittering keys.
Hushed were the children's voices, and
 every eye grew dim,
As, floating from lip and finger, arose the
 "Vesper Hymn."

Catharine, child of a neighbor, curly and
 rosy-red,
(Wedded since, and a widow, — something
 like ten years dead,)
Hearing a gush of music such as none be-
 fore,
Steals from her mother's chamber and
 peeps at the open door.

Just as the "Jubilate" in threaded whis-
 per dies,
"Open it! open it, lady!" the little
 maiden cries,
(For she thought 't was a singing creature
 caged in a box she heard,)
"Open it! open it, lady! and let me see
 the *bird!*"

MIDSUMMER

HERE! sweep these foolish leaves away,
I will not crush my brains to-day!
Look! are the southern curtains drawn?
Fetch me a fan, and so begone!

Not that, — the palm-tree's rustling leaf
Brought from a parching coral-reef!
Its breath is heated; — I would swing
The broad gray plumes, — the eagle's
 wing.

I hate these roses' feverish blood! —
Pluck me a half-blown lily-bud,
A long-stemmed lily from the lake,
Cold as a coiling water-snake.

Rain me sweet odors on the air,
And wheel me up my Indian chair,
And spread some book not overwise
Flat out before my sleepy eyes.

Who knows it not — this dead recoil
Of weary fibres stretched with toil, —
The pulse that flutters faint and low
When Summer's seething breezes blow!

O Nature! bare thy loving breast,
And give thy child one hour of rest, —
One little hour to lie unseen
Beneath thy scarf of leafy green!

So, curtained by a singing pine,
Its murmuring voice shall blend with mine,
Till, lost in dreams, my faltering lay
In sweeter music dies away.

DE SAUTY

AN ELECTRO-CHEMICAL ECLOGUE

The first messages received through the sub-
marine cable were sent by an electrical expert,
a mysterious personage who signed himself De
Sauty.

Professor   *Blue-Nose*

PROFESSOR

TELL me, O Provincial! speak, Ceruleo-
 Nasal!
Lives there one De Sauty extant now
 among you,
Whispering Boanerges, son of silent thun-
 der,
 Holding talk with nations?

Is there a De Sauty ambulant on Tellus,
Bifid-cleft like mortals, dormient in night-
 cap,
Having sight, smell, hearing, food-receiv-
 ing feature
 Three times daily patent?

Breathes there such a being, O Ceruleo-
 Nasal?
Or is he a *mythus*, — ancient word for
 "humbug,"
Such as Livy told about the wolf that wet-
 nursed
 Romulus and Remus?

Was he born of woman, this alleged De
    Sauty ?
Or a living product of galvanic action,
Like the *acarus* bred in Crosse's flint-solu-
    tion ?
    Speak, thou Cyano-Rhinal !

BLUE–NOSE

Many things thou askest, jackknife-bearing
    stranger,
Much-conjecturing   mortal,   pork-and-
    treacle-waster !
Pretermit thy whittling, wheel thine ear-
    flap toward me,
    Thou shalt hear them answered.

When the charge galvanic tingled through
    the cable,
At the polar focus of the wire electric
Suddenly appeared a white-faced man
    among us:
    Called himself " De Sauty."

As the small opossum held in pouch mater-
    nal
Grasps the nutrient organ whence the term
    mammalia,
So the unknown stranger held the wire
    electric,
    Sucking in the current.

When the current strengthened, bloomed
    the pale-faced stranger, —
Took no drink nor victual, yet grew fat
    and rosy, —
And from time to time, in sharp articulation,
    Said, " *All right !* De Sauty."

From the lonely station passed the utter-
    ance, spreading
Through the pines and hemlocks to the
    groves of steeples,
Till the land was filled with loud reverber-
    ations
    Of " *All right !* De Sauty."

When the current slackened, drooped the
    mystic stranger, —
Faded, faded, faded, as the stream grew
    weaker, —
Wasted to a shadow, with a hartshorn
    odor
    Of disintegration.

Drops of deliquescence glistened on his
    forehead,
Whitened round his feet the dust of efflo-
    rescence,
Till one Monday morning, when the flow
    suspended,
    There was no De Sauty.

Nothing but a cloud of elements organic,
C. O. H. N. Ferrum, Chlor. Flu. Sil.
    Potassa,
Calc.   Sod.   Phosph.   Mag.   Sulphur,
    Mang. (?) Alumin. (?) Cuprum, (?)
    Such as man is made of.

Born of stream galvanic, with it he had
    perished !
There is no De Sauty now there is no
    current !
Give us a new cable, then again we 'll hear
    him
    Cry, " *All right !* De Sauty."

POEMS FROM THE POET AT THE BREAKFAST-TABLE

1871–1872

HOMESICK IN HEAVEN

Most people love this world more than they are willing to confess, and it is hard to conceive ourselves weaned from it so as to feel no emotion at the thought of its most sacred recollections, — even after a sojourn of years, as we should count the lapse of earthly time, — in the realm where, sooner or later, all tears shall be wiped away. I hope, therefore, the title of my lines will not frighten those who are little accustomed to think of men and women as beings in any state but the present.

THE DIVINE VOICE

Go seek thine earth-born sisters, — thus
    the Voice
  That all obey, — the sad and silent
    three;
These only, while the hosts of Heaven re-
    joice,
  Smile never; ask them what their sor-
    rows be;

And when the secret of their griefs they
    tell,
  Look on them with thy mild, half-human
    eyes;
Say what thou wast on earth; thou
    knowest well;
  So shall they cease from unavailing
    sighs.

THE ANGEL

Why thus, apart, — the swift-winged
    herald spake, —
Sit ye with silent lips and unstrung lyres
While the trisagion's blending chords
    awake
  In shouts of joy from all the heavenly
    choirs ?

THE FIRST SPIRIT

Chide not thy sisters, — thus the answer
    came; —
  Children of earth, our half - weaned
    nature clings
To earth's fond memories, and her
    whispered name
  Untunes our quivering lips, our saddened
    strings;

For there we loved, and where we love is
    home,
  Home that our feet may leave, but not
    our hearts,
Though o'er us shine the jasper-lighted
    dome: —
  The chain may lengthen, but it never
    parts !

Sometimes a sunlit sphere comes rolling
    by,
  And then we softly whisper, — *can it be?*
And leaning toward the silvery orb, we try
  To hear the music of its murmuring sea;

To catch, perchance, some flashing glimpse
    of green,
  Or breathe some wild-wood fragrance,
    wafted through
The opening gates of pearl, that fold be-
    tween
  The blinding splendors and the change-
    less blue.

THE ANGEL

Nay, sister, nay ! a single healing leaf
  Plucked from the bough of yon twelve-
    fruited tree
Would soothe such anguish, — deeper
    stabbing grief
  Has pierced thy throbbing heart —

THE FIRST SPIRIT

Ah, woe is me !

I from my clinging babe was rudely torn;
  His tender lips a loveless bosom pressed;
Can I forget him in my life new born ?
  Oh that my darling lay upon my breast !

THE ANGEL

And thou ? —

THE SECOND SPIRIT

I was a fair and youthful bride,

The kiss of love still burns upon my cheek,
He whom I worshipped, ever at my side, —
  Him through the spirit realm in vain I
    seek.

Sweet faces turn their beaming eyes on
    mine;
  Ah ! not in these the wished-for look I
    read;
Still for that one dear human smile I pine;
  Thou and none other ! — is the lover's
    creed.

THE ANGEL

And whence *thy* sadness in a world of bliss
  Where never parting comes, nor mourn-
    er's tear ?
Art thou, too, dreaming of a mortal's kiss
  Amid the seraphs of the heavenly
    sphere ?

THE THIRD SPIRIT

Nay, tax not me with passion's wasting fire;
  When the swift message set my spirit
    free,
Blind, helpless, lone, I left my gray-haired
    sire;
  My friends were many, he had none save
    me.

I left him, orphaned, in the starless night;
  Alas, for him no cheerful morning's
    dawn !
I wear the ransomed spirit's robe of white,
  Yet still I hear him moaning, *She is gone!*

THE ANGEL

Ye know me not, sweet sisters ? — All in
  vain

Ye seek your lost ones in the shapes they
    wore;
The flower once opened may not bud again,
  The fruit once fallen finds the stem no
    more.

Child, lover, sire, — yea, all things loved
    below, —
  Fair pictures damasked on a vapor's
    fold, —
Fade like the roseate flush, the golden
    glow,
  When the bright curtain of the day is
    rolled.

I was the babe that slumbered on *thy* breast,
  And, sister, mine the lips that called *thee*
    bride.
Mine were the silvered locks *thy* hand ca-
    ressed,
  That faithful hand, my faltering foot-
    step's guide !

Each changing form, frail vesture of decay,
  The soul unclad forgets it once hath
    worn,
Stained with the travel of the weary day,
  And shamed with rents from every way-
    side thorn.

To lie, an infant, in *thy* fond embrace, —
  To come with love's warm kisses back to
    thee, —
To show *thine* eyes thy gray-haired father's
    face,
  Not Heaven itself could grant; this may
    not be !

Then spread your folded wings, and leave
    to earth
  The dust once breathing ye have mourned
    so long,
Till Love, new risen, owns his heavenly
    birth,
  And sorrow's discords sweeten into song !

FANTASIA

THE YOUNG GIRL'S POEM

Kiss mine eyelids, beauteous Morn,
Blushing into life new-born !
Lend me violets for my hair,
And thy russet robe to wear,

And thy ring of rosiest hue
Set in drops of diamond dew !

Kiss my cheek, thou noontide ray,
From my Love so far away !
Let thy splendor streaming down
Turn its pallid lilies brown,
Till its darkening shades reveal
Where his passion pressed its seal !

Kiss my lips, thou Lord of light,
Kiss my lips a soft good-night !
Westward sinks thy golden car;
Leave me but the evening star,
And my solace that shall be,
Borrowing all its light from thee !

AUNT TABITHA

THE YOUNG GIRL'S POEM

WHATEVER I do, and whatever I say,
Aunt Tabitha tells me that is n't the way;
When *she* was a girl (forty summers ago)
Aunt Tabitha tells me they never did so.

Dear aunt ! If I only would take her ad-
    vice !
But I like my own way, and I find it *so* nice !
And besides, I forget half the things I am
    told;
But they all will come back to me — when
    I am old.

If a youth passes by, it may happen, no
    doubt,
He may chance to look in as I chance to
    look out;
She would never endure an impertinent
    stare, —
It is *horrid*, she says, and I must n't sit
    there.

A walk in the moonlight has pleasures, I
    own,
But it is n't quite safe to be walking alone;
So I take a lad's arm, — just for safety,
    you know, —
But Aunt Tabitha tells me *they* did n't do so.

How wicked we are, and how good they
    were then !
They kept at arm's length those detestable
    men;

What an era of virtue she lived in ! — But
    stay —
Were the *men* all such rogues in Aunt
    Tabitha's day ?

If the men *were* so wicked, I 'll ask my papa
How he dared to propose to my darling
    mamma;
Was he like the rest of them ?   Goodness !
    Who knows ?
And what shall *I* say, if a wretch should
    propose ?

I am thinking if Aunt knew so little of
    sin,
What a wonder Aunt Tabitha's aunt must
    have been !
And her grand-aunt — it scares me — how
    shockingly sad
That we girls of to-day are so frightfully
    bad !

A martyr will save us, and nothing else can;
Let *me* perish — to rescue some wretched
    young man !
Though when to the altar a victim I go,
Aunt Tabitha 'll tell me *she* never did so !

WIND–CLOUDS AND STAR–DRIFTS

FROM THE YOUNG ASTRONOMER'S POEM

I

AMBITION

ANOTHER clouded night; the stars are hid,
The orb that waits my search is hid with
    them.
Patience ! Why grudge an hour, a month,
    a year,
To plant my ladder and to gain the round
That leads my footsteps to the heaven of
    fame,
Where waits the wreath my sleepless mid-
    nights won ?
Not the stained laurel such as heroes wear
That withers when some stronger conquer-
    or's heel
Treads down their shrivelling trophies in
    the dust;
But the fair garland whose undying green
Not time can change, nor wrath of gods or
    men !

With quickened heart-beats I shall hear
    the tongues
That speak my praise; but better far the
    sense
That in the unshaped ages, buried deep
In the dark mines of unaccomplished time
Yet to be stamped with morning's royal die
And coined in golden days, — in those dim
    years
I shall be reckoned with the undying dead,
My name emblazoned on the fiery arch,
Unfading till the stars themselves shall
    fade.
Then, as they call the roll of shining
    worlds,
Sages of race unborn in accents new
Shall count me with the Olympian ones of
    old,
Whose glories kindle through the midnight
    sky:
Here glows the God of Battles; this recalls
The Lord of Ocean, and yon far-off sphere
The Sire of Him who gave his ancient
    name
To the dim planet with the wondrous rings;
Here flames the Queen of Beauty's silver
    lamp,
And there the moon-girt orb of mighty
    Jove;
But *this*, unseen through all earth's æons
    past,
A youth who watched beneath the western
    star
Sought in the darkness, found, and shewed
    to men;
Linked with his name thenceforth and
    evermore !
So shall that name be syllabled anew
In all the tongues of all the tribes of men:
I that have been through immemorial years
Dust in the dust of my forgotten time
Shall live in accents shaped of blood-warm
    breath,
Yea, rise in mortal semblance, newly born
In shining stone, in undecaying bronze,
And stand on high, and look serenely down
On the new race that calls the earth its own.

Is this a cloud, that, blown athwart my
    soul,
Wears a false seeming of the pearly stain
Where worlds beyond the world their
    mingling rays
Blend in soft white, — a cloud that, born
    of earth,

Would cheat the soul that looks for light
    from heaven ?
Must every coral-insect leave his sign
On each poor grain he lent to build the
    reef,
As Babel's builders stamped their sunburnt
    clay,
Or deem his patient service all in vain ?
What if another sit beneath the shade
Of the broad elm I planted by the way, —
What if another heed the beacon light
I set upon the rock that wrecked my
    keel, —
Have I not done my task and served my
    kind ?
Nay, rather act thy part, unnamed, un-
    known,
And let Fame blow her trumpet through
    the world
With noisy wind to swell a fool's renown,
Joined with some truth he stumbled blindly
    o'er,
Or coupled with some single shining deed
That in the great account of all his days
Will stand alone upon the bankrupt sheet
His pitying angel shows the clerk of
    Heaven.
The noblest service comes from nameless
    hands,
And the best servant does his work unseen.
Who found the seeds of fire and made
    them shoot,
Fed by his breath, in buds and flowers of
    flame ?
Who forged in roaring flames the ponder-
    ous stone,
And shaped the moulded metal to his need ?
Who gave the dragging car its rolling
    wheel,
And tamed the steed that whirls its circling
    round ?
All these have left their work and not their
    names, —
Why should I murmur at a fate like theirs ?
This is the heavenly light; the pearly stain
Was but a wind-cloud drifting o'er the
    stars !

II

REGRETS

Brief glimpses of the bright celestial
    spheres,
False lights, false shadows, vague, uncer-
    tain gleams,

Pale vaporous mists, wan streaks of lurid
flame,
The climbing of the upward-sailing cloud,
The sinking of the downward-falling star, —
All these are pictures of the changing
moods
Borne through the midnight stillness of my
soul.

Here am I, bound upon this pillared rock,
Prey to the vulture of a vast desire
That feeds upon my life. — I burst my bands
And steal a moment's freedom from the
beak,
The clinging talons and the shadowing
plumes;
Then comes the false enchantress, with her
song;
" Thou wouldst not lay thy forehead in the
dust
Like the base herd that feeds and breeds
and dies!
Lo, the fair garlands that I weave for
thee,
Unchanging as the belt Orion wears,
Bright as the jewels of the seven-starred
Crown,
The spangled stream of Berenice's hair ! "
And so she twines the fetters with the
flowers
Around my yielding limbs, and the fierce
bird
Stoops to his quarry, — then to feed his
rage
Of ravening hunger I must drain my blood
And let the dew-drenched, poison-breeding
night
Steal all the freshness from my fading
cheek,
And leave its shadows round my caverned
eyes.
All for a line in some unheeded scroll;
All for a stone that tells to gaping clowns,
" Here lies a restless wretch beneath a
clod
Where squats the jealous nightmare men
call Fame ! "

I marvel not at him who scorns his kind
And thinks not sadly of the time foretold
When the old hulk we tread shall be a
wreck,
A slag, a cinder drifting through the sky
Without its crew of fools ! We live too
long,

And even so are not content to die,
But load the mould that covers up our
bones
With stones that stand like beggars by the
road
And show death's grievous wound and ask
for tears;
Write our great books to teach men who
we are,
Sing our fine songs that tell in artful
phrase
The secrets of our lives, and plead and
pray
For alms of memory with the after time,
Those few swift seasons while the earth
shall wear
Its leafy summers, ere its core grows cold
And the moist life of all that breathes
shall die;
Or as the new-born seer, perchance more
wise,
Would have us deem, before its growing
mass,
Pelted with star-dust, stoned with meteor-
balls,
Heats like a hammered anvil, till at last
Man and his works and all that stirred it-
self
Of its own motion, in the fiery glow
Turns to a flaming vapor, and our orb
Shines a new sun for earths that shall be
born.

I am as old as Egypt to myself,
Brother to them that squared the pyramids
By the same stars I watch. I read the
page
Where every letter is a glittering world,
With them who looked from Shinar's clay-
built towers,
Ere yet the wanderer of the Midland sea
Had missed the fallen sister of the seven.
I dwell in spaces vague, remote, unknown,
Save to the silent few, who, leaving earth,
Quit all communion with their living time.
I lose myself in that ethereal void,
Till I have tired my wings and long to fill
My breast with denser air, to stand, to
walk
With eyes not raised above my fellow-men.
Sick of my unwalled, solitary realm,
I ask to change the myriad lifeless worlds
I visit as mine own for one poor patch
Of this dull spheroid and a little breath
To shape in word or deed to serve my kind.

Was ever giant's dungeon dug so deep,
Was ever tyrant's fetter forged so strong,
Was e'er such deadly poison in the draught
The false wife mingles for the trusting fool,
As he whose willing victim is himself
Digs, forges, mingles, for his captive soul?

III

SYMPATHIES

The snows that glittered on the disk of
    Mars
Have melted, and the planet's fiery orb
Rolls in the crimson summer of its year;
But what to me the summer or the snow
Of worlds that throb with life in forms un-
    known,
If life indeed be theirs; I heed not these.
My heart is simply human; all my care
For them whose dust is fashioned like mine
    own,
These ache with cold and hunger, live in
    pain,
And shake with fear of worlds more full
    of woe;
There may be others worthier of my love,
But such I know not save through these I
    know.

There are two veils of language, hid be-
    neath
Whose sheltering folds, we dare to be our-
    selves;
And not that other self which nods and
    smiles
And babbles in our name; the one is Prayer,
Lending its licensed freedom to the tongue
That tells our sorrows and our sins to
    Heaven;
The other, Verse, that throws its spangled
    web
Around our naked speech and makes it
    bold.
I, whose best prayer is silence; sitting
    dumb
In the great temple where I nightly serve
Him who is throned in light, have dared to
    claim
The poet's franchise, though I may not hope
To wear his garland; hear me while I tell
My story in such form as poets use,
But breathed in fitful whispers, as the wind
Sighs and then slumbers, wakes and sighs
    again.

Thou Vision, floating in the breathless air
Between me and the fairest of the stars,
I tell my lonely thoughts as unto thee.
Look not for marvels of the scholar's pen
In my rude measure; I can only show
A slender-margined, unillumined page,
And trust its meaning to the flattering eye
That reads it in the gracious light of love.
Ah, would thou clothe thyself in breathing
    shape
And nestle at my side, my voice should
    lend
Whate'er my verse may lack of tender
    rhythm
To make thee listen.
                        I have stood entranced
When, with her fingers wandering o'er the
    keys,
The white enchantress with the golden hair
Breathed all her soul through some un-
    valued rhyme;
Some flower of song that long had lost its
    bloom;
Lo! its dead summer kindled as she sang!
The sweet contralto, like the ringdove's coo,
Thrilled it with brooding, fond, caressing
    tones,
And the pale minstrel's passion lived again,
Tearful and trembling as a dewy rose
The wind has shaken till it fills the air
With light and fragrance.   Such the won-
    drous charm
A song can borrow when the bosom throbs
That lends it breath.
                        So from the poet's lips
His verse sounds doubly sweet, for none
    like him
Feels every cadence of its wave-like flow;
He lives the passion over, while he reads,
That shook him as he sang his lofty strain,
And pours his life through each resounding
    line,
As ocean, when the stormy winds are
    hushed,
Still rolls and thunders through his billowy
    caves.

IV

MASTER AND SCHOLAR

Let me retrace the record of the years
That made me what I am.   A man most
    wise,
But overworn with toil and bent with age,

Sought me to be his scholar, — me, run
 wild
From books and teachers, — kindled in my
 soul
The love of knowledge; led me to his tower,
Showed me the wonders of the midnight
 realm
His hollow sceptre ruled, or seemed to rule,
Taught me the mighty secrets of the
 spheres,
Trained me to find the glimmering specks
 of light
Beyond the unaided sense, and on my chart
To string them one by one, in order due,
As on a rosary a saint his beads.
I was his only scholar; I became
The echo to his thought; whate'er he knew
Was mine for asking; so from year to year
We wrought together, till there came a time
When I, the learner, was the master half
Of the twinned being in the dome-crowned
 tower.

Minds roll in paths like planets; they re-
 volve,
This in a larger, that a narrower ring,
But round they come at last to that same
 phase,
That selfsame light and shade they showed
 before.
I learned his annual and his monthly tale,
His weekly axiom and his daily phrase,
I felt them coming in the laden air,
And watched them laboring up to vocal
 breath,
Even as the first-born at his father's board
Knows ere he speaks the too familiar jest
Is on its way, by some mysterious sign
Forewarned, the click before the striking
 bell.

He shrivelled as I spread my growing
 leaves,
Till trust and reverence changed to pitying
 care;
He lived for me in what he once had been,
But I for him, a shadow, a defence,
The guardian of his fame, his guide, his
 staff,
Leaned on so long he fell if left alone.
I was his eye, his ear, his cunning hand,
Love was my spur and longing after fame,
But his the goading thorn of sleepless age
That sees its shortening span, its lengthen-
 ing shades,

That clutches what it may with eager grasp,
And drops at last with empty, outstretched
 hands.
All this he dreamed not. He would sit
 him down
Thinking to work his problems as of old,
And find the star he thought so plain a
 blur,
The columned figures labyrinthine wilds
Without my comment, blind and senseless
 scrawls
That vexed him with their riddles; he
 would strive
And struggle for a while, and then his eye
Would lose its light, and over all his mind
The cold gray mist would settle; and ere-
 long
The darkness fell, and I was left alone.

V

ALONE

Alone! no climber of an Alpine cliff,
No Arctic venturer on the waveless sea,
Feels the dread stillness round him as it
 chills
The heart of him who leaves the slumber-
 ing earth
To watch the silent worlds that crowd the
 sky.

Alone! And as the shepherd leaves his
 flock
To feed upon the hillside, he meanwhile
Finds converse in the warblings of the
 pipe
Himself has fashioned for his vacant hour,
So have I grown companion to myself,
And to the wandering spirits of the air
That smile and whisper round us in our
 dreams.
Thus have I learned to search if I may
 know
The whence and why of all beneath the
 stars
And all beyond them, and to weigh my life
As in a balance, — poising good and ill
Against each other, — asking of the Power
That flung me forth among the whirling
 worlds,
If I am heir to any inborn right,
Or only as an atom of the dust
That every wind may blow where'er it will.

VI

QUESTIONING

I am not humble; I was shown my place,
Clad in such robes as Nature had at hand;
Took what she gave, not chose; I know no
    shame,
No fear for being simply what I am.
I am not proud, I hold my every breath
At Nature's mercy.   I am as a babe
Borne in a giant's arms, he knows not
    where;
Each several heart-beat, counted like the
    coin
A miser reckons, is a special gift
As from an unseen hand; if that withhold
Its bounty for a moment, I am left
A clod upon the earth to which I fall.

Something I find in me that well might
    claim
The love of beings in a sphere above
This doubtful twilight world of right and
    wrong;
Something that shows me of the selfsame
    clay
That creeps or swims or flies in humblest
    form.
Had I been asked, before I left my bed
Of shapeless dust, what clothing I would
    wear,
I would have said, More angel and less
    worm;
But for their sake who are even such as I,
Of the same mingled blood, I would not
    choose
To hate that meaner portion of myself
Which makes me brother to the least of
    men.

I dare not be a coward with my lips
Who dare to question all things in my soul;
Some men may find their wisdom on their
    knees,
Some prone and grovelling in the dust like
    slaves;
Let the meek glowworm glisten in the dew;
I ask to lift my taper to the sky
As they who hold their lamps above their
    heads,
Trusting the larger currents up aloft,
Rather than crossing eddies round their
    breast,
Threatening with every puff the flickering
    blaze.

My life shall be a challenge, not a truce!
This is my homage to the mightier powers,
To ask my boldest question, undismayed
By muttered threats that some hysteric
    sense
Of wrong or insult will convulse the throne
Where wisdom reigns supreme; and if I
    err,
They all must err who have to feel their
    way
As bats that fly at noon; for what are we
But creatures of the night, dragged forth
    by day,
Who needs must stumble, and with stam-
    mering steps
Spell out their paths in syllables of pain?

Thou wilt not hold in scorn the child who
    dares
Look up to Thee, the Father, — dares to
    ask
More than thy wisdom answers.   From thy
    hand
The worlds were cast; yet every leaflet
    claims
From that same hand its little shining
    sphere
Of star-lit dew; thine image, the great sun
Girt with his mantle of tempestuous flame,
Glares in mid-heaven; but to his noontide
    blaze
The slender violet lifts its lidless eye,
And from his splendor steals its fairest
    hue,
Its sweetest perfume from his scorching
    fire.

VII

WORSHIP

From my lone turret as I look around
O'er the green meadows to the ring of blue,
From slope, from summit, and from half-
    hid vale
The sky is stabbed with dagger-pointed
    spires,
Their gilded symbols whirling in the wind,
Their brazen tongues proclaiming to the
    world,
"Here truth is sold, the only genuine ware;
See that it has our trade-mark!   You will
    buy
Poison instead of food across the way,
The lies of —— " this or that, each several
    name

The standard's blazon and the battle-cry
Of some true-gospel faction, and again
The token of the Beast to all beside.
And grouped round each I see a huddling
    crowd
Alike in all things save the words they use;
In love, in longing, hate and fear the same.

Whom do we trust and serve? We speak
    of one
And bow to many; Athens still would find
The shrines of all she worshipped safe
    within
Our tall barbarian temples, and the thrones
That crowned Olympus mighty as of old.
The god of music rules the Sabbath choir;
The lyric muse must leave the sacred nine
To help us please the dilettante's ear;
Plutus limps homeward with us, as we
    leave
The portals of the temple where we knelt
And listened while the god of eloquence
(Hermes of ancient days, but now disguised
In sable vestments) with that other god
Somnus, the son of Erebus and Nox,
Fights in unequal contest for our souls;
The dreadful sovereign of the under-world
Still shakes his sceptre at us, and we hear
The baying of the triple-throated hound;
Eros is young as ever, and as fair
The lovely Goddess born of ocean's foam.

These be thy gods, O Israel! Who is he,
The one ye name and tell us that ye serve,
Whom ye would call me from my lonely
    tower
To worship with the many-headed throng?
Is it the God that walked in Eden's grove
In the cool hour to seek our guilty sire?
The God who dealt with Abraham as the
    sons
Of that old patriarch deal with other men?
The jealous God of Moses, one who feels
An image as an insult, and is wroth
With him who made it and his child un-
    born?
The God who plagued his people for the sin
Of their adulterous king, beloved of
    him, —
The same who offers to a chosen few
The right to praise him in eternal song
While a vast shrieking world of endless woe
Blends its dread chorus with their raptur-
    ous hymn?
Is this the God ye mean, or is it he

Who heeds the sparrow's fall, whose loving
    heart
Is as the pitying father's to his child,
Whose lesson to his children is "Forgive,"
Whose plea for all, "They know not what
    they do"?

VIII

MANHOOD

I claim the right of knowing whom I serve,
Else is my service idle; He that asks
My homage asks it from a reasoning soul.
To crawl is not to worship; we have
    learned
A drill of eyelids, bended neck and knee,
Hanging our prayers on hinges, till we ape
The flexures of the many-jointed worm.
Asia has taught her Allahs and salaams
To the world's children, — we have grown
    to men!
We who have rolled the sphere beneath
    our feet
To find a virgin forest, as we lay
The beams of our rude temple, first of all
Must frame its doorway high enough for
    man
To pass unstooping; knowing as we do
That He who shaped us last of living forms
Has long enough been served by creeping
    things,
Reptiles that left their footprints in the
    sand
Of old sea-margins that have turned to
    stone,
And men who learned their ritual; we de-
    mand
To know Him first, then trust Him and
    then love
When we have found Him worthy of our
    love,
Tried by our own poor hearts and not be-
    fore;
He must be truer than the truest friend,
He must be tenderer than a woman's love,
A father better than the best of sires;
Kinder than she who bore us, though we
    sin
Oftener than did the brother we are told
We — poor ill-tempered mortals — must
    forgive,
Though seven times sinning threescore
    times and ten.

This is the new world's gospel: Be ye men !
Try well the legends of the children's time;
Ye are the chosen people, God has led
Your steps across the desert of the deep
As now across the desert of the shore;
Mountains are cleft before you as the sea
Before the wandering tribe of Israel's sons;
Still onward rolls the thunderous caravan,
Its coming printed on the western sky,
A cloud by day, by night a pillared flame;
Your prophets are a hundred unto one
Of them of old who cried, " Thus saith the
    Lord; "
They told of cities that should fall in heaps,
But yours of mightier cities that shall rise
Where yet the lonely fishers spread their
    nets,
Where hides the fox and hoots the midnight
    owl;
The tree of knowledge in your garden grows
Not single, but at every humble door;
Its branches lend you their immortal food,
That fills you with the sense of what ye
    are,
No servants of an altar hewed and carved
From senseless stone by craft of human
    hands,
Rabbi, or dervish, brahmin, bishop, bonze,
But masters of the charm with which they
    work
To keep your hands from that forbidden
    tree !

Ye that have tasted that divinest fruit,
Look on this world of yours with opened
    eyes !
Ye are as gods ! Nay, makers of your
    gods, —
Each day ye break an image in your shrine
And plant a fairer image where it stood:
Where is the Moloch of your fathers' creed,
Whose fires of torment burned for span-
    long babes ?
Fit object for a tender mother's love !
Why not ? It was a bargain duly made
For these same infants through the surety's
    act
Intrusted with their all for earth and
    heaven,
By Him who chose their guardian, knowing
    well
His fitness for the task, — this, even this,
Was the true doctrine only yesterday
As thoughts are reckoned, — and to-day
    you hear

In words that sound as if from human
    tongues
Those monstrous, uncouth horrors of the
    past
That blot the blue of heaven and shame the
    earth
As would the saurians of the age of slime,
Awaking from their stony sepulchres
And wallowing hateful in the eye of day !

IX

RIGHTS

What am I but the creature Thou hast
    made ?
What have I save the blessings Thou hast
    lent ?
What hope I but thy mercy and thy love ?
Who but myself shall cloud my soul with
    fear ?
Whose hand protect me from myself but
    thine ?
  I claim the rights of weakness, I, the
    babe,
Call on my sire to shield me from the ills
That still beset my path, not trying me
With snares beyond my wisdom or my
    strength,
He knowing I shall use them to my harm,
And find a tenfold misery in the sense
That in my childlike folly I have sprung
The trap upon myself as vermin use,
Drawn by the cunning bait to certain doom.
Who wrought the wondrous charm that
    leads us on
To sweet perdition, but the selfsame power
That set the fearful engine to destroy
His wretched offspring (as the Rabbis tell),
And hid its yawning jaws and treacherous
    springs
In such a show of innocent sweet flowers
It lured the sinless angels and they fell ?
  Ah ! He who prayed the prayer of all
    mankind
Summed in those few brief words the
    mightiest plea
For erring souls before the courts of
    heaven, —
Save us from being tempted, — lest we fall !

If we are only as the potter's clay
Made to be fashioned as the artist wills,
And broken into shards if we offend

The eye of Him who made us, it is well;
Such love as the insensate lump of clay
That spins upon the swift-revolving wheel
Bears to the hand that shapes its growing
    form, —
Such love, no more, will be our hearts' re-
    turn
To the great Master-workman for his
    care, —
Or would be, save that this, our breathing
    clay,
Is intertwined with fine innumerous threads
That make it conscious in its framer's
    hand;
And this He must remember who has filled
These vessels with the deadly draught of
    life, —
Life, that means death to all it claims.
    Our love
Must kindle in the ray that streams from
    heaven,
A faint reflection of the light divine;
The sun must warm the earth before the
    rose
Can show her inmost heart-leaves to the
    sun.

He yields some fraction of the Maker's right
Who gives the quivering nerve its sense of
    pain;
Is there not something in the pleading eye
Of the poor brute that suffers, which ar-
    raigns
The law that bids it suffer?   Has it not
A claim for some remembrance in the book
That fills its pages with the idle words
Spoken of men?   Or is it only clay,
Bleeding and aching in the potter's hand,
Yet all his own to treat it as He will
And when He will to cast it at his feet,
Shattered, dishonored, lost forevermore?
My dog loves me, but could he look beyond
His earthly master, would his love extend
To Him who —   Hush! I will not doubt
    that He
Is better than our fears, and will not wrong
The least, the meanest of created things!

He would not trust me with the smallest
    orb
That circles through the sky; He would
    not give
A meteor to my guidance; would not leave
The coloring of a cloudlet to my hand;
He locks my beating heart beneath its bars

And keeps the key himself; He measures
    out
The draughts of vital breath that warm
    my blood,
Winds up the springs of instinct which un-
    coil,
Each in its season; ties me to my home,
My race, my time, my nation, and my
    creed
So closely that if I but slip my wrist
Out of the band that cuts it to the bone,
Men say, "He hath a devil;" He has lent
All that I hold in trust, as unto one
By reason of his weakness and his years
Not fit to hold the smallest shred in fee
Of those most common things he calls his
    own, —
And yet — my Rabbi tells me — He has
    left
The care of that to which a million worlds
Filled with unconscious life were less than
    naught,
Has left that mighty universe, the Soul
To the weak guidance of our baby hands,
Let the foul fiends have access at their will,
Taking the shape of angels, to our hearts, —
Our hearts already poisoned through and
    through
With the fierce virus of ancestral sin;
Turned us adrift with our immortal charge,
To wreck ourselves in gulfs of endless woe.
If what my Rabbi tells me is the truth
Why did the choir of angels sing for joy?
Heaven must be compassed in a narrow
    space,
And offer more than room enough for all
That pass its portals; but the under-world,
The godless realm, the place where demons
    forge
Their fiery darts and adamantine chains,
Must swarm with ghosts that for a little
    while
Had worn the garb of flesh, and being heirs
Of all the dulness of their stolid sires,
And all the erring instincts of their tribe,
Nature's own teaching, rudiments of "sin,"
Fell headlong in the snare that could not
    fail
To trap the wretched creatures shaped of
    clay
And cursed with sense enough to lose their
    souls!
  Brother, thy heart is troubled at my
    word;
Sister, I see the cloud is on thy brow.

He will not blame me, He who sends not
    peace,
But sends a sword, and bids us strike amain
At Error's gilded crest, where in the van
Of earth's great army, mingling with the
    best
And bravest of its leaders, shouting loud
The battle-cries that yesterday have led
The host of Truth to victory, but to-day
Are watchwords of the laggard and the
    slave,
He leads his dazzled cohorts. God has
    made
This world a strife of atoms and of spheres;
With every breath I sigh myself away
And take my tribute from the wandering
    wind
To fan the flame of life's consuming fire;
So, while my thought has life, it needs
    must burn,
And, burning, set the stubble-fields ablaze,
Where all the harvest long ago was reaped
And safely garnered in the ancient barns.
But still the gleaners, groping for their
    food,
Go blindly feeling through the close-shorn
    straw,
While the young reapers flash their glitter-
    ing steel
Where later suns have ripened nobler
    grain !

X

TRUTHS

The time is racked with birth-pangs; every
    hour
Brings forth some gasping truth, and truth
    newborn
Looks a misshapen and untimely growth,
The terror of the household and its shame,
A monster coiling in its nurse's lap
That some would strangle, some would only
    starve;
But still it breathes, and passed from hand
    to hand,
And suckled at a hundred half-clad breasts,
Comes slowly to its stature and its form,
Calms the rough ridges of its dragon-
    scales,
Changes to shining locks its snaky hair,
And moves transfigured into angel guise,
Welcomed by all that cursed its hour of
    birth,

And folded in the same encircling arms
That cast it like a serpent from their hold !

If thou wouldst live in honor, die in peace,
Have the fine words the marble-workers
    learn
To carve so well, upon thy funeral-stone,
And earn a fair obituary, dressed
In all the many-colored robes of praise,
Be deafer than the adder to the cry
Of that same foundling truth, until it
    grows
To seemly favor, and at length has won
The smiles of hard-mouthed men and
    light-lipped dames;
Then snatch it from its meagre nurse's
    breast,
Fold it in silk and give it food from gold;
So shalt thou share its glory when at last
It drops its mortal vesture, and, revealed
In all the splendor of its heavenly form,
Spreads on the startled air its mighty
    wings !

Alas ! how much that seemed immortal
    truth
That heroes fought for, martyrs died to
    save,
Reveals its earth-born lineage, growing old
And limping in its march, its wings un-
    plumed,
Its heavenly semblance faded like a dream !
    Here in this painted casket, just un-
    sealed,
Lies what was once a breathing shape like
    thine,
Once loved as thou art loved; there beamed
    the eyes
That looked on Memphis in its hour of
    pride,
That saw the walls of hundred-gated
    Thebes,
And all the mirrored glories of the Nile.
See how they toiled that all-consuming time
Might leave the frame immortal in its
    tomb;
Filled it with fragrant balms and odorous
    gums
That still diffuse their sweetness through
    the air,
And wound and wound with patient fold
    on fold
The flaxen bands thy hand has rudely torn !
Perchance thou yet canst see the faded stain
Of the sad mourner's tear.

XI

IDOLS

But what is this?
The sacred beetle, bound upon the breast
Of the blind heathen! Snatch the curious
prize,
Give it a place among thy treasured spoils,
Fossil and relic, — corals, encrinites,
The fly in amber and the fish in stone,
The twisted circlet of Etruscan gold,
Medal, intaglio, poniard, poison-ring, —
Place for the Memphian beetle with thine
hoard!

Ah! longer than thy creed has blest the
world
This toy, thus ravished from thy brother's
breast,
Was to the heart of Mizraim as divine,
As holy, as the symbol that we lay
On the still bosom of our white-robed dead,
And raise above their dust that all may
know
Here sleeps an heir of glory. Loving
friends,
With tears of trembling faith and choking
sobs,
And prayers to those who judge of mortal
deeds,
Wrapped this poor image in the cerement's
fold
That Isis and Osiris, friends of man,
Might know their own and claim the ran-
somed soul.

An idol? Man was born to worship such!
An idol is an image of his thought;
Sometimes he carves it out of gleaming
stone,
And sometimes moulds it out of glittering
gold,
Or rounds it in a mighty frescoed dome,
Or lifts it heavenward in a lofty spire,
Or shapes it in a cunning frame of words,
Or pays his priest to make it day by day;
For sense must have its god as well as soul;
A new-born Dian calls for silver shrines,
And Egypt's holiest symbol is our own,
The sign we worship as did they of old
When Isis and Osiris ruled the world.

Let us be true to our most subtle selves,
We long to have our idols like the rest.

Think! when the men of Israel had their
God
Encamped among them, talking with their
chief,
Leading them in the pillar of the cloud
And watching o'er them in the shaft of fire,
They still must have an image; still they
longed
For somewhat of substantial, solid form
Whereon to hang their garlands, and to fix
Their wandering thoughts and gain a
stronger hold
For their uncertain faith, not yet assured
If those same meteors of the day and night
Were not mere exhalations of the soil.
Are we less earthly than the chosen race?
Are we more neighbors of the living God
Than they who gathered manna every morn,
Reaping where none had sown, and heard
the voice
Of him who met the Highest in the mount,
And brought them tables, graven with His
hand?
Yet these must have their idol, brought
their gold,
That star-browed Apis might be god again;
Yea, from their ears the women brake the
rings
That lent such splendors to the gypsy brown
Of sunburnt cheeks, — what more could
woman do
To show her pious zeal? They went astray,
But nature led them as it leads us all.
We too, who mock at Israel's golden calf
And scoff at Egypt's sacred scarabee,
Would have our amulets to clasp and kiss,
And flood with rapturous tears, and bear
with us
To be our dear companions in the dust;
Such magic works an image in our souls!

Man is an embryo; see at twenty years
His bones, the columns that uphold his
frame
Not yet cemented, shaft and capital,
Mere fragments of the temple incomplete.
At twoscore, threescore, is he then full
grown?
Nay, still a child, and as the little maids
Dress and undress their puppets, so he tries
To dress a lifeless creed, as if it lived,
And change its raiment when the world
cries shame!
We smile to see our little ones at play
So grave, so thoughtful, with maternal care

Nursing the wisps of rags they call their
  babes; —
Does He not smile who sees us with the
  toys
We call by sacred names, and idly feign
To be what we have called them ?   He is
  still
The Father of this helpless nursery-brood,
Whose second childhood joins so close its
  first,
That in the crowding, hurrying years be-
  tween
We scarce have trained our senses to their
  task
Before the gathering mist has dimmed our
  eyes,
And with our hollowed palm we help our
  ear,
And trace with trembling hand our wrin-
  kled names,
And then begin to tell our stories o'er,
And see — not hear — the whispering lips
  that say,
"You know —— ? Your father knew him.
  — This is he,
Tottering and leaning on the hireling's
  arm," —
And so, at length, disrobed of all that
  clad
The simple life we share with weed and
  worm,
Go to our cradles, naked as we came.

XII

LOVE

What if a soul redeemed, a spirit that
  loved
While yet on earth and was beloved in
  turn,
And still remembered every look and tone
Of that dear earthly sister who was left
Among the unwise virgins at the gate, —
Itself admitted with the bridegroom's
  train, —
What if this spirit redeemed, amid the
  host
Of chanting angels, in some transient lull
Of the eternal anthem, heard the cry
Of its lost darling, whom in evil hour
Some wilder pulse of nature led astray
And left an outcast in a world of fire,
Condemned to be the sport of cruel fiends,

Sleepless, unpitying, masters of the skill
To wring the maddest ecstasies of pain
From worn-out souls that only ask to die, —
Would it not long to leave the bliss of
  heaven, —
Bearing a little water in its hand
To moisten those poor lips that plead in
  vain
With Him we call our Father ?   Or is all
So changed in such as taste celestial joy
They hear unmoved the endless wail of
  woe;
The daughter in the same dear tones that
  hushed
Her cradle slumbers; she who once had
  held
A babe upon her bosom from its voice
Hoarse with its cry of anguish, yet the
  same ?

No ! not in ages when the Dreadful Bird
Stamped his huge footprints, and the Fear-
  ful Beast
Strode with the flesh about those fossil
  bones
We build to mimic life with pygmy hands,—
Not in those earliest days when men ran
  wild
And gashed each other with their knives of
  stone,
When their low foreheads bulged in ridgy
  brows
And their flat hands were callous in the
  palm
With walking in the fashion of their sires,
Grope as they might to find a cruel god
To work their will on such as human wrath
Had wrought its worst to torture, and had
  left
With rage unsated, white and stark and
  cold,
Could hate have shaped a demon more
  malign
Than him the dead men mummied in their
  creed
And taught their trembling children to
  adore !
  Made in *his* image !   Sweet and gracious
  souls
Dear to my heart by nature's fondest
  names,
Is not your memory still the precious mould
That lends its form to Him who hears my
  prayer ?
Thus only I behold Him, like to them,

Long-suffering, gentle, ever slow to wrath,
If wrath it be that only wounds to heal,
Ready to meet the wanderer ere he reach
The door he seeks, forgetful of his sin,
Longing to clasp him in a father's arms,
And seal his pardon with a pitying tear !

Four gospels tell their story to mankind,
And none so full of soft, caressing words
That bring the Maid of Bethlehem and her
    Babe
Before our tear-dimmed eyes, as his who
    learned
In the meek service of his gracious art
The tones which, like the medicinal balms
That calm the sufferer's anguish, soothe
    our souls.
Oh that the loving woman, she who sat
So long a listener at her Master's feet,
Had left us Mary's Gospel, — all she heard
Too sweet, too subtle for the ear of man !
Mark how the tender-hearted mothers read
The messages of love between the lines
Of the same page that loads the bitter
    tongue
Of him who deals in terror as his trade
With threatening words of wrath that
    scorch like flame !
They tell of angels whispering round the
    bed
Of the sweet infant smiling in its dream,
Of lambs enfolded in the Shepherd's arms,
Of Him who blessed the children; of the
    land
Where crystal rivers feed unfading flowers,
Of cities golden-paved with streets of pearl,
Of the white robes the winged creatures
    wear,
The crowns and harps from whose melodi-
    ous strings
One long, sweet anthem flows forever-
    more !

We too had human mothers, even as Thou,
Whom we have learned to worship as
    remote
From mortal kindred, wast a cradled babe.
The milk of woman filled our branching
    veins,
She lulled us with her tender nursery-
    song,
And folded round us her untiring arms,
While the first unremembered twilight
    year
Shaped us to conscious being; still we feel

Her pulses in our own, — too faintly feel;
Would that the heart of woman warmed
    our creeds !

Not from the sad-eyed hermit's lonely cell,
Not from the conclave where the holy
    men
Glare on each other, as with angry eyes
They battle for God's glory and their own,
Till, sick of wordy strife, a show of hands
Fixes the faith of ages yet unborn, —
Ah, not from these the listening soul can
    hear
The Father's voice that speaks itself
    divine !
Love must be still our Master; till we
    learn
What he can teach us of a woman's heart,
We know not His whose love embraces all.

EPILOGUE TO THE BREAK-FAST-TABLE SERIES

AUTOCRAT — PROFESSOR — POET

AT A BOOKSTORE

Anno Domini 1972

A CRAZY bookcase, placed before
A low-price dealer's open door;
Therein arrayed in broken rows
A ragged crew of rhyme and prose,
The homeless vagrants, waifs, and strays
Whose low estate this line betrays
(Set forth the lesser birds to lime)
YOUR CHOICE AMONG THESE BOOKS 1
    DIME !

Ho ! dealer; for its motto's sake
This scarecrow from the shelf I take;
Three starveling volumes bound in one,
Its covers warping in the sun.
Methinks it hath a musty smell,
I like its flavor none too well,
But Yorick's brain was far from dull,
Though Hamlet pah ! 'd, and dropped his
    skull.

Why, here comes rain ! The sky grows
    dark, —
Was that the roll of thunder ? Hark !
The shop affords a safe retreat,
A chair extends its welcome seat,

The tradesman has a civil look
(I 've paid, impromptu, for my book),
The clouds portend a sudden shower, —
I 'll read my purchase for an hour.

. . . .

What have I rescued from the shelf ?
A Boswell, writing out himself !
For though he changes dress and name,
The man beneath is still the same,
Laughing or sad, by fits and starts,
One actor in a dozen parts,
And whatsoe'er the mask may be,
The voice assures us, *This is he.*

I say not this to cry him down;
I find my Shakespeare in his clown,
His rogues the selfsame parent own;
Nay ! Satan talks in Milton's tone !
Where'er the ocean inlet strays,
The salt sea wave its source betrays;
Where'er the queen of summer blows,
She tells the zephyr, " I 'm the rose ! "

And his is not the playwright's page;
His table does not ape the stage;
What matter if the figures seen
Are only shadows on a screen,
He finds in them his lurking thought,
And on their lips the words he sought,
Like one who sits before the keys
And plays a tune himself to please.

And was he noted in his day ?
Read, flattered, honored ?   Who shall say ?

Poor wreck of time the wave has cast
To find a peaceful shore at last,
Once glorying in thy gilded name
And freighted deep with hopes of fame,
Thy leaf is moistened with a tear,
The first for many a long, long year !

For be it more or less of art
That veils the lowliest human heart
Where passion throbs, where friendship
        glows,
Where pity's tender tribute flows,
Where love has lit its fragrant fire,
And sorrow quenched its vain desire,
For me the altar is divine,
Its flame, its ashes, — all are mine !

And thou, my brother, as I look
And see thee pictured in thy book,
Thy years on every page confessed
In shadows lengthening from the west,
Thy glance that wanders, as it sought
Some freshly opening flower of thought,
Thy hopeful nature, light and free,
I start to find myself in thee !

. . . .

Come, vagrant, outcast, wretch forlorn
In leather jerkin stained and torn,
Whose talk has filled my idle hour
And made me half forget the shower,
I 'll do at least as much for you,
Your coat I 'll patch, your gilt renew,
Read you — perhaps — some other time.
Not bad, my bargain !   Price one dime !

SONGS OF MANY SEASONS

1862–1874

OPENING THE WINDOW

THUS I lift the sash, so long
Shut against the flight of song;
All too late for vain excuse, —
Lo, my captive rhymes are loose!

Rhymes that, flitting through my brain,
Beat against my window-pane,
Some with gayly colored wings,
Some, alas! with venomed stings.

Shall they bask in sunny rays?
Shall they feed on sugared praise?
Shall they stick with tangled feet
On the critic's poisoned sheet?

Are the outside winds too rough?
Is the world not wide enough?
Go, my wingèd verse, and try, —
Go, like Uncle Toby's fly!

PROGRAMME

OCTOBER 7, 1874

READER — gentle — if so be
Such still live, and live for me,
Will it please you to be told
What my tenscore pages hold?

Here are verses that in spite
Of myself I needs must write,
Like the wine that oozes first
When the unsqueezed grapes have burst.

Here are angry lines, "too hard!"
Says the soldier, battle-scarred.
Could I smile his scars away
I would blot the bitter lay,

Written with a knitted brow,
Read with placid wonder now.

Throbbed such passion in my heart?
Did his wounds once really smart?

Here are varied strains that sing
All the changes life can bring,
Songs when joyous friends have met,
Songs the mourner's tears have wet.

See the banquet's dead bouquet,
Fair and fragrant in its day;
Do they read the selfsame lines, —
He that fasts and he that dines?

Year by year, like milestones placed,
Mark the record Friendship traced.
Prisoned in the walls of time
Life has notched itself in rhyme:

As its seasons slid along,
Every year a notch of song,
From the June of long ago,
When the rose was full in blow,

Till the scarlet sage has come
And the cold chrysanthemum.
Read, but not to praise or blame;
Are not all our hearts the same?

For the rest, they take their chance, —
Some may pay a passing glance;
Others, — well, they served a turn, —
Wherefore written, would you learn?

Not for glory, not for pelf,
Not, be sure, to please myself,
Not for any meaner ends, —
Always "by request of friends."

Here's the cousin of a king, —
Would I do the civil thing?
Here's the first-born of a queen:
Here's a slant-eyed Mandarin.

Would I polish off Japan ?
Would I greet this famous man,
Prince or Prelate, Sheik or Shah ? —
Figaro çi and Figaro là !

Would I just this once comply ? —
So they teased and teased till I
(Be the truth at once confessed)
Wavered — yielded — did my best.

Turn my pages, — never mind
If you like not all you find;
Think not all the grains are gold
Sacramento's sand-banks hold.

Every kernel has its shell,
Every chime its harshest bell,
Every face its weariest look,
Every shelf its emptiest book,

Every field its leanest sheaf,
Every book its dullest leaf,
Every leaf its weakest line, —
Shall it not be so with mine ?

Best for worst shall make amends,
Find us, keep us, leave us friends
Till, perchance, we meet again.
Benedicite. — Amen!

IN THE QUIET DAYS

AN OLD-YEAR SONG

As through the forest, disarrayed
By chill November, late I strayed,
A lonely minstrel of the wood
Was singing to the solitude:
I loved thy music, thus I said,
When o'er thy perch the leaves were
  spread;
Sweet was thy song, but sweeter now
Thy carol on the leafless bough.
  Sing, little bird ! thy note shall cheer
  The sadness of the dying year.

When violets pranked the turf with blue
And morning filled their cups with dew,
Thy slender voice with rippling trill
The budding April bowers would fill,
Nor passed its joyous tones away
When April rounded into May:
  Thy life shall hail no second dawn, —
  Sing, little bird ! the spring is gone.

And I remember — welladay ! —
Thy full-blown summer roundelay,
As when behind a broidered screen
Some holy maiden sings unseen:
With answering notes the woodland rung,
And every treetop found a tongue.
  How deep the shade ! the groves how
    fair !
  Sing, little bird ! the woods are bare.

The summer's throbbing chant is done
And mute the choral antiphon;
The birds have left the shivering pines

To flit among the trellised vines,
Or fan the air with scented plumes
Amid the love-sick orange-blooms,
  And thou art here alone, — alone, —
  Sing, little bird ! the rest have flown.

The snow has capped yon distant hill,
At morn the running brook was still,
From driven herds the clouds that rise
Are like the smoke of sacrifice;
Erelong the frozen sod shall mock
The ploughshare, changed to stubborn
  rock,
  The brawling streams shall soon be
    dumb, —
  Sing, little bird ! the frosts have come.

Fast, fast the lengthening shadows creep,
The songless fowls are half asleep,
The air grows chill, the setting sun
May leave thee ere thy song is done,
The pulse that warms thy breast grow cold,
Thy secret die with thee, untold:
  The lingering sunset still is bright, —
  Sing, little bird ! 't will soon be night.

DOROTHY Q.

A FAMILY PORTRAIT

I cannot tell the story of Dorothy Q. more
simply in prose than I have told it in verse,
but I can add something to it.

Dorothy was the daughter of Judge Edmund
Quincy, and the aunt of Josiah Quincy, junior,
the young patriot and orator who died just
before the American Revolution, of which he

was one of the most eloquent and effective promoters. The son of the latter, Josiah Quincy, the first mayor of Boston bearing that name, lived to a great age, one of the most useful and honored citizens of his time.

The canvas of the painting was so much decayed that it had to be replaced by a new one, in doing which the rapier thrust was of course filled up.

GRANDMOTHER'S mother: her age, I guess,
Thirteen summers, or something less;
Girlish bust, but womanly air;
Smooth, square forehead with uprolled
    hair;
Lips that lover has never kissed;
Taper fingers and slender wrist;
Hanging sleeves of stiff brocade;
So they painted the little maid.

On her hand a parrot green
Sits unmoving and broods serene.
Hold up the canvas full in view, —
Look! there's a rent the light shines
    through,
Dark with a century's fringe of dust, —
That was a Red-Coat's rapier-thrust!
Such is the tale the lady old,
Dorothy's daughter's daughter, told.

Who the painter was none may tell, —
One whose best was not over well;
Hard and dry, it must be confessed,
Flat as a rose that has long been pressed;
Yet in her cheek the hues are bright,
Dainty colors of red and white,
And in her slender shape are seen
Hint and promise of stately mien.

Look not on her with eyes of scorn, —
Dorothy Q. was a lady born!
Ay! since the galloping Normans came,
England's annals have known her name;
And still to the three-hilled rebel town
Dear is that ancient name's renown,
For many a civic wreath they won,
The youthful sire and the gray-haired son.

O Damsel Dorothy! Dorothy Q.!
Strange is the gift that I owe to you;
Such a gift as never a king
Save to daughter or son might bring, —
All my tenure of heart and hand,
All my title to house and land;
Mother and sister and child and wife
And joy and sorrow and death and life!

What if a hundred years ago
Those close-shut lips had answered No,
When forth the tremulous question came
That cost the maiden her Norman name,
And under the folds that look so still
The bodice swelled with the bosom's thrill?
Should I be I, or would it be
One tenth another, to nine tenths me?

Soft is the breath of a maiden's YES:
Not the light gossamer stirs with less;
But never a cable that holds so fast
Through all the battles of wave and blast,
And never an echo of speech or song
That lives in the babbling air so long!
There were tones in the voice that whis-
    pered then
You may hear to-day in a hundred men.

O lady and lover, how faint and far
Your images hover, — and here we are,
Solid and stirring in flesh and bone, —
Edward's and Dorothy's — all their own, —
A goodly record for Time to show
Of a syllable spoken so long ago! —
Shall I bless you, Dorothy, or forgive
For the tender whisper that bade me
    live?

It shall be a blessing, my little maid!
I will heal the stab of the Red-Coat's
    blade,
And freshen the gold of the tarnished
    frame,
And gild with a rhyme your household
    name;
So you shall smile on us brave and bright
As first you greeted the morning's light,
And live untroubled by woes and fears
Through a second youth of a hundred
    years.

THE ORGAN-BLOWER

DEVOUTEST of my Sunday friends,
The patient Organ-blower bends;
I see his figure sink and rise,
(Forgive me, Heaven, my wandering
    eyes!)
A moment lost, the next half seen,
His head above the scanty screen,
Still measuring out his deep salaams
Through quavering hymns and panting
    psalms.

No priest that prays in gilded stole,
To save a rich man's mortgaged soul;
No sister, fresh from holy vows,
So humbly stoops, so meekly bows;
His large obeisance puts to shame
The proudest genuflecting dame,
Whose Easter bonnet low descends
With all the grace devotion lends.

O brother with the supple spine,
How much we owe those bows of thine !
Without thine arm to lend the breeze,
How vain the finger on the keys !
Though all unmatched the player's skill,
Those thousand throats were dumb and
    still:
Another's art may shape the tone,
The breath that fills it is thine own.

Six days the silent Memnon waits
Behind his temple's folded gates;
But when the seventh day's sunshine falls
Through rainbowed windows on the walls,
He breathes, he sings, he shouts, he fills
The quivering air with rapturous thrills;
The roof resounds, the pillars shake,
And all the slumbering echoes wake !

The Preacher from the Bible-text
With weary words my soul has vexed
(Some stranger, fumbling far astray
To find the lesson for the day);
He tells us truths too plainly true,
And reads the service all askew, —
Why, why the — mischief — can't he look
Beforehand in the service-book ?

But thou, with decent mien and face,
Art always ready in thy place;
Thy strenuous blast, whate'er the tune,
As steady as the strong monsoon;
Thy only dread a leathery creak,
Or small residual extra squeak,
To send along the shadowy aisles
A sunlit wave of dimpled smiles.

Not all the preaching, O my friend,
Comes from the church's pulpit end !
Not all that bend the knee and bow
Yield service half so true as thou !
One simple task performed aright,
With slender skill, but all thy might,
Where honest labor does its best,
And leaves the player all the rest.

This many-diapasoned maze,
Through which the breath of being strays,
Whose music makes our earth divine,
Has work for mortal hands like mine.
My duty lies before me.   Lo,
The lever there !   Take hold and blow !
And He whose hand is on the keys
Will play the tune as He shall please.

AFTER THE FIRE

[The great Boston fire occurred November
9–10, 1872.]

WHILE far along the eastern sky
I saw the flags of Havoc fly,
As if his forces would assault
The sovereign of the starry vault
And hurl Him back the burning rain
That seared the cities of the plain,
I read as on a crimson page
The words of Israel's sceptred sage: —

For riches make them wings, and they
Do as an eagle fly away.

O vision of that sleepless night,
What hue shall paint the mocking light
That burned and stained the orient skies
Where peaceful morning loves to rise,
As if the sun had lost his way
And dawned to make a second day, —
Above how red with fiery glow,
How dark to those it woke below !

On roof and wall, on dome and spire,
Flashed the false jewels of the fire;
Girt with her belt of glittering panes,
And crowned with starry-gleaming vanes,
Our northern queen in glory shone
With new-born splendors not her own,
And stood, transfigured in our eyes,
A victim decked for sacrifice !

The cloud still hovers overhead,
And still the midnight sky is red;
As the lost wanderer strays alone
To seek the place he called his own,
His devious footprints sadly tell
How changed the pathways known so
    well;
The scene, how new !   The tale, how old
Ere yet the ashes have grown cold !

Again I read the words that came
Writ in the rubric of the flame:
Howe'er we trust to mortal things,
Each hath its pair of folded wings;
Though long their terrors rest unspread
Their fatal plumes are never shed;
At last, at last, they stretch in flight,
And blot the day and blast the night !

Hope, only Hope, of all that clings
Around us, never spreads her wings;
Love, though he break his earthly chain,
Still whispers he will come again;
But Faith that soars to seek the sky
Shall teach our half-fledged souls to fly,
And find, beyond the smoke and flame,
The cloudless azure whence they came !

AT THE PANTOMIME

18—: REWRITTEN 1874

THE house was crammed from roof to floor,
Heads piled on heads at every door;
Half dead with August's seething heat
I crowded on and found my seat,
My patience slightly out of joint,
My temper short of boiling-point,
Not quite at *Hate mankind as such*,
Nor yet at *Love them overmuch*.

Amidst the throng the pageant drew
Were gathered Hebrews not a few,
Black-bearded, swarthy, — at their side
Dark, jewelled women, orient-eyed:
If scarce a Christian hopes for grace
Who crowds one in his narrow place,
What will the savage victim do
Whose ribs are kneaded by a Jew ?

Next on my left a breathing form
Wedged up against me, close and warm;
The beak that crowned the bistred face
Betrayed the mould of Abraham's race, —
That coal-black hair, that smoke-brown
          hue, —
Ah, cursèd, unbelieving Jew !
I started, shuddering, to the right,
And squeezed — a second Israelite !

Then woke the evil brood of rage
That slumber, tongueless, in their cage;
I stabbed in turn with silent oaths
The hook-nosed kite of carrion clothes,
The snaky usurer, him that crawls
And cheats beneath the golden balls,

Moses and Levi, all the horde,
Spawn of the race that slew its Lord.

Up came their murderous deeds of old,
The grisly story Chaucer told,
And many an ugly tale beside
Of children caught and crucified;
I heard the ducat-sweating thieves
Beneath the Ghetto's slouching eaves,
And, thrust beyond the tented green,
The lepers cry, " Unclean !   Unclean ! "

The show went on, but, ill at ease,
My sullen eye it could not please,
In vain my conscience whispered, " Shame !
Who but their Maker is to blame ? "
I thought of Judas and his bribe,
And steeled my soul against their tribe:
My neighbors stirred; I looked again
Full on the younger of the twain.

A fresh young cheek whose olive hue
The mantling blood shows faintly through;
Locks dark as midnight, that divide
And shade the neck on either side;
Soft, gentle, loving eyes that gleam
Clear as a starlit mountain stream; —
So looked that other child of Shem,
The Maiden's Boy of Bethlehem !

And thou couldst scorn the peerless blood
That flows unmingled from the Flood, —
Thy scutcheon spotted with the stains
Of Norman thieves and pirate Danes !
The New World's foundling, in thy pride
Scowl on the Hebrew at thy side,
And lo ! the very semblance there
The Lord of Glory deigned to wear !

I see that radiant image rise,
The flowing hair, the pitying eyes,
The faintly crimsoned cheek that shows
The blush of Sharon's opening rose, —
Thy hands would clasp his hallowed feet
Whose brethren soil thy Christian seat,
Thy lips would press his garment's hem
That curl in wrathful scorn for them !

A sudden mist, a watery screen,
Dropped like a veil before the scene;
The shadow floated from my soul,
And to my lips a whisper stole, —
" Thy prophets caught the Spirit's flame,
From thee the Son of Mary came,
With thee the Father deigned to dwell, —
Peace be upon thee, Israel ! "

A BALLAD OF THE BOSTON TEA-PARTY

The tax on tea, which was considered so odious and led to the act on which *A Ballad of the Boston Tea Party* is founded, was but a small matter, only twopence in the pound. But it involved a principle of taxation, to which the Colonies would not submit. Their objection was not to the amount, but the claim. The East India Company, however, sent out a number of tea-ships to different American ports, three of them to Boston.

The inhabitants tried to send them back, but in vain. The captains of the ships had consented, if permitted, to return with their cargoes to England, but the consignees refused to discharge them from their obligations, the custom house to give them a clearance for their return, and the governor to grant them a passport for going by the fort. It was easily seen that the tea would be gradually landed from the ships lying so near the town, and that if landed it would be disposed of, and the purpose of establishing the monopoly and raising a revenue effected. To prevent the dreaded consequence, a number of armed men, disguised like Indians, boarded the ships and threw their whole cargoes of tea into the dock. About seventeen persons boarded the ships in Boston harbor, and emptied three hundred and forty-two chests of tea. Among these "Indians" was Major Thomas Melville, the same who suggested to me the poem, *The Last Leaf*.

Read at a meeting of the Massachusetts Historical Society in 1874.

No! never such a draught was poured
  Since Hebe served with nectar
The bright Olympians and their Lord,
  Her over-kind protector, —
Since Father Noah squeezed the grape
  And took to such behaving
As would have shamed our grandsire ape
  Before the days of shaving, —
No! ne'er was mingled such a draught
  In palace, hall, or arbor,
As freemen brewed and tyrants quaffed
  That night in Boston Harbor!
It kept King George so long awake
  His brain at last got addled,
It made the nerves of Britain shake,
  With sevenscore millions saddled;
Before that bitter cup was drained,
  Amid the roar of cannon,
The Western war-cloud's crimson stained
  The Thames, the Clyde, the Shannon;

Full many a six-foot grenadier
  The flattened grass had measured,
And many a mother many a year
  Her tearful memories treasured;
Fast spread the tempest's darkening pall,
  The mighty realms were troubled,
The storm broke loose, but first of all
  The Boston teapot bubbled!

An evening party, — only that,
  No formal invitation,
No gold-laced coat, no stiff cravat,
  No feast in contemplation,
No silk-robed dames, no fiddling band,
  No flowers, no songs, no dancing, —
A tribe of red men, axe in hand, —
  Behold the guests advancing!
How fast the stragglers join the throng,
  From stall and workshop gathered!
The lively barber skips along
  And leaves a chin half-lathered;
The smith has flung his hammer down, —
  The horseshoe still is glowing;
The truant tapster at the Crown
  Has left a beer-cask flowing;
The cooper's boys have dropped the adze,
  And trot behind their master;
Up run the tarry ship-yard lads, —
  The crowd is hurrying faster, —
Out from the Millpond's purlieus gush
  The streams of white-faced millers,
And down their slippery alleys rush
  The lusty young Fort-Hillers;
The ropewalk lends its 'prentice crew, —
  The tories seize the omen:
" Ay, boys, you 'll soon have work to do
  For England's rebel foemen,
'King Hancock,' Adams, and their gang,
  That fire the mob with treason, —
When these we shoot and those we hang
  The town will come to reason."

On — on to where the tea-ships ride!
  And now their ranks are forming, —
A rush, and up the Dartmouth's side
  The Mohawk band is swarming!
See the fierce natives! What a glimpse
  Of paint and fur and feather,
As all at once the full-grown imps
  Light on the deck together!
A scarf the pigtail's secret keeps,
  A blanket hides the breeches, —
And out the cursèd cargo leaps,
  And overboard it pitches!

O woman, at the evening board
  So gracious, sweet, and purring,
So happy while the tea is poured,
  So blest while spoons are stirring,
What martyr can compare with thee,
  The mother, wife, or daughter,
That night, instead of best Bohea,
  Condemned to milk and water !

Ah, little dreams the quiet dame
  Who plies with rock and spindle
The patient flax, how great a flame
  Yon little spark shall kindle !
The lurid morning shall reveal
  A fire no king can smother
Where British flint and Boston steel
  Have clashed against each other !
Old charters shrivel in its track,
  His Worship's bench has crumbled,
It climbs and clasps the union-jack,
  Its blazoned pomp is humbled,
The flags go down on land and sea
  Like corn before the reapers;
So burned the fire that brewed the tea
  That Boston served her keepers !

The waves that wrought a century's wreck
  Have rolled o'er whig and tory;
The Mohawks on the Dartmouth's deck
  Still live in song and story;
The waters in the rebel bay
  Have kept the tea-leaf savor;
Our old North-Enders in their spray
  Still taste a Hyson flavor;

And Freedom's teacup still o'erflows
  With ever fresh libations,
To cheat of slumber all her foes
  And cheer the wakening nations !

NEARING THE SNOW–LINE

1870

SLOW toiling upward from the misty vale,
  I leave the bright enamelled zones be-
      low;
  No more for me their beauteous bloom
      shall glow,
Their lingering sweetness load the morning
      gale;
Few are the slender flowerets, scentless,
      pale,
  That on their ice-clad stems all trembling
      blow
  Along the margin of unmelting snow;
Yet with unsaddened voice thy verge I hail,
  White realm of peace above the flower-
      ing line;
Welcome thy frozen domes, thy rocky
      spires !
  O'er thee undimmed the moon-girt
      planets shine,
On thy majestic altars fade the fires
That filled the air with smoke of vain de-
      sires,
  And all the unclouded blue of heaven is
      thine !

IN WAR TIME

TO CANAAN

A PURITAN WAR-SONG

AUGUST 12, 1862

This poem, published anonymously in the
Boston *Evening Transcript*, was claimed by
several persons, three, if I remember correctly,
whose names I have or have had, but never
thought it worth while to publish.

WHERE are you going, soldiers,
  With banner, gun, and sword ?
We're marching South to Canaan
  To battle for the Lord !

What Captain leads your armies
  Along the rebel coasts ?
The Mighty One of Israel,
  His name is Lord of Hosts !
To Canaan, to Canaan
  The Lord has led us forth,
To blow before the heathen walls
  The trumpets of the North !

What flag is this you carry
  Along the sea and shore ?
The same our grandsires lifted up, —
  The same our fathers bore !
In many a battle's tempest
  It shed the crimson rain, —

What God has woven in his loom
  Let no man rend in twain !
    To Canaan, to Canaan
    The Lord has led us forth,
    To plant upon the rebel towers
    The banners of the North !

What troop is this that follows,
  All armed with picks and spades ?
These are the swarthy bondsmen, —
  The iron-skin brigades !
They 'll pile up Freedom's breastwork,
  They 'll scoop out rebels' graves;
Who then will be their owner
  And march them off for slaves ?
    To Canaan, to Canaan
    The Lord has led us forth,
    To strike upon the captive's chain
    The hammers of the North !

What song is this you 're singing ?
  The same that Israel sung
When Moses led the mighty choir,
  And Miriam's timbrel rung !
To Canaan ! To Canaan !
  The priests and maidens cried:
To Canaan ! To Canaan !
  The people's voice replied.
    To Canaan, to Canaan
    The Lord has led us forth,
    To thunder through its adder dens
    The anthems of the North !

When Canaan's hosts are scattered,
  And all her walls lie flat,
What follows next in order ?
  The Lord will see to that !
We 'll break the tyrant's sceptre, —
  We 'll build the people's throne, —
When half the world is Freedom's,
  Then all the world 's our own !
    To Canaan, to Canaan
    The Lord has led us forth,
    To sweep the rebel threshing-floors,
    A whirlwind from the North !

"THUS SAITH THE LORD, I OFFER THEE THREE THINGS"

1862

In poisonous dens, where traitors hide
  Like bats that fear the day,
While all the land our charters claim

Is sweating blood and breathing flame,
Dead to their country's woe and shame,
  The recreants whisper Stay !

In peaceful homes, where patriot fires
  On Love's own altars glow,
The mother hides her trembling fear,
The wife, the sister, checks a tear,
To breathe the parting word of cheer,
  Soldier of Freedom, Go !

In halls where Luxury lies at ease,
  And Mammon keeps his state,
Where flatterers fawn and menials crouch,
The dreamer, startled from his couch,
Wrings a few counters from his pouch,
  And murmurs faintly Wait !

In weary camps, on trampled plains
  That ring with fife and drum,
The battling host, whose harness gleams
Along the crimson-flowing streams,
Calls, like a warning voice in dreams,
  We want you, Brother ! Come !

Choose ye whose bidding ye will do, —
  To go, to wait, to stay !
Sons of the Freedom-loving town,
Heirs of the Fathers' old renown,
The servile yoke, the civic crown,
  Await your choice To-day !

The stake is laid ! O gallant youth
  With yet unsilvered brow,
If Heaven should lose and Hell should
    win,
On whom shall lie the mortal sin,
That cries aloud, *It might have been ?*
  God calls you — answer NOW.

NEVER OR NOW

AN APPEAL

1862

Listen, young heroes ! your country is
    calling !
  Time strikes the hour for the brave and
    the true !
Now, while the foremost are fighting and
    falling,
  Fill up the ranks that have opened for
    you !

You whom the fathers made free and de-
fended,
Stain not the scroll that emblazons their
fame!
You whose fair heritage spotless descended,
Leave not your children a birthright of
shame!

Stay not for questions while Freedom
stands gasping!
Wait not till Honor lies wrapped in his
pall!
Brief the lips' meeting be, swift the hands'
clasping, —
"Off for the wars!" is enough for them
all!

Break from the arms that would fondly
caress you!
Hark! 't is the bugle-blast, sabres are
drawn!
Mothers shall pray for you, fathers shall
bless you,
Maidens shall weep for you when you
are gone!

Never or now! cries the blood of a nation,
Poured on the turf where the red rose
should bloom;
Now is the day and the hour of salva-
tion, —
Never or now! peals the trumpet of
doom!

Never or now! roars the hoarse-throated
cannon
Through the black canopy blotting the
skies;
Never or now! flaps the shell-blasted pen-
non
O'er the deep ooze where the Cumber-
land lies!

From the foul dens where our brothers are
dying,
Aliens and foes in the land of their
birth, —
From the rank swamps where our martyrs
are lying
Pleading in vain for a handful of earth, —

From the hot plains where they perish out-
numbered,
Furrowed and ridged by the battle-field's
plough,

Comes the loud summons; too long you
have slumbered,
Hear the last Angel-trump, — Never or
Now!

HYMN

WRITTEN FOR THE GREAT CENTRAL FAIR
IN PHILADELPHIA, 1864

[This hymn was to have been sung at the
Inaugural Ceremonies June 7, but an accident to
the singers' platform prevented its use in that
form.]

FATHER, send on Earth again
Peace and good-will to men;
Yet, while the weary track of life
Leads thy people through storm and strife,
Help us to walk therein.

Guide us through the perilous path;
Teach us love that tempers wrath;
Let the fountain of mercy flow
Alike for helpless friend and foe,
Children all of Thine.

God of grace, hear our call;
Bless our gifts, Giver of all;
The wounded heal, the captive restore,
And make us a nation evermore
Faithful to Freedom and Thee.

ONE COUNTRY

1865

ONE country! Treason's writhing asp
Struck madly at her girdle's clasp,
And Hatred wrenched with might and main
To rend its welded links in twain,
While Mammon hugged his golden calf
Content to take one broken half,
While thankless churls stood idly by
And heard unmoved a nation's cry!

One country! "Nay," — the tyrant crew
Shrieked from their dens, — "it shall be
two!
Ill bodes to us this monstrous birth,
That scowls on all the thrones of earth,
Too broad yon starry cluster shines,
Too proudly tower the New-World pines,
Tear down the 'banner of the free,'
And cleave their land from sea to sea!"

One country still, though foe and "friend"
Our seamless empire strove to rend;
Safe ! safe ! though all the fiends of hell
Join the red murderers' battle-yell !
What though the lifted sabres gleam,
The cannons frown by shore and stream, —
The sabres clash, the cannons thrill,
In wild accord, One country still !

One country ! in her stress and strain
We heard the breaking of a chain !
Look where the conquering Nation swings
Her iron flail, — its shivered rings !
Forged by the rebels' crimson hand,
That bolt of wrath shall scourge the land
Till Peace proclaims on sea and shore
One Country now and evermore !

GOD SAVE THE FLAG !

1865

WASHED in the blood of the brave and the
    blooming,
  Snatched from the altars of insolent foes,
Burning with star-fires, but never consuming,
  Flash its broad ribbons of lily and rose.

Vainly the prophets of Baal would rend it,
  Vainly his worshippers pray for its fall;
Thousands have died for it, millions defend
    it,
  Emblem of justice and mercy to all:

Justice that reddens the sky with her terrors,
  Mercy that comes with her white-handed
    train,
Soothing all passions, redeeming all errors,
  Sheathing the sabre and breaking the
    chain.

Borne on the deluge of old usurpations,
  Drifted our Ark o'er the desolate seas,
Bearing the rainbow of hope to the nations,
  Torn from the storm-cloud and flung to
    the breeze !

God bless the Flag and its loyal defenders,
  While its broad folds o'er the battle-field
    wave,
Till the dim star-wreath rekindle its splen-
    dors,
  Washed from its stains in the blood of
    the brave !

HYMN

AFTER THE PASSAGE OF THE THIRTEENTH
AMENDMENT

1863

GIVER of all that crowns our days,
With grateful hearts we sing thy praise;
Through deep and desert led by Thee,
Our promised land at last we see.

Ruler of Nations, judge our cause !
If we have kept thy holy laws,
The sons of Belial curse in vain
The day that rends the captive's chain.

Thou God of vengeance ! Israel's Lord !
Break in their grasp the shield and sword,
And make thy righteous judgments known
Till all thy foes are overthrown !

Then, Father, lay thy healing hand
In mercy on our stricken land;
Lead all its wanderers to the fold,
And be their Shepherd as of old.

So shall one Nation's song ascend
To Thee, our Ruler, Father, Friend,
While Heaven's wide arch resounds again
With Peace on earth, good-will to men !

HYMN

FOR THE FAIR AT CHICAGO

1865

O GOD ! in danger's darkest hour,
  In battle's deadliest field,
Thy name has been our Nation's tower,
  Thy truth her help and shield.

Our lips should fill the air with praise,
  Nor pay the debt we owe,
So high above the songs we raise
  The floods of mercy flow.

Yet Thou wilt hear the prayer we speak,
  The song of praise we sing, —
Thy children, who thine altar seek
  Their grateful gifts to bring.

Thine altar is the sufferer's bed,
  The home of woe and pain,
The soldier's turfy pillow, red
  With battle's crimson rain.

No smoke of burning stains the air,
  No incense-clouds arise;
Thy peaceful servants, Lord, prepare
  A bloodless sacrifice.

Lo! for our wounded brothers' need,
  We bear the wine and oil;
For us they faint, for us they bleed,
  For them our gracious toil!

O Father, bless the gifts we bring!
  Cause Thou thy face to shine,
Till every nation owns her King,
  And all the earth is thine.

UNDER THE WASHINGTON ELM, CAMBRIDGE

APRIL 27, 1861

EIGHTY years have passed, and more,
  Since under the brave old tree
Our fathers gathered in arms, and swore
They would follow the sign their banners
    bore,
  And fight till the land was free.

Half of their work was done,
  Half is left to do, —
Cambridge, and Concord, and Lexington!
When the battle is fought and won,
  What shall be told of you?

Hark! — 't is the south-wind moans, —
  Who are the martyrs down?
Ah, the marrow was true in your children's
    bones
That sprinkled with blood the cursèd stones
  Of the murder-haunted town!

What if the storm-clouds blow?
  What if the green leaves fall?
Better the crashing tempest's throe
Than the army of worms that gnawed be-
    low;
  Trample them one and all!

Then, when the battle is won,
  And the land from traitors free,
Our children shall tell of the strife begun
When Liberty's second April sun
  Was bright on our brave old tree!

FREEDOM, OUR QUEEN

LAND where the banners wave last in the
    sun,
Blazoned with star-clusters, many in one,
Floating o'er prairie and mountain and sea;
Hark! 't is the voice of thy children to
  thee!

Here at thine altar our vows we renew
Still in thy cause to be loyal and true, —
True to thy flag on the field and the wave,
Living to honor it, dying to save!

Mother of heroes! if perfidy's blight
Fall on a star in thy garland of light,
Sound but one bugle-blast! Lo! at the
    sign
Armies all panoplied wheel into line!

Hope of the world! thou hast broken its
  chains, —
Wear thy bright arms while a tyrant re-
  mains,
Stand for the right till the nations shall
  own
Freedom their sovereign, with Law for her
  throne!

Freedom! sweet Freedom! our voices re-
  sound,
Queen by God's blessing, unsceptred, un-
  crowned!
Freedom, sweet Freedom, our pulses re-
  peat,
Warm with her life-blood, as long as they
  beat!

Fold the broad banner-stripes over her
  breast, —
Crown her with star-jewels Queen of the
  West!
Earth for her heritage, God for her friend,
She shall reign over us, world without
  end!

ARMY HYMN

"OLD HUNDRED"

O LORD of Hosts ! Almighty King !
Behold the sacrifice we bring !
To every arm thy strength impart,
Thy spirit shed through every heart !

Wake in our breasts the living fires,
The holy faith that warmed our sires;
Thy hand hath made our Nation free;
To die for her is serving Thee.

Be Thou a pillared flame to show
The midnight snare, the silent foe;
And when the battle thunders loud,
Still guide us in its moving cloud.

God of all Nations ! Sovereign Lord !
In thy dread name we draw the sword,
We lift the starry flag on high
That fills with light our stormy sky.

From treason's rent, from murder's stain,
Guard Thou its folds till Peace shall
    reign, —
Till fort and field, till shore and sea,
Join our loud anthem, PRAISE TO THEE !

PARTING HYMN

" DUNDEE "

FATHER of Mercies, Heavenly Friend,
    We seek thy gracious throne;
To Thee our faltering prayers ascend,
    Our fainting hearts are known !

From blasts that chill, from suns that
        smite,
    From every plague that harms;
In camp and march, in siege and fight,
    Protect our men-at-arms !

Though from our darkened lives they take
    What makes our life most dear,
We yield them for their country's sake
    With no relenting tear.

Our blood their flowing veins will shed,
    Their wounds our breasts will share;
Oh, save us from the woes we dread,
    Or grant us strength to bear !

Let each unhallowed cause that brings
    The stern destroyer cease,
Thy flaming angel fold his wings,
    And seraphs whisper Peace !

Thine are the sceptre and the sword,
    Stretch forth thy mighty hand, —
Reign Thou our kingless nation's Lord,
    Rule Thou our throneless land !

THE FLOWER OF LIBERTY

WHAT flower is this that greets the morn,
Its hues from Heaven so freshly born ?
With burning star and flaming band
It kindles all the sunset land:
Oh tell us what its name may be, —
Is this the Flower of Liberty ?
    It is the banner of the free,
    The starry Flower of Liberty !

In savage Nature's far abode
Its tender seed our fathers sowed;
The storm-winds rocked its swelling bud,
Its opening leaves were streaked with
        blood,
Till lo ! earth's tyrants shook to see
The full-blown Flower of Liberty !
    Then hail the banner of the free,
    The starry Flower of Liberty !

Behold its streaming rays unite,
One mingling flood of braided light, —
The red that fires the Southern rose,
With spotless white from Northern snows,
And, spangled o'er its azure, see
The sister Stars of Liberty !
    Then hail the banner of the free,
    The starry Flower of Liberty !

The blades of heroes fence it round,
Where'er it springs is holy ground;
From tower and dome its glories spread;
It waves where lonely sentries tread;
It makes the land as ocean free,
And plants an empire on the sea !
    Then hail the banner of the free,
    The starry Flower of Liberty !

Thy sacred leaves, fair Freedom's flower,
Shall ever float on dome and tower,
To all their heavenly colors true,
In blackening frost or crimson dew. —

And God love us as we love thee,
Thrice holy Flower of Liberty !
Then hail the banner of the free,
The starry FLOWER OF LIBERTY !

THE SWEET LITTLE MAN

DEDICATED TO THE STAY-AT-HOME
RANGERS

Now, while our soldiers are fighting our
battles,
Each at his post to do all that he can,
Down among rebels and contraband chat-
tels,
What are you doing, my sweet little man ?

All the brave boys under canvas are sleep-
ing,
All of them pressing to march with the
van,
Far from the home where their sweethearts
are weeping;
What are you waiting for, sweet little
man ?

You with the terrible warlike mustaches,
Fit for a colonel or chief of a clan,
You with the waist made for sword-belts
and sashes,
Where are your shoulder-straps, sweet
little man ?

Bring him the buttonless garment of
woman !
Cover his face lest it freckle and tan;
Muster the Apron-String Guards on the
Common,
That is the corps for the sweet little
man !

Give him for escort a file of young misses,
Each of them armed with a deadly rattan;
They shall defend him from laughter and
hisses,
Aimed by low boys at the sweet little
man.

All the fair maidens about him shall cluster,
Pluck the white feathers from bonnet
and fan,
Make him a plume like a turkey-wing
duster, —
That is the crest for the sweet little man !

Oh, but the Apron-String Guards are the
fellows !
Drilling each day since our troubles be-
gan, —
" Handle your walking-sticks !" " Shoulder
umbrellas !"
That is the style for the sweet little man !

Have we a nation to save ? In the first
place
Saving ourselves is the sensible plan, —
Surely the spot where there 's shooting 's
the worst place
Where I can stand, says the sweet little
man.

Catch me confiding my person with stran-
gers !
Think how the cowardly Bull-Runners
ran !
In the brigade of the Stay-at-Home Rangers
Marches my corps, says the sweet little
man.

Such was the stuff of the Malakoff-takers,
Such were the soldiers that scaled the
Redan;
Truculent housemaids and bloodthirsty
Quakers,
Brave not the wrath of the sweet little
man !

Yield him the sidewalk, ye nursery maid-
ens !
Sauve qui peut! Bridget, and right
about ! Ann; —
Fierce as a shark in a school of menhadens,
See him advancing, the sweet little man !

When the red flails of the battle-field's
threshers
Beat out the continent's wheat from its
bran,
While the wind scatters the chaffy seceshers,
What will become of our sweet little
man ?

When the brown soldiers come back from
the borders,
How will he look while his features they
scan ?
How will he feel when he gets marching
orders,
Signed by his lady love ? sweet little
man !

Fear not for him, though the rebels expect
    him, —
  Life is too precious to shorten its span;
Woman her broomstick shall raise to pro-
    tect him,
    Will she not fight for the sweet little
    man ?

Now then, nine cheers for the Stay-at-Home
    Ranger !
  Blow the great fish-horn and beat the
    big pan !
First in the field that is farthest from
    danger,
    Take your white-feather plume, sweet
    little man !

UNION AND LIBERTY

FLAG of the heroes who left us their glory,
  Borne through their battle-fields' thun-
    der and flame,
Blazoned in song and illumined in story,
  Wave o'er us all who inherit their fame !
    Up with our banner bright,
    Sprinkled with starry light,
  Spread its fair emblems from mountain
    to shore,
    While through the sounding sky
    Loud rings the Nation's cry, —
UNION AND LIBERTY ! ONE EVERMORE !

Light of our firmament, guide of our Na-
    tion,
  Pride of her children, and honored afar,

Let the wide beams of thy full constellation
  Scatter each cloud that would darken
    a star !
    Up with our banner bright, etc.

Empire unsceptred ! what foe shall assail
    thee,
  Bearing the standard of Liberty's van ?
Think not the God of thy fathers shall fail
    thee,
  Striving with men for the birthright of
    man !
    Up with our banner bright, etc.

Yet if, by madness and treachery blighted,
  Dawns the dark hour when the sword
    thou must draw,
Then with the arms of thy millions united,
  Smite the bold traitors to Freedom and
    Law !
    Up with our banner bright, etc.

Lord of the Universe ! shield us and guide
    us,
  Trusting Thee always, through shadow
    and sun !
Thou hast united us, who shall divide us ?
  Keep us, oh keep us the MANY IN ONE !
    Up with our banner bright,
    Sprinkled with starry light,
  Spread its fair emblems from mountain
    to shore,
    While through the sounding sky
    Loud rings the Nation's cry, —
UNION AND LIBERTY ! ONE EVERMORE !

SONGS OF WELCOME AND FAREWELL

AMERICA TO RUSSIA

AUGUST 17, 1866

Read by Hon. G. V. Fox at a dinner given to
the Mission from the United States, St. Peter-
burg.

THOUGH watery deserts hold apart
  The worlds of East and West,
Still beats the selfsame human heart
  In each proud Nation's breast.

Our floating turret tempts the main
  And dares the howling blast

To clasp more close the golden chain
  That long has bound them fast.

In vain the gales of ocean sweep,
  In vain the billows roar
That chafe the wild and stormy steep
  Of storied Elsinore.

She comes ! She comes ! her banners dip
  In Neva's flashing tide,
With greetings on her cannon's lip,
  The storm-god's iron bride !

Peace garlands with the olive-bough
  Her thunder-bearing tower,

And plants before her cleaving prow
  The sea-foam's milk-white flower.

No prairies heaped their garnered store
  To fill her sunless hold,
Not rich Nevada's gleaming ore
  Its hidden caves infold,

But lightly as the sea-bird swings
  She floats the depths above,
A breath of flame to lend her wings,
  Her freight a people's love !

When darkness hid the starry skies
  In war's long winter night,
One ray still cheered our straining eyes,
  The far-off Northern light !

And now the friendly rays return
  From lights that glow afar,
Those clustered lamps of Heaven that
  burn
  Around the Western Star.

A nation's love in tears and smiles
  We bear across the sea,
O Neva of the banded isles,
  We moor our hearts in thee !

WELCOME TO THE GRAND DUKE ALEXIS

MUSIC HALL, DECEMBER 6, 1871

Sung to the Russian national air by the children of the public schools.

SHADOWED so long by the storm-cloud of
    danger,
  Thou whom the prayers of an empire
    defend,
Welcome, thrice welcome ! but not as a
    stranger,
  Come to the nation that calls thee its
    friend !

Bleak are our shores with the blasts of
    December,
  Fettered and chill is the rivulet's flow;
Throbbing and warm are the hearts that
    remember
  Who was our friend when the world was
    our foe.

Look on the lips that are smiling to greet
    thee,
  See the fresh flowers that a people has
    strewn:
Count them thy sisters and brothers that
    meet thee;
  Guest of the Nation, her heart is thine
    own !

Fires of the North, in eternal communion,
  Blend your broad flashes with evening's
    bright star !
God bless the Empire that loves the Great
    Union;
  Strength to her people ! Long life to
    the Czar !

AT THE BANQUET TO THE GRAND DUKE ALEXIS

DECEMBER 9, 1871

ONE word to the guest we have gathered
    to greet !
The echoes are longing that word to re-
    peat, —
It springs to the lips that are waiting to part,
For its syllables spell themselves first in
    the heart.

Its accents may vary, its sound may be
    strange,
But it bears a kind message that nothing
    can change;
The dwellers by Neva its meaning can tell,
For the smile, its interpreter, shows it full
    well.

That word ! How it gladdened the Pilgrim
    of yore
As he stood in the snow on the desolate
    shore !
When the shout of the sagamore startled
    his ear
In the phrase of the Saxon, 't was music
    to hear !

Ah, little could Samoset offer our sire, —
The cabin, the corn-cake, the seat by the
    fire;
He had nothing to give, — the poor lord
    of the land, —
But he gave him a WELCOME, — his heart
    in his hand !

The tribe of the sachem has melted away,
But the word that he spoke is remembered
to-day,
And the page that is red with the record
of shame
The tear-drops have whitened round Samo-
set's name.

The word that he spoke to the Pilgrim of
old
May sound like a tale that has often been
told;
But the welcome we speak is as fresh as
the dew, —
As the kiss of a lover, that always is new!

Ay, Guest of the Nation! each roof is
thine own
Through all the broad continent's star-ban-
nered zone;
From the shore where the curtain of morn
is uprolled,
To the billows that flow through the gate-
way of gold.

The snow-crested mountains are calling
aloud;
Nevada to Ural speaks out of the cloud,
And Shasta shouts forth, from his throne
in the sky,
To the storm-splintered summits, the peaks
of Altai!

You must leave him, they say, till the sum-
mer is green!
Both shores are his home, though the
waves roll between;
And then we'll return him, with thanks
for the same,
As fresh and as smiling and tall as he
came.

But ours is the region of arctic delight;
We can show him auroras and pole-stars
by night;
There's a Muscovy sting in the ice-tem-
pered air,
And our firesides are warm and our maid-
ens are fair.

The flowers are full-blown in the garlanded
hall, —
They will bloom round his footsteps wher-
ever they fall;

For the splendors of youth and the sun-
shine they bring
Make the roses believe 't is the summons
of Spring.

One word of our language he needs must
know well,
But another remains that is harder to
spell;
We shall speak it so ill, if he wishes to
learn
How we utter *Farewell*, he will have to
return!

AT THE BANQUET TO THE CHINESE EMBASSY

AUGUST 21, 1868

BROTHERS, whom we may not reach
Through the veil of alien speech,
Welcome! welcome! eyes can tell
What the lips in vain would spell, —
Words that hearts can understand,
Brothers from the Flowery Land!

We, the evening's latest born,
Hail the children of the morn!
We, the new creation's birth,
Greet the lords of ancient earth,
From their storied walls and towers
Wandering to these tents of ours!

Land of wonders, fair Cathay,
Who long hast shunned the staring day,
Hid in mists of poet's dreams
By thy blue and yellow streams, —
Let us thy shadowed form behold, —
Teach us as thou didst of old.

Knowledge dwells with length of days;
Wisdom walks in ancient ways:
Thine the compass that could guide
A nation o'er the stormy tide,
Scourged by passions, doubts, and fears,
Safe through thrice a thousand years!

Looking from thy turrets gray
Thou hast seen the world's decay, —
Egypt drowning in her sands, —
Athens rent by robbers' hands, —
Rome, the wild barbarian's prey,
Like a storm-cloud swept away:

Looking from thy turrets gray
Still we see thee.   Where are they ?
And lo ! a new-born nation waits,
Sitting at the golden gates
That glitter by the sunset sea, —
Waits with outspread arms for thee !

Open wide, ye gates of gold,
To the Dragon's banner-fold !
Builders of the mighty wall,
Bid your mountain barriers fall !
So may the girdle of the sun
Bind the East and West in one,

Till Mount Shasta's breezes fan
The snowy peaks of Ta Sieue-Shan, —
Till Erie blends its waters blue
With the waves of Tung-Ting-Hu, —
Till deep Missouri lends its flow
To swell the rushing Hoang-Ho !

AT THE BANQUET TO THE JAPANESE EMBASSY

AUGUST 2, 1872

WE welcome you, Lords of the Land of
the Sun !
The voice of the many sounds feebly
through one;
Ah ! would 't were a voice of more musical
tone,
But the dog-star is here, and the song-
birds have flown.

And what shall I sing that can cheat you
of smiles,
Ye heralds of peace from the Orient isles ?
If only the Jubilee — Why did you wait ?
You are welcome, but oh ! you 're a little
too late !

We have greeted our brothers of Ireland
and France,
Round the fiddle of Strauss we have joined
in the dance,
We have lagered Herr Saro, that fine-
looking man,
And glorified Godfrey, whose name it is
Dan.

What a pity ! we 've missed it and you 've
missed it too,
We had a day ready and waiting for you;

We 'd have shown you — provided, of
course, you had come —
You 'd have heard — no, you would n't,
because it was dumb.

And then the great organ ! The chorus's
shout !
Like the mixture teetotalers call "Cold
without " —
A mingling of elements, strong, but not
sweet;
And the drum, just referred to, that "could
n't be beat."

The shrines of our pilgrims are not like
your own,
Where white Fusiyama lifts proudly its cone,
(The snow-mantled mountain we see on
the fan
That cools our hot cheeks with a breeze
from Japan.)

But ours the wide temple where worship is
free
As the wind of the prairie, the wave of the
sea;
You may build your own altar wherever
you will,
For the roof of that temple is over you still.

One dome overarches the star-bannered
shore;
You may enter the Pope's or the Puritan's
door,
Or pass with the Buddhist his gateway of
bronze,
For a priest is but Man, be he bishop or
bonze.

And the lesson we teach with the sword
and the pen
Is to all of God's children, " We also are
men !
If you wrong us we smart, if you prick us
we bleed,
If you love us, no quarrel with color or
creed ! "

You 'll find us a well-meaning, free-spoken
crowd,
Good - natured enough, but a little too
loud, —
To be sure, there is always a bit of a row
When we choose our Tycoon, and especially
now.

You 'll take it all calmly, — we want you
　　to see
What a peaceable fight such a contest can
　　be,
And of one thing be certain, however it
　　ends,
You will find that our voters have chosen
　　your friends.

If the horse that stands saddled is first in
　　the race,
You will greet your old friend with the
　　weed in his face;
And if the white hat and the White House
　　agree,
You 'll find H. G. really as loving as he.

But oh, what a pity — once more I must
　　say —
That we could not have joined in a " Japan-
　　ese day " !
Such greeting we give you to-night as we
　　can;
Long life to our brothers and friends of
　　Japan !

The Lord of the mountain looks down from
　　his crest
As the banner of morning unfurls in the
　　West;
The Eagle was always the friend of the
　　Sun;
You are welcome ! — The song of the cage-
　　bird is done.

BRYANT'S SEVENTIETH BIRTH-DAY

NOVEMBER 3, 1864

O EVEN-HANDED Nature ! we confess
This life that men so honor, love, and bless
Has filled thine olden measure.　Not the
　　less

We count the precious seasons that remain;
Strike not the level of the golden grain,
But heap it high with years, that earth
　　may gain

What heaven can lose, — for heaven is rich
　　in song:
Do not all poets, dying, still prolong
Their broken chants amid the seraph throng,

Where, blind no more, Ionia's bard is seen,
And England's heavenly minstrel sits be-
　　tween
The Mantuan and the wan-cheeked Floren-
　　tine ?

This was the first sweet singer in the
　　cage
Of our close-woven life.　A new-born age
Claims in his vesper song its heritage:

Spare us, oh spare us long our heart's de-
　　sire !
Moloch, who calls our children through the
　　fire,
Leaves us the gentle master of the lyre.

We count not on the dial of the sun
The hours, the minutes, that his sands have
　　run;
Rather, as on those flowers that one by
　　one

From earliest dawn their ordered bloom
　　display
Till evening's planet with her guiding ray
Leads in the blind old mother of the day,

We reckon by his songs, each song a
　　flower,
The long, long daylight, numbering hour
　　by hour,
Each breathing sweetness like a bridal
　　bower.

His morning glory shall we e'er forget ?
His noontide's full-blown lily coronet ?
His evening primrose has not opened yet;

Nay, even if creeping Time should hide the
　　skies
In midnight from his century-laden eyes,
Darkened like his who sang of Paradise,

Would not some hidden song-bud open
　　bright
As the resplendent cactus of the night
That floods the gloom with fragrance and
　　with light ?

How can we praise the verse whose music
　　flows
With solemn cadence and majestic close,
Pure as the dew that filters through the
　　rose ?

How shall we thank him that in evil days
He faltered never, — nor for blame, nor
  praise,
Nor hire, nor party, shamed his earlier
  lays ?

But as his boyhood was of manliest hue,
So to his youth his manly years were true,
All dyed in royal purple through and
  through !

He for whose touch the lyre of Heaven is
  strung
Needs not the flattering toil of mortal
  tongue:
Let not the singer grieve to die unsung !

Marbles forget their message to mankind:
In his own verse the poet still we find,
In his own page his memory lives enshrined,

As in their amber sweets the smothered
  bees, —
As the fair cedar, fallen before the breeze,
Lies self-embalmed amidst the mouldering
  trees.

Poets, like youngest children, never grow
Out of their mother's fondness. Nature
  so
Holds their soft hands, and will not let
  them go,

Till at the last they track with even feet
Her rhythmic footsteps, and their pulses
  beat .
Twinned with her pulses, and their lips re-
  peat

The secrets she has told them, as their
  own:
Thus is the inmost soul of Nature known,
And the rapt minstrel shares her awful
  throne !

O lover of her mountains and her woods,
Her bridal chamber's leafy solitudes,
Where Love himself with tremulous step
  intrudes,

Her snows fall harmless on thy sacred
  fire:
Far be the day that claims thy sounding
  lyre
To join the music of the angel choir !

Yet, since life's amplest measure must be
  filled,
Since throbbing hearts must be forever
  stilled,
And all must fade that evening sunsets gild,

Grant, Father, ere he close the mortal eyes
That see a Nation's reeking sacrifice,
Its smoke may vanish from these blackened
  skies !

Then, when his summons comes, since come
  it must,
And, looking heavenward with unfaltering
  trust,
He wraps his drapery round him for the
  dust,

His last fond glance will show him o'er his
  head
The Northern fires beyond the zenith
  spread
In lambent glory, blue and white and
  red, —

The Southern cross without its bleeding
  load,
The milky way of peace all freshly strowed,
And every white-throned star fixed in its
  lost abode !

A FAREWELL TO AGASSIZ

[Written on the eve of Agassiz's journey to
Brazil in 1865.]

How the mountains talked together,
Looking down upon the weather,
When they heard our friend had planned his
Little trip among the Andes !
How they 'll bare their snowy scalps
To the climber of the Alps
When the cry goes through their passes,
"Here comes the great Agassiz !"
"Yes, I 'm tall," says Chimborazo,
"But I wait for him to say so, —
That 's the only thing that lacks, — he
Must see me, Cotopaxi !"
"Ay ! ay !" the fire-peak thunders,
"And he must view my wonders !
I 'm but a lonely crater
Till I have him for spectator !"
The mountain hearts are yearning,
The lava-torches burning,
The rivers bend to meet him,

The forests bow to greet him,
It thrills the spinal column
Of fossil fishes solemn,
And glaciers crawl the faster
To the feet of their old master !
Heaven keep him well and hearty,
Both him and all his party !
From the sun that broils and smites,
From the centipede that bites,
From the hail-storm and the thunder,
From the vampire and the condor,
From the gust upon the river,
From the sudden earthquake shiver,
From the trip of mule or donkey,
From the midnight howling monkey,
From the stroke of knife or dagger,
From the puma and the jaguar,
From the horrid boa-constrictor
That has scared us in the pictur',
From the Indians of the Pampas
Who would dine upon their grampas,
From every beast and vermin
That to think of sets us squirmin',
From every snake that tries on
The traveller his p'ison,
From every pest of Natur',
Likewise the alligator,
And from two things left behind him, —
(Be sure they 'll try to find him,)
The tax-bill and assessor, —
Heaven keep the great Professor !
May he find, with his apostles,
That the land is full of fossils,
That the waters swarm with fishes
Shaped according to his wishes,
That every pool is fertile
In fancy kinds of turtle,
New birds around him singing,
New insects, never stinging,
With a million novel data
About the articulata,
And facts that strip off all husks
From the history of mollusks.

And when, with loud Te Deum,
He returns to his Museum,
May he find the monstrous reptile
That so long the land has kept ill
By Grant and Sherman throttled,
And by Father Abraham bottled,
(All specked and streaked and mottled
With the scars of murderous battles,
Where he clashed the iron rattles
That gods and men he shook at,)
For all the world to look at !

God bless the great Professor !
And Madam, too, God bless her !
Bless him and all his band,
On the sea and on the land,
Bless them head and heart and hand,
Till their glorious raid is o'er,
And they touch our ransomed shore !
Then the welcome of a nation,
With its shout of exultation,
Shall awake the dumb creation,
In the form that once it wore
And the shapes of buried æons
Join the living creature's pæans,
Till the fossil echoes roar;
While the mighty megalosaurus
Leads the palæozoic chorus, —
With a bass like ocean's roar
God bless the great Professor,
And the land his proud possessor, —
Bless them now and evermore !

AT A DINNER TO ADMIRAL FARRAGUT

JULY 6, 1865

Now, smiling friends and shipmates all,
Since half our battle 's won,
A broadside for our Admiral !
Load every crystal gun !
Stand ready till I give the word, —
You won't have time to tire, —
And when that glorious name is heard,
Then hip ! hurrah ! and fire !

Bow foremost sinks the rebel craft, —
Our eyes not sadly turn
And see the pirates huddling aft
To drop their raft astern :
Soon o'er the sea-worm's destined prey
The lifted wave shall close, —
So perish from the face of day
All Freedom's banded foes !

But ah ! what splendors fire the sky !
What glories greet the morn !
The storm-tost banner streams on high,
Its heavenly hues new-born !
Its red fresh dyed in heroes' blood,
Its peaceful white more pure,
To float unstained o'er field and flood
While earth and seas endure !

All shapes before the driving blast
Must glide from mortal view;

Black roll the billows of the past
  Behind the present's blue,
Fast, fast, are lessening in the light
  The names of high renown, —
Van Tromp's proud besom fades from
    sight,
  And Nelson's half hull down !

Scarce one tall frigate walks the sea
  Or skirts the safer shores
Of all that bore to victory
  Our stout old commodores;
Hull, Bainbridge, Porter, — where are
    they ?
  The waves their answer roll,
" Still bright in memory's sunset ray, —
  God rest each gallant soul ! "

A brighter name must dim their light
  With more than noontide ray,
The Sea-King of the " River Fight,"
  The Conqueror of the Bay, —
Now then the broadside ! cheer on cheer
  To greet him safe on shore !
Health, peace, and many a bloodless year
  To fight his battles o'er !

AT A DINNER TO GENERAL GRANT

JULY 31, 1865

WHEN treason first began the strife
  That crimsoned sea and shore,
The Nation poured her hoarded life
  On Freedom's threshing-floor;
From field and prairie, east and west,
  From coast and hill and plain,
The sheaves of ripening manhood pressed
  Thick as the bearded grain.

Rich was the harvest; souls as true
  As ever battle tried ;
But fiercer still the conflict grew,
  The floor of death more wide;
Ah, who forgets that dreadful day
  Whose blot of grief and shame
Four bitter years scarce wash away
  In seas of blood and flame ?

Vain, vain the Nation's lofty boasts,
  Vain all her sacrifice !
" Give me a man to lead my hosts,
  O God in heaven ! " she cries.

While Battle whirls his crushing flail,
  And plies his winnowing fan, —
Thick flies the chaff on every gale, —
  She cannot find her man !

Bravely they fought who failed to win, —
  Our leaders battle-scarred, —
Fighting the hosts of hell and sin,
  But devils die always hard !
Blame not the broken tools of God
  That helped our sorest needs;
Through paths that martyr feet have trod
  The conqueror's steps He leads.

But now the heavens grow black with
    doubt,
  The ravens fill the sky,
" Friends " plot within, foes storm with-
    out,
  Hark, — that despairing cry,
" Where is the heart, the hand, the brain
  To dare, to do, to plan ? "
The bleeding Nation shrieks in vain, —
  She has not found her man !

A little echo stirs the air, —
  Some tale, whate'er it be,
Of rebels routed in their lair
  Along the Tennessee.
The little echo spreads and grows,
  And soon the trump of Fame
Has taught the Nation's friends and foes
  The " man on horseback " 's name.

So well his warlike wooing sped,
  No fortress might resist
His billets-doux of lisping lead,
  The bayonets in his fist, —
With kisses from his cannons' mouth
  He made his passion known
Till Vicksburg, vestal of the South,
  Unbound her virgin zone.

And still where'er his banners led
  He conquered as he came,
The trembling hosts of treason fled
  Before his breath of flame,
And Fame's still gathering echoes grew
  Till high o'er Richmond's towers
The starry fold of Freedom flew,
  And all the land was ours.

Welcome from fields where valor fought
  To feasts where pleasure waits;

A Nation gives you smiles unbought
  At all her opening gates !
Forgive us when we press your hand, —
  Your war-worn features scan, —
God sent you to a bleeding land;
  Our Nation found its man !

TO H. W. LONGFELLOW

BEFORE HIS DEPARTURE FOR EUROPE, MAY 27, 1868

OUR Poet, who has taught the Western
    breeze
To waft his songs before him o' er the
    seas,
Will find them wheresoe'er his wander-
    ings reach
Borne on the spreading tide of English
    speech
Twin with the rhythmic waves that kiss the
    farthest beach.

Where shall the singing bird a stranger
    be
That finds a nest for him in every
    tree ?
How shall he travel who can never go
Where his own voice the echoes do not
    know,
Where his own garden flowers no longer
    learn to grow ?

Ah ! gentlest soul ! how gracious, how
    benign
Breathes through our troubled life that
    voice of thine,
Filled with a sweetness born of happier
    spheres,
That wins and warms, that kindles, soft-
    ens, cheers,
That calms the wildest woe and stays the
    bitterest tears !

Forgive the simple words that sound
    like praise;
The mist before me dims my gilded
    phrase;
Our speech at best is half alive and cold,
And save that tenderer moments make
    us bold
Our whitening lips would close, their tru-
    est truth untold.

We who behold our autumn sun be-
    low
The Scorpion's sign, against the Archer's
    bow,
Know well what parting means of friend
    from friend;
After the snows no freshening dews de-
    scend,
And what the frost has marred, the sun-
    shine will not mend.

So we all count the months, the weeks,
    the days,
That keep thee from us in unwonted
    ways,
Grudging to alien hearths our widowed
    time;
And one has shaped a breath in artless
    rhyme
That sighs, " We track thee still through
    each remotest clime."

What wishes, longings, blessings, prayers
    shall be
The more than golden freight that floats
    with thee !
And know, whatever welcome thou shalt
    find, —
Thou who hast won the hearts of half
    mankind, —
The proudest, fondest love thou leavest
    still behind !

TO CHRISTIAN GOTTFRIED EHRENBERG

FOR HIS " JUBILÆUM " AT BERLIN, NO-VEMBER 5, 1868

This poem was written at the suggestion of
Mr. George Bancroft, the historian.

THOU who hast taught the teachers of man-
    kind
How from the least of things the might-
    iest grow,
What marvel jealous Nature made thee
    blind,
Lest man should learn what angels long
    to know ?
Thou in the flinty rock, the river's flow,
  In the thick-moted sunbeam's sifted
    light

Hast trained thy downward-pointed tube
to show
  Worlds within worlds unveiled to mortal
  sight,
Even as the patient watchers of the
  night, —
  The cyclope gleaners of the fruitful
  skies, —
Show the wide misty way where heaven is
  white
  All paved with suns that daze our won-
  dering eyes.

Far o'er the stormy deep an empire lies,
  Beyond the storied islands of the blest,
That waits to see the lingering day-star
  rise;
  The forest-cinctured Eden of the West;
Whose queen, fair Freedom, twines her
  iron crest
  With leaves from every wreath that mor-
  tals wear,
But loves the sober garland ever best
  That science lends the sage's silvered
  hair; —
Science, who makes life's heritage more
  fair,
  Forging for every lock its mastering
  key,
Filling with life and hope the stagnant
  air,
  Pouring the light of Heaven o'er land
  and sea !
From her unsceptred realm we come to
  thee,
  Bearing our slender tribute in our hands;
Deem it not worthless, humble though it
  be,
  Set by the larger gifts of older lands:
The smallest fibres weave the strongest
  bands, —
  In narrowest tubes the sovereign nerves
  are spun, —
A little cord along the deep sea-sands
  Makes the live thought of severed na-
  tions one:
Thy fame has journeyed westering with
  the sun,
  Prairies and lone sierras know thy name

And the long day of service nobly done
  That crowns thy darkened evening with
  its flame !

One with the grateful world, we own thy
  claim, —
  Nay, rather claim our right to join the
  throng
Who come with varied tongues, but hearts
  the same,
  To hail thy festal morn with smiles and
  song;
Ah, happy they to whom the joys belong
  Of peaceful triumphs that can never die
From History's record, — not of gilded
  wrong,
  But golden truths that, while the world
  goes by
With all its empty pageant, blazoned high
  Around the Master's name forever shine!
So shines thy name illumined in the sky, —
  Such joys, such triumphs, such remem-
  brance thine !

A TOAST TO WILKIE COLLINS

FEBRUARY 16, 1874

THE painter's and the poet's fame
Shed their twinned lustre round his name,
To gild our story-teller's art,
Where each in turn must play his part.

What scenes from Wilkie's pencil sprung,
The minstrel saw but left unsung !
What shapes the pen of Collins drew,
No painter clad in living hue !

But on our artist's shadowy screen
A stranger miracle is seen
Than priest unveils or pilgrim seeks, —
The poem breathes, the picture speaks !

And so his double name comes true,
They christened better than they knew,
And Art proclaims him twice her son, —
Painter and poet, both in one !

MEMORIAL VERSES

FOR THE SERVICES IN MEMORY OF ABRAHAM LINCOLN

CITY OF BOSTON, JUNE 1, 1865

CHORAL: "LUTHER'S JUDGMENT HYMN"

O THOU of soul and sense and breath
    The ever-present Giver,
Unto thy mighty Angel, Death,
    All flesh thou dost deliver;
What most we cherish we resign,
For life and death alike are thine,
    Who reignest Lord forever!

Our hearts lie buried in the dust
    With him so true and tender,
The patriot's stay, the people's trust,
    The shield of the offender;
Yet every murmuring voice is still,
As, bowing to thy sovereign will,
    Our best-loved we surrender.

Dear Lord, with pitying eye behold
    This martyr generation,
Which thou, through trials manifold,
    Art showing thy salvation!
Oh let the blood by murder spilt
Wash out thy stricken children's guilt
    And sanctify our nation!

Be thou thy orphaned Israel's friend,
    Forsake thy people never,
In One our broken Many blend,
    That none again may sever!
Hear us, O Father, while we raise
With trembling lips our song of praise,
    And bless thy name forever!

FOR THE COMMEMORATION SERVICES

CAMBRIDGE, JULY 21, 1865

FOUR summers coined their golden light in leaves,
    Four wasteful autumns flung them to the gale,

Four winters wore the shroud the tempest weaves,
    The fourth wan April weeps o'er hill and vale;

And still the war-clouds scowl on sea and land,
    With the red gleams of battle staining through,
When lo! as parted by an angel's hand,
    They open, and the heavens again are blue!

Which is the dream, the present or the past?
    The night of anguish or the joyous morn?
The long, long years with horrors overcast,
    Or the sweet promise of the day new-born?

Tell us, O father, as thine arms infold
    Thy belted first-born in their fast embrace,
Murmuring the prayer the patriarch breathed of old, —
    "Now let me die, for I have seen thy face!"

Tell us, O mother, — nay, thou canst not speak,
    But thy fond eyes shall answer, brimmed with joy, —
Press thy mute lips against the sunbrowned cheek,
    Is this a phantom, — thy returning boy?

Tell us, O maiden, — ah, what canst thou tell
    That Nature's record is not first to teach, —
The open volume all can read so well,
    With its twin rose-hued pages full of speech?

And ye who mourn your dead, — how sternly true
    The crushing hour that wrenched their lives away,
Shadowed with sorrow's midnight veil for you,
    For them the dawning of immortal day!

Dream-like these years of conflict, not a
    dream !
Death, ruin, ashes tell the awful tale,
Read by the flaming war-track's lurid
    gleam:
    No dream, but truth that turns the na-
        tions pale !

For on the pillar raised by martyr hands
    Burns the rekindled beacon of the right,
Sowing its seeds of fire o'er all the lands, —
    Thrones look a century older in its light !

Rome had her triumphs; round the con-
    queror's car
    The ensigns waved, the brazen clarions
        blew,
And o'er the reeking spoils of bandit war
    With outspread wings the cruel eagles
        flew;

Arms, treasures, captives, kings in clanking
    chains
    Urged on by trampling cohorts bronzed
        and scarred,
And wild-eyed wonders snared on Libyan
    plains,
    Lion and ostrich and camelopard.

Vain all that prætors clutched, that consuls
    brought
    When Rome's returning legions crowned
        their lord;
Less than the least brave deed these hands
    have wrought,
    We clasp, unclinching from the bloody
        sword.

Theirs was the mighty work that seers
    foretold;
    They know not half their glorious toil
        has won,
For this is Heaven's same battle, — joined
    of old
    When Athens fought for us at Mara-
        thon !

Behold a vision none hath understood !
    The breaking of the Apocalyptic seal;
Twice rings the summons. — Hail and fire
    and blood !
    Then the third angel blows his trumpet-
        peal.

Loud wail the dwellers on the myrtled
    coasts,
    The green savannas swell the maddened
        cry,
And with a yell from all the demon hosts
    Falls the great star called Wormwood
        from the sky !

Bitter it mingles with the poisoned flow
    Of the warm rivers winding to the shore,
Thousands must drink the waves of death
    and woe,
    But the star Wormwood stains the heav-
        ens no more !

Peace smiles at last; the Nation calls her
    sons
    To sheathe the sword; her battle-flag
        she furls,
Speaks in glad thunders from unshotted
    guns,
    No terror shrouded in the smoke-wreath's
        curls.

O ye that fought for Freedom, living, dead,
    One sacred host of God's anointed Queen,
For every holy drop your veins have shed
    We breathe a welcome to our bowers of
        green !

Welcome, ye living ! from the foeman's
    gripe
    Your country's banner it was yours to
        wrest, —
Ah, many a forehead shows the banner-
    stripe,
    And stars, once crimson, hallow many a
        breast.

And ye, pale heroes, who from glory's bed
    Mark when your old battalions form in
        line,
Move in their marching ranks with noise-
    less tread,
    And shape unheard the evening counter-
        sign,

Come with your comrades, the returning
    brave;
    Shoulder to shoulder they await you here;
These lent the life their martyr-brothers
    gave, —
    Living and dead alike forever dear !

EDWARD EVERETT

"OUR FIRST CITIZEN"

Read at the meeting of the Massachusetts
Historical Society, January 30, 1865.

WINTER'S cold drift lies glistening o'er his
    breast ;
  For him no spring shall bid the leaf un-
    fold :
What Love could speak, by sudden grief
    oppressed,
  What swiftly summoned Memory tell, is
    told.

Even as the bells, in one consenting chime,
  Filled with their sweet vibrations all
    the air,
So joined all voices, in that mournful time,
  His genius, wisdom, virtues, to declare.

What place is left for words of measured
    praise,
  Till calm-eyed History, with her iron
    pen,
Grooves in the unchanging rock the final
    phrase
  That shapes his image in the souls of
    men ?

Yet while the echoes still repeat his name,
  While countless tongues his full-orbed
    life rehearse,
Love, by his beating pulses taught, will
    claim
  The breath of song, the tuneful throb of
    verse, —

Verse that, in ever-changing ebb and flow,
  Moves, like the laboring heart, with rush
    and rest,
Or swings in solemn cadence, sad and
    slow,
  Like the tired heaving of a grief-worn
    breast.

This was a mind so rounded, so complete,
  No partial gift of Nature in excess,
That, like a single stream where many
    meet,
  Each separate talent counted something
    less.

A little hillock, if it lonely stand,
  Holds o'er the fields an undisputed
    reign;
While the broad summit of the table-land
  Seems with its belt of clouds a level
    plain.

Servant of all his powers, that faithful
    slave,
  Unsleeping Memory, strengthening with
    his toils,
To every ruder task his shoulder gave,
  And loaded every day with golden spoils.

Order, the law of Heaven, was throned
    supreme
  O'er action, instinct, impulse, feeling,
    thought;
True as the dial's shadow to the beam,
  Each hour was equal to the charge it
    brought.

Too large his compass for the nicer skill
  That weighs the world of science grain
    by grain;
All realms of knowledge owned the mas-
    tering will
  That claimed the franchise of its whole
    domain.

Earth, air, sea, sky, the elemental fire,
  Art, history, song, — what meanings lie
    in each
Found in his cunning hand a stringless lyre,
  And poured their mingling music through
    his speech.

Thence flowed those anthems of our festal
    days,
  Whose ravishing division held apart
The lips of listening throngs in sweet
    amaze,
  Moved in all breasts the selfsame human
    heart.

Subdued his accents, as of one who tries
  To press some care, some haunting sad-
    ness down;
His smile half shadow; and to stranger
    eyes
  The kingly forehead wore an iron crown.

He was not armed to wrestle with the
    storm,

To fight for homely truth with vulgar
 power;
Grace looked from every feature, shaped
 his form, —
The rose of Academe, — the perfect
 flower !

Such was the stately scholar whom we
 knew
In those ill days of soul-enslaving calm,
Before the blast of Northern vengeance
 blew
Her snow-wreathed pine against the
 Southern palm.

Ah, God forgive us ! did we hold too cheap
 The heart we might have known, but
  would not see,
And look to find the nation's friend asleep
 Through the dread hour of her Geth-
  semane ?

That wrong is past ; we gave him up to
 Death
With all a hero's honors round his name ;
As martyrs coin their blood, he coined his
 breath,
 And dimmed the scholar's in the pa-
  triot's fame.

So shall we blazon on the shaft we raise, —
 Telling our grief, our pride, to unborn
  years, —
" He who had lived the mark of all men's
 praise
Died with the tribute of a Nation's tears."

SHAKESPEARE

TERCENTENNIAL CELEBRATION

APRIL 23, 1864

" WHO claims our Shakespeare from that
 realm unknown,
 Beyond the storm-vexed islands of the
  deep,
Where Genoa's roving mariner was blown?
 Her twofold Saint's-day let our England
  keep ;
Shall warring aliens share her holy task ? "
 The Old World echoes ask.

O land of Shakespeare ! ours with all thy
 past,
 Till these last years that make the sea
  so wide,
Think not the jar of battle's trumpet-blast
 Has dulled our aching sense to joyous
  pride
In every noble word thy sons bequeathed
 The air our fathers breathed !

War-wasted, haggard, panting from the
 strife,
 We turn to other days and far-off lands,
Live o'er in dreams the Poet's faded life,
 Come with fresh lilies in our fevered
  hands
To wreathe his bust, and scatter purple
 flowers, —
 Not his the need, but ours !

We call those poets who are first to mark
 Through earth's dull mist the coming of
  the dawn, —
Who see in twilight's gloom the first pale
 spark,
 While others only note that day is gone;
For him the Lord of light the curtain rent
 That veils the firmament.

The greatest for its greatness is half known,
 Stretching beyond our narrow quadrant-
  lines, —
As in that world of Nature all outgrown
 Where Calaveras lifts his awful pines,
And cast from Mariposa's mountain-wall
 Nevada's cataracts fall.

Yet heaven's remotest orb is partly ours,
 Throbbing its radiance like a beating
  heart;
In the wide compass of angelic powers
 The instinct of the blindworm has its part;
So in God's kingliest creature we behold
 The flower our buds infold.

With no vain praise we mock the stone-
 carved name
 Stamped once on dust that moved with
  pulse and breath,
As thinking to enlarge that amplest fame
 Whose undimmed glories gild the night
  of death:
We praise not star or sun; in these we see
 Thee, Father, only thee !

Thy gifts are beauty, wisdom, power, and
    love:
  We read, we reverence on this human
    soul, —
Earth's clearest mirror of the light above, —
  Plain as the record on thy prophet's scroll,
When o'er his page the effluent splendors
    poured,
    Thine own " Thus saith the Lord ! "

This player was a prophet from on high,
  Thine own elected.   Statesman, poet,
    sage,
For him thy sovereign pleasure passed them
    by;
  Sidney's fair youth, and Raleigh's ripened
    age,
Spenser's chaste soul, and his imperial
    mind
    Who taught and shamed mankind.

Therefore we bid our hearts' Te Deum
    rise,
  Nor fear to make thy worship less divine,
And hear the shouted choral shake the
    skies,
    Counting all glory, power, and wisdom
    thine;
For thy great gift thy greater name adore,
    And praise thee evermore !

In this dread hour of Nature's utmost
    need,
  Thanks for these unstained drops of
    freshening dew !
Oh, while our martyrs fall, our heroes bleed,
  Keep us to every sweet remembrance
    true,
Till from this blood-red sunset springs new-
    born
    Our Nation's second morn !

IN MEMORY OF JOHN AND ROBERT WARE

Read at the annual meeting of the Massa-
chusetts Medical Society, May 25, 1864.

No mystic charm, no mortal art,
  Can bid our loved companions stay;
The bands that clasp them to our heart
Snap in death's frost and fall apart;
    Like shadows fading with the day,
      They pass away.

The young are stricken in their pride,
  The old, long tottering, faint and fall;
Master and scholar, side by side,
Through the dark portals silent glide,
    That open in life's mouldering wall
      And close on all.

Our friend's, our teacher's task was done,
  When Mercy called him from on high;
A little cloud had dimmed the sun,
The saddening hours had just begun,
    And darker days were drawing nigh:
      'T was time to die.

A whiter soul, a fairer mind,
  A life with purer course and aim,
A gentler eye, a voice more kind,
We may not look on earth to find.
    The love that lingers o'er his name
      Is more than fame.

These blood-red summers ripen fast;
  The sons are older than the sires;
Ere yet the tree to earth is cast,
The sapling falls before the blast;
    Life's ashes keep their covered fires, —
      Its flame expires.

Struck by the noiseless, viewless foe,
  Whose deadlier breath than shot or shell
Has laid the best and bravest low,
His boy, all bright in morning's glow,
    That high-souled youth he loved so well,
      Untimely fell.

Yet still he wore his placid smile,
  And, trustful in the cheering creed
That strives all sorrow to beguile,
Walked calmly on his way awhile:
    Ah, breast that leans on breaking reed
      Must ever bleed !

So they both left us, sire and son,
  With opening leaf, with laden bough:
The youth whose race was just begun,
The wearied man whose course was run,
    Its record written on his brow,
      Are brothers now.

Brothers ! — The music of the sound
  Breathes softly through my closing strain;
The floor we tread is holy ground,
Those gentle spirits hovering round,
    While our fair circle joins again
      Its broken chain.

HUMBOLDT'S BIRTHDAY

CENTENNIAL CELEBRATION, SEPTEMBER
14, 1869

BONAPARTE, AUGUST 15, 1769. — HUMBOLDT,
SEPTEMBER 14, 1769

ERE yet the warning chimes of midnight
　　sound,
　Set back the flaming index of the year,
Track the swift-shifting seasons in their
　　round
　　Through fivescore circles of the swinging
　　　sphere !

Lo, in yon islet of the midland sea
　That cleaves the storm-cloud with its
　　snowy crest,
The embryo-heir of Empires yet to be,
　A month-old babe upon his mother's
　　breast.

Those little hands that soon shall grow so
　　strong
　In their rude grasp great thrones shall
　　rock and fall,
Press her soft bosom, while a nursery song
　Holds the world's master in its slender
　　thrall.

Look ! a new crescent bends its silver bow;
　A new-lit star has fired the eastern sky;
Hark ! by the river where the lindens blow
　A waiting household hears an infant's cry.

This, too, a conqueror ! His the vast do-
　　main,
　Wider than widest sceptre - shadowed
　　lands;
Earth and the weltering kingdom of the
　　main
　Laid their broad charters in his royal
　　hands.

His was no taper lit in cloistered cage,
　Its glimmer borrowed from the grove or
　　porch;
He read the record of the planet's page
　By Etna's glare and Cotopaxi's torch.

He heard the voices of the pathless woods;
　On the salt steppes he saw the starlight
　　shine;

He scaled the mountain's windy solitudes,
　And trod the galleries of the breathless
　　mine.

For him no fingering of the love-strung
　　lyre,
　No problem vague, by torturing school-
　　men vexed;
He fed no broken altar's dying fire,
　Nor skulked and scowled behind a
　　Rabbi's text.

For God's new truth he claimed the kingly
　　robe
　That priestly shoulders counted all their
　　own,
Unrolled the gospel of the storied globe
　And led young Science to her empty
　　throne.

While the round planet on its axle spins
　One fruitful year shall boast its double
　　birth,
And show the cradles of its mighty twins,
　Master and Servant of the sons of earth.

Which wears the garland that shall never
　　fade,
　Sweet with fair memories that can never
　　die ?
Ask not the marbles where their bones are
　　laid,
　But bow thine ear to hear thy brothers'
　　cry: —

" Tear up the despot's laurels by the root,
　Like mandrakes, shrieking as they quit
　　the soil !
Feed us no more upon the blood-red fruit
　That sucks its crimson from the heart of
　　Toil !

" We claim the food that fixed our mortal
　　fate, —
　Bend to our reach the long-forbidden
　　tree !
The angel frowned at Eden's eastern
　　gate, —
　Its western portal is forever free !

" Bring the white blossoms of the waning
　　year,
　Heap with full hands the peaceful con-
　　queror's shrine

Whose bloodless triumphs cost no sufferer's
    tear !
  Hero of knowledge, be our tribute
    thine ! "

POEM

AT THE DEDICATION OF THE HALLECK MONUMENT, JULY 8, 1869

SAY not the Poet dies !
  Though in the dust he lies,
He cannot forfeit his melodious breath,
  Unsphered by envious death !
Life drops the voiceless myriads from its
    roll;
  Their fate he cannot share,
  Who, in the enchanted air
Sweet with the lingering strains that
    Echo stole,
Has left his dearer self, the music of his
    soul !

  We o'er his turf may raise
  Our notes of feeble praise,
And carve with pious care for after eyes
  The stone with " Here he lies;"
He for himself has built a nobler shrine,
  Whose walls of stately rhyme
  Roll back the tides of time,
While o'er their gates the gleaming tab-
    lets shine
That wear his name inwrought with many
    a golden line !

  Call not our Poet dead,
  Though on his turf we tread !
Green is the wreath their brows so long
    have worn, —
  The minstrels of the morn,
Who, while the Orient burned with new-
    born flame,
  Caught that celestial fire
  And struck a Nation's lyre !
These taught the western winds the
    poet's name;
Theirs the first opening buds, the maiden
    flowers of fame !

  Count not our Poet dead !
  The stars shall watch his bed,
The rose of June its fragrant life re-
    new
  His blushing mound to strew,

And all the tuneful throats of summer
    swell
  With trills as crystal-clear
  As when he wooed the ear
Of the young muse that haunts each
    wooded dell,
With songs of that " rough land " he loved
    so long and well !

  He sleeps; he cannot die !
  As evening's long-drawn sigh,
Lifting the rose-leaves on his peaceful
    mound,
  Spreads all their sweets around,
So, laden with his song, the breezes blow
  From where the rustling sedge
  Frets our rude ocean's edge
To the smooth sea beyond the peaks of
    snow.
His soul the air enshrines and leaves but
    dust below !

HYMN

FOR THE CELEBRATION AT THE LAYING OF THE CORNER-STONE OF HARVARD MEMORIAL HALL, CAMBRIDGE, OCTOBER 6, 1870

NOT with the anguish of hearts that are
    breaking
  Come we as mourners to weep for our
    dead;
Grief in our breasts has grown weary of
    aching,
  Green is the turf where our tears we
    have shed.

While o'er their marbles the mosses are
    creeping,
  Stealing each name and its legend away,
Give their proud story to Memory's keep-
    ing,
  Shrined in the temple we hallow to-day.

Hushed are their battle-fields, ended their
    marches,
  Deaf are their ears to the drum-beat of
    morn, —
Rise from the sod, ye fair columns and
    arches !
  Tell their bright deeds to the ages un-
    born !

Emblem and legend may fade from the
  portal,
  Keystone may crumble and pillar may
  fall;
They were the builders whose work is im-
  mortal,
  Crowned with the dome that is over us
  all !

HYMN

FOR THE DEDICATION OF MEMORIAL HALL AT CAMBRIDGE, JUNE 23, 1874

WHERE, girt around by savage foes,
Our nurturing Mother's shelter rose,
Behold, the lofty temple stands,
Reared by her children's grateful hands !

Firm are the pillars that defy
The volleyed thunders of the sky;
Sweet are the summer wreaths that twine
With bud and flower our martyrs' shrine.

The hues their tattered colors bore
Fall mingling on the sunlit floor
Till evening spreads her spangled pall,
And wraps in shade the storied hall.

Firm were their hearts in danger's hour,
Sweet was their manhood's morning flower
Their hopes with rainbow hues were
  bright, —
How swiftly winged the sudden night !

O Mother ! on thy marble page
Thy children read, from age to age,
The mighty word that upward leads
Through noble thought to nobler deeds.

TRUTH, heaven-born TRUTH, their fearless
  guide,
Thy saints have lived, thy heroes died;
Our love has reared their earthly shrine,
Their glory be forever thine !

HYMN

AT THE FUNERAL SERVICES OF CHARLES SUMNER, APRIL 29, 1874

SUNG BY MALE VOICES TO A NATIONAL AIR OF HOLLAND

ONCE more, ye sacred towers,
  Your solemn dirges sound;
Strew, loving hands, the April flowers,
  Once more to deck his mound.
  A nation mourns its dead,
  Its sorrowing voices one,
As Israel's monarch bowed his head
  And cried, "My son ! My son !"

Why mourn for him ? — For him
  The welcome angel came
Ere yet his eye with age was dim
  Or bent his stately frame;
  His weapon still was bright,
  His shield was lifted high
To slay the wrong, to save the right, —
  What happier hour to die ?

Thou orderest all things well;
  Thy servant's work was done;
He lived to hear Oppression's knell,
  The shouts for Freedom won.
  Hark ! from the opening skies
  The anthem's echoing swell, —
"O mourning Land, lift up thine eyes !
  God reigneth.   All is well !"

RHYMES OF AN HOUR

AN IMPROMPTU

AT THE WALCKER DINNER UPON THE COMPLETION OF THE GREAT ORGAN FOR BOSTON MUSIC HALL IN 1863

I ASKED three little maidens who heard the
  organ play,
Where all the music came from that stole
  our hearts away:

"I know," — said fair-haired Edith, — "it
  was the autumn breeze
That whistled through the hollows of all
  those silver trees."

"No, child !" — said keen-eyed Clara, —
  "it is a lion's cage, —
They woke him out of slumber, —I heard
  him roar and rage."

"Nay," — answered soft-voiced Anna, —
  "'t was thunder that you heard,
And after that came sunshine and singing
  of a bird."

"Hush, hush, you little children, for all of
  you are wrong,"
I said, "my pretty darlings, — it was no
  earthly song;
A band of blessed angels has left the
  heavenly choirs,
And what you heard last evening were
  seraph lips and lyres!"

ADDRESS

FOR THE OPENING OF THE FIFTH AV-
ENUE THEATRE, NEW YORK, DECEM-
BER 3, 1873

HANG out our banners on the stately
  tower!
It dawns at last — the long-expected hour!
The steep is climbed, the star-lit summit
  won,
The builder's task, the artist's labor done;
Before the finished work the herald stands,
And asks the verdict of your lips and
  hands!

Shall rosy daybreak make us all forget
The golden sun that yester-evening set?
Fair was the fabric doomed to pass away
Ere the last headaches born of New Year's
  Day;
With blasting breath the fierce destroyer
  came
And wrapped the victim in his robes of
  flame;
The pictured sky with redder morning
  blushed,
With scorching streams the naiad's foun-
  tain gushed,
With kindling mountains glowed the fune-
  ral pyre,
Forests ablaze and rivers all on fire, —
The scenes dissolved, the shriveling curtain
  fell, —
Art spread her wings and sighed a long
  farewell!

Mourn o'er the Player's melancholy
  plight, —
Falstaff in tears, Othello deadly white, —
Poor Romeo reckoning what his doublet
  cost,
And Juliet whimpering for her dresses
  lost, —
Their wardrobes burned their salaries all
  undrawn,
Their cues cut short, their occupation
  gone!

"Lie there in dust," the red-winged de-
  mon cried,
"Wreck of the lordly city's hope and
  pride!"
Silent they stand, and stare with vacant
  gaze,
While o'er the embers leaps the fitful
  blaze;
When, lo! a hand, before the startled
  train,
Writes in the ashes, "It shall rise again, —
Rise and confront its elemental foes!"
The word was spoken, and the walls arose,
And ere the seasons round their brief ca-
  reer
The new-born temple waits the unborn
  year.

Ours was the toil of many a weary day
Your smiles, your plaudits, only can repay;
We are the monarchs of the painted
  scenes,
You, you alone the real Kings and Queens!
Lords of the little kingdom where we
  meet,
We lay our gilded sceptres at your feet,
Place in your grasp our portal's silvered
  keys
With one brief utterance: *We have tried
to please.*
Tell us, ye sovereigns of the new domain,
Are you content — or have we toiled in
  vain?

With no irreverent glances look around
The realm you rule, for this is haunted
  ground!
Here stalks the Sorcerer, here the Fairy
  trips,
Here limps the Witch with malice-work-
  ing lips,
The Graces here their snowy arms entwine,
Here dwell the fairest sisters of the
  Nine, —
She who, with jocund voice and twinkling
  eye,

Laughs at the brood of follies as they fly;
She of the dagger and the deadly bowl,
Whose charming horrors thrill the trem-
    bling soul;
She who, a truant from celestial spheres,
In mortal semblance now and then appears,
Stealing the fairest earthly shape she
    can —
Sontag or Nilsson, Lind or Malibran;
With these the spangled houri of the
    dance, —
What shaft so dangerous as her melting
    glance,
As poised in air she spurns the earth below,
And points aloft her heavenly-minded toe!

What were our life, with all its rents and
    seams,
Stripped of its purple robes, our waking
    dreams ?
The poet's song, the bright romancer's page,
The tinselled shows that cheat us on the
    stage
Lead all our fancies captive at their will;
Three years or threescore, we are children
    still.
The little listener on his father's knee,
With wandering Sindbad ploughs the
    stormy sea,
With Gotham's sages hears the billows roll
(Illustrious trio of the venturous bowl,
Too early shipwrecked, for they died too
    soon
To see their offspring launch the great
    balloon) ;
Tracks the dark brigand to his mountain
    lair,
Slays the grim giant, saves the lady fair,
Fights all his country's battles o'er again
From Bunker's blazing height to Lundy's
    Lane;
Floats with the mighty captains as they
    sailed,
Before whose flag the flaming red-cross
    paled,
And claims the oft-told story of the scars
Scarce yet grown white, that saved the
    stripes and stars !

Children of later growth, we love the
    PLAY,
We love its heroes, be they grave or gay,
From squeaking, peppery, devil-defying
    Punch

To roaring Richard with his camel-hunch;
Adore its heroines, those immortal dames,
Time's only rivals, whom he never tames,
Whose youth, unchanging, lives while
    thrones decay
(Age spares the Pyramids — and Déjazet);
The saucy - aproned, razor - tongued sou-
    brette,
The blond-haired beauty with the eyes of
    jet,
The gorgeous Beings whom the viewless
    wires
Lift to the skies in strontian-crimsoned
    fires,
And all the wealth of splendor that awaits
The throng that enters those Elysian gates.

See where the hurrying crowd impatient
    pours,
With noise of trampling feet and flapping
    doors,
Streams to the numbered seat each paste-
    board fits
And smooths its caudal plumage as it sits ;
Waits while the slow musicians saunter
    in,
Till the bald leader taps his violin;
Till the old overture we know so well,
Zampa or Magic Flute or William Tell,
Has done its worst — then hark ! the
    tinkling bell !
The crash is o'er — the crinkling curtain
    furled,
And lo ! the glories of that brighter world !

Behold the offspring of the Thespian
    cart,
This full-grown temple of the magic art,
Where all the conjurers of illusion meet,
And please us all the more, the more they
    cheat.
These are the wizards and the witches too
Who win their honest bread by cheating
    you
With cheeks that drown in artificial tears
And lying skull-caps white with seventy
    years,
Sweet-tempered matrons changed to scold-
    ing Kates,
Maids mild as moonbeams crazed with
    murderous hates,
Kind, simple souls that stab and slash and
    slay
And stick at nothing, if it's in the play !

Would all the world told half as harm-
 less lies !
Would all its real fools were half as wise
As he who blinks through dull Dundreary's
 eyes !
Would all the unhanged bandits of the age
Were like the peaceful ruffians of the
 stage !
Would all the cankers wasting town and
 state,
The mob of rascals, little thieves and
 great,
Dealers in watered milk and watered
 stocks,
Who lead us lambs to pasture on the
 rocks, —
Shepherds — Jack Sheppards — of their
 city flocks, —
The rings of rogues that rob the luckless
 town,
Those evil angels creeping up and down
The Jacob's ladder of the treasury stairs,—
Not stage, but real Turpins and Ma-
 caires, —
Could doff, like us, their knavery with
 their clothes,
And find it easy as forgetting oaths !

Welcome, thrice welcome to our virgin
 dome,
The Muses' shrine, the Drama's new-found
 home !
Here shall the Statesman rest his weary
 brain,
The worn-out Artist find his wits again;
Here Trade forget his ledger and his cares,
And sweet communion mingle Bulls and
 Bears;
Here shall the youthful Lover, nestling
 near
The shrinking maiden, her he holds most
 dear,
Gaze on the mimic moonlight as it falls
On painted groves, on sliding canvas walls,
And sigh, "My angel ! What a life of
 bliss
We two could live in such a world as
 this ! "
Here shall the timid pedants of the schools,
The gilded boors, the labor-scorning fools,
The grass-green rustic and the smoke-
 dried cit,
Feel each in turn the stinging lash of wit,
And as it tingles on some tender part
Each find a balsam in his neighbor's smart;

So every folly prove a fresh delight
As in the picture of our play to-night.

Farewell ! The Players wait the Prompt-
 er's call;
Friends, lovers, listeners ! Welcome one
 and all !

A SEA DIALOGUE

NOVEMBER 10, 1864

Cabin Passenger   *Man at Wheel*

CABIN PASSENGER

FRIEND, you seem thoughtful. I not won-
 der much
That he who sails the ocean should be sad.
I am myself reflective. When I think
Of all this wallowing beast, the Sea, has
 sucked
Between his sharp thin lips, the wedgy
 waves,
What heaps of diamonds, rubies, emeralds,
 pearls;
What piles of shekels, talents, ducats,
 crowns,
What bales of Tyrian mantles, Indian
 shawls,
Of laces that have blanked the weavers'
 eyes,
Of silken tissues, wrought by worm and
 man,
The half-starved workman, and the well-
 fed worm;
What marbles, bronzes, pictures, parch-
 ments, books;
What many-lobuled, thought-engendering
 brains;
Lie with the gaping sea-shells in his
 maw, —
I, too, am silent; for all language seems
A mockery, and the speech of man is vain.
O mariner, we look upon the waves
And they rebuke our babbling. "Peace!"
 they say, —
"Mortal, be still ! " My noisy tongue is
 hushed,
And with my trembling finger on my lips
My soul exclaims in ecstasy —

MAN AT WHEEL

                              Belay !

CABIN PASSENGER

Ah yes! " Delay," — it calls, " nor haste to
    break
The charm of stillness with an idle word! "
O mariner, I love thee, for thy thought
Strides even with my own, nay, flies be-
    fore.
Thou art a brother to the wind and wave;
Have they not music for thine ear as
    mine,
When the wild tempest makes thy ship his
    lyre,
Smiting a cavernous basso from the
    shrouds
And climbing up his gamut through the
    stays,
Through buntlines, bowlines, ratlines, till
    it shrills
An alto keener than the locust sings,
And all the great Æolian orchestra
Storms out its mad sonata in the gale ?
Is not the scene a wondrous and —

MAN AT WHEEL

                    Avast !

CABIN PASSENGER

Ah yes, a vast, a vast and wondrous scene !
I see thy soul is open as the day
That holds the sunshine in its azure bowl
To all the solemn glories of the deep.
Tell me, O mariner, dost thou never feel
The grandeur of thine office, — to control
The keel that cuts the ocean like a knife
And leaves a wake behind it like a seam
In the great shining garment of the world ?

MAN AT WHEEL

Belay y'r jaw, y' swab ! y' hoss-marine !
    (*To the Captain.*)
Ay. ay, Sir ! Stiddy, Sir ! Sou'wes' b'sou' !

CHANSON WITHOUT MUSIC

BY THE PROFESSOR EMERITUS OF DEAD
AND LIVE LANGUAGES

PHI BETA KAPPA. — CAMBRIDGE, 1867

You bid me sing, — can I forget
    The classic ode of days gone by, —

How belle Fifine and jeune Lisette
    Exclaimed, " Anacreōn, gerōn ei " ?
" Regardez donc," those ladies said, —
    " You 're getting bald and wrinkled **too:**
When summer's roses all are shed,
    Love 's nullum ite, voyez-vous ! "

In vain ce brave Anacreon's cry,
    " Of Love alone my banjo sings "
(Erōta mounon). " Etiam si, —
    Eh b'en ? " replied the saucy things, —
" Go find a maid whose hair is gray,
    And strike your lyre, — we sha'n't com-
        plain:
But parce nobis, s'il vous plaît, —
    Voilà Adolphe ! Voilà Eugène ! "

Ah, jeune Lisette ! Ah, belle Fifine !
    Anacreon's lesson all must learn;
O kairos oxūs; Spring is green,
    But Acer Hyems waits his turn !
I hear you whispering from the dust,
    " Tiens, mon cher, c'est toujours so, —
The brightest blade grows dim with rust,
    The fairest meadow white with snow ! "

You do not mean it ! *Not* encore ?
    Another string of playday rhymes ?
You 've heard me — nonne est ? — before,
    Multoties, — more than twenty times;
Non possum, — vraiment, — pas du tout,
    I cannot ! I am loath to shirk;
But who will listen if I do,
    My memory makes such shocking work ?

Ginōsko. Scio. Yes, I 'm told
    Some ancients like my rusty lay,
As Grandpa Noah loved the old
    Red-sandstone march of Jubal's day.
I used to carol like the birds,
    But time my wits has quite unfixed,
Et quoad verba, — for my words, —
    Ciel ! Eheu ! Whe-ew ! — how they 're
        mixed !

Mehercle ! Zeu ! Diable ! how
    My thoughts were dressed when I was
        young,
But tempus fugit ! see them now
    Half clad in rags of every tongue !
O philoi, fratres, chers amis !
    I dare not court the youthful Muse,
For fear her sharp response should be,
    " Papa Anacreon, please excuse ! "

Adieu ! I 've trod my annual track
　How long ! — let others count the miles, —
And peddled out my rhyming pack
　To friends who always paid in smiles.
So, laissez-moi ! some youthful wit
　No doubt has wares he wants to show;
And I am asking, " Let me sit,"
　Dum ille clamat, " Dos pou sto ! "

FOR THE CENTENNIAL DINNER

OF THE PROPRIETORS OF BOSTON PIER,
OR THE LONG WHARF, APRIL 16, 1873

DEAR friends, we are strangers; we never
　before
Have suspected what love to each other we
　bore;
But each of us all to his neighbor is dear,
Whose heart has a throb for our time-
　honored pier.

As I look on each brother proprietor's
　face,
I could open my arms in a loving em-
　brace;
What wonder that feelings, undreamed of
　so long,
Should burst all at once in a blossom of
　song !

While I turn my fond glance on the mon-
　arch of piers,
Whose throne has stood firm through his
　eightscore of years,
My thought travels backward and reaches
　the day
When they drove the first pile on the edge
　of the bay.

See ! The joiner, the shipwright, the smith
　from his forge,
The redcoat, who shoulders his gun for
　King George,
The shopman, the 'prentice, the boys from
　the lane,
The parson, the doctor with gold-headed
　cane,

Come trooping down King Street, where
　now may be seen
The pulleys and ropes of a mighty ma-
　chine;

The weight rises slowly; it drops with a
　thud;
And, lo ! the great timber sinks deep in
　the mud !

They are gone, the stout craftsmen that
　hammered the piles,
And the square-toed old boys in the three-
　cornered tiles;
The breeches, the buckles, have faded
　from view,
And the parson's white wig and the ribbon-
　tied queue.

The redcoats have vanished; the last gren-
　adier
Stepped into the boat from the end of our
　pier;
They found that our hills were not easy to
　climb,
And the order came, " Countermarch,
　double-quick time ! "

They are gone, friend and foe, — anchored
　fast at the pier,
Whence no vessel brings back its pale
　passengers here;
But our wharf, like a lily, still floats on the
　flood,
Its breast in the sunshine, its roots in the
　mud.

Who — who that has loved it so long and
　so well —
The flower of his birthright would barter
　or sell ?
No: pride of the bay, while its ripples shall
　run,
You shall pass, as an heirloom, from father
　to son !

Let me part with the acres my grandfather
　bought,
With the bonds that my uncle's kind leg-
　acy brought,
With my bank - shares, — old " Union,"
　whose ten per cent stock
Stands stiff through the storms as the Ed-
　dystone rock;

With my rights (or my wrongs) in the
　" Erie," — alas !
With my claims on the mournful and
　" Mutual Mass.; "

With my " Phil. Wil. and Balt.," with my
    " C. B. and Q.; "
But I never, no never, will sell out of
    you.

We drink to thy past and thy future to-
    day,
Strong right arm of Boston, stretched out
    o'er the bay.
May the winds waft the wealth of all na-
    tions to thee,
And thy dividends flow like the waves of
    the sea !

A POEM SERVED TO ORDER

PHI BETA KAPPA, JUNE 26, 1873

THE Caliph ordered up his cook,
And, scowling with a fearful look
    That meant, — We stand no gammon, —
"To-morrow, just at two," he said,
" Hassan, our cook, will lose his head,
    Or serve us up a salmon."

" Great sire," the trembling *chef* replied,
" Lord of the Earth and all beside,
    Sun, Moon, and Stars, and so on " —
(Look in *Eōthen*, — there you 'll find
A list of titles. Never mind ;
    I have n't time to go on :)

" Great sire," and so forth, thus he spoke,
" Your Highness must intend a joke;
    It does n't stand to reason
For one to order salmon brought,
Unless that fish is sometimes caught,
    And also is in season.

" Our luck of late is shocking bad,
In fact, the latest catch we had
    (We kept the matter shady),
But, hauling in our nets, — alack !
We found no salmon, but a sack
    That held your honored Lady ! "

" Allah is great ! " the Caliph said,
" My poor Zuleika, you are dead,
    I once took interest in you."
" Perhaps, my Lord, you 'd like to know
We cut the lines and let her go."
    " Allah be praised ! Continue."

" It is n't hard one's hook to bait,
And, squatting down, to watch and wait,
    To see the cork go under;
At last suppose you 've got your bite,
You twitch away with all your might, —
    You 've hooked an eel, by thunder ! "

The Caliph patted Hassan's head :
" Slave, thou hast spoken well," he said,
    " And won thy master's favor.
Yes; since what happened t' other morn
The salmon of the Golden Horn
    Might have a doubtful flavor.

" That last remark about the eel
Has also justice that we feel
    Quite to our satisfaction.
To-morrow we dispense with fish,
And, for the present, if you wish,
    You 'll keep your bulbous fraction."

" Thanks ! thanks ! " the grateful *chef* re-
    plied,
His nutrient feature showing wide
    The gleam of arches dental:
" To cut my head off would n't pay,
I find it useful every day,
    As well as ornamental."

———

Brothers, I hope you will not fail
To see the moral of my tale
    And kindly to receive it.
You know your anniversary pie
Must have its crust, though hard and
    dry,
    And some prefer to leave it.

How oft before these youths were born
I 've fished in Fancy's Golden Horn
    For what the Muse might send me !
How gayly then I cast the line,
When all the morning sky was mine,
    And Hope her flies would lend me !

And now I hear our despot's call,
And come, like Hassan, to the hall, —
    If there 's a slave, I am one, —
My bait no longer flies, but worms !
I 've caught — Lord bless me ! how he
    squirms !
    An eel, and not a salmon !

THE FOUNTAIN OF YOUTH

READ AT THE MEETING OF THE HAR-
VARD ALUMNI ASSOCIATION, JUNE 25,
1873

The fount the Spaniard sought in vain
  Through all the land of flowers
Leaps glittering from the sandy plain
  Our classic grove embowers;
Here youth, unchanging, blooms and smiles,
  Here dwells eternal spring,
And warm from Hope's elysian isles
  The winds their perfume bring.

Here every leaf is in the bud,
  Each singing throat in tune,
And bright o'er evening's silver flood
  Shines the young crescent moon.
What wonder Age forgets his staff
  And lays his glasses down
And gray-haired grandsires look and laugh
  As when their locks were brown!

With ears grown dull and eyes grown dim
  They greet the joyous day
That calls them to the fountain's brim
  To wash their years away.
What change has clothed the ancient sire
  In sudden youth? For, lo!
The Judge, the Doctor, and the Squire
  Are Jack and Bill and Joe!

And be his titles what they will,
  In spite of manhood's claim
The graybeard is a school-boy still
  And loves his school-boy name;
It calms the ruler's stormy breast
  Whom hurrying care pursues,
And brings a sense of peace and rest,
  Like slippers after shoes.

And what are all the prizes won
  To youth's enchanted view?
And what is all the man has done
  To what the boy may do?
O blessed fount, whose waters flow
  Alike for sire and son,
That melts our winter's frost and snow
  And makes all ages one!

I pledge the sparkling fountain's tide,
  That flings its golden shower
With age to fill and youth to guide,
  Still fresh in morning flower!

Flow on with ever-widening stream,
  In ever-brightening morn, —
Our story's pride, our future's dream,
  The hope of times unborn!

NO TIME LIKE THE OLD TIME

1865

There is no time like the old time, when
  you and I were young,
When the buds of April blossomed, and the
  birds of spring-time sung!
The garden's brightest glories by summer
  suns are nursed,
But oh, the sweet, sweet violets, the flowers
  that opened first!

There is no place like the old place, where
  you and I were born,
Where we lifted first our eyelids on the
  splendors of the morn
From the milk-white breast that warmed
  us, from the clinging arms that bore,
Where the dear eyes glistened o'er us that
  will look on us no more!

There is no friend like the old friend, who
  has shared our morning days,
No greeting like his welcome, no homage
  like his praise:
Fame is the scentless sunflower, with gaudy
  crown of gold;
But friendship is the breathing rose, with
  sweets in every fold.

There is no love like the old love, that we
  courted in our pride;
Though our leaves are falling, falling, and
  we 're fading side by side,
There are blossoms all around us with the
  colors of our dawn,
And we live in borrowed sunshine when the
  day-star is withdrawn.

There are no times like the old times, —
  they shall never be forgot!
There is no place like the old place, — keep
  green the dear old spot!
There are no friends like our old friends, —
  may Heaven prolong their lives!
There are no loves like our old loves, —
  God bless our loving wives!

A HYMN OF PEACE

SUNG AT THE "JUBILEE," JUNE 15, 1869,
TO THE MUSIC OF KELLER'S "AMERI-
CAN HYMN"

ANGEL of Peace, thou hast wandered too
    long !
  Spread thy white wings to the sunshine
    of love !
Come while our voices are blended in
    song, —
  Fly to our ark like the storm-beaten
    dove !
Fly to our ark on the wings of the dove, —
  Speed o'er the far-sounding billows of
    song,
Crowned with thine olive-leaf garland of
    love, —
  Angel of Peace, thou hast waited too long!

Joyous we meet, on this altar of thine
  Mingling the gifts we have gathered for
    thee,

Sweet with the odors of myrtle and pine,
  Breeze of the prairie and breath of the
    sea, —
Meadow and mountain and forest and
    sea !
  Sweet is the fragrance of myrtle and
    pine,
Sweeter the incense we offer to thee,
  Brothers, once more round this altar of
    thine !

Angels of Bethlehem, answer the strain !
  Hark ! a new birth-song is filling the
    sky ! —
Loud as the storm-wind that tumbles the
    main
  Bid the full breath of the organ re-
    ply, —
Let the loud tempest of voices reply, —
  Roll its long surge like the earth-shaking
    main !
Swell the vast song till it mounts to the
    sky ! —
  Angels of Bethlehem, echo the strain !

BUNKER-HILL BATTLE AND OTHER POEMS

1874-1877

GRANDMOTHER'S STORY OF BUNKER-HILL BATTLE

AS SHE SAW IT FROM THE BELFRY

The story of Bunker Hill battle is told as literally in accordance with the best authorities as it would have been if it had been written in prose instead of in verse. I have often been asked what steeple it was from which the little group I speak of looked upon the conflict. To this I answer that I am not prepared to speak authoritatively, but that the reader may take his choice among all the steeples standing at that time in the northern part of the city. Christ Church in Salem Street is the one I always think of, but I do not insist upon its claim. As to the personages who made up the small company that followed the old corporal, it would be hard to identify them, but by ascertaining where the portrait by Copley is now to be found, some light may be thrown on their personality.

Daniel Malcolm's gravestone, splintered by British bullets, may be seen in the Copp's Hill burial-ground.

'T is like stirring living embers when, at
    eighty, one remembers
All the achings and the quakings of "the
    times that tried men's souls;"
When I talk of *Whig* and *Tory*, when I
    tell the *Rebel* story,
To you the words are ashes, but to me
    they 're burning coals.

I had heard the muskets' rattle of the
    April running battle;
Lord Percy's hunted soldiers, I can see
    their red coats still;
But a deadly chill comes o'er me, as the
    day looms up before me,
When a thousand men lay bleeding on the
    slopes of Bunker's Hill.

'T was a peaceful summer's morning,
    when the first thing gave us warn-
    ing
Was the booming of the cannon from the
    river and the shore:
"Child," says grandma, "what 's the mat-
    ter, what is all this noise and clat-
    ter?
Have those scalping Indian devils come to
    murder us once more?"

Poor old soul! my sides were shaking in
    the midst of all my quaking,
To hear her talk of Indians when the guns
    began to roar:
She had seen the burning village, and the
    slaughter and the pillage,
When the Mohawks killed her father with
    their bullets through his door.

Then I said, "Now, dear old granny, don't
    you fret and worry any,
For I 'll soon come back and tell you
    whether this is work or play;
There can't be mischief in it, so I won't
    be gone a minute" —
For a minute then I started. I was gone
    the livelong day.

No time for bodice-lacing or for looking-
    glass grimacing;
Down my hair went as I hurried, tumbling
    half-way to my heels;
God forbid your ever knowing, when
    there 's blood around her flowing,
How the lonely, helpless daughter of a
    quiet household feels!

In the street I heard a thumping; and I
    knew it was the stumping
Of the Corporal, our old neighbor, on that
    wooden leg he wore,

With a knot of women round him, — it was
    lucky I had found him,
So I followed with the others, and the Cor-
    poral marched before.

They were making for the steeple, — the
    old soldier and his people;
The pigeons circled round us as we climbed
    the creaking stair.
Just across the narrow river — oh, so close
    it made me shiver ! —
Stood a fortress on the hill-top that but
    yesterday was bare.

Not slow our eyes to find it; well we knew
    who stood behind it,
Though the earthwork hid them from us,
    and the stubborn walls were dumb:
Here were sister, wife, and mother, looking
    wild upon each other,
And their lips were white with terror as
    they said, THE HOUR HAS COME !

The morning slowly wasted, not a morsel
    had we tasted,
And our heads were almost splitting with
    the cannons' deafening thrill,
When a figure tall and stately round the
    rampart strode sedately;
It was PRESCOTT, one since told me; he
    commanded on the hill.

Every woman's heart grew bigger when
    we saw his manly figure,
With the banyan buckled round it, stand-
    ing up so straight and tall;
Like a gentleman of leisure who is stroll-
    ing out for pleasure,
Through the storm of shells and cannon-
    shot he walked around the wall.

At eleven the streets were swarming, for
    the redcoats' ranks were forming;
At noon in marching order they were
    moving to the piers;
How the bayonets gleamed and glistened,
    as we looked far down, and listened
To the trampling and the drum-beat of the
    belted grenadiers !

At length the men have started, with a
    cheer (it seemed faint-hearted),
In their scarlet regimentals, with their
    knapsacks on their backs,

And the reddening, rippling water, as after
    a sea-fight's slaughter,
Round the barges gliding onward blushed
    like blood along their tracks.

So they crossed to the other border, and
    again they formed in order;
And the boats came back for soldiers, came
    for soldiers, soldiers still:
The time seemed everlasting to us women
    faint and fasting,
At last they 're moving, marching, marching
    proudly up the hill.

We can see the bright steel glancing all
    along the lines advancing, —
Now the front rank fires a volley, — they
    have thrown away their shot;
For behind their earthwork lying, all the
    balls above them flying,
Our people need not hurry; so they wait
    and answer not.

Then the Corporal, our old cripple (he would
    swear sometimes and tipple), —
He had heard the bullets whistle (in the
    old French war) before, —
Calls out in words of jeering, just as if they
    all were hearing, —
And his wooden leg thumps fiercely on the
    dusty belfry floor : —

" Oh ! fire away, ye villains, and earn King
    George's shillin's,
But ye 'll waste a ton of powder afore a
    ' rebel ' falls;
You may bang the dirt and welcome, they 're
    as safe as Dan'l Malcolm
Ten foot beneath the gravestone that you 've
    splintered with your balls ! "

In the hush of expectation, in the awe and
    trepidation
Of the dread approaching moment, we are
    well-nigh breathless all;
Though the rotten bars are failing on the
    rickety belfry railing,
We are crowding up against them like the
    waves against a wall.

Just a glimpse (the air is clearer), they are
    nearer, — nearer, — nearer,
When a flash — a curling smoke-wreath —
    then a crash — the steeple shakes —

The deadly truce is ended; the tempest's
   shroud is rended;
Like a morning mist it gathered, like a
   thundercloud it breaks !

Oh the sight our eyes discover as the blue-
   black smoke blows over !
The red-coats stretched in windrows as a
   mower rakes his hay;
Here a scarlet heap is lying, there a head-
   long crowd is flying
Like a billow that has broken and is shiv-
   ered into spray.

Then we cried, "The troops are routed !
   they are beat — it can't be doubted !
God be thanked, the fight is over ! " — Ah !
   the grim old soldier's smile !
"Tell us, tell us why you look so ? " (we
   could hardly speak, we shook so), —
"Are they beaten ? *Are* they beaten ?
   ARE they beaten ? " — "Wait a
   while."

Oh the trembling and the terror ! for too
   soon we saw our error:
They are baffled, not defeated; we have
   driven them back in vain;
And the columns that were scattered, round
   the colors that were tattered,
Toward the sullen, silent fortress turn their
   belted breasts again.

All at once, as we are gazing, lo the roofs
   of Charlestown blazing !
They have fired the harmless village; in an
   hour it will be down !
The Lord in heaven confound them, rain
   his fire and brimstone round them, —
The robbing, murdering red-coats, that
   would burn a peaceful town !

They are marching, stern and solemn; we
   can see each massive column
As they near the naked earth-mound with
   the slanting walls so steep.
Have our soldiers got faint-hearted, and in
   noiseless haste departed?
Are they panic-struck and helpless ? Are
   they palsied or asleep ?

Now ! the walls they 're almost under !
   scarce a rod the foes asunder !
Not a firelock flashed against them ! up
   the earthwork they will swarm !

But the words have scarce been spoken,
   when the ominous calm is broken,
And a bellowing crash has emptied all the
   vengeance of the storm !

So again, with murderous slaughter, pelted
   backwards to the water,
Fly Pigot's running heroes and the
   frightened braves of Howe;
And we shout, " At last they 're done for,
   it 's their barges they have run for:
They are beaten, beaten, beaten; and the
   battle 's over now ! "

And we looked, poor timid creatures, on
   the rough old soldier's features,
Our lips afraid to question, but he knew
   what we would ask :
"Not sure," he said; "keep quiet, — once
   more, I guess, they 'll try it —
Here 's damnation to the cut-throats ! " —
   then he handed me his flask,

Saying, " Gal, you 're looking shaky; have
   a drop of old Jamaiky;
I 'm afeard there 'll be more trouble afore
   the job is done; "
So I took one scorching swallow; dreadful
   faint I felt and hollow,
Standing there from early morning when
   the firing was begun.

All through those hours of trial I had
   watched a calm clock dial,
As the hands kept creeping, creeping, —
   they were creeping round to four,
When the old man said, " They 're forming
   with their bagonets fixed for storm-
   ing:
It 's the death-grip that 's a-coming, — they
   will try the works once more."

With brazen trumpets blaring, the flames
   behind them glaring,
The deadly wall before them, in close array
   they come;
Still onward, upward toiling, like a dragon's
   fold uncoiling, —
Like the rattlesnake's shrill warning the
   reverberating drum !

Over heaps all torn and gory — shall I tell
   the fearful story,
How they surged above the breastwork, as
   a sea breaks over a deck;

How, driven, yet scarce defeated, our worn-
    out men retreated,
With their powder-horns all emptied, like
    the swimmers from a wreck ?

It has all been told and painted; as for me,
    they say I fainted,
And the wooden - legged old Corporal
    stumped with me down the stair:
When I woke from dreams affrighted the
    evening lamps were lighted, —
On the floor a youth was lying; his bleeding
    breast was bare.

And I heard through all the flurry, " Send
    for WARREN ! hurry ! hurry !
Tell him here 's a soldier bleeding, and
    he 'll come and dress his wound ! "
Ah, we knew not till the morrow told its
    tale of death and sorrow,
How the starlight found him stiffened on
    the dark and bloody ground.

Who the youth was, what his name was,
    where the place from which he came
    was,
Who had brought him from the battle, and
    had left him at our door,
He could not speak to tell us; but 't was
    one of our brave fellows,
As the homespun plainly showed us which
    the dying soldier wore.

For they all thought he was dying, as they
    gathered round him crying, —
And they said, " Oh, how they 'll miss him ! "
    and, " What *will* his mother do ? "
Then, his eyelids just unclosing like a child's
    that has been dozing,
He faintly murmured, " Mother ! " — and
    — I saw his eyes were blue.

" Why, grandma, how you 're winking ! "
    Ah, my child, it sets me thinking
Of a story not like this one. Well, he
    somehow lived along;
So we came to know each other, and I
    nursed him like a — mother,
Till at last he stood before me, tall, and
    rosy-cheeked, and strong.

And we sometimes walked together in the
    pleasant summer weather, —
" Please to tell us what his name was ? "
    Just your own, my little dear, —

There 's his picture Copley painted: we be-
    came so well acquainted,
That — in short, that 's why I 'm grandma,
    and you children all are here !

AT THE "ATLANTIC" DINNER

DECEMBER 15, 1874

I SUPPOSE it 's myself that you 're making
    allusion to
And bringing the sense of dismay and con-
    fusion to.
Of course *some* must speak, — they are al-
    ways selected to,
But pray what 's the reason that I am ex-
    pected to ?
I 'm not fond of wasting my breath as those
    fellows do
That want to be blowing forever as bellows
    do;
Their legs are uneasy, but why will you jog
    any
That long to stay quiet beneath the mahog-
    any ?

Why, why call *me* up with your battery of
    flatteries ?
You say " He writes poetry," — that 's what
    the matter is !
" It costs him no trouble — a pen full of
    ink or two
And the poem is done in the time of a
    wink or two;
As for thoughts — never mind — take the
    ones that lie uppermost,
And the rhymes used by Milton and Byron
    and Tupper most;
The lines come so easy ! at one end he jin-
    gles 'em,
At the other with capital letters he shingles
    'em, —
Why, the thing writes itself, and before
    he 's half done with it
He hates to stop writing, he has such good
    fun with it ! "

Ah, that is the way in which simple ones
    go about
And draw a fine picture of things they
    don't know about !
We all know a kitten, but come to a cata-
    mount
The beast is a stranger when grown up to
    that amount,

(A stranger we rather prefer should n't
　visit us,
A *felis* whose advent is far from felici-
　tous.)
The boy who can boast that his trap has
　just got a mouse
Must n't draw it and write underneath
　" hippopotamus; "
Or say unveraciously, " This is an ele-
　phant," —
Don't think, let me beg, these examples
　irrelevant, —
What they mean is just this — that a thing
　to be painted well
Should always be something with which
　we 're acquainted well.

You call on your victim for " things he has
　plenty of, —
Those copies of verses no doubt at least
　twenty of;
His desk is crammed full, for he always
　keeps writing 'em
And reading to friends as his way of de-
　lighting 'em ! "
I tell you this writing of verses means busi-
　ness, —
It makes the brain whirl in a vortex of
　dizziness:
You think they are scrawled in the languor
　of laziness —
I tell you they 're squeezed by a spasm of
　craziness,
A fit half as bad as the staggering vertigos
That seize a poor fellow and down in the
　dirt he goes !

And therefore it chimes with the word's
　etymology
That the sons of Apollo are great on apol-
　ogy,
For the writing of verse is a struggle mys-
　terious
And the gayest of rhymes is a matter that 's
　serious.
For myself, I 'm relied on by friends in ex-
　tremities,
And I don't mind so much if a comfort to
　them it is;
'T is a pleasure to please, and the straw
　that can tickle us
Is a source of enjoyment though slightly
　ridiculous.

I am up for a — something — and since
　I 've begun with it,

I must give you a toast now before I have
　done with it.
Let me pump at my wits as they pumped
　the Cochituate
That moistened — it may be — the very
　last bit you ate:
Success to our publishers, authors and
　editors,
To our debtors good luck, — pleasant
　dreams to our creditors;
May the monthly grow yearly, till all we
　are groping for
Has reached the fulfilment we 're all of us
　hoping for ;
Till the bore through the tunnel — it makes
　me let off a sigh
To think it may possibly ruin my pro-
　phecy —
Has been punned on so often 't will never
　provoke again
One mild adolescent to make the old joke
　again;
Till abstinent, all-go-to-meeting society
Has forgotten the sense of the word ine-
　briety;
Till the work that poor Hannah and Bridget
　and Phillis do
The humanized, civilized female gorillas do;
Till the roughs, as we call them, grown
　loving and dutiful,
Shall worship the true and the pure and
　the beautiful,
And, preying no longer as tiger and vulture
　do,
All read the " Atlantic " as persons of cul-
　ture do !

"LUCY"

FOR HER GOLDEN WEDDING, OCTOBER 18, 1875

[The subject of this poem was a familiar fig-
ure in the household of Dr. Holmes's father, and
was married while living there to a farmer.]

" Lucy." — The old familiar name
　Is now, as always, pleasant,
Its liquid melody the same
　Alike in past or present;
Let others call you what they will,
　I know you 'll let me use it;
To me your name is Lucy still,
　I cannot bear to lose it.

What visions of the past return
　With Lucy's image blended !

What memories from the silent urn
  Of gentle lives long ended !
What dreams of childhood's fleeting morn,
  What starry aspirations,
That filled the misty days unborn
  With fancy's coruscations !

Ah, Lucy, life has swiftly sped
  From April to November;
The summer blossoms all are shed
  That you and I remember;
But while the vanished years we share
  With mingling recollections,
How all their shadowy features wear
  The hue of old affections !

Love called you.   He who stole your heart
  Of sunshine half bereft us;
Our household's garland fell apart
  The morning that you left us;
The tears of tender girlhood streamed
  Through sorrow's opening sluices;
Less sweet our garden's roses seemed,
  Less blue its flower-de-luces.

That old regret is turned to smiles,
  That parting sigh to greeting;
I send my heart-throb fifty miles,
  Through every line 't is beating;
God grant you many and happy years,
  Till when the last has crowned you
The dawn of endless day appears,
  And heaven is shining round you !

HYMN

FOR THE INAUGURATION OF THE
STATUE OF GOVERNOR ANDREW,
HINGHAM, OCTOBER 7, 1875

BEHOLD the shape our eyes have known !
It lives once more in changeless stone;
So looked in mortal face and form
Our guide through peril's deadly storm.

But hushed the beating heart we knew,
That heart so tender, brave, and true,
Firm as the rooted mountain rock,
Pure as the quarry's whitest block !

Not his beneath the blood-red star
To win the soldier's envied scar;
Unarmed he battled for the right,
In Duty's never-ending fight.

Unconquered will, unslumbering eye,
Faith such as bids the martyr die,
The prophet's glance, the master's hand
To mould the work his foresight planned,

These were his gifts; what Heaven had
    lent
For justice, mercy, truth, he spent,
First to avenge the traitorous blow,
And first to lift the vanquished foe.

Lo, thus he stood; in danger's strait
The pilot of the Pilgrim State !
Too large his fame for her alone, —
A nation claims him as her own !

A MEMORIAL TRIBUTE

READ AT THE MEETING HELD AT MUSIC
HALL, FEBRUARY 8, 1876, IN MEMORY
OF DR. SAMUEL G. HOWE

I

LEADER of armies, Israel's God,
  Thy soldier's fight is won !
Master, whose lowly path he trod,
  Thy servant's work is done !

No voice is heard from Sinai's steep
  Our wandering feet to guide;
From Horeb's rock no waters leap;
  No Jordan's waves divide;

No prophet cleaves our western sky
  On wheels of whirling fire;
No shepherds hear the song on high
  Of heaven's angelic choir:

Yet here as to the patriarch's tent
  God's angel comes a guest;
He comes on heaven's high errand sent,
  In earth's poor raiment drest.

We see no halo round his brow
  Till love its own recalls,
And, like a leaf that quits the bough,
  The mortal vesture falls.

In autumn's chill declining day,
  Ere winter's killing frost,
The message came; so passed away
  The friend our earth has lost.

Still, Father, in thy love we trust;
  Forgive us if we mourn
The saddening hour that laid in dust
  His robe of flesh outworn.

II

How long the wreck-strewn journey seems
  To reach the far-off past
That woke his youth from peaceful dreams
  With Freedom's trumpet-blast !

Along her classic hillsides rung
  The Paynim's battle-cry,
And like a red-cross knight he sprung
  For her to live or die.

No trustier service claimed the wreath
  For Sparta's bravest son;
No truer soldier sleeps beneath
  The mound of Marathon;

Yet not for him the warrior's grave
  In front of angry foes;
To lift, to shield, to help, to save,
  The holier task he chose.

He touched the eyelids of the blind,
  And lo ! the veil withdrawn,
As o'er the midnight of the mind
  He led the light of dawn.

He asked not whence the fountains roll
  No traveller's foot has found,
But mapped the desert of the soul
  Untracked by sight or sound.

What prayers have reached the sapphire
    throne,
  By silent fingers spelt,
For him who first through depths unknown
  His doubtful pathway felt,

Who sought the slumbering sense that lay
  Close shut with bolt and bar,
And showed awakening thought the ray
  Of reason's morning star !

Where'er he moved, his shadowy form
  The sightless orbs would seek,
And smiles of welcome light and warm
  The lips that could not speak.

No labored line, no sculptor's art,
  Such hallowed memory needs;

His tablet is the human heart,
  His record loving deeds.

III

The rest that earth denied is thine, —
  Ah, is it rest ? we ask,
Or, traced by knowledge more divine,
  Some larger, nobler task ?

Had but those boundless fields of blue
  One darkened sphere like this;
But what has heaven for thee to do
  In realms of perfect bliss ?

No cloud to lift, no mind to clear,
  No rugged path to smooth,
No struggling soul to help and cheer,
  No mortal grief to soothe !

Enough; is there a world of love,
  No more we ask to know;
The hand will guide thy ways above
  That shaped thy task below.

JOSEPH WARREN, M. D.

1875

TRAINED in the holy art whose lifted shield
  Wards off the darts a never-slumbering
    foe,
  By hearth and wayside lurking, waits to
    throw,
Oppression taught his helpful arm to wield
The slayer's weapon: on the murderous field
  The fiery bolt he challenged laid him low,
  Seeking its noblest victim.   Even so
The charter of a nation must be sealed!
  The healer's brow the hero's honors
    crowned,
From lowliest duty called to loftiest deed.
  Living, the oak-leaf wreath his temples
    bound;
Dying, the conqueror's laurel was his meed,
Last on the broken ramparts' turf to bleed
  Where Freedom's victory in defeat was
    found.

OLD CAMBRIDGE

JULY 3, 1875

[Upon the occasion of the Centennial cele-
bration of Washington's taking command of

the American army. It was on this occasion
that Lowell read his ode, *Under the Old
Elm.*]

AND can it be you 've found a place
Within this consecrated space,
    That makes so fine a show,
For one of Rip Van Winkle's race ?
    And is it really so ?
Who wants an old receipted bill ?
Who fishes in the Frog-pond still ?
Who digs last year's potato hill ? —
    That 's what he 'd like to know !

And were it any spot on earth
Save this dear home that gave him birth
    Some scores of years ago,
He had not come to spoil your mirth
    And chill your festive glow;
But round his baby-nest he strays,
With tearful eye the scene surveys,
His heart unchanged by changing days, —
    That 's what he 'd have you know.

Can you whose eyes not yet are dim
Live o'er the buried past with him,
    And see the roses blow
When white-haired men were Joe and Jim
    Untouched by winter's snow ?
Or roll the years back one by one
As Judah's monarch backed the sun,
And see the century just begun ? —
    That 's what he 'd like to know !

I come, but as the swallow dips,
Just touching with her feather-tips
    The shining wave below,
To sit with pleasure-murmuring lips
    And listen to the flow
Of Elmwood's sparkling Hippocrene,
To tread once more my native green,
To sigh unheard, to smile unseen, —
    That 's what I 'd have you know.

But since the common lot I 've shared
(We all are sitting " unprepared,"
    Like culprits in a row,
Whose heads are down, whose necks are
        bared
    To wait the headsman's blow),
I 'd like to shift my task to you,
By asking just a thing or two
About the good old times I knew, —
    Here 's what I want to know:

The yellow meetin' house — can you tell
Just where it stood before it fell
    Prey of the vandal foe, —
Our dear old temple, loved so well,
    By ruthless hands laid low ?
Where, tell me, was the Deacon's pew ?
Whose hair was braided in a queue ?
(For there were pig-tails not a few,) —
    That 's what I 'd like to know.

The bell — can you recall its clang ?
And how the seats would slam and bang ?
    The voices high and low ?
The basso's trump before he sang ?
    The viol and its bow ?
Where was it old Judge Winthrop sat ?
Who wore the last three-cornered hat ?
Was Israel Porter lean or fat ? —
    That 's what I 'd like to know.

Tell where the market used to be
That stood beside the murdered tree ?
    Whose dog to church would go ?
Old Marcus Reemie, who was he ?
    Who were the brothers Snow ?
Does not your memory slightly fail
About that great September gale ? —
Whereof one told a moving tale,
    As Cambridge boys should know.

When Cambridge was a simple town,
Say just when Deacon William Brown
    (Last door in yonder row),
For honest silver counted down,
    His groceries would bestow ? —
For those were days when money meant
Something that jingled as you went, —
No hybrid like the nickel cent,
    I 'd have you all to know,

But quarter, ninepence, pistareen,
And fourpence hapennies in between,
    All metal fit to show,
Instead of rags in stagnant green,
    The scum of debts we owe;
How sad to think such stuff should be
Our Wendell's cure-all recipe, —
Not Wendell H., but Wendell P., —
    The one you all must know !

I question — but you answer not —
Dear me ! and have I quite forgot
    How fivescore years ago,

Just on this very blessed spot,
  The summer leaves below,
Before his homespun ranks arrayed
In green New England's elm-bough shade
The great Virginian drew the blade
  King George full soon should know !

O George the Third ! you found it true
Our George was more than *double you*,
  For nature made him so.
Not much an empire's crown can do
  If brains are scant and slow, —
Ah, not like that his laurel crown
Whose presence gilded with renown
Our brave old Academic town,
  As all her children know !

So here we meet with loud acclaim
To tell mankind that here he came,
  With hearts that throb and glow;
Ours is a portion of his fame
  Our trumpets needs must blow !
On yonder hill the Lion fell,
But here was chipped the eagle's shell, —
That little hatchet did it well,
  As all the world shall know !

WELCOME TO THE NATIONS

PHILADELPHIA, JULY 4, 1876

BRIGHT on the banners of lily and rose
  Lo! the last sun of our century sets !
Wreathe the black cannon that scowled on
    our foes,
  All but her friendships the nation for-
    gets !
  All but her friends and their welcome
    forgets !
These are around her; but where are her
    foes ?
  Lo, while the sun of her century sets,
Peace with her garlands of lily and rose !

Welcome ! a shout like the war trumpet's
    swell
  Wakes the wild echoes that slumber
    around !
Welcome! it quivers from Liberty's bell;
  Welcome ! the walls of her temple re-
    sound !
  Hark! the gray walls of her temple re-
    sound !
Fade the far voices o'er hillside and dell;

Welcome ! still whisper the echoes
    around;
Welcome ! still trembles on Liberty's bell !

Thrones of the continent ! isles of the
    sea !
  Yours are the garlands of peace we en-
    twine;
Welcome, once more, to the land of the
    free,
  Shadowed alike by the palm and the
    pine;
  Softly they murmur, the palm and the
    pine,
" Hushed is our strife, in the land of the
    free ; "
  Over your children their branches en-
    twine,
Thrones of the continents ! isles of the sea !

A FAMILIAR LETTER

TO SEVERAL CORRESPONDENTS

YES, write, if you want to, there 's nothing
    like trying;
  Who knows what a treasure your casket
    may hold ?
I 'll show you that rhyming 's as easy as
    lying,
  If you' ll listen to me while the art I un-
    fold.

Here 's a book full of words; one can
    choose as he fancies,
  As a painter his tint, as a workman his
    tool;
Just think ! all the poems and plays and
    romances
  Were drawn out of this, like the fish
    from a pool !

You can wander at will through its sylla-
    bled mazes,
  And take all you want, — not a copper
    they cost, —
What is there to hinder your picking out
    phrases
  For an epic as clever as " Paradise
    Lost " ?

Don't mind if the index of sense is at zero,
  Use words that run smoothly, whatever
    they mean;

Leander and Lilian and Lillibullero
  Are much the same thing in the rhyming
    machine.

There are words so delicious their sweet-
  ness will smother
That boarding-school flavor of which
  we 're afraid, —
There is "lush " is a good one, and " swirl "
  is another, —
Put both in one stanza, its fortune is
  made.

With musical murmurs and rhythmical
  closes
You can cheat us of smiles when you 've
  nothing to tell;
You hand us a nosegay of milliner's roses,
And we cry with delight, " Oh, how
  sweet they *do* smell ! "

Perhaps you will answer all needful condi-
  tions
For winning the laurels to which you
  aspire,
By docking the tails of the two preposi-
  tions
I' the style o' the bards you so greatly
  admire.

As for subjects of verse, they are only too
  plenty
For ringing the changes on metrical
  chimes;
A maiden, a moonbeam, a lover of twenty
Have filled that great basket with bush-
  els of rhymes.

Let me show you a picture — 't is far from
  irrelevant —
By a famous old hand in the arts of de-
  sign;
'T is only a photographed sketch of an
  elephant, —
The name of the draughtsman was Rem-
  brandt of Rhine.

How easy ! no troublesome colors to lay
  on,
It can't have fatigued him, — no, not in
  the least, —
A dash here and there with a hap-hazard
  crayon,
And there stands the wrinkled-skinned,
  baggy-limbed beast.

Just so with your verse, — 't is as easy as
  sketching, —
You can reel off a song without knitting
  your brow,
As lightly as Rembrandt a drawing or
  etching;
It is nothing at all, if you only know how.

Well; imagine you 've printed your volume
  of verses:
Your forehead is wreathed with the gar-
  land of fame,
Your poems the eloquent school-boy re-
  hearses,
Her album the school-girl presents for
  your name;

Each morning the post brings you auto-
  graph letters;
You 'll answer them promptly, — an
  hour is n't much
For the honor of sharing a page with your
  betters,
With magistrates, members of Congress,
  and such.

Of course you 're delighted to serve the
  committees
That come with requests from the coun-
  try all round,
You would grace the occasion with poems
  and ditties
When they 've got a new schoolhouse,
  or poorhouse, or pound.

With a hymn for the saints and a song for
  the sinners,
You go and are welcome wherever you
  please;
You 're a privileged guest at all manner of
  dinners,
You 've a seat on the platform among
  the grandees.

At length your mere presence becomes a
  sensation,
Your cup of enjoyment is filled to its brim
With the pleasure Horatian of digitmon-
  stration,
As the whisper runs round of " That 's
  he ! " or " That 's him ! "

But remember, O dealer in phrases sono-
  rous,
So daintily chosen, so tunefully matched,

Though you soar with the wings of the
  cherubim o'er us,
The *ovum* was human from which you
  were hatched.

No will of your own with its puny compul-
  sion
  Can summon the spirit that quickens the
  lyre;
It comes, if at all, like the Sibyl's convul-
  sion
  And touches the brain with a finger of
  fire.

So perhaps, after all, it's as well to be
  quiet
  If you've nothing you think is worth
  saying in prose,
As to furnish a meal of their cannibal diet
  To the critics, by publishing, as you pro-
  pose.

But it's all of no use, and I'm sorry I've
  written, —
  I shall see your thin volume some day
  on my shelf;
For the rhyming tarantula surely has bit-
  ten,
  And music must cure you, so pipe it
  yourself.

UNSATISFIED

"Only a housemaid!" She looked from
  the kitchen, —
  Neat was the kitchen and tidy was she;
There at her window a sempstress sat
  stitching;
  "Were I a sempstress, how happy I'd
  be!"

"Only a Queen!" She looked over the
  waters, —
  Fair was her kingdom and mighty was
  she;
There sat an Empress, with Queens for
  her daughters;
  "Were I an Empress, how happy I'd
  be!"

Still the old frailty they all of them trip in!
  Eve in her daughters is ever the same;
Give her all Eden, she sighs for a pippin;
  Give her an Empire, she pines for a
  name!

HOW THE OLD HORSE WON THE BET

DEDICATED BY A CONTRIBUTOR TO THE
COLLEGIAN, 1830, TO THE EDITORS
OF THE HARVARD ADVOCATE, 1876

Unquestionably there is something a little
like extravagance in *How the Old Horse won
the Bet*, which taxes the credulity of experi-
enced horsemen. Still there have been a good
many surprises in the history of the turf and
the trotting course.

The Godolphin Arabian was taken from ig-
noble drudgery to become the patriarch of the
English racing stock.

Old Dutchman was transferred from between
the shafts of a cart to become a champion of
the American trotters in his time.

"Old Blue," a famous Boston horse of the
early decades of this century, was said to trot
a mile in less than three minutes, but I do not
find any exact record of his achievements.

Those who have followed the history of the
American trotting horse are aware of the won-
derful development of speed attained in these
last years. The lowest time as yet recorded is
by Maud S., in 2.08¾.

'Twas on the famous trotting-ground,
The betting men were gathered round
From far and near; the "cracks" were
  there
Whose deeds the sporting prints declare:
The swift g. m., Old Hiram's nag,
The fleet s. h., Dan Pfeiffer's brag,
With these a third — and who is he
That stands beside his fast b. g.?
Budd Doble, whose catarrhal name
So fills the nasal trump of fame.
There too stood many a noted steed
Of Messenger and Morgan breed;
Green horses also, not a few;
Unknown as yet what they could do;
And all the hacks that know so well
The scourgings of the Sunday swell.

Blue are the skies of opening day;
The bordering turf is green with May;
The sunshine's golden gleam is thrown
On sorrel, chestnut, bay, and roan;
The horses paw and prance and neigh,
Fillies and colts like kittens play,
And dance and toss their rippled **manes**
Shining and soft as silken skeins;
Wagons and gigs are ranged about,

And fashion flaunts her gay turn-out;
Here stands — each youthful Jehu's
    dream —
The jointed tandem, ticklish team !
And there in ampler breadth expand
The splendors of the four-in-hand;
On faultless ties and glossy tiles
The lovely bonnets beam their smiles;
(The style 's the man, so books avow;
The style 's the woman, anyhow);
From flounces frothed with creamy lace
Peeps out the pug-dog's smutty face,
Or spaniel rolls his liquid eye,
Or stares the wiry pet of Skye, —
O woman, in your hours of ease
So shy with us, so free with these !

"Come on ! I 'll bet you two to one
I 'll make him do it !" "Will you ?
    Done !"

What was it who was bound to do ?
I did not hear and can't tell you, —
Pray listen till my story 's through.
Scarce noticed, back behind the rest,
By cart and wagon rudely prest,
The parson's lean and bony bay
Stood harnessed in his one-horse shay —
Lent to his sexton for the day;
(A funeral — so the sexton said;
His mother's uncle's wife was dead.)

Like Lazarus bid to Dives' feast,
So looked the poor forlorn old beast;
His coat was rough, his tail was bare,
The gray was sprinkled in his hair;
Sportsmen and jockeys knew him not,
And yet they say he once could trot
Among the fleetest of the town,
Till something cracked and broke him
    down, —
The steed's, the statesman's, common lot !
"And are we then so soon forgot ?"
Ah me ! I doubt if one of you
Has ever heard the name "Old Blue,"
Whose fame through all this region rung
In those old days when I was young !

"Bring forth the horse !" Alas ! he
    showed
Not like the one Mazeppa rode;
Scant-maned, sharp-backed, and shaky-
    kneed,
The wreck of what was once a steed,

Lips thin, eyes hollow, stiff in joints;
Yet not without his knowing points.
The sexton laughing in his sleeve,
As if 't were all a make-believe,
Led forth the horse, and as he laughed
Unhitched the breeching from a shaft,
Unclasped the rusty belt beneath,
Drew forth the snaffle from his teeth,
Slipped off his head-stall, set him free
From strap and rein, — a sight to see !

So worn, so lean in every limb,
It can't be they are saddling him !
It is ! his back the pig-skin strides
And flaps his lank, rheumatic sides;
With look of mingled scorn and mirth
They buckle round the saddle-girth;
With horsy wink and saucy toss
A youngster throws his leg across,
And so, his rider on his back,
They lead him, limping, to the track,
Far up behind the starting-point,
To limber out each stiffened joint.

As through the jeering crowd he past,
One pitying look Old Hiram cast;
"Go it, ye cripple, while ye can !"
Cried out unsentimental Dan;
"A Fast-Day dinner for the crows !"
Budd Doble's scoffing shout arose.

Slowly, as when the walking-beam
First feels the gathering head of steam,
With warning cough and threatening
    wheeze
The stiff old charger crooks his knees;
At first with cautious step sedate,
As if he dragged a coach of state;
He 's not a colt; he knows full well
That time is weight and sure to tell;
No horse so sturdy but he fears
The handicap of twenty years.

As through the throng on either hand
The old horse nears the judges' stand,
Beneath his jockey's feather-weight
He warms a little to his gait,
And now and then a step is tried
That hints of something like a stride.

"Go !" — Through his ear the summons
    stung
As if a battle-trump had rung;
The slumbering instincts long unstirred

Start at the old familiar word;
It thrills like flame through every limb, —
What mean his twenty years to him?
The savage blow his rider dealt
Fell on his hollow flanks unfelt;
The spur that pricked his staring hide
Unheeded tore his bleeding side;
Alike to him are spur and rein, —
He steps a five-year-old again!

Before the quarter pole was past,
Old Hiram said, "He's going fast."
Long ere the quarter was a half,
The chuckling crowd had ceased to laugh;
Tighter his frightened jockey clung
As in a mighty stride he swung,
The gravel flying in his track,
His neck stretched out, his ears laid back,
His tail extended all the while
Behind him like a rat-tail file!
Off went a shoe, — away it spun,
Shot like a bullet from a gun;
The quaking jockey shapes a prayer
From scraps of oaths he used to swear;
He drops his whip, he drops his rein,
He clutches fiercely for a mane;
He 'll lose his hold — he sways and reels —
He 'll slide beneath those trampling heels!
The knees of many a horseman quake,
The flowers on many a bonnet shake,
And shouts arise from left and right,
"Stick on! Stick on!" "Hould tight!
    Hould tight!"
"Cling round his neck and don't let go —
That pace can't hold — there! steady!
    whoa!"
But like the sable steed that bore
The spectral lover of Lenore,
His nostrils snorting foam and fire,
No stretch his bony limbs can tire;
And now the stand he rushes by,
And "Stop him! — stop him!" is the
    cry.
Stand back! he 's only just begun —
He 's having out three heats in one!

"Don't rush in front! he 'll smash your
    brains;
But follow up and grab the reins!"
Old Hiram spoke. Dan Pfeiffer heard,
And sprang impatient at the word;
Budd Doble started on his bay,
Old Hiram followed on his gray,
And off they spring, and round they go,

The fast ones doing "all they know."
Look! twice they follow at his heels,
As round the circling course he wheels,
And whirls with him that clinging boy
Like Hector round the walls of Troy;
Still on, and on, the third time round!
They 're tailing off! they 're losing ground!
Budd Doble's nag begins to fail!
Dan Pfeiffer's sorrel whisks his tail!
And see! in spite of whip and shout,
Old Hiram's mare is giving out!
Now for the finish! at the turn,
The old horse — all the rest astern —
Comes swinging in, with easy trot;
By Jove! he 's distanced all the lot!

That trot no mortal could explain;
Some said, "Old Dutchman come again!"
Some took his time, — at least they tried,
But what it was could none decide;
One said he could n't understand
What happened to his second hand;
One said 2.10; *that* could n't be —
More like two twenty-two or three;
Old Hiram settled it at last;
"The time was two — too dee-vel-ish fast!"

The parson's horse had won the bet;
It cost him something of a sweat;
Back in the one-horse shay he went;
The parson wondered what it meant,
And murmured, with a mild surprise
And pleasant twinkle of the eyes,
"That funeral must have been a trick,
Or corpses drive at double-quick;
I should n't wonder, I declare,
If brother — Jehu — made the prayer!"

And this is all I have to say
About that tough old trotting bay,
Huddup! Huddup! G'lang! Good day!

Moral for which this tale is told:
A horse *can* trot, for all he 's old.

AN APPEAL FOR "THE OLD SOUTH"

"While stands the Coliseum, Rome shall stand;
When falls the Coliseum, Rome shall fall."

[Written in the spirit of *Old Ironsides*.
There was danger that the historic church in
Boston would be destroyed, since it stood on

land very valuable for commercial purposes, and the congregation worshipping in it had built a new meeting-house in the dwelling-house part of the city. The building was saved almost wholly through the intervention of public-spirited women, headed by Mrs. Mary Hemenway, who not only contributed most of the money needed, but afterward made the church the centre of important work in the teaching of history.]

FULL sevenscore years our city's pride —
  The comely Southern spire —
Has cast its shadow, and defied
  The storm, the foe, the fire;
Sad is the sight our eyes behold;
  Woe to the three-hilled town,
When through the land the tale is told —
  " The brave ' Old South ' is down ! "

Let darkness blot the starless dawn
  That hears our children tell,
" Here rose the walls, now wrecked and
    gone,
  Our fathers loved so well;
Here, while his brethren stood aloof,
  The herald's blast was blown
That shook St. Stephen's pillared roof
  And rocked King George's throne !

" The home-bound wanderer of the main
  Looked from his deck afar,
To where the gilded, glittering vane
  Shone like the evening star,
And pilgrim feet from every clime
  The floor with reverence trod,
Where holy memories made sublime
  The shrine of Freedom's God ! "

The darkened skies, alas ! have seen
  Our monarch tree laid low,
And spread in ruins o'er the green,
  But Nature struck the blow;
No scheming thrift its downfall planned,
  It felt no edge of steel,
No soulless hireling raised his hand
  The deadly stroke to deal.

In bridal garlands, pale and mute,
  Still pleads the storied tower;
These are the blossoms, but the fruit
  Awaits the golden shower;
The spire still greets the morning sun, —
  Say, shall it stand or fall ?
Help, ere the spoiler has begun !
  Help, each, and God help all !

THE FIRST FAN

READ AT A MEETING OF THE BOSTON BRIC-À-BRAC CLUB, FEBRUARY 21, 1877

WHEN rose the cry "Great Pan is dead ! "
  And Jove's high palace closed its portal,
The fallen gods, before they fled,
  Sold out their frippery to a mortal.

" To whom ? " you ask. I ask of you.
  The answer hardly needs suggestion;
Of course it was the Wandering Jew, —
  How could you put me such a question ?

A purple robe, a little worn,
  The Thunderer deigned himself to offer;
The bearded wanderer laughed in scorn, —
  You know he always was a scoffer.

" Vife shillins ! 't is a monstrous price;
  Say two and six and further talk shun."
" Take it," cried Jove; " we can't be
    nice, —
  'T would fetch twice that at Leonard's
    auction."

The ice was broken; up they came,
  All sharp for bargains, god and goddess,
Each ready with the price to name
  For robe or head-dress, scarf or bodice.

First Juno, out of temper, too, —
  Her queenly forehead somewhat cloudy;
Then Pallas in her stockings blue,
  Imposing, but a little dowdy.

The scowling queen of heaven unrolled
  Before the Jew a threadbare turban:
" Three shillings." " One. 'T will suit
    some old
  Terrific feminine suburban."

But as for Pallas, — how to tell
  In seemly phrase a fact so shocking ?
She pointed, — pray excuse me, — well,
  She pointed to her azure stocking.

And if the honest truth were told,
  Its heel confessed the need of darning;
" Gods ! " low-bred Vulcan cried, " be-
    hold !
  There ! that 's what comes of too much
    larning ! "

Pale Proserpine came groping round,
  Her pupils dreadfully dilated
With too much living underground —
  A residence quite overrated;

" This kerchief 's what you want, I know, —
  Don't cheat poor Venus of her cestus, —
You 'll find it handy when you go
  To — you know where; it 's pure as-
    bestus."

Then Phœbus of the silver bow,
  And Hebe, dimpled as a baby,
And Dian with the breast of snow,
  Chaser and chased — and caught, it may
    be:

One took the quiver from her back,
  One held the cap he spent the night in,
And one a bit of *bric-à-brac*,
  Such as the gods themselves delight in.

Then Mars, the foe of human kind,
  Strode up and showed his suit of armor;
So none at last was left behind
  Save Venus, the celestial charmer.

Poor Venus ! What had she to sell ?
  For all she looked so fresh and jaunty,
Her wardrobe, as I blush to tell,
  Already seemed but quite too scanty.

Her gems were sold, her sandals gone, —
  She always would be rash and flighty, —
Her winter garments all in pawn,
  Alas for charming Aphrodite !

The lady of a thousand loves,
  The darling of the old religion,
Had only left of all the doves
  That drew her car one fan-tailed pigeon.

How oft upon her finger-tips
  He perched, afraid of Cupid's arrow,
Or kissed her on the rosebud lips,
  Like Roman Lesbia's loving sparrow !

" My bird, I want your train," she cried;
  " Come, don't let 's have a fuss about it;
I 'll make it beauty's pet and pride,
  And you 'll be better off without it.

" So vulgar ! Have you noticed, pray,
  An earthly belle or dashing bride walk,

And how her flounces track her way,
  Like slimy serpents on the sidewalk ?

" A lover's heart it quickly cools;
  In mine it kindles up enough rage
To wring their necks.   How can such fools
  Ask men to vote for woman suffrage ? "

The goddess spoke, and gently stripped
  Her bird of every caudal feather;
A strand of gold-bright hair she clipped,
  And bound the glossy plumes together,

And lo, the Fan ! for beauty's hand,
  The lovely queen of beauty made it;
The price she named was hard to stand,
  But Venus smiled: the Hebrew paid it.

Jove, Juno, Venus, where are you ?
  Mars, Mercury, Phœbus, Neptune, Sat-
    urn ?
But o'er the world the Wandering Jew
  Has borne the Fan's celestial pattern.

So everywhere we find the Fan, —
  In lonely isles of the Pacific,
In farthest China and Japan, —
  Wherever suns are sudorific.

Nay, even the oily Esquimaux
  In summer court its cooling breezes, —
In fact, in every clime 't is so,
  No matter if it fries or freezes.

And since from Aphrodite's dove
  The pattern of the fan was given,
No wonder that it breathes of love
  And wafts the perfumed gales of heaven !

Before this new Pandora's gift
  In slavery woman's tyrant kept her,
But now he kneels her glove to lift, —
  The fan is mightier than the sceptre.

The tap it gives how arch and sly !
  The breath it wakes how fresh and
    grateful !
Behind its shield how soft the sigh !
  The whispered tale of shame how fateful !

Its empire shadows every throne
  And every shore that man is tost on;
It rules the lords of every zone,
  Nay, even the bluest blood of Boston !

But every one that swings to-night,
  Of fairest shape, from farthest region,
May trace its pedigree aright
  To Aphrodite's fan-tailed pigeon.

TO RUTHERFORD BIRCHARD HAYES

AT THE DINNER TO THE PRESIDENT, BOSTON, JUNE 27, 1877

How to address him ? awkward, it is true:
Call him " Great Father," as the Red Men
    do ?
Borrow some title ? this is not the place
That christens men Your Highness and
    Your Grace;
We tried such names as these awhile, you
    know,
But left them off a century ago.

His Majesty ? We 've had enough of that:
Besides, that needs a crown; he wears a
    hat.
What if, to make the nicer ears content,
We say His Honesty, the President ?

Sir, we believed you honest, truthful, brave,
When to your hands their precious trust
    we gave,
And we have found you better than we knew,
Braver, and not less honest, not less true !
So every heart has opened, every hand
Tingles with welcome, and through all the
    land
All voices greet you in one broad acclaim,
Healer of strife ! Has earth a nobler
    name ?

What phrases mean you do not need to
    learn;
We must be civil, and they serve our turn:
" Your most obedient humble " means —
    means what ?
Something the well-bred signer just is not.
Yet there are tokens, sir, you must believe;
There is one language never can deceive:
The lover knew it when the maiden smiled;
The mother knows it when she clasps her
    child;
Voices may falter, trembling lips turn pale,
Words grope and stumble; this will tell
    their tale
Shorn of all rhetoric, bare of all pretence,

But radiant, warm, with Nature's eloquence.
Look in our eyes ! Your welcome waits
    you there, —
North, South, East, West, from all and
    everywhere !

THE SHIP OF STATE

A SENTIMENT

This " sentiment " was read on the same occasion as the *Family Record*, which immediately follows it. The latter poem is the dutiful tribute of a son to his father and his father's ancestors, residents of Woodstock [Connecticut] from its first settlement. [The occasion was the celebration of the Fourth of July, 1877, in accordance with a custom established at Woodstock by Mr. H. C. Bowen.]

THE Ship of State ! above her skies are
    blue,
But still she rocks a little, it is true,
And there *are* passengers whose faces white
Show they don't feel as happy as they
    might;
Yet on the whole her crew are quite content,
Since its wild fury the typhoon has spent,
And willing, if her pilot thinks it best,
To head a little nearer south by west.
And this they feel: the ship came too near
    wreck,
In the long quarrel for the quarter-deck,
Now when she glides serenely on her way, —
The shallows past where dread explosives
    lay, —
The stiff obstructive's churlish game to try:
Let sleeping dogs and still torpedoes lie !
And so I give you all the Ship of State;
Freedom's last venture is her priceless
    freight;
God speed her, keep her, bless her, while
    she steers
Amid the breakers of unsounded years;
Lead her through danger's paths with even
    keel,
And guide the honest hand that holds her
    wheel !

A FAMILY RECORD

NOT to myself this breath of vesper song,
Not to these patient friends, this kindly
    throng,
Not to this hallowed morning, though it be

Our summer Christmas, Freedom's jubilee,
When every summit, topmast, steeple,
    tower,
That owns her empire spreads her starry
    flower,
Its blood-streaked leaves in heaven's be-
    nignant dew
Washed clean from every crimson stain
    they knew, —
No, not to these the passing thrills belong
That steal my breath to hush themselves
    with song.
    These moments all are memory's; I have
        come
To speak with lips that rather should be
    dumb;
For what are words? At every step I
    tread
The dust that wore the footprints of the
    dead
But for whose life my life had never known
This faded vesture which it calls its own.
Here sleeps my father's sire, and they who
    gave
That earlier life here found their peaceful
    grave.
In days gone by I sought the hallowed
    ground;
Climbed yon long slope; the sacred spot I
    found
Where all unsullied lies the winter snow,
Where all ungathered spring's pale violets
    blow,
And tracked from stone to stone the
    Saxon name
That marks the blood I need not blush to
    claim,
Blood such as warmed the Pilgrim sons of
    toil,
Who held from God the charter of the soil.
    I come an alien to your hills and plains,
Yet feel your birthright tingling in my
    veins;
Mine are this changing prospect's sun and
    shade,
In full-blown summer's bridal pomp ar-
    rayed;
Mine these fair hillsides and the vales be-
    tween;
Mine the sweet streams that lend their
    brightening green;
I breathed your air — the sunlit landscape
    smiled;
I touch your soil — it knows its children's
    child;

Throned in my heart your heritage is mine;
I claim it all by memory's right divine!
    Waking, I dream. Before my vacant
        eyes
In long procession shadowy forms arise;
Far through the vista of the silent years
I see a venturous band; the pioneers,
Who let the sunlight through the forest's
    gloom,
Who bade the harvest wave, the garden
    bloom.
Hark! loud resounds the bare-armed set-
    tler's axe, —
See where the stealthy panther left his
    tracks!
As fierce, as stealthy creeps the skulking
    foe
With stone-tipped shaft and sinew-corded
    bow;
Soon shall he vanish from his ancient reign,
Leave his last cornfield to the coming train,
Quit the green margin of the wave he
    drinks,
For haunts that hide the wild-cat and the
    lynx.

    But who the Youth his glistening axe
        that swings
To smite the pine that shows a hundred
    rings?
His features? — something in his look I
    find
That calls the semblance of my race to
    mind.
His name? — my own; and that which
    goes before
The same that once the loved disciple bore.
Young, brave, discreet, the father of a line
Whose voiceless lives have found a voice
    in mine;
Thinned by unnumbered currents though
    they be,
Thanks for the ruddy drops I claim from
    thee!

    The seasons pass; the roses come and go;
Snows fall and melt; the waters freeze and
    flow;
The boys are men; the girls, grown tall
    and fair,
Have found their mates; a gravestone here
    and there
Tells where the fathers lie; the silvered
    hair
Of some bent patriarch yet recalls the time

That saw his feet the northern hillside
climb,
A pilgrim from the pilgrims far away,
The godly men, the dwellers by the bay.
On many a hearthstone burns the cheerful
fire;
The schoolhouse porch, the heavenward
pointing spire
Proclaim in letters every eye can read,
Knowledge and Faith, the new world's sim-
ple creed.
   Hush ! 't is the Sabbath's silence-stricken
morn:
No feet must wander through the tasselled
corn;
No merry children laugh around the door,
No idle playthings strew the sanded floor;
The law of Moses lays its awful ban
On all that stirs; here comes the tithing-
man !
   At last the solemn hour of worship
calls;
Slowly they gather in the sacred walls;
Man in his strength and age with knotted
staff,
And boyhood aching for its week-day
laugh,
The toil-worn mother with the child she
leads,
The maiden, lovely in her golden beads, —
The popish symbols round her neck she
wears,
But on them counts her lovers, not her
prayers, —
Those youths in homespun suits and rib-
boned queues,
Whose hearts are beating in the high-
backed pews.
   The pastor rises; looks along the seats
With searching eye; each wonted face he
meets;
Asks heavenly guidance; finds the chapter's
place
That tells some tale of Israel's stubborn
race;
Gives out the sacred song; all voices join,
For no *quartette* extorts their scanty coin;
Then while both hands their black-gloved
palms display,
Lifts his gray head, and murmurs, " Let us
pray ! "
   And pray he does ! as one that never
fears
To plead unanswered by the God that hears;
What if he dwells on many a fact as though

Some things Heaven knew not which it
ought to know, —
Thanks God for all his favors past, and yet,
Tells Him there 's something He must not
forget;
Such are the prayers his people love to
hear, —
See how the Deacon slants his listening ear !
   What ! look once more ! Nay, surely
there I trace
The hinted outlines of a well-known face !
Not those the lips for laughter to beguile,
Yet round their corners lurks an embryo
smile,
The same on other lips my childhood knew
That scarce the Sabbath's mastery could
subdue.
Him too my lineage gives me leave to
claim, —
The good, grave man that bears the Psalm-
ist's name.

   And still in ceaseless round the seasons
passed;
Spring piped her carol; Autumn blew his
blast;
Babes waxed to manhood; manhood shrunk
to age;
Life's worn-out players tottered off the
stage;
The few are many; boys have grown to men
Since Putnam dragged the wolf from Pom-
fret's den;
Our new-old Woodstock is a thriving town;
Brave are her children; faithful to the
crown;
Her soldiers' steel the savage redskin
knows;
Their blood has crimsoned his Canadian
snows.
And now once more along the quiet vale
Rings the dread call that turns the mothers
pale;
Full well they know the valorous heat that
runs
In every pulse-beat of their loyal sons;
Who would not bleed in good King George's
cause
When England's lion shows his teeth and
claws ?
   With glittering firelocks on the village
green
In proud array a martial band is seen;
You know what names those ancient rosters
hold, —

Whose belts were buckled when the drum-
beat rolled, —
But mark their Captain! tell us, who is
he?
On his brown face that same old look I
see!
Yes! from the homestead's still retreat he
came,
Whose peaceful owner bore the Psalmist's
name;
The same his own. Well, Israel's glorious
king
Who struck the harp could also whirl the
sling, —
Breathe in his song a penitential sigh
And smite the sons of Amalek hip and
thigh:
These shared their task; one deaconed out
the psalm,
One slashed the scalping hell-hounds of
Montcalm;
The praying father's pious work is done,
Now sword in hand steps forth the fighting
son.
On many a field he fought in wilds afar;
See on his swarthy cheek the bullet's scar!
There hangs a murderous tomahawk; be-
neath,
Without its blade, a knife's embroidered
sheath;
Save for the stroke his trusty weapon dealt
His scalp had dangled at their owner's
belt;
But not for him such fate; he lived to see
The bloodier strife that made our nation
free,
To serve with willing toil, with skilful
hand,
The war-worn saviors of the bleeding land.
His wasting life to others' needs he gave, —
Sought rest in home and found it in the
grave.
See where the stones life's brief memorials
keep,
The tablet telling where he "fell on
sleep,"—
Watched by a winged cherub's rayless
eye, —
A scroll above that says we all must die, —
Those saddening lines beneath, the "Night-
Thoughts" lent:
So stands the Soldier's, Surgeon's monu-
ment.
Ah! at a glance my filial eye divines
The scholar son in those remembered lines.

The Scholar Son. His hand my foot-
steps led.
No more the dim unreal past I tread.
O thou whose breathing form was once so
dear,
Whose cheering voice was music to my ear,
Art thou not with me as my feet pursue
The village paths so well thy boyhood
knew,
Along the tangled margin of the stream
Whose murmurs blended with thine in-
fant dream,
Or climb the hill, or thread the wooded vale,
Or seek the wave where gleams yon dis-
tant sail,
Or the old homestead's narrowed bounds
explore,
Where sloped the roof that sheds the rains
no more,
Where one last relic still remains to tell
Here stood thy home, — the memory-haunt-
ed well,
Whose waters quench a deeper thirst than
thine,
Changed at my lips to sacramental wine, —
Art thou not with me, as I fondly trace
The scanty records of thine honored race,
Call up the forms that earlier years have
known,
And spell the legend of each slanted stone?
With thoughts of thee my loving verse
began,
Not for the critic's curious eye to scan,
Not for the many listeners, but the few
Whose fathers trod the paths my fathers
knew;
Still in my heart thy loved remembrance
burns;
Still to my lips thy cherished name returns;
Could I but feel thy gracious presence near
Amid the groves that once to thee were
dear!
Could but my trembling lips with mortal
speech
Thy listening ear for one brief moment
reach!
How vain the dream! The pallid voyager's
track
No sign betrays; he sends no message back.
No word from thee since evening's shadow
fell
On thy cold forehead with my long fare-
well, —
Now from the margin of the silent sea,
Take my last offering ere I cross to thee!

THE IRON GATE AND OTHER POEMS

1877–1881

THE IRON GATE

[Read at the Breakfast given in honor of Dr. Holmes's Seventieth Birthday by the publishers of the *Atlantic Monthly*, Boston, December 3, 1879.]

WHERE is this patriarch you are kindly greeting?
  Not unfamiliar to my ear his name,
Nor yet unknown to many a joyous meeting
  In days long vanished, — is he still the same,

Or changed by years, forgotten and forgetting,
  Dull-eared, dim-sighted, slow of speech and thought,
Still o'er the sad, degenerate present fretting,
  Where all goes wrong, and nothing as it ought?

Old age, the graybeard! Well, indeed, I know him, —
  Shrunk, tottering, bent, of aches and ills the prey;
In sermon, story, fable, picture, poem,
  Oft have I met him from my earliest day:

In my old Æsop, toiling with his bundle, —
  His load of sticks, — politely asking Death,
Who comes when called for, — would he lug or trundle
  His fagot for him? — he was scant of breath.

And sad " Ecclesiastes, or the Preacher," —
  Has he not stamped the image on my soul,
In that last chapter, where the worn-out Teacher
  Sighs o'er the loosened cord, the broken bowl?

Yes, long, indeed, I 've known him at a distance,
  And now my lifted door-latch shows him here;
I take his shrivelled hand without resistance,
  And find him smiling as his step draws near.

What though of gilded baubles he bereaves us,
  Dear to the heart of youth, to manhood's prime;
Think of the calm he brings, the wealth he leaves us,
  The hoarded spoils, the legacies of time!

Altars once flaming, still with incense fragrant,
  Passion's uneasy nurslings rocked asleep,
Hope's anchor faster, wild desire less vagrant,
  Life's flow less noisy, but the stream how deep!

Still as the silver cord gets worn and slender,
  Its lightened task-work tugs with lessening strain,
Hands get more helpful, voices, grown more tender,
  Soothe with their softened tones the slumberous brain.

Youth longs and manhood strives, but age remembers,
  Sits by the raked-up ashes of the past,

Spreads its thin hands above the whitening
    embers
    That warm its creeping life-blood till
        the last.

Dear to its heart is every loving token
    That comes unbidden ere its pulse grows
        cold,
Ere the last lingering ties of life are
        broken,
    Its labors ended and its story told.

Ah, while around us rosy youth rejoices,
    For us the sorrow-laden breezes sigh,
And through the chorus of its jocund voices
    Throbs the sharp note of misery's hope-
        less cry.

As on the gauzy wings of fancy flying
    From some far orb I track our watery
        sphere,
Home of the struggling, suffering, doubt-
        ing, dying,
    The silvered globule seems a glistening
        tear.

But Nature lends her mirror of illusion
    To win from saddening scenes our age-
        dimmed eyes,
And misty day-dreams blend in sweet con-
        fusion
    The wintry landscape and the summer
        skies.

So when the iron portal shuts behind us,
    And life forgets us in its noise and whirl,
Visions that shunned the glaring noonday
        find us,
    And glimmering starlight shows the
        gates of pearl.

I come not here your morning hour to sad-
        den,
    A limping pilgrim, leaning on his staff, —
I, who have never deemed it sin to gladden
    This vale of sorrows with a wholesome
        laugh.

If word of mine another's gloom has
        brightened,
    Through my dumb lips the heaven-sent
        message came;
If hand of mine another's task has lightened,
    It felt the guidance that it dares not
        claim.

But, O my gentle sisters, O my brothers,
    These thick-sown snow-flakes hint of
        toil's release;
These feebler pulses bid me leave to others
    The tasks once welcome; evening asks
        for peace.

Time claims his tribute; silence now is
        golden;
    Let me not vex the too long suffering
        lyre;
Though to your love untiring still beholden,
    The curfew tells me — cover up the fire.

And now with grateful smile and accents
        cheerful,
    And warmer heart than look or word
        can tell,
In simplest phrase — these traitorous eyes
        are tearful —
    Thanks, Brothers, Sisters, — Children,
        — and farewell!

VESTIGIA QUINQUE RETROR-SUM

AN ACADEMIC POEM

1829–1879

Read at the Commencement Dinner of the
Alumni of Harvard University, June 25, 1879.

WHILE fond, sad memories all around
    us throng,
Silence were sweeter than the sweetest song;
Yet when the leaves are green and heaven
    is blue,
The choral tribute of the grove is due,
And when the lengthening nights have
    chilled the skies,
We fain would hear the song-bird ere he
    flies,
And greet with kindly welcome, even as
    now,
The lonely minstrel on his leafless bough.

This is our golden year, — its golden
    day;
Its bridal memories soon must pass away;
Soon shall its dying music cease to ring,
And every year must loose some silver
    string,

Till the last trembling chords no longer
thrill, —
Hands all at rest and hearts forever still.

A few gray heads have joined the form-
ing line;
We hear our summons, — " Class of
'Twenty-Nine ! "
Close on the foremost, and, alas, how few !
Are these " The Boys " our dear old Mother
knew ?
Sixty brave swimmers. Twenty — some-
thing more —
Have passed the stream and reached this
frosty shore !

How near the banks these fifty years di-
vide
When memory crosses with a single stride !
'T is the first year of stern " Old Hick-
ory " 's rule
When our good Mother lets us out of
school,
Half glad, half sorrowing, it must be con-
fessed,
To leave her quiet lap, her bounteous breast,
Armed with our dainty, ribbon-tied degrees,
Pleased and yet pensive, exiles and A. B.'s.

Look back, O comrades, with your faded
eyes,
And see the phantoms as I bid them rise.
Whose smile is that ? Its pattern Nature
gave,
A sunbeam dancing in a dimpled wave;
KIRKLAND alone such grace from Heaven
could win,
His features radiant as the soul within;
That smile would let him through Saint
Peter's gate
While sad-eyed martyrs had to stand and
wait.
Here flits mercurial *Farrar;* standing there,
See mild, benignant, cautious, learned *Ware,*
And sturdy, patient, faithful, honest *Hedge,*
Whose grinding logic gave our wits their
edge;
Ticknor, with honeyed voice and courtly
grace;
And *Willard,* larynxed like a double bass;
And *Channing,* with his bland, superior
look,
Cool as a moonbeam on a frozen brook,
While the pale student, shivering in his
shoes,

Sees from his theme the turgid rhetoric
ooze;
And the born soldier, fate decreed to wreak
His martial manhood on a class in Greek,
Popkin! How that explosive name recalls
The grand old Busby of our ancient halls !
Such faces looked from Skippon's grim
platoons,
Such figures rode with Ireton's stout dra-
goons;
He gave his strength to learning's gentle
charms,
But every accent sounded " Shoulder
arms ! "

Names, — empty names ! Save only
here and there
Some white-haired listener, dozing in his
chair,
Starts at the sound he often used to hear,
And upward slants his Sunday-sermon ear.

And we — our blooming manhood we re-
gain;
Smiling we join the long Commencement
train,
One point first battled in discussion hot, —
Shall we wear gowns ? and settled: *We will
not.*
How strange the scene, — that noisy boy-
debate
Where embryo-speakers learn to rule the
State !
This broad-browed youth, sedate and sober-
eyed,
Shall wear the ermined robe at Taney's
side;
And he, the stripling, smooth of face and
slight,
Whose slender form scarce intercepts the
light,
Shall rule the Bench where Parsons gave
the law,
And sphinx-like sat uncouth, majestic
Shaw !
Ah, many a star has shed its fatal ray
On names we loved — our brothers —
where are they ?
Nor these alone; our hearts in silence
claim
Names not less dear, unsyllabled by fame.

How brief the space ! and yet it sweeps
us back
Far, far along our new-born history's track !

Five strides like this; — the sachem rules
    the land;
The Indian wigwams cluster where we
    stand.

    The second. Lo! a scene of deadly
      strife —
A nation struggling into infant life;
Not yet the fatal game at Yorktown won
Where failing Empire fired its sunset gun.
LANGDON sits restless in the ancient chair, —
Harvard's grave Head, — these echoes
    heard his prayer
When from yon mansion, dear to memory
    still,
The banded yeomen marched for Bunker's
    Hill.
Count on the grave triennial's thick-starred
    roll
What names were numbered on the length-
    ening scroll, —
Not unfamiliar in our ears they ring, —
Winthrop, Hale, Eliot, Everett, Dexter,
    Tyng.

    Another stride. Once more at 'twenty-
      nine, —
GOD SAVE KING GEORGE, the Second of his
    line!
And is *Sir Isaac* living? Nay, not so, —
He followed *Flamsteed* two short years
    ago, —
And what about the little hump-backed
    man
Who pleased the bygone days of good
    Queen Anne?
What, *Pope?* another book he's just put
    out, —
"The Dunciad," — witty, but profane, no
    doubt.
Where's *Cotton Mather?* he was always
    here.
And so he would be, but he died last year.
Who is this preacher our Northampton
    claims,
Whose rhetoric blazes with sulphureous
    flames
And torches stolen from Tartarean mines?
Edwards, the salamander of divines.
A deep, strong nature, pure and undefiled;
Faith, firm as his who stabbed his sleeping
    child;
Alas for him who blindly strays apart,
And seeking God has lost his human heart!

Fall where they might, no flying cinders
    caught
These sober halls where WADSWORTH
    ruled and taught.

    One footstep more; the fourth receding
      stride
Leaves the round century on the nearer
    side.
GOD SAVE KING CHARLES! God knows
    that pleasant knave
His grace will find it hard enough to save.
Ten years and more, and now the Plague,
    the Fire,
Talk of all tongues, at last begin to tire;
One fear prevails, all other frights forgot, —
White lips are whispering, — hark! *The
    Popish Plot!*
Happy New England, from such troubles
    free
In health and peace beyond the stormy sea!
No Romish daggers threat her children's
    throats,
No gibbering nightmare mutters " *Titus
    Oates;* "
Philip is slain, the Quaker graves are
    green,
Not yet the witch has entered on the scene;
Happy our Harvard; pleased her graduates
    four;
URIAN OAKES the name their parchments
    bore.

    Two centuries past, our hurried feet
      arrive
At the last footprint of the scanty five;
Take the fifth stride; our wandering eyes
    explore
A tangled forest on a trackless shore;
Here, where we stand, the savage sorcerer
    howls,
The wild cat snarls, the stealthy gray wolf
    prowls,
The slouching bear, perchance the tramp-
    ling moose
Starts the brown squaw and scares her red
    pappoose;
At every step the lurking foe is near;
His Demons reign; God has no temple
    here!

    Lift up your eyes! behold these pictured
    walls;
Look where the flood of western glory falls

Through the great sunflower disk of blaz-
ing panes
In ruby, saffron, azure, emerald stains;
With reverent step the marble pavement
tread
Where our proud Mother's martyr-roll is
read;
See the great halls that cluster, gathering
round
This lofty shrine with holiest memories
crowned;
See the fair Matron in her summer bower,
Fresh as a rose in bright perennial flower;
Read on her standard, always in the van,
"TRUTH,"—the one word that makes a
slave a man;
Think whose the hands that fed her altar-
fires,
Then count the debt we owe our scholar-
sires!

Brothers, farewell! the fast declining ray
Fades to the twilight of our golden day;
Some lesson yet our wearied brains may
learn,
Some leaves, perhaps, in life's thin volume
turn.
How few they seem as in our waning age
We count them backwards to the title-
page!
Oh let us trust with holy men of old
Not all the story here begun is told;
So the tired spirit, waiting to be freed,
On life's last leaf with tranquil eye shall
read
By the pale glimmer of the torch reversed,
Not *Finis*, but *The End of Volume First!*

MY AVIARY

THROUGH my north window, in the wintry
weather,—
My airy oriel on the river shore,—
I watch the sea-fowl as they flock together
Where late the boatman flashed his
dripping oar.

The gull, high floating, like a sloop un-
laden,
Lets the loose water waft him as it will;
The duck, round-breasted as a rustic
maiden,
Paddles and plunges, busy, busy still.

I see the solemn gulls in council sitting
On some broad ice-floe pondering long
and late,
While overhead the home-bound ducks are
flitting,
And leave the tardy conclave in debate,

Those weighty questions in their breasts re-
volving
Whose deeper meaning science never
learns,
Till at some reverend elder's look dis-
solving,
The speechless senate silently adjourns.

But when along the waves the shrill north-
easter
Shrieks through the laboring coaster's
shrouds "Beware!"
The pale bird, kindling like a Christmas
feaster
When some wild chorus shakes the vinous
air,

Flaps from the leaden wave in fierce re-
joicing,
Feels heaven's dumb lightning thrill his
torpid nerves,
Now on the blast his whistling plumage
poising,
Now wheeling, whirling in fantastic
curves.

Such is our gull; a gentleman of leisure,
Less fleshed than feathered; bagged
you'll find him such;
His virtue silence; his employment pleas-
ure;
Not bad to look at, and not good for
much.

What of our duck? He has some high-
bred cousins,—
His Grace the Canvas-back, My Lord
the Brant,—
Anas and *Anser*,—both served up by
dozens,
At Boston's *Rocher*, half-way to Na-
hant.

As for himself, he seems alert and thriv-
ing,—
Grubs up a living somehow—what, who
knows?

Crabs ? mussels ? weeds ? — Look quick !
    there 's one just diving !
Flop ! Splash ! his white breast glistens
    — down he goes !

And while he 's under — just about a min-
    ute —
I take advantage of the fact to say
His fishy carcase has no virtue in it
    The gunning idiot's worthless hire to pay.

He knows you ! " sportsmen " from subur-
    ban alleys,
Stretched under seaweed in the treacher-
    ous punt;
Knows every lazy, shiftless lout that sallies
    Forth to waste powder — as *he* says, to
    " hunt."

I watch you with a patient satisfaction,
    Well pleased to discount your predes-
    tined luck;
The float that figures in your sly transac-
    tion
    Will carry back a goose, but not a duck.

Shrewd is our bird; not easy to outwit him !
    Sharp is the outlook of those pin-head
    eyes;
Still, he is mortal and a shot may hit him,
    One cannot always miss him if he tries.

Look ! there 's a young one, dreaming not
    of danger;
    Sees a flat log come floating down the
    stream;
Stares undismayed upon the harmless
    stranger;
    Ah ! were all strangers harmless as they
    seem !

Habet ! a leaden shower his breast has shat-
    tered;
    Vainly he flutters, not again to rise;
His soft white plumes along the waves are
    scattered;
    Helpless the wing that braved the tem-
    pest lies.

He sees his comrades high above him flying
    To seek their nests among the island
    reeds;
Strong is their flight; all lonely he is lying
    Washed by the crimsoned water as he
    bleeds.

O Thou who carest for the falling spar-
    row,
    Canst Thou the sinless sufferer's pang
    forget ?
Or is thy dread account-book's page so
    narrow
    Its one long column scores thy creatures'
    debt ?

Poor gentle guest, by nature kindly
    cherished,
    A world grows dark with thee in blinding
    death;
One little gasp — thy universe has per-
    ished,
    Wrecked by the idle thief who stole thy
    breath !

Is this the whole sad story of creation,
    Lived by its breathing myriads o'er and
    o'er, —
One glimpse of day, then black annihila-
    tion, —
    A sunlit passage to a sunless shore ?

Give back our faith, ye mystery-solving
    lynxes !
    Robe us once more in heaven-aspiring
    creeds !
Happier was dreaming Egypt with her
    sphinxes,
    The stony convent with its cross and
    beads !

How often gazing where a bird reposes,
    Rocked on the wavelets, drifting with
    the tide,
I lose myself in strange metempsychosis
    And float a sea-fowl at a sea-fowl's side;

From rain, hail, snow in feathery mantle
    muffled,
    Clear-eyed, strong-limbed, with keenest
    sense to hear
My mate soft murmuring, who, with plumes
    unruffled,
    Where'er I wander still is nestling near;

The great blue hollow like a garment o'er
    me;
    Space all unmeasured, unrecorded time;
While seen with inward eye moves on be-
    fore me
    Thought's pictured train in wordless
    pantomime.

A voice recalls me. — From my window
    turning
  I find myself a plumeless biped still;
No beak, no claws, no sign of wings dis-
    cerning, —
  In fact with nothing bird-like but my
    quill.

ON THE THRESHOLD

INTRODUCTION TO A COLLECTION OF
POEMS BY DIFFERENT AUTHORS

An usher standing at the door
  I show my white rosette;
A smile of welcome, nothing more,
  Will pay my trifling debt;
Why should I bid you idly wait
Like lovers at the swinging gate?

Can I forget the wedding guest?
  The veteran of the sea?
In vain the listener smites his breast, —
  "There was a ship," cries he!
Poor fasting victim, stunned and pale,
He needs must listen to the tale.

He sees the gilded throng within,
  The sparkling goblets gleam,
The music and the merry din
  Through every window stream,
But there he shivers in the cold
Till all the crazy dream is told.

Not mine the graybeard's glittering eye
  That held his captive still
To hold my silent prisoners by
  And let me have my will;
Nay, *I* were like the three-years' child,
To think you could be so beguiled!

My verse is but the curtain's fold
  That hides the painted scene,
The mist by morning's ray unrolled
  That veils the meadow's green,
The cloud that needs must drift away
To show the rose of opening day.

See, from the tinkling rill you hear
  In hollowed palm I bring
These scanty drops, but ah, how near
  The founts that heavenward spring!
Thus, open wide the gates are thrown,
And founts and flowers are all your own!

TO GEORGE PEABODY

PEABODY, 1866

Bankrupt! our pockets inside out!
  Empty of words to speak his praises!
Worcester and Webster up the spout!
  Dead broke of laudatory phrases!
Yet why with flowery speeches tease,
  With vain superlatives distress him?
Has language better words than these?
  The friend of all his race, God
    bless him!

A simple prayer — but words more sweet
  By human lips were never uttered,
Since Adam left the country seat
  Where angel wings around him flut-
    tered.
The old look on with tear-dimmed eyes,
  The children cluster to caress him,
And every voice unbidden cries,
  The friend of all his race, God
    bless him!

AT THE PAPYRUS CLUB

A lovely show for eyes to see
  I looked upon this morning, —
A bright-hued, feathered company
  Of nature's own adorning;
But ah! those minstrels would not sing
  A listening ear while I lent, —
The lark sat still and preened his wing,
  The nightingale was silent;
I longed for what they gave me not —
  Their warblings sweet and fluty,
But grateful still for all I got
  I thanked them for their beauty.

A fairer vision meets my view
  Of Claras, Margarets, Marys,
In silken robes of varied hue,
  Like bluebirds and canaries;
The roses blush, the jewels gleam,
  The silks and satins glisten,
The black eyes flash, the blue eyes beam,
  We look — and then we listen:
Behold the flock we cage to-night —
  Was ever such a capture?
To see them is a pure delight;
  To hear them — ah! what rapture!

Methinks I hear Delilah's laugh
  At Samson bound in fetters;
" *We* captured ! " shrieks each lovelier half,
  " Men think themselves *our* betters !
We push the bolt, we turn the key
  On warriors, poets, sages,
Too happy, all of them, to be
  Locked in our golden cages ! "

Beware ! the boy with bandaged eyes
  Has flung away his blinder;
He 's lost his mother — so he cries —
  And here he knows he 'll find her:
The rogue ! 't is but a new device, —
  Look out for flying arrows
Whene'er the birds of Paradise
  Are perched amid the sparrows!

FOR WHITTIER'S SEVENTIETH BIRTHDAY

DECEMBER 17, 1877

I BELIEVE that the copies of verses I 've
  spun,
Like Scheherezade's tales, are a thousand
  and one;
You remember the story, — those mornings
  in bed, —
'T was the turn of a copper, — a tale or a
  head.

A doom like Scheherezade's falls upon me
In a mandate as stern as the Sultan's de-
  cree:
I 'm a florist in verse, and what *would* peo-
  ple say
If I came to a banquet without my bou-
  quet ?

It is trying, no doubt, when the company
  knows
Just the look and the smell of each lily and
  rose,
The green of each leaf in the sprigs that I
  bring,
And the shape of the bunch and the knot
  of the string.

Yes, — "the style is the man," and the
  nib of one's pen
Makes the same mark at twenty, and three-
  score and ten;

It is so in all matters, if truth may be told;
Let one look at the cast he can tell you the
  mould.

How we all know each other ! no use in
  disguise;
Through the holes in the mask comes the
  flash of the eyes;
We can tell by his — somewhat — each one
  of our tribe,
As we know the old hat which we cannot
  describe.

Though in Hebrew, in Sanscrit, in Choctaw
  you write,
Sweet singer who gave us the Voices of
  Night,
Though in buskin or slipper your song may
  be shod,
Or the velvety verse that Evangeline trod,

We shall say, "You can't cheat us, — we
  know it is you,"
There is one voice like that, but there can-
  not be two,
Maëstro, whose chant like the dulcimer
  rings:
And the woods will be hushed while the
  nightingale sings.

And he, so serene, so majestic, so true,
Whose temple hypæthral the planets shine
  through,
Let us catch but five words from that mys-
  tical pen,
We should know our one sage from all
  children of men.

And he whose bright image no distance
  can dim,
Through a hundred disguises we can't mis-
  take him,
Whose play is all earnest, whose wit is the
  edge
(With a beetle behind) of a sham-splitting
  wedge.

Do you know whom we send you, Hidalgos
  of Spain ?
Do you know your old friends when you
  see them again ?
Hosea was Sancho ! you Dons of Madrid,
But Sancho that wielded the lance of the
  Cid !

And the wood-thrush of Essex, — you know
    whom I mean,
Whose song echoes round us while he sits
    unseen,
Whose heart-throbs of verse through our
    memories thrill
Like a breath from the wood, like a breeze
    from the hill,

So fervid, so simple, so loving, so pure,
We hear but one strain and our verdict is
    sure, —
Thee cannot elude us, — no further we
    search, —
'T is Holy George Herbert cut loose from
    his church !

We think it the voice of a seraph that
    sings, —
Alas ! we remember that angels have
    wings, —
What story is this of the day of his birth ?
Let him live to a hundred ! we want him
    on earth !

One life has been paid him (in gold) by
    the sun ;
One account has been squared and another
    begun;
But he never will die if he lingers be-
    low
Till we 've paid him in love half the bal-
    ance we owe !

TWO SONNETS: HARVARD

At the meeting of the New York Harvard
Club, February 21, 1878.

"CHRISTO ET ECCLESIÆ." 1700

To GOD'S ANOINTED AND HIS CHOSEN
    FLOCK :
  So ran the phrase the black-robed con-
    clave chose
To guard the sacred cloisters that arose
Like David's altar on Moriah's rock.
Unshaken still those ancient arches mock
  The ram's-horn summons of the windy
    foes
  Who stand like Joshua's army while it
    blows
And wait to see them toppling with the
    shock.

Christ and the Church. *Their* church,
    whose narrow door
Shut out the many, who if over bold
Like hunted wolves were driven from
    the fold,
Bruised with the flails these godly zealots
    bore,
  Mindful that Israel's altar stood of old
Where echoed once Araunah's threshing-
    floor.

1643   "VERITAS."   1878

TRUTH: So the frontlet's older legend ran,
  On the brief record's opening page dis-
    played;
  Not yet those clear-eyed scholars were
    afraid
Lest the fair fruit that wrought the woe of
    man
By far Euphrates — where our sire began
  His search for truth, and, seeking, was
    betrayed —
  Might work new treason in their forest
    shade,
Doubling the curse that brought life's
    shortened span.
Nurse of the future, daughter of the past,
  That stern phylactery best becomes thee
    now:
  Lift to the morning star thy marble
    brow !
Cast thy brave truth on every warring
    blast !
  Stretch thy white hand to that forbidden
    bough,
And let thine earliest symbol be thy last !

THE COMING ERA

THEY tell us that the Muse is soon to fly
    hence,
  Leaving the bowers of song that once
    were dear,
Her robes bequeathing to her sister, Science,
  The groves of Pindus for the axe to
    clear.

Optics will claim the wandering eye of
    fancy,
  Physics will grasp imagination's wings,
Plain fact exorcise fiction's necromancy,
  The workshop hammer where the min-
    strel sings.

No more with laughter at Thalia's frolics
　Our eyes shall twinkle till the tears run
　　down,
But in her place the lecturer on hydraulics
　Spout forth his watery science to the
　　town.

No more our foolish passions and affections
　The tragic Muse with mimic grief shall
　　try,
But, nobler far, a course of vivisections
　Teach what it costs a tortured brute to
　　die.

The unearthed monad, long in buried rocks
　　hid,
　Shall tell the secret whence our being
　　came;
The chemist show us death is life's black
　　oxide,
　Left when the breath no longer fans its
　　flame.

Instead of crack-brained poets in their at-
　　tics
　Filling thin volumes with their flowery
　　talk,
There shall be books of wholesome mathe-
　　matics;
　The tutor with his blackboard and his
　　chalk.

No longer bards with madrigal and sonnet
　Shall woo to moonlight walks the rib-
　　boned sex,
But side by side the beaver and the bonnet
　Stroll, calmly pondering on some prob-
　　lem's x.

The sober bliss of serious calculation
　Shall mock the trivial joys that fancy
　　drew,
And, oh, the rapture of a solved equation, —
　One selfsame answer on the lips of two !

So speak in solemn tones our youthful sages,
　Patient, severe, laborious, slow, exact,
As o'er creation's protoplasmic pages
　They browse and munch the thistle crops
　　of fact.

And yet we 've sometimes found it rather
　　pleasant
　To dream again the scenes that Shake-
　　speare drew, —

To walk the hill-side with the Scottish
　　peasant
　Among the daisies wet with morning's
　　dew;

To leave awhile the daylight of the real,
　Led by the guidance of the master's
　　hand,
For the strange radiance of the far ideal, —
　" The light that never was on sea or
　　land."

Well, Time alone can lift the future's cur-
　　tain, —
　Science may teach our children all she
　　knows,
But Love will kindle fresh young hearts,
　　't is certain,
　And June will not forget her blushing
　　rose.

And so, in spite of all that Time is bring-
　　ing, —
　Treasures of truth and miracles of art,
Beauty and Love will keep the poet sing-
　　ing,
　And song still live, the science of the
　　heart.

IN RESPONSE

Breakfast at the Century Club, New York,
May, 1879.

SUCH kindness ! the scowl of a cynic would
　　soften,
　His pulse beat its way to some eloquent
　　word,
Alas ! my poor accents have echoed too
　　often,
　Like that Pinafore music you 've some
　　of you heard.

Do you know me, dear strangers — the
　　hundredth time comer
　At banquets and feasts since the days of
　　my Spring ?
Ah ! would I could borrow one rose of my
　　Summer,
　But this is a leaf of my Autumn I bring.

I look at your faces, — I 'm sure there are
　　some from
　The three-breasted mother I count as my
　　own;

You think you remember the place you
  have come from,
  But how it has changed in the years that
  have flown !

Unaltered, 't is true, is the hall we call
  " Funnel,"
  Still fights the " Old South " in the
  battle for life,
But we 've opened our door to the West
  through the tunnel,
  And we 've cut off Fort Hill with our
  Amazon knife.

You should see the new Westminster Bos-
  ton has builded, —
  Its mansions, its spires, its museums of
  arts, —
You should see the great dome we have
  gorgeously gilded, —
  'T is the light of our eyes, 't is the joy of
  our hearts.

When first in his path a young asteroid
  found it,
  As he sailed through the skies with the
  stars in his wake,
He thought 't was the sun, and kept
  circling around it
  Till Edison signalled, " You 've made a
  mistake."

We are proud of our city, — her fast-grow-
  ing figure,
  The warp and the woof of her brain and
  her hands, —
But we 're proudest of all that her heart
  has grown bigger,
  And warms with fresh blood as her gir-
  dle expands.

One lesson the rubric of conflict has taught
  her:
  Though parted awhile by war's earth-
  rending shock,
The lines that divide us are written in
  water,
  The love that unites us cut deep in the
  rock.

As well might the Judas of treason en-
  deavor
  To write his black name on the disk of
  the sun
As try the bright star-wreath that binds us
  to sever

And blot the fair legend of " Many in
  One."

We love YOU, tall sister, the stately, the
  splendid, —
  The banner of empire floats high on your
  towers,
Yet ever in welcome your arms are ex-
  tended, —
  We share in your splendors, your glory
  is ours.

Yes, Queen of the Continent ! All of us
  own thee, —
  The gold-freighted argosies flock at thy
  call,
The naiads, the sea-nymphs have met to
  enthrone thee,
  But the Broadway of one is the Highway
  of all !

I thank you. Three words that can hardly
  be mended,
  Though phrases on phrases their elo-
  quence pile,
If you hear the heart's throb with their
  eloquence blended,
  And read all they mean in a sunshiny
  smile.

FOR THE MOORE CENTENNIAL CELEBRATION

MAY 28, 1879

I

ENCHANTER of Erin, whose magic has
  bound us,
  Thy wand for one moment we fondly
  would claim,
Entranced while it summons the phantoms
  around us
  That blush into life at the sound of thy
  name.

The tell-tales of memory wake from their
  slumbers, —
  I hear the old song with its tender
  refrain, —
What passion lies hid in those honey-voiced
  numbers !
  What perfume of youth in each exquisite
  strain !

The home of my childhood comes back as
    a vision, —
    Hark! Hark! A soft chord from its
        song-haunted room, —
'T is a morning of May, when the air is
    Elysian, —
    The syringa in bud and the lilac in
        bloom, —

We are clustered around the "Clementi"
    piano, —
    There were six of us then, — there are
        two of us now, —
She is singing — the girl with the silver
    soprano —
    How "The Lord of the Valley" was false
        to his vow;

"Let Erin remember" the echoes are
    calling;
    Through "The Vale of Avoca" the
        waters are rolled;
"The Exile" laments while the night-dews
    are falling;
    "The Morning of Life" dawns again as
        of old.

But ah! those warm love-songs of fresh
    adolescence!
    Around us such raptures celestial they
        flung
That it seemed as if Paradise breathed its
    quintessence
    Through the seraph-toned lips of the
        maiden that sung!

Long hushed are the chords that my boy-
    hood enchanted
    As when the smooth wave by the angel
        was stirred,
Yet still with their music is memory
    haunted,
    And oft in my dreams are their melodies
        heard.

I feel like the priest to his altar return-
    ing, —
    The crowd that was kneeling no longer
        is there,
The flame has died down, but the brands
    are still burning,
    And sandal and cinnamon sweeten the
        air.

II

The veil for her bridal young Summer is
    weaving
    In her azure-domed hall with its tapes-
        tried floor,
And Spring the last tear-drop of May-dew
    is leaving
    On the daisy of Burns and the shamrock
        of Moore.

How like, how unlike, as we view them to-
    gether,
    The song of the minstrels whose record
        we scan, —
One fresh as the breeze blowing over the
    heather,
    One sweet as the breath from an oda-
        lisque's fan!

Ah, passion can glow mid a palace's splendor;
    The cage does not alter the song of the
        bird;
And the curtain of silk has known whispers
    as tender
    As ever the blossoming hawthorn has
        heard.

No fear lest the step of the soft-slippered
    Graces
    Should fright the young Loves from their
        warm little nest,
For the heart of a queen, under jewels and
    laces,
    Beats time with the pulse in the peasant
        girl's breast!

Thrice welcome each gift of kind Nature's
    bestowing!
    Her fountain heeds little the goblet we
        hold;
Alike, when its musical waters are flowing,
    The shell from the seaside, the chalice
        of gold.

The twins of the lyre to her voices had
    listened;
    Both laid their best gifts upon Liberty's
        shrine;
For Coila's loved minstrel the holly-wreath
    glistened;
    For Erin's the rose and the myrtle en-
        twine.

And while the fresh blossoms of summer
are braided
    For the sea-girdled, stream-silvered,
    lake-jewelled isle,
While her mantle of verdure is woven un-
faded,
    While Shannon and Liffey shall dimple
    and smile,

The land where the staff of Saint Patrick
was planted,
    Where the shamrock grows green from
    the cliffs to the shore,
The land of fair maidens and heroes un-
daunted,
    Shall wreathe her bright harp with the
    garlands of Moore !

TO JAMES FREEMAN CLARKE

APRIL 4, 1880

I BRING the simplest pledge of love,
    Friend of my earlier days;
Mine is the hand without the glove,
    The heart-beat, not the phrase.

How few still breathe this mortal air
    We called by school-boy names !
You still, whatever robe you wear,
    To me are always James.

That name the kind apostle bore
    Who shames the sullen creeds,
Not trusting less, but loving more,
    And showing faith by deeds.

What blending thoughts our memories
share !
    What visions yours and mine
Of May-days in whose morning air
    The dews were golden wine,

Of vistas bright with opening day,
    Whose all-awakening sun
Showed in life's landscape, far away,
    The summits to be won !

The heights are gained.   Ah, say not so
    For him who smiles at time,
Leaves his tired comrades down below,
    And only lives to climb !

His labors, — will they ever cease, —
    With hand and tongue and pen ?
Shall wearied Nature ask release
    At threescore years and ten ?

Our strength the clustered seasons tax, —
    For him new life they mean;
Like rods around the lictor's axe
    They keep him bright and keen.

The wise, the brave, the strong, we know, —
    We mark them here or there,
But he, — we roll our eyes, and lo !
    We find him everywhere !

With truth's bold cohorts, or alone,
    He strides through error's field;
His lance is ever manhood's own,
    His breast is woman's shield.

Count not his years while earth has need
    Of souls that Heaven inflames
With sacred zeal to save, to lead, —
    Long live our dear Saint James !

WELCOME TO THE CHICAGO COMMERCIAL CLUB

JANUARY 14, 1880

CHICAGO sounds rough to the maker of
    verse;
One comfort we have — Cincinnati sounds
    worse;
If we only were licensed to say Chicagó !
But Worcester and Webster won't let us,
    you know.

No matter, we songsters must sing as we
    can;
We can make some nice couplets with Lake
    Michigan,
And what more resembles a nightingale's
    voice,
Than the oily trisyllable, sweet Illinois ?

Your waters are fresh, while our harbor is
    salt,
But we know you can't help it — it is n't
    your fault;
Our city is old and your city is new,
But the railroad men tell us we 're greener
    than you.

You have seen our gilt dome, and no doubt
    you 've been told
That the orbs of the universe round it are
    rolled;
But I 'll own it to you, and I ought to know
    best,
That this is n't quite true of all stars of
    the West.

You 'll go to Mount Auburn, — we 'll show
    you the track, —
And can stay there, — unless you prefer to
    come back;
And Bunker's tall shaft you can climb if
    you will,
But you 'll puff like a paragraph praising
    a pill.

You must see — but you *have* seen — our
    old Faneuil Hall,
Our churches, our school-rooms, our sam-
    ple-rooms, all;
And, perhaps, though the idiots must have
    their jokes,
You have found our good people much like
    other folks.

There are cities by rivers, by lakes, and by
    seas,
Each as full of itself as a cheese-mite of
    cheese;
And a city will brag as a game-cock will
    crow:
Don't your cockerels at home — just a
    little, you know ?

But we 'll crow for you now — here 's a
    health to the boys,
Men, maidens, and matrons of fair Illi-
    nois,
And the rainbow of friendship that arches
    its span
From the green of the sea to the blue
    Michigan !

AMERICAN ACADEMY CENTEN-
NIAL CELEBRATION

MAY 26, 1880

SIRE, son, and grandson; so the century
    glides;
    Three lives, three strides, three foot-
      prints in the sand;

Silent as midnight's falling meteor slides
    Into the stillness of the far-off land;
      How dim the space its little arc has
      spanned !

See on this opening page the names re-
    nowned
    Tombed in these records on our dusty
      shelves,
Scarce on the scroll of living memory
    found,
    Save where the wan-eyed antiquarian
      delves;
    Shadows they seem; ah, what are we
      ourselves ?

Pale ghosts of Bowdoin, Winthrop, Wil-
    lard, West,
    Sages of busy brain and wrinkled brow,
Searchers of Nature's secrets unconfessed,
    Asking of all things Whence and Why
      and How —
    What problems meet your larger vision
      now ?

Has Gannett tracked the wild Aurora's
    path ?
    Has Bowdoin found his all-surrounding
      sphere ?
What question puzzles ciphering Philo-
    math ?
    Could Williams make the hidden causes
      clear
    Of the Dark Day that filled the land
      with fear ?

Dear ancient school-boys ! Nature taught
    to them
    The simple lessons of the star and
      flower,
Showed them strange sights; how on a
    single stem, —
    Admire the marvels of Creative
      Power ! —
Twin apples grew, one sweet, the other
    sour;

How from the hill-top where our eyes be-
    hold
    In even ranks the plumed and bannered
      maize
Range its long columns, in the days of old
    The live volcano shot its angry blaze, —
    Dead since the showers of Noah's watery
    days;

How, when the lightning split the mighty
    rock,
  The spreading fury of the shaft was
    spent !
How the young scion joined the alien stock,
  And when and where the homeless swal-
    lows went
    To pass the winter of their discontent.

Scant were the gleanings in those years of
    dearth;
  No Cuvier yet had clothed the fossil
    bones
That slumbered, waiting for their second
    birth;
  No Lyell read the legend of the stones;
  Science still pointed to her empty
    thrones.

Dreaming of orbs to eyes of earth un-
    known,
  Herschel looked heavenwards in the
    starlight pale;
Lost in those awful depths he trod alone,
  Laplace stood mute before the lifted
    veil;
  While home-bred Humboldt trimmed
    his toy ship's sail.

No mortal feet these loftier heights had
    gained
  Whence the wide realms of Nature we
    descry;
In vain their eyes our longing fathers
    strained
  To scan with wondering gaze the sum-
    mits high
  That far beneath their children's foot-
    paths lie.

Smile at their first small ventures as we
    may,
  The school-boy's copy shapes the schol-
    ar's hand,
Their grateful memory fills our hearts to-
    day;
  Brave, hopeful, wise, this bower of peace
    they planned,
  While war's dread ploughshare scarred
    the suffering land.

Child of our children's children yet un-
    born,
  When on this yellow page you turn your
    eyes,

Where the brief record of this May-day
    morn
  In phrase antique and faded letters lies,
  How vague, how pale our flitting ghosts
    will rise !

Yet in our veins the blood ran warm and
    red,
  For us the fields were green, the skies
    were blue,
Though from our dust the spirit long has
    fled,
  We lived, we loved, we toiled, we
    dreamed like you,
  Smiled at our sires and thought how
    much we knew.

Oh might our spirits for one hour return,
  When the next century rounds its hun-
    dredth ring,
All the strange secrets it shall teach to
    learn,
  To hear the larger truths its years shall
    bring,
  Its wiser sages talk, its sweeter minstrels
    sing !

THE SCHOOL-BOY

Read at the Centennial Celebration of the
foundation of Phillips Academy, Andover.

1778–1878

THESE hallowed precincts, long to mem-
    ory dear,
Smile with fresh welcome as our feet draw
    near;
With softer gales the opening leaves are
    fanned,
With fairer hues the kindling flowers ex-
    pand,
The rose-bush reddens with the blush of
    June,
The groves are vocal with their minstrels'
    tune,
The mighty elm, beneath whose arching
    shade
The wandering children of the forest
    strayed,
Greets the bright morning in its bridal
    dress,
And spreads its arms the gladsome dawn
    to bless.

Is it an idle dream that nature shares
Our joys, our griefs, our pastimes, and our
    cares ?
Is there no summons when, at morning's
    call,
The sable vestments of the darkness fall ?
Does not meek evening's low-voiced *Ave*
    blend
With the soft vesper as its notes ascend ?
Is there no whisper in the perfumed air
When the sweet bosom of the rose is bare ?
Does not the sunshine call us to rejoice ?
Is there no meaning in the storm-cloud's
    voice ?
No silent message when from midnight
    skies
Heaven looks upon us with its myriad eyes ?

Or shift the mirror; say our dreams
    diffuse
O'er life's pale landscape their celestial
    hues,
Lend heaven the rainbow it has never
    known,
And robe the earth in glories not its own,
Sing their own music in the summer breeze,
With fresher foliage clothe the stately
    trees,
Stain the June blossoms with a livelier dye
And spread a bluer azure on the sky, —
Blest be the power that works its lawless
    will
And finds the weediest patch an Eden
    still;
No walls so fair as those our fancies build, —
No views so bright as those our visions
    gild !

So ran my lines, as pen and paper met,
The truant goose-quill travelling like Plan-
    chette;
Too ready servant, whose deceitful ways
Full many a slipshod line, alas ! betrays;
Hence of the rhyming thousand not a few
Have builded worse — a great deal — than
    they knew.

What need of idle fancy to adorn
Our mother's birthplace on her birthday
    morn ?
Hers are the blossoms of eternal spring,
From these green boughs her new-fledged
    birds take wing,
These echoes hear their earliest carols sung,
In this old nest the brood is ever young.

If some tired wanderer, resting from his
    flight,
Amid the gay young choristers alight,
These gather round him, mark his faded
    plumes
That faintly still the far-off grove per-
    fumes,
And listen, wondering if some feeble note
Yet lingers, quavering in his weary throat:—
I, whose fresh voice yon red-faced temple
    knew,
What tune is left me, fit to sing to you ?
Ask not the grandeurs of a labored song,
But let my easy couplets slide along;
Much could I tell you that you know too
    well;
Much I remember, but I will not tell;
Age brings experience; graybeards oft are
    wise,
But oh ! how sharp a youngster's ears and
    eyes !

My cheek was bare of adolescent down
When first I sought the academic town;
Slow rolls the coach along the dusty road,
Big with its filial and parental load;
The frequent hills, the lonely woods are
    past,
The school-boy's chosen home is reached
    at last.
I see it now, the same unchanging spot,
The swinging gate, the little garden plot,
The narrow yard, the rock that made its
    floor,
The flat, pale house, the knocker-garnished
    door,
The small, trim parlor, neat, decorous, chill,
The strange, new faces, kind, but grave
    and still;
Two, creased with age, — or what I then
    called age, —
Life's volume open at its fiftieth page;
One, a shy maiden's, pallid, placid, sweet
As the first snowdrop, which the sunbeams
    greet;
One, the last nursling's; slight she was,
    and fair,
Her smooth white forehead warmed with
    auburn hair;
Last came the virgin Hymen long had
    spared,
Whose daily cares the grateful household
    shared,
Strong, patient, humble; her substantial
    frame

Stretched the chaste draperies I forbear to
name.
   Brave, but with effort, had the school-
boy come
To the cold comfort of a stranger's home;
How like a dagger to my sinking heart
Came the dry summons, " It is time to part;
Good-by ! " " Goo—ood-by ! " one fond
maternal kiss. . . .
Homesick as death ! Was ever pang like
this ? . . .
Too young as yet with willing feet to stray
From the tame fireside, glad to get away, —
Too old to let my watery grief appear, —
And what so bitter as a swallowed tear !
   One figure still my vagrant thoughts
pursue;
First boy to greet me, Ariel, where are you ?
Imp of all mischief, heaven alone knows how
You learned it all, — are you an angel now,
Or tottering gently down the slope of years,
Your face grown sober in the vale of tears ?
Forgive my freedom if you are breathing
still;
If in a happier world, I know you will.
You were a school-boy — what beneath the
sun
So like a monkey ?   I was also one.
   Strange, sure enough, to see what curi-
ous shoots
The nursery raises from the study's roots !
In those old days the very, very good
Took up more room — a little — than they
should;
Something too much one's eyes encountered
then
Of serious youth and funeral-visaged men;
The solemn elders saw life's mournful
half, —
Heaven sent this boy, whose mission was to
laugh,
Drollest of buffos, Nature's odd protest,
A catbird squealing in a blackbird's nest.
   Kind, faithful Nature ! While the sour-
eyed Scot —
Her cheerful smiles forbidden or forgot —
Talks only of his preacher and his kirk, —
Hears five-hour sermons for his Sunday
work, —
Praying and fasting till his meagre face
Gains its due length, the genuine sign of
grace, —
An Ayrshire mother in the land of Knox
Her embryo poet in his cradle rocks; —
Nature, long shivering in her dim eclipse,

Steals in a sunbeam to those baby lips;
So to its home her banished smile returns,
And Scotland sweetens with the song of
Burns !

   The morning came; I reached the classic
hall;
A clock-face eyed me, staring from the
wall;
Beneath its hands a printed line I read:
YOUTH IS LIFE'S SEED-TIME: so the clock-
face said:
Some took its counsel, as the sequel
showed, —
Sowed, — their wild oats, — and reaped as
they had sowed.
   How all comes back ! the upward slant-
ing floor, —
The masters' thrones that flank the central
door, —
The long, outstretching alleys that divide
The rows of desks that stand on either
side, —
The staring boys, a face to every desk,
Bright, dull, pale, blooming, common, pic-
turesque.
   Grave is the Master's look; his forehead
wears
Thick rows of wrinkles, prints of worrying
cares;
Uneasy lie the heads of all that rule,
His most of all whose kingdom is a school.
Supreme he sits; before the awful frown
That bends his brows the boldest eye goes
down;
Not more submissive Israel heard and
saw
At Sinai's foot the Giver of the Law.
   Less stern he seems, who sits in equal
state
On the twin throne and shares the empire's
weight;
Around his lips the subtle life that plays
Steals quaintly forth in many a jesting
phrase;
A lightsome nature, not so hard to chafe,
Pleasant when pleased; rough-handled, not
so safe;
Some tingling memories vaguely I recall,
But to forgive him.   God forgive us all !

   One yet remains, whose well-remembered
name
Pleads in my grateful heart its tender
claim;

His was the charm magnetic, the bright
　　look
That sheds its sunshine on the dreariest
　　book;
A loving soul to every task he brought
That sweetly mingled with the lore he
　　taught;
Sprung from a saintly race that never could
From youth to age be anything but good,
His few brief years in holiest labors spent,
Earth lost too soon the treasure heaven had
　　lent.
Kindest of teachers, studious to divine
Some hint of promise in my earliest line,
These faint and faltering words thou canst
　　not hear
Throb from a heart that holds thy memory
　　dear.
　　As to the traveller's eye the varied plain
Shows through the window of the flying
　　train,
A mingled landscape, rather felt than seen,
A gravelly bank, a sudden flash of green,
A tangled wood, a glittering stream that
　　flows
Through the cleft summit where the cliff
　　once rose,
All strangely blended in a hurried gleam,
Rock, wood, waste, meadow, village, hill-
　　side, stream, —
So, as we look behind us, life appears,
Seen through the vista of our bygone years.
　　Yet in the dead past's shadow-filled do-
　　main,
Some vanished shapes the hues of life re-
　　tain;
Unbidden, oft, before our dreaming eyes
From the vague mists in memory's path
　　they rise.
So comes his blooming image to my view,
The friend of joyous days when life was
　　new,
Hope yet untamed, the blood of youth un-
　　chilled,
No blank arrear of promise unfulfilled,
Life's flower yet hidden in its sheltering
　　fold,
Its pictured canvas yet to be unrolled.
His the frank smile I vainly look to greet,
His the warm grasp my clasping hand
　　should meet;
How would our lips renew their school-boy
　　talk,
Our feet retrace the old familiar walk !

For thee no more earth's cheerful morning
　　shines
Through the green fringes of the tented
　　pines;
Ah me ! is heaven so far thou canst not
　　hear,
Or is thy viewless spirit hovering near,
A fair young presence, bright with morn-
　　ing's glow,
The fresh-cheeked boy of fifty years ago ?
　　Yes, fifty years, with all their circling
　　suns,
Behind them all my glance reverted runs;
Where now that time remote, its griefs, its
　　joys,
Where are its gray-haired men, its bright-
　　haired boys ?
Where is the patriarch time could hardly
　　tire, —
The good old, wrinkled, immemorial
　　" squire " ?
(An honest treasurer, like a black-plumed
　　swan,
Not every day our eyes may look upon.)
Where the tough champion who, with Cal-
　　vin's sword,
In wordy conflicts battled for the Lord ?
Where the grave scholar, lonely, calm,
　　austere,
Whose voice like music charmed the listen-
　　ing ear,
Whose light rekindled, like the morning
　　star
Still shines upon us through the gates ajar ?
Where the still, solemn, weary, sad-eyed
　　man,
Whose care-worn face my wandering eyes
　　would scan, —
His features wasted in the lingering strife
With the pale foe that drains the student's
　　life ?
Where my old friend, the scholar, teacher,
　　saint,
Whose creed, some hinted, showed a speck
　　of taint;
He broached his own opinion, which is not
Lightly to be forgiven or forgot;
Some riddle's point, — I scarce remember
　　now, —
Homo*i*-, perhaps, where they said homo*o*-ou.
(If the unlettered greatly wish to know
Where lies the difference betwixt *oi* and *o*,
Those of the curious who have time may
　　search

Among the stale conundrums of their
    church.)
Beneath his roof his peaceful life I shared,
And for his modes of faith I little cared, —
I, taught to judge men's dogmas by their
    deeds,
Long ere the days of india-rubber creeds.

Why should we look one common faith
    to find,
Where one in every score is color-blind ?
If here on earth they know not red from
    green,
Will they see better into things unseen !
Once more to time's old graveyard I
    return
And scrape the moss from memory's
    pictured urn.
Who, in these days when all things go by
    steam,
Recalls the stage-coach with its four-horse
    team ?
Its sturdy driver, — who remembers him ?
Or the old landlord, saturnine and grim,
Who left our hill-top for a new abode
And reared his sign-post farther down the
    road ?
Still in the waters of the dark Shawshine
Do the young bathers splash and think
    they 're clean ?
Do pilgrims find their way to Indian Ridge,
Or journey onward to the far-off bridge,
And bring to younger ears the story back
Of the broad stream, the mighty Merrimac ?
Are there still truant feet that stray beyond
These circling bounds to Pomp's or
    Haggett's Pond,
Or where the legendary name recalls
The forest's earlier tenant, — "Deerjump
    Falls " ?

Yes, every nook these youthful feet ex-
    plore,
Just as our sires and grandsires did of
    yore;
So all life's opening paths, where nature
    led
Their father's feet, the children's children
    tread.
Roll the round century's fivescore years
    away,
Call from our storied past that earliest day
When great Eliphalet (I can see him
    now, —
Big name, big frame, big voice, and beet-
    ling brow),

Then *young* Eliphalet, — ruled the rows of
    boys
In homespun gray or old-world cordu-
    roys, —
And save for fashion's whims, the benches
    show
The selfsame youths, the very boys we
    know.
Time works strange marvels: since I trod
    the green
And swung the gates, what wonders I have
    seen !
But come what will, — the sky itself may
    fall, —
As things of course the boy accepts them
    all.
The prophet's chariot, drawn by steeds of
    flame,
For daily use our travelling millions claim;
The face we love a sunbeam makes our
    own;
No more the surgeon hears the sufferer's
    groan;
What unwrit histories wrapped in darkness
    lay
Till shovelling Schliemann bared them to
    the day !
Your Richelieu says, and says it well, my
    lord,
The pen is (sometimes) mightier than the
    sword;
Great is the goosequill, say we all; Amen !
Sometimes the spade is mightier than the
    pen;
It shows where Babel's terraced walls were
    raised,
The slabs that cracked when Nimrod's
    palace blazed,
Unearths Mycenæ, rediscovers Troy, —
Calmly he listens, that immortal boy.
A new Prometheus tips our wands with
    fire,
A mightier Orpheus strains the whispering
    wire,
Whose lightning thrills the lazy winds out-
    run
And hold the hours as Joshua stayed the
    sun, —
So swift, in truth, we hardly find a place
For those dim fictions known as time and
    space.
Still a new miracle each year supplies, —
See at his work the chemist of the skies,
Who questions Sirius in his tortured rays
And steals the secret of the solar blaze;

Hush! while the window-rattling bugles play
The nation's airs a hundred miles away!
That wicked phonograph! hark! how it swears!
Turn it again and make it say its prayers!
And was it true, then, what the story said
Of Oxford's friar and his brazen head?
While wondering Science stands, herself perplexed
At each day's miracle, and asks "What next?"
The immortal boy, the coming heir of all,
Springs from his desk to "urge the flying ball,"
Cleaves with his bending oar the glassy waves,
With sinewy arm the dashing current braves,
The same bright creature in these haunts of ours
That Eton shadowed with her "antique towers."

Boy! Where is he? the long-limbed youth inquires,
Whom his rough chin with manly pride inspires;
Ah, when the ruddy cheek no longer glows,
When the bright hair is white as winter snows,
When the dim eye has lost its lambent flame,
Sweet to his ear will be his school-boy name!
Nor think the difference mighty as it seems
Between life's morning and its evening dreams;
Fourscore, like twenty, has its tasks and toys;
In earth's wide school-house all are girls and boys.

Brothers, forgive my wayward fancy. Who
Can guess beforehand what his pen will do?
Too light my strain for listeners such as these,
Whom graver thoughts and soberer speech shall please.
Is he not here whose breath of holy song
Has raised the downcast eyes of Faith so long?
Are they not here, the strangers in your gates,

For whom the wearied ear impatient waits, —
The large-brained scholars whom their toils release, —
The bannered heralds of the Prince of Peace?

Such was the gentle friend whose youth unblamed
In years long past our student-benches claimed;
Whose name, illumined on the sacred page,
Lives in the labors of his riper age;
Such he whose record time's destroying march
Leaves uneffaced on Zion's springing arch:
Not to the scanty phrase of measured song,
Cramped in its fetters, names like these belong;
One ray they lend to gild my slender line, —
Their praise I leave to sweeter lips than mine.

Homes of our sires, where Learning's temple rose,
While yet they struggled with their banded foes,
As in the West thy century's sun descends,
One parting gleam its dying radiance lends.
Darker and deeper though the shadows fall
From the gray towers on Doubting Castle's wall,
Though Pope and Pagan re-array their hosts,
And her new armor youthful Science boasts,
Truth, for whose altar rose this holy shrine,
Shall fly for refuge to these bowers of thine;
No past shall chain her with its rusted vow,
No Jew's phylactery bind her Christian brow,
But Faith shall smile to find her sister free,
And nobler manhood draw its life from thee.

Long as the arching skies above thee spread,
As on thy groves the dews of heaven are shed,
With currents widening still from year to year,

And deepening channels, calm, untroubled,
    clear,
Flow the twin streamlets from thy sacred
    hill —
Pieria's fount and Siloam's shaded rill !

THE SILENT MELODY

"BRING me my broken harp," he said;
  "We both are wrecks, — but as ye
    will, —
Though all its ringing tones have fled,
  Their echoes linger round it still ;
It had some golden strings, I know,
But that was long — how long ! — ago.

"I cannot see its tarnished gold,
  I cannot hear its vanished tone,
Scarce can my trembling fingers hold
  The pillared frame so long their own;
We both are wrecks, — awhile ago
It had some silver strings, I know,

"But on them Time too long has played
  The solemn strain that knows no change,
And where of old my fingers strayed
  The chords they find are new and
    strange, —
Yes ! iron strings, — I know, — I know, —
We both are wrecks of long ago.

"We both are wrecks, — a shattered
    pair, —
  Strange to ourselves in time's dis-
    guise . . .
What say ye to the lovesick air
  That brought the tears from Marian's
    eyes?
Ay ! trust me, — under breasts of snow
Hearts could be melted long ago !

"Or will ye hear the storm-song's crash
  That from his dreams the soldier woke,
And bade him face the lightning flash
  When battle's cloud in thunder
    broke ? . . .
Wrecks, — nought but wrecks ! — the time
    was when
We two were worth a thousand men ! "

And so the broken harp they bring
  With pitying smiles that none could
    blame;

Alas ! there 's not a single string
  Of all that filled the tarnished frame !
But see ! like children overjoyed,
  His fingers rambling through the void !

"I clasp thee ! Ay . . . mine ancient
    lyre . . .
  Nay, guide my wandering fingers. . . .
    There !
They love to dally with the wire
  As Isaac played with Esau's hair. . . .
Hush ! ye shall hear the famous tune
That Marian called the Breath of June ! "

And so they softly gather round:
  Rapt in his tuneful trance he seems:
His fingers move: but not a sound !
  A silence like the song of dreams. . . .
"There ! ye have heard the air," he cries,
"That brought the tears from Marian's
    eyes ! "

Ah, smile not at his fond conceit,
  Nor deem his fancy wrought in vain;
To him the unreal sounds are sweet, —
  No discord mars the silent strain
Scored on life's latest, starlit page —
The voiceless melody of age.

Sweet are the lips of all that sing,
  When Nature's music breathes unsought,
But never yet could voice or string
  So truly shape our tenderest thought
As when by life's decaying fire
Our fingers sweep the stringless lyre !

OUR HOME—OUR COUNTRY

FOR THE TWO HUNDRED AND FIFTI-
ETII ANNIVERSARY OF THE SETTLE-
MENT OF CAMBRIDGE, MASS., DE-
CEMBER 28, 1880

YOUR home was mine, — kind Nature's
    gift;
  My love no years can chill;
In vain their flakes the storm-winds sift,
The snowdrop hides beneath the drift,
  A living blossom still.

Mute are a hundred long-famed lyres,
  Hushed all their golden strings;
Once lay the coldest bosom fires,
One song, one only, never tires
  While sweet-voiced memory sings.

No spot so lone but echo knows
    That dear familiar strain;
In tropic isles, on arctic snows,
Through burning lips its music flows
    And rings its fond refrain.

From Pisa's tower my straining sight
    Roamed wandering leagues away,
When lo ! a frigate's banner bright,
The starry blue, the red, the white,
    In far Livorno's bay.

Hot leaps the life-blood from my heart,
    Forth springs the sudden tear;
The ship that rocks by yonder mart
Is of my land, my life, a part, —
    Home, home, sweet home, is here !

Fades from my view the sunlit scene, —
    My vision spans the waves;
I see the elm-encircled green,
The tower, — the steeple, — and, between,
    The field of ancient graves.

There runs the path my feet would tread
    When first they learned to stray;
There stands the gambrel roof that spread
Its quaint old angles o'er my head
    When first I saw the day.

The sounds that met my boyish ear
    My inward sense salute, —
The woodnotes wild I loved to hear, —
The robin's challenge, sharp and clear, —
    The breath of evening's flute.

The faces loved from cradle days, —
    Unseen, alas, how long !
As fond remembrance round them plays,
Touched with its softening moonlight rays,
    Through fancy's portal throng.

And see ! as if the opening skies
    Some angel form had spared
Us wingless mortals to surprise,
The little maid with light-blue eyes,
    White necked and golden haired !

So rose the picture full in view
    I paint in feebler song;
Such power the seamless banner knew
Of red and white and starry blue
    For exiles banished long.

Oh, boys, dear boys, who wait as men
    To guard its heaven-bright folds,
Blest are the eyes that see again
That banner, seamless now, as then, —
    The fairest earth beholds !

Sweet was the Tuscan air and soft
    In that unfading hour,
And fancy leads my footsteps oft
Up the round galleries, high aloft
    On Pisa's threatening tower.

And still in Memory's holiest shrine
    I read with pride and joy,
" For me those stars of empire shine;
That empire's dearest home is mine;
    I am a Cambridge boy ! "

POEM

AT THE CENTENNIAL ANNIVERSARY
DINNER OF THE MASSACHUSETTS
MEDICAL SOCIETY, JUNE 8, 1881

THREE paths there be where Learning's
    favored sons,
Trained in the schools which hold her fa-
    vored ones,
Follow their several stars with separate
    aim;
Each has its honors, each its special claim.
Bred in the fruitful cradle of the East,
First, as of oldest lineage, comes the Priest;
The Lawyer next, in wordy conflict strong,
Full armed to battle for the right, — or
    wrong;
Last, he whose calling finds its voice in
    deeds,
Frail Nature's helper in her sharpest needs.
    Each has his gifts, his losses and his
        gains,
    Each his own share of pleasures and of
        pains;
No life-long aim with steadfast eye pursued
Finds a smooth pathway all with roses
    strewed;
Trouble belongs to man of woman born, —
Tread where he may, his foot will find its
    thorn.

Of all the guests at life's perennial feast,
Who of her children sits above the Priest ?
For him the broidered robe, the carven
    seat,

Pride at his beck, and beauty at his feet,
For him the incense fumes, the wine is
    poured,
Himself a God, adoring and adored !
His the first welcome when our hearts
    rejoice,
His in our dying ear the latest voice,
Font, altar, grave, his steps on all attend,
Our staff, our stay, our all but heavenly
    friend !
  Where is the meddling hand that dares
    to probe
The secret grief beneath his sable robe ?
How grave his port ! how every gesture
    tells
Here truth abides, here peace forever
    dwells;
Vex not his lofty soul with comments vain;
Faith asks no questions; silence, ye pro-
    fane !
  Alas ! too oft while all is calm without
The stormy spirit wars with endless *doubt* ;
This is the mocking spectre, scarce con-
    cealed
Behind tradition's bruised and battered
    shield.
He sees the sleepless critic, age by age,
Scrawl his new readings on the hallowed
    page,
The wondrous deeds that priests and pro-
    phets saw
Dissolved in legend, crystallized in law,
And on the soil where saints and martyrs
    trod
Altars new builded to the Unknown God;
His shrines imperilled, his evangels torn, —
He dares not limp, but ah ! how sharp his
    thorn !
  Yet while God's herald questions as he
    reads
The outworn dogmas of his ancient creeds,
Drops from his ritual the exploded verse,
Blots from its page the Athanasian curse,
Though by the critic's dangerous art per-
    plexed,
His holy life is Heaven's unquestioned text;
That shining guidance doubt can never
    mar, —
The pillar's flame, the light of Bethlehem's
    star !

Strong is the moral blister that will draw
Laid on the conscience of the Man of Law
Whom blindfold Justice lends her eyes to
    see

Truth in the scale that holds his promised
    fee.
What ! Has not every lie its truthful
    side,
Its honest fraction, not to be denied ?
Per contra, — ask the moralist, — in sooth
Has not a lie its share in every truth ?
Then what forbids an honest man to try
To find the truth that lurks in every lie,
And just as fairly call on truth to yield
The lying fraction in its breast concealed ?
So the worst rogue shall claim a ready
    friend
His modest virtues boldly to defend,
And he who shows the record of a saint
See himself blacker than the devil could
    paint.
  What struggles to his captive soul be-
    long
Who loves the right, yet combats for the
    wrong,
Who fights the battle he would fain re-
    fuse,
And wins, well knowing that he ought to
    lose,
Who speaks with glowing lips and look
    sincere
In spangled words that make the worse
    appear
The better reason; who, behind his mask,
Hides his true self and blushes at his
    task, —
What quips, what quillets cheat the in-
    ward scorn
That mocks such triumph ? Has he not
    his thorn ?
  Yet stay thy judgment; were thy life
    the prize,
Thy death the forfeit, would thy cynic
    eyes
See fault in him who bravely dares de-
    fend
The cause forlorn, the wretch without a
    friend ?
Nay, though the rightful side is wisdom's
    choice,
Wrong has its rights and claims a cham-
    pion's voice ;
Let the strong arm be lifted for the weak,
For the dumb lips the fluent pleader
    speak; —
When with warm "rebel" blood our
    street was dyed
Who took, unawed, the hated hirelings'
    side ?

No greener civic wreath can Adams claim,
No brighter page the youthful Quincy's
   name !

   How blest is he who knows no meaner
      strife
Than Art's long battle with the foes of
   life !
No doubt assails him, doing still his best,
And trusting kindly Nature for the rest;
No mocking conscience tears the thin dis-
   guise
That wraps his breast, and tells him that
   he lies.
He comes: the languid sufferer lifts his
   head
And smiles a welcome from his weary
   bed;
He speaks: what music like the tones that
   tell,
" Past is the hour of danger, — all is
   well ! "
How can he feel the petty stings of grief
Whose · cheering presence always brings
   relief ?
What ugly dreams can trouble his repose
Who yields himself to soothe another's
   woes ?
   Hour after hour the busy day has found
The good physician on his lonely round;
Mansion and hovel, low and lofty door,
He knows, his journeys every path ex-
   plore, —
Where the cold blast has struck with
   deadly chill
The sturdy dweller on the storm-swept
   hill,
Where by the stagnant marsh the sicken-
   ing gale
Has blanched the poisoned tenants of the
   vale,
Where crushed and maimed the bleeding
   victim lies,
Where madness raves, where melancholy
   sighs,
And where the solemn whisper tells too
   plain
That all his science, all his art, were vain.
   How sweet his fireside when the day is
      done
And cares have vanished with the setting
   sun !
Evening at last its hour of respite brings
And on his couch his weary length he
   flings.

Soft be thy pillow, servant of mankind,
Lulled by an opiate Art could never find;
Sweet be thy slumber, — thou hast earned
   it well, —
Pleasant thy dreams !   Clang ! goes the
   midnight bell !
   Darkness and storm ! the home is far
      away
That waits his coming ere the break of day;
The snow-clad pines their wintry plumage
   toss, —
Doubtful the frozen stream his road must
   cross;
Deep lie the drifts, the slanted heaps have
   shut
The hardy woodman in his mountain hut, —
Why should thy softer frame the tempest
   brave ?
Hast thou no life, no health, to lose or
   save ?
Look ! read the answer in his patient
   eyes, —
For him no other voice when suffering
   cries;
Deaf to the gale that all around him blows,
A feeble whisper calls him, — and he goes.
   Or seek the crowded city, — summer's
      heat
Glares burning, blinding, in the narrow
   street,
Still, noisome, deadly, sleeps the enven-
   omed air,
Unstirred the yellow flag that says " Be-
   ware ! "
Tempt not thy fate, — one little moment's
   breath
Bears on its viewless wing the seeds of
   death;
Thou at whose door the gilded chariots
   stand,
Whose dear-bought skill unclasps the
   miser's hand,
Turn from thy fatal quest, nor cast away
That life so precious; let a meaner prey
Feed the destroyer's hunger; live to bless
Those happier homes that need thy care no
   less !
   Smiling he listens; has he then a charm
Whose magic virtues peril can disarm ?
No safeguard his; no amulet he wears,
Too well he knows that Nature never
   spares
Her truest servant, powerless to defend
From her own weapons her unshrinking
   friend.

He dares the fate the bravest well might
    shun,
Nor asks reward save only Heaven's
    " Well done ! "
  Such are the toils, the perils that he
    knows,
Days without rest and nights without re-
    pose,
Yet all unheeded for the love he bears
His art, his kind, whose every grief he
    shares.
  Harder than these to know how small
    the part
Nature's proud empire yields to striving
    Art;
How, as the tide that rolls around the
    sphere
Laughs at the mounds that delving arms
    uprear, —
Spares some few roods of oozy earth, but
    still
Wastes and rebuilds the planet at its will,
Comes at its ordered season, night or noon,
Led by the silver magnet of the moon, —
So life's vast tide forever comes and goes,
Unchecked, resistless, as it ebbs and flows.
  Hardest of all, when Art has done her
    best,
To find the cuckoo brooding in her nest;
The shrewd adventurer, fresh from parts
    unknown,
Kills off the patients Science thought her
    own;
Towns from a nostrum-vender get their
    name,
Fences and walls the cure-all drug pro-
    claim,
Plasters and pads the willing world be-
    guile,
Fair Lydia greets us with astringent smile,
Munchausen's fellow-countryman unlocks
His new Pandora's globule-holding box,
And as King George inquired, with puzzled
    grin,
" How — how the devil get the apple in ? "
So we ask how, — with wonder-opening
    eyes, —
Such pygmy pills can hold such giant lies!
  Yes, sharp the trials, stern the daily
    tasks
That suffering Nature from her servant
    asks;
His the kind office dainty menials scorn,
His path how hard, — at every step a
    thorn !

What does his saddening, restless slavery
    buy ?
What save a right to live, a chance to die, —
To live companion of disease and pain,
To die by poisoned shafts untimely slain ?
  Answer from hoary eld, majestic shades,—
From Memphian courts, from Delphic col-
    onnades,
Speak in the tones that Persia's despot
    heard
When nations treasured every golden word
The wandering echoes wafted o'er the seas,
From the far isle that held Hippocrates;
And thou, best gift that Pergamus could
    send
Imperial Rome, her noblest Cæsar's friend,
Master of masters, whose unchallenged
    sway
Not bold Vesalius dared to disobey;
Ye who while prophets dreamed of dawn-
    ing times
Taught your rude lessons in Salerno's
    rhymes,
And ye, the nearer sires, to whom we owe
The better share of all the best we know,
In every land an ever-growing train,
Since wakening Science broke her rusted
    chain, —
Speak from the past, and say what prize
    was sent
To crown the toiling years so freely spent !
  List while they speak:
                    In life's uneven road
Our willing hands have eased our brothers'
    load;
One forehead smoothed, one pang of tor-
    ture less,
One peaceful hour a sufferer's couch to
    bless,
The smile brought back to fever's parching
    lips,
The light restored to reason in eclipse,
Life's treasure rescued like a burning brand
Snatched from the dread destroyer's waste-
    ful hand;
Such were our simple records day by day,
For gains like these we wore our lives away.
In toilsome paths our daily bread we sought,
But bread from heaven attending angels
    brought;
Pain was our teacher, speaking to the
    heart,
Mother of pity, nurse of pitying art;
Our lesson learned, we reached the peace-
    ful shore

Where the pale sufferer asks our aid no
    more, —
These gracious words our welcome, our
    reward:
Ye served your brothers; ye have served
    your Lord !

HARVARD

[Read at Commencement Dinner, July 1,
1880. The author had that day received
from his Alma Mater the degree of Doctor of
Laws.]

CHANGELESS in beauty, rose-hues on her
    cheek,
Old walls, old trees, old memories all
    around
Lend her unfading youth their charm an-
    tique
And fill with mystic light her holy ground.
Here the lost dove her leaf of promise
    found
While the new morning showed its blush-
    ing streak
Far o'er the waters she had crossed to seek
The bleak, wild shore in billowy forests
    drowned.
Mother of scholars ! on thy rising throne
Thine elder sisters look benignant down;
England's proud twins, and they whose
    cloisters own

The fame of Abelard, the scarlet gown
That laughing Rabelais wore, not yet out-
    grown —
And on thy forehead place the New World's
    crown.

RHYMES OF A LIFE–TIME

FROM the first gleam of morning to the
    gray
    Of peaceful evening, lo, a life unrolled !
    In woven pictures all its changes told,
Its lights, its shadows, every flitting ray,
Till the long curtain, falling, dims the day,
    Steals from the dial's disk the sunlight's
        gold,
    And all the graven hours grow dark and
        cold
Where late the glowing blaze of noontide
    lay.
Ah ! the warm blood runs wild in youthful
    veins, —
    Let me no longer play with painted fire;
    New songs for new-born days ! I would
        not tire
The listening ears that wait for fresher
    strains
In phrase new - moulded, new - forged
    rhythmic chains,
    With plaintive measures from a worn-out
        lyre.

BEFORE THE CURFEW

AT MY FIRESIDE

ALONE, beneath the darkened sky,
  With saddened heart and unstrung lyre,
I heap the spoils of years gone by,
And leave them with a long-drawn sigh,
Like drift-wood brands that glimmering
    lie,
  Before the ashes hide the fire.

Let not these slow declining days
  The rosy light of dawn outlast;
Still round my lonely hearth it plays,
And gilds the east with borrowed rays,
While memory's mirrored sunset blaze
  Flames on the windows of the past.
  March 1, 1888.

AT THE SATURDAY CLUB

About the time when these papers [*The Autocrat*] were published, the Saturday Club was founded, or, rather, found itself in existence, without any organization, almost without parentage. It was natural enough that such men as Emerson, Longfellow, Agassiz, Peirce, with Hawthorne, Motley, Sumner, when within reach, and others who would be good company for them, should meet and dine together once in a while, as they did, in point of fact, every month, and as some who are still living, with other and newer members, still meet and dine. If some of them had not admired each other they would have been exceptions in the world of letters and science. The club deserves being remembered for having no constitution or by-laws, for making no speeches, reading no papers, observing no ceremonies, coming and going at will without remark, and acting out, though it did not proclaim the motto, "Shall I not take mine ease in mine inn?" There was and is nothing of the Bohemian element about this club, but it has had many good times and not a little good talking.

THIS is our place of meeting; opposite
That towered and pillared building: look
    at it;
King's Chapel in the Second George's day,
Rebellion stole its regal name away, —
Stone Chapel sounded better; but at last
The poisoned name of our provincial past
Had lost its ancient venom; then once more
Stone Chapel was King's Chapel as before.
(So let rechristened North Street, when it
    can,
Bring back the days of Marlborough and
    Queen Anne!)
  Next the old church your wandering eye
    will meet —
A granite pile that stares upon the street —
Our civic temple; slanderous tongues have
    said
Its shape was modelled from St. Botolph's
    head,
Lofty, but narrow; jealous passers-by
Say Boston always held her head too high.
  Turn half-way round, and let your look
    survey
The white façade that gleams across the
    way, —
The many-windowed building, tall and wide,
The palace-inn that shows its northern side
In grateful shadow when the sunbeams
    beat
The granite wall in summer's scorching
    heat.
This is the place; whether its name you
    spell
Tavern, or caravansera, or hotel.
Would I could steal its echoes! you should
    find
Such store of vanished pleasures brought to
    mind:
Such feasts! the laughs of many a jocund
    hour
That shook the mortar from King George's
    tower;
Such guests! What famous names its record
    boasts,

Whose owners wander in the mob of ghosts !
Such stories ! Every beam and plank is
    filled
With juicy wit the joyous talkers spilled,
Ready to ooze, as once the mountain pine
The floors are laid with oozed its turpen-
    tine !

A month had flitted since The Club had
    met;
The day came round; I found the table set,
The waiters lounging round the marble
    stairs,
Empty as yet the double row of chairs.
I was a full half hour before the rest,
Alone, the banquet-chamber's single guest.
So from the table's side a chair I took,
And having neither company nor book
To keep me waking, by degrees there crept
A torpor over me, — in short, I slept.
    Loosed from its chain, along the wreck-
        strown track
Of the dead years my soul goes travelling
    back;
My ghosts take on their robes of flesh; it
    seems
Dreaming is life; nay, life less life than
    dreams,
So real are the shapes that meet my eyes.
They bring no sense of wonder, no surprise,
No hint of other than an earth-born source;
All seems plain daylight, everything of
    course.
    How dim the colors are, how poor and
        faint
This palette of weak words with which I
    paint !
Here sit my friends; if I could fix them so
As to my eyes they seem, my page would
    glow
Like a queen's missal, warm as if the brush
Of Titian or Velasquez brought the flush
Of life into their features. *Ay de mi !*
If syllables were pigments, you should see
Such breathing portraitures as never man
Found in the Pitti or the Vatican.

    Here sits our POET, Laureate, if you will.
Long has he worn the wreath, and wears it
    still.
Dead ? Nay, not so; and yet they say his
    bust
Looks down on marbles covering royal dust,
Kings by the Grace of God, or Nature's
    grace;

Dead ! No ! Alive ! I see him in his
    place,
Full-featured, with the bloom that heaven
    denies
Her children, pinched by cold New Eng-
    land skies,
Too often, while the nursery's happier few
Win from a summer cloud its roseate hue.
Kind, soft-voiced, gentle, in his eye there
    shines
The ray serene that filled Evangeline's.
    Modest he seems, not shy; content to
        wait
Amid the noisy clamor of debate
The looked-for moment when a peaceful
    word
Smooths the rough ripples louder tongues
    have stirred.
In every tone I mark his tender grace
And all his poems hinted in his face;
What tranquil joy his friendly presence
    gives !
How could I think him dead ? He lives !
    He lives !

    There, at the table's further end I see
In his old place our Poet's *vis-à-vis*,
The great PROFESSOR, strong, broad-shoul-
    dered, square,
In life's rich noontide, joyous, debonair.
His social hour no leaden care alloys,
His laugh rings loud and mirthful as a
    boy's, —
That lusty laugh the Puritan forgot, —
What ear has heard it and remembers not ?
How often, halting at some wide crevasse
Amid the windings of his Alpine pass,
High up the cliffs, the climbing moun-
    taineer,
Listening the far-off avalanche to hear,
Silent, and leaning on his steel-shod staff,
Has heard that cheery voice, that ringing
    laugh,
From the rude cabin whose nomadic walls
Creep with the moving glacier as it crawls !
    How does vast Nature lead her living
        train
In ordered sequence through that spacious
    brain,
As in the primal hour when Adam named
The new-born tribes that young creation
    claimed ! —
How will her realm be darkened, losing
    thee,
Her darling, whom we call *our* AGASSIZ !

But who is he whose massive frame be-
lies
The maiden shyness of his downcast eyes ?
Who broods in silence till, by questions
pressed,
Some answer struggles from his laboring
breast ?
An artist Nature meant to dwell apart,
Locked in his studio with a human heart,
Tracking its caverned passions to their lair,
And all its throbbing mysteries laying bare.
Count it no marvel that he broods alone
Over the heart he studies, — 't is his own;
So in his page, whatever shape it wear,
The Essex wizard's shadowed self is there,—
The great ROMANCER, hid beneath his veil
Like the stern preacher of his sombre tale;
Virile in strength, yet bashful as a girl,
Prouder than Hester, sensitive as Pearl.

From his mild throng of worshippers
released,
Our Concord Delphi sends its chosen priest,
Prophet or poet, mystic, sage, or seer,
By every title always welcome here.
Why that ethereal spirit's frame describe ?
You know the race-marks of the Brahmin
tribe, —
The spare, slight form, the sloping shoul-
der's droop,
The calm, scholastic mien, the clerkly
stoop,
The lines of thought the sharpened features
wear,
Carved by the edge of keen New England
air.
List ! for he speaks ! As when a king
would choose
The jewels for his bride, he might refuse
This diamond for its flaw, — find that less
bright
Than those, its fellows, and a pearl less
white
Than fits her snowy neck, and yet at last,
The fairest gems are chosen, and made
fast
In golden fetters; so, with light delays
He seeks the fittest word to fill his phrase;
Nor vain nor idle his fastidious quest,
His chosen word is sure to prove the best.
Where in the realm of thought, whose
air is song,
Does he, the Buddha of the West, belong ?
He seems a wingèd Franklin, sweetly wise,
Born to unlock the secrets of the skies;

And which the nobler calling, — if 't is fair
Terrestrial with celestial to compare, —
To guide the storm-cloud's elemental flame,
Or walk the chambers whence the light-
ning came,
Amidst the sources of its subtile fire,
And steal their effluence for his lips and
lyre ?
If lost at times in vague aerial flights,
None treads with firmer footstep when he
lights;
A soaring nature, ballasted with sense,
Wisdom without her wrinkles or pretence,
In every Bible he has faith to read,
And every altar helps to shape his creed.
Ask you what name this prisoned spirit
bears
While with ourselves this fleeting breath it
shares ?
Till angels greet him with a sweeter one
In heaven, on earth we call him EMERSON.

I start; I wake; the vision is withdrawn;
Its figures fading like the stars at dawn;
Crossed from the roll of life their cher-
ished names,
And memory's pictures fading in their
frames;
Yet life is lovelier for these transient gleams
Of buried friendships; blest is he who
dreams !

OUR DEAD SINGER

H. W. L.

PRIDE of the sister realm so long our own,
  We claim with her that spotless fame of
  thine,
  White as her snow and fragrant as her
  pine !
Ours was thy birthplace, but in every zone
Some wreath of song thy liberal hand has
  thrown
  Breathes perfume from its blossoms,
  that entwine
  Where'er the dewdrops fall, the sun-
  beams shine,
On life's long path with tangled cares o'er-
  grown.
Can Art thy truthful counterfeit com-
  mand, —
  The silver-haloed features, tranquil,
  mild, —

Soften the lips of bronze as when they
smiled,
Give warmth and pressure to the marble
hand ?
Seek the lost rainbow in the sky it spanned !
Farewell, sweet Singer ! Heaven re-
claims its child.

Carved from the block or cast in clinging
mould,
Will grateful Memory fondly try her
best
The mortal vesture from decay to wrest;
His look shall greet us, calm, but ah, how
cold !
No breath can stir the brazen drapery's fold,
No throb can heave the statue's stony
breast;
" He is not here, but risen," will stand
confest
In all we miss, in all our eyes behold.
How Nature loved him ! On his placid
brow,
Thought's ample dome, she set the sacred
sign
That marks the priesthood of her holiest
shrine,
Nor asked a leaflet from the laurel's bough
That envious Time might clutch or disallow,
To prove her chosen minstrel's song
divine.

On many a saddened hearth the evening
fire
Burns paler as the children's hour draws
near, —
That joyous hour his song made doubly
dear, —
And tender memories touch the faltering
choir.
He sings no more on earth; our vain desire
Aches for the voice we loved so long to
hear
In Dorian flute-notes breathing soft and
clear, —
The sweet contralto that could never tire.
Deafened with listening to a harsher strain,
The Mænad's scream, the stark barba-
rian's cry,
Still for those soothing, loving tones we
sigh;
Oh, for our vanished Orpheus once again !
The shadowy silence hears us call in vain !
His lips are hushed; his song shall never
die.

TWO POEMS TO HARRIET BEECHER STOWE

ON HER SEVENTIETH BIRTHDAY, JUNE 14, 1882

I. AT THE SUMMIT

SISTER, we bid you welcome, — we who
stand
On the high table-land;
We who have climbed life's slippery Alpine
slope,
And rest, still leaning on the staff of hope,
Looking along the silent Mer de Glace,
Leading our footsteps where the dark cre-
vasse
Yawns in the frozen sea we all must pass, —
Sister, we clasp your hand !

Rest with us in the hour that Heaven has
lent
Before the swift descent.
Look ! the warm sunbeams kiss the glitter-
ing ice;
See ! next the snow-drift blooms the edel-
weiss;
The mated eagles fan the frosty air;
Life, beauty, love, around us everywhere,
And, in their time, the darkening hours
that bear
Sweet memories, peace, content.

Thrice welcome ! shining names our missals
show
Amid their rubrics' glow,
But search the blazoned record's starry line,
What halo's radiance fills the page like
thine ?
Thou who by some celestial clue couldst
find
The way to all the hearts of all mankind,
On thee, already canonized, enshrined,
What more can Heaven bestow !

II. THE WORLD'S HOMAGE

IF every tongue that speaks her praise
For whom I shape my tinkling phrase
Were summoned to the table,
The vocal chorus that would meet
Of mingling accents harsh or sweet,
From every land and tribe, would beat
The polyglots at Babel.

Briton and Frenchman, Swede and Dane,
Turk, Spaniard, Tartar of Ukraine,
  Hidalgo, Cossack, Cadi,
High Dutchman and Low Dutchman, too,
The Russian serf, the Polish Jew,
Arab, Armenian, and Mantchoo,
  Would shout, " We know the lady ! "

Know her ! Who knows not Uncle Tom
And her he learned his gospel from
  Has never heard of Moses;
Full well the brave black hand we know
That gave to freedom's grasp the hoe
That killed the weed that used to grow
  Among the Southern roses.

When Archimedes, long ago,
Spoke out so grandly, " *dos pou sto* —
  Give me a place to stand on,
I 'll move your planet for you, now," —
He little dreamed or fancied how
The *sto* at last should find its *pou*
  For woman's faith to land on.

Her lever was the wand of art,
Her fulcrum was the human heart,
  Whence all unfailing aid is;
She moved the earth ! Its thunders pealed,
Its mountains shook, its temples reeled,
The blood-red fountains were unsealed,
  And Moloch sunk to Hades.

All through the conflict, up and down
Marched Uncle Tom and Old John Brown,
  One ghost, one form ideal;
And which was false and which was true,
And which was mightier of the two,
The wisest sibyl never knew,
  For both alike were real.

Sister, the holy maid does well
Who counts her beads in convent cell,
  Where pale devotion lingers;
But she who serves the sufferer's needs,
Whose prayers are spelt in loving deeds,
May trust the Lord will count her beads
  As well as human fingers.

When Truth herself was Slavery's slave,
Thy hand the prisoned suppliant gave
  The rainbow wings of fiction.
And Truth who soared descends to-day
Bearing an angel's wreath away,
Its lilies at thy feet to lay
  With Heaven's own benediction.

A WELCOME TO DR. BENJAMIN APTHORP GOULD

ON HIS RETURN FROM SOUTH AMERICA

AFTER FIFTEEN YEARS DEVOTED TO CATA-
LOGUING THE STARS OF THE SOUTHERN
HEMISPHERE

Read at the Dinner given at the Hotel Ven-
dome, May 6, 1885.

ONCE more Orion and the sister Seven
  Look on thee from the skies that hailed
    thy birth, —
How shall we welcome thee, whose home
    was heaven,
  From thy celestial wanderings back to
    earth ?

Science has kept her midnight taper burn-
    ing
  To greet thy coming with its vestal
    flame;
Friendship has murmured, " When art thou
    returning ? "
  " Not yet ! Not yet ! " the answering
    message came.

Thine was unstinted zeal, unchilled devo-
    tion,
  While the blue realm had kingdoms to
    explore, —
Patience, like his who ploughed the unfur-
    rowed ocean,
  Till o'er its margin loomed San Salva-
    dor.

Through the long nights I see thee ever
    waking,
  Thy footstool earth, thy roof the hemi-
    sphere,
While with thy griefs our weaker hearts
    are aching,
  Firm as thine equatorial's rock-based
    pier.

The souls that voyaged the azure depths
    before thee
  Watch with thy tireless vigils, all un-
    seen, —
Tycho and Kepler bend benignant o'er
    thee,
  And with his toy-like tube the Floren-
    tine, —

He at whose word the orb that bore him
    shivered
  To find her central sovereignty disowned,
While the wan lips of priest and pontiff
    quivered,
  Their jargon stilled, their Baal disen-
    throned.

Flamsteed and Newton look with brows
    unclouded,
  Their strife forgotten with its faded
    scars, —
(Titans, who found the world of space too
    crowded
  To walk in peace among its myriad
    stars).

All cluster round thee, — seers of earliest
    ages,
  Persians, Ionians, Mizraim's learned
    kings,
From the dim days of Shinar's hoary sages
  To his who weighed the planet's fluid
    rings.

And we, for whom the northern heavens
    are lighted,
  For whom the storm has passed, the sun
    has smiled,
Our clouds all scattered, all our stars
    united,
  We claim thee, clasp thee, like a long-
    lost child.

Fresh from the spangled vault's o'er-arch-
    ing splendor,
  Thy lonely pillar, thy revolving dome,
In heartfelt accents, proud, rejoicing, ten-
    der,
  We bid thee welcome to thine earthly
    home !

TO FREDERICK HENRY HEDGE

AT A DINNER GIVEN HIM ON HIS
EIGHTIETH BIRTHDAY, DECEMBER 12,
1885

With a bronze statuette of John of Bologna's
Mercury, presented by a few friends.

FIT emblem for the altar's side,
  And him who serves its daily need,
The stay, the solace, and the guide
  Of mortal men, whate'er his creed !

Flamen or Auspex, Priest or Bonze,
  He feeds the upward-climbing fire,
Still teaching, like the deathless bronze,
  Man's noblest lesson, — to aspire.

Hermes lies prone by fallen Jove,
  Crushed are the wheels of Krishna's car,
And o'er Dodona's silent grove
  Streams the white ray from Bethlehem's
    star.

Yet snatched from Time's relentless clutch,
  A godlike shape, that human hands
Have fired with Art's electric touch,
  The herald of Olympus stands.

Ask not what ore the furnace knew;
  Love mingled with the flowing mass,
And lends its own unchanging hue,
  Like gold in Corinth's molten brass.

Take then our gift; this airy form
  Whose bronze our benedictions gild,
The hearts of all its givers warm
  With love by freezing years unchilled.

With eye undimmed, with strength unworn,
  Still toiling in your Master's field,
Before you wave the growths unshorn,
  Their ripened harvest yet to yield.

True servant of the Heavenly Sire,
  To you our tried affection clings,
Bids you still labor, still aspire,
  But clasps your feet and steals their
    wings.

TO JAMES RUSSELL LOWELL

THIS is your month, the month of "perfect
    days,"
Birds in full song and blossoms all ablaze.
Nature herself your earliest welcome
    breathes,
Spreads every leaflet, every bower in-
    wreathes;
Carpets her paths for your returning feet,
Puts forth her best your coming steps to
    greet;
And Heaven must surely find the earth in
    tune
When Home, sweet Home, exhales the
    breath of June.

These blessed days are waning all too fast,
And June's bright visions mingling with the past;
Lilacs have bloomed and faded, and the rose
Has dropped its petals, but the clover blows,
And fills its slender tubes with honeyed sweets;
The fields are pearled with milk-white margarites;
The dandelion, which you sang of old,
Has lost its pride of place, its crown of gold,
But still displays its feathery-mantled globe,
Which children's breath or wandering winds unrobe.
These were your humble friends; your opened eyes
Nature had trained her common gifts to prize;
Not Cam nor Isis taught you to despise
Charles, with his muddy margin and the harsh,
Plebeian grasses of the reeking marsh.
New England's home-bred scholar, well you knew
Her soil, her speech, her people, through and through,
And loved them ever with the love that holds
All sweet, fond memories in its fragrant folds.
Though far and wide your wingèd words have flown,
Your daily presence kept you all our own,
Till, with a sorrowing sigh, a thrill of pride,
We heard your summons, and you left our side
For larger duties and for tasks untried.

How pleased the Spaniards for a while to claim
This frank Hidalgo with the liquid name,
Who stored their classics on his crowded shelves
And loved their Calderon as they did themselves!
Before his eyes what changing pageants pass!
The bridal feast how near the funeral mass!
The death-stroke falls, — the Misereres wail;

The joy-bells ring, — the tear-stained cheeks unveil,
While, as the playwright shifts his pictured scene,
The royal mourner crowns his second queen.

From Spain to Britain is a goodly stride, —
Madrid and London long-stretched leagues divide.
What if I send him, "Uncle S., says he,"
To my good cousin whom he calls "J. B."?
A nation's servants go where they are sent, —
He heard his Uncle's orders, and he went.
By what enchantments, what alluring arts,
Our truthful James led captive British hearts, —
Whether his shrewdness made their statesmen halt,
Or if his learning found their Dons at fault,
Or if his virtue was a strange surprise,
Or if his wit flung star-dust in their eyes, —
Like honest Yankees we can simply guess;
But that he did it all must needs confess.
England herself without a blush may claim
Her only conqueror since the Norman came.
Eight years an exile! What a weary while
Since first our herald sought the mother isle!
His snow-white flag no churlish wrong has soiled, —
He left unchallenged, he returns unspoiled.

Here let us keep him, here he saw the light, —
His genius, wisdom, wit, are ours by right;
And if we lose him our lament will be
We have "five hundred" — not "as good as he."

TO JOHN GREENLEAF WHITTIER

ON HIS EIGHTIETH BIRTHDAY

1887

FRIEND, whom thy fourscore winters leave more dear
Than when life's roseate summer on thy cheek

Burned in the flush of manhood's manliest
    year,
Lonely, how lonely ! is the snowy peak
Thy feet have reached, and mine have
    climbed so near !
Close on thy footsteps 'mid the landscape
    drear
I stretch my hand thine answering grasp to
    seek,
Warm with the love no rippling rhymes
    can speak !
Look backward ! From thy lofty height
    survey
Thy years of toil, of peaceful victories
    won,
Of dreams made real, largest hopes out-
    run !
Look forward ! Brighter than earth's
    morning ray
Streams the pure light of Heaven's unset-
    ting sun,
The unclouded dawn of life's immortal
    day !

PRELUDE TO A VOLUME PRINTED IN RAISED LET-TERS FOR THE BLIND

DEAR friends, left darkling in the long
    eclipse
That veils the noonday, — you whose
    finger-tips
A meaning in these ridgy leaves can find
Where ours go stumbling, senseless, help-
    less, blind,
This wreath of verse how dare I offer you
To whom the garden's choicest gifts are
    due ?
The hues of all its glowing beds are ours,
Shall you not claim its sweetest-smelling
    flowers ?

Nay, those I have I bring you, — at their
    birth
Life's cheerful sunshine warmed the grate-
    ful earth ;
If my rash boyhood dropped some idle
    seeds,
And here and there you light on saucy
    weeds
Among the fairer growths, remember still
Song comes of grace, and not of human
    will:

We get a jarring note when most we try,
Then strike the chord we know not how or
    why;
Our stately verse with too aspiring art
Oft overshoots and fails to reach the
    heart,
While the rude rhyme one human throb
    endears
Turns grief to smiles, and softens mirth to
    tears.
Kindest of critics, ye whose fingers read,
From Nature's lesson learn the poet's
    creed;
The queenly tulip flaunts in robes of flame,
The wayside seedling scarce a tint may
    claim,
Yet may the lowliest leaflets that unfold
A dewdrop fresh from heaven's own chalice
    hold.

BOSTON TO FLORENCE

Sent to "The Philological Circle" of Flor-
ence for its meeting in commemoration of
Dante, January 27, 1881, the anniversary of
his first condemnation.

PROUD of her clustering spires, her new-
    built towers,
  Our Venice, stolen from the slumbering
    sea,
  A sister's kindliest greeting wafts to
    thee,
Rose of Val d' Arno, queen of all its
    flowers !
Thine exile's shrine thy sorrowing love em-
    bowers,
  Yet none with truer homage bends the
    knee,
  Or stronger pledge of fealty brings, than
    we,
Whose poets make thy dead Immortal
    ours.
Lonely the height, but ah, to heaven how
    near !
  Dante, whence flowed that solemn verse
    of thine
  Like the stern river from its Apennine
Whose name the far-off Scythian thrilled
    with fear :
Now to all lands thy deep-toned voice is
    dear,
  And every language knows the Song
    Divine !

AT THE UNITARIAN FESTIVAL

MARCH 8 AND JUNE 1, 1882

THE waves unbuild the wasting shore;
  Where mountains towered the billows
    sweep,
Yet still their borrowed spoils restore,
  And build new empires from the deep.
So while the floods of thought lay waste
  The proud domain of priestly creeds,
Its heaven-appointed tides will haste
  To plant new homes for human needs.
Be ours to mark with hearts unchilled
  The change an outworn church deplores;
The legend sinks, but Faith shall build
  A fairer throne on new-found shores.

POEM

FOR THE TWO HUNDRED AND FIFTIETH ANNIVERSARY OF THE FOUNDING OF HARVARD COLLEGE

TWICE had the mellowing sun of autumn
    crowned
The hundredth circle of his yearly round,
When, as we meet to-day, our fathers met:
That joyous gathering who can e'er forget,
When Harvard's nurslings, scattered far
    and wide,
Through mart and village, lake's and
    ocean's side,
Came, with one impulse, one fraternal
    throng,
And crowned the hours with banquet,
    speech, and song ?

Once more revived in fancy's magic glass,
I see in state the long procession pass:
Tall, courtly, leader as by right divine,
Winthrop, our Winthrop, rules the mar-
    shalled line,
Still seen in front, as on that far-off day
His ribboned baton showed the column's
    way.
Not all are gone who marched in manly
    pride
And waved their truncheons at their lead-
    er's side;
Gray, Lowell, Dixwell, who his empire
    shared,
These to be with us envious Time has
    spared.

Few are the faces, so familiar then,
Our eyes still meet amid the haunts of
    men;
Scarce one of all the living gathered there,
Whose unthinned locks betrayed a silver
    hair,
Greets us to-day, and yet we seem the
    same
As our own sires and grandsires, save in
    name.
There are the patriarchs, looking vaguely
    round
For classmates' faces, hardly known if
    found;
See the cold brow that rules the busy mart;
Close at its side the pallid son of art,
Whose purchased skill with borrowed
    meaning clothes,
And stolen hues, the smirking face he
    loathes.
Here is the patient scholar; in his looks
You read the titles of his learned books;
What classic lore those spidery crow's-feet
    speak !
What problems figure on that wrinkled
    cheek !
For never thought but left its stiffened
    trace,
Its fossil footprint, on the plastic face,
As the swift record of a raindrop stands,
Fixed on the tablet of the hardening sands.
On every face as on the written page
Each year renews the autograph of age;
One trait alone may wasting years defy, —
The fire still lingering in the poet's eye,
While Hope, the siren, sings her sweetest
    strain, —
Non omnis moriar is its proud refrain.

Sadly we gaze upon the vacant chair;
He who should claim its honors is not
    there, —
Otis, whose lips the listening crowd en-
    thrall
That press and pack the floor of Boston's
    hall.
But Kirkland smiles, released from toil
    and care
Since the silk mantle younger shoulders
    wear, —
Quincy's, whose spirit breathes the self-
    same fire
That filled the bosom of his youthful sire,
Who for the altar bore the kindled torch
To freedom's temple, dying in its porch.

Three grave professions in their sons appear,
Whose words well studied all well pleased
　　will hear:
Palfrey, ordained in varied walks to shine,
Statesman, historian, critic, and divine;
Solid and square behold majestic Shaw,
A mass of wisdom and a mine of law;
Warren, whose arm the doughtiest war-
　　riors fear,
Asks of the startled crowd to lend its ear, —
Proud of his calling, him the world loves
　　best,
Not as the coming, but the parting guest.

Look on that form, — with eye dilating scan
The stately mould of nature's kingliest man !
Tower-like he stands in life's unfaded prime;
Ask you his name ?　None asks a second
　　time !
He from the land his outward semblance
　　takes,
Where storm-swept mountains watch o'er
　　slumbering lakes.
See in the impress which the body wears
How its imperial might the soul declares:
The forehead's large expansion, lofty, wide,
That locks unsilvered vainly strive to hide;
The lines of thought that plough the sober
　　cheek;
Lips that betray their wisdom ere they speak
In tones like answers from Dodona's grove;
An eye like Juno's when she frowns on Jove.
I look and wonder; will he be content —
This man, this monarch, for the purple
　　meant —
The meaner duties of his tribe to share,
Clad in the garb that common mortals
　　wear ?
Ah, wild Ambition, spread thy restless
　　wings,
Beneath whose plumes the hidden œstrum
　　stings;
Thou whose bold flight would leave earth's
　　vulgar crowds,
And like the eagle soar above the clouds,
Must feel the pang that fallen angels know
When the red lightning strikes thee from
　　below !

Less bronze, more silver, mingles in the
　　mould
Of him whom next my roving eyes behold;
His, more the scholar's than the statesman's
　　face,
Proclaims him born of academic race.

Weary his look, as if an aching brain
Left on his brow the frozen prints of pain;
His voice far-reaching, grave, sonorous,
　　owns
A shade of sadness in its plaintive tones,
Yet when its breath some loftier thought
　　inspires
Glows with a heat that every bosom fires.
Such Everett seems; no chance-sown wild
　　flower knows
The full-blown charms of culture's double
　　rose, —
Alas, how soon, by death's unsparing frost,
Its bloom is faded and its fragrance lost !

Two voices, only two, to earth belong,
Of all whose accents met the listening
　　throng:
Winthrop, alike for speech and guidance
　　framed,
On that proud day a twofold duty claimed;
One other yet, — remembered or forgot, —
Forgive my silence if I name him not.
Can I believe it ?　I, whose youthful voice
Claimed a brief gamut, — notes not over
　　choice, —
Stood undismayed before the solemn throng,
And *propria voce* sung that saucy song
Which even in memory turns my soul
　　aghast, —
Felix audacia was the verdict cast.

What were the glory of these festal days
Shorn of their grand illumination's blaze ?
Night comes at last with all her starry train
To find a light in every glittering pane.
From " Harvard's " windows see the sudden
　　flash, —
Old " Massachusetts " glares through every
　　sash;
From wall to wall the kindling splendors
　　run
Till all is glorious as the noonday sun.

How to the scholar's mind each object
　　brings
What some historian tells, some poet sings !
The good gray teacher whom we all re-
　　vered —
Loved, honored, laughed at, and by fresh-
　　men feared,
As from old " Harvard," where its light
　　began,
From hall to hall the clustering splendors
　　ran —

Took down his well-worn Æschylus and
  read,
Lit by the rays a thousand tapers shed,
How the swift herald crossed the leagues
  between
Mycenæ's monarch and his faithless queen;
And thus he read, — my verse but ill dis-
  plays
The Attic picture, clad in modern phrase:

On Ida's summit flames the kindling pile,
And Lemnos answers from his rocky isle;
From Athos next it climbs the reddening skies,
Thence where the watch-towers of Macistus
  rise.
The sentries of Mesapius in their turn
Bid the dry heath in high-piled masses burn,
Cithæron's crag the crimson billows stain,
Far Ægiplanctus joins the fiery train.
Thus the swift courier through the pathless
  night
Has gained at length the Arachnœan height,
Whence the glad tidings, borne on wings of
  flame,
" Ilium has fallen ! " reach the royal dame.

So ends the day; before the midnight stroke
The lights expiring cloud the air with
  smoke;
While these the toil of younger hands em-
  ploy,
The slumbering Grecian dreams of smoul-
  dering Troy.

As to that hour with backward steps I turn,
Midway I pause: behold a funeral urn !
Ah, sad memorial ! known but all too well
The tale which thus its golden letters tell:

This dust, once breathing, changed its joyous
  life
For toil and hunger, wounds and mortal
  strife ;
Love, friendship, learning's all-prevailing
  charms,
For the cold bivouac and the clash of arms.
The cause of freedom won, a race enslaved
Called back to manhood, and a nation saved,
These sons of Harvard, falling ere their
  prime,
Leave their proud memory to the coming time.

While in their still retreats our scholars
  turn
The mildewed pages of the past, to learn

With endless labor of the sleepless brain
What once has been and ne'er shall be
  again,
We reap the harvest of their ceaseless toil
And find a fragrance in their midnight oil.
But let a purblind mortal dare the task
The embryo future of itself to ask,
The world reminds him, with a scornful
  laugh,
That times have changed since Prospero
  broke his staff.
Could all the wisdom of the schools foretell
The dismal hour when Lisbon shook and
  fell,
Or name the shuddering night that toppled
  down
Our sister's pride, beneath whose mural
  crown
Scarce had the scowl forgot its angry lines,
When earth's blind prisoners fired their
  fatal mines ?
  New realms, new worlds, exulting Science
  claims,
Still the dim future unexplored remains;
Her trembling scales the far-off planet
  weigh,
Her torturing prisms its elements betray,—
We know what ores the fires of Sirius
  melt,
What vaporous metals gild Orion's belt;
Angels, archangels, may have yet to learn
Those hidden truths our heaven-taught
  eyes discern;
Yet vain is Knowledge, with her mystic
  wand,
To pierce the cloudy screen and read be-
  yond;
Once to the silent stars the fates were
  known,
To us they tell no secrets but their own.

At Israel's altar still we humbly bow,
But where, oh where, are Israel's prophets
  now ?
Where is the sibyl with her hoarded leaves ?
Where is the charm the weird enchantress
  weaves ?
No croaking raven turns the auspex pale,
No reeking altars tell the morrow's tale;
The measured footsteps of the Fates are
  dumb,
Unseen, unheard, unheralded, they come,
Prophet and priest and all their following
  fail.
Who then is left to rend the future's veil ?

Who but the poet, he whose nicer sense
No film can baffle with its slight defence,
Whose finer vision marks the waves that
    stray,
Felt, but unseen, beyond the violet ray ? —
Who, while the storm-wind waits its dark-
    ening shroud,
Foretells the tempest ere he sees the
    cloud, —
Stays not for time his secrets to reveal,
But reads his message ere he breaks the
    seal.
So Mantua's bard foretold the coming day
Ere Bethlehem's infant in the manger lay;
The promise trusted to a mortal tongue
Found listening ears before the angels
    sung.
So while his load the creeping pack-horse
    galled,
While inch by inch the dull canal-boat
    crawled,
Darwin beheld a Titan from "afar
Drag the slow barge or drive the rapid car,"
That panting giant fed by air and flame,
The mightiest forges task their strength to
    tame.

Happy the poet ! him no tyrant fact
Holds in its clutches to be chained and
    racked;
Him shall no mouldy document convict,
No stern statistics gravely contradict;
No rival sceptre threats his airy throne;
He rules o'er shadows, but he reigns alone.
Shall I the poet's broad dominion claim
Because you bid me wear his sacred name
For these few moments ? Shall I boldly
    clash
My flint and steel, and by the sudden flash
Read the fair vision which my soul descries
Through the wide pupils of its wondering
    eyes ?
List then awhile; the fifty years have sped;
The third full century's opened scroll is
    spread,
Blank to all eyes save his who dimly sees
The shadowy future told in words like
    these:

How strange the prospect to my sight ap-
    pears,
Changed by the busy hands of fifty years !
Full well I know our ocean-salted Charles,
Filling and emptying through the sands
    and marls

That wall his restless stream on either bank,
Not all unlovely when the sedges rank
Lend their coarse veil the sable ooze to
    hide
That bares its blackness with the ebbing
    tide.
In other shapes to my illumined eyes
Those ragged margins of our stream arise:
Through walls of stone the sparkling wa-
    ters flow,
In clearer depths the golden sunsets glow,
On purer waves the lamps of midnight
    gleam,
That silver o'er the unpolluted stream.
Along his shores what stately temples rise,
What spires, what turrets, print the shad-
    owed skies !
Our smiling Mother sees her broad domain
Spread its tall roofs along the western
    plain;
Those blazoned windows' blushing glories
    tell
Of grateful hearts that loved her long and
    well;
Yon gilded dome that glitters in the sun
Was Dives' gift, — alas, his only one !
These buttressed walls enshrine a banker's
    name,
That hallowed chapel hides a miser's
    shame;
Their wealth they left, — their memory
    cannot fade
Though age shall crumble every stone they
    laid.
    Great lord of millions, — let me call thee
    great,
Since countless servants at thy bidding
    wait, —
Richesse oblige: no mortal must be blind
To all but self, or look at human kind
Laboring and suffering, — all its want and
    woe, —
Through sheets of crystal, as a pleasing
    show
That makes life happier for the chosen
    few
Duty for whom is something not to do.
    When thy last page of life at length is
    filled,
What shall thine heirs to keep thy memory
    build ?
Will piles of stone in Auburn's mournful
    shade
Save from neglect the spot where thou art
    laid ?

Nay, deem not thus; the sauntering stran-
ger's eye
Will pass unmoved thy columned tombstone
by,
No memory wakened, not a teardrop shed,
Thy name uncared for and thy date unread.
But if thy record thou indeed dost prize,
Bid from the soil some stately temple
rise, —
Some hall of learning, some memorial
shrine,
With names long honored to associate
thine:
So shall thy fame outlive thy shattered
bust
When all around thee slumber in the dust.
Thus England's Henry lives in Eton's
towers,
Saved from the spoil oblivion's gulf de-
vours;
Our later records with as fair a fame
Have wreathed each uncrowned benefac-
tor's name;
The walls they reared the memories still
retain
That churchyard marbles try to keep in
vain.
In vain the delving antiquary tries
To find the tomb where generous Harvard
lies:
Here, here, his lasting monument is found,
Where every spot is consecrated ground !
O'er Stoughton's dust the crumbling stone
decays,
Fast fade its lines of lapidary praise;
There the wild bramble weaves its ragged
nets,
There the dry lichen spreads its gray ro-
settes;
Still in yon walls his memory lives un-
spent,
Nor asks a braver, nobler monument.
Thus Hollis lives, and Holden, honored,
praised,
And good Sir Matthew, in the halls they
raised;
Thus live the worthies of these later times,
Who shine in deeds, less brilliant, grouped
in rhymes.
Say, shall the Muse with faltering steps
retreat,
Or dare these names in rhythmic form re-
peat ?
Why not as boldly as from Homer's lips
The long array of Argive battle-ships ?

When o'er our graves a thousand years
have past
(If to such date our threatened globe shall
last)
These classic precincts, myriad feet have
pressed,
Will show on high, in beauteous garlands
dressed,
Those honored names that grace our later
day, —
Weld, Matthews, Sever, Thayer, Austin,
Gray,
Sears, Phillips, Lawrence, Hemenway, —
to the list
Add Sanders, Sibley, — all the Muse has
missed.

Once more I turn to read the pictured page
Bright with the promise of the coming age.
Ye unborn sons of children yet unborn,
Whose youthful eyes shall greet that far-off
morn,
Blest are those eyes that all undimmed be-
hold
The sights so longed for by the wise of old.
From high-arched alcoves, through re-
sounding halls,
Clad in full robes majestic Science calls,
Tireless, unsleeping, still at Nature's feet,
Whate'er she utters fearless to repeat,
Her lips at last from every cramp released
That Israel's prophet caught from Egypt's
priest.
I see the statesman, firm, sagacious, bold,
For life's long conflict cast in amplest
mould;
Not his to clamor with the senseless throng
That shouts unshamed, " Our party, right
or wrong,"
But in the patriot's never-ending fight
To side with Truth, who changes wrong to
right.
I see the scholar; in that wondrous time
Men, women, children, all can write in
rhyme.
These four brief lines addressed to youth
inclined
To idle rhyming in his notes I find:

Who writes in verse that should have writ in
prose
Is like a traveller walking on his toes;
Happy the rhymester who in time has found
The heels he lifts were made to touch the
ground.

I see gray teachers, — on their work intent,
Their lavished lives, in endless labor spent,
Had closed at last in age and penury
    wrecked,
Martyrs, not burned, but frozen in neglect,
Save for the generous hands that stretched
    in aid
Of worn-out servants left to die half paid.
Ah, many a year will pass, I thought, ere
    we
Such kindly forethought shall rejoice to
    see, —
Monarchs are mindful of the sacred debt
That cold republics hasten to forget.
    I see the priest, — if such a name he
        bears
Who without pride his sacred vestment
    wears;
And while the symbols of his tribe I seek
Thus my first impulse bids me think and
    speak:

Let not the mitre England's prelate wears
Next to the crown whose regal pomp it
    shares,
Though low before it courtly Christians
    bow,
Leave its red mark on Younger England's
    brow.
We love, we honor, the maternal dame,
But let her priesthood wear a modest name,
While through the waters of the Pilgrim's
    bay
A new-born Mayflower shows her keels the
    way.
Too old grew Britain for her mother's
    beads, —
Must we be necklaced with her children's
    creeds ?
Welcome alike in surplice or in gown
The loyal lieges of the Heavenly Crown !
We greet with cheerful, not submissive,
    mien
A sister church, but not a mitred Queen !

A few brief flutters, and the unwilling
    Muse,
Who feared the flight she hated to refuse,
Shall fold the wings whose gayer plumes
    are shed,
Here where at first her half-fledged pin-
    ions spread.
    Well I remember in the long ago
How in the forest shades of Fontainebleau,

Strained through a fissure in a rocky cell,
One crystal drop with measured cadence
    fell.
Still, as of old, forever bright and clear,
The fissured cavern drops its wonted tear,
And wondrous virtue, simple folk aver,
Lies in that teardrop of *la roche qui pleure.*
    Of old I wandered by the river's side
Between whose banks the mighty waters
    glide,
Where vast Niagara, hurrying to its fall,
Builds and unbuilds its ever-tumbling wall;
Oft in my dreams I hear the rush and roar
Of battling floods, and feel the trembling
    shore,
As the huge torrent, girded for its leap,
With bellowing thunders plunges down the
    steep.
    Not less distinct, from memory's pic-
        tured urn,
The gray old rock, the leafy woods, return;
Robed in their pride the lofty oaks appear,
And once again with quickened sense I
    hear,
Through the low murmur of the leaves
    that stir,
The tinkling teardrop of *la roche qui pleure.*

So when the third ripe century stands com-
    plete,
As once again the sons of Harvard meet,
Rejoicing, numerous as the seashore sands,
Drawn from all quarters, — farthest dis-
    tant lands,
Where through the reeds the scaly saurian
    steals,
Where cold Alaska feeds her floundering
    seals,
Where Plymouth, glorying, wears her iron
    crown,
Where Sacramento sees the suns go down;
Nay, from the cloisters whence the refluent
    tide
Wafts their pale students to our Mother's
    side, —
Mid all the tumult that the day shall
    bring,
While all the echoes shout, and roar, and
    ring,
These tinkling lines, oblivion's easy prey,
Once more emerging to the light of day,
Not all unpleasing to the listening ear
Shall wake the memories of this bygone
    year,

Heard as I hear the measured drops that
flow
From the gray rock of wooded Fontaine-
bleau.

Yet, ere I leave, one loving word for all
Those fresh young lives that wait our
Mother's call:
  One gift is yours, kind Nature's richest
  dower, —
Youth, the fair bud that holds life's opening
flower,
Full of high hopes no coward doubts en-
chain,
With all the future throbbing in its brain,
And mightiest instincts which the beating
heart
Fills with the fire its burning waves impart.
  O joyous youth, whose glory is to dare, —
Thy foot firm planted on the lowest stair,
Thine eye uplifted to the loftiest height
Where Fame stands beckoning in the rosy
light,
Thanks for thy flattering tales, thy fond
deceits,
Thy loving lies, thy cheerful smiling cheats !
Nature's rash promise every day is broke, —
A thousand acorns breed a single oak,
The myriad blooms that make the orchard
gay
In barren beauty throw their lives away;
Yet shall we quarrel with the sap that
yields
The painted blossoms which adorn the fields,
When the fair orchard wears its May-day
suit
Of pink-white petals, for its scanty fruit ?
Thrice happy hours, in hope's illusion
dressed,
In fancy's cradle nurtured and caressed,
Though rich the spoils that ripening years
may bring,
To thee the dewdrops of the Orient cling, —
Not all the dye-stuffs from the vats of truth
Can match the rainbow on the robes of
youth !

Dear unborn children, to our Mother's trust
We leave you, fearless, when we lie in dust:
While o'er these walls the Christian banner
waves
From hallowed lips shall flow the truth
that saves;
While o'er those portals *Veritas* you read

No church shall bind you with its human
creed.
Take from the past the best its toil has
won,
But learn betimes its slavish ruts to shun.
Pass the old tree whose withered leaves are
shed,
Quit the old paths that error loved to tread,
And a new wreath of living blossoms seek,
A narrower pathway up a loftier peak;
Lose not your reverence, but unmanly fear
Leave far behind you, all who enter here !

As once of old from Ida's lofty height
The flaming signal flashed across the night,
So Harvard's beacon sheds its unspent rays
Till every watch-tower shows its kindling
blaze.
Caught from a spark and fanned by every
gale,
A brighter radiance gilds the roofs of Yale;
Amherst and Williams bid their flambeaus
shine,
And Bowdoin answers through her groves
of pine;
O'er Princeton's sands the far reflections
steal,
Where mighty Edwards stamped his iron
heel;
Nay, on the hill where old beliefs were
bound
Fast as if Styx had girt them nine times
round,
Bursts such a light that trembling souls
inquire
If the whole church of Calvin is on fire !
Well may they ask, for what so brightly
burns
As a dry creed that nothing ever learns ?
Thus link by link is knit the flaming chain
Lit by the torch of Harvard's hallowed
plain.

Thy son, thy servant, dearest Mother mine,
Lays this poor offering on thy holy shrine,
An autumn leaflet to the wild winds tost,
Touched by the finger of November's frost,
With sweet, sad memories of that earlier
day,
And all that listened to my first-born lay,
With grateful heart this glorious morn I
see, —
Would that my tribute worthier were of
thee !

POST-PRANDIAL

PHI BETA KAPPA

WENDELL PHILLIPS, ORATOR; CHARLES GOD-
FREY LELAND, POET

1881

"THE Dutch have taken Holland," — so
 the school-boys used to say;
The Dutch have taken Harvard, — no doubt
 of that to-day !
For the Wendells were low Dutchmen, and
 all their vrows were Vans;
And the Breitmanns are high Dutchmen,
 and here is honest Hans.

Mynheers, you both are welcome ! Fair
 cousin Wendell P.,
Our ancestors were dwellers beside the
 Zuyder Zee;
Both Grotius and Erasmus were country-
 men of we,
And Vondel was our namesake, though he
 spelt it with a V.

It is well old Evert Jansen sought a dwell-
 ing over sea
On the margin of the Hudson, where he
 sampled you and me
Through our grandsires and great-grand-
 sires, for you would n't quite agree
With the steady-going burghers along the
 Zuyder Zee.

Like our Motley's John of Barnveld, you
 have always been inclined
To speak, — well, — somewhat frankly, —
 to let us know your mind,
And the Mynheers would have told you to
 be cautious what you said,
Or else that silver tongue of yours might
 cost your precious head.

But we 're very glad you 've kept it; it was
 always Freedom's own,
And whenever Reason chose it she found
 a royal throne;
You have whacked us with your sceptre;
 our backs were little harmed,
And while we rubbed our bruises we owned
 we had been charmed.

And you, our *quasi* Dutchman, what wel-
 come should be yours
For all the wise prescriptions that work
 your laughter-cures ?
"Shake before taking"? — not a bit, —
 the bottle-cure 's a sham;
Take before shaking, and you 'll find it
 shakes your diaphragm.

"Hans Breitmann gif a barty, — vhere is
 dot barty now ? "
On every shelf where wit is stored to
 smooth the careworn brow !
A health to stout Hans Breitmann ! How
 long before we see
Another Hans as handsome, — as bright a
 man as he !

THE FLÂNEUR

BOSTON COMMON, DECEMBER 6, 1882

DURING THE TRANSIT OF VENUS

I LOVE all sights of earth and skies,
From flowers that glow to stars that shine;
The comet and the penny show,
All curious things, above, below,
Hold each in turn my wandering eyes:
I claim the Christian Pagan's line,
Humani nihil, — even so, —
And is not human life divine ?

When soft the western breezes blow,
And strolling youths meet sauntering maids,
I love to watch the stirring trades
Beneath the Vallombrosa shades
Our much-enduring elms bestow;
The vender and his rhetoric's flow,
That lambent stream of liquid lies;
The bait he dangles from his line,
The gudgeon and his gold-washed prize.
I halt before the blazoned sign
That bids me linger to admire
The drama time can never tire,
The little hero of the hunch,
With iron arm and soul of fire,
And will that works his fierce desire, —
Untamed, unscared, unconquered Punch !
My ear a pleasing torture finds
In tones the withered sibyl grinds, —
The *dame sans merci's* broken strain,
Whom I erewhile, perchance, have known,

When Orleans filled the Bourbon throne,
A siren singing by the Seine.

But most I love the tube that spies
The orbs celestial in their march;
That shows the comet as it whisks
Its tail across the planets' disks,
As if to blind their blood-shot eyes;
Or wheels so close against the sun
We tremble at the thought of risks
Our little spinning ball may run,
To pop like corn that children parch,
From summer something overdone,
And roll, a cinder, through the skies.

Grudge not to-day the scanty fee
To him who farms the firmament,
To whom the Milky Way is free;
Who holds the wondrous crystal key,
The silent Open Sesame
That Science to her sons has lent;
Who takes his toll, and lifts the bar
That shuts the road to sun and star.
If Venus only comes to time,
(And prophets say she must and shall,)
To-day will hear the tinkling chime
Of many a ringing silver dime,
For him whose optic glass supplies
The crowd with astronomic eyes, —
The Galileo of the Mall.

Dimly the transit morning broke;
The sun seemed doubting what to do,
As one who questions how to dress,
And takes his doublets from the press,
And halts between the old and new.
Please Heaven he wear his suit of blue,
Or don, at least, his ragged cloak,
With rents that show the azure through !

I go the patient crowd to join
That round the tube my eyes discern,
The last new-comer of the file,
And wait, and wait, a weary while,
And gape, and stretch, and shrug, and
        smile,
(For each his place must fairly earn,
Hindmost and foremost, in his turn,)
Till hitching onward, pace by pace,
I gain at last the envied place,
And pay the white exiguous coin:
The sun and I are face to face;
He glares at me, I stare at him;
And lo ! my straining eye has found
A little spot that, black and round,

Lies near the crimsoned fire-orb's rim.
O blessed, beauteous evening star,
Well named for her whom earth adores, —
The Lady of the dove-drawn car, —
I know thee in thy white simar;
But veiled in black, a rayless spot,
Blank as a careless scribbler's blot,
Stripped of thy robe of silvery flame, —
The stolen robe that Night restores
When Day has shut his golden doors, —
I see thee, yet I know thee not;
And canst thou call thyself the same ?

A black, round spot, — and that is all ;
And such a speck our earth would be
If he who looks upon the stars
Through the red atmosphere of Mars
Could see our little creeping ball
Across the disk of crimson crawl
As I our sister planet see.

And art thou, then, a world like ours,
Flung from the orb that whirled our own
A molten pebble from its zone ?
How must thy burning sands absorb
The fire-waves of the blazing orb,
Thy chain so short, thy path so near,
Thy flame-defying creatures hear
The maelstroms of the photosphere !
And is thy bosom decked with flowers
That steal their bloom from scalding show-
        ers ?
And hast thou cities, domes, and towers,
And life, and love that makes it dear,
And death that fills thy tribes with fear ?

Lost in my dream, my spirit soars
Through paths the wandering angels know;
My all-pervading thought explores
The azure ocean's lucent shores;
I leave my mortal self below,
As up the star-lit stairs I climb,
And still the widening view reveals
In endless rounds the circling wheels
That build the horologe of time.
New spheres, new suns, new systems gleam;
The voice no earth-born echo hears
Steals softly on my ravished ears:
I hear them " singing as they shine " —
A mortal's voice dissolves my dream:
My patient neighbor, next in line,
Hints gently there are those who wait.
O guardian of the starry gate,
What coin shall pay this debt of mine ?
Too slight thy claim, too small the fee

That bids thee turn the potent key
The Tuscan's hand has placed in thine.
Forgive my own the small affront,
The insult of the proffered dime;
Take it, O friend, since this thy wont,
But still shall faithful memory be
A bankrupt debtor unto thee,
And pay thee with a grateful rhyme.

AVE

PRELUDE TO "ILLUSTRATED POEMS"

FULL well I know the frozen hand has come
That smites the songs of grove and garden
    dumb,
And chills sad autumn's last chrysanthe-
    mum;

Yet would I find one blossom, if I might,
Ere the dark loom that weaves the robe of
    white
Hides all the wrecks of summer out of sight.

Sometimes in dim November's narrowing
    day,
When all the season's pride has passed
    away,
As mid the blackened stems and leaves we
    stray,

We spy in sheltered nook or rocky cleft
A starry disk the hurrying winds have left,
Of all its blooming sisterhood bereft:

Some pansy, with its wondering baby eyes —
Poor wayside nursling ! — fixed in blank
    surprise
At the rough welcome of unfriendly skies;

Or golden daisy, — will it dare disclaim
The lion's tooth, to wear this gentler name ?
Or blood-red salvia, with its lips aflame:

The storms have stripped the lily and the
    rose,
Still on its cheek the flush of summer
    glows,
And all its heart-leaves kindle as it blows.

So had I looked some bud of song to find
The careless winds of autumn left behind,
With these of earlier seasons' growth to
    bind.

Ah me ! my skies are dark with sudden
    grief,
A flower lies faded on my garnered sheaf;
Yet let the sunshine gild this virgin leaf, —

The joyous, blessed sunshine of the past,
Still with me, though the heavens are
    overcast, —
The light that shines while life and memory
    last.

Go, pictured rhymes, for loving readers
    meant!
Bring back the smiles your jocund morning
    lent,
And warm their hearts with sunbeams yet
    unspent !

KING'S CHAPEL

READ AT THE TWO HUNDREDTH ANNI-VERSARY

Is it a weanling's weakness for the past
    That in the stormy, rebel-breeding town,
Swept clean of relics by the levelling blast,
Still keeps our gray old chapel's name of
    "King's,"
Still to its outworn symbols fondly clings, —
    Its unchurched mitres and its empty
    crown ?

Poor harmless emblems ! All has shrunk
    away
    That made them gorgons in the patriot's
    eyes;
The priestly plaything harms us not to-day;
The gilded crown is but a pleasing show,
An old-world heirloom, left from long ago,
    Wreck of the past that memory bids us
    prize.

Lightly we glance the fresh-cut marbles o'er;
    Those two of earlier date our eyes en-
    thrall:
The proud old Briton's by the western door,
And hers, the Lady of Colonial days,
Whose virtues live in long-drawn classic
    phrase, —
    The fair Francesca of the southern wall.

Ay ! those were goodly men that Reynolds
    drew,
    And stately dames our Copley's canvas
    holds,

To their old Church, their Royal Master,
    true,
Proud of the claim their valiant sires had
    earned,
That "gentle blood," not lightly to be
    spurned,
    Save by the churl ungenerous Nature
    moulds.

All vanished ! It were idle to complain
    That ere the fruits shall come the flowers
    must fall;
Yet somewhat we have lost amidst our
    gain,
Some rare ideals time may not restore, —
The charm of courtly breeding, seen no
    more,
    And reverence, dearest ornament of all.

Thus musing, to the western wall I came,
    Departing: lo ! a tablet fresh and fair,
Where glistened many a youth's remem-
    bered name
In golden letters on the snow-white stone, —
Young lives these aisles and arches once
    have known,
    Their country's bleeding altar might not
    spare.

These died that we might claim a soil un-
    stained,
    Save by the blood of heroes; their be-
    quests
A realm unsevered and a race unchained.
Has purer blood through Norman veins
    come down
From the rough knights that clutched the
    Saxon's crown
    Than warmed the pulses in these faith-
    ful breasts ?

These, too, shall live in history's deathless
    page,
    High on the slow-wrought pedestals of
    fame,
Ranged with the heroes of remoter age;
They could not die who left their nation free,
Firm as the rock, unfettered as the sea,
    Its heaven unshadowed by the cloud of
    shame.

While on the storied past our memory
    dwells,
    Our grateful tribute shall not be de-
    nied, —

The wreath, the cross of rustling immor-
    telles ;
And willing hands shall clear each darken-
    ing bust,
As year by year sifts down the clinging
    dust
    On Shirley's beauty and on Vassal's
    pride.

But for our own, our loved and lost, we bring
    With throbbing hearts and tears that
    still must flow,
In full-heaped hands, the opening flowers
    of spring,
Lilies half-blown, and budding roses, red
As their young cheeks, before the blood
    was shed
    That lent their morning bloom its gener-
    ous glow.

Ah, who shall count a rescued nation's
    debt,
    Or sum in words our martyrs' silent
    claims ?
Who shall our heroes' dread exchange for-
    get, —
All life, youth, hope, could promise to
    allure
For all that soul could brave or flesh en-
    dure ?
    They shaped our future; we but carve
    their names.

HYMN

FOR THE SAME OCCASION

SUNG BY THE CONGREGATION TO THE TUNE
OF TALLIS'S EVENING HYMN

O'ERSHADOWED by the walls that climb,
    Piled up in air by living hands,
A rock amid the waves of time,
    Our gray old house of worship stands.

High o'er the pillared aisles we love
    The symbols of the past look down;
Unharmed, unharming, throned above,
    Behold the mitre and the crown !

Let not our younger faith forget
    The loyal souls that held them dear;
The prayers we read their tears have wet,
    The hymns we sing they loved to hear.

The memory of their earthly throne
　Still to our holy temple clings,
But here the kneeling suppliants own
　One only Lord, the King of kings.

Hark ! while our hymn of grateful praise
　The solemn echoing vaults prolong,
The far-off voice of earlier days
　Blends with our own in hallowed song:

To Him who ever lives and reigns,
　Whom all the hosts of heaven adore,
Who lent the life his breath sustains,
　Be glory now and evermore !

HYMN — THE WORD OF PROM-ISE

(BY SUPPOSITION)

AN HYMN SET FORTH TO BE SUNG BY THE GREAT ASSEMBLY AT NEWTOWN, [MASS.] MO. 12. I. 1636

Written by OLIVER WENDELL HOLMES, *eldest son of Rev.* ABIEL HOLMES, *eighth Pastor of the First Church in Cambridge, Massachusetts.*

LORD, Thou hast led us as of old
　Thine Arm led forth the chosen Race
Through Foes that raged, through Floods
　　that roll'd,
　To Canaan's far-off Dwelling-Place.

Here is Thy bounteous Table spread,
　Thy Manna falls on every Field,
Thy Grace our hungering Souls hath fed,
　Thy Might hath been our Spear and
　　Shield.

Lift high Thy Buckler, Lord of Hosts !
　Guard Thou Thy Servants, Sons and
　　Sires,
While on the Godless heathen Coasts
　They light Thine Israel's Altar-fires !

The salvage Wilderness remote
　Shall hear Thy Works and Wonders
　　sung;
So from the Rock that Moses smote
　The Fountain of the Desart sprung.

Soon shall the slumbering Morn awake,
　From wandering Stars of Errour freed,
When Christ the Bread of Heaven shall
　　break
　For Saints that own a common Creed.

The Walls that fence His Flocks apart
　Shall crack and crumble in Decay,
And every Tongue and every Heart
　Shall welcome in the new-born Day.

Then shall His glorious Church rejoice
　His Word of Promise to recall, —
ONE SHELTERING FOLD, ONE SHEPHERD'S
　　VOICE,
　ONE GOD AND FATHER OVER ALL !

HYMN

READ AT THE DEDICATION OF THE OLIVER WENDELL HOLMES HOSPITAL AT HUDSON, WISCONSIN

JUNE 7, 1887

ANGEL of love, for every grief
　Its soothing balm thy mercy brings,
For every pang its healing leaf,
　For homeless want, thine outspread wings.

Enough for thee the pleading eye,
　The knitted brow of silent pain;
The portals open to a sigh
　Without the clank of bolt or chain.

Who is our brother ?　He that lies
　Left at the wayside, bruised and sore:
His need our open hand supplies,
　His welcome waits him at our door.

Not ours to ask in freezing tones
　His race, his calling, or his creed;
Each heart the tie of kinship owns,
　When those are human veins that bleed.

Here stand the champions to defend
　From every wound that flesh can feel;
Here science, patience, skill, shall blend
　To save, to calm, to help, to heal.

Father of Mercies !　Weak and frail,
　Thy guiding hand thy children ask;
Let not the Great Physician fail
　To aid us in our holy task.

Source of all truth, and love, and light,
　That warm and cheer our earthly days,
Be ours to serve Thy will aright,
　Be Thine the glory and the praise !

ON THE DEATH OF PRESIDENT GARFIELD

I

FALLEN with autumn's falling leaf
  Ere yet his summer's noon was past,
Our friend, our guide, our trusted chief, —
  What words can match a woe so vast !

And whose the chartered claim to speak
  The sacred grief where all have part,
Where sorrow saddens every cheek
  And broods in every aching heart ?

Yet Nature prompts the burning phrase
  That thrills the hushed and shrouded
    hall,
The loud lament, the sorrowing praise,
  The silent tear that love lets fall.

In loftiest verse, in lowliest rhyme,
  Shall strive unblamed the minstrel
    choir, —
The singers of the new-born time,
  And trembling age with outworn lyre.

No room for pride, no place for blame, —
  We fling our blossoms on the grave,
Pale, — scentless, — faded, — all we claim,
  This only, — what we had we gave.

Ah, could the grief of all who mourn
  Blend in one voice its bitter cry,
The wail to heaven's high arches borne
  Would echo through the caverned sky.

II

O happiest land, whose peaceful choice
  Fills with a breath its empty throne !
God, speaking through thy people's voice,
  Has made that voice for once his own.

No angry passion shakes the state
  Whose weary servant seeks for rest,
And who could fear that scowling hate
  Would strike at that unguarded breast ?

He stands, unconscious of his doom,
  In manly strength, erect, serene;
Around him Summer spreads her bloom;
  He falls, — what horror clothes the scene !

How swift the sudden flash of woe
  Where all was bright as childhood's
    dream !
As if from heaven's ethereal bow
  Had leaped the lightning's arrowy gleam.

Blot the foul deed from history's page;
  Let not the all-betraying sun
Blush for the day that stains an age
  When murder's blackest wreath was
    won.

III

Pale on his couch the sufferer lies,
  The weary battle-ground of pain:
Love tends his pillow; Science tries
  Her every art, alas ! in vain.

The strife endures how long ! how long !
  Life, death, seem balanced in the scale,
While round his bed a viewless throng
  Await each morrow's changing tale.

In realms the desert ocean parts
  What myriads watch with tear-filled
    eyes,
His pulse-beats echoing in their hearts,
  His breathings counted with their sighs !

Slowly the stores of life are spent,
  Yet hope still battles with despair ;
Will Heaven not yield when knees are
    bent ?
    Answer, O thou that hearest prayer !

But silent is the brazen sky;
  On sweeps the meteor's threatening
    train,
Unswerving Nature's mute reply,
  Bound in her adamantine chain.

Not ours the verdict to decide
  Whom death shall claim or skill shall
    save;
The hero's life though Heaven denied,
  'It gave our land a martyr's grave.

Nor count the teaching vainly sent
  How human hearts their griefs may
    share, —
The lesson woman's love has lent,
  What hope may do, what faith can
    bear !

Farewell! the leaf-strown earth enfolds
  Our stay, our pride, our hopes, our fears,
And autumn's golden sun beholds
  A nation bowed, a world in tears.

THE GOLDEN FLOWER

WHEN Advent dawns with lessening days,
  While earth awaits the angels' hymn;
When bare as branching coral sways
  In whistling winds each leafless limb;
When spring is but a spendthrift's dream,
  And summer's wealth a wasted dower,
Nor dews nor sunshine may redeem, —
  Then autumn coins his Golden Flower.

Soft was the violet's vernal hue,
  Fresh was the rose's morning red,
Full-orbed the stately dahlia grew, —
  All gone! their short-lived splendors
    shed.
The shadows, lengthening, stretch at noon;
  The fields are stripped, the groves are
    dumb;
The frost-flowers greet the icy moon, —
  Then blooms the bright chrysanthemum.

The stiffening turf is white with snow,
  Yet still its radiant disks are seen
Where soon the hallowed morn will show
  The wreath and cross of Christmas
    green;
As if in autumn's dying days
  It heard the heavenly song afar,
And opened all its glowing rays,
  The herald lamp of Bethlehem's star.

Orphan of summer, kindly sent
  To cheer the fading year's decline,
In all that pitying Heaven has lent
  No fairer pledge of hope than thine.
Yes! June lies hid beneath the snow,
  And winter's unborn heir shall claim
For every seed that sleeps below
  A spark that kindles into flame.

Thy smile the scowl of winter braves,
  Last of the bright-robed, flowery train,
Soft sighing o'er the garden graves,
  " Farewell! farewell! we meet again!"
So may life's chill November bring
  Hope's golden flower, the last of all,
Before we hear the angels sing
  Where blossoms never fade and fall!

YOUTH

[Read at the celebration of the thirty-first anniversary of the Boston Young Men's Christian Union, May 31, 1882.]

WHY linger round the sunken wrecks
  Where old Armadas found their graves?
Why slumber on the sleepy decks
  While foam and clash the angry waves?
Up! when the storm-blast rends the clouds,
  And winged with ruin sweeps the gale,
Young feet must climb the quivering
    shrouds,
  Young hands must reef the bursting
    sail!

Leave us to fight the tyrant creeds
  Who felt their shackles, feel their scars;
The cheerful sunlight little heeds
  The brutes that prowled beneath the
    stars;
The dawn is here, the day star shows
  The spoils of many a battle won,
But sin and sorrow still are foes
  That face us in the morning sun.

Who sleeps beneath yon bannered mound
  The proudly sorrowing mourner seeks,
The garland-bearing crowd surrounds?
  A light-haired boy with beardless cheeks!
'T is time this "fallen world" should
    rise;
  Let youth the sacred work begin!
What nobler task, what fairer prize
  Than earth to save and Heaven to win?

HAIL, COLUMBIA!

1798

THE FIRST VERSE OF THE SONG

BY JOSEPH HOPKINSON

"HAIL, Columbia! Happy land!
  Hail, ye heroes, heaven-born band,
  Who fought and bled in Freedom's cause,
  Who fought and bled in Freedom's cause,
And when the storm of war was gone
Enjoy'd the peace your valor won.
  Let independence be our boast,
  Ever mindful what it cost;
  Ever grateful for the prize,
  Let its altar reach the skies.

"Firm — united — let us be,
Rallying round our Liberty;
As a band of brothers join'd,
Peace and safety we shall find."

. . . .

ADDITIONAL VERSES

WRITTEN AT THE REQUEST OF THE COMMIT-
TEE FOR THE CONSTITUTIONAL CENTENNIAL
CELEBRATION AT PHILADELPHIA, 1887

LOOK our ransomed shores around,
Peace and safety we have found !
  Welcome, friends who once were foes !
  Welcome, friends who once were foes,
To all the conquering years have gained, —
A nation's rights, a race unchained !
  Children of the day new-born,
  Mindful of its glorious morn,
  Let the pledge our fathers signed
  Heart to heart forever bind !

While the stars of heaven shall burn,
While the ocean tides return,
Ever may the circling sun
Find the Many still are One !

Graven deep with edge of steel,
Crowned with Victory's crimson seal,
  All the world their names shall read !
  All the world their names shall read,
Enrolled with his, the Chief that led
The hosts whose blood for us was shed.
  Pay our sires their children's debt,
  Love and honor, nor forget
  Only Union's golden key
  Guards the Ark of Liberty !

While the stars of heaven shall burn,
While the ocean tides return,
Ever may the circling sun
Find the Many still are One !

Hail, Columbia ! strong and free,
Throned in hearts from sea to sea !
  Thy march triumphant still pursue !
  Thy march triumphant still pursue
With peaceful stride from zone to zone,
Till Freedom finds the world her own !
  Blest in Union's holy ties,
  Let our grateful song arise,
  Every voice its tribute lend,
  All in loving chorus blend !

While the stars in heaven shall burn,
While the ocean tides return,
Ever shall the circling sun
Find the Many still are One !

POEM

FOR THE DEDICATION OF THE FOUNTAIN
AT STRATFORD-ON-AVON, PRESENTED
BY GEORGE W. CHILDS, OF PHILADEL-
PHIA

[Dated August 29, 1887.]

WELCOME, thrice welcome is thy silvery
    gleam,
    Thou long-imprisoned stream !
Welcome the tinkle of thy crystal beads
As plashing raindrops to the flowery
    meads,
As summer's breath to Avon's whispering
    reeds !
From rock-walled channels, drowned in
    rayless night,
    Leap forth to life and light;
Wake from the darkness of thy troubled
    dream,
And greet with answering smile the morn-
    ing's beam !

No purer lymph the white-limbed Naiad
    knows
    Than from thy chalice flows;
Not the bright spring of Afric's sunny
    shores,
Starry with spangles washed from golden
    ores,
Nor glassy stream Bandusia's fountain
    pours,
Nor wave translucent where Sabrina fair
    Braids her loose-flowing hair,
Nor the swift current, stainless as it rose
Where chill Arveiron steals from Alpine
    snows.

Here shall the traveller stay his weary feet
    To seek thy calm retreat;
Here at high noon the brown-armed reaper
    rest;
Here, when the shadows, lengthening from
    the west,
Call the mute song-bird to his leafy nest,
Matron and maid shall chat the cares away
    That brooded o'er the day,

While flocking round them troops of chil-
dren meet,
And all the arches ring with laughter
sweet.

Here shall the steed, his patient life who
spends
In toil that never ends,
Hot from his thirsty tramp o'er hill and
plain,
Plunge his red nostrils, while the torturing
rein
Drops in loose loops beside his floating
mane;
Nor the poor brute that shares his master's
lot
Find his small needs forgot, —
Truest of humble, long-enduring friends,
Whose presence cheers, whose guardian
care defends!

Here lark and thrush and nightingale shall
sip,
And skimming swallows dip,
And strange shy wanderers fold their lus-
trous plumes
Fragrant from bowers that lent their sweet
perfumes
Where Pæstum's rose or Persia's lilac
blooms;
Here from his cloud the eagle stoop to
drink
At the full basin's brink,
And whet his beak against its rounded lip,
His glossy feathers glistening as they drip.

Here shall the dreaming poet linger long,
Far from his listening throng, —
Nor lute nor lyre his trembling hand shall
bring;
Here no frail Muse shall imp her crippled
wing,
No faltering minstrel strain his throat to
sing !
These hallowed echoes who shall dare to
claim
Whose tuneless voice would shame,
Whose jangling chords with jarring notes
would wrong
The nymphs that heard the Swan of Avon's
song ?

What visions greet the pilgrim's raptured
eyes !
What ghosts made real rise!

The dead return, — they breathe, — they
live again,
Joined by the host of Fancy's airy train,
Fresh from the springs of Shakespeare's
quickening brain !
The stream that slakes the soul's diviner
thirst
Here found the sunbeams first;
Rich with his fame, not less shall memory
prize
The gracious gift that humbler wants sup-
plies.

O'er the wide waters reached the hand
that gave
To all this bounteous wave,
With health and strength and joyous beauty
fraught;
Blest be the generous pledge of friendship,
brought
From the far home of brothers' love, un-
bought!
Long may fair Avon's fountain flow, en-
rolled
With storied shrines of old,
Castalia's spring, Egeria's dewy cave,
And Horeb's rock the God of Israel clave!

Land of our fathers, ocean makes us two,
But heart to heart is true !
Proud is your towering daughter in the West,
Yet in her burning life-blood reign confest
Her mother's pulses beating in her breast.
This holy fount, whose rills from heaven
descend,
Its gracious drops shall lend, —
Both foreheads bathed in that baptismal
dew,
And love make one the old home and the
new !

TO THE POETS WHO ONLY READ AND LISTEN

WHEN evening's shadowy fingers fold
The flowers of every hue,
Some shy, half-opened bud will hold
Its drop of morning's dew.

Sweeter with every sunlit hour
The trembling sphere has grown,
Till all the fragrance of the flower
Becomes at last its own.

We that have sung perchance may find
  Our little meed of praise,
And round our pallid temples bind
  The wreath of fading bays:

Ah, Poet, who has never spent
  Thy breath in idle strains,
For thee the dewdrop morning lent
  Still in thy heart remains;

Unwasted, in its perfumed cell
  It waits the evening gale;
Then to the azure whence it fell
  Its lingering sweets exhale.

FOR THE DEDICATION OF THE NEW CITY LIBRARY, BOSTON

NOVEMBER 26, 1888

PROUDLY, beneath her glittering dome,
  Our three-hilled city greets the morn;
Here Freedom found her virgin home, —
  The Bethlehem where her babe was
    born.

The lordly roofs of traffic rise
  Amid the smoke of household fires;
High o'er them in the peaceful skies
  Faith points to heaven her clustering
    spires.

Can Freedom breathe if ignorance reign ?
  Shall Commerce thrive where anarchs
    rule ?
Will Faith her half-fledged brood retain
  If darkening counsels cloud the school ?

Let in the light ! from every age
  Some gleams of garnered wisdom pour,
And, fixed on thought's electric page,
  Wait all their radiance to restore.

Let in the light ! in diamond mines
  Their gems invite the hand that delves;
So learning's treasured jewels shine
  Ranged on the alcove's ordered shelves.

From history's scroll the splendor streams,
  From science leaps the living ray;
Flashed from the poet's glowing dreams
  The opal fires of fancy play.

Let in the light ! these windowed walls
  Shall brook no shadowing colonnades,
But day shall flood the silent halls
  Till o'er yon hills the sunset fades.

Behind the ever open gate
  No pikes shall fence a crumbling throne,
No lackeys cringe, no courtiers wait, —
  This palace is the people's own !

Heirs of our narrow-girdled past,
  How fair the prospect we survey,
Where howled unheard the wintry blast
  And rolled unchecked the storm-swept
    bay !

These chosen precincts, set apart
  For learned toil and holy shrines,
Yield willing homes to every art
  That trains, or strengthens, or refines.

Here shall the sceptred mistress reign
  Who heeds her meanest subject's call,
Sovereign of all their vast domain,
  The queen, the handmaid of them all !

TO JAMES RUSSELL LOWELL

AT THE DINNER GIVEN IN HIS HONOR AT THE TAVERN CLUB, ON HIS SEVEN- TIETH BIRTHDAY, FEBRUARY 22, 1889

A HEALTH to him whose double wreath
    displays
The critic's ivy and the poet's bays;
Who stayed not till with undisputed claim
The civic garland filled his meed of fame;
True knight of Freedom, ere her doubtful
    cause
Rose from the dust to meet the world's
    applause,
His country's champion on the bloodless
    field
Where truth and manhood stand for spear
    and shield !

Who is the critic ? He who never skips
The luckless passage where his author slips;
Slides o'er his merits, stumbles at his
    faults,
Calls him a cripple if he sometimes halts.
Rich in the caustic epithets that sting,
The venom-vitriol malice loves to fling;

His quill a feathered fang at hate's com-
mand,
His ink the product of his poison-gland, —
Is this the critic? Call him not a snake, —
This noxious creature, — for the reptile's
sake!
He is the critic who is first to mark
The star of genius when its glimmering
spark
First pricks the sky, not waiting to pro-
claim
Its coming glory till it bursts in flame.
He is the critic whose divining rod
Tells where the waters hide beneath the sod;
Whom studious search through varied lore
has taught
The streams, the rills, the fountain-heads,
of thought;
Who, if some careless phrase, some slip-
shod clause,
Crack Priscian's skull or break Quintil-
ian's laws,
Points out the blunder in a kindly way,
Nor tries his larger wisdom to display.
Where will you seek him? Wander far
and wide,
Then turn and find him seated at your
side!

Who is the poet? He who matches
rhymes
In the last fashion of the new-born times;
Sweats over sonnets till the toil seems
worse
Than Heaven intended in the primal
curse;
Work, duties, pleasures, every claim for-
gets,
To shape his rondeaus and his triolets?
Or is it he whose random venture throws
His lawless whimseys into moonstruck
prose,
Where they who worship the barbarian's
creed
Will find a rhythmic cadence as they read,
As the pleased rustic hears a tune, or
thinks
He hears a tune, in every bell that clinks?
Are these the poets? Though their pens
should blot
A thousand volumes, surely such are not.
Who *is* the poet? He whom Nature
chose
In that sweet season when she made the
rose.

Though with the changes of our colder
clime
His birthday will come somewhat out of
time,
Through all the shivering winter's frost
and chill,
The bloom and fragrance cling around it
still.
He is the poet who can stoop to read
The secret hidden in a wayside weed;
Whom June's warm breath with child-
like rapture fills,
Whose spirit "dances with the daffodils;"
Whom noble deeds with noble thoughts in-
spire
And lend his verse the true Promethean fire;
Who drinks the waters of enchanted
streams
That wind and wander through the land of
dreams;
For whom the unreal is the real world,
Its fairer flowers with brighter dews im-
pearled.
He looks a mortal till he spreads his
wings, —
He seems an angel when he soars and sings!
Behold the poet! Heaven his days pro-
long,
Whom Elmwood's nursery cradled into
song!

Who is the patriot? He who deftly
bends
To every shift that serves his private ends,
His face all smiling while his conscience
squirms,
His back as limber as a canker worm's;
Who sees his country floundering through
a drift,
Nor stirs a hand the laboring wheel to
lift,
But trusts to Nature's leisure-loving law,
And waits with patience for the snow to
thaw?
Or is he one who, called to conflict,
draws
His trusty weapon in his country's cause;
Who, born a poet, grasps his trenchant
rhymes
And strikes unshrinking at the nation's
crimes;
Who in the days of peril learns to teach
The wisest lessons in the homeliest speech;
Whose plain good sense, alive with tingling
wit,

Can always find a handle that will fit;
Who touches lightly with Ithuriel spear
The toad close squatting at the people's
    ear,
And bids the laughing, scornful world de-
    scry
The masking demon, the incarnate lie?
This, this is he his country well may say
Is fit to share her savior's natal day!
    Think not the date a worn-out king
      assigned
As Life's full measure holds for all man-
    kind;
Shall Gladstone, crowned with eighty
    years, withdraw?
See, nearer home, the Lion of the Law —
How Court Street trembles when he leaves
    his den,
Clad in the pomp of *four* score years and
    ten!

Once more the health of Nature's favored
    son,
The poet, critic, patriot, all in one;
Health, honor, friendship, ever round him
    wait
In life's fair field beyond the seven-barred
    gate!

BUT ONE TALENT

YE who yourselves of larger worth esteem
Than common mortals, listen to my dream,
And learn the lesson of life's cozening
    cheat,
    The coinage of conceit.

— The angel, guardian of my youth and
    age,
Spread out before me an account-book's
    page,
Saying, "This column marks what thou
    dost owe, —
    The gain thou hast to show."

"Spirit," I said, "I know, alas! too well
How poor the tale thy record has to tell.
Much I received, — the little I have
    brought
    Seems by its side as naught.

"Five talents, all of Ophir's purest gold,
These five fair caskets ranged before thee
    hold;

The first can show a few poor shekels' gain,
    The rest unchanged remain.

"Bringing my scanty tribute, overawed,
To Him who reapeth where He hath not
    strawed,
I tremble like a culprit when I count
    My whole vast debt's amount.

"What will He say to one from whom
    were due
Ten talents, when he comes with less than
    two?
What can I do but shudder and await
    The slothful servant's fate?"

— As looks a mother on an erring child,
The angel looked me in the face and
    smiled:
"How couldst thou, reckoning with thy-
    self, contrive
    To count thy talents five?

"These caskets which thy flattering fan-
    cies gild
Not all with Ophir's precious ore are
    filled;
Thy debt is slender, for thy gift was small:
    One talent, — that was all.

"This second casket, with its grave pre-
    tence,
Is weighty with thine IGNORANCE, dark
    and dense,
Save for a single glowworm's glimmering
    light
    To mock its murky night

"The third conceals the DULNESS that was
    thine.
How could thy mind its lack of wit di-
    vine?
Let not what Heaven assigned thee bring
    thee blame;
    Thy want is not thy shame.

"The fourth, so light to lift, so fair to see,
Is filled to bursting with thy VANITY,
The vaporous breath that kept thy hopes
    alive
    By counting one as five.

"These held but little, but the fifth held
    less, —
Only blank vacuum, naked nothingness,

An idiot's portion.　He who gave it knows
　　Its claimant nothing owes.

" Thrice happy pauper he whose last ac-
　　count
Shows on the debtor side the least amount!
The more thy gifts, the more thou needs
　　must pay
　　　　On life's dread reckoning day."

— Humbled, not grieving to be undeceived,
I woke, from fears of hopeless debt re-
　　lieved:
For sparing gifts but small returns are
　　due, —
　　　　Thank Heaven I had so few !

FOR THE WINDOW IN ST. MARGARET'S

IN MEMORY OF A SON OF ARCHDEACON
FARRAR

AFAR he sleeps whose name is graven here,
　　Where loving hearts his early doom de-
　　plore;
Youth, promise, virtue, all that made him
　　dear
　　Heaven lent, earth borrowed, sorrowing
　　to restore.

JAMES RUSSELL LOWELL

1819–1891

THOU shouldst have sung the swan-song
　　for the choir
　　That filled our groves with music till the
　　day
Lit the last hilltop with its reddening fire,
　　And evening listened for thy lingering
　　lay.

But thou hast found thy voice in realms afar
　　Where strains celestial blend their notes
　　with thine;
Some cloudless sphere beneath a happier
　　star
　　Welcomes the bright-winged spirit we
　　resign.

How Nature mourns thee in the still retreat
　　Where passed in peace thy love-enchanted
　　hours !

Where shall she find an eye like thine to
　　greet
　　Spring's earliest footprints on her open-
　　ing flowers ?

Have the pale wayside weeds no fond re-
　　gret
　　For him who read the secrets they enfold?
Shall the proud spangles of the field for-
　　get
　　The verse that lent new glory to their
　　gold ?

And ye whose carols wooed his infant ear,
　　Whose chants with answering woodnotes
　　he repaid,
Have ye no song his spirit still may hear
　　From Elmwood's vaults of overarching
　　shade ?

Friends of his studious hours, who thronged
　　to teach
　　The deep-read scholar all your varied
　　lore,
Shall he no longer seek your shelves to
　　reach
　　The treasure missing from his world-
　　wide store ?

———

This singer whom we long have held so
　　dear
　　Was Nature's darling, shapely, strong,
　　and fair ;
Of keenest wit, of judgment crystal-clear,
　　Easy of converse, courteous, debonair,

Fit for the loftiest or the lowliest lot,
　　Self-poised, imperial, yet of simplest
　　ways;
At home alike in castle or in cot,
　　True to his aim, let others blame or
　　praise.

Freedom he found an heirloom from his
　　sires;
　　Song, letters, statecraft, shared his years
　　in turn;
All went to feed the nation's altar-fires
　　Whose mourning children wreathe his
　　funeral urn.

He loved New England, — people, lan-
　　guage, soil,
　　Unweaned by exile from her arid breast.

Farewell awhile, white - handed son of
toil,
  Go with her brown-armed laborers to thy
rest.

Peace to thy slumber in the forest shade !
  Poet and patriot, every gift was thine;
Thy name shall live while summers bloom
and fade,
  And grateful Memory guard thy leafy
shrine !

IN MEMORY OF JOHN GREEN-LEAF WHITTIER

DECEMBER 17, 1807 — SEPTEMBER 7, 1892

THOU, too, hast left us.   While with heads
bowed low,
  And sorrowing hearts, we mourned our
summer's dead,
The flying season bent its Parthian bow,
  And yet again our mingling tears were
shed.

Was Heaven impatient that it could not
wait
  The blasts of winter for earth's fruits to
fall ?
Were angels crowding round the open
gate
  To greet the spirits coming at their
call ?

Nay, let not fancies, born of old be-liefs,
  Play with the heart-beats that are throb-bing still,
And waste their outworn phrases on the
griefs,
  The silent griefs that words can only
chill.

For thee, dear friend, there needs no high-wrought lay,
  To shed its aureole round thy cherished
name, —
Thou whose plain, home-born speech of
Yea and Nay
  Thy truthful nature ever best became.

Death reaches not a spirit such as thine, —
  It can but steal the robe that hid thy
wings;

Though thy warm breathing presence we
resign,
  Still in our hearts its loving semblance
clings.

Peaceful thy message, yet for struggling
right, —
  When Slavery's gauntlet in our face was
flung, —
While timid weaklings watched the dubi-ous fight
  No herald's challenge more defiant rung.

Yet was thy spirit tuned to gentle themes
  Sought in the haunts thy humble youth
had known.
Our stern New England's hills and vales
and streams, —
  Thy tuneful idyls made them all their own.

The wild flowers springing from thy native
sod
  Lent all their charms thy new-world
song to fill, —
Gave thee the mayflower and the golden-rod
  To match the daisy and the daffodil.

In the brave records of our earlier time
  A hero's deed thy generous soul inspired,
And many a legend, told in ringing rhyme,
  The youthful soul with high resolve has
fired.

Not thine to lean on priesthood's broken
reed;
  No barriers caged thee in a bigot's fold;
Did zealots ask to syllable thy creed,
  Thou saidst "Our Father," and thy creed
was told.

Best loved and saintliest of our singing
train,
  Earth's noblest tributes to thy name be-long.
A lifelong record closed without a stain,
  A blameless memory shrined in deathless
song.

Lift from its quarried ledge a flawless
stone;
  Smooth the green turf and bid the tablet
rise,
And on its snow-white surface carve alone
  These words, — he needs no more, —
    HERE WHITTIER LIES.

TO THE TEACHERS OF AMERICA

[During a session in Boston of the National Educational Association, in February, 1893, Mr. Houghton and other publishers gave a reception for the purpose of introducing resident authors to the members of the association. It was on this occasion, February 23, 1893, that Dr. Holmes read the following verses.]

TEACHERS of teachers ! Yours the task,
Noblest that noble minds can ask,
High up Aonia's murmurous mount,
To watch, to guard the sacred fount
  That feeds the streams below;
To guide the hurrying flood that fills
A thousand silvery rippling rills
  In ever-widening flow.

Rich is the harvest from the fields
That bounteous Nature kindly yields,
But fairer growths enrich the soil
Ploughed deep by thought's unwearied toil
  In Learning's broad domain.
And where the leaves, the flowers, the
    fruits,
Without your watering at the roots,
  To fill each branching vein ?

Welcome ! the Author's firmest friends,
Your voice the surest Godspeed lends.
Of you the growing mind demands
The patient care, the guiding hands,
  Through all the mists of morn.
And knowing well the future's need,
Your prescient wisdom sows the seed
  To flower in years unborn.

HYMN

WRITTEN FOR THE TWENTY-FIFTH ANNI-
VERSARY OF THE REORGANIZATION OF
THE BOSTON YOUNG MEN'S CHRISTIAN
UNION, MAY 31, 1893

TUNE, " DUNDEE "

OUR Father ! while our hearts unlearn
  The creeds that wrong thy name,
Still let our hallowed altars burn
  With Faith's undying flame !

Not by the lightning-gleams of wrath
  Our souls thy face shall see,

The star of Love must light the path
  That leads to Heaven and Thee.

Help us to read our Master's will
  Through every darkening stain
That clouds his sacred image still,
  And see Him once again,

The brother man, the pitying friend
  Who weeps for human woes,
Whose pleading words of pardon blend
  With cries of raging foes.

If 'mid the gathering storms of doubt,
  Our hearts grow faint and cold,
The strength we cannot live without
  Thy love will not withhold.

Our prayers accept; our sins forgive;
  Our youthful zeal renew;
Shape for us holier lives to live,
  And nobler work to do !

FRANCIS PARKMAN

SEPTEMBER 16, 1823 — NOVEMBER 8, 1893

Read at the memorial meeting of the Massachusetts Historical Society.

HE rests from toil; the portals of the
    tomb
  Close on the last of those unwearying
    hands
That wove their pictured webs in His-
    tory's loom,
  Rich with the memories of three mighty
    lands.

One wrought the record of the Royal Pair
  Who saw the great Discoverer's sail un-
    furled,
Happy his more than regal prize to share,
  The spoils, the wonders, of the sunset
    world.

There, too, he found his theme; upreared
    anew,
  Our eyes beheld the vanished Aztec
    shrines,
And all the silver splendors of Peru
  That lured the conqueror to her fatal
    mines.

Nor less remembered he who told the tale
  Of empire wrested from the strangling
    sea;
Of Leyden's woe, that turned his readers
    pale,
  The price of unborn freedom yet to be;

Who taught the New World what the Old
    could teach;
  Whose silent hero, peerless as our
    own,
By deeds that mocked the feeble breath of
    speech
  Called up to life a State without a
    Throne.

As year by year his tapestry unrolled,
  What varied wealth its growing length
    displayed !
What long processions flamed in cloth of
    gold !
  What stately forms their flowing robes
    arrayed !

Not such the scenes our later craftsman
    drew;
  Not such the shapes his darker pattern
    held;
A deeper shadow lent its sober hue,
  A sadder tale his tragic task compelled.

He told the red man's story; far and wide
  He searched the unwritten annals of his
    race;
He sat a listener at the Sachem's side,
  He tracked the hunter through his wild-
    wood chase.

High o'er his head the soaring eagle
    screamed;
  The wolf's long howl rang nightly;
    through the vale

Tramped the lone bear; the panther's eye-
    balls gleamed;
  The bison's gallop thundered on the gale.

Soon o'er the horizon rose the cloud of
    strife, —
  Two proud, strong nations battling for
    the prize, —
Which swarming host should mould a na-
    tion's life,
  Which royal banner float the western
    skies.

Long raged the conflict; on the crimson sod
  Native and alien joined their hosts in
    vain;
The lilies withered where the Lion trod,
  Till Peace lay panting on the ravaged
    plain.

A nobler task was theirs who strove to win
  The blood-stained heathen to the Chris-
    tian fold,
To free from Satan's clutch the slaves of
    sin;
  Their labors, too, with loving grace he
    told.

Halting with feeble step, or bending o'er
  The sweet-breathed roses which he loved
    so well,
While through long years his burdening
    cross he bore,
  From those firm lips no coward accents
    fell.

A brave, bright memory ! his the stainless
    shield
  No shame defaces and no envy mars !
When our far future's record is unsealed,
  His name will shine among its morning
    stars.

POEMS FROM OVER THE TEACUPS

TO THE ELEVEN LADIES

WHO PRESENTED ME WITH A SILVER
LOVING CUP ON THE TWENTY-NINTH
OF AUGUST, M DCCC LXXXIX

"WHO gave this cup?"   The secret thou
　　wouldst steal
Its brimming flood forbids it to reveal:
No mortal's eye shall read it till he first
　　Cool the red throat of thirst.

If on the golden floor one draught remain,
Trust me, thy careful search will be in
　　vain;
Not till the bowl is emptied shalt thou
　　know
　　The names enrolled below.

Deeper than Truth lies buried in her well
Those modest names the graven letters spell
Hide from the sight; but wait, and thou
　　shalt see
　　Who the good angels be

Whose bounty glistens in the beauteous gift
That friendly hands to loving lips shall
　　lift:
Turn the fair goblet when its floor is dry, —
　　Their names shall meet thine eye.

Count thou their number on the beads of
　　Heaven:
Alas! the clustered Pleiads are but seven;
Nay, the nine sister Muses are too few, —
　　The Graces must add two.

"For whom this gift?"   For one who all
　　too long
Clings to his bough among the groves of
　　song;
Autumn's last leaf, that spreads its faded
　　wing
　　To greet a second spring.

Dear friends, kind friends, whate'er the
　　cup may hold,
Bathing its burnished depths, will change
　　to gold:
Its last bright drop let thirsty Mænads
　　drain,
　　Its fragrance will remain.

Better love's perfume in the empty bowl
Then wine's nepenthe for the aching soul ;
Sweeter than song that ever poet sung,
　　It makes an old heart young !

THE PEAU DE CHAGRIN OF STATE STREET

How beauteous is the bond
In the manifold array
Of its promises to pay,
While the eight per cent it gives
And the rate at which one lives
　　Correspond !

But at last the bough is bare
Where the coupons one by one
Through their ripening days have run,
And the bond, a beggar now,
Seeks investment anyhow,
　　Anywhere !

CACOETHES SCRIBENDI

IF all the trees in all the woods were men;
And each and every blade of grass a pen;
If every leaf on every shrub and tree
Turned to a sheet of foolscap ; every sea
Were changed to ink, and all earth's living
　　tribes
Had nothing else to do but act as scribes,
And for ten thousand ages, day and night,
The human race should write, and write,
　　and write,

Till all the pens and paper were used up,
And the huge inkstand was an empty cup,
Still would the scribblers clustered round
its brink
Call for more pens, more paper, and more
ink.

THE ROSE AND THE FERN

LADY, life's sweetest lesson wouldst thou
learn,
Come thou with me to Love's enchanted
bower:
High overhead the trellised roses burn;
Beneath thy feet behold the feathery
fern, —
A leaf without a flower.

What though the rose leaves fall? They
still are sweet,
And have been lovely in their beauteous
prime,
While the bare frond seems ever to re-
peat,
" For us no bud, no blossom, wakes to greet
The joyous flowering time ! "

Heed thou the lesson. Life has leaves to
tread
And flowers to cherish; summer round
thee glows ;
Wait not till autumn's fading robes are
shed,
But while its petals still are burning red
Gather life's full-blown rose !

I LIKE YOU AND I LOVE YOU

I LIKE YOU met I LOVE YOU, face to face;
The path was narrow, and they could not
pass.
I LIKE YOU smiled; I LOVE YOU cried,
Alas !
And so they halted for a little space.

"Turn thou and go before," I LOVE YOU
said,
" Down the green pathway, bright with
many a flower;
Deep in the valley, lo ! my bridal bower
Awaits thee." But I LIKE YOU shook his
head.

Then while they lingered on the span-wide
shelf
That shaped a pathway round the rocky
ledge,
I LIKE YOU bared his icy dagger's edge,
And first he slew I LOVE YOU, — then him-
self.

LA MAISON D'OR

(BAR HARBOR)

FROM this fair home behold on either side
The restful mountains or the restless sea:
So the warm sheltering walls of life divide
Time and its tides from still eternity.

Look on the waves: their stormy voices
teach
That not on earth may toil and struggle
cease.
Look on the mountains: better far than
speech
Their silent promise of eternal peace.

TOO YOUNG FOR LOVE

Too young for love ?
Ah, say not so !
Tell reddening rosebuds not to blow !
Wait not for spring to pass away, —
Love's summer months begin with May !
Too young for love ?
Ah, say not so !
Too young ? Too young ?
Ah, no ! no ! no !

Too young for love ?
Ah, say not so,
While daisies bloom and tulips glow !
June soon will come with lengthened day
To practise all love learned in May.
Too young for love ?
Ah, say not so !
Too young ? Too young ?
Ah, no ! no ! no !

THE BROOMSTICK TRAIN ; OR, THE RETURN OF THE WITCHES

If there are any anachronisms or other inac-
curacies in this story, the reader will please to
remember that the narrator's memory is liable
to be at fault, and if the event recorded inter-

ests him, will not worry over any little slips or stumbles.

The terrible witchcraft drama of 1692 has been seriously treated, as it well deserves to be. The story has been told in two large volumes by the Rev. Charles Wentworth Upham, and in a small and more succinct volume, based upon his work, by his daughter-in-law, Caroline E. Upham.

The delusion, commonly spoken of as if it belonged to Salem, was more widely diffused through the towns of Essex County. Looking upon it as a pitiful and long dead and buried superstition, I trust my poem will no more offend the good people of Essex County than Tam O'Shanter worries the honest folk of Ayrshire.

The localities referred to are those with which I am familiar in my drives about Essex County.

LOOK out ! Look out, boys ! Clear the
　　track !
The witches are here ! They 've all come
　　back !
They hanged them high, — No use ! No
　　use !
What cares a witch for a hangman's noose ?
They buried them deep, but they would n't
　　lie still,
For cats and witches are hard to kill;
They swore they should n't and would n't
　　die, —
Books said they did, but they lie ! they lie !

A couple of hundred years, or so,
They had knocked about in the world below,
When an Essex Deacon dropped in to call,
And a homesick feeling seized them all;
For he came from a place they knew full
　　well,
And many a tale he had to tell.
They longed to visit the haunts of men,
To see the old dwellings they knew again,
And ride on their broomsticks all around
Their wide domain of unhallowed ground.

In Essex county there 's many a roof
Well known to him of the cloven hoof;
The small square windows are full in view
Which the midnight hags went sailing
　　through,
On their well-trained broomsticks mounted
　　high,
Seen like shadows against the sky;
Crossing the track of owls and bats,
Hugging before them their coal-black cats.

Well did they know, those gray old wives,
The sights we see in our daily drives:
Shimmer of lake and shine of sea,
Browne's bare hill with its lonely tree,
(It was n't then as we see it now,
With one scant scalp-lock to shade its
　　brow;)
Dusky nooks in the Essex woods,
Dark, dim, Dante-like solitudes,
Where the tree-toad watches the sinuous
　　snake
Glide through his forests of fern and
　　brake;
Ipswich River; its old stone bridge;
Far off Andover's Indian Ridge,
And many a scene where history tells
Some shadow of bygone terror dwells, —
Of " Norman's Woe " with its tale of
　　dread,
Of the Screeching Woman of Marblehead,
(The fearful story that turns men pale:
Don't bid me tell it, — my speech would
　　fail.)

Who would not, will not, if he can,
Bathe in the breezes of fair Cape Ann, —
Rest in the bowers her bays enfold,
Loved by the sachems and squaws of old ?
Home where the white magnolias bloom,
Sweet with the bayberry's chaste perfume,
Hugged by the woods and kissed by the
　　sea !
Where is the Eden like to thee ?
For that " couple of hundred years, or
　　so,"
There had been no peace in the world be-
　　low;
The witches still grumbling, " It is n't
　　fair !
Come, give us a taste of the upper air !
We 've had enough of your sulphur springs,
And the evil odor that round them clings;
We long for a drink that is cool and
　　nice, —
Great buckets of water with Wenham ice;
We 've served you well up-stairs, you
　　know;
You 're a good old — fellow — come, let us
　　go ! ' "

I don't feel sure of his being good,
But he happened to be in a pleasant
　　mood, —
As fiends with their skins full sometimes
　　are, —

(He 'd been drinking with "roughs" at a
Boston bar.)
So what does he do but up and shout
To a graybeard turnkey, "Let 'em out !"

To mind his orders was all he knew;
The gates swung open, and out they flew.
"Where are our broomsticks ?" the bel-
dams cried.
"Here are your broomsticks," an imp re-
plied.
"They 've been in — the place you know —
so long
They smell of brimstone uncommon strong;
But they 've gained by being left alone, —
Just look, and you 'll see how tall they 've
grown."
"And where is my cat ?" a vixen squalled.
"Yes, where are our cats ?" the witches
bawled,
And began to call them all by name:
As fast as they called the cats, they came:
There was bob-tailed Tommy and long-
tailed Tim,
And wall-eyed Jacky and green-eyed Jim,
And splay-foot Benny and slim-legged
Beau,
And Skinny and Squally, and Jerry and
Joe,
And many another that came at call, —
It would take too long to count them all.
All black, — one could hardly tell which
was which,
But every cat knew his own old witch;
And she knew hers as hers knew her, —
Ah, did n't they curl their tails and purr !

No sooner the withered hags were free
Than out they swarmed for a midnight
spree;
I could n't tell all they did in rhymes,
But the Essex people had dreadful times.
The Swampscott fishermen still relate
How a strange sea-monster stole their bait;
How their nets were tangled in loops and
knots,
And they found dead crabs in their lobster-
pots.
Poor Danvers grieved for her blasted crops,
And Wilmington mourned over mildewed
hops.
A blight played havoc with Beverly
beans, —
It was all the work of those hateful queans !
A dreadful panic began at "Pride's,"

Where the witches stopped in their mid-
night rides,
And there rose strange rumors and vague
alarms
'Mid the peaceful dwellers at Beverly
Farms.

Now when the Boss of the Beldams found
That without his leave they were ramping
round,
He called, — they could hear him twenty
miles,
From Chelsea beach to the Misery Isles;
The deafest old granny knew his tone
Without the trick of the telephone.
"Come here, you witches ! Come here !"
says he, —
"At your games of old, without asking
me !
I 'll give you a little job to do
That will keep you stirring, you godless
crew !"

They came, of course, at their master's call,
The witches, the broomsticks, the cats, and
all;
He led the hags to a railway train
The horses were trying to drag in vain.
"Now, then," says he, "you 've had your
fun,
And here are the cars you 've got to run.
The driver may just unhitch his team,
We don't want horses, we don't want
steam;
You may keep your old black cats to hug,
But the loaded train you 've got to lug."

Since then on many a car you 'll see
A broomstick plain as plain can be;
On every stick there 's a witch astride, —
The string you see to her leg is tied.
She will do a mischief if she can,
But the string is held by a careful man,
And whenever the evil-minded witch
Would cut some caper, he gives a twitch.
As for the hag, you can't see her,
But hark ! you can hear her black cat's
purr,
And now and then, as a car goes by,
You may catch a gleam from her wicked
eye.
Often you 've looked on a rushing train,
But just what moved it was not so plain.
It could n't be those wires above,
For they could neither pull nor shove;

Where was the motor that made it go
You could n't guess, *but now you know.*

Remember my rhymes when you ride again
On the rattling rail by the broomstick
    train !

TARTARUS

WHILE in my simple gospel creed
That " God is Love " so plain I read,
Shall dreams of heathen birth affright
My pathway through the coming night ?
Ah, Lord of life, though spectres pale
Fill with their threats the shadowy vale,
With Thee my faltering steps to aid,
How can I dare to be afraid ?

Shall mouldering page or fading scroll
Outface the charter of the soul ?
Shall priesthood's palsied arm protect
The wrong our human hearts reject,
And smite the lips whose shuddering cry
Proclaims a cruel creed a lie ?
The wizard's rope we disallow
Was justice once, — is murder now !

Is there a world of blank despair,
And dwells the Omnipresent there ?
Does He behold with smile serene
The shows of that unending scene,
Where sleepless, hopeless anguish lies,
And, ever dying, never dies ?
Say, does He hear the sufferer's groan,
And is that child of wrath his own ?

O mortal, wavering in thy trust,
Lift thy pale forehead from the dust !
The mists that cloud thy darkened eyes
Fade ere they reach the o'erarching skies !
When the blind heralds of despair
Would bid thee doubt a Father's care,
Look up from earth, and read above
On heaven's blue tablet, GOD IS LOVE !

AT THE TURN OF THE ROAD

THE glory has passed from the goldenrod's
    plume,
The purple-hued asters still linger in
    bloom:
The birch is bright yellow, the sumachs
    are red,
The maples like torches aflame overhead.

But what if the joy of the summer is past,
And winter's wild herald is blowing his
    blast ?
For me dull November is sweeter than
    May,
For my love is its sunshine, — she meets
    me to-day !

Will she come ? Will the ring-dove re-
    turn to her nest ?
Will the needle swing back from the east
    or the west ?
At the stroke of the hour she will be at her
    gate;
A friend may prove laggard, — love never
    comes late.

Do I see her afar in the distance ? Not
    yet.
Too early ! Too early ! She could not
    forget !
When I cross the old bridge where the
    brook overflowed,
She will flash full in sight at the turn of
    the road.

I pass the low wall where the ivy entwines;
I tread the brown pathway that leads
    through the pines;
I haste by the boulder that lies in the field,
Where her promise at parting was lovingly
    sealed.

Will she come by the hillside or round
    through the wood ?
Will she wear her brown dress or her
    mantle and hood ?
The minute draws near, — but her watch
    may go wrong;
My heart *will* be asking, What keeps her so
    long ?

Why doubt for a moment ? More shame
    if I do !
Why question ? Why tremble ? Are an-
    gels more true ?
She would come to the lover who calls her
    his own
Though she trod in the track of a whirling
    cyclone !

I crossed the old bridge ere the minute had
    passed.
I looked: lo ! my Love stood before me at
    last.

Her eyes, how they sparkled, her cheeks,
    how they glowed,
As we met, face to face, at the turn of the
    road !

INVITÂ MINERVÂ

I find the burden and restrictions of rhyme more and more troublesome as I grow older. There are times when it seems natural enough to employ that form of expression, but it is only occasionally; and the use of it as a vehicle of the commonplace is so prevalent that one is not much tempted to select it as the medium for his thoughts and emotions. The art of rhyming has almost become a part of a high-school education, and its practice is far from being an evidence of intellectual distinction. Mediocrity is as much forbidden to the poet in our days as it was in those of Horace, and the immense majority of the verses written are stamped with hopeless mediocrity.

When one of the ancient poets found he was trying to grind out verses which came unwillingly, he said he was writing *Invitâ Minervâ*.

Vex not the Muse with idle prayers, —
    She will not hear thy call;
She steals upon thee unawares,
    Or seeks thee not at all.

Soft as the moonbeams when they sought
    Endymion's fragrant bower,
She parts the whispering leaves of thought
    To show her full-blown flower.

For thee her wooing hour has passed,
    The singing birds have flown,
And winter comes with icy blast
    To chill thy buds unblown.

Yet, though the woods no longer thrill
    As once their arches rung,
Sweet echoes hover round thee still
    Of songs thy summer sung.

Live in thy past; await no more
    The rush of heaven-sent wings;
Earth still has music left in store
    While Memory sighs and sings.

READINGS OVER THE TEACUPS

FIVE STORIES AND A SEQUEL

[IN his volume, *Songs in Many Keys*, Dr. Holmes had a division, *Pictures from Occasional Poems*. He discarded his sub-title in the River-side Edition, but took from the group under that title five stories and reproduced them in a new setting under the above title.]

TO MY OLD READERS

YOU know " The Teacups," that congenial set
Which round the Teapot you have often met;
The grave DICTATOR, him you knew of old, —
Knew as the shepherd of another fold:
Grayer he looks, less youthful, but the same
As when you called him by a different name.
   Near him the MISTRESS, whose experienced skill
Has taught her duly every cup to fill;
" Weak; " " strong; " " cool; " " lukewarm; " " hot as you can pour; "
" No sweetening ; " " sugared; " " two lumps; " " one lump more."
   Next, the PROFESSOR, whose scholastic phrase
At every turn the teacher's tongue betrays,
Trying so hard to make his speech precise
The captious listener finds it overnice.
   Nor be forgotten our ANNEXES twain,
Nor HE, the owner of the squinting brain,
Which, while its curious fancies we pursue,
Oft makes us question, " Are we crackbrained too ? "
   Along the board our growing list extends,
As one by one we count our clustering friends, —
The youthful DOCTOR waiting for his share
Of fits and fevers when his crown gets bare;
In strong, dark lines our square-nibbed pen should draw
The lordly presence of the MAN OF LAW;
Our bashful TUTOR claims a humbler place,
A lighter touch, his slender form to trace.
Mark the fair lady he is seated by, —
Some say he is her lover, — some deny, —
Watch them together, — time alone can show
If dead-ripe friendship turns to love or no.
Where in my list of phrases shall I seek
The fitting words of NUMBER FIVE to speak ?
Such task demands a readier pen than mine, —
What if I steal the Tutor's Valentine ?
   Why should I call her gracious, winning, fair ?
Why with the loveliest of her sex compare ?
Those varied charms have many a Muse inspired, —
At last their worn superlatives have tired;
Wit, beauty, sweetness, each alluring grace,
All these in honeyed verse have found their place ;
I need them not, — two little words I find
Which hold them all in happiest form combined ;
No more with baffled language will I strive, —
All in one breath I utter: Number Five !
   Now count our teaspoons — if you care to learn
How many tinkling cups were served in turn, —
Add all together, you will find them ten, —
Our young MUSICIAN joined us now and then.

Our bright DELILAH you must needs re-
call,
The comely handmaid, youngest of us all;
Need I remind you how the little maid
Came at a pinch to our Professor's aid, —
Trimmed his long locks with unrelenting
shears
And eased his looks of half a score of
years ?

Sometimes, at table, as you well must
know,
The stream of talk will all at once run low,
The air seems smitten with a sudden chill,
The wit grows silent and the gossip still;
This was our poet's chance, the hour of
need,
When rhymes and stories we were used to
read.
  One day a whisper round the teacups
stole, —
" No scrap of paper in the silver bowl ! "
(Our " poet's corner " may I not expect
My kindly reader still may recollect ?)
  " What ! not a line to keep our souls
alive ? "
Spoke in her silvery accents Number Five.
"No matter, something we must find to
read, —
Find it or make it, — yes, we must in-
deed !
Now I remember I have seen at times
Some curious stories in a book of rhymes, —
How certain secrets, long in silence sealed,
In after days were guessed at or revealed.
Those stories, doubtless, some of you must
know, —
They all were written many a year ago;
But an old story, be it false or true,
Twice told, well told, is twice as good as
new;
Wait but three sips and I will go myself,
And fetch the book of verses from its
shelf."
  No time was lost in finding what she
sought, —
Gone but one moment, — lo ! the book is
brought.
  "Now, then, Professor, fortune has de-
creed
That you, this evening, shall be first to
read, —
Lucky for us that listen, for in fact
Who reads this poem must know how to
act."

Right well she knew that in his greener
age
He had a mighty hankering for the stage.
The patient audience had not long to wait;
Pleased with his chance, he smiled and
took the bait;
Through his wild hair his coaxing fingers
ran, —
He spread the page before him and began.

THE BANKER'S SECRET

[When first published this bore the title *The
Banker's Dinner.*]

THE Banker's dinner is the stateliest
feast
The town has heard of for a year, at least;
The sparry lustres shed their broadest
blaze,
Damask and silver catch and spread the
rays;
The florist's triumphs crown the daintier
spoil
Won from the sea, the forest, or the soil;
The steaming hot-house yields its largest
pines,
The sunless vaults unearth their oldest
wines;
With one admiring look the scene survey,
And turn a moment from the bright dis-
play.

  Of all the joys of earthly pride or power,
What gives most life, worth living, in an
hour ?
When Victory settles on the doubtful
fight
And the last foeman wheels in panting
flight,
No thrill like this is felt beneath the sun;
Life's sovereign moment is a battle won.
  But say what next ? To shape a Senate's
choice,
By the strong magic of the master's voice;
To ride the stormy tempest of debate
That whirls the wavering fortunes of the
state.
  Third in the list, the happy lover's prize
Is won by honeyed words from women's
eyes.
If some would have it first instead of third,
So let it be, — I answer not a word.

The fourth, — sweet readers, let the
    thoughtless half
Have its small shrug and inoffensive
    laugh;
Let the grave quarter wear its virtuous
    frown,
The stern half-quarter try to scowl us
    down;
But the last eighth, the choice and sifted
    few,
Will hear my words, and, pleased, confess
    them true.

    Among the great whom Heaven has
        made to shine,
How few have learned the art of arts, —
    to dine !
Nature, indulgent to our daily need,
Kind-hearted mother ! taught us all to
    feed;
But the chief art, — how rarely Nature
    flings
This choicest gift among her social kings !
Say, man of truth, has life a brighter hour
Than waits the chosen guest who knows
    his power ?
    He moves with ease, itself an angel
        charm, —
Lifts with light touch my lady's jewelled
    arm,
Slides to his seat, half leading and half led,
Smiling but quiet till the grace is said,
Then gently kindles, while by slow degrees
Creep softly out the little arts that please;
Bright looks, the cheerful language of the
    eye,
The neat, crisp question and the gay
    reply, —
Talk light and airy, such as well may pass
Between the rested fork and lifted glass; —
With play like this the earlier evening flies,
Till rustling silks proclaim the ladies rise.
    His hour has come, — he looks along
        the chairs,
As the Great Duke surveyed his iron
    squares.
That 's the young traveller, — is n't much
    to show, —
Fast on the road, but at the table slow.
Next him, — you see the author in his
    look, —
His forehead lined with wrinkles like a
    book, —
Wrote the great history of the ancient
    Huns, —

Holds back to fire among the heavy guns.
Oh, there 's our poet seated at his side,
Beloved of ladies, soft, cerulean-eyed.
Poets are prosy in their common talk,
As the fast trotters, for the most part,
    walk.
And there 's our well-dressed gentleman,
    who sits,
By right divine, no doubt, among the wits,
Who airs his tailor's patterns when he
    walks,
The man that often speaks, but never talks.
Why should he talk, whose presence lends
    a grace
To every table where he shows his face ?
He knows the manual of the silver fork,
Can name his claret — if he sees the cork, —
Remark that " White-top " was considered
    fine,
But swear the " Juno " is the better wine; —
Is not this talking ? Ask Quintilian's rules;
If they say No, the town has many fools.
Pause for a moment, — for our eyes behold
The plain unsceptred king, the man of gold,
The thrice illustrious threefold million-
    naire;
Mark his slow-creeping, dead, metallic
    stare;
His eyes, dull glimmering, like the balance-
    pan
That weighs its guinea as he weighs his
    man.
Who 's next ? An artist in a satin tie
Whose ample folds defeat the curious eye.
And there 's the cousin, — must be asked,
    you know, —
Looks like a spinster at a baby-show.
Hope he is cool, — they set him next the
    door, —
And likes his place, between the gap and
    bore.
Next comes a Congressman, distinguished
    guest !
We don't count him, — they asked him
    with the rest;
And then some white cravats, with well-
    shaped ties,
And heads above them which their owners
    prize.

    Of all that cluster round the genial
        board,
Not one so radiant as the banquet's lord.
Some say they fancy, but they know not
    why,

A shade of trouble brooding in his eye,
Nothing, perhaps, — the rooms are over-
hot, —
Yet see his cheek, — the dull-red burning
spot, —
Taste the brown sherry which he does not
pass, —
Ha ! That is brandy; see him fill his glass !
But not forgetful of his feasting friends,
To each in turn some lively word he sends;
See how he throws his baited lines about,
And plays his men as anglers play their
trout.

With the dry sticks all bonfires are be-
gun;
Bring the first fagot, proser number one !
A question drops among the listening crew
And hits the traveller, pat on Timbuctoo.
We're on the Niger, somewhere near its
source, —
Not the least hurry, take the river's course
Through Kissi, Foota, Kankan, Bammakoo,
Bambarra, Sego, so to Timbuctoo,
Thence down to Youri; — stop him if we
can,
We can't fare worse, — wake up the Con-
gressman !
The Congressman, once on his talking legs,
Stirs up his knowledge to its thickest dregs;
Tremendous draught for dining men to
quaff !
Nothing will choke him but a purpling
laugh.
A word, — a shout, — a mighty roar, — 't is
done;
Extinguished; lassoed by a treacherous pun.
A laugh is priming to the loaded soul;
The scattering shots become a steady roll,
Broke by sharp cracks that run along the
line,
The light artillery of the talker's wine.
The kindling goblets flame with golden
dews,
The hoarded flasks their tawny fire diffuse,
And the Rhine's breast-milk gushes cold
and bright,
Pale as the moon and maddening as her
light;
With crimson juice the thirsty southern sky
Sucks from the hills where buried armies
lie,
So that the dreamy passion it imparts
Is drawn from heroes' bones and lovers'
hearts.

But lulls will come; the flashing soul
transmits
Its gleams of light in alternating fits.
The shower of talk that rattled down amain
Ends in small patterings like an April's
rain;
The voices halt; the game is at a stand;
Now for a solo from the master-hand !
'T is but a story, — quite a simple
thing, —
An *aria* touched upon a single string,
But every accent comes with such a grace
The stupid servants listen in their place,
Each with his waiter in his lifted hands,
Still as a well-bred pointer when he stands.
A query checks him: " Is he quite exact ? "
(This from a grizzled, square-jawed man
of fact.)
The sparkling story leaves him to his fate,
Crushed by a witness, smothered with a
date,
As a swift river, sown with many a star,
Runs brighter, rippling on a shallow bar.
The smooth divine suggests a graver doubt;
A neat quotation bowls the parson out;
Then, sliding gayly from his own display,
He laughs the learned dulness all away.
So, with the merry tale and jovial song,
The jocund evening whirls itself along,
Till the last chorus shrieks its loud *encore*,
And the white neckcloths vanish through
the door.

One savage word ! — The menials know
its tone,
And slink away; the master stands alone.
" Well played, by —— ;" breathe not what
were best unheard;
His goblet shivers while he speaks the
word, —
" If wine tells truth, — and so have said
the wise, —
It makes me laugh to think how brandy
lies !
Bankrupt to - morrow, — millionnaire to-
day, —
The farce is over, — now begins the play ! "
The spring he touches lets a panel glide;
An iron closet lurks beneath the slide,
Bright with such treasures as a search
might bring
From the deep pockets of a truant king.
Two diamonds, eyeballs of a god of bronze,
Bought from his faithful priest, a pious
bonze,

A string of brilliants; rubies, three or four;
Bags of old coin and bars of virgin ore;
A jewelled poniard and a Turkish knife,
Noiseless and useful if we come to strife.
  Gone ! As a pirate flies before the wind,
And not one tear for all he leaves behind !
From all the love his better years have
    known
Fled like a felon, — ah ! but not alone !
The chariot flashes through a lantern's
    glare, —
Oh the wild eyes ! the storm of sable hair !
Still to his side the broken heart will
    cling, —
The bride of shame, the wife without the
    ring:
Hark, the deep oath, — the wail of fren-
    zied woe, —
Lost ! lost to hope of Heaven and peace
    below !

He kept his secret; but the seed of crime
Bursts of itself in God's appointed time.
The lives he wrecked were scattered far
    and wide;
One never blamed nor wept, — she only
    died.
None knew his lot, though idle tongues
    would say
He sought a lonely refuge far away,
And there, with borrowed name and al-
    tered mien,
He died unheeded, as he lived unseen.
The moral market had the usual chills
Of Virtue suffering from protested bills;
The White Cravats, to friendship's mem-
    ory true,
Sighed for the past, surveyed the future
    too;
Their sorrow breathed in one expressive
    line, —
" Gave pleasant dinners; who has got his
    wine ? "

The reader paused, — the Teacups knew
    his ways, —
He, like the rest, was not averse to praise.
Voices and hands united; every one
Joined in approval : " Number Three, well
    done ! "

" Now for the Exile's story; if my wits
Are not at fault, his curious record fits
Neatly as sequel to the tale we 've heard;

Not wholly wild the fancy, nor absurd
That this our island hermit well might be
That story's hero, fled from over sea.
Come, Number Seven, we would not have
    you strain
The fertile powers of that inventive brain.
Read us ' The Exile's Secret; ' there 's
    enough
Of dream-like fiction and fantastic stuff
In the strange web of mystery that invests
The lonely isle where sea birds build their
    nests."

" Lies ! naught but lies ! " so Number
    Seven began, —
No harm was known of that secluded man.
He lived alone, — who would n't if he
    might,
And leave the rogues and idiots out of
    sight ?
A foolish story, — still, I 'll do my best, —
The house was real, — don't believe the
    rest.
How could a ruined dwelling last so long
Without its legends shaped in tale and
    song ?
Who was this man of whom they tell the
    lies ?
Perhaps — why not ? — NAPOLEON ! in dis-
    guise, —
So some said, kidnapped from his ocean
    coop,
Brought to this island in a coasting sloop, —
Meanwhile a sham Napoleon in his place
Played Nap. and saved Sir Hudson from
    disgrace.
Such was one story; others used to say,
" No, — not Napoleon, — it was Marshal
    Ney."
" Shot ? " Yes, no doubt, but not with balls
    of lead,
But balls of pith that never shoot folks
    dead.
He wandered round, lived South for many
    a year,
At last came North and fixed his dwelling
    here.
Choose which you will of all the tales that
    pile
Their mingling fables on the tree-crowned
    isle.
  Who wrote this modest version I suppose
That truthful Teacup, our Dictator, knows;
Made up of various legends, it would seem,
The sailor's yarn, the crazy poet's dream.

Such tales as this, by simple souls received,
At first are stared at and at last believed;
From threads like this the grave historians try
To weave their webs, and never know they lie.
Hear, then, the fables that have gathered round
The lonely home an exiled stranger found.

THE EXILE'S SECRET

[Originally entitled *The Island Ruin*.]

YE that have faced the billows and the spray
Of good St. Botolph's island-studded bay,
As from the gliding bark your eye has scanned
The beaconed rocks, the wave-girt hills of sand,
Have ye not marked one elm-o'ershadowed isle,
Round as the dimple chased in beauty's smile, —
A stain of verdure on an azure field,
Set like a jewel in a battered shield?
Fixed in the narrow gorge of Ocean's path,
Peaceful it meets him in his hour of wrath;
When the mailed Titan, scourged by hissing gales,
Writhes in his glistening coat of clashing scales,
The storm-beat island spreads its tranquil green,
Calm as an emerald on an angry queen.
So fair when distant should be fairer near;
A boat shall waft us from the outstretched pier.
The breeze blows fresh; we reach the island's edge,
Our shallop rustling through the yielding sedge.
No welcome greets us on the desert isle;
Those elms, far-shadowing, hide no stately pile:
Yet these green ridges mark an ancient road;
And lo! the traces of a fair abode;
The long gray line that marks a garden-wall,
And heaps of fallen beams, — fire-branded all.

Who sees unmoved, a ruin at his feet,
The lowliest home where human hearts have beat?
Its hearthstone, shaded with the bistre stain
A century's showery torrents wash in vain;
Its starving orchard, where the thistle blows
And mossy trunks still mark the broken rows;
Its chimney-loving poplar, oftenest seen
Next an old roof, or where a roof has been;
Its knot-grass, plantain, — all the social weeds,
Man's mute companions, following where he leads;
Its dwarfed, pale flowers, that show their straggling heads,
Sown by the wind from grass-choked garden-beds;
Its woodbine, creeping where it used to climb;
Its roses, breathing of the olden time;
All the poor shows the curious idler sees,
As life's thin shadows waste by slow degrees,
Till naught remains, the saddening tale to tell,
Save home's last wrecks, — the cellar and the well?

And whose the home that strews in black decay
The one green-glowing island of the bay?
Some dark-browed pirate's, jealous of the fate
That seized the strangled wretch of " Nix's Mate"?
Some forger's, skulking in a borrowed name,
Whom Tyburn's dangling halter yet may claim?
Some wan-eyed exile's, wealth and sorrow's heir,
Who sought a lone retreat for tears and prayer?
Some brooding poet's, sure of deathless fame,
Had not his epic perished in the flame?
Or some gray wooer's, whom a girlish frown
Chased from his solid friends and sober town?
Or some plain tradesman's, fond of shade and ease,
Who sought them both beneath these quiet trees?

Why question mutes no question can un-
  lock,
Dumb as the legend on the Dighton rock?
One thing at least these ruined heaps de-
  clare, —
They were a shelter once; a man lived
  there.

  But where the charred and crumbling
    records fail,
Some breathing lips may piece the half-
  told tale;
No man may live with neighbors such as
  these,
Though girt with walls of rock and angry
  seas,
And shield his home, his children, or his
  wife,
His ways, his means, his vote, his creed,
  his life,
From the dread sovereignty of Ears and
  Eyes
And the small member that beneath them
  lies.
  They told strange things of that myste-
    rious man;
Believe who will, deny them such as can;
Why should we fret if every passing sail
Had its old seaman talking on the rail?
The deep-sunk schooner stuffed with
  Eastern lime,
Slow wedging on, as if the waves were
  slime;
The knife-edged clipper with her ruffled
  spars,
The pawing steamer with her mane of
  stars,
The bull-browed galliot butting through
  the stream,
The wide-sailed yacht that slipped along
  her beam,
The deck-piled sloops, the pinched chebacco-
  boats,
The frigate, black with thunder-freighted
  throats,
All had their talk about the lonely man;
And thus, in varying phrase, the story ran.
  His name had cost him little care to
    seek,
Plain, honest, brief, a decent name to
  speak,
Common, not vulgar, just the kind that
  slips
With least suggestion from a stranger's
  lips.

His birthplace England, as his speech
  might show,
Or his hale cheek, that wore the red-
  streak's glow;
His mouth sharp-moulded; in its mirth or
  scorn
There came a flash as from the milky corn,
When from the ear you rip the rustling
  sheath,
And the white ridges show their even teeth.
His stature moderate, but his strength con-
  fessed,
In spite of broadcloth, by his ample breast;
Full-armed, thick-handed; one that had
  been strong,
And might be dangerous still, if things
  went wrong.
He lived at ease beneath his elm-trees'
  shade,
Did naught for gain, yet all his debts were
  paid;
Rich, so 't was thought, but careful of his
  store;
Had all he needed, claimed to have no more.

  But some that lingered round the isle at
    night
Spoke of strange stealthy doings in their
  sight;
Of creeping lonely visits that he made
To nooks and corners, with a torch and
  spade.
Some said they saw the hollow of a cave;
One, given to fables, swore it was a grave;
Whereat some shuddered, others boldly
  cried,
Those prowling boatmen lied, and knew
  they lied.
  They said his house was framed with
    curious cares,
Lest some old friend might enter unawares;
That on the platform at his chamber's door
Hinged a loose square that opened through
  the floor;
Touch the black silken tassel next the bell,
Down, with a crash, the flapping trap-door
  fell;
Three stories deep the falling wretch would
  strike,
To writhe at leisure on a boarder's pike.
  By day armed always; double-armed at
    night,
His tools lay round him; wake him such
  as might.
A carbine hung beside his India fan,

His hand could reach a Turkish ataghan;
Pistols, with quaint-carved stocks and bar-
  rels gilt,
Crossed a long dagger with a jewelled hilt;
A slashing cutlass stretched along the
  bed; —
All this was what those lying boatmen said.
  Then some were full of wondrous stories
    told
Of great oak chests and cupboards full of
    gold;
Of the wedged ingots and the silver bars
That cost old pirates ugly sabre-scars;
How his laced wallet often would disgorge
The fresh-faced guinea of an English
    George,
Or sweated ducat, palmed by Jews of yore,
Or double Joe, or Portuguese moidore;
And how his finger wore a rubied ring
Fit for the white-necked play-girl of a king.
But these fine legends, told with staring
    eyes,
Met with small credence from the old and
    wise.

  Why tell each idle guess, each whisper
    vain ?
Enough: the scorched and cindered beams
    remain.
He came, a silent pilgrim to the West,
Some old-world mystery throbbing in his
    breast;
Close to the thronging mart he dwelt alone;
He lived ; he died.   The rest is all un-
    known.

  Stranger, whose eyes the shadowy isle
    survey,
As the black steamer dashes through the
    bay,
Why ask his buried secret to divine ?
He was thy brother; speak, and tell us
    thine !

  Silence at first, a kind of spell-bound
    pause;
Then all the Teacups tinkled their applause;
When that was hushed no sound the still-
    ness broke
Till once again the soft-voiced lady spoke:

  "The Lover's Secret, — surely that must
    need
The youngest voice our table holds to read.

Which of our two 'Annexes' shall we
    choose ?
Either were charming, neither will refuse;
But choose we must, — what better can we
    do
Than take the younger of the youthful
    two ? "
  True to the primal instinct of her sex,
" Why, that means me," half whispered
    each Annex.
" What if it does ? " the voiceless question
    came,
That set those pale New England cheeks
    aflame;
" Our old-world scholar may have ways to
    teach
Of Oxford English, Britain's purest
    speech, —
She shall be youngest, — youngest *for to-
    day*, —
Our dates we 'll fix hereafter as we may;
All rights reserved, — the words we know so
    well,
That guard the claims of books which never
    sell."
  The British maiden bowed a pleased as-
    sent,
Her two long ringlets swinging as she bent;
The glistening eyes her eager soul looked
    through
Betrayed her lineage in their Saxon blue.
Backward she flung each too obtrusive curl
And thus began, — the rose-lipped English
    girl.

THE LOVER'S SECRET

[When first published this poem was entitled
The Mysterious Illness.]

  WHAT ailed young Lucius ? Art had
    vainly tried
To guess his ill, and found herself defied.
The Augur plied his legendary skill;
Useless; the fair young Roman languished
    still.
His chariot took him every cloudless day
Along the Pincian Hill or Appian Way;
They rubbed his wasted limbs with sul-
    phurous oil,
Oozed from the far-off Orient's heated soil;
They led him tottering down the steamy
    path
Where bubbling fountains filled the ther-
    mal bath;

Borne in his litter to Egeria's cave,
They washed him, shivering, in her icy
　　wave.
They sought all curious herbs and costly
　　stones,
They scraped the moss that grew on dead
　　men's bones,
They tried all cures the votive tablets
　　taught,
Scoured every place whence healing drugs
　　were brought,
O'er Thracian hills his breathless couriers
　　ran,
His slaves waylaid the Syrian caravan.
　　At last a servant heard a stranger speak
A new chirurgeon's name; a clever Greek,
Skilled in his art; from Pergamus he came
To Rome but lately; GALEN was the name.
The Greek was called: a man with piercing
　　eyes,
Who must be cunning, and who might be
　　wise.
He spoke but little, — if they pleased, he
　　said,
He 'd wait awhile beside the sufferer's bed.
So by his side he sat, serene and calm,
His very accents soft as healing balm;
Not curious seemed, but every movement
　　spied,
His sharp eyes searching where they seemed
　　to glide;
Asked a few questions, — what he felt, and
　　where ?
" A pain just here," " A constant beating
　　there."
Who ordered bathing for his aches and
　　ails ?
" Charmis, the water-doctor from Mar-
　　seilles."
What was the last prescription in his case ?
" A draught of wine with powdered chryso-
　　prase."
Had he no secret grief he nursed alone ?
A pause ; a little tremor ; answer, —
　　" None."
　　Thoughtful, a moment, sat the cunning
　　leech,
And muttered " Eros ! " in his native
　　speech.
　　In the broad atrium various friends
　　await
The last new utterance from the lips of
　　fate;
Men, matrons, maids, they talk the ques-
　　tion o'er,

And, restless, pace the tessellated floor.
Not unobserved the youth so long had
　　pined
By gentle-hearted dames and damsels
　　kind;
One with the rest, a rich Patrician's pride,
The lady Hermia, called " the golden-
　　eyed; "
The same the old Proconsul fain must woo,
Whom, one dark night, a masked sicarius
　　slew;
The same black Crassus over roughly
　　pressed
To hear his suit, — the Tiber knows the
　　rest.
(Crassus was missed next morning by his
　　set;
Next week the fishers found him in their
　　net.)
She with the others paced the ample hall,
Fairest, alas ! and saddest of them all.
　　At length the Greek declared, with puz-
　　zled face,
Some strange enchantment mingled in the
　　case,
And naught would serve to act as counter-
　　charm
Save a warm bracelet from a maiden's arm.
Not every maiden's, — many might be
　　tried;
Which not in vain, experience must de-
　　cide.
Were there no damsels willing to attend
And do such service for a suffering friend ?
　　The message passed among the waiting
　　crowd,
First in a whisper, then proclaimed aloud.
Some wore no jewels ; some were disin-
　　clined,
For reasons better guessed at than defined;
Though all were saints, — at least pro-
　　fessed to be, —
The list all counted, there were named but
　　three.
　　The leech, still seated by the patient's
　　side,
Held his thin wrist, and watched him,
　　eagle-eyed.
　　Aurelia first, a fair-haired Tuscan girl,
Slipped off her golden asp, with eyes of
　　pearl.
His solemn head the grave physician
　　shook;
The waxen features thanked her with a
　　look.

Olympia next, a creature half divine,
Sprung from the blood of old Evander's
   line,
Held her white arm, that wore a twisted
   chain
Clasped with an opal-sheeny cymophane.
In vain, O daughter! said the baffled
   Greek.
The patient sighed the thanks he could not
   speak.
   Last, Hermia entered; look, that sudden
   start!
The pallium heaves above his leaping
   heart;
The beating pulse, the cheek's rekindled
   flame,
Those quivering lips, the secret all pro-
   claim.
The deep disease long throbbing in the
   breast,
The dread enchantment, all at once con-
   fessed!
The case was plain; the treatment was be-
   gun;
And Love soon cured the mischief he had
   done.
   Young Love, too oft thy treacherous
   bandage slips
Down from the eyes it blinded to the lips!
Ask not the Gods, O youth, for clearer
   sight,
But the bold heart to plead thy cause
   aright.
And thou, fair maiden, when thy lovers
   sigh,
Suspect thy flattering ear, but trust thine
   eye;
And learn this secret from the tale of old:
No love so true as love that dies untold.

"Bravo, Annex!" they shouted, every
   one,—
"Not Mrs. Kemble's self had better done."
"Quite so," she stammered in her awk-
   ward way,—
Not just the thing, but something she
   must say.

The teaspoon chorus tinkled to its close
When from his chair the MAN OF LAW
   arose,
Called by her voice whose mandate all
   obeyed,

And took the open volume she displayed.
Tall, stately, strong, his form begins to own
Some slight exuberance in its central
   zone,—
That comely fulness of the growing girth
Which fifty summers lend the sons of
   earth.
A smooth, round disk about whose margin
   stray,
Above the temples, glistening threads of
   gray;
Strong, deep-cut grooves by toilsome de-
   cades wrought
On brow and mouth, the battle-fields of
   thought;
A voice that lingers in the listener's ear,
Grave, calm, far-reaching, every accent
   clear,—
(Those tones resistless many a foreman
   knew
That shaped their verdict ere the twelve
   withdrew;)
A statesman's forehead, athlete's throat
   and jaw,
Such the proud semblance of the Man of
   Law.
His eye just lighted on the printed leaf,
Held as a practised pleader holds his brief.
One whispered softly from behind his cup,
"He does not read,—his book is wrong
   side up!
He knows the story that it holds by
   heart,—
So like his own! How well he'll act his
   part!"
   Then all were silent; not a rustling fan
Stirred the deep stillness as the voice
   began.

THE STATESMAN'S SECRET

[Formerly *The Disappointed Statesman.*]

WHO of all statesmen is his country's
   pride,
Her councils' prompter and her leaders'
   guide?
He speaks; the nation holds its breath to
   hear;
He nods, and shakes the sunset hemisphere.
Born where the primal fount of Nature
   springs
By the rude cradles of her throneless
   kings,

In his proud eye her royal signet flames,
By his own lips her Monarch she proclaims.
  Why name his countless triumphs, whom
      to meet
Is to be famous, envied in defeat ?
The keen debaters, trained to brawls and
    strife,
Who fire one shot, and finish with the
    knife,
Tried him but once, and, cowering in their
    shame,
Ground their hacked blades to strike at
    meaner game.
The lordly chief, his party's central stay,
Whose lightest word a hundred votes obey,
Found a new listener seated at his side,
Looked in his eye, and felt himself defied,
Flung his rash gauntlet on the startled floor,
Met the all - conquering, fought, — and
    ruled no more.
  See where he moves, what eager crowds
      attend !
What shouts of thronging multitudes as-
    cend !
If this is life, — to mark with every hour
The purple deepening in his robes of
    power,
To see the painted fruits of honor fall
Thick at his feet, and choose among them
    all,
To hear the sounds that shape his spread-
    ing name
Peal through the myriad organ-stops of
    fame,
Stamp the lone isle that spots the seaman's
    chart,
And crown the pillared glory of the mart,
To count as peers the few supremely wise
Who mark their planet in the angels'
    eyes, —
If this is life —
          What savage man is he
Who strides alone beside the sounding sea ?
Alone he wanders by the murmuring shore,
His thoughts as restless as the waves that
    roar;
Looks on the sullen sky as stormy-browed
As on the waves yon tempest-brooding
    cloud,
Heaves from his aching breast a wailing
    sigh,
Sad as the gust that sweeps the clouded sky.
Ask him his griefs; what midnight demons
    plough
The lines of torture on his lofty brow;

Unlock those marble lips, and bid them
    speak
The mystery freezing in his bloodless
    cheek.
  His secret ? Hid beneath a flimsy word;
One foolish whisper that ambition heard;
And thus it spake: "Behold yon gilded
    chair,
The world's one vacant throne, — thy place
    is there !"
  Ah, fatal dream ! What warning spec-
    tres meet
In ghastly circle round its shadowy seat !
Yet still the Tempter murmurs in his ear
The maddening taunt he cannot choose but
    hear:
"Meanest of slaves, by gods and men ac-
    curst,
He who is second when he might be first !
Climb with bold front the ladder's topmost
    round,
Or chain thy creeping footsteps to the
    ground !"
  Illustrious Dupe ! Have those majestic
    eyes
Lost their proud fire for such a vulgar
    prize ?
Art thou the last of all mankind to know
That party-fights are won by aiming low ?
Thou, stamped by Nature with her royal
    sign,
That party-hirelings hate a look like thine ?
Shake from thy sense the wild delusive
    dream !
Without the purple, art thou not supreme ?
And soothed by love unbought, thy heart
    shall own
A nation's homage nobler than its throne !

Loud rang the plaudits; with them rose the
    thought,
"Would he had learned the lesson he has
    taught !"
Used to the tributes of the noisy crowd,
The stately speaker calmly smiled and
    bowed;
The fire within a flushing cheek betrayed,
And eyes that burned beneath their pent-
    house shade.

  "The clock strikes ten, the hours are
    flying fast, —
Now, Number Five, we've kept you till
    the last !"

What music charms like those caressing tones
Whose magic influence every listener owns, —
Where all the woman finds herself expressed,
And Heaven's divinest effluence breathes confessed ?
Such was the breath that wooed our ravished ears,
Sweet as the voice a dreaming vestal hears;
Soft as the murmur of a brooding dove,
It told the mystery of a mother's love.

THE MOTHER'S SECRET

[Originally *A Mother's Secret.*]

How sweet the sacred legend — if unblamed
In my slight verse such holy things are named —
Of Mary's secret hours of hidden joy,
Silent, but pondering on her wondrous boy !
Ave, Maria ! Pardon, if I wrong
Those heavenly words that shame my earthly song !
The choral host had closed the Angel's strain
Sung to the listening watch on Bethlehem's plain,
And now the shepherds, hastening on their way,
Sought the still hamlet where the Infant lay.
They passed the fields that gleaning Ruth toiled o'er, —
They saw afar the ruined threshing-floor
Where Moab's daughter, homeless and forlorn,
Found Boaz slumbering by his heaps of corn;
And some remembered how the holy scribe,
Skilled in the lore of every jealous tribe,
Traced the warm blood of Jesse's royal son
To that fair alien, bravely wooed and won.
So fared they on to seek the promised sign,
That marked the anointed heir of David's line.
At last, by forms of earthly semblance led,
They found the crowded inn, the oxen's shed.
No pomp was there, no glory shone around
On the coarse straw that strewed the reeking ground ;
One dim retreat a flickering torch betrayed, —
In that poor cell the Lord of Life was laid !
The wondering shepherds told their breathless tale
Of the bright choir that woke the sleeping vale;
Told how the skies with sudden glory flamed,
Told how the shining multitude proclaimed,
"Joy, joy to earth ! Behold the hallowed morn !
In David's city Christ the Lord is born !
'Glory to God !' let angels shout on high,
'Good-will to men !' the listening earth reply !"
They spoke with hurried words and accents wild ;
Calm in his cradle slept the heavenly child.
No trembling word the mother's joy revealed, —
One sigh of rapture, and her lips were sealed;
Unmoved she saw the rustic train depart,
But kept their words to ponder in her heart.

Twelve years had passed; the boy was fair and tall,
Growing in wisdom, finding grace with all.
The maids of Nazareth, as they trooped to fill
Their balanced urns beside the mountain rill,
The gathered matrons, as they sat and spun,
Spoke in soft words of Joseph's quiet son.
No voice had reached the Galilean vale
Of star-led kings, or awe-struck shepherd's tale;
In the meek, studious child they only saw
The future Rabbi, learned in Israel's law.
So grew the boy, and now the feast was near
When at the Holy Place the tribes appear.
Scarce had the home-bred child of Nazareth seen
Beyond the hills that girt the village green;
Save when at midnight, o'er the starlit sands,
Snatched from the steel of Herod's murdering bands,

A babe, close folded to his mother's breast,
Through Edom's wilds he sought the shel-
    tering West.
    Then Joseph spake: "Thy boy hath
    largely grown;
Weave him fine raiment, fitting to be
    shown;
Fair robes beseem the pilgrim, as the priest;
Goes he not with us to the holy feast?"
    And Mary culled the flaxen fibres white;
Till eve she spun; she spun till morning
    light.
The thread was twined; its parting meshes
    through
From hand to hand her restless shuttle
    flew,
Till the full web was wound upon the
    beam;
Love's curious toil, — a vest without a
    seam!
    They reach the Holy Place, fulfil the days
To solemn feasting given, and grateful
    praise.
At last they turn, and far Moriah's height
Melts in the southern sky and fades from
    sight.
All day the dusky caravan has flowed
In devious trails along the winding road;
(For many a step their homeward path
    attends,
And all the sons of Abraham are as
    friends.)
Evening has come, — the hour of rest and
    joy, —
Hush! Hush! That whisper, — "Where
    is Mary's boy?"
    Oh, weary hour! Oh, aching days that
    passed
Filled with strange fears each wilder than
    the last, —
The soldier's lance, the fierce centurion's
    sword,
The crushing wheels that whirl some Ro-
    man lord,
The midnight crypt that sucks the captive's
    breath,
The blistering sun on Hinnom's vale of
    death!
    Thrice on his cheek had rained the
    morning light;
Thrice on his lips the mildewed kiss of
    night,
Crouched by a sheltering column's shining
    plinth,
Or stretched beneath the odorous terebinth.

    At last, in desperate mood, they sought
    once more
The Temple's porches, searched in vain
    before;
They found him seated with the ancient
    men, —
The grim old rufflers of the tongue and
    pen, —
Their bald heads glistening as they clus-
    tered near,
Their gray beards slanting as they turned
    to hear,
Lost in half-envious wonder and surprise
That lips so fresh should utter words so
    wise.
    And Mary said, — as one who, tried too
    long,
Tells all her grief and half her sense of
    wrong, —
"What is this thoughtless thing which
    thou hast done?
Lo, we have sought thee sorrowing, O my
    son!"
    Few words he spake, and scarce of filial
    tone,
Strange words, their sense a mystery yet
    unknown;
Then turned with them and left the holy
    hill,
To all their mild commands obedient still.
    The tale was told to Nazareth's sober men,
And Nazareth's matrons told it oft again;
The maids retold it at the fountain's side,
The youthful shepherds doubted or de-
    nied;
It passed around among the listening
    friends,
With all that fancy adds and fiction lends,
Till newer marvels dimmed the young re-
    nown
Of Joseph's son, who talked the Rabbis
    down.
    But Mary, faithful to its lightest word,
Kept in her heart the sayings she had
    heard,
Till the dread morning rent the Temple's
    veil,
And shuddering earth confirmed the won-
    drous tale.

Youth fades; love droops; the leaves of
    friendship fall:
A mother's secret hope outlives them all.

Hushed was the voice, but still its accents
        thrilled
The throbbing hearts its lingering sweet-
        ness filled.
The simple story which a tear repays
Asks not to share the noisy breath of
        praise.
A trance-like stillness, — scarce a whisper
        heard,
No tinkling teaspoon in its saucer stirred;
A deep-drawn sigh that would not be sup-
        pressed,
A sob, a lifted kerchief told the rest.

"Come now, Dictator," so the lady spoke,
"You too must fit your shoulder to the
        yoke;
You'll find there's something, doubtless,
        if you look,
To serve your purpose, — so, now take the
        book."
        "Ah, my dear lady, you must know full
        well,
'Story, God bless you, I have none to tell.'
To those five stories which these pages hold
You all have listened, — every one is told.
There's nothing left to make you smile or
        weep, —
A few grave thoughts may work you off to
        sleep."

THE SECRET OF THE STARS

    Is man's the only throbbing heart that
        hides
The silent spring that feeds its whispering
        tides?
Speak from thy caverns, mystery-breeding
        Earth,
Tell the half-hinted story of thy birth,
And calm the noisy champions who have
        thrown
The book of types against the book of
        stone!

    Have ye not secrets, ye refulgent spheres,
No sleepless listener of the starlight hears?
In vain the sweeping equatorial pries
Through every world-sown corner of the
        skies,
To the far orb that so remotely strays
Our midnight darkness is its noonday
        blaze;
In vain the climbing soul of creeping man

Metes out the heavenly concave with a
        span,
Tracks into space the long-lost meteor's
        trail,
And weighs an unseen planet in the scale;
Still o'er their doubts the wan-eyed watch-
        ers sigh,
And Science lifts her still unanswered cry:
"Are all these worlds, that speed their
        circling flight,
Dumb, vacant, soulless, — baubles of the
        night?
Warmed with God's smile and wafted by
        his breath,
To weave in ceaseless round the dance of
        Death?
Or rolls a sphere in each expanding zone,
Crowned with a life as varied as our own?"

    Maker of earth and stars! If thou hast
        taught
By what thy voice hath spoke, thy hand
        hath wrought,
By all that Science proves, or guesses true,
More than thy poet dreamed, thy prophet
        knew, —
The heavens still bow in darkness at thy
        feet,
And shadows veil thy cloud-pavilioned seat!
    Not for ourselves we ask thee to reveal
One awful word beneath the future's
        seal;
What thou shalt tell us, grant us strength
        to bear;
What thou withholdest is thy single care.
Not for ourselves; the present clings too
        fast,
Moored to the mighty anchors of the past;
But when, with angry snap, some cable
        parts,
The sound re-echoing in our startled
        hearts, —
When, through the wall that clasps the
        harbor round,
And shuts the raving ocean from its bound,
Shattered and rent by sacrilegious hands,
The first mad billow leaps upon the sands, —
Then to the Future's awful page we turn,
And what we question hardly dare to learn.
    Still let us hope! for while we seem to
        tread
The time-worn pathway of the nations dead,
Though Sparta laughs at all our warlike
        deeds,
And buried Athens claims our stolen creeds,

Though Rome, a spectre on her broken throne,
Beholds our eagle and recalls her own,
Though England fling her pennons on the breeze
And reign before us Mistress of the seas, —
While calm-eyed History tracks us circling round
Fate's iron pillar where they all were bound,
Still in our path a larger curve she finds,
The spiral widening as the chain unwinds !
Still sees new beacons crowned with brighter flame
Than the old watch-fires, like, but not the same !
No shameless haste shall spot with bandit-crime
Our destined empire snatched before its time.
Wait, — wait, undoubting, for the winds have caught
From our bold speech the heritage of thought ;
No marble form that sculptured truth can wear
Vies with the image shaped in viewless air ;
And thought unfettered grows through speech to deeds,
As the broad forest marches in its seeds.
What though we perish ere the day is won ?
Enough to see its glorious work begun !
The thistle falls before a trampling clown,
But who can chain the flying thistle-down ?
Wait while the fiery seeds of freedom fly,
The prairie blazes when the grass is dry !
 What arms might ravish, leave to peaceful arts,
Wisdom and love shall win the roughest hearts ;
So shall the angel who has closed for man
The blissful garden since his woes began

Swing wide the golden portals of the West,
And Eden's secret stand at length confessed !

The reader paused ; in truth he thought it time, —
Some threatening signs accused the drowsy rhyme.
The Mistress nodded, the Professor dozed,
The two Annexes sat with eyelids closed, —
Not *sleeping*, — no ! But when one shuts one's eyes,
That one hears better no one, sure, denies.
The Doctor whispered in Delilah's ear,
Or seemed to whisper, for their heads drew near.
Not all the owner's efforts could restrain
The wild vagaries of the squinting brain, —
Last of the listeners Number Five alone
The patient reader still could call his own.

"Teacups, arouse ! " 'T was thus the spell I broke ;
The drowsy started and the slumberers woke.
"The sleep I promised you have now enjoyed,
Due to your hour of labor well employed.
Swiftly the busy moments have been passed ;
This, our first 'Teacups,' must not be our last.
Here, on this spot, now consecrated ground,
The Order of 'The Teacups ' let us found !
By winter's fireside and in summer's bower
Still shall it claim its ever-welcome hour,
In distant regions where our feet may roam
The magic teapot find or make a home ;
Long may its floods their bright infusion pour,
Till time and teacups both shall be no more ! "

ADDITIONAL POEMS

1838—1894 AND UNDATED

AN UNPUBLISHED POEM

FOR THE BOSTON SOCIETY OF MEDICAL
IMPROVEMENT

FEBRUARY 7, 1838?

THIS evening hour which grateful mem-
ory spares
From evening toil and unrequited cares ;
These curling lips, these joy revealing
eyes,
These mirthful tones, re-echoing as they
rise,
These friendly pledges on this festal
shrine,
The glistening goblet and the flowing
wine,
This genial influence which the coldest
heart
Warms to receive and opens to impart,
Mock the poor Art who does her subjects
wrong
And steals from Pleasure all she wastes in
Song.
Yet since you ask this feeble hand to
strew
Wreathes on the flowers and diamonds on
the snow,
Take all it bears, and if the gift offend,
Condemn the Poet — spare ! oh ! spare
the friend !

Yes, while I speak, some magic wand
appears
Shapes the long past, oh ! say not happier
years,
The lawless fancies, yet untaught to know
The charms of reason, or the scourge of
woe ;
The boyish dreams now melting into air ;
The virgin forms, alas ! no longer fair ;

The scattered friends, with many a tear
resigned,
Once all our own, now mingled with man-
kind ;
Since, save in memory, ye appear no more
In the bright present, let the Past live
o'er.
Still in the heart, some lingering spark
remains —
You cannot chase it from the shrinking
veins.
Grief comes too early ; Pleasure ne'er too
late.
Snatch the fair blossom, whatsoe'er its
date ;
If youth still charms thee, mirth is justly
thine ;
If age has chilled thee, lo ! — the gen-
erous wine !

Oh ! thoughtless revellers ! when you set
my task,
How little dreamed you of the toil you
asked.
How shall I please you ? — I, a grave
young man,
Whose fate is drudgery on " the useful
plan."
How can I coax you, smooth you, comb
you down,
And cheat your frontals of that awful
frown —
Portentous scowl ! which marks in every
age
The blistering, clystering, tooth-extract-
ing sage ?
A verse too polished will not stick at all ;
The worst back scratcher is a billiard ball.
A rhyme too rugged would not hit the
point,
Its loose legs wriggling in and out of joint.
Shall I be serious, touching, lachrymose ;

Mix tears with wine and give you all a dose ?
But well-filled stomachs have not room for grief,
For sips and sighs, for porter and roast beef.
Shall I be learned, and with punch and claw,
Dig stumps of Greek from every Ancient's jaw ?
But who quotes Cuvier when he feasts on snipe,
Or reads Gastritis when his wife cooks tripe ?
Not all the wisdom of recorded time
Can change one titbit to concocted chyme.
Not all the schools from Berkshire to the Nile
Can melt one sausage into milky chyle.
Nor all the Galens since Deucalion's flood
Change lifeless pudding into living blood.

Then Heavenly Muse, avert thy rolling eyes,
Lest in their sight unlicked creations rise ;
Or should those linger in the wanton air,
Pull off thy girdle and unbind thy hair ;
Come not like Juno to such scenes as this ;
Too proud to play with, and too prim to kiss ;
But wild and careless as some slip-shod maid,
Oh ! classic Broad street, in thy fragrant shade,
With braidless ringlets, tangled, tumbling down,
And blue-veined bosom gleaming through her gown,
And all the lovelier for a casual streak
Of smutty semblance in her damask cheek ;
Nor over conscious should her flounces fly
To Love's half tide-mark, when his waves are high.

Our noble Art, what countless shoals invade,
Some as a science, many as a trade.
In every column quackery has its line ;
From every corner stares the Doctor's sign ;
From every shore the straining vessel tugs

Ill-scented balsams, stomach turning drugs.
The keels of commerce clear the farthest surge,
Lest some old beldam want her morning purge.
The seaman wanders on his venturous route
To turn a baby's stomach inside out.
Rich were the Queen of yon hepatic isle
With half her subjects squander on their bile ;
Rich were Van Buren, could he pay his bills
With half his people waste on Brandreth's pills,
Or with their products fill his farmers' carts
With tare and tret for reproductive parts.

If one great truth defies the skeptic's scorn
That truth is this — that children must be born ;
If one great maxim, man dare not deny,
That maxim is — that mortal man must die.
If long experience be not all a trick,
Who dares to say that mortals can't be sick ?
These solemn truths, by thinking minds allowed,
Lift the stern reasoner above the vulgar crowd.
From every truth some vast conclusion flows —
Truth is the pump, and reason is its nose ;
Its handle, logic ; work it, and it brings
Transcendent streams from transcendental springs.

Heaven surely ordered on Creation's morn
This mighty law — that children must be born.
Hence came the science, thou dost show so well
With white fore finger — Madame Lachapelle ;
Hence came the forceps, hence the screw to pinch
The soul's own viscus to half an inch ;
Hence came the weapons, which the embryos bore

Left in the lurch, their brains escaped
before, —
A trivial damage, since so oft we find
That babes grow up, who left their brains
behind —
Hence came the fillet, whence the infant
wretch
Mistakes the midwife for her friend Jack
Ketch ;
Hence came the lever, which the toothless
fry
Take for a crowbar, when the monsters
pry ;
Hence the scooped pinchers, with the
fangs between,
Skull-crushing Davis — thy divine ma-
chine —
Hence all the " claptraps," potent to ex-
tract
The hero struggling in his closing act.

So the stout foetus, kicking and alive
Leaps from the fundus for his final dive ;
Tired of the prison where his legs were
curled,
He pants like Rasselas for a wider world.
No more to him their wonted joys afford
The fringed placenta and the knotted
cord ;
No longer liberal of his filial thanks,
He drums his minuets on his mother's
flanks ;
But nobly daring, seeks the air to find
Through paths untrodden, spite of waves
or wind.
Hush decent muse and leave such things
as these
To modest Maygrier and concise Dewees.
As some green school girl, who at morn
forgets,
Lost in strange thoughts her wanton pan-
talets,
Squats, stoops and straddles, while the
passers stare
Alas ! unconscious that her limbs are
bare,
So thou, forgetful that another spies
Things which escape thy unsuspecting
eyes
Would'st freak and gambol while thy
neighbors see
The white warm flesh above thy gartered
knee.

Thus with the entrance of the first born
man
The reign of Science o'er the earth began.
Nurse of his weakness, soother of his
woes,
She waits and watches till his sorrows
close ;
Nor yet she leaves him when the undying
mind
Flits from his clay and leaves the frame
behind.

If thou should'st wonder that mankind
must die,
Ask the Curator of our Museum, why ?
When man's immortal, who had ever seen
The stomach, colon, kidneys, pancreas,
spleen ?
Each pickled viscus, every varnished
bone,
Seducing scirrhus and attractive stone ?
Lost to the world, had never come to
grace
Our well filled phials in their padlocked
case.
Unknown to fame had Morgagni sighed
And Louis floated down oblivion's tide.
On " Brunner's glands " no cheering ray
had shone,
And " Peyer " claimed no " patches " but
his own.
Science untaught her scalpel to employ.
Had seen no Ileum since the days of
Troy ;
And man the ruler of the storms and tides
Had groped in ignorance of his own in-
sides.
Thus the same art that caught our earliest
breath
Lives with our life and lasts beyond our
death.
Man, ever curious, still would seek to
save
Some wreck of Knowledge from the wait-
ing grave.
Yet keen-eyed searcher into Nature's
laws,
Slight not the suffering while thou reck'st
the cause.
How poor the solace, when thy patients
die,
To tell the mourners *all* the reasons why.
Love linked with Knowledge crowns thy
angel art ;

Gold buys thy science ; Heaven rewards
  thy heart.

Between two breaths, what worlds of an-
  guish lie ;
The first short gasp, the last and long
  drawn sigh.
Thou who hast aided with coercive
  thumbs
The red-legged infant, kicking as it
  comes ;
Thou who hast tracked each doubtful
  lesion home
With probe and scissors, knife and entero-
  tome ;
Short is the opening ; short the closing
  scene ;
But a long drama fills the stage between.
Nor deem it strange, since every season
  flings
Its sun or cloud on life's unguarded
  springs ;
Since song or science, love of fame, or
  truth,
All feed like vampires on the brow of
  youth ;
Since the red goblet shakes the hand that
  grasps
And hot-cheeked beauty wastes the form
  she clasps ;
One half mankind should spend their time
  to make
The pills and draughts the other half
  must take.
Oh ! fertile source of never failing wealth,
Mysterious faith ! thou alchemist of
  health ;
But for thy wand, how vainly should we
  strive
To cure the world and keep ourselves
  alive !
Not all the fruit the yellow harvest yields,
When the curved sickle sweeps the rus-
  tling fields ;
Not all the stores the deep-sunk vessel
  brings
When India's breezes swell her perfumed
  wings :
Not all the gems, whose wild Auroras
  shine
Through the black darkness of Golconda's
  mine,
Can match the profits thou dost still dis-
  pense

To thy best favorites — Ease and Im-
  pudence,
Who find Golconda in a case of gout
Or rich Potosi in a baby's clout ;
And gather ingots, ever fresh and hot
Smelt, but not smelted, in a chamber-pot.

Small is the *learning* which the patients
  ask
When the grave Doctor ventures on his
  task ;
To greet the Quack admiring hundreds
  come,
Whose wisdom centers in his fife and
  drum ;
Why should'st *thou study,* if thou canst
  obtain
A wig, a gig, an eye glass or a cane ?
Greenest of greenhorns, know that drugs
  like these
Are the best weapons to subdue disease.
Should'st thou not flourish by enacting
  lies,
Step into print, good friend, and adver-
  tise ;
And in the " Post," the " Herald," or the
  " Sun "
Thus let thine honest manifestoes run :
That great physician, learned Dr. C.
F. R. S., Staff-surgeon and M.D. —
Lately from London ; now at number
  " four "
Left side of North Street (Don't mistake
  the door),
May be consulted for life's various ills ;
Where's also sold the patent " Pickwick
  Pills."
What grieves the Doctor, is that all man-
  kind
To their own good should be so shocking
  blind.
He could not stand it, but relief imparts
The grateful feeling of a thousand hearts ;
His fee is nothing ; 'tis his conscious skill,
Backed by the virtues of the " Pickwick
  Pill,"
That prompts the Doctor to dispense his
  cure
To all mankind, and also to the poor.
What is dyspepsia ? When the humors
  vile,
The cardiac sphincter closes on the bile.
What cures dyspepsia ? — Why, the Doc-
  tor's skill,

Consult by letter, and enclose a bill.
What's fluor albus ? 'Tis a term we know
From "albus"—white, and "fluor,"
    Greek, to flow.
'Tis the great pest of lovely woman's
    life—
Females treated through the Doctor's
    wife.
What's gonorrhoea ? — A disease so called
From "gonor"—water, and from
    "rhea"—scald.
In some rash moment, when unguarded
    youth
Strays from the path of reason and of
    truth,
The poison enters, the disease is hatched ;
See your case cured, not plastered up and
    patched.
N.B. — No money till the patient's cured.
P. S. — The utmost secrecy insured.
Observe ! the Doctor has a private door ;
Green blinds, no steps, back stairs, and
    second floor.
Of testimonials, which have come in
    heaps,
But two small cartloads now the Doctor
    keeps ;
They were too numerous for the public
    eyes ;
Hence the small number which he now
    supplies.
John Smith of Boston — aged "thirty-
    five"
Is much surprised to find himself alive,
Which justly owing, as he thinks must be,
Half to his Maker, half to Doctor C.
Had a stuffed feeling, used to wake in
    starts,
Had wind and rumbling in the inward
    parts,
Had swelled stomach, used to vomit
    some,
Was often squeamish, thought his brains
    were numb,
Had fell away, could not digest his food,
Had tried all physics — nothing did him
    good —
In short was dying with his numerous ills,
"Cured by three doses of the Pickwick
    Pills."
The Doctor's skill, the sluggard clergy
    owns,
As in this note from Reverend Judas
    Jones :

"Dear Sir, The blessing of the Lord at-
    tend
You and your ointment, called ' The loaf-
    er's friend,'
My worthy wife, the partner of my toils,
Like Job of old, has suffered from the
    ' boils,'
Some on her fingers, wherewithal she
    knits,
Some on her person, whereupon she sits,
Which quite unfit her, when her ail re-
    turns,
To do her duties by her small concerns.
Since times are hard, and earthly comforts
    dear,
And Gospel harvests come but once a
    year,
With my good deacon, I resolved to halve
One precious box of your unrivalled salve.
With heaven's kind blessing, and one
    hearty rub,
We chased away this leprous Beelzebub.
Enough was left to cure our warts and
    styes,
And six great pimples on my handmaid's
    thighs.
Please send three boxes, by the earliest
    hand
To Judas Jones, your servant at com-
    mand.
P. S. Your pills have cured my baby's
    fits ;
I'll write particulars if the Lord permits."

The following letter sent to Doctor C.
Comes from Barrabas Waterpot, M. D. :
"Dear Sir, The duties which I owe man-
    kind,
Have made it proper I should speak my
    mind ;
And while my breast an honest conscience
    fills,
I can but praise the patent "Pickwick
    Pills."
I have no interest in the pills at stake
And never sell them and but rarely take.
Fit for the welfare of a suffering race,
Their many virtues, I now feebly trace :
When taken *fasting*, they the strength
    maintain ;
When on *full stomach*, they deplete the
    brain ;
One pill relieves the almost drowning
    thirst ;

Two, keep one sober, though he drink to
    burst.
One pill a week cures Phthisis and the
    Gout ;
One half a pill will keep the measles out.
Rubbed on the fingers they destroy the
    itch ;
Worn next the skin, Lumbago and the
    stitch,
Though, like a corkscrew they the bowels
    search,
A curious fact — *they never work in
    church !*
Small children take them with advantage
    great,
As also *ladies* in a certain state.
In short, this medicine every want fulfils,
I give no physic but the " Pickwick Pills."
Please print this letter, which of use may
    be,
(Signed) Barrabas Waterpot, M. D."

Here's a small postscript Doctor C. left
    out
Of small importance to the public doubt :
" The pills sell briskly — twenty gross or
    more,
Send a fresh parcel to the grocer's store ;
Put in *more jalap ;* never mind expense,
Folks must be *griped* or *grudge their fifty
    cents.*
Put up two sizes, one three times as small,
For little brats ; the big ones *kill* them
    all.
I want my pay, you poison pounding
    knave
Send me good bills — How like the D–1
    you shave."
All this well printed, and with bigger type
Words like *Dyspepsia, Liver, Humor,
    Gripe,*
Two solid columns in the " Times " would
    fill
And make thy fortune by the " Pickwick
    Pill."

But thou, poor dreamer, who hast rashly
    thought
To live by knowledge which thy bloom
    has bought ;
Thou who hast waited with a martyr's
    smile —
Hope gently whispering — " Yet a
    while" —

Too proud to stoop beneath thy nobler
    aim,
While prostrate meanness crawls to
    wealth and fame ;
Thou, all unfriended, while a thousand
    fools
Vaunt their raw cousins, reeking from the
    schools,
Go, scorn the art that every boon denies,
'Till age sits glassy in thy sunken eyes ;
Go, scorn the treasury which withholds its
    store
Till hope grows cold, and blessings bless
    no more.

Peace to our banquet ; let me not pro-
    long,
Its nearest moments with my idle song.
This measured tread of ever marching
    rhyme,
Like clockwork, pleases only for a time ;
Too long repeated makes our heart so
    sick
We cut the weights to stop its tedious
    click.
Let sweeter strains our opening hearts
    inspire,
The listening echoes tremble round the
    lyre.
Dance Bacchus ! hours of labor come
    again,
To lock the rivets of our loosened chain.
Shine, star of evening, with thy *steadiest*
    ray,
To guide us homeward on our *devious*
    way.

SUNG AT THE HUNT

NAUSHON ISLAND

NOVEMBER 1? 1838

Ye Colonels Councillors and Squires
That You may all remember
The hunting of the Island deer
That happened this November,

I've written out a little song
To give you decent warning
Between the first and second gongs
All of a Thursday morning —
    morning, morning, all of a Thursday
    morning.

At 7 Oclock on Tuesday morn
They roused each ancient dreamer
With hunting gun & powder horn
To go on board the steamer

So when they got us all on board
They made the water boil and
In half a shake they had us down
Upon the *little Island*
   Island, Island, upon the *little Island*

The Governor & his suite were there
To bid us welcome gaily
With broad brimmed hat & long tailed
    coat
Which is his habit daily.

The air was soft, the sky was blue
The Isle was all before us
And whelp and hound were baying round
All joining in the chorus
   chorus, chorus, all joining in the chorus

But just before We took our stand,
We all went in the closet
When each pet bank beneath our ribs
Received a small deposit

And when the lunch was stowed below
And fingers all were wipéd
We stroked that little pig you know
That is so very stripéd.
   stripéd, stripéd, that is so very stripéd.

Then off we sett to scour the woods
With our unhappy drivers
Uncertain if the deer or they
Would be the days survivors

But having safely met at last
And all our laurels housing
The knowing ones made bets on wine
And there was some carousing
   carousing, carousing, and there was
    some carousing

The first days victim was a Doe
Shot by Nantucket Upton
They say he dodged a little though
Or else his toes she trod on

Then Clifford thought that he must fire
Peabody fain would hit too
With William, Holmes & many more
But all their Does were dittos
   dittos, dittos, but all their Does were
    dittos

On Wednesday morn the doctors twain
Went in a new direction
For once they could not kill 'twas plain
So took to resurrection

And with them in the little boat
The Speaker too did seat him
Perhaps 'twas by a special vote
That body rose to meet him
   to meet him, to meet him, that body
    rose to meet him

The second day now blazed away
Each doubled barrelled hero
They made the number up to ten
If ten is one and Zero

The night before We drank until
The wines ran from our scuppers
Which made us on the second night
Like Deacons at their suppers
   suppers, suppers, like Deacons at their
    suppers

Tomorrow I shall add a verse
To finish out the story
In which I shall at length rehearse
The Candidates for glory

Long live the glorious Governor
For whom my song was written
I should have finished it tonight
But that I was frost bitten
   bitten, bitten, but that I was frost
    bitten

AT DARTMOUTH

PHI BETA KAPPA, JULY 24, 1839

THESE tranquil shades, where Nature un-
    confined
Flings her green drapery on the mountain
    wind,
These smiling hillsides, which our river
    queen
Wreathes in wild blossoms as she winds
    between,
If dear to those who never learned to
    stray
Far from the shadows where their cradles
    lay —
How sweet to him whom many a wind has
    blown
To shores less loved if lovelier than his
    own !

How soft to him whose weary feet have
    trod
The burning pavement, is the dewy sod —
How fair to him is every nameless flower
Whose painted disk recalls some infant
    hour ;
How free to him the wide horizon
    seems —
How glad the music of the mountain
    streams —
How pure the breeze whose restless wings
    have fanned
The tossing fringes of his forest land —
While rose lipped Summer robes in all her
    charms
The living landscape locked in Nature's
    arms.
If scenes like these the wanderer's heart
    inspire
With lingering sparkles of forgotten fire,
If tired with tumult and the noisy strife
That chokes with dust the crowded paths
    of life
He turns with rapture from the thronging
    street
To rest and silence in their calm retreat
Not so with all. The maid in russet gown,
The blue frocked plough boy, pant alike
    for town,
The solemn umpires of our health and
    laws
Who ask more patients, practice or ap-
    plause,
Nay, the grave preacher, who for meagre
    hire
Quotes Greek and Latin to astound the
    squire
Filled with high visions as the rattling
    mail
Rolls with its burden from their quiet
    vale
Forgetting patients, practice, parish, all
Dream of some ' opening ' — some invit-
    ing ' call ' —
Alas ! Too anxious for an ampler space
To flourish, flutter, sputter or grimace —
Or in the phrase that suits a saintly ear
To be more useful in a wider sphere.

From the still hamlet to the noisy mart
The home of Nature to the throne of Art
As led by fate the wanderer's footsteps
    tend
What varied colors oer the landscape
    blend !

What changing scenes the curious eye will
    find
To strike the senses or enchain the
    mind ! —
If themes like these can stay the wheels
    of time
Forged by rude memory into ruder rhyme
Some listless moments may be whiled
    away
By the dull cadence of my slipshod lay.
Tis summer's noon — and blazing fiercely
    down
The dazzling sunbeams gild the glittering
    town
Bathed in their light, from every lofty
    spire
Its wheeling symbol burns in starry fire
Each sombre turret lifted calm and high
Prints its cold outline on the sultry sky, —
Mingling and glimmering in the flickering
    glow
Palace and hovel spread their roofs be-
    low —
So gleams the surface, but surveyed more
    near
Its fancied glories melt and disappear ;
The baffled winds that stagnate ere they
    meet
Scarce lift the dust that strews the arid
    street.
No clustering foliage checks the burning
    ray
But scanty awnings line the glaring
    way —
From gaping windows mingling sounds
    arise —
The nurse that threatens and the child
    that cries
The flute's hoarse lisp that speaks some
    shop boy's art
Who kills an hour by murdering poor
    Mozart
The clink of hammers — not on warriors'
    mails,
But closing rivets in disjointed pails
The clash of steel — of most unwarlike
    knives —
From plates — not breast-plates — taking
    meals, not lives ;
The hiss of fountains — soda founts alas !
That pour their treasures at so much a
    glass
So bursts the chorus led sublimely off
By lusty infants, black with hooping
    cough

While the vexed pavement by the cart
    wheel ground
Growls a rough bass to swell the mighty
    sound,
And loud and long the jarring discord
    rings
Like the last crash of all created things !

— Turn to the spot where Nature's laws
    maintain
Their ancient empire over hill and plain
Look when the forest waving wild and
    high
Braids its deep fringes on the sultry
    sky —
In those calm depths no living sound is
    heard
Save the light carol of the summer bird
Or the low rustling of the leafy crest
Whose plaited shelter screens his rocking
    nest
Or whispering waters, which with languid
    flow
Steal in soft channels through the flowers
    below ; —
Hush ! for thy voice will wrong the peace-
    ful scene
Where all is shadowy, solemn and serene.
Around thy pathway floats the trailing
    vine
And breathes the fragrance of the balmy
    pine
Beneath thy feet the perfumed turf is
    spread
Fresh with the dew those glossy leaves
    have shed,
Through the dark tracery that above thee
    bends
In checkered gleams the trembling ray
    descends —
Look — breathe — and listen ! Say, if
    mortal power
With gold and purple clothed thy lonely
    bower
Smoothed the rude soil and chained the
    wandering stream
And bared the wild flowers to the noon-
    tide beam
Would all it lavished from its wealth
    repay
The tangled sweetness which it swept
    away ?

— The dead of winter ! chained in ice and
    snow

The wreck of autumn slumbers dark and
    low
The silent streamlet fills its frozen bed
As if still lingering by the flowers it fed.
The jagged hemlock splintered in the
    storm
Frowns oer the forest with its crested
    form
The strong armed oak, his garlands cast
    aside
Stands like an athlete in his naked pride
The slanting sunbeam glimmers faint and
    chill
O'er the choked valley and the whitened
    hill,
The leaf has faded and the bird has flown
And all is voiceless — Death is Lord
    alone !

— Not such the scene where man usurps
    the sway
To change with art the empire of decay
For him no winter bids the blushing rose
Shrink from the breeze beneath the drift-
    ing snows
Nay, the frail nurseling torn from tropic
    skies
Warmed by his care the arctic storm defies
His tendriled vines their purple orbs dis-
    play
Ere the first violet dares the breath of
    May
The golden cone that loads the dark-
    leaved pine
Breathes with the fragrance of the burn-
    ing vine
The bright plumed prisoner waves his
    yellow wing
Amidst the blossoms of an endless spring
So wills the pleasure of imperial Man
As if in mockery of his Maker's plan.
Nor less transformed the midnight hours
    that call
The gay and fair to many a gilded hall
While the hoarse wind is raving hoarsely
    round
From yon bright scene the merry voices
    sound
The blazing lustre sheds its radiance o'er
Those graceful shapes that trip the
    bounding floor
What though the storm is raging fierce
    and wild —
No wind is rude to fortune's favored
    child —

Round her white neck the circling jewels
glow
Like sparkling flashes on the moonlight
snow
No envious drapery oer its beauty weaves
Blanched to the whiteness of the lily's
leaves
That fragile form no ruder robes enfold
Than the flowered tissue clasped with
fretted gold
Those twinkling feet, in slenderest satin
bound
Trace their light circles guiltless of a
sound
The curtained walls the wreathes of sum-
mer wear
And faint with fragrance breathes the
balmy air
And flushing maidens court the gale that
swings
The close drawn curtain on its gilded
wings —
— Strong is gray Winter — for his arms
can rend
The living rock and bid the forest bend,
But man is mightier for he scales his
throne
And breaks his sceptre to extend his own !

— Is man the same, where'er his fortune
falls,
Left to himself, or caged in crowded
walls ?
Ask the pert cockney, who, the pink of
town
Greets some rough cousin, raw, and just
come down —
Ask the stout rustic when the cit descends
With gloves and cane among his country
friends !
" John " — says the first " That hat of
yours was made
" About the time that Noah's keel was
laid —
" Who built that coat ? The bill was
monstrous large
" If extra puckers made a separate charge
" Don't swing that stick — how every
body stares
" Pray did you think the town was full of
bears
" Why, how you stamp — who ventured
to abuse
" The feet of man with such a pair of
shoes ?

" Look there ! Why bless me ! — Now,
upon my word —
" Those cotton stockings — aren't they
too absurd,
" And that striped waistcoat and that
checked cravat
" Upon my honor but you *are* a flat ! "
" Tom " says the rustic, when, the greet-
ing past,
He gets the cockney on his farm at last —
" You're mighty knowing — don't you
think you know
" How to thresh wheat ? — or would you
rather mow ?
" There — take that stick — that's what
we call a flail
" Don't break your head — what makes
you look so pale ?
" Ah — there you have it — pray don't
make me laugh.
" Hit where you will you'll scatter lots of
chaff !
" Well then, the scythe — come — gently
— don't be rash
" Take off those gloves — ah — there's an
ugly gash —
" Come home with me — next time I'll
show you how
" Walk straight along and never fear the
cow
" Keep those French boots from off my
uncut grass
" I'm sorry, Cousin, but you *are* an ass !

— From dress and manners if we turn to
find
The graver contrasts of the inward mind
How vast the gulf our wondering eye
must scan
From clashing crowds to isolated man !

— Few are the cares the simple rustic
knows,
So calm the current of his being flows ;
The changing hues that paint the living
scene
With autumn's brown or spring's rekin-
dled green
The fruits and herbage as by turns they
yield
Their ripened treasures in his cultured
field
The flight of birds that chase their shift-
ing clime

These are his dials for the lapse of time.
Far from the world, no jarring tones intrude
To break the stillness of his solitude —
His wayward fancies few are found to share
And ceaseless toil demands his daily care —
Few are his sorrows — such as Heaven ordained
And soothed by tears unseen and unrestrained.
His pleasures tranquil, yet not loved the less
Than the brief raptures wooed by wild excess ;
When from his arm its manly strength has past
Life's wasting flame burns gently to the last
Taught by long years, his trembling lips inform
The listening reapers of the rising storm —
Bent down with age, and tottering to his tomb
His eye still gladdens in the summer's bloom —
Slowly he fades, while faces fresh and fair
Crowd with sweet smiles around his ancient chair
Till by kind hands his reverend form is laid
In the still churchyard where so oft he strayed
By those he loved he finds his lowly bed,
And oer his mound the grassy turf is spread,
His life unwritten on the roles of fame,
But love still lingering oer his humble name.

— But who is he, whose shattered form appears
Bowed by long care and sapped by wasting years ?
Through the dense mart that ancient shape is known
The halls of trade those feeble accents own
In these dark walls the busy years have sped
Whose winters whiten on his trembling head

The field, the forest, and the mountain stream
To him are shadows of his boyhood's dream
The narrow circle where his footsteps range
These strips of pavement centering in exchange ;
That stony glance no artful words beguile —
He looks and hears, while others speak and smile ;
If this be man, how changed by selfish toil
From man the monarch of the virgin soil !

— Yet scorn not him whose withered hands uphold
In thin cold grasp the dynasty of gold ; —
He speaks — his accents, wafted oer the seas
Blend with the sigh of India's farthest breeze —
His quivering fingers trace a single line,
And bar and bolt obey the mighty sign
Through steel and stone the silent mandate goes
And sunless vaults their golden hoards disclose ;
Yet in his garb the sneering stranger's eye
Reads the rude marks of threadbare poverty
And the gay spendthrift with contemptuous air
Crowds from the walk the humble millionaire —
The lord of wealth, which Fortune when she gave
Cramped with one shackle — ' thou shalt be a slave
A slave to toil that ceases but with life
One sleepless task one ever wearing strife
Till o'er thy grave the curse and blessing blends
Of smiling heirs and unremembered friends !
Can this be all that queenly Commerce brings
When o'er the deep she spreads her myriad wings —
To grasp the means without the will to use

Less pleased with gain than anxious not
　　to lose
To wean the sense from all that Heaven
　　bestows
And coin to gold each drop of blood that
　　flows ?
If such the gift her glittering robes con-
　　ceal
Trust not thy fate to fortune's rolling
　　wheel —
The lavished treasures of the earth and
　　sky
Around, above thee, and beneath thee lie
For thee they blossom, and for thee they
　　shine,
Unbought by suffering, they at least are
　　thine !

— At every step some little trace we find
That varying habits print upon the
　　mind ;
The simpler rustic talks with sense pro-
　　found
On all the marvels of the country round,
Whose horse is dead — who stole his
　　neighbor's hen —
Whose dog kills sheep — whose pig has
　　left his pen —
Who staid from church, and what the
　　deacon said —
Whose child is sick — whose grandpapa
　　is dead,
Whose farm is mortgaged for his bar-
　　room bills
Whose desperate case was cured by
　　Brandreth's pills
Whose buxom lady rules her passive
　　spouse —
Whose milder helpmeet milks her hus-
　　band's cows —
And themes like these, whose mighty
　　rumor rolls
Through the small world of half a thou-
　　sand souls.
Not so the gossips of the striving town
Where every mail with news is breaking
　　down
Then every hour some pleasing tale
　　attends
Or precious scandal which the journal
　　lends ; —
For them no fire is worthy of the name
If scores of buildings do not sink in
　　flame —

Morn brings its murder with their break-
　　fast rolls
Noon leaves a steamboat thumping on
　　the shoals
The evening paper tells them whereabout
Some thief broke in or chicken pox broke
　　out
Or how some worthy of undoubted
　　wealth
Has struck for Texas — to restore his
　　health —
(His land of promise, but of small de-
　　light
To the blank holders of his notes at
　　sight)
Duels and deaths, the wedding and the
　　puff —
Tales for the tender, slanders for the
　　tough,
A web of fact, which fancy weaves at will
Through the sly shuttle of a scribbler's
　　quill :
That is the draught that simple truth
　　supplies
And tart the flavor of unmingled lies ;
Like soda powders wrapped in white and
　　blue
To make them sparkle you must mix the
　　two.
— So reeks the city with eternal tales
Of births, deaths, weddings, fires, wrecks,
　　riots, gales.
The poet's caution would be idle there —
" Nil admirari " — you must never stare ;
Tell an old townsman that you just have
　　learned
On Monday next our planet will be
　　burned,
To him the tidings will not bring sur-
　　prise,
Nor chalky cheeks, nor saucer spreading
　　eyes ; —
" 'Twill beat the fireworks," he perhaps
　　will say
" That made such fun on Independence
　　day,"
Or if a tradesman will express a hope
Ashes will fall and sink the price of
　　soap !

— As some vast lake where thousand
　　currents tend
And chafe and glitter as their waters
　　blend

Now fresh and stainless from their mountain home,
Now by rough channels scourged to eddying foam
Or darkly turbid, as with sullen toil
They sweep in shadow through the loosening soil
Flung from tall cliffs in many a bright cascade
Or creeping voiceless through the leafy shade,
So in the scene of man's tumultuous strife
Mingle and melt the murmuring waves of life.

— There he that basks in fortune's noontide blaze
Spreads his gay honors to the vulgar gaze
There the pale artist writes his lowly name
And faints for bread to feed the vulture fame
There haggard vice secures her last retreat
And shameless hearts grow harder as they meet
There the lost exile, friendless and alone
Broods o'er his grief unknowing and unknown
There passion's victim in the careless throng
In deepening guilt forgets her girlhood's wrong
And pallid shapes unnoticed as they fade
With trembling lips implore the stranger's aid
And wearied age, unconscious of repose,
And sickly childhood, born to want and woes
Joined by stern fate in one tumultuous sphere
In one dark vortex roll and disappear.

— Between two breaths what worlds of anguish lie
The first short gasp, the last and long drawn sigh ;
If thou would'st hear the ceaseless groans that rise
And count the tears that fall from joyless eyes
And read the lines of misery and despair

Seek the wide city — thou wilt find them there.
Turn to yon dome whose dreary arches spread
Their sullen shelter o'er the wanderer's head —
Where the last act of life's poor drama ends
In the cold walls that sorrowing mercy lends.
That sinewy shape, whose shrunken forms reveal
The strength once centering in its nerves of steel,
In fruitless toil its stormy day has past
To ask a grave from charity at last.
— Yon whitelipped child who wastes by slow degrees
The heir of want and nurseling of disease
He whose chilled infancy hath never known
One accent kinder than the stranger's tone
Matured untimely by the frost of grief
Seared in his spring as autumn's stricken leaf —
Read the mute question in his sunken eye
That asks in terror — 'tell me — must I die ? '

And there — deserted in her hour of woe —
The death shade darkening o'er her cheek of snow —
(That cheek whose freshness was her fatal dower
And lured the spoiler in its rosier hour)
The wasted form and weary heart are laid
Of one who loved — and loving was betrayed.
Fair as the roses that around her grew
And bathed her tresses in their perfumed dew
She sprung in beauty, and her native wild
Smiled as in welcome o'er the lovely child.
— And snows and summers passed oer hill and plain
And rolling years renewed the golden grain
On Anna's brow they left their ripening trace —

Changed mirth to calm and sprightliness
  to grace,
But taught too little save the dangerous
  creed
That conscious beauty learns too soon to
  read.
— And who is he whose step is ever near,
Whose low breathed accents meet the
  maiden's ear
Who bends and smiles, and courts with
  flattering lies
Melts in feigned tears and breathes in
  artful sighs
Why change her features when his name
  is heard
Why heaves her bosom at his lightest
  word
Alas, she deems that faithless heart her
  own —
She hears but love in every studied tone
And wondering eyes remark her altered
  air
And busy tongues their scanty hints com-
  pare —
A breath — a whisper — doubts — suspi-
  cion — shame —
And shuddering virtue wept oer Anna's
  name!
Dark are the paths her hurrying steps
  will share
From shame to guilt, from anguish to
  despair
Soon from her cheek shall fade its sullied
  bloom
And every hope look forward to the
  tomb —
That hour has come — its sands are fall-
  ing fast
Forget her frailty for it is the last.
— Can this be slumber? Yet its mur-
  murs seem
Like the wild visions of a troubled
  dream —
" Come — come " — she   whispers — " I
  have waited long —
" Indeed I love thee though thou didst
  me wrong —
" Thou dost not know me — I am pale
  and worn,
" And those long tresses, once thy pride,
  are shorn —
" Nay, do not blame me, for the nights
  were cold
" And we were starving, and they gave
  me gold —

" He took the food and warmed him at
  the flame
" And lisped his thanks to him I dared
  not name
" Thou neer hast seen him — look — how
  sweetly fair
" O'er his white forehead waves his flaxen
  hair
" Come to my arms — and art thou liv-
  ing still
" I thought thee dead — thy little hand
  is chill
" Thou hast been slumbering where the
  night wind blew
" And on thy ringlets shines the icy dew
" Oh God how heavy on my aching
  breast
" Weighs thy cold cheek — I pray thee
  let me rest
" The shadows darken and the sun is
  gone
" Sleep, sleep, sweet angel till the day
  star's dawn
" I too must slumber " — Yes to wake no
  more
Thy dreams are ended and thy sorrows
  oer !

Not ours to trace the endless shapes
  that rise
As o'er the stage the living scenery flies
A fertile subject is a dangerous thing
A patent pump in sweet Castalia's spring
That sucks and pours in one eternal
  stream
And damns the poet with his drowning
  theme.

O sovereign Patience ! more than mor-
  tal power
Whose smile can cheat each leaden
  footed hour
Not winged like Hope, but rising calm
  and sure
Strong to resist and faithful to endure,
Spread thy mute influence o'er these
  wearied walls
One little moment ere the curtain falls.
If Sleep, thy sister, lend her drowsy
  charms
And feebler heads nod heavy in her arms,
Let Fancy cheat them with delicious
  dreams
Of seraph minstrels and celestial
  themes, —

Then shall they murmur as they yawn and wake
That *was* a poem — there is no mistake !

Look then once more, but pass the meaner throng
And turn to those that claim a loftier song
Cold were the heart and lifeless were the hand
That left unsung the daughters of the land
Yet ah how vain the labor to compare
And crown but one where all are passing fair
How long untired would lingering fancy dwell
On every grace that marks the city bell
How melt in rapture oer the rustic maid
The flying Daphne of the woodland shade
While each was balanced in the poet's lay
And both united stole his heart away !

— Ye artless nymphs, like fleeting shadows seen
As with thy steps ye print the village green
Or at your windows, bending o'er the wheel
In one stray glance your bashful charms reveal
Look not in envy at the gems that crown
The glittering maidens of the gilded town ; —
With borrowed light the labored diamond glows
But Heaven's own blushes paint the breathing rose
Learn from the flower in native grace to shine
And love the garden better than the mine —
Trust in old paths — respect the ancient creeds
And wear unchanged your mother's golden beads !

— Yet ere we part this home of Science claims
One passing tribute to her hallowed names
Years roll on years in darkness and decay

Youth chills to age and age dissolves away
Yet though the lamp of burning mind expire
Hope waits and watches oer the central fire
Rude were the hands that reared this ancient shrine
Beneath the shadow of the storm-swept pine
They toiled and slept, but brighter summers shone
To nurse the seeds their humble faith had sown.

— Long shall the day-dream of romance pursue
Thy starlit wanderer in his frail canoe
And the rapt student in the twilight beam
Trace his dark shadow down the winding stream.

And he whose voice these classic shades have known
When first it deepened into manhood's tone
Whose ripening fame the wandering breezes bore
From the far prairie to the foaming shore
To other breasts shall light the deathless flame
That flings its halo round his patriot name
And warm and wake the rustic heart that thrills
To those deep accents from his granite hills !
— Here, Holy Science, may thy sceptre reign
Long as the mountains gird thy grassy plain
Still to thy courts may thronging footsteps tend
Still at thy feet may learning's pilgrims bend
Alike unheeding from thy Heaven built tower
The scoff of ignorance and the scowl of power
While ever watching round thy radiant throne
Truth, Freedom, Virtue claim thee as their own.

HUNTING–SONG FOR 1839

NAUSHON

YE hunters of New England
　Who bear the rusty guns
Your fathers shot the redcoats with,
　And left them to their sons !
With all your firelocks blaze away
　Before the bucks are gone,
As you aim at the game
　In the woods of old Naushon,
Where the shot are flying right and left
In the woods of old Naushon.

Our sportsmen are proverbial
　Among the ducks and loons,
And greatly feared of quadrupeds,
　From mammoths down to coons.
With double barrels loaded high,
　Their triggers both are drawn,
As they clang and they bang
　In the woods of old Naushon,
Where the bucks are leaping through the
　　leaves
　In the woods of old Naushon.

New England's trusty sportsmen
　Shall leave their wives so dear,
To hunt with our brave Governor
　For many a happy year.
Then, then, ye gallant gentlemen,
　When ancient corks are drawn,
Fill the toast to the host
　In the hall of old Naushon,
While the wine is flowing bright and free
In the hall of old Naushon.

TO A. L. J.

MARCH 6, 1840

ONE word — and that so softly fell
　That Love alone could catch the sound,
But all that virgin lips might tell
　Was in that little whisper found.
The breath had melted on the air —
　The form had passed, the smile had
　　flown.
I　sought　thee — but　thou　wast　not
　　there —
　Yet, Dearest ! I was not alone —

Still side by side we seemed to stray
　Beneath those bleak and leafless trees
Where balmy blossoms soon shall play
　Wreathed by the gentle April breeze —
Still side by side we wandered slow
　Unconscious through the busy throng
And still in accents soft and low
　We murmured as we passed along.

If He who bids the spring renew
　Her jewels like a blushing bride
And sprinkles with the morning dew
　The moss upon the mountain's side
Stoops from his azure throne above
　To paint the frail and thankless flowers
O smiles he not on hope and love
　When first they bloom in hearts like
　　ours ?

Darkness and silence ! all around
　Dissolves the midnight's sable tide —
Yet still I tread on any ground
　With thee still trembling at my side.
Come — come sweet shadow — roam no
　　more.
　Is not this lonely house thy own !
O let me dream the morning o'er —
　Nay Dearest I am not alone.

TO A. L. J.

MAY 22, 1840

O DEAREST, may each coming year
　More calm and cloudless shine
Than this of mingling love and fear
　The first that calls thee mine !

Still lightening like the morning beams
　Still spreading like the flowers
May all yet locked in golden dreams
　Wake in the coming hours.

In one deep tide our lives must flow
　O may they ever blend
When bright with joy or dark with woe
　Unruffled to the end.

TO A. L. J.

MAY 30, 1840

WHEN skims the summer moon on high
　Her starry train around her glowing

When waves are bright and breezes sigh
  Through the dark foliage softly flowing
Then like the voice that breathes around
  Shall be the gentle name thou bearest
The first my trembling accents found —
  And thou shalt be *Amelia,* dearest.

When to thy girlhood's simpler years
  With tranquil pulse thy heart is turning
And she who watched thy smiles and
    tears —
  Her midnight lamp above thee burning
Comes to thee as in days gone by
  Ere of her fondness death bereft
    thee —
Thou shalt be little *Ámelie* —
  The name her silent lips have left thee.

When winter wears her snowy crest
  And dark the angry waves are swelling
And love has made his peaceful nest
  Within our little quiet dwelling
We will not heed the blustering storm
  Though all without is bleak and chilly
But keep our fireside bright and warm
  And change Amelia into *Milly.*

A SCINTILLA

AT THE DINNER AFTER THE
INAUGURATION OF JARED SPARKS
HARVARD COLLEGE, JUNE 6, 1849

THE TASK

TWELVE well-crammed lines, firm, juicy,
    marrowy, sweet,
No bone or trimmings, nothing here but
    meat,
With rhyme run through them like a
    golden skewer.
Taste might approve and patience may
    endure.

THE EXECUTION

Long live old Harvard ! Lo, her rushing
    train
Greets a new sign-board stretched across
    the plain ,
While the bell rings — (and that the bell
    shall do
Till Charles shall drop his worn-out
    channel through,) —

It gently hints to every cur that barks,
Here comes the engine, — don't you see
    the Sparks ?

How changed the scene ! The forest path
    is clear ;
That mighty engine finds no *Indian
    here !*
The world's great teachers quit their na-
    tive Alps
To fill the skulls once trembling for their
    scalps,
When the red neighbors of our ancient
    school
Let their own wig*wams* others' wigs to
    cool !

A VISION OF LIFE

SEPTEMBER 27, 1849

THE well-known weakness of the rhym-
    ing race
Is to be ready in and out of place ;
No bashful glow, no timid begging off,
No sudden hoarseness, no discordant
    cough
(Those coy excuses which your singers
    plead,
When faintly uttering : " No, I can't,
    indeed ")
Impedes your rhymster in his prompt
    career.
Give him but hint ; and *won't* the muse
    appear !

So, without blushing, when they asked,
    I came —
I whom the plough-share, not the quill,
    should claim —
The rural nymphs that on my labors
    smile
May mend my fence, but cannot mend
    my style.
The winged horse disdains my sober
    team,
And teeming fancy must forget to dream.
I harrow fields and not the hearts of
    men ;
Pigs, and not poems, claim my humble
    pen.
And then to enter on so new a stage,
With the fair critics of this captious age,

Might lead a sceptic to the rude surmise
That cits, turned rustics, are not other-
    wise ;
Or the bright verdure of the pastoral
    scene
Had changed my hue, and made me very
    green.

A few brief words that, fading as they
    fall,
Like the frail garlands of a banquet hall,
May lend one glow, one breath of fra-
    grance pour,
Ere swept ungathered from the silent
    floor.
Such is my offering for your festal day :
These sprigs of rhyme ; this metrical
    bouquet.

O my sweet sisters — let me steal the
    name
Nearest to love and most remote from
    blame —
How brief an hour of fellowship ensures
The heart's best homage at a shrine like
    yours.
As o'er your band our kindling glances
    fall,
It seems a life-time since I've known you
    all !
Yet on each face, where youthful graces
    blend,
Our partial memory still revives a
    friend ;
The forms once loved, the features once
    adored,
In her new picture nature has restored.

Those golden ringlets, rippling as they
    flow,
We wreathed with blossoms many years
    ago.
Seasons have wasted ; but remembered
    yet,
There gleams the lily through those
    braids of jet.
Cheeks that have faded, worn by slow
    decay,
Have caught new blushes from the morn-
    ing's ray.
That simple ribbon, crossed upon the
    breast,
Wakes a poor heart that sobbed itself to
    rest ;

Aye, thus she wore it ; tell me not she
    died,
With that fair phantom floating by my
    side.
'T is as of old : why ask the vision's
    name :
All, to the white robe's folding, is the
    same ;
On that white bosom burns the self-same
    rose.

Oh, dear illusion, how thy magic power
Works with two charms — a maiden and
    a flower !
Then blame me not if, lost in memory's
    dream,
I cheat your hopes of some expansive
    theme.
When the pale starlight fills the evening
    dim,
A misty mantle folds our river's brim.
In those white wreaths, how oft the wan-
    derer sees
Half real shapes, the playthings of the
    breeze.
While every image in the darkening tide
Fades from its breast, unformed and un-
    descried.
Thus, while I stand among your starry
    train,
My gathering fancies turn to mist again.
O'er time's dark wave aerial shadows
    play,
But all the living landscape melts away.

WYCLIFFE

THE Avon to the Severn runs,
The Severn to the sea ;
And Wycliffe's dust shall spread abroad,
Wide as the waters be.

LETTER TO THE GOVERNOR

WILLIAM W. SWAIN

TELL me, Dear Governor, what shall I
    do for you,
How can you ask me to write something
    new for you —
I, who am working myself to an atomy
Over my lectures in odious Anatomy ?
Surely your breast cannot hold such a
    stony part

While I'm engaged on my Sketches of
Bony part
That you refuse to accept an apology —
Guilt I confess, but I plead Osteology.
What if I came ; Why the pavement
would fly at me.
Bucks would start up and insist on a shy
at me.
Science suspending her habeas corpusses
While I was shooting or looking at por-
pusses
— But there's a secret, Alas ! that I'm
splitting with ;
Guns do not suit me there's danger of
killing with.
Deer are such dears that I gladly would
kiss 'em all,
Treat 'em like ladies — and thats why I
Miss 'em all ;
Fishing is getting too rough for my feel-
ing heart
Though catching eels is a branch of the
'ealing art ;
Then as to feasting, it doesn't agree with
me
Each single goblet is equal to three with
me
Wine is my foe, though I still am a
friend of it —
Hock becomes hic with a cup at the end
of it —
And if I sit where the bumpers are bub-
bling,
While I am looking each Cork seems a
D(o)ublin !
— Fairest of Islands the birds ever light
about
Thine are the beauties for angels to write
about ;
Kindest of hearts that a button e'er burst
over
Thine are the virtues that saints would
cry first over !
Blessings fall on you both, thick as the
snow does,
Till your last doe shall be do. with the
dodos !

PLEASURE REMEMBERED

NAUSHON, NOVEMBER 19, 1850

DEAR are our smiling pleasures while they
last,

But dearer sighs are wafted from the
past.
O'er the bright present with its arching
bowers
The vines, luxuriant, trail their fruit and
flowers ;
In memory's vaults uncounted summers
shine,
Their purple clusters changed to beaming
wine !
Snatched from its stem, amidst the vul-
gar strife
The grape may cool the fiery thirst of
life,
But the rich goblet that in peace we
drain
Turns to sweet visions in the dreaming
brain.

TO JULIA WARD HOWE

JANUARY 1, 1854

IF I were one, O Minstrel wild,
That held "the golden cup"
Not unto thee, Art's stolen child,
My hand should yield it up ;

Why should I waste its gold on one
That holds a guerdon bright —
A chalice, flashing in the sun
Of perfect chrysolite.

And shaped on such a swelling sphere
As if some God has pressed
Its flowing crystal, soft and clear
On Hebe's virgin breast ?

What though the bitter grapes of earth
Have mingled in its wine,
The stolen fruits of heavenly birth
Have made its hue divine.

Oh, Lady, there are charms that win
Their way to magic bowers,
And they that weave them enter in
In spite of mortal powers ;

And hearts that seek the chapel's floor
Will throb the long aisle through,
Though none are waiting at the door
To sprinkle holy dew !

I, sitting in the portal gray
Of Art's cathedral dim,
Can see thee, passing in to pray
And sing thy first-born hymn ; —

Hold out thy hand ! these scanty drops
Come from a hallowed stream,
Its sands, a poet's crumbling hopes,
Its mist, his fading dream.

Pass on. Around the inmost shrine
A few faint tapers burn ;
This altar, priestess, shall be thine
To light and watch in turn ;

Above it smiles the Mother Maid,
It leans on Love and Art,
And in its glowing depth is laid
The first true woman's heart !

LETTER TO THE CONNECTICUT STATE MEDICAL SOCIETY

MARCH 23, 1855

IF schoolboy memory does not serve me
    wrong,
The God of Physic was the God of Song,
Whence cunning slander on the lips of
    some,
Declares his best prescription was a *hum*,
Though modern skill disowns the pun,
Medicine and Music still are one.

Health to the great Musician ! Him
    whose art
Steals through the senses to the coldest
    heart.
Not his to flourish on the pipe or lute,
The horn, the fife, the flageolet, or flute ;
He blows no trumpet, draws no bow, nor
    sings ;
He only plays — the "harp of thousand
    strings."

TO J. R. L.

MAY 29, 1855

HOSEA Biglow's folks is gone
    Down east to see his Uncle Franklin

He's lame to home — he's spilt the bone
    That keeps the sinnews of the ankle in

He'd like to come and see ye all
    And says he's greatly disappinted
But taint so serious arter all
    As Hosey's sorter double jinted

Hosea he don't drink no toast
    But tadpoles and Cochituate water
He says you're jail-birds eenamost
    For swallerin what you hadnt oughter

Besides he says he kinder thinks
    The police comes and takes the leavins
And cal'clates when theyve done their
    drinks
    They'll go and peach on Pason Stevens.

TO J. R. L. FROM HOMER WILBUR

MAY 29, 1855

THE Reverend Homer Wilbur sends
    His best respects to brother Lowell
Would come to meet him with his friends
    If Homer Junior was not so ill
Is loath to trouble Brother L.
    Desires to send his special blessing
A note of several things as well
    H. W.'s anxious for possessing.

A pocket copy — if its found
    Of all the earlier Christian fathers
" Daimōn, or Satan's Arm unbound "
    A missing tract of Cotton Mather's
Item a lock of Wickliff's hair
    And Calvins book on Revelation
Please ask if Reverend Jubb can spare
    His Peddlingtonian dissertation

Likewise a portrait of the lad
    The ninth or tenth of Smithfields mar-
    tyrs
I send my own (which cant be had)
    To trade with in the way of barter
The Lord be with my youthful friend
    And save his lot from all disaster —
Please dont forget it when you send
    To pay the postage for your pastor.

FROM AN AFTER–DINNER SPEECH

MASSACHUSETTS MEDICAL SOCIETY

JUNE 27, 1855

As the river of New England
  That is flowing at our side,
No rock can stay from running
  To meet the salt sea-tide ;
So roll our art's deep current
  By many a grateful shore,
Till life has reached the ocean
  That pain shall vex no more.

As the mountain of New England
  In the far off northern sky
Looks down upon the river
  That wanders murmuring by,
So from her cloud-capped turret
  Let solemn art look down
On fashion's lying whisper
  And folly's idle frown.

As the bright star of evening
  Plays on the mountain's crest,
Glancing from every streamlet
  That sparkles on its breast ;
So let the heavenly splendors
  Of truth's white star be found
Still shining fairest in us
  While all is dark around !

CAMILLA

AUGUST 9, 1855

THE gray robe trailing round her feet,
  She smiled and took the slippered stir-
    rup
(A smile as sparkling, rosy, sweet,
  As soda, drawn with strawberry
    syrup) ; —
Now, gallant, now ! be strong and
    calm, —
  The graceful toilet is completed, —
Her foot is in thy hollowed palm —
  One little spring, and she is seated !

No foot-print on the grass was seen,
  The clover hardly bent beneath her,
I knew not if she pressed the green,
  Or floated over it in ether ;

Why, such an airy, fairy thing
  Should carry ballast in her pocket, —
God bless me ! If I help her spring
  She'll shoot up heavenward like a
    rocket.

Ah, fatal doubt ! The sleepless power
  That chains the orbs of light together,
Bends on its stem the slenderest flower
  That lifts its plume from turf or
    heather ;
Clasp, lady, clasp the bridle rein !
  The filly stands — holds hard upon
    her !
Twine fast those fingers in her mane,
  Or all is lost — excepting honor !

Earth stretched his arms to snatch his
    prize,
  The fairies shouted "Stand from
    under ! "
The violets shut their purple eyes,
  The naked daisies stared in wonder :
One moment. — Seated in her pride,
  Those arms shall try in vain to win
    her ;
" Earth claims her not," the fairies cried,
  " She has so little of it in her ! "

TWO POEMS FOR THE FESTIVAL OF ST. STEPHEN'S PARISH

PITTSFIELD, AUGUST 9, 1855

I

A DOLLAR'S WORTH

MOTTO

IF man, or boy, or dolt, or scholar
  Will break this seal, he pays his
    dollar ;
But if he reads a single minute,
  He'll find a dollar's worth within it.

LETTER

Listen to me and I will try
To tell you what a dollar will buy.

A dollar will buy a Voter's conscience,
Or a book of " Fiftieth thousand " non-
    sense ;

Or a ticket to hear a Prima Donna,
Or a fractional part of a statesman's
   honor ;

It will buy a tree to sit in the shade of
Or half the cotton a tournure's made of.

It will buy a glass of rum or gin
At a Deacon's store or a Temperance inn,
(The Deacon will show you how to mix it
Or the Temperance Landlord stay and fix
   it.)

It will buy a painting at Burbank's hall
That will frighten the spiders from off
   the wall ;

Or a dozen teaspoons of medium size,
That will do for an Agricultural prize.

It will buy four tickets to Barnum's
   show —
(Late firm of Pharaoh, Herod & Co.)

Or get you a paper that brings by mail
Its weekly " Original thrilling tale " —
Of which the essential striking plot
Is a daddy that's rich and a youth that's
   not,
Who seeking in vain for Papa's consent,
Runs off with his daughter — the poor
   old gent !
The Governor's savage ; at last relents
And leaves them a million in cash and
   rents.

Or a Hair-wash, patent, and warranted
   too,
That will turn your whiskers from gray
   to blue,
And dye old three score as good as new ;
So that your wife will open her eyes
And treat you with coolness, and then
   surprise,
And at last, as you're sidling up to her,
Cry " I'll call my husband, you saucy
   cur ! "

Or a monochrome landscape, done in an
   hour,
That looks like a ceiling stained in a
   shower ;

Or a ride to Lenox through mire and
   clay,

Where you may see, through the live
   long day,
Scores of women with couples of men
Trudging up hill — and down again.

This is what a dollar will do,
With many things as strange but true ;
This very dollar I've got from you —
P. S. We shouldn't mind if you made it
   two.

II

FAITH

MOTTO

FAITH is the conquering Angel's crown ;
   Who hopes for grace must ask it ;
Look shrewdly ere you lay me down,
   I'm Portia's leaden casket.

LETTER

Fair lady, whosoe'er thou art,
   Turn this poor leaf with tenderest care,
And — hush, O hush thy beating heart —
   The One thou lovest will be there !

Alas ! not loved by thee alone,
   Thine idol, ever prone to range ;
To-day, all thine, to-morrow flown,
   Frail thing that every hour may
      change.

Yet, when that truant course is done,
   If thy lost wanderer reappear,
Press to thy heart thy only One
   That nought can make more truly
      dear !

POSTSCRIPT

Fair lady, lift thine eyes and tell
   If this is not a truthful letter ;
This is the one (1) thou lovest well,
   And nought (0) can make thee love it
      better (10).
Though fickle, do not think it strange
   That such a friend is worth possessing,
For one that gold can never change
   Is Heaven's own dearest earthly bless-
      ing.

CRIMEA

THERE is a weeping by England's hun-
   dred streams,
   By Severn, and Thames, and Trent ;

And o'er the graves of her trampled
braves,
The queen of the sea is bent.

One lesson shall serve the haughty isle,
Girt round with stately towers ;
Thank God that the blow which lays her
low,
Comes not from a hand of ours.

INTRODUCTION

FOR THE MEETING OF THE BURNS CLUB

JANUARY 25, 1856

I HAVE come with the rest, I can hardly
tell why,
With a line I will read you before it is
dry.
I know I've no business among you, full
well,
But I'm here, notwithstanding, and how,
I will tell.

It was not a billet beginning " Dear Sir ;"
No missive like that would have coaxed
me to stir ;
Nor a ticket, announcing the " on " and
the " at,"
And " requesting the honor," — 'twas
better than that.

It was done by a visit, from one that you
know,
Whose smile is unchilled by life's season
of snow,
Whose voice is so winning, resist as you
may,
You must do what it says, for it will
have its way.

It is true that at first I began to suggest
I should sit like a stranger apart from the
rest ;
But he said : " To no clan is our banquet
confined,
For the heart of the poet belongs to
mankind."

Then I timidly asked, " Can I run, at a
pinch,

If our friends from the old world have
learned how to lynch ? "
For I thought with dismay of the Know-
Nothing Crew,
And I fancied a yell — " He's a Know-
Nothing too ! "

I thought of old Porteous, of Hare and
of Burke ;
I remembered the witches of Alloway
Kirk ; —
" Why bless you," he said with a smile,
" if you're *cotched,*
You will never be killed, you will only
be *Scotched !* "

So I came, and I'm here, with a line as I
said ;
I don't mean the verses that just have
been read,
But the ones in my pocket, and so, if
you please,
You shall hear them at once if you'll
pardon me these.

FOR THE HARVARD MEDICAL SCHOOL

I TOLD him I wouldn't — by George, and
I meant it
It's six o'clock now and too late to repent
it, —
Why need he come trying to wheedle
and flatter me ?
Confound that Professor of morbid Anat-
omy !

I swore that I would n't — I cant commit
perjury —
— There's a rap at my door — the Pro-
fessor of Surgery —
He'd like to know whether I shall not
read something —
Why, haven't I sworn that I will be a
dumb thing ?

" I am told," he replies, " there are strong
expectations
Of one of your rhyming tintinnabula-
tions, — "
I don't care, says I, what they told you
about it —
I myself — on the highest authority, —
doubt it,

It's a quarter past six, and its out of the question —
It will just interrupt duodenal diges-
tion —
For writing carotids and vertebrals taxes
I want all my blood for my caliac axis.

This stoning of frogs to the boy pretty sport is
As the hill paddy said in articulo mortis,
And its pleasant no doubt while one's filling his pharynx
To call for a tune from another man's larynx.

I told him I wouldn't — I mean to stick to it
In spite of J. B. S. J. — he can't make me do it —
Go — bid your old skeletons open their throttles,
Or stir up the babes in your alcohol bottles !

No, no ! you can't do it ! don't think I'm half-witted
Like alcohol babies whose brains were omitted !
You don't suppose mine are beginning to soften ?
They would if I did as you'd have me so often.

— " So often ! *How* often ? No need we should tell you, —
It is not the lips of the living compel you — "
Ah no ! from the shadows that hover around us
I hear in the accents of friendship that bound us, —

" Come now for the voice to which fondly we listened
Some years before half these young fel-
lows were christened
It will cost you an hour, it will soothe us a minute
Though nothing but love and good na-
ture are in it."

Have I broken my oath like a traitor false-hearted ?
It was made to the living and the de-
parted ;

I turn to the past from the bloom of the present
That charming old lady is always so pleasant !

But this is no place for the sage that remembers, —
We want the bright flame, not the ashes and embers, —
We ask but for smiles, not for tear drops to tickle, —
Come, J. B. S. J. show a baby in pickle !

AT A DINNER TO AGASSIZ

MAY 28, 1857?

THE larches are green, and the lilacs have blown,
And over the hillsides young summer has shone ;
So joyous, so glowing the welcome we bring, —
As warm as our summer, as fresh as our spring !

No breath from the glacier shall waft us its chill.
Though Jung-frau remembers her van-
quisher still ;
Our skies have an azure as deep as his own,
And bright eyes have beamed for him, blue as the Rhone.

We clasp him once more to the heart of the West ;
The rose of the Alps is for Liberty's breast.
A home for his thought like the cloud-
rending peak,
His smile like the sunbeam that rests on its cheek !

A SONG FOR THE WIDOW

MASSACHUSETTS MEDICAL BENEVOLENT
SOCIETY

JULY 30, 1857

WE drink to-night to eyes once bright,
While Hope still told her story,

That lost their gleam in the noontide
    beam,
  Like the blue of the morning-glory !

CHORUS

  Then drink to-night to eyes once
      bright,
    While Heaven is bending o'er us
  To catch the song our lips prolong,
    And angels join our chorus.

Let the sparkles pass o'er the brimming
    glass,
  With summer's life-blood glowing,
As the fire-flies shine through the tangled
    vine
  Where the purple grapes are growing.
                                    CHORUS

Though faint the spark that gilds our
    dark
  With love instead of learning,
'Tis the red that shows ere the rose-bud
    blows,
  Now its inmost heart is burning !
                                    CHORUS

If wine can bring, from Mercy's spring,
  One drop for Sorrow's daughter,
Why then 'tis clear, we need not fear —
  Our wine has changed to water.

CHORUS

  Then while we drink, the saints shall
      wink
    That stand as sentries o'er us,
  And the angels' eyes shall close like-
      wise,
    Till they wake to join our chorus.

SONG AT THE HUNT

NAUSHON ISLAND

SEPTEMBER 21, 1857

As o'er the goblets crystal brink
  The rosy blood is rushing
Our lips must have a health to drink
  To save our cheeks from blushing

We shall not pledge our young tonight
  If We've our wits about us

Their blood is warm, their hearts are
    light
  They're well enough without us

The old ! what simpletons are they
  That leave their youth behind them ?
We drink their better sense — but stay !
  We don't know where to find them.

The ladies ? shall our goblets ring
  For mothers wives & daughters ?
Our hearts, without the " Eagles Wing "
  Have flown across the waters

And as the river holds the skies
  With all their starry splendor
Each cup is bright with beaming eyes
  As pure, as true, as tender.

But look in silence on the wine
  For if the word were spoken
The liquid mirror where they shine
  Would be forever broken

So then for fear We die of thirst
  Before we lift the sluices
We'll drink the health that mingles first,
  With summer's golden juices

The Youth that holds his court today
  And spreads his household banner
Long live the gallant, generous, gay
  Lord of the Ocean Manor !

Though like the Island where he reigns
  His frame by fate is anchored
Love still runs laughing through the
    veins
  That rust has never cankered.

And like the rock that breasts the sea
  Life's sunlit waves shall find him
Till Heaven's soft whisper sets him free
  And Angel hands unbind him.

THE HUNT

NAUSHON, 1857

NOT a buck was shot nor a doe nor a
    faun
  As from desire to dream they hurried,

Though the huntsmen were dragged from
    their beds by dawn
  And the deer were terribly worried.

They crawled back slowly at fall of night
  At a funeral trot returning,
As they steered their course by the dim
    red light
  Where the Captain's cheroot was burn-
    ing.

Short, not sweet, were the words they
    said
  As they smoked in silent sorrow,
But they swore that the deer must all be
    dead,
  And they'd try again tomorrow.

No wish for a saddle or haunch was
    heard ;
  They did not care a button,
They said with a grin how they all
    preferred
  A leg of the island mutton.

Little they spoke, as they jogged in the
    road
  But they kept up a mighty thinking
Of the wagon showing its empty load,
  And the folks are staring and winking.

They thought, as they sadly removed the
    caps
  From the useless shot and powder,
How they'd better have staid at home,
    perhaps,
  And plied with their spoons at chowder.

Slowly and solemnly, one by one,
  They entered and told their story,
The hearing whereof brought lots of fun
  With a plentiful lack of glory —

TO JAMES JACKSON, M. D.

WITH A GIFT OF SILVER SALT–CELLARS

THIS shrine a precious gift enfolds ;
  Look, when its lids unclose,
Not on the shining cross it holds,
  But on the love it shows.

What though the silvered brow may seem
  Amid the youthful throng
A little farther down the stream
  That bears us all along ;

Those murmuring waves are mute to-
    day,
  The stream forgets to run,
The brown locks mingle with the gray,
  And all our hearts are one.

Ah, could we bring earth's sweetest song
  And bear its brightest gold,
The gift our grateful hearts would wrong,
  Our love were still untold.

OUR SECOND SELVES

LOOK with me through this magic glass,
And see the people as they pass !
As each in turn we bring in view,
We thought him one, but find him two ;
A double shape, a twin-like pair,
But one of flesh and one of air, —
The first a vulgar mortal elf, —
The second what he thinks himself !

Our magic glass has curious tricks, —
Yon slender youth of five feet six
Struts like a peacock in the sun, —
His second self is six feet one !
And he with features all awry,
Whose sweetest smile makes children cry,
Walks not alone, but always near
That lovely youth the " Belvidere " !

My lady's cheek can boast no more
The cranberry white and pink it wore ;
And where her shining locks divide
The parting line is all too wide, —
(That fatal sign which still reveals
The   track   of   Time's   remorseless
    wheels, —
In short, if all the truth were told,
She's — Hush ! a lady's never old !

We lift our glass ; what youthful bride
Walks blooming at my lady's side ?
Where'er she moves is always seen
This sweet young figure, just eighteen,
Fresh as Love's Goddess from the sea, —
Who can this lovely image be ?
O, that's my lady, as she seems
When waking, of herself she dreams !

Give some poor lecturer leave to spout,
And sit an hour to hear him out
Look through our eye-glass at the
  chair —
Lo ! Tully seated with him there !
Nay spare the wretch that frozen sneer
Or melt it with one pitying tear,
When the lean, black-coat crow has
  cawed
And wonders why they dont applaud.

Shadow and substance ; so we glide,
Life's double spectres, side by side,
Till o'er us peals the passing bell, —
And which is real who can tell ?
God grant that in some happier sphere
These flitting shapes may reappear
Each fairer than its earthly dreams
And be as to itself it seems !

VARIATIONS ON AN ARIA

HARVARD MUSICAL ASSOCIATION

JANUARY 18, 1858

ONE molten cluster let me claim
  Of grapes that wore the purple stain, —
No maddening draught of scorching
  flame
But leaf and blossom-filtered rain,
  Sweet with the musky earth's perfume,
  Red with the burning glow of dawn,
Still flower-like in its breath and
  bloom, —
  The soul of summers dead and gone !

Ah, not alone their sunsets lie
  Dissolved in this empurpled glow,
But sounds and shapes that will not die
  Run with its current's crimson flow !
The music of the silent tongue, —
  The flying hand that swept the keys, —
The broken lute, the harp unstrung, —
  We listen and we look for these.

Hark ! while the dimpling fount is
  stirred,
  The far off echoes move their wings,
And through the quivering past is heard
  The murmur of its myriad strings.
Once more that old remembered strain !
  The Prima Donna's locust-cry !

And hush for memory breathes again
  Some lost " Pierian " melody !

And so we will not call him thief
  Nor hold him guilty of a sin
Who plucks away one ivy-leaf
  Or smoothes the panther's spotted
  skin ;
For if we steal the brightest wine
  We do the thyrsus little wrong,
Since all the jewels of the vine
  Were thrown her by the God of Song !

ADIEUX À LA VIE

FROM THE FRENCH OF NICOLAS GILBERT

AT life's gay banquet placed, a poor un-
  happy guest,
  One day I pass then disappear ;
I die, and on the tomb where I at length
  shall rest
  No friend shall come to shed a tear.

LES BOHÉMIENS

FROM THE FRENCH OF BÉRANGER

WIZARDS, jugglers, thieving crew, —
  Refuse drawn
    From the nations gone, —
Wizards, jugglers, thieving crew,
Merry Gipsies, whence come you ?

Whence we come ? There's none may
  know.
    Swallows come,
    But where their home ?
Whence we come ? There's none may
  know
Who shall tell us where we go ?

From country, law and monarch free,
    Such a lot
    Who envies not ?
From country, law and monarch free
Man is blest one day in three.

Free-born babes we greet the day, —
    Church's rite
    Denied us quite, —

Free-born babes we greet the day,
To sound of fife and roundelay.

Our young feet are unconfined
        Here below
        Where follies grow,—
Our young feet are unconfined
By swaddling bands of errors blind.

Good people at whose cost we thieve
        In juggling book
        Will always look ;
Good people at whose cost we thieve
In sorcerers and in saints believe.

If Plutus meets our tramping band,
        Charity !
        We gaily cry ;
If Plutus meets our tramping band,
We sing and hold him out our hand.

Hapless birds whom God has blest
        Hunted down
        Through every town,—
Hapless birds whom God has blest
Deep in forests hangs our nest.

Love, without his torch, at night
        Bids us meet
        In union sweet ;
Love, without his torch, at night
Binds us to his chariot's flight.

Thine eye can never stir again,
        Learned sage
        Of slenderest gauge,—
Thine eye can never stir again
From thy old steeple's rusty vane.

Seeing is having. Here we go !
        Life that's free
        Is ecstasy.
Seeing is having. Here we go !
Who sees all, conquers all below.

But still in every place they cry,
        Join the strife
        Or lag through life;
But still in every place they cry,
'Thou'rt born, good-day ; thou diest,
        good-bye.'

When we die, both young and old,
        Great and small,
        God save us all !

When we die, both young and old,
To the doctors all are sold.

We are neither rich nor proud ;
        Laws we scorn
        For freedom born ;
We are neither rich nor proud,—
Have no cradle, roof or shroud.

But, trust us, we are merry still ;
        Lord or priest
        Greatest or least :
But, trust us, we are merry still ;
'Tis happiness to have our will.

Yes, trust us, we are merry still
        Lord or priest
        Greatest or least
Yes, trust us, we are merry still :
'Tis happiness to have our will.

ANSWER TO A TEETOTALER

        Who was it, I pray,
        On the wedding day
        Of the Galilean's daughter
        With a touch divine
        Turned into wine
        Six buckets of *filtered* water ?

THE EXAMINATION

I

Come you Professors, young and old
        Disperse yourselves around
And straight prepare to answer square
        The questions we propound !
Speak out aloud before the crowd
        And so we all shall see
If you have wit that makes you fit
        To ask for our degree !
        O Professors !
        Professors, don't be shy
We'll put you through, so don't look
        blue,
        Unless we turn you by !

II

Call Number one.—Professor *Bones.*
        Take down his age and name.
Now ask your questions, brother Jones.
        Professor, hear the same.

Here, take your place, look in my face,
  Stand up upon your legs
And tell me why it's all a lie
  That men are hatched from eggs ?
    O Professor
  Professor, can't you tell ?
  I rather guess that you'll confess
    The ovum is a *sell*.

III

What do you say ? You all vote *Nay*.
  Professor Bones may go.
Professor Bougie, you'll proceed
  To tell us what you know.
Explain this fact. When you extract
  A polyp or a wen,
Why are you drest in all your best,
  Among these plain young men ?
    O Professor !
  Professor, can't you tell ?
  Why when you take a tumour out
  You needs must *cut a swell !*

IV

Professor Bougie, stand aside,
  We cannot let you in.
Professor Squills, Professor Pills,
  With you we will begin.
Pray tell us why, when people lie
  In fevers, sick abed,
In your prescriptions you employ
  A language that is dead ?
    O Professors !
  Professors, don't you know ?
  Because its what the dead folks talk
  Where all your patients go !

V

Vote, brothers ! So, you all say No !
  Rejected both the two !
Professor Gasbag take the stand
  And try what you can do.
If SH, KO, HO, N,
  And — AN, OS, E
Are brought in contact, please explain
  What will the product be ?
    O Professor !
  Professor, can't you tell ?
  There is, no doubt you'll soon find out
  There'll be a mighty smell !

VI

Now don't be vexed, but call the next, —
  Curator ! won't you come ?

He's always found a stirring round
  In that old museum !
When Typhoid fever's getting well
  Pray tell us why you find
That Peyers glands are like a boot
  A cobbler mends behind ?
    O Professor ?
  How badly you must feel !
  The healing of a patch is like
  The patching of a heel !

VII

You all say No ! it is no go !
  We can no longer dwell
And so we mean to call the Dean.
  Professor Fontanel !
You know full well as people tell
  The branch that you profess :
Why is the gravid matrix like
  To Adams his Express ?
    O Professor
  The reason I will state :
Because they both *contract* to make
  Delivery of freight !

VIII

He can't get in ! they're all turned by !
  Now boys, what shall we do ?
Remember this, how you may miss
  When they get hold of you !
So don't condemn, but pity them
  And give them their degree.
For if we're kind to folks we find
  That folks are kind to we !
    O Professors !
  Remember if you please
How kind we've been to let you in
  And make us all M.D.'s !

PENITENTIA

FEBRUARY 27, 1860

SWEET cousin, if too hard I hit,
To any fine I will submit.
Drench me with teacups of Souchong
Redder than garnets, upas-strong, —
Drug me with coffee, make me drain
Huge bowls of Hyson, Slumber's bane,
Too happy for my pardon's sake
To lie till morning, wide awake.

By all the firefly sparks that fill
The twilight groves of Shady hill, —

(Faint emblems of the gleams that flit
And sparkle through a woman's wit,)
By every smile on woman's face, —
By all that makes my Cousin Grace, —
By every Nymph of cakes and tea
If I said *wasp* — I *meant a bee.*

Alas ! we have been friends so long
But tongues are sharp, and tea is strong
And words are sudden, and minds are
    weak,
And to be thoughtless when we speak
Is to be human. —
        Chase away
This silly stinging " wasp ", I pray,
And on the next Triennial see
If you are not declared A. B.

TO E. AND L. A. WITH A PEAR

THE Prophet for his thirsting flock
  Bade streams of water flow ;
The new enchanter smites the rock
  And fruits of Eden glow.

Like goes to like ; this beauty seeks
  The great and good and fair,
And finds at length, with blushing cheeks,
  A second *matchless pair.*

A LETTER TO ELIZA

IF any other son of Adam
Owns my whole name, respected Madam,
Except one boy, who's now in college,
It's quite beyond my sphere of knowl-
    edge.
A thousand pounds against a guinea
I never looked on Old Virginny
The whole Dominion to an acre
I never knew your " Dr Baker," —
Whoso describes my hair as sable
Has told a — horizontal fable ;
— *Who is* this saucy youth that tries a
Base trick upon my friend Eliza ?

STAR–SPANGLED BANNER

EXTRA STANZA

WHEN our Land is illumined with Lib-
  erty's smile,

If a foe from within strike a blow at her
  glory,
Down, down with the traitor that dares
  to defile
The flag of her stars and the page of her
  story !
By the millions unchained, when our
  birthright was gained,
We will keep her bright blazon forever
  unstained !
And the star-spangled banner in triumph
  shall wave
While the land of the free is the home of
  the brave.

TRUMPET SONG

THE battle-drum's loud rattle is rending
  the air,
The troopers all are mounted, their
  sabres are bare :
The guns are unlimbered, the bayonets
  shine,
Hark ! hark ! 'tis the trumpet-call !
  wheel into line !
    Ta ra ! ta ta ta !
    Trum trum, tra ra ra ra !
    Beat drums, and blow trumpets !
    Hurrah, boys, hurrah !

March onward, soldiers, onward, the
  strife is begun,
Loud bellowing rolls the boom of the
  black-throated gun ;
The rifles are cracking, the torn banners
  toss,
The sabres are clashing, the bayonets
  cross !
    Ta ra ! ta ta ta ! , etc.

Down with the leaguing liars, the traitors
  to their trust,
Who trampled the fair charter of Free-
  dom in dust !
They falter, they waver, they scatter,
  they run,
The field is our own, and the battle is
  won !
    Ta ra ! ta ta ta ! , etc.

God save our mighty people, and prosper
  our cause !

We're fighting for our nation, our land,
    and our laws !
Though tyrants may hate us, their
    threats we defy,
And drum-beat and trumpet shall peal
    our reply !
        Ta ra ! ta ta ta ! , etc.

WITH TWELVE AUTOGRAPHS

JANUARY 26, 1864

THIS is Autograph number one,
The first of a dozen I've just begun.

This is Autograph number two,
Written, my lady, express for you.

This is Autograph number three,
Warranted genuine. Signed by me

This is Autograph number four.
Shouldn't you think it would be a bore ?

This is Autograph number five, —
Fifth of a dozen — if I survive.

This is Autograph number six.
(You pays your money and takes your
    picks.)

This is Autograph number seven.
(More than half of 'em done, thank
    heaven !)

This is Autograph number eight.
" Fond of writing 'em ? " *Pas si bête !*

This is Autograph number nine.
It is, and it isn't, both yours and mine.

This is Autograph number ten.
Six volumes written with this same pen.

This is Autograph number eleven.
Warranted his by whom 'tis given.

This is Autograph twelfth and last.
What is so pleasant as trouble past ?

WEARY

FEBRUARY 17, 1864

PEACE ! Shall we ever hear that blissful
    sound
And see the raging steeds of War un-
    bound ?
Our streams run blood, our fields are
    crimson mire,
Smoke hides the sun, the night is red
    with fire, —
    How long, O Lord, how long ?

As one that sleeping moans but knows
    not why
Till at the last he wakes with sudden
    cry —
I, slumbering, woke to hear a Nation's
    prayer
Piercing the death-chilled, sorrow-laden
    air
    How long, O Lord, how long ?

Patience ! the fire must burn the root of
    shame ;
The tears of anguished souls must quench
    the flame.
God led his people to the promised shore
Through the long desert — we will ask no
    more
    How long, O Lord, how long ?

SONG OF WELCOME TO THE RUSSIAN FLEET

JUNE 8, 1864

SEA-BIRDS of Muscovy, rest in our waters,
    Fold your white wings by our rock-
        girded shore ;
While with glad voices its sons and its
    daughters
    Welcome the friends ye have wafted us
        o'er.

Sea-kings of Neva, our hearts throb your
    greeting !
    Deep as the anchors your frigates let
        fall ;
Down to the fount where our life-pulse is
    beating,

Sink the kind accents you bear to us
all.

Fires of the North, in eternal com-
munion,
Blend your broad flashes with eve-
ning's bright star !
God bless the Empire that loves the
great Union !
Strength to her people ! Long life to
the Czar !

AN OLD GRADUATE'S VERSES

PHI BETA KAPPA DINNER, HARVARD
JULY 21, 1864

A PEACEFUL haven while the deep is
seething,
An alcove's cobwebs while the flags are
flaunting,
A spot of tranquil shade for quiet breath-
ing
While all the haggard, hurried world is
panting ;

Hard by, a church-yard full of soundest
sleepers,
Old square-browed Presidents with wis-
dom brimming,
Long " deaded " tutors and clean swept
up sweepers,
And the slim youths of promise,
drowned in swimming ;

Old trees, the saplings of the Revolution,
That heard the banging of the " Live-
ly's " cannon, —
The first salute that hailed the " Con-
stitution," —
The broadsides of the " Chesapeake "
and " Shannon";

Old halls, each building youth's eternal
palace,
Stirring and sparkling still with fresh
newcomers,
As the last vintage fills the same old
chalice

That held the life-blood of a hundred
summers ;

Old teachers, abstracts of the mouldy
centuries,
Sines, xs, accents, etched on all their
features,
Old beldames slopping through the windy
entries
With pail and besom, — obsoletest
creatures !

Old legends of our fathers' fathers' follies,
Born of hot youth and blood-inflaming
revel, —
The midnight leap from Harvard's roof
to Hollis, —
The sinful words that summoned up
the Devil ;

Prayer bells — brief toilets — limited la-
vation —
Sharp run of tardy saints to *Pater
noster,*
Where worship mingles with the contem-
plation
Of doubtful record on the morning's
roster ;

The long, long grind of daily recitation
Chalk, blackboard, " pony," prompter,
all in action
The prisoned hour of stifling condensa-
tion,
The final gush, rush, flush of rarefac-
tion.

These are the old, old tangled recollec-
tions
That Time in strange confusion blends
and mingles
Till with the wakened thrill of young
affections
The marrow in the bones of Memory
tingles !

These weave the dream, the beatific
vision
That haunts our busy day, our toil-
bought slumbers,
Here are the blissful shades, the bowers
Elysian,
And these the brightest hours our eve-
ning numbers !

PRELUDE

NAUSHON ISLAND, NOVEMBER 1864

O THOU who lovest best the song
    Of bird that never sang in cage,
Such as the wood-notes that belong
    To this, our Island Song-book's page !

O'er its fair field the fancy flits
    That never bounden book confined,
And on its perch the warbler sits
    Whom leaden chains could never bind.

As when the birds in copse and glen,
    From   oaken   bough   and   beechen
        spray, —
Thrush, robin, sparrow, bobolink, wren,
    Blackbird and bluebird, finch and
        jay, —

With joyous clamor wake the morn
    And startle all the leafy woods,
So thrill those poet-voices, born
    In Nature's sea-girt solitudes !

Ah, happy seasons, lapsing sweet
    Amid those bowers of peace and rest,
Where all the songsters loved to meet
    And carol round the king-bird's nest,

Your flowers are dust, your suns have
        set,
    Yet here they still shall bloom and
        shine,
Till Love and Friendship both forget
    They knelt before the Island shrine !

THE JUBILEE

Nauticus loquitur

I'VE heerd some talk of a Jubilee
To celebrate " our " " victory " ; —
Now I'm a chap as follers the sea,
'n' f'r 'z I know, nob'dy'll listen t'me,
B't I'll tell y' jest what's my idee.

When you 'n' a felalh 'z got your grip,
Before y've settled it which can whip,
I won't say nothin'. You let her rip !
Knock him to splinters, chip by chip !

I tell y', shipmates 'n' lan'sm'n too,
There's chaps aboard th't's 'z good 'z
        you, —
'Twas God A'mighty that made her
    crew !
FOLKS is FOLKS ! 'n' that's 'z true
'z that land is black 'n' water blue !

Come tell us, shipmates, ef y' can,
Was there ever a crew sence th' worl'
    began
That sech a wallopin' had to stan'
'z them poor fellahs th't tried t' man
The great Chicago catamaran ?

Wahl, this is what y've had t' do, —
T' lick 'em, — but not t' drown 'em too !
There's some good fellahs, 'n' not a few
That's a swimmin' about, all chilled 'n'
    blue,
'n' wants t' be h'isted aboard o' you !

Come, drowning foes ! your friends we'll
    be, —
We've licked ! Haw ! haw ! You're
    licked ! Hee ! hee !
Hooraw for you ! Horraw for we !
We'll wait till the whole wide land is
    free,
And then we'll have our JUBILEE !

TO JOHN PIERPONT

APRIL 6, 1865

LOVE, honour, reverence are the meed we
    owe
To him who in the press of younger men,
Toiling with head, heart, hand, with
    tongue and pen,
Treads his firm pathway through the
    blinding snow,
Singing in cheery tones that long ago
Our fathers heard : Not less melodious,
    when
Ten winters lie on three score years and
    ten,
And still life's unchilled fountains over-
    flow !
Though paler seems the faithful watch
    tower's light
In the rich dawn that kindles all the day,
Still in our grateful memory lives the ray

Of the lone flambeau, blazing through
    the night
Now while the heavens, in new-born
    splendours bright
Shine o'er a ransomed people's opening
    way.

TO THE HARVARD ASSOCIATION OF NEW YORK CITY

FEBRUARY 20, 1866

SHE to whose faithful breast each child
    is dear
    Hears the far murmur of your voices
      meeting, —
Ah sweetest music to her loving ear !
    And sends a mother's greeting.

When first enrobed her radiant form she
    dressed
    TRUTH was the pearl that on her fore-
      head glistened, —
FREEDOM her message to the virgin West,
    And the whole world has listened.

Whate'er she gave you, — learning, sci-
    ence, art, —
    Shed from the mystic tree whose leaves
      are letters,
One gift excelled them all — a manly
    heart
    Freed from all earthly fetters.

Guard well the pearl of Harvard, all too
    white
    For the coarse hands to clutch that buy
      and barter, —
Conquer with Freedom in her life-long
    fight
    Or fall her noble martyr !

FOR A MONUMENT

I

INSENSIBILITY to pain
During a surgical operation
First produced at the Mass.
General Hospital
In Boston
By the use of Sulphuric Ether
in October 1846

To commemorate this event
A citizen of Boston
Has caused this monument to be erected
A.D. 1866

II

These dews of mercy Heaven in pity
    shed
To lap in peaceful dreams the sufferer's
    head,
To calm the lingering throb of mortal
    strife,
And smooth the path that leads from life
    to life.

III

God wrought the marvel of our Mother's
    birth
While Adam slumbered, painless, on the
    earth ;
Her living daughters bless the gracious
    power
That soothes the pang of woman's sor-
    rowing hour.

IV

Too cold the stone, the shaping hand too
    rude
Though only mortals asked our gratitude,
Thy glories, Father, in Thy servants
    shine, —
For all our blessings all the praise be
    Thine !

FOR LONGFELLOW'S BIRTHDAY

FEBRUARY 27, 1867

IN gentle bosoms tried and true
    How oft the thought will be,
" Dear friend, shall I remember you,
    Or you remember me ? "

But thou, sweet singer of the West,
    Whose song in every zone
Has soothed some aching grief to rest
    And made some heart thine own,

Whene'er thy tranquil sun descends, —
    Far, far that evening be, —

What mortal tongue may count the friends
  That shall remember thee ?

ON RECEIVING A STOLEN APPLE

WE owe, alas ! to woman's sin
  The woes with which we grapple ; —
To think that all our plagues came in
  For one poor stolen apple !
And still we love the darling thief
  Whose rosy fingers stole it ; —
Her weakness brought the world to grief,
  Her smiles alone console it !
— I take the " stolen " fruit you leave, —
  (Forgive me, Maid and Madam,)
It makes me dream that you are Eve,
  And wish that I were Adam !

A WREATH OF FLOWERS

THIS wreath of flowers that bids thee wait
A moment at the trellised gate
Shall lure thee to enchanted ground
Where all the singing birds are found,
Where flows the fount that never fails, —
The Garden of the Nightingales !

— Behold the slender star that lifts
The fringe of Winter's narrowing drifts ;
The violet that with open wings
Lights where the first-born verdure springs ;
The bell-wort, swinging in the breeze
As if to call the wandering bees
To taste the honeyed lymph that shines
Globed in the clustering columbines.

— These heaven-kissed darlings never know
How sweet their breath, how bright their glow
They win the charm they never seek,
The perfume and the painted cheek,
Feel in their veins the morning's flame
Nor ask the sunbeam whence it came.

— Traced in the blossom's silken fold
Is not the Poet's story told ?
Then grudge not to his flowering lays

The humble violet's meed of praise
For beauty, Nature's sweet surprise
Must read itself in other's eyes,
And till the welcome echoes ring
The song-birds hardly know they sing.

CATULLUS: DE ARRIO, LXXXII

ARRIUS says *ch*ommoda for commoda ;
*H*insidias for insidias he must say.
Counting his language wonderful polite
He says *h*insidias with all his might.
Just so, I think, his mother used to do,
His uncle, grandsire and his grandam too.
At length, to Syria sent, our Arrius goes
And so our ears obtain a brief repose ;
Soft, smooth once more becomes each self-same word,
When all at once the horrid tale is heard
Ionia's wave, since Arrius came must be,
No more the Ionian, but the *H*ionian Sea !

THE RELUCTANT MINSTREL

MY Lord the King, — the minstrel swore
I sing at banquet board no more
Not for the stranger from afar —
No ! were it Emperor, King or Czar
Or my Lord the Bishop of Zanzibar
Will I straighten leg on feasting floor !

For who would waste laborious days
And toilsome nights on idle lays
That win some little word of praise
Pleasing or *clever, neat,* or *nice,*
Brief as the candelabrum's blaze
And shrivel with the dead bouquets ?
Tonight too cheap at any price,
Tomorrow like the fair device
The artist shaped in sugared ice,
The frozen Cupid's melting kiss —
— An immortality like this
I hold it rather gain to miss.

And so the Singer would not sing
But stood before My Lord the King
Mute as a lyre without a string !
Great Captains came from over sea
Ladies and Lords of high degree
But never a song for them had he !

A mighty gathering there was seen
Came many a king and many a queen
With little princes packed between —
All Europe's monarchs to a man
The Great Mikado from Japan
Likewise the Shah from Teheran.

Well known the Singer was to these
To hear him they had crossed the seas ;
They knelt upon their royal knees ; —
" O sing now, Minstrel, sing now, please !
And you shall claim what boon you
    wish "
The bard stood silent as a fish.

The King of England then laid down
A diamond plucked from off his crown
— Would pay the ransom of a town, —
" Take this, he said, and fill your purse,
But Oh ! for Heaven's sweet sake, re-
    hearse
Some stanzas of your charming verse."

The Sultan would not be outdone
The Emperor, Brother of the Sun
Khedives and Caliphs, every one
The Shah, the Czar and all the rest
From North and South and East and
    West
Threw down the gems they loved the
    best.

For who would waste laborious days
And toilsome nights on idle lays
That win some little word of praise
As " pleasing," " clever " " neat " or
    " nice "
Then shrivel with the dead bouquets ?
Tonight too cheap at any price
Tomorrow like the fair device
The artist shaped in sugared ice —
To vanish while the candles blaze !
The doves that cooed in frosty bliss —
Cupid with frozen bow and quiver
(A little boy whose melting kiss
Would make a Lapland lover shiver —)
I hold it rather gain to miss
An immortality like this !

And so the Singer would not sing,
But stood before my Lord the King
Mute as a lyre without a string
Great Captains came from over sea
Ladies and Lords of high degree —
But never a song for them had he.

WIND-CLOUDS AND STAR-DRIFTS

ADDITIONAL LINES

— They had their choice, you say, their
    will was free,
And nothing hindered each and every one
From thinking always as he should have
    thought
From doing always as he should have
    done.
So had he found the right and saved his
    soul
Look you, this choosing seems a simple
    thing
But could we always choose as we would
    choose,
When nothing seems to bind us in our
    choice
What painters, sculptors, poets, we might
    be !
— Lay me those flakes of color thus and
    so —
Here are the brush and palette, — you
    are free —
Make me a picture such as Raphael
    drew !
Here are the block and chisel, you may
    work
Just as you will with them, — choose well
    your strokes,
You'll find the Queen of beauty in the
    stone !
Spread open on your desk the ample
    page
That holds the treasures of our English
    tongue ;
You have your choice of each and every
    word ;
And you are free to place them as you
    will ;
Write me a play like Hamlet, or a song
Like his who sang of Eden and its woe !
    Lend me your patience O ye solemn
    stars

THE TOOTHACHE

How well I remember through years that
    have gone
The hour when the first of my molars
    was drawn !

I often have sung of the day-dreams of
    youth,
But oh ! its dread nightmare, — that
    pulling a tooth !

It had ached all the day, it had ached
    all the night
As morning came on it redoubled its
    spite
It jumped like a bull-frog — it beat like
    a drum
Till I shrieked "I can stand it no longer
    — I vum ! "

So I sprang from my bed with a series of
    howls
One eye sticking out of my head like an
    owl's
The other poor optic was closed as in
    sleep, —
In fact my poor peeper was tight as a
    peep

Then rushed the whole household to an-
    swer my call
Aunts sisters and mammy and granny
    and all
With plasters and lotions and potions
    and drops
And camphor and cajeput, laudanum and
    hops.

So they drugged and they doctored and
    bandaged my cheek
(Still out of one corner I managed to
    speak ;)
"Have the camphor and cajeput made
    it all well ? "
No ! It aches like — a word I prefer not
    to tell

Alas there was nothing could solace my
    pain.
Hops camphor and cajeput all were in
    vain,
But they kept at it stoutly with more of
    the same —
And so things went on till the Governor
    came.

"Let me see it ! " he said: then all quak-
    ing with fear
I just opened my mouth — it was under
    my ear —
He gave but one look — Ah ha ! there's
    no doubt

We must go to the doctor's it's got to
    come out !

So we started at once — as we got to the
    door
"Papa ! I exclaimed, it is aching no
    more
Let us not waste our money, but go to
    the shop
That's next to the doctors and purchase
    a top.

Done aching ! the Governor says with a
    grin —
A rogue in the halter repents of his sin
That grinder's a humbug — it can't tell
    the truth
When its scared there is nothing will lie
    like a tooth.

Then he rapped — And we hadn't a sec-
    ond to wait
For a doctor's a fish and a patient's the
    bait,
And before I knew what I was doing and
    where,
I was seated — my head on the back of
    the chair.

How I wished he was dead or I'd never
    been born
As he poked in my mouth with his finger
    of horn !
And he fumbled and the next thing I saw
Was a damnable tool with a horrible
    claw !

The next I remember was "Stop ! Let
    me go ! "
And a yell as of murder committing, —
    Oh ! Oh !
For I thought he was pulling my head by
    the roots
And its fangs were clenched under the
    soles of my boots.

That wrench of the key ! I remember it
    yet
'Tis a moment it takes a whole life to
    forget ;
The swelling soon went, but a terrible
    while
Elapsed ere my cheek was relaxed in a
    smile.

The moral sticks out like a pawnbroker's
    sign,

It projects from my verse like an upper
    canine ;
There is something to say for the pleas-
    ures of youth
But its terrible drawback is drawing a
    tooth !

And thus I conclude — for my story is
    told —
It is good to be young, but it's best to be
    old
For we're curst with twelve molars that
    all must be drawn
And we never have peace till the last of
    them's gone.

CHARADE

My name declares my date to be
    The morning of a Christian year,
Though motherless, as all agree,
    I am a mother, it is clear,
A father too, without dispute,
    And when my son comes, — he's a
    fruit.
And not to puzzle you too much,
    'T was I gave Holland to the Dutch.

IN T. G. A.'S ALBUM

FEBRUARY 22, 1874

Who that can pluck the flower will
    choose the weed,
    Leave the sweet rose and gather
    blooms less fair ?
And who my homely verse will stay to
    read
    Straying enchanted through this bright
    parterre
When morning's herald lifts his purple
    bell
    And spring's young violet woos the
    wanderer's eye ?
Nay ! let me seek the fallen leaves that
    tell
    Of beggared winter's footstep drawing
    nigh
There shall my shred of song enshrouded
    lie,
    A leaf that dropped in memory's flow-
    ery dell ;

The breath of friendship stirred it and
    it fell
Tinged with the loving hue of autumn's
    fond farewell !

TELEGRAM TO THE BOHEMIAN CLUB: SAN FRANCISCO

MIDNIGHT, FEBRUARY 28, 1874

Message from San Francisco ! Whisper
    low,
Asleep in bed an hour or so ago,
While on his peaceful pillow he declines,
Say to his friend who sent these loving
    lines :
" Silent, unanswering, still to friendship
    true,
He smiles in slumber, for he dreams of
    you."

CHARADE

1876

Parted ! Alas, it brings my first to
    mind ;
    My second doubles every tear that's
    shed ;
My whole why task your laboring brain
    to find
    Since being what it is 'twere best un-
    said.

Parted ! the rip brings *needles* to my
    mind ;
    S makes *tear tears,* so doubles each
    that's shed ;
Needless, my whole, why task your brain
    to find
    Since, being needless, it were best un-
    said ?

A RHYMED RIDDLE

FEBRUARY 14, 1876

" I'm going to *blank*," with failing breath,
    The fallen gladiator said ;

Unconquered, he " consents to death ; "
One gasp — the hero soul has fled.
" I'm going to *blank*," the school-boy
    cried ;
    Two sugared sweets his hands dis-
        play, —
Like snow-flakes in the ocean-tide
    They vanish, melted both away.
Tell with one verb, or I'll tell you,
    What each was just about to do.

"OVER THE RIVER"

A NEW VERSION, WITH INSTRUMENTAL
ACCOMPANIMENT

THE ungloved fingers of dainty Spring
    Are peeping from· tree and shrub ;
I see the flash of the blue-bird's wing,
Their welcome carol the robin's sing.
    I hear their — rub a dub rub dub rub
    Rub a dub dub dub DUB !

Ha ! What is the sound that smites mine
    ear ?
Rub a dub rub dub dub !
The dull concussions approach more
    near —
Yes ! over the river the drums I hear —
    Rub a dub rub a dub rub dub rub,
    Rub a dub dub dub DUB !

All through the winter the shores were
    dumb, —
Rub a dub rub dub dub !
Now the sweet breath of spring has
    come, —
Horror of horrors ! once more that
    drum !
    Rub a dub rub a dub rub dub rub
    Rub a dub dub dub DUB !

Talk of the rhyme of the " conduct-
    air." —
Rub a dub rub dub dub !
This would have made meek Moses
    swear,
And Job by hand fulls pull out his
    hair, —
    Rub a dub rub a dub rub dub rub
    Rub a dub dub dub DUB !

Always the same old thumping chime !
    Rub a dub rub dub dub !
Rub a dub rub a dub goes my rhyme,
Rub a dub beat both legs in time,
    Rub a dub rub a dub rub dub rub
    Rub a dub dub dub DUB !

Mother is holding her splitting head, —
    Rub a dub rub dub dub !
Baby sits bolt upright in bed,
Screeching as if to wake the dead, —
    Rub a dub rub a dub rub dub rub !
    Rub a dub dub dub DUB !

What if a shotted gun they tried, —
    Rub a dub rub dub dub !
And swore that they wouldn't be denied.
Because they fired from the other side ?
    Rub a dub rub a dub rub dub rub
    Rub a dub dub dub DUB !

Mayor of Cantabridge, what shall we
    do ?
Rub a dub rub dub dub !
Drummers are many and poets few ;
Can't you make use of a halter or two ?
    Rub a dub rub a dub rub dub rub,
    Rub a dub dub dub DUB !

Or is there a — rub a dub — one could
    mix, —
Rub a dub rub dub dub !
Their goose to cook and their flint to fix
And send these drummers across the
    Styx —
    Rub a dub rub a dub rub dub rub
    Rub a dub dub dub DUB !

Do it, your Honor, we humbly pray, —
    Rub a dub rub dub dub !
They've murdered our ears in the shock-
    ingest way ;
Where murderers go I needn't say —
    Rub a dub rub a dub rub dub rub,
    Rub a dub dub dub DUB !

But stave their drum-heads before they
    go —
Rub a dub rub dub dub !
Or they'll teach Old — rub a dub — down
    below
A trick of torture he mustn't know, —
    Rub a dub rub a dub rub dub rub
    Rub a dub dub dub DUB !

MY EXCUSE FOR NOT WRITING

JUNE 9, 1876

You ask me to write you some verses !
Not I
While the Crab and the Lion are lords of
the sky —
Nay, wait till the Virgin gives place to
the Scales
And the first leaves of autumn are swept
by the gales.

If you'll give me a spade in the earth I
will delve
If you'll lend me a hatchet I'll clutch at
its helve
If you'll find me a knife there are
branches to prune
But a pen makes me shudder — a goose-
quill in June !

I have laid all my papers and books on
the shelf
Why scribble while nature is writing
herself
Each grass-blade a letter that sparkles
with dew
And flowers for her capitals, gold red and
blue ?

I can read all day long from those pages
of green
Whose characters lay through the winter
unseen
Till out at the summons of sunshine they
came
Like the words of a love-letter held to
the flame

But to write in dead phrases ! the roses
have blown
Shall I sprinkle their damask with Eau
de Cologne ?
Shall I mock the sweet season of blos-
soming bowers
With a milliner's nosegay of calico flow-
ers ?

While the spice of the sassafras clings to
my lips
While the axe I have chopped with
smells sweet of the chips

While the turtles lie basking on fence
rails and logs
While the meadows resound with the
chorus of frogs

While the lily-pad greenbacks their
promise display
Of the silver and gold that the lilies will
pay,
While heavy the nest of the oriole swings
While Nature's gay *buffo,* the bobolink
sings

Excuse me, dear friend ; in your quest
after verse
You may have gone farther — you can't
have fared worse.
I send you my blessing, 'tis all that I
can —
In the lazy, limp month of the flowers
and the fan.

TO J. R. N.

SEPTEMBER 22, 1876

SEE what the artist's hand could do
To clothe these winged words !
So Nature lends each loveliest hue
To deck her darling birds.

Why turn the leaves for aught beside
Your pleasure to prolong ?
'Tis not the brightest plumes that hide
The throats of sweetest song.

TO J. R. L.

JULY 14, 1877

GOOD bye ! Good bye ! We cannot mend
The homely Saxon phrase.
May God be with you, parting friend
We love too well to praise.

We lose you as we lose the light
On yonder steep that burns ;
For us on shore awhile tis bright
Then to the wave it turns.

What though we miss the lofty blaze
Our eyes have learned to hail, —

More welcome still its widening rays
   To many a wandering sail.

So, though we miss your light awhile,
   We will not vainly sigh,
But falter with a sorrowing smile
   Dear friend Good bye ! Good bye !

THE GOLDEN CALENDAR

TO J. G. W.

Count not the years that hoarding Time
   has told,
Save by the starry memories in their
   train ;
Not by the vacant moons that wax and
   wane,
Nor all the season's changing robes en-
   fold :
Look on the life whose record is un-
   rolled !
Bid thought, word, action, breathe, burn,
   strive again,
Bid the freed captive clank his broken
   chain !
Old altars flame whose ashes scarce are
   cold,
So will we count thy years and months
   and days,
Poet whose heart-strings thrill upon thy
   lyre,
Whose kindling spirit lent like Hecla's
   fire
Its heat to Freedom's faint auroral blaze,
But waste no words the loving soul to
   tire
That finds its life in duty, not in praise !

MAY IT PLEASE YOUR HONORS' WORSHIPS

FOR THE SUFFOLK BAR ASSOCIATION

JANUARY 8, 1879

May it please your Honors' Worships,
   since I'm on the witness stand,

I will speak the truth — So help me !
   See, I'm holding up my hand !
I'm a Doctor, not a Lawyer, — I'm aware
   it's very queer,
And the Court has asked the question
   How a Doctor came in here.

Now I hope you will believe him ; he
   will try to be exact —
How he came here is the question, for
   he can't deny the fact ;
Every minute he's been listening for a
   general scream and shout
Here's a wolf among the lambkins —
   throw him over ! turn him out !

Don't be scared ! He can't do mischief,
   even were he so inclined,
For he comes without his weapons — he
   has left them all behind —
His decoctions, his infusions, all his plas-
   ters, all his pills,
All his lotions, all his potions, all his
   vaccinating quills.

It's himself that shakes and shivers, as
   full well indeed he may,
When he sees the Law all round him in
   its terrible array,
With its warrants, its indictments, its pre-
   sentments and its writs,
And its sheriffs and its constables that
   scare folks into fits.

How he came here is the question ; he
   had said so once before,
But the Law loves repetition up to
   twenty times or more ;
'Tis the question *How he came here,* or
   to make it still more plain,
Here he came and *How's* the question ;
   thus he states the case again.

He was brought in on a *capias,* he would
   have you understand,
And the mandate is *no exeat* until he
   shows his hand
So he opens it before you ; keep your
   places ! pray be calm !
'Tis a strange sight for you lawyers ;
   there is nothing in its palm !

There may have been some blunder, such
   as magistrates will make,

It may need a writ of error, if we find
  there's a mistake,
But the jurists and the medicine-men
  their phrases so have fixed
That there *is* some little reason why
  their callings should get mixed.

Take an action of ejectment — 'tis the
  commonest of things —
In a case of over-feeding just that same
  your doctor brings,
And the lawyer, *vice versa,* in the courts
  of ancient time
Wrote prescriptions for his clients how to
  purge themselves — of crime.

How many learned counsellors, with Di-
  gests on their shelves,
Go complaining to their doctors that
  they can't digest, themselves !
When you talk of Magna Charta, I
  should like to ask of you
What without their *Habeas corpus* poor
  anatomists would do ?

But my scroll is growing, lengthening,
  and you're asking for relief
From a paper that resembled what a law-
  yer calls his *brief,*
And of all the calm assumptions the
  coolest one by far
Were to say " I do the talking for the
  deaf-mutes of the Bar."

What's a Doctor's or Professor's to a
  jury-lawyer's tongue ?
'Tis a pitch-pipe to a fog-horn ; tis a
  spigot to a bung ;
Says a Doctor to a patient " Run your
  tongue out to the roots ; "
To a jury-lawyer never, for it reaches to
  his boots !

I am honest, though I say so ; I am
  modest, that is clear ;
Do you ask to know the reason ; Well,
  I studied Law a year.
So I've said my say, Your Honor, and
  you gentry of the Laws,
And await my jury's verdict. — Please
  to call another cause.

THE ALBUM FIEND

APRIL 6, 1880

" ONE verse," she says, — " four glittering
  lines —
A solitaire, — just one." —
'Tis finished ; every facet shines
A star that mocks the sun.

" *One* earring ! that were frightful,
  sure, —
What Muse would wear but one,
Were that the blazing Koh-i-noor ?
One more, since you've begun ! "

So, once again, with weary sigh —
'Twere vain my fate to shun —
I rack my brain and roll my eye ;
My album task is done !

Done ! when those daughters fill their
  sieve,
When rivers cease to run,
When imps turn angels, then believe
Your album task is done !

ALMA MATER

HARVARD CLUB, NEW YORK, FEBRUARY 21, 1882

YES, home is sweet ! and yet we needs
  must sigh,
  Restless until our longing souls have
    found
  Some realm beyond the fireside's nar-
    row bound
Where slippered ease and sleepy comfort
  lie, —
Some fair ideal form that cannot die
  By age dismantled and by change un-
    crowned,
  Else life creeps circling in the self-
    same round,
And the low ceiling hides the lofty sky.
Ah, then to thee our truant hearts return,
  Dear Mother, *Alma, Casta* — spotless,
    kind !
  Thy sacred walls a larger home we find,

And still for thee thy wandering children
  yearn,
While with undying fires thine altars
  burn
  Where all our holiest memories rest
  enshrined.

AT THE UNITARIAN FESTIVAL

JUNE 1, 1882

THE waves unbuild the wasting shore ;
  Where mountains towered the billows
  sweep,
Yet still their borrowed spoils restore
  And raise new empires from the deep.
So, while the floods of thought lay waste
  The old domain of chartered creeds,
Its heaven-appointed tides will haste
  To shape new homes for human needs.

Be ours to mark with hearts unchilled
  The change an outworn age deplores ;
The legend sinks, but Faith shall build
  A fairer throne on new-found shores.
The star shall glow in Western skies
  That shone o'er Bethlehem's hallowed
  shrine,
And once again the temple rise
  That crowned the rock of Palestine.

Not when the wondering shepherds
  bowed
  Did angels sing their latest song,
Nor yet to Israel's kneeling crowd
  Did heaven's sacred dome belong, —
Let priest and prophet have their dues,
  The Levite counts but half a man,
Whose proud "salvation of the Jews"
  Shuts out the good Samaritan !

Though scattered far the flock may
  stray,
  His own the shepherd still shall
  claim, —
The saints who never learned to pray, —
  The friends who never spoke his name.
Dear Master, while we hear thy voice
  That says, "The truth shall make you
  free,"
Thy servants still by loving choice,
  Oh, keep us faithful unto thee !

RESPONSE TO A TOAST

BOSTON BAR ASSOCIATION

JANUARY 30, 1883

HIS Honor's father yet remains
His proud paternal posture firm in ;
But, while his right he still maintains
To wield the household rod and reins,
He bows before the filial ermine.

What curious tales has life in store,
With all its must-be's and its may-be's !
The sage of eighty years and more
Once crept a nursling, on the floor, —
Kings, conquerors, judges, — all were
  babies.

The fearless soldier, who has faced
The serried bayonet's gleam appalling,
For nothing save a pin misplaced
The peaceful nursery has disgraced
With hours of unheroic bawling.

The mighty monarch, whose renown
Fills up the stately page historic,
Has howled and wakened half the town,
And finished off by gulping down
His castor-oil or paregoric.

The justice, who, in gown and cap,
Condemns a wretch to strangulation,
Has scratched his nurse and spilled his
  pap
And sprawled across his mother's lap
For wholesome law's administration.

Ah, life has many a reef to shun
Before in port we drop our anchor,
But when its course is proudly run,
Look aft ! for there the work was done.
Life owes its headway to the spanker !

Yon seat of Justice well might awe
The fairest manhood's half-blown sum-
  mer, —
There Parsons scourged the laggard law,
There reigned and ruled majestic
  Shaw, —
What ghosts to hail the last new-comer !

One cause of fear I faintly name, —
The dread lest duty's dereliction

Shall give so rarely cause for blame
Our guileless voters will exclaim,
"No need of human jurisdiction!"

What keeps the doctor's trade alive?
Bad air, bad water,—more's the pity!
But lawyers walk where doctors drive,
And starve in streets where surgeons
     thrive
Our Boston is so pure a city.

What call for judge or court, indeed,
When righteousness prevails so through
     it?
Our virtuous car conductors need
Only a card whereon they read
"Do right! It's naughty not to do it!"

The whirligig of time goes round
And changes all things but affection;
One blessed comfort may be found
In Heaven's broad statute, which has
     bound
Each household to its head's protection.

If e'er aggrieved, attacked, accused,
A sire may claim a son's devotion
To shield his innocence abused,
As old Anchises freely used
His offspring's legs for locomotion.

You smile. You did not come to weep,
Nor I my weakness to be showing;
And these gay stanzas, slight and cheap,
Have served their simple use—to keep
A father's eyes from overflowing.

DOROTHY QUINCY UPHAM

JUNE 7, 1883

DEAR little Dorothy, Dorothy Q.,
What can I find to write to you?
You have two U's in your name, it's true,
And mine is adorned with a double-u;
But there's this difference in the U's,
That one you will stand a chance to lose
When a happy man of the bearded sex
Shall make it Dorothy Q. + X.

May Heaven smile bright on the blissful
     day
That teaches this lesson in Algebra!

When the orange blossoms crown your
     head,
Then read what your old great-uncle
     said,
And remember how in your baby-time
He scribbled a scrap of idle rhyme,—
Idle, it may be—but kindly, too,
For the little lady, Dorothy Q.

TO J. R. L. HOMEWARD BOUND

JUNE 15, 1885

[BRAVE Bird o' fredum] what a sight it
     were
   To see thee in our waters yet appeare
[After] those flights upon the banks of
     Thames
   That so did take [all England with]
     our James.
   *Ben Jonson in memory of Shake-
   speare.*

Adapted by O. W. H.

TO MARK TWAIN

ON HIS FIFTIETH BIRTHDAY

NOVEMBER 23, 1885

AH Clemens, when I saw thee last,—
   We both of us were younger,—
How fondly mumbling o'er the past
   Is Memory's toothless hunger!

So fifty years have fled, they say,
   Since first you took to drinking,—
I mean in Nature's milky way,—
   Of course no ill I'm thinking.

But while on life's uneven road
   Your track you've been pursuing,
What fountains from your wit have
     flowed—
   What drinks you have been brewing!

I know whence all your magic came,—
   Your secret I've discovered,—
The source that fed your inward flame—
   The dreams that round you hovered:

Before you learned to bite or munch
  Still kicking in your cradle,
The Muses mixed a bowl of punch
  And Hebe seized the ladle.

Dear babe, whose fiftieth year to-day
  Your ripe half-century rounded,
Your books the precious draught betray
  The laughing Nine compounded.

So mixed the sweet, the sharp, the strong,
  Each finds its faults amended,
The virtues that to each belong
  In happier union blended.

And what the flavor can surpass
  Of sugar, spirit, lemons ?
So while one health fills every glass
  Mark Twain for Baby Clemens !

TO YOUTHFUL RHYMESTERS

So youthful rhymesters when a poet sings
Feel at their shoulders for the envied
    wings
Flap their bare arms, cry " can " and
    wonder why
They like the song birds cannot sing and
    fly.

Beware, young dreamer ! he that hopes
    to climb
To fame and fortune up the stairs of
    rhyme
Too oft will find his weary feet have
    found
A creaking treadmill travelling round and
    round
While on its path the world of action
    goes
And leaves its prizes with the men of
    prose.
Ill is the bough that yields the laurel
    wreath —
Its drip is poison to the herbs beneath —
And many an idle youth and bitter maid
Have seen their virtues languish in its
    shade
Though vain the task their fated course
    to stem
This bitter lesson I commend to them :
Who writes in verse that should have
    writ in prose

Is like a traveller walking on his toes, —
Happy the rhymester who in time has
    found
The heels he lifts were made to touch
    the ground.

FOR MISS HOWELLS' ALBUM

APRIL 24, 1887

It is winter with me now, —
Not a pippin on the bough
  Save a single " froze-n-thaw " ;
Spread your lap and it shall fall, —
It's an apple after all,
  Though it's neither roast nor raw.

So my verse its life has lost
In its battles with the frost
  And I fear the branch will break
While the leafless tree I climb
For this " froze-n-thaw " of rhyme
  For a dear young maiden's sake.

TO THE REVEREND S. F. SMITH, D. D.

AUTHOR OF "MY COUNTRY 'TIS OF THEE," ON HIS EIGHTIETH BIRTHDAY

OCTOBER 21, 1888

While through the land the strains re-
    sound
  What added fame can love impart
To him who touched the string that
    found
  Its echoes in a Nation's heart ?

No stormy ode, no fiery march,
  His gentle memory shall prolong,
But on fair Freedom's climbing arch,
  He shed the light of hallowed song.

Full many a poet's labored lines
  A country's creeping waves will hide, —
The verse a people's love enshrines
  Stands like the rock that breasts the
    tide.

Time wrecks the proudest piles we
    raise,—
  The towers, the domes, the temples
    fall ;
The fortress ever crumbles and decays,—
  One breath of song outlasts them all.

CENTENNIAL OF
WASHINGTON'S INAUGURAL

APRIL 30, 1889

SCEPTRES and thrones the morning realms
    have tried ;
Earth for the people kept her sunset side.
Arts, manners, creeds the teeming Orient
    gave ;
Freedom, the gift that freights the re-
    fluent wave,
Pays with one priceless pearl the guerdon
    due,
And leaves the Old World debtor to the
    New.

Long as the watch-towers of our crown-
    less Queen
Front the broad oceans that she sits be-
    tween,
May her proud sons their plighted faith
    maintain,
And guard unbroken Union's lengthening
    chain,—
Union, our peaceful sovereign, she alone
Can make or keep the western world our
    own !

TO SARAH WHITMAN

FROM Nature's precious quarry sought,
By hands untiring slowly wrought,
Behold the smooth translucent sphere,
As friendship's pledge made doubly
    dear !

What stone so clear has mortal found ?
What figure like its faultless round ?
All else must try some flaw to screen,—
But here perfection's self is seen.

Come thou, my birth-day's fair surprise,
And fill with light my fading eyes !
Close to the clock thy place shall be,—
The clock that chimes " Remember
    me ! "

Thrice welcome, blessed, beauteous gift !
Thy silent speech our souls shall lift
Like thee unchanging to endure
Full-orbed, forever bright and pure.

THE LIVING DYNAMO

EDWARD EVERETT HALE

APRIL 18, 1892

NIGHT after night the incandescent arc
Has fought its dazzling battle with the
    dark,
Our doubtful paths with purest ray il-
    lumed,
Untired, undimmed, unswerving, uncon-
    sumed.

A slender wire the living light conveys
That startles midnight with its noonday
    blaze.
Through that same channel streams the
    giant force
That whirls the wheels along their clank-
    ing course
When, like a mail-clad monster o'er the
    plain,
With clash and clamor sweeps the broom-
    stick train.

Whence gains the wondrous wire its two-
    fold dower,
Its double heritage of light and power ?
Ask of the motor-man,— he ought to
    know,—
And he will tell you " from the dynamo."
And what, again, the dynamo inspires ?
" A mighty engine, urged by quickening
    fires."

When I behold that large, untiring brain
Which seventy winters have assailed in
    vain
Toiling, still toiling at its endless task,
With patience such as Sisyphus might
    ask,
To flood the paths of ignorance with
    light,

To speed the progress of the struggling
  right,
Its burning pulses borrowed from a heart
That claims in every grist a brother's
  part,
My lips repeat with reverence " Even
  so —
This is in truth a living Dynamo ! "

Be ours to heed its lessons while we
  may,
Look up for light to guide our devious
  way —
Look forward bravely, look not weakly
  back
The past is done with, mind the coming
  track ;
Look in with searching eye and courage
  stout,
But when temptation comes look out !
  look out !

Heaven grant all blessings time and earth
  can give
To him whose life has taught us how to
  live
Till on the golden dial of the spheres
The twentieth century counts its gather-
  ing years,
While many a birthday tells its cheerful
  tale,
And the round hundredth shouts All
  hail ! All hail !

POEM ON THE OCCASION
OF THE PRESENTATION
OF MY PORTRAIT TO THE
PHILADELPHIA COLLEGE
OF PHYSICIANS

APRIL 30, 1892

" How came I here?" The portrait thus
  might speak, —
The crimson mantling in its canvas
  cheek, —
" Here in this concourse of the grave
  and wise
Who look upon me with inquiring eyes,
As on some homeless wanderer, caught
  astray ?
An *error loci,* Boerhaave would say.

Is this great hive of industry my home ?
Where is the Common ? Where my
  gilded dome ?
Where the Old South ? The Frog pond ?
  Most of all,
My sacred temple, Freedom's Faneuil
  Hall ? "

No answer comes ; no trick of human art
Can force those fixed unmoving lips
  apart.
He whom the picture shadows must ex-
  plain
This lawless inroad on a strange domain.
Were it *my* votive offering, meant to
  show
My grateful sense of all the debts I owe
To your fair city, its unlooked-for face
Might find no caviller to dispute its
  place.
Yet though the friendly offering is not
  mine
It bears my benediction to the shrine
Where, if it meets a welcome, longer yet
Will stretch the column which displays
  my debt.
Friends of my earlier manhood, ever
  dear
Whose lives, whose labors all were cen-
  tred here
How bright each figure stands before me
  now
With eyes undimmed and fair unwrin-
  kled brow,
As when, with life before us yet untried,
We walked the " Latin Quarter " side
  by side
Through halls of death, through palaces
  of pain
That cast their shadows on the turbid
  Seine.

When o'er our coffee, at the old " Pro-
  cope,"
Smiling we cast each other's horoscope
Daring the future's dubious path to scan,
Gerhard, your Gerhard was the coming
  man.
Strong-brained, strong-willed, inquiring,
  patient, wise,
He looked on truth with achromatic
  eyes ;
Sure to succeed, for Nature, like a maid,

Loves best the lovers who are not afraid,
Lends them her hand to lead them where
    they please,
And trusts them boldly with her master-
    keys
Behold, unfading on the rolls of fame.
Typhus and Typhoid stamped with Ger-
    hard's name.
Look on the stately form at Gerhard's
    side
He too shall live to be his city's pride.
Tall, manly, quiet, grave, but not austere,
Not slow of wit, a little dull of ear,
Him we predestined to the place he
    won, —
Norris, The Quaker City's noble son.
Armed with the skill that science renders
    sure
His look, his touch, were half his pa-
    tients' cure ;
What need his merits I should further
    tell ?
His record stands ; your pages know it
    well.

Still wandering, lonely, mid the funeral
    urns
To one loved name my saddening
    thought returns
Less to the many known, but to the few
A precious memory, — *Stewardson*, to
    you.
Through many a league we two together
    fared,
The traveller's comforts and discomforts
    shared,
When hills and valleys parted distant
    towns,
Long ere the railway smoothed their ups
    and downs.
In all the trials wearying days could
    bring
No fretful utterance ever left its sting.
Pity it was that, chased by pallid fears,
He walked in shadow through his morn-
    ing years,
Talked of his early doom, and then, and
    then
Lived on, and on, past three score years
    and ten.
Too shy, perhaps too timid for success
He fought life's battle bravely not the
    less, —
Others left prouder memories, none more
    dear, —

For those a sigh, for Stewardson a tear.

Well, years rolled on, we went our several
    ways
Not unrewarded with our meed of
    praise ;
Time took the weight and measure of
    our brains
Set us our tasks and paid us for our
    pains
At length (our side-locks fast were turn-
    ing gray)
He brought our art that all-important
    day
When here our Aesculapian Congress
    met.
(Its second gathering, you will not for-
    get.)
I with the crowd your far-famed city
    sought,
Pleased to behold the schools where
    Rush had taught,
Where Wistar labored and where Horner
    led
His thirsting flock to Surgery's fountain-
    head.
What kindly welcome with the rest I
    shared, —
A little pleased, — perhaps a little scared,
When *Chapman* hugged me in his huge
    embrace
With praise that lit a bonfire in my
    face, —
When *Francis*, guest at *Mitchell's* gen-
    erous board,
My humble name across the table
    roared,
Coupled with one which figures on the
    roll
Of England's poets, — bless his worthy
    soul !
Garth, — good Sir Samuel, whose poetic
    spark
Scarce seen by day, still glimmers in the
    dark.

These flitting phantoms of the past sur-
    vive
While grateful Memory keeps her fires
    alive.
Friends of the days that fear and anguish
    knew
My heart records a deeper debt to you.
To this kind refuge, hallowed evermore,
Her shattered sufferers fond affection
    bore.

Full many a father tracked his bleeding
son
Fresh from the murderous conflict, lost
or won,
Strayed through some quiet ward, and
looking round,
In pity's sheltering arms the lost was
found.

Enough ! Enough ! these eyes will over-
flow
In sweet remembrance of the debt I
owe, —
A debt 'twould bankrupt gratitude to
pay, —
But Heaven perhaps will hear me when
I pray
Peace to your borders ! Long may sci-
ence reign
Supreme, unchallenged o'er her old do-
main !
While sons as worthy as their sires of
old
Her borrowed sceptre still unbroken hold
Till a new Rush shall teach his time to
think,
An unborn Leidy find the missing link.

TO J. M. F. ON HIS EIGHTIETH BIRTHDAY

FEBRUARY 23, 1893

I KNOW thee well. From olden time
Thou hadst a weakness for a rhyme.
And wilt with gracious smile excuse
The languor of a laggard muse,
Whose gait betrays in every line
The weight of years outnumbering thine.
And who will care for blame or praise,
When love each syllable betrays ?

The seven-barred gate has long been
past,
The eighth tall decade cleared at last ;
But when its topmost bar is crossed
Think not that life its charm hath lost ;
Ginger will still be hot in mouth,
And winter winds blow sometimes south,
And youth might almost long to take
A slice of fourscore's frosted cake.

Thrice welcome to the chosen band,
Culled from the crowd by Nature's
hand :

No warmer heart for us shall beat,
No freer hand in friendship meet.
Long may he breathe our mortal air,
For heaven has souls enough to spare.
Lay at his feet the fairest flowers —
Thank God he still is Earth's and ours.

ELLEN TERRY

HOMMAGE DE L'AUTEUR

JANUARY 17, 1894

SUR la scène
Toujours la Reine
Sans diadème
Encore la même

VERSION OF A FRAGMENT OF SAPPHO

GODLIKE the mortal seems to me
Nay greater than divinity
Who sits by thee and all the while
Can hear thy pleasant laugh and see
thy smile !
From me such vision steals my soul
away
My tongue is palsied, — I have
naught to say
A subtile flame
Runs through each fibre of my
joined frame,
My ears are ringing and my sight
grows dim
Cold drops of sweat bedew each
trembling limb
My face grows white and every laboring
breath
Seems like the gasping harbinger of
death.

THE COMBINATION

THOU wear'st a padlock on thy heart,
  A lock without a key ;
And none shall force its clasp apart
  Save only he
Who gets its mystic letters in a row,
  And so
  Is lord of thee !
  What may they be ?

Try these four letters, G, O, L and D !
It has not stirred.
Now try L, O, V, E — ah ! that's the
    word !

EPITAPH

I

FROM his far isle the gentle stranger
    came
Who taught our lips to love his liquid
    name,
Found a new home beneath our western
    sky
Won all our hearts and left us but to die.

EPITAPH

II

NOT his the Buddhist's creed, the Chris-
    tian's name,
Between two open doors a wind-blown
    flame ;
His was the largest faith, the heaven-
    born creed
That shaped his life in thought, in
    speech, in deed.

ILLUSION

How oft, as children, on the stage
    We've seen with wonder-opening eyes
A withered beldame bent with age —
    The kindly fairy in disguise !

Not yet betrayed, through many a scene
    She creeps around with cloak and cane,
So truthful in her speech and mien
    To doubt her wrinkles were profane.

With trembling voice and tottering feet
    She limps along from act to act
Still genuine in her thin deceit
    To simple eyes ; an honest fact.

What e'er the sable robe conceals
    No truant fold of gauze betrays,
No straying border yet reveals
    The gorgeous mantle's hidden blaze.

Four acts and something more have
    past —
    Still virtue seems the losing side —
Each wrong more crushing than the
    last —
    When lo ! The sable robes divide ;

The villain flies — the maiden kneels —
    Behold ! in angel splendors drest
From plume crowned head to spangled
    heels
    The great enchantress stands confest !

IN THE DEAD SEASON

CAMBRIDGE

IN the dead season when the boughs are
    bare
And chill from Labrador the wild winds
    blow
Beneath these outstretched arms that
    show so fair
In hanging sleeves that Summer bids
    them wear
A pilgrim round his birth-place wander-
    ing slow
As wayward memory led him here or
    there,
With lingering footsteps tracked the vir-
    gin snow.

Stripped of his royal vestments, naked,
    lone,
The immemorial monarch of the plain
Sat crownless, shivering on his marble
    throne ;
Full many a bitter winter had he known
And shook his leaves in many a blinding
    rain
And felt his far-stretched rootlets tug
    and strain
When the roof-rending hurricane had
    blown.

Then he whom cradle memories lured to
    stray
Beneath the shadeless boughs that idly
    spread
Their net of crossing branches, tangled
    spray,
Against the sky's round hollow, dull and
    gray

With clouds portending tempest, over-
  head,
Saw the Greek page before him where
  he read
" As forest-leaves the tribes of men de-
  cay."

The mighty deeds whereof the world
  hath sung
As each slow-moving century led its
  train
Art, History, Verse have shaped and
  told and sung
Vain all the toil of chisel, pencil, tongue
Image   and   record   and   resounding
  strain —
Vain is the sweetest lyre that hand hath
  strung
Marble and scroll and canvas, all are
  vain.

From dark abysses burst the ravening
  tides
And grind with foaming jaws the wasting
  land
O'er sunken Tyre the conqueror's trireme
  rides
To shineless night the bannered navy
  glides
Memnon sinks voiceless in the Lybian
  sand
Through Balbec's arch the giant key-
  stone slides
The sceptre falls from mummied Phar-
  oah's hand.

Earth, like a worn out medal shews no
  more
Her date and superscription ; whence
  she came
Spinning her endless circles o'er and
  o'er
Turning the shore to sea, the sea to
  shore,
Forever changing, evermore the same,
Paving with mountain peaks her ocean
  floor,
No sage may guess, no prophet may
  proclaim.

Still wandering on he reached the holy
  ground
Where, under mossy slab and slanted
  stone

And shining obelisk and swelling mound
The silent generations slumber round
The village fathers modest Fame had
  known
Captains and Deacons, mighty men re-
  nowned
Whose crumbling bones the churchyard
  calls its own.

And with them mingled some of statelier
  name,
The ruffled Tory true to church and
  crown,
Esquire and Colonel ; and the lofty
  dame
Whose glistening satin puts our pride
  to shame
As Copley's canvas hands her proudly
  down ;
And grand divines whose Presidential
  fame
Once filled the grave old Academic
  town.

LOVE

WHILE sunset stains the windows of the
  west
  In parting glory drest,
Ere yet the evening star leads in the
  hours
That hush all voices in their leafy
  bowers
  Save the lone bird's that shuns the
  light ;
Ere in the burning chamber of the night
  With sacramental rite
Of dewdrops on the cerements of the
  flowers
  Its burden dropped, its sins confessed
Our long drawn day is laid at length at
  rest
We, flung together as the seeds are
  thrown
  The sower's hand has strown,
But clinging as the iron sands that feel
The soul-like effluence of the enchanted
  steel,
  We whom the years have tried
And clustered closer, striving to divide,
  Beside our altar kneel
And thank the gracious Power that made
  our own

The sacred gift of love the best that life
has known.

For what has life but love when all is
told ?
Fame ? pleasure ? empire ? gold ?
Fame breeds the worm that gnaws its
greenest leaves ;
Pleasure is hope that smiles and still
deceives ;
Power ! target of envenomed cares !
Gold ! See the rippled brow the ash-
hued hairs
Its hoarding vassal wears !
A sable woof the loom of fate inweaves
With every web by time unrolled ;
Love, only love it wraps in snow-white
fold.

THE POET GROWS OLD

How I cut the fresh branches of suc-
culent rhyme
In the spring of my years, my asparagus
time !
To clip them, to bind them, how light
was the toil,
As each morning they sprouted afresh
from the soil !

Spring passed, still my pages of silver-
shod lines
Filled up like the pods on my marrow
fat vines ;
Uncared for they grew and unasked for
they came, —
The peas and the poems, — with both
'twas the same.

And when the last crop on the meadow
was mown,
When the apples were ripe, when the
song-birds had flown,
My harvest of verse was awaiting me
still
For the corn-field stood ready my basket
to fill.

But winter has come with his icicle-
spear
And built his white throne on the grave
of the year
The blossoms are snowflakes he flings to
the gale

And the seed that he casts in the furrow
is hail.

The fields are all bare and the harvest
is o'er
I come with my sickle and basket no
more ;
But a rusty old spade, and I prospect
around
For the bread-fruit of Erin that grows
underground.

TO AN AUTOGRAPH COLLECTOR

WHEN next you wish an autograph, I
hope
You'll furnish *paper, stamp* and *envel-
ope* ;
Why, when you tax a hard-worked weary
man,
Not save him all the trouble that you
can ?

TO A BRIGHT BOY

I TRUST my counsel you will heed —
You're almost too quick witted ;
Your brain is like a fiery steed
That needs to be well bitted
Don't treat it like a wooden toy
A child may safely play with ;
You'd better hold it tight, my boy,
Or you'll be run away with !

TO CORINNA

STAR of my childhood, long withdrawn
And veiled to me in midnight shade,
Still glowing on the mists of morn
Thine early light can never fade.
Thy glance perchance has lightly past
And wondered at my altered brow,
But thou as when I saw thee last
So are thy breathing features now.
The same dark hair — the same wild
eye —
The voice like dying music's flow —
All seems as in the days gone by

Though woman's heart beats warm
  below
Our paths have parted far and wide,
  They met but for a single hour,
But winds that roam the troubled tide
  Still bear the fragrance of the flower
Thus to my memory thou hast been —
  Thus to my future thou shalt be ;

Though chance may dash her waves be-
  tween
  They cannot part my dreams from thee
And by thy pathway dark or bright
  Fair girl, it yet may give thee joy
To know that thou hast touched with
  light
  The visions of a nameless boy.

APPENDIX

APPENDIX

I. VERSES FROM THE OLDEST PORTFOLIO

FROM THE "COLLEGIAN," 1830, ILLUS-
TRATED ANNUALS, ETC.

Nescit vox missa reverti. — HORAT. *Ars Poetica.*
Ab iis quæ non adjuvant quam mollissime oportet
pedem referre. — QUINTILIAN, L. VI. C. 4.

THESE verses have always been printed in
my collected poems, and as the best of them
may bear a single reading, I allow them to
appear, but in a less conspicuous position than
the other productions. A chick, before his
shell is off his back, is hardly a fair subject
for severe criticism. If one has written any-
thing worth preserving, his first efforts may be
objects of interest and curiosity. Other young
authors may take encouragement from seeing
how tame, how feeble, how commonplace were
the rudimentary attempts of the half-fledged
poet. If the boy or youth had anything in
him, there will probably be some sign of it in
the midst of his imitative mediocrities and am-
bitious failures.

These "first verses" of mine, written before
I was sixteen, have little beyond a common
academy boy's ordinary performance. Yet a
kindly critic said there was one line which
showed a poetical quality : —

> "The boiling ocean trembled into calm."

One of these poems — the reader may guess
which — won fair words from Thackeray. The
Spectre Pig was a wicked suggestion which
came into my head after reading Dana's *Buc-
caneer.* Nobody seemed to find it out, and I
never mentioned it to the venerable poet, who
might not have been pleased with the parody.

This is enough to say of these unvalued
copies of verses.

FIRST VERSES

PHILLIPS ACADEMY, ANDOVER, MASS., 1824 OR
1825

Translation from The Æneid, Book I.

THE god looked out upon the troubled deep
Waked into tumult from its placid sleep ;
The flame of anger kindles in his eye

As the wild waves ascend the lowering sky ;
He lifts his head above their awful height
And to the distant fleet directs his sight,
Now borne aloft upon the billow's crest,
Struck by the bolt or by the winds oppressed,
And well he knew that Juno's vengeful ire
Frowned from those clouds and sparkled in that
    fire.
On rapid pinions as they whistled by
He calls swift Zephyrus and Eurus nigh :
Is this your glory in a noble line
To leave your confines and to ravage mine ?
Whom I — but let these troubled waves sub
    side —
Another tempest and I'll quell your pride !
Go — bear our message to your master's ear,
That wide as ocean I am despot here ;
Let him sit monarch in his barren caves,
I wield the trident and control the waves !
  He said, and as the gathered vapors break
The swelling ocean seemed a peaceful lake ;
To lift their ships the graceful nymphs essayed
And the strong trident lent its powerful aid ;
The dangerous banks are sunk beneath the
    main,
And the light chariot skims the unruffled plain.
As when sedition fires the public mind,
And maddening fury leads the rabble blind,
The blazing torch lights up the dread alarm,
Rage points the steel and fury nerves the arm,
Then, if some reverend sage appear in sight,
They stand — they gaze, and check their head-
    long flight, —
He turns the current of each wandering breast
And hushes every passion into rest, —
Thus by the power of his imperial arm
The boiling ocean trembled into calm ;
With flowing reins the father sped his way
And smiled serene upon rekindled day.

THE MEETING OF THE DRYADS

Written after a general pruning of the trees
around Harvard College. A little poem, on a
similar occasion, may be found in the works of
Swift, from which, perhaps, the idea was bor-
rowed; although I was as much surprised as
amused to meet with it some time after writing
the following lines.

IT was not many centuries since,
  When, gathered on the moonlit green,
Beneath the Tree of Liberty,
  A ring of weeping sprites was seen.

The freshman's lamp had long been dim,
  The voice of busy day was mute,
And tortured Melody had ceased
  Her sufferings on the evening flute.

They met not as they once had met,
  To laugh o'er many a jocund tale :
But every pulse was beating low,
  And every cheek was cold and pale.

There rose a fair but faded one,
  Who oft had cheered them with her song ;
She waved a mutilated arm,
  And silence held the listening throng.

" Sweet friends," the gentle nymph began,
  " From opening bud to withering leaf,
One common lot has bound us all,
  In every change of joy and grief.

" While all around has felt decay,
  We rose in ever-living prime,
With broader shade and fresher green,
  Beneath the crumbling step of Time.

" When often by our feet has past
  Some biped, Nature's walking whim,
Say, have we trimmed one awkward shape,
  Or lopped away one crooked limb ?

" Go on, fair Science ; soon to thee
  Shall Nature yield her idle boast ;
Her vulgar fingers formed a tree,
  But thou hast trained it to a post.

" Go, paint the birch's silver rind,
  And quilt the peach with softer down ;
Up with the willow's trailing threads,
  Off with the sunflower's radiant crown !

" Go, plant the lily on the shore,
  And set the rose among the waves,
And bid the tropic bud unbind
  Its silken zone in arctic caves ;

" Bring bellows for the panting winds,
  Hang up a lantern by the moon,
And give the nightingale a fife,
  And lend the eagle a balloon !

" I cannot smile, — the tide of scorn,
  That rolled through every bleeding vein,
Comes kindling fiercer as it flows
  Back to its burning source again.

" Again in every quivering leaf
  That moment's agony I feel,
When limbs, that spurned the northern blast,
  Shrunk from the sacrilegious steel.

" A curse upon the wretch who dared
  To crop us with his felon saw !
May every fruit his lip shall taste
  Lie like a bullet in his maw.

" In every julep that he drinks,
  May gout, and bile, and headache be ;

And when he strives to calm his pain,
  May colic mingle with his tea.

" May nightshade cluster round his path,
  And thistles shoot, and brambles cling ;
May blistering ivy scorch his veins,
  And dogwood burn, and nettles sting.

" On him may never shadow fall,
  When fever racks his throbbing brow,
And his last shilling buy a rope
  To hang him on my highest bough ! "

She spoke ; — the morning's herald beam
  Sprang from the bosom of the sea,
And every mangled sprite returned
  In sadness to her wounded tree.

THE MYSTERIOUS VISITOR

THERE was a sound of hurrying feet,
  A tramp on echoing stairs,
There was a rush along the aisles, —
  It was the hour of prayers.

And on, like Ocean's midnight wave,
  The current rolled along,
When, suddenly, a stranger form
  Was seen amidst the throng.

He was a dark and swarthy man,
  That uninvited guest ;
A faded coat of bottle-green
  Was buttoned round his breast.

There was not one among them all
  Could say from whence he came ;
Nor beardless boy, nor ancient man,
  Could tell that stranger's name.

All silent as the sheeted dead,
  In spite of sneer and frown,
Fast by a gray-haired senior's side
  He sat him boldly down.

There was a look of horror flashed
  From out the tutor's eyes ;
When all around him rose to pray,
  The stranger did not rise !

A murmur broke along the crowd,
  The prayer was at an end ;
With ringing heels and measured tread,
  A hundred forms descend.

Through sounding aisle, o'er grating stair,
  The long procession poured,
Till all were gathered on the seats
  Around the Commons board.

That fearful stranger ! down he sat,
  Unasked, yet undismayed ;
And on his lip a rising smile
  Of scorn or pleasure played.

He took his hat and hung it up,
  With slow but earnest air ;

He stripped his coat from off his back,
  And placed it on a chair.

Then from his nearest neighbor's side
  A knife and plate he drew;
And, reaching out his hand again,
  He took his teacup too.

How fled the sugar from the bowl!
  How sunk the azure cream!
They vanished like the shapes that float
  Upon a summer's dream.

A long, long draught, — an outstretched hand, —
  And crackers, toast, and tea,
They faded from the stranger's touch,
  Like dew upon the sea.

Then clouds were dark on many a brow,
  Fear sat upon their souls,
And, in a bitter agony,
  They clasped their buttered rolls.

A whisper trembled through the crowd, —
  Who could the stranger be?
And some were silent, for they thought
  A cannibal was he.

What if the creature should arise, —
  For he was stout and tall, —
And swallow down a sophomore,
  Coat, crow's-foot, cap, and all!

All sullenly the stranger rose;
  They sat in mute despair;
He took his hat from off the peg,
  His coat from off the chair.

Four freshmen fainted on the seat,
  Six swooned upon the floor;
Yet on the fearful being passed,
  And shut the chapel door.

There is full many a starving man,
  That walks in bottle green,
But never more that hungry one
  In Commons hall was seen.

Yet often at the sunset hour,
  When tolls the evening bell,
The freshman lingers on the steps,
  That frightful tale to tell.

THE TOADSTOOL

THERE's a thing that grows by the fainting
      flower,
And springs in the shade of the lady's bower;
The lily shrinks, and the rose turns pale,
When they feel its breath in the summer gale,
And the tulip curls its leaves in pride,
And the blue-eyed violet starts aside;
But the lily may flaunt, and the tulip stare,
For what does the honest toadstool care?

She does not glow in a painted vest,
And she never blooms on the maiden's breast;
But she comes, as the saintly sisters do,
In a modest suit of a Quaker hue.
And, when the stars in the evening skies
Are weeping dew from their gentle eyes,
The toad comes out from his hermit cell,
The tale of his faithful love to tell.

Oh, there is light in her lover's glance,
That flies to her heart like a silver lance;
His breeches are made of spotted skin,
His jacket is tight, and his pumps are thin;
In a cloudless night you may hear his song,
As its pensive melody floats along,
And, if you will look by the moonlight fair,
The trembling form of the toad is there.

And he twines his arms round her slender stem,
In the shade of her velvet diadem;
But she turns away in her maiden shame,
And will not breathe on the kindling flame;
He sings at her feet through the livelong night,
And creeps to his cave at the break of light;
And whenever he comes to the air above,
His throat is swelling with baffled love.

THE SPECTRE PIG

A BALLAD

IT was the stalwart butcher man,
  That knit his swarthy brow,
And said the gentle Pig must die,
  And sealed it with a vow.

And oh! it was the gentle Pig
  Lay stretched upon the ground,
And ah! it was the cruel knife
  His little heart that found.

They took him then, those wicked men,
  They trailed him all along:
They put a stick between his lips,
  And through his heels a thong;

And round and round an oaken beam
  A hempen cord they flung,
And, like a mighty pendulum,
  All solemnly he swung!

Now say thy prayers, thou sinful man,
  And think what thou hast done,
And read thy catechism well,
  Thou bloody-minded one;

For if his sprite should walk by night,
  It better were for thee,
That thou wert mouldering in the ground,
  Or bleaching in the sea.

It was the savage butcher then,
  That made a mock of sin,
And swore a very wicked oath,
  He did not care a pin.

It was the butcher's youngest son, —
  His voice was broke with sighs,
And with his pocket-handkerchief
  He wiped his little eyes;

All young and ignorant was he,
  But innocent and mild,
And, in his soft simplicity,
  Out spoke the tender child: —

"Oh, father, father, list to me;
  The Pig is deadly sick,
And men have hung him by his heels,
  And fed him with a stick."

It was the bloody butcher then,
  That laughed as he would die,
Yet did he soothe the sorrowing child,
  And bid him not to cry; —

"Oh, Nathan, Nathan, what's a Pig,
  That thou shouldst weep and wail?
Come, bear thee like a butcher's child,
  And thou shalt have his tail!"

It was the butcher's daughter then,
  So slender and so fair,
That sobbed as if her heart would break,
  And tore her yellow hair;

And thus she spoke in thrilling tone, —
  Fast fell the tear-drops big: —
"Ah! woe is me! Alas! Alas!
  The Pig! The Pig! The Pig!"

Then did her wicked father's lips
  Make merry with her woe,
And call her many a naughty name,
  Because she whimpered so.

Ye need not weep, ye gentle ones,
  In vain your tears are shed,
Ye cannot wash his crimson hand,
  Ye cannot soothe the dead.

The bright sun folded on his breast
  His robes of rosy flame,
And softly over all the west
  The shades of evening came.

He slept, and troops of murdered Pigs
  Were busy with his dreams;
Loud rang their wild, unearthly shrieks,
  Wide yawned their mortal seams.

The clock struck twelve; the Dead hath
    heard;
  He opened both his eyes,
And sullenly he shook his tail
  To lash the feeding flies.

One quiver of the hempen cord, —
  One struggle and one bound, —
With stiffened limb and leaden eye,
  The Pig was on the ground!

And straight towards the sleeper's house
  His fearful way he wended;
And hooting owl and hovering bat
  On midnight wing attended.

Back flew the bolt, up rose the latch,
  And open swung the door,
And little mincing feet were heard
  Pat, pat along the floor.

Two hoofs upon the sanded floor,
  And two upon the bed;
And they are breathing side by side,
  The living and the dead!

"Now wake, now wake, thou butcher man!
  What makes thy cheek so pale?
Take hold! take hold! thou dost not fear
  To clasp a spectre's tail?"

Untwisted every winding coil;
  The shuddering wretch took hold,
All like an icicle it seemed,
  So tapering and so cold.

"Thou com'st with me, thou butcher man!" —
  He strives to loose his grasp,
But, faster than the clinging vine,
  Those twining spirals clasp:

And open, open swung the door,
  And, fleeter than the wind,
The shadowy spectre swept before,
  The butcher trailed behind.

Fast fled the darkness of the night,
  And morn rose faint and dim;
They called full loud, they knocked full long,
  They did not waken him.

Straight, straight towards that oaken beam,
  A trampled pathway ran;
A ghastly shape was swinging there, —
  It was the butcher man.

TO A CAGED LION

Poor conquered monarch! though that haughty
    glance
  Still speaks thy courage unsubdued by time,
And in the grandeur of thy sullen tread
  Lives the proud spirit of thy burning clime: —
Fettered by things that shudder at thy roar,
Torn from thy pathless wilds to pace this nar-
    row floor!

Thou wast the victor, and all nature shrunk
  Before the thunders of thine awful wrath;
The steel-armed hunter viewed thee from afar,
  Fearless and trackless in thy lonely path!
The famished tiger closed his flaming eye,
And crouched and panted as thy step went
    by!

Thou art the vanquished, and insulting man
  Bars thy broad bosom as a sparrow's wing;
His nerveless arms thine iron sinews bind,
  And lead in chains the desert's fallen king;
Are these the beings that have dared to twine
  Their feeble threads around those limbs of
      thine?

So must it be; the weaker, wiser race,
  That wields the tempest and that rides the
      sea,
Even in the stillness of thy solitude
  Must teach the lesson of its power to thee;
And thou, the terror of the trembling wild,
Must bow thy savage strength, the mockery of
  a child!

THE STAR AND THE WATER-LILY

THE sun stepped down from his golden throne,
  And lay in the silent sea,
And the Lily had folded her satin leaves,
  For a sleepy thing was she;
What is the Lily dreaming of?
  Why crisp the waters blue?
See, see, she is lifting her varnished lid!
  Her white leaves are glistening through!

The Rose is cooling his burning cheek
  In the lap of the breathless tide; —
The Lily hath sisters fresh and fair,
  That would lie by the Rose's side;
He would love her better than all the rest,
  And he would be fond and true; —
But the Lily unfolded her weary lids,
  And looked at the sky so blue.

Remember, remember, thou silly one,
  How fast will thy summer glide,
And wilt thou wither a virgin pale,
  Or flourish a blooming bride?
"Oh, the Rose is old, and thorny, and cold,
  And he lives on earth," said she;
"But the Star is fair and he lives in the air,
  And he shall my bridegroom be."

But what if the stormy cloud should come,
  And ruffle the silver sea?
Would he turn his eye from the distant sky,
  To smile on a thing like thee?
Oh no, fair Lily, he will not send
  One ray from his far-off throne;
The winds shall blow, and the waves shall
      flow,
  And thou wilt be left alone.

There is not a leaf on the mountain-top,
  Nor a drop of evening dew,
Nor a golden sand on the sparkling shore,
  Nor a pearl in the waters blue,
That he has not cheered with his fickle smile,
  And warmed with his faithless beam, —
And will he be true to a pallid flower,
  That floats on the quiet stream?

Alas for the Lily! she would not heed,
  But turned to the skies afar,
And bared her breast to the trembling ray
  That shot from the rising star;
The cloud came over the darkened sky,
  And over the waters wide:
She looked in vain through the beating rain,
  And sank in the stormy tide.

ILLUSTRATION OF A PICTURE

"A SPANISH GIRL IN REVERIE"

SHE twirled the string of golden beads,
  That round her neck was hung, —
My grandsire's gift; the good old man
  Loved girls when he was young;
And, bending lightly o'er the cord,
  And turning half away,
With something like a youthful sigh,
  Thus spoke the maiden gray: —

"Well, one may trail her silken robe,
  And bind her locks with pearls,
And one may wreathe the woodland rose
  Among her floating curls;
And one may tread the dewy grass,
  And one the marble floor,
Nor half-hid bosom heave the less,
  Nor broidered corset more!

"Some years ago, a dark-eyed girl
  Was sitting in the shade, —
There's something brings her to my mind
  In that young dreaming maid, —
And in her hand she held a flower,
  A flower, whose speaking hue
Said, in the language of the heart,
  'Believe the giver true.'

"And, as she looked upon its leaves,
  The maiden made a vow
To wear it when the bridal wreath
  Was woven for her brow;
She watched the flower, as, day by day,
  The leaflets curled and died;
But he who gave it never came
  To claim her for his bride.

"Oh, many a summer's morning glow
  Has lent the rose its ray,
And many a winter's drifting snow
  Has swept its bloom away;
But she has kept that faithless pledge
  To this, her winter hour,
And keeps it still, herself alone,
  And wasted like the flower."

Her pale lip quivered, and the light
  Gleamed in her moistening eyes; —
I asked her how she liked the tints
  In those Castilian skies?
"She thought them misty, — 't was perhaps
  Because she stood too near;"
She turned away, and as she turned
  I saw her wipe a tear.

A ROMAN AQUEDUCT

THE sun-browned girl, whose limbs recline
  When noon her languid hand has laid
Hot on the green flakes of the pine,
  Beneath its narrow disk of shade;

As, through the flickering noontide glare,
  She gazes on the rainbow chain
Of arches, lifting once in air
  The rivers of the Roman's plain; —

Say, does her wandering eye recall
  The mountain-current's icy wave, —
Or for the dead one tear let fall,
  Whose founts are broken by their grave?

From stone to stone the ivy weaves
  Her braided tracery's winding veil,
And lacing stalks and tangled leaves
  Nod heavy in the drowsy gale.

And lightly floats the pendent vine,
  That swings beneath her slender bow,
Arch answering arch, — whose rounded line
  Seems mirrored in the wreath below.

How patient Nature smiles at Fame!
  The weeds, that strewed the victor's way,
Feed on his dust to shroud his name,
  Green where his proudest towers decay.

See, through that channel, empty now,
  The scanty rain its tribute pours, —
Which cooled the lip and laved the brow
  Of conquerors from a hundred shores.

Thus bending o'er the nation's bier,
  Whose wants the captive earth supplied,
The dew of Memory's passing tear
  Falls on the arches of her pride!

FROM A BACHELOR'S PRIVATE JOURNAL

SWEET Mary, I have never breathed
  The love it were in vain to name;
Though round my heart a serpent wreathed,
  I smiled, or strove to smile, the same.

Once more the pulse of Nature glows
  With faster throb and fresher fire,
While music round her pathway flows,
  Like echoes from a hidden lyre.

And is there none with me to share
  The glories of the earth and sky?
The eagle through the pathless air
  Is followed by one burning eye.

Ah no! the cradled flowers may wake,
  Again may flow the frozen sea,

From every cloud a star may break, —
  There comes no second spring to me.

Go, — ere the painted toys of youth
  Are crushed beneath the tread of years;
Ere visions have been chilled to truth,
  And hopes are washed away in tears.

Go, — for I will not bid thee weep, —
  Too soon my sorrows will be thine,
And evening's troubled air shall sweep
  The incense from the broken shrine.

If Heaven can hear the dying tone
  Of chords that soon will cease to thrill,
The prayer that Heaven has heard alone
  May bless thee when those chords are still.

LA GRISETTE

AH, Clemence! when I saw thee last
  Trip down the Rue de Seine,
And turning, when thy form had past,
  I said, "We meet again," —
I dreamed not in that idle glance
  Thy latest image came,
And only left to memory's trance
  A shadow and a name.

The few strange words my lips had taught
  Thy timid voice to speak,
Their gentler signs, which often brought
  Fresh roses to thy cheek,
The trailing of thy long loose hair
  Bent o'er my couch of pain,
All, all returned, more sweet, more fair:
  Oh, had we met again!

I walked where saint and virgin keep
  The vigil lights of Heaven,
I knew that thou hadst woes to weep,
  And sins to be forgiven;
I watched where Genevieve was laid,
  I knelt by Mary's shrine,
Beside me low, soft voices prayed;
  Alas! but where was thine?

And when the morning sun was bright,
  When wind and wave were calm,
And flamed, in thousand-tinted light,
  The rose of Notre Dame,
I wandered through the haunts of men,
  From Boulevard to Quai,
Till, frowning o'er Saint Etienne,
  The Pantheon's shadow lay.

In vain, in vain; we meet no more,
  Nor dream what fates befall;
And long upon the stranger's shore
  My voice on thee may call,
When years have clothed the line in moss
  That tells thy name and days,
And withered, on thy simple cross,
  The wreaths of Père-la-Chaise!

OUR YANKEE GIRLS

Let greener lands and bluer skies,
  If such the wide earth shows,
With fairer cheeks and brighter eyes,
  Match us the star and rose ;
The winds that lift the Georgian's veil,
  Or wave Circassia's curls,
Waft to their shores the sultan's sail, —
  Who buys our Yankee girls ?

The gay grisette, whose fingers touch
  Love's thousand chords so well ;
The dark Italian, loving much,
  But more than *one* can tell ;
And England's fair-haired, blue-eyed dame,
  Who binds her brow with pearls ; —
Ye who have seen them, can they shame
  Our own sweet Yankee girls ?

And what if court or castle vaunt
  Its children loftier born ? —
Who heeds the silken tassel's flaunt
  Beside the golden corn ?
They ask not for the dainty toil
  Of ribboned knights and earls,
The daughters of the virgin soil,
  Our freeborn Yankee girls !

By every hill whose stately pines
  Wave their dark arms above
The home where some fair being shines,
  To warm the wilds with love,
From barest rock to bleakest shore
  Where farthest sail unfurls,
That stars and stripes are streaming o'er, —
  God bless our Yankee girls !

L'INCONNUE

Is thy name Mary, maiden fair ?
  Such should, methinks, its music be ;
The sweetest name that mortals bear
  Were best befitting thee ;
And she to whom it once was given,
Was half of earth and half of heaven.

I hear thy voice, I see thy smile,
  I look upon thy folded hair ;
Ah ! while we dream not they beguile,
  Our hearts are in the snare ;
And she who chains a wild bird's wing
Must start not if her captive sing.

So, lady, take the leaf that falls,
  To all but thee unseen, unknown :
When evening shades thy silent walls,
  Then read it all alone ;
In stillness read, in darkness seal,
Forget, despise, but not reveal !

STANZAS

Strange ! that one lightly whispered tone
  Is far, far sweeter unto me,
Than all the sounds that kiss the earth,
  Or breathe along the sea ;

But, lady, when thy voice I greet,
Not heavenly music seems so sweet.

I look upon the fair blue skies,
  And naught but empty air I see ;
But when I turn me to thine eyes,
  It seemeth unto me
Ten thousand angels spread their wings
Within those little azure rings.

The lily hath the softest leaf
  That ever western breeze hath fanned,
But thou shalt have the tender flower,
  So I may take thy hand ;
That little hand to me doth yield
More joy than all the broidered field.

O lady ! there be many things
  That seem right fair, below, above ;
But sure not one among them all
  Is half so sweet as love ; —
Let us not pay our vows alone,
But join two altars both in one.

LINES BY A CLERK

Oh ! I did love her dearly,
  And gave her toys and rings,
And I thought she meant sincerely,
  When she took my pretty things.
But her heart has grown as icy
  As a fountain in the fall,
And her love, that was so spicy,
  It did not last at all.

I gave her once a locket,
  It was filled with my own hair,
And she put it in her pocket
  With very special care.
But a jeweller has got it, —
  He offered it to me, —
And another that is not it
  Around her neck I see.

For my cooings and my billings
  I do not now complain,
But my dollars and my shillings
  Will never come again ;
They were earned with toil and sorrow,
  But I never told her that,
And now I have to borrow,
  And want another hat.

Think, think, thou cruel Emma,
  When thou shalt hear my woe,
And know my sad dilemma,
  That thou hast made it so.
See, see my beaver rusty,
  Look, look upon this hole,
This coat is dim and dusty ;
  Oh let it rend thy soul !

Before the gates of fashion
  I daily bent my knee,
But I sought the shrine of passion,
  And found my idol, — thee.

Though never love intenser
　　Had bowed a soul before it,
Thine eye was on the censer,
　　And not the hand that bore it.

THE PHILOSOPHER TO HIS LOVE

DEAREST, a look is but a ray
Reflected in a certain way;
A word, whatever tone it wear,
Is but a trembling wave of air;
A touch, obedience to a clause
In nature's pure material laws.

The very flowers that bend and meet,
In sweetening others, grow more sweet;
The clouds by day, the stars by night,
Inweave their floating locks of light;
The rainbow, Heaven's own forehead's braid,
Is but the embrace of sun and shade.

How few that love us have we found!
How wide the world that girds them round!
Like mountain streams we meet and part,
Each living in the other's heart,
Our course unknown, our hope to be
Yet mingled in the distant sea.

But Ocean coils and heaves in vain,
Bound in the subtle moonbeam's chain;
And love and hope do but obey
Some cold, capricious planet's ray,
Which lights and leads the tide it charms
To Death's dark caves and icy arms.

Alas! one narrow line is drawn,
That links our sunset with our dawn;
In mist and shade life's morning rose,
And clouds are round it at its close;
But ah! no twilight beam ascends
To whisper where that evening ends.

Oh! in the hour when I shall feel
Those shadows round my senses steal,
When gentle eyes are weeping o'er
The clay that feels their tears no more,
Then let thy spirit with me be,
Or some sweet angel, likest thee!

THE POET'S LOT

WHAT is a poet's love? —
　　To write a girl a sonnet,
To get a ring, or some such thing,
　　And fustianize upon it.

What is a poet's fame? —
　　Sad hints about his reason,
And sadder praise from garreteers,
　　To be returned in season.

Where go the poet's lines? —
　　Answer, ye evening tapers!
Ye auburn locks, ye golden curls,
　　Speak from your folded papers!

Child of the ploughshare, smile;
　　Boy of the counter, grieve not,
Though muses round thy trundle-bed
　　Their broidered tissue weave not.

The poet's future holds
　　No civic wreath above him;
Nor slated roof, nor varnished chaise,
　　Nor wife nor child to love him.

Maid of the village inn,
　　Who workest woe on satin,
(The grass in black, the graves in green,
　　The epitaph in Latin,)

Trust not to them who say,
　　In stanzas, they adore thee;
Oh rather sleep in churchyard clay,
　　With urn and cherub o'er thee!

TO A BLANK SHEET OF PAPER

WAN-VISAGED thing! thy virgin leaf
　　To me looks more than deadly pale,
Unknowing what may stain thee yet, —
　　A poem or a tale.

Who can thy unborn meaning scan?
　　Can Seer or Sibyl read thee now?
No, — seek to trace the fate of man
　　Writ on his infant brow.

Love may light on thy snowy cheek,
　　And shake his Eden-breathing plumes;
Then shalt thou tell how Lelia smiles,
　　Or Angelina blooms.

Satire may lift his bearded lance,
　　Forestalling Time's slow-moving scythe,
And, scattered on thy little field,
　　Disjointed bards may writhe.

Perchance a vision of the night,
　　Some grizzled spectre, gaunt and thin,
Or sheeted corpse, may stalk along,
　　Or skeleton may grin!

If it should be in pensive hour
　　Some sorrow-moving theme I try,
Ah, maiden, how thy tears will fall,
　　For all I doom to die!

But if in merry mood I touch
　　Thy leaves, then shall the sight of thee
Sow smiles as thick on rosy lips
　　As ripples on the sea.

The Weekly press shall gladly stoop
　　To bind thee up among its sheaves;
The Daily steal thy shining ore,
　　To gild its leaden leaves.

Thou hast no tongue, yet thou canst speak,
　　Till distant shores shall hear the sound;

Thou hast no life, yet thou canst breathe
Fresh life on all around.

Thou art the arena of the wise,
The noiseless battle-ground of fame ;
The sky where halos may be wreathed
Around the humblest name.

Take, then, this treasure to thy trust,
To win some idle reader's smile,
Then fade and moulder in the dust,
Or swell some bonfire's pile.

TO THE PORTRAIT OF "A GENTLE-MAN"

IN THE ATHENÆUM GALLERY

It may be so, — perhaps thou hast
A warm and loving heart ;
I will not blame thee for thy face,
Poor devil as thou art.

That thing thou fondly deem'st a nose,
Unsightly though it be, —
In spite of all the cold world's scorn,
It may be much to thee.

Those eyes, — among thine elder friends
Perhaps they pass for blue, —
No matter, — if a man can see,
What more have eyes to do ?

Thy mouth, — that fissure in thy face,
By something like a chin, —
May be a very useful place
To put thy victual in.

I know thou hast a wife at home,
I know thou hast a child,
By that subdued, domestic smile
Upon thy features mild.

That wife sits fearless by thy side,
That cherub on thy knee ;
They do not shudder at thy looks,
They do not shrink from thee.

Above thy mantel is a hook, —
A portrait once was there;
It was thine only ornament, —
Alas ! that hook is bare.

She begged thee not to let it go,
She begged thee all in vain;
She wept, — and breathed a trembling prayer
To meet it safe again.

It was a bitter sight to see
That picture torn away;
It was a solemn thought to think
What all her friends would say !

And often in her calmer hours,
And in her happy dreams,
Upon its long-deserted hook
The absent portrait seems.

Thy wretched infant turns his head
In melancholy wise,
And looks to meet the placid stare
Of those unbending eyes.

I never saw thee, lovely one, —
Perchance I never may ;
It is not often that we cross
Such people in our way ;

But if we meet in distant years,
Or on some foreign shore,
Sure I can take my Bible oath,
I 've seen that face before.

THE BALLAD OF THE OYSTERMAN

It was a tall young oysterman lived by the river-side,
His shop was just upon the bank, his boat was on the tide ;
The daughter of a fisherman, that was so straight and slim,
Lived over on the other bank, right opposite to him.

It was the pensive oysterman that saw a lovely maid,
Upon a moonlight evening, a-sitting in the shade ;
He saw her wave her handkerchief, as much as if to say,
"I 'm wide awake, young oysterman, and all the folks away."

Then up arose the oysterman, and to himself said he,
"I guess I 'll leave the skiff at home, for fear that folks should see ;
I read it in the story-book, that, for to kiss his dear,
Leander swam the Hellespont, — and I will swim this here."

And he has leaped into the waves, and crossed the shining stream,
And he has clambered up the bank, all in the moonlight gleam ;
Oh there were kisses sweet as dew, and words as soft as rain, —
But they have heard her father's step, and in he leaps again !

Out spoke the ancient fisherman, — "Oh, what was that, my daughter ? "
" 'T was nothing but a pebble, sir, I threw into the water."
" And what is that, pray tell me, love, that paddles off so fast ? "
" It 's nothing but a porpoise, sir, that 's been a-swimming past."

Out spoke the ancient fisherman, — "Now bring
    me my harpoon!
I 'll get into my fishing-boat, and fix the fellow
    soon."
Down fell that pretty innocent, as falls a snow-
    white lamb,
Her hair drooped round her pallid cheeks, like
    seaweed on a clam.

Alas for those two loving ones! she waked not
    from her swound,
And he was taken with the cramp, and in the
    waves was drowned;
But Fate has metamorphosed them, in pity of
    their woe,
And now they keep an oyster-shop for mer-
    maids down below.

A NOONTIDE LYRIC

THE dinner-bell, the dinner-bell
    Is ringing loud and clear;
Through hill and plain, through street and lane,
    It echoes far and near;
From curtained hall and whitewashed stall,
    Wherever men can hide,
Like bursting waves from ocean caves,
    They float upon the tide.

I smell the smell of roasted meat!
    I hear the hissing fry!
The beggars know where they can go,
    But where, oh where shall I?
At twelve o'clock men took my hand,
    At two they only stare,
And eye me with a fearful look,
    As if I were a bear!

The poet lays his laurels down,
    And hastens to his greens;
The happy tailor quits his goose,
    To riot on his beans;
The weary cobbler snaps his thread,
    The printer leaves his pi;
His very devil hath a home,
    But what, oh what have I?

Methinks I hear an angel voice,
    That softly seems to say:
"Pale stranger, all may yet be well,
    Then wipe thy tears away;
Erect thy head, and cock thy hat,
    And follow me afar,
And thou shalt have a jolly meal,
    And charge it at the bar."

I hear the voice! I go! I go!
    Prepare your meat and wine!
They little heed their future need
    Who pay not when they dine.
Give me to-day the rosy bowl,
    Give me one golden dream, —
To-morrow kick away the stool,
    And dangle from the beam!

THE HOT SEASON

THE folks, that on the first of May
    Wore winter coats and hose,
Began to say, the first of June,
    "Good Lord! how hot it grows!"
At last two Fahrenheits blew up,
    And killed two children small,
And one barometer shot dead
    A tutor with its ball!

Now all day long the locusts sang
    Among the leafless trees;
Three new hotels warped inside out,
    The pumps could only wheeze;
And ripe old wine, that twenty years
    Had cobwebbed o'er in vain,
Came spouting through the rotten corks
    Like Joly's best champagne!

The Worcester locomotives did
    Their trip in half an hour;
The Lowell cars ran forty miles
    Before they checked the power;
Roll brimstone soon became a drug,
    And loco-focos fell;
All asked for ice, but everywhere
    Saltpetre was to sell.

Plump men of mornings ordered tights,
    But, ere the scorching noons,
Their candle-moulds had grown as loose
    As Cossack pantaloons!
The dogs ran mad, — men could not try
    If water they would choose;
A horse fell dead, — he only left
    Four red-hot, rusty shoes!

But soon the people could not bear
    The slightest hint of fire;
Allusions to caloric drew
    A flood of savage ire;
The leaves on heat were all torn out
    From every book at school,
And many blackguards kicked and caned,
    Because they said, "Keep cool!"

The gas-light companies were mobbed,
    The bakers all were shot,
The penny press began to talk
    Of lynching Doctor Nott;
And all about the warehouse steps
    Were angry men in droves,
Crashing and splintering through the doors
    To smash the patent stoves!

The abolition men and maids
    Were tanned to such a hue,
You scarce could tell them from their friends,
    Unless their eyes were blue;
And, when I left, society
    Had burst its ancient guards,
And Brattle Street and Temple Place
    Were interchanging cards!

A PORTRAIT

A STILL, sweet, placid, moonlight face,
 And slightly nonchalant,
Which seems to claim a middle place
 Between one's love and aunt,
Where childhood's star has left a ray
 In woman's sunniest sky,
As morning dew and blushing day
 On fruit and blossom lie.

And yet, — and yet I cannot love
 Those lovely lines on steel ;
They beam too much of heaven above,
 Earth's darker shades to feel ;
Perchance some early weeds of care
 Around my heart have grown,
And brows unfurrowed seem not fair,
 Because they mock my own.

Alas ! when Eden's gates were sealed,
 How oft some sheltered flower
Breathed o'er the wanderers of the field,
 Like their own bridal bower ;
Yet, saddened by its loveliness,
 And humbled by its pride,
Earth's fairest child they could not bless, —
 It mocked them when they sighed.

AN EVENING THOUGHT

WRITTEN AT SEA

IF sometimes in the dark blue eye,
 Or in the deep red wine,
Or soothed by gentlest melody,
 Still warms this heart of mine,
Yet something colder in the blood,
 And calmer in the brain,
Have whispered that my youth's bright flood
 Ebbs, not to flow again.

If by Helvetia's azure lake,
 Or Arno's yellow stream,
Each star of memory could awake,
 As in my first young dream,
I know that when mine eye shall greet
 The hillsides bleak and bare,
That gird my home, it will not meet
 My childhood's sunsets there.

Oh, when love's first, sweet, stolen kiss
 Burned on my boyish brow,
Was that young forehead worn as this ?
 Was that flushed cheek as now ?
Were that wild pulse and throbbing heart
 Like these, which vainly strive,
In thankless strains of soulless art,
 To dream themselves alive ?

Alas ! the morning dew is gone,
 Gone ere the full of day ;
Life's iron fetter still is on,
 Its wreaths all torn away ;

Happy if still some casual hour
 Can warm the fading shrine,
Too soon to chill beyond the power
 Of love, or song, or wine !

"THE WASP" AND "THE HORNET"

THE two proud sisters of the sea,
 In glory and in doom ! —
Well may the eternal waters be
 Their broad, unsculptured tomb !
The wind that rings along the wave,
 The clear, unshadowed sun,
Are torch and trumpet o'er the brave,
 Whose last green wreath is won !

No stranger-hand their banners furled,
 No victor's shout they heard ;
Unseen, above them ocean curled,
 Save by his own pale bird ;
The gnashing billows heaved and fell ;
 Wild shrieked the midnight gale ;
Far, far beneath the morning swell
 Were pennon, spar, and sail.

The land of Freedom ! Sea and shore
 Are guarded now, as when
Her ebbing waves to victory bore
 Fair barks and gallant men ;
Oh, many a ship of prouder name
 May wave her starry fold,
Nor trail, with deeper light of fame,
 The paths they swept of old !

"QUI VIVE?"

"*Qui vive?*" The sentry's musket rings ;
 The channelled bayonet gleams ;
High o'er him, like a raven's wings
 The broad tricolored banner flings
Its shadow, rustling as it swings
 Pale in the moonlight beams ;
Pass on ! while steel-clad sentries keep
Their vigil o'er the monarch's sleep,
 Thy bare, unguarded breast
Asks not the unbroken, bristling zone
That girds yon sceptred trembler's throne ;
 Pass on, and take thy rest !

" *Qui vive?*" How oft the midnight air
 That startling cry has borne !
How oft the evening breeze has fanned
The banner of this haughty land,
O'er mountain snow and desert sand,
 Ere yet its folds were torn !
Through Jena's carnage flying red,
Or tossing o'er Marengo's dead,
 Or curling on the towers
Where Austria's eagle quivers yet,
And suns the ruffled plumage, wet
 With battle's crimson showers !

" *Qui vive?*" And is the sentry's cry, —
 The sleepless soldier's hand, —
Are these — the painted folds that fly

And lift their emblems, printed high
On morning mist and sunset sky —
 The guardians of a land?
No! If the patriot's pulses sleep,
How vain the watch that hirelings keep, —
 The idle flag that waves,
When Conquest, with his iron heel,
Treads down the standards and the steel
 That belt the soil of slaves!

A SOUVENIR

Yes, lady! I can ne'er forget,
That once in other years we met;
Thy memory may perchance recall
A festal eve, a rose-wreathed hall,
Its tapers' blaze, its mirrors' glance,
Its melting song, its ringing dance; —
Why, in thy dream of virgin joy,
Shouldst thou recall a pallid boy?

Thine eye had other forms to seek,
Why rest upon his bashful cheek?
With other tones thy heart was stirred,
Why waste on him a gentle word?
We parted, lady, — all night long
Thine ear to thrill with dance and song, —
And I — to weep that I was born
A thing thou scarce wouldst deign to scorn.

And, lady! now that years have past,
My bark has reached the shore at last;
The gales that filled her ocean wing,
Have chilled and shrunk thy hasty spring,
And eye to eye, and brow to brow,
I stand before thy presence now; —
Thy lip is smoothed, thy voice is sweet,
Thy warm hand offered when we meet.

Nay, lady! 't is not now for me
To droop the lid or bend the knee.
I seek thee, — oh thou dost not shun;
I speak, — thou listenest like a nun;
I ask thy smile, — thy lip uncurls,
Too liberal of its flashing pearls;
Thy tears, — thy lashes sing again, —
My Hebe turns to Magdalen!

O changing youth! that evening hour
Looked down on ours, — the bud — the flower:
Thine faded in its virgin soil,
And mine was nursed in tears and toil;
Thy leaves were withering, one by one,
While mine were opening to the sun.
Which now can meet the cold and storm,
With freshest leaf and hardiest form?

Ay, lady! that once haughty glance
Still wanders through the glittering dance,
And ask in vain from others' pride,
The charity thine own denied;
And as thy fickle lips could learn
To smile and praise, — that used to spurn,
So the last offering on thy shrine .
Shall be this flattering lay of mine!

THE DYING SENECA

He died not as the martyr dies,
 Wrapped in his living shroud of flame;
He fell not as the warrior falls,
 Gasping upon the field of fame ;
A gentler passage to the grave,
The murderer's softened fury gave.

Rome's slaughtered sons and blazing piles
 Had tracked the purpled demon's path,
And yet another victim lived
 To fill the fiery scroll of wrath ;
Could not imperial vengeance spare
His furrowed brow and silver hair?

The field was sown with noble blood,
 The harvest reaped in burning tears,
When, rolling up its crimson flood,
 Broke the long-gathering tide of years ;
His diadem was rent away,
And beggars trampled on his clay.

None wept, — none pitied ; — they who knelt
 At morning by the despot's throne,
At evening dashed the laurelled bust,
 And spurned the wreaths themselves had
 strown ;
The shout of triumph echoed wide,
The self-stung reptile writhed and died !

THE LAST PROPHECY OF CASSANDRA

The sun is fading in the skies,
 And evening shades are gathering fast ;
Fair city, ere that sun shall rise,
 Thy night hath come, — thy day is past !

Ye know not, — but the hour is nigh ;
 Ye will not heed the warning breath ;
No vision strikes your clouded eye,
 To break the sleep that wakes in death.

Go, age, and let thy withered cheek
 Be wet once more with freezing tears ;
And bid thy trembling sorrow speak,
 In accents of departed years.

Go, child, and pour thy sinless prayer
 Before the everlasting throne ;
And He, who sits in glory there,
 May stoop to hear thy silver tone.

Go, warrior, in thy glittering steel,
 And bow thee at the altar's side ;
And bid thy frowning gods reveal
 The doom their mystic counsels hide.

Go, maiden, in thy flowing veil,
 And bare thy brow, and bend thy knee ;
When the last hopes of mercy fail,
 Thy God may yet remember thee.

Go, as thou didst in happier hours,
 And lay thine incense on the shrine ;

And greener leaves, and fairer flowers,
  Around the sacred image twine.

I saw them rise, — the buried dead, —
  From marble tomb and grassy mound ;
I heard the spirits' printless tread,
  And voices not of earthly sound.

I looked upon the quivering stream,
  And its cold wave was bright with flame ;
And wild, as from a fearful dream,
  The wasted forms of battle came.

Ye will not hear, — ye will not know, —
  Ye scorn the maniac's idle song ;
Ye care not ! but the voice of woe
  Shall thunder loud, and echo long.

Blood shall be in your marble halls,
  And spears shall glance, and fire shall glow;
Ruin shall sit upon your walls,
  But ye shall lie in death below.

Ay, none shall live, to hear the storm
  Around their blackened pillars sweep ;
To shudder at the reptile's form,
  Or scare the wild bird from her sleep.

TO MY COMPANIONS

MINE ancient chair ! thy wide-embracing arms
  Have clasped around me even from a boy :
Hadst thou a voice to speak of years gone by,
  Thine were a tale of sorrow and of joy,
Of fevered hopes and ill-foreboding fears,
And smiles unseen, and unrecorded tears.

And thou, my table ! though unwearied time
  Hath set his signet on thine altered brow,
Still can I see thee in thy spotless prime,
  And in my memory thou art living now ;
Soon must thou slumber with forgotten things,
The peasant's ashes and the dust of kings.

Thou melancholy mug ! thy sober brown
  Hath something pensive in its evening hue,
Not like the things that please the tasteless
    clown,
  With gaudy streaks of orange and of blue ;
And I must love thee, for thou art mine own,
Pressed by my lip, and pressed by mine alone.

My broken mirror ! faithless, yet beloved,
  Thou who canst smile, and smile alike on all,
Oft do I leave thee, oft again return,
  I scorn the siren, but obey the call ;
I hate thy falsehood, while I fear thy truth,
But most I love thee, flattering friend of youth.

Primeval carpet ! every well-worn thread
  Has slowly parted with its virgin dye ;
I saw thee fade beneath the ceaseless tread,
  Fainter and fainter in mine anxious eye ;
So flies the color from the brightest flower,
And heaven's own rainbow lives but for an
    hour.

I love you all ! there radiates from our own,
  A soul that lives in every shape we see ;
There is a voice, to other ears unknown,
  Like echoed music answering to its key.
The dungeoned captive hath a tale to tell,
Of every insect in his lonely cell ;
And these poor frailties have a simple tone,
That breathes in accents sweet to me alone.

II. ADDITIONAL VERSES FROM THE OLDEST PORTFOLIO

1822—1833

"PERDIDI DIEM." TIBERIUS

JULY 25, 1822

"I've lost a day," old Tibby said,
Then sighed and groaned, and went to bed.
This monarch, as they said of old,
Knew time was worth much more than gold.
I'm of this sage opinion too,
And think this man judged pretty true.
— But now, my friends, I'll bid good bye,
For you are tired — and so am I.

CHARITABLE ANN

CHARITABLE Ann —
Give this poor man —
As much as you can —
A little meat
And bread to eat
And a shady seat —

HASTY PUDDING

MAY 2, 1828

FOR soon appeared the smiling pot
Brimful of pudding, smoking hot
With ready step and joyful faces
The glad providers took their places
Soon as their bowls and spoons they found
To make all *square* they helped us *round*
Two different ways their footsteps tend
For one *began* at either *end*
And therefore these providers seem
To *carry things* to *the extreme*

SERENADE

THE moon is up, and soft and bright,
  And tender is her light in June,
For is this not a lovely night,
  And is not that a splendid moon ?

Oh, that you knew how often, love,
  When I was in the tropic sea,
My eyes were on the moon above
  While thought was wandering back to thee.

And when we lost the polar star,
    Far southward of the central line,
To you I struck the soft guitar,
    And was your moonlight song like mine?

For mine was love, as still it is;
    And shall it be forever crost,
And must I in a night like this
    But sigh to find "Love's Labour Lost"?

TO M. C. D.

I THANK thee for the silken prize —
    So sweetly shines its heavenly blue
That one might think thine own bright eyes
    Had kindled the celestial hue
Or that a cloud from heaven had strayed,
And tinged it with its softest shade.

As round the vaulted dome of night
    A thousand radiant cressets shine
So flame these points of silver light
    That bound the azure circles line
And brighter seem the rays to me
Because their lustre came from thee.

In every collar's loosened tie —
    In every stitch that time shall strain —
When night obscures my troubled sky
    Those stars shall scatter light again —
O then shall grateful memory turn
And think of her who bade them burn.

P. S.

My gratitude will never cool,
    My sister says so too.
I fear that when she sees a fool
    She'll always think of you

BURIAL OF A MAIDEN AT SEA

O LAY her in the stormy grave,
    And soft her slumbers be,
Her pillow is the mountain wave,
    Her tomb the boundless sea.

Old Ocean round the maiden's breast
    His mantle green shall fold,
And angels guard her silent rest
    Beneath the waters cold.

Still shall the angry tempests sweep,
    The ceaseless tide shall flow;
But wind, nor wave, shall break her sleep
Who lies in peace below.

Farewell! The waves are closing fast
    Around thy fading form;
O may thy spirit find at last,
    A home without a storm.

THE LOVER'S RETURN

"O, TELL me, my daughter, why is it, that
    now
There's a tear in thine eye, and a cloud on
    thy brow?
Thy footsteps no longer are light in the vale,
And the cheek, once so rosy, is haggard and
    pale.

"I will bring thee, my daughter, a garland so
    fair,
To entwine in the locks of thy dark waving
    hair."
"Its freshness will fade, and its bloom will
    decay,
Then weave me no wreaths that will wither
    away."

"I will bring thee a gem, that shall sparkle
    as bright
As the planet that flames on the girdle of
    night."
"I ask not thy jewels, their splendor is vain,
They will soothe not my slumbers, will ease
    not my pain."

"Oh weep not, my daughter, while others are
    gay,
It is not for thee to be grieving to day;
Let sorrow no longer o'ershadow thy charms,
For thy long absent lover has come to thine
    arms."

The gloom passed away from the brow of his
    child;
Full deeply she crimsoned, but sweetly she
    smiled;
And soon by her lover, the maiden did stand,
With a wreath in her tresses, a gem on her
    hand.

FORGOTTEN AGES

HARVARD COLLEGE EXHIBITION

APRIL 28, 1829

FROM yon high chamber, on whose naked
    walls
The slanting ray of rosy morning falls —
Where kind Aurora showers her earliest
    beams
To wake the sleeper from delusive dreams —
Where playful zephyrs riot through the floor
Laugh at the cracks and revel round the
    door —
From that bright home the poet gladly flies
To meet the radiance of these brighter eyes.
    What various beauties crowd upon my
    sight
Flash from the left and sparkle from the
    right.

The matron's sweetness and the maiden's
   bloom —
The flaunting ribband and the waving
   plume —
Blushes that saucers never owned before
And looks unpurchased from the fancy-
   store —
In queenly pride the lofty head-dress towers
And bonnets blossom with unfading
   flowers —
Their different charms the smiling sisters
   blend,
All nature gives, and all that art can lend.
— O envious time, could not thy chariot stay
A moment longer on its silent way?
Must all they glories burst upon the eye,
Like angel's pinions, only as they fly!
How short our empire on this little stage!
How swift these moments in the train of age!
In vain the light that beauty sheds around
To stay our footsteps on the enchanted
   ground.
Time waves his wand — the short-lived
   pageant flies
And other hours, and other forms arise.
— As fades the memory of an idle day
The name of ages hastens to decay:
Wrapped in the past, in darkness disappears
The gleam of moments and the light of years.
— O where, forgotten in the silent shade
Are all the forms, that once had being, laid?
Where sunk the palace and where fell the
   throne
On which the sun of ancient splendor shone?
Nations have been where we may look in vain
For one frail remnant on the voiceless plain.
Unchecked the mind around the desert flows
Where proud Ambition's lofty turrets rose.
Some wasted slowly into dull decay
Till stone by stone, their grandeur dropped
   away.
The conqueror came, and in a single hour
Fell the bright trophies of imperial power.
Some sank beneath the red volcanic wave
And after ages trod their burning grave —
The surge has rolled o'er many an ancient
   shore
And Ocean sweeps where man has reigned
   before.
— Quenched is the lustre of the glancing
   eye —
Cold is the heart that once beat warm and
   high —
The lips that nature only formed for smiles
Lie in the ashes of their buried piles.
In thousand paths the subtle shafts have fled
And none is left — the herald of the dead.
The torch of famine seared the dying land,
The warrior fell beneath another's hand.
And slow disease hath wasted many a form,
That rode in triumph on the battle-storm.
— They sleep, unconscious that the hour has
   come
When all that echoed to their voice is dumb;
Alike to them if o'er their dark repose
The forest blossoms or the ocean flows.

The hand of spring their funeral chaplet
   weaves,
And autumn strews them with his withered
   leaves;
Or wildly murmuring round their stormy
   home
The towering billow stoops its crest of foam.
In vain they bade their mausoleums rise,
And reared their pillars till they reached the
   skies.
No stone is rescued from the dust to tell
Where once they stood and where at last they
   fell
— O'er other lands that wore the crown of
   old
The shroud of age is gathering fold by fold.
But still half-lost amid the deepening gloom
The dying sun-beam plays around their
   tomb.
   Though art has risen from her native clime
All is not darkened in the clouds of time;
We trace her brightness in the lingering glow
Her foot has kindled while it walked below.
The stately relics of departed pride —
The temple mouldering by its builder's side.
The prostrate column and the fallen shrine
Point to the days that saw their glory shine,
And tell the stranger on their hallowed
   ground
That man is crumbling in the soil around.
And some have lived, if that be life which
   Fame,
When all is dust, can lavish on a name;
Still rings the harp that Athens loved to hear
And bright-eyed Thalia woos the modern's
   ear.
But they who called her from the mountain-
   steep —
Can music wake them from their silent
   sleep? —
— And we, the children of a later birth,
The transient monarchs of this changing
   earth,
We too shall pass and leave no single trace
To fix our memory on some future race.
Our heroes glory in the crimson wreath
Their hands have wrested from the brow of
   death
They little see it, in their fevered dream,
Torn by the ripple of the noiseless stream:
Our rulers frame their statutes for the free
Of after ages that shall never be.
The luckless votaries of Apollo's lyre
Catch far more real than poetic fire;
And vainly scatter from their pictured urns,
Not "thoughts that breathe," but "many a
   word that burns."
— So flies a moment, and so rolls an age,
Monarchs and poets quit alike the stage;
They leave at last their sceptre and their
   crown,
We gently bow and lay our laurels down.
If our young Muse has managed to beguile
Her fairer sisters of one favoring smile —
If hard-heeled students and if booted boys
Will aid her exit with their flattering noise —

If sterner age will spare the humble lays
And kindly pardon what it cannot praise,
Though e'er tomorrow it shall be forgot,
That she has hovered round this little spot,
Without a murmur that her feeble wings
Must share the fate of empires and of kings,
No longer fluttering in your wearied sight,
She folds her mantle and she takes her flight.

A POEM

HARVARD COLLEGE COMMENCEMENT

AUGUST 26, 1829

As the proud champion in the days of old
Ere the deep thunders for the onset rolled
Turned to the ranks where beauty's bright
array
Rose like the crescent on the brow of day
And sought through all the glowing forms to
trace
His own fair lady in the crowded place
To ask the favour of one gentle sigh —
To claim one tribute from her glancing eye
So would we turn, in anxious hope to find
Some pitying symptoms from the fair and
kind
And ask for mercy as we humbly bow
Down at their feet our laurel cinctured brow.

— And this dread moment is at last our own
And we are left unpitied and alone
With beating heart and trembling hands to
dare
The idle glance — the stern unwavering stare
The sneers of youth — the darker frown of
age
The schoolboy critic and the solemn sage
The pensive miss who listens as she sighs
For "golden ringlets" and for "sunny skies"
The nameless being whose existence fills
What would be vacuum in his faultless gills
The sober people that consult the time
And think of dinner in despite of rhyme
And those that crowd around the sacred door
To see the place they never saw before.

— Fair creatures kindling with a starlike
glow
The hallowed precincts of the lofty row
Since ye are straining all your eyes to scan
The curves and angles of our outer man
And we all quivering with disdain must feel
Your curious looks that creep from crown to
heel
Since fate's dark pleasure has decreed to day
That you must hear what we shall choose to
say
To make at once the mutual compact fair
We turn to you and find our subject there.

— We be your subject lisps the miss of ten
Why poets are as impudent as men !
We be your subject ! cries the shrinking belle
This horrid bonnet ! but the gown looks
well —
Pray did he think we wanted to be seen
In Cupid's name what does the creature
mean ?
The married lady hints that she allows
No such remarks from her well managed
spouse
Or whispers glancing at her wedding ring
I wish my husband had said such a thing.

— Bid all your fans their slender veils expand
Knit the fair brow and clench the little hand
The timid miss is happy ere she flies
To light her taper in your flashing eyes.

— There sits the wife — and though a wife
may seem
A curious subject for the poet's dream
Yet there is something in that gentle name
That wakes the slumbers of the soul to flame.
When the last angel winged his silent way
From earth's dark shadows to a brighter day
Yet erring man of heavenly forms bereft
Could thank his God that one at least was
left.
O had our mother like the modern Eves
Robed her fair brow in those luxuriant sleeves
Then had poor Adam like their husbands
known
How hard his fortune who is all alone
And walked in sorrow by his blooming bride
Some twenty paces from the lady's side.

— On yonder seat — but Fancy says beware
Nor wake the vengeance that is slumbering
there
By all your prospects, as you hope to claim
A lasting record on the page of fame
Tread not too rashly on the sacred ground
Where the soft votary of the muse is found.
The time has been when nature's simple child
Was free and fearless in his forest wild
His lovely savage in her native grace
Asked not the aid of ribbons or of lace
She read no novels poems or reviews
And men were happy in the want of blues.
The times have changed — the steps of
womankind
Are first and foremost in the march of mind
The housewife's manual sleeps upon the
shelves
They read — they write — they criticise
themselves.
Turn for a moment to that youthful fair
With dovelike aspect and with gentle air
Who softly flutters with her little fan
And looks as much like fainting as she can.
If you have seen — and by a victim's tears
The sight is common in these latter years
A fair haired maiden who forever sought
For what she called "a sweet poetic thought"
Who wrote in lines that jingled at their ends
And kept an album for her private friends
Then gentle hearer you indeed have seen
The female monster that our verses mean.

Trust not the light of her insidious smile
Tis but the splendour of your funeral pile
Though all the graces in her pout appear
That pink leaved album follows in the rear.

— Nor there alone the fleeting muse require
To waste the glimmer of her waning fire
While lips like thine celestial beauty claim
The worthless offering of her feeble flame.
Fairest of beings, if thy melting eyes
Have caught the azure of the summer skies
Or the pure spirit send its flashes through
The kindling shadows of a darker hue
If oer thy forehead parts the raven fold
Or the bright tresses float in liquid gold
We own thy influence and we bow to thee
The atheist's God — the despot of the free
We coldly bend at many a prouder throne
But the heart's homage — it is all thine own.

— Our time is past — we may not stay to
        raise
The idle paeans of unneeded praise
If the poor graduate's ever frugal board
Shall soon or late so strange a thing afford
One classic tribute shall at least be thine —
The deepest bumper of the brightest wine —

TO S — L —

YET wert thou false — in vain the smiles
    That played in light around thee
A seraph in an icy chain
    That sparkled while it bound thee

I can forget thee — all hath fled
    Save one half buried gleam
Of what thou wast — and what thou art
    Shall be a nameless dream —

RHYMED CHRONICLE

THE Praeses has a weekly *row*,
    I think they call it a *levee*,
And people say it's very fine;
    I'm sure it's flat enough to me.
Judge Story's bought a horse in town;
    The law school every day grows bigger;
And Sukey Lenox — I forgot,
    I've told you all about the nigger.
One fellow lately came from Maine,
    And now there is another comer;
And one is Upton called by name.
    And t'other one is christened Dummer.
The undergraduates have made
    Proposals for a monthly paper,
Which I am very much afraid
    Will end in something worse than vapor.

I wish I had a little room, —
    It makes my heart feel very sadly,
When I have so much news to tell
    To crowd it up so very badly.
The folks have bolted up the doors,

And I have bolted down my supper.
My pony threw me t'other day
    And very nearly broke my crupper.
Get *Blackwood's Magazine* and read
    The story of the modern Gyges;
And if you ride a coltish steed
    Be careful of your "os coxygis."
The college servant took some books
    And laid the mischief to the students,
But as it happened to be false
    We thought him guilty of impudence.

SELECTIONS FROM THE NEWS-PAPERS

A TAX on hemp has been proposed —
    By convicts in the county prison —
Strange facts have lately been disclosed —
    From which we learn that pork has risen.

A black was taken Friday last —
    Stealing Sir Francis Bacon's phrases —
Within a single year have past —
    A coach and several handsome chaises.

She was a stale and starch old maid —
    The prettiest ever man set eyes on —
So very killing it was said —
    Three worthy butchers died by poison.

Two hundred casks of shingle nails —
    Were brought last autumn to the
        hammer —
The secretary, say the mails —
    Is publishing a work on grammar.

A farce is acting at the South —
    In the Virginia Convention —
A lady with the sweetest mouth —
    Said things too scandalous to mention.

The razors made by Smith and Son —
    Are said to be extremely cutting —
A steady man of twenty-one —
    Would like to get a place for strutting.

The sermon preached on Sunday night —
    Has been accused of taking purses —
Missing, a puppy nearly white —
    Addicted much to writing verses.

A subterranean arch was found —
    By men at work upon the steeple —
There now are lying in the pound —
    Great numbers of the starving people.

A maid too false, and yet too fair —
    Was roundly whipped for picking
        pockets —
Just landed, thirty bales of hair —
    Much used for bracelets and for lockets.

A fellow has been seen of late —
    Extremely regular at meeting —
And turkey in its present state —
    Is very pleasant, wholesome eating.

People who do not make their wills —
Require a copious ablution —
The celebrated bilious pills —
Have done tremendous execution.

AN ENIGMA

I

IN light, in shade, its changing form appears,
Now clothed in blushes, and now bathed in
tears;
It spreads its wings upon the summer air,
And sits in silence on the mountain bare;
Wrapped in the shadows of its gloomy breast,
The springs of life, the fires of vengeance,
rest;
It floats in kindness, and it flies in wrath,
And skies grow darker in its awful path;
It paints the petal of the dying flower,
It shakes the temple, and it rocks the tower!
Its shaft strikes down the lovely and the
brave;
Yet will it turn and weep upon their grave.

ENIGMA

II

IT came unheard, and darkness veiled its
birth,
The child of heaven, yet only seen on earth;
It lay half hidden in the folded leaves,
The sleeping floweret round her bosom
weaves,
And when the moonbeam touched it from
afar,
It shone and sparkled like a fallen star;
But ah, it trembled in the breath of day,
And softly faded like a dream away.
Such was its fate — and thus, without a
stain,
It came to earth, and sought the skies again;
A rosy cradle, and a golden shroud,
Born in a flower, and dying in A CLOUD.

RUNAWAY BALLADS

I

WAKE from thy slumbers, Isabel, the stars
are in the sky,
And night has hung her silver lamp, to light
our altar by;
The flowers have closed their fading leaves,
and droop upon the plain,
O wake thee, and their dying hues shall blush
to life again.

In such a sacred hour as this, how beams the
eye of love,
When all is mellowed shade below, and all is
light above;

And oh, how soft a maiden's sigh melts on the
midnight air,
When scarce a wanton zephyr breathes, to
wave her silken hair.

The rattle of the soldier's steel has left the
silent hall,
The mastiff slumbers at the gate, the sentry
on the wall;
And there, by many a stately barge, that
rocks upon the tide,
A bark is floating on the waves and dancing
by their side.

And when before the flowing wind she spreads
her eagle wings,
And like a halcyon, from her breast the
shivered billow flings;
Though many a prouder pendant flies before
the ocean breeze,
No keel can track her foaming path, that
sweeps the sparkling seas.

Then come to me, my lovely one, and haste
we far away,
And we will reach the distant isle before the
break of day;
Let not thy gentle eyes grow dim, thy rosy
cheek grow pale,
For thou shalt find a beating heart beneath a
warrior's mail.

II

GET up! get up! Miss Polly Jones, the
tandem's at the door;
Get up, and shake your lovely bones, it's
twelve o'clock and more,
The chaises they have rattled by, and nothing
stirs around,
And all the world, but you and I, are moving
safe and sound.

I broke a drunken watchman's nap, and he
began to mutter,
I gave him just a gentle tap, that helped him
to the gutter;
The cur-dog growled an ugly growl, and
grinned a bitter grin;
I tipped the beast a rat's-bane pill, to keep
his music in.

When Squaretoes stumps about the house,
and doesn't find you there,
And all the folks are in a touse, my eyes!
how dad will stare!
He locked and double-locked the door, and
saw you safe abed,
And never dreamed a jailor's paw could
scratch a booby's head.

Come hurry! hurry! Polly Jones, it is no
time to snooze;
Don't stop for t'other petticoat, nor fidget
for your shoes;
I have a quilted wrapper here, your tender
limbs to fold,

It's growing mighty chilly, dear, and I shall
catch a cold.

I've got my gouty uncle's bay, and trotting
Peggy too,
I've lined their tripes with oats and hay, and
now for love and you;
The lash is curling in the air, and I am at
your side,
To-morrow you are Mrs. Snaggs, my bold
and blooming bride.

ROMANCE

O! SHE was a maid of a laughing eye,
And she lived in a garret cold and high;
And he was a threadbare, whiskered beau,
And he lived in a cellar damp and low.

But the rosy boy of the cherub wing
Hath many a shaft for his slender string,
And the youth below and the maid above
Were touched with the flaming darts of love.

And she would wake from her troubled sleep,
O'er his tender billet-doux to weep;
Or stand like a statue cold and fair,
And gaze on a lock of his bright red hair.

And he who was late so tall and proud,
With his step so firm and his laugh so loud;
His beard grew long and his face grew thin,
As he pined in solitude over his gin.

But one soft night in the month of June,
As she lay in the light of a cloudless moon,
A voice came floating soft and clear,
To the startled maiden's listening ear.

O then from her creaking couch she sprung,
And her tangled tresses back she flung;
She looked from the window far below,
And he stood beneath — her whiskered beau!

She did not start with a foolish frown,
But she packed her trunk, and she scamper'd
down;
And there was her lover tall and true,
In his threadbare coat of the brightest blue.

The star that rose in the evening shade
Looked sadly down on a weeping maid;
The sun that came in his morning pride
Shed golden light on a laughing bride.

SCENES FROM AN UNPUBLISHED PLAY

I

(BACK-ROOM AT PORTER'S — DICK, SOLUS.)

I AM not well to-night — methinks the fumes
Of overheated punch have something dimmed
The cerebellum or pineal gland,
Or where the soul sits regent. Strange that
things

Born of the grosser elements of earth
Should cloud the mind's own heaven with
fantasies!
I am no baby — look upon that leg
All laced with steely sinews — see that arm,
Embossed with swelling muscle — and this
shape
Of nature's best expansion — were they made
But to be sneered at by the grinning imps
That leave the dotard's slumbers visionless,
To play their antics in the teeth of manhood?
(Fellow, another measure of your com-
pound,
And be less liberal of your aqueous tincture.)
A man who hath been elbowed out of office,
A poet who hath sown some score of verses,
And reaped one sorry sentence of damnation,
Look down i' the mouth, and feel unutter-
ably —
But one who is not plagued with corporal
evils,
Who feels not hungry, save at dinner time,
And is not snarled at by the world about him,
Can do but little, save to fume and fret
At air-born hydras of imagination.
And yet, in these same most degenerate days,
There be some things that do much gall a
man.
(Looking at his boots.)
Methinks the polish of these nether casings
Is not so radiant as it was of old —
Perhaps the varlet who doth give them lustre
Hath ta'en to reading of philosophy,
For learning has of late put off her wings,
And creeps along with beggars in the dust. —
Why, I have seen a kitchen-nurtured wench,
With feet that seemed like mountain
pedestals,
And fingers redder than the peony,
Who tripped so daintily upon the earth,
As she were stepping on Elysian flowers;
And did so dally with the household stuff,
As if a saucepan were an instrument
Fit for the music of angelic choirs.
She'd quote you loving ditties by the hour,
And scribble verses in your Sunday bible,
And talk to you of starlight, and of flowers,
And mind, and metaphysics. Out upon
them —
I'd rather have a Patagonian savage,
One that can grapple with the mountain bear,
And eat him as a Christian eats a chicken,
Than such a mincing thing to wait upon me.
Fellow, here's money for thine aliments,
I must away.
(Exit.)

II

(DICK, SOLUS WITH A NEWSPAPER. —
SMOKING PITCHER ON THE TABLE)

No murders and no robberies, — speeches —
speeches,

Column on column one eternal speech;
Now I had rather read your pirate-stories,
Of men minced up and shovelled overboard,
Your slitting throats, and knocking out of brains,
And such well-spiced misdoings —
(Enter TOM.)
                         Save you, Tom,
How goes your nothingship, — and gentle Julia,
How does she fare, — the lady of thy love.
Tom.   Her good old grandam's dead —
Dick.   Why then the devil
May sharpen up his claws to deal with her;
She was a potent vixen in her day.
Tom.   Be pleased to tread less rudely on the ashes
Of one that was a woman. You are wont
To speak unfitly of the fairest thing
That stepped on Eden's roses. Why should man
Scoff at the creatures he was made to love?
It is as if the iron-fibred oak
Should tear the clasping tendrils. —
Dick.   Save your nonsense
To feed your starving poetry withal;
I hate to see resuscitated thoughts
Come sneaking back to life in ladies's albums.
Pray talk to me as if I were a man, —
Look, — do I wear a petticoat or breeches?
Have I long locks? Is this a woman's foot?
Is aught of silver in these brazen tones?
Fill up your glass, — here's to thy sanity.
Tom.   O beast! You drink as if you were a Titan,
Just hot from Etna. What would Julia say,
If she could dream of such abominations!
Dick.   Would she might taste this punch!
I much opine
She'd soon forswear her ghostly milk and water.
O thou art good! 't would vivify a statue,
Could statue but its marble lips unclose:
I would I were upon an ocean of thee —
A bowl my boat — a ladle for mine oar:
Green islands in the ever-blooming south
Should scatter flowers upon thee — and the fires
That roll and flash in earth's unfathomed bosom,
Should keep thee steaming hot. That's poetry.
Tom.   Insensate wretch; can nothing stir thy soul,
But tempests brewed from earthly elements?
No light break through thy darkness, save a gleam,
The offspring of corruption? Is there nought
Can cheat thee for a moment of thy grossness?
Dick.   He's talking big, — I'll wake the imp within him. (Aside.)
I cannot blame thee — nay, I pity thee
For such unseemly license of thy tongue;
Touched in the brain, — I feared it might be so;
'T was wrong — it was most cruel in the girl,

To play so false a game. Who would have thought it, —
A coach, a parson, and a man in whiskers.
Tom.   Oh devil! what! speak, let me hear it all —
Not Julia! Parson! whiskers! tell me all,
And I will love thee.
Dick.   Who has spoke of Julia?
Are there no women in the world but Julia?
I was but thinking of an ancient spinster,
Miss Sally or Miss Celia Somebody,
That ran away from Time to play with Cupid.
Tom.   Lend me your kerchief — I am much exhausted:
What if I'd drawn that razor —
Dick.   There'd have been
Another tombstone, and a lie upon it.
I would have dressed you an obituary,
That should be really decent, and have written
With mine own hands a fancy epitaph.
Tom.   Come, you are caustic, — but you know my nature.
I'll show thee something for thine age to dream of,
A token of her beauty and her love;
Look at that auburn ringlet, boy, and think
On what a peerless brow it must have floated!
Her own white fingers did unweave the ray
From the soft coronal of light and beauty.
Dick.   Call you that auburn? it is hardly crimson.
There is a something of Aurora red —
A something like to filaments of flame, —
And yet they are not cobwebs in their texture,
Right thick and rosy.
Tom.   Ha! what is't you say?
Take that to help you in your rhetoric.
(Striking DICK.)
Dick.   Infant! I will not beat thee. Here's a chair.
And here's a neckcloth — yes, and here's a towel,
And I will truss thee like a callow goose.
(Tying him to the chair.)
So, thou art fixed, thou paralytic tiger —
I'm sorry to have been so rough with thee,
How is it, do you call it auburn still?
Tom.   Were every muscle beaten to a pulp,
And my bones powdered, I would call it auburn.
Dick.   There's tragedy! It shall be auburn, then.
Hark, there's a step with something leaden in it,
As one that is not full of merriment, —
I'll fling my cloak upon you — there, keep still.
Tom.   I'm d——dly battered, an' it please the Tutor.
(Enter TUTOR.)
Tutor.   Men ye are troublous, — there has been a noise,
As of exceeding vehement discussion.

If ye must talk of controverted things,
Wait till your beards do give you gravity.
(Exit.)

III

(DICK, solus.)

Ay — if a viper coiled upon her doorstep —
If the broad river were a stream of fire
And I must cross it on a raft of tinder —
If Cerberus stood keeper of the toll,
And I were penniless — I'd see the girl.
A vixen and a jilt — but still I love her.
An arrant baggage, who would tear my
    letters
To paper up her hair — but still I love her.
Not that the rose is fairer on her cheek,
Not that the light is brighter in her eye,
Than half the seraph sisterhood can boast.
Where lurks the influence that thus can steal,
Like the sweet music of a prisoned lyre,
Through all the marble barriers of the heart?
So are we tempered, that we know not why
We love or hate, we follow or we shun.
Is it in outward seeming? do we stoop
To meet the bending statute? do we press
The lips that glow unbreathing on the
    canvas?
Nay, are there not a thousand living shapes
That are like shadows to the listless soul,
Lifeless and pulseless? yet we turn from them
To one less fair, and think her born of heaven.
Who sees the bow when Love lets loose the
    shaft?
A plague upon the nice anatomy
That cuts up feeling into curves and angles.
Her eye is blue — and so too is her bonnet —
Her forehead white — so is a sheet of
    paper —
Her hair is golden — I can buy enough
Of just such hair to fill a bushel basket —
Her voice is smooth — why so is milk and
    water;
And this is what you get for analyzing.
But take her in the whole, form, voice, and
    motion,
I love the compound. — If she loves not me,
Why, she has lost a — might pretty fellow;
A six-foot man, with most effulgent whiskers,
And two good hands to put in empty pockets.
I wonder how my grandam stood the frost.
How the old spider hangs upon her cobweb!
They say her will is made, and when she
    tumbles,
Perhaps a pension to her gray-beard tom-cat,
Some small *post mortem* acts of piety,
To crutch her poor rheumatic soul upon,
And I shall dust the dear old lady's guineas.
Ha! when we rattle in our own good tandem,
And crack the ivory-handled whip we paid
    for,
There'll be a stir among the plumes and
    ribbons!
Lightly he treads who steps on golden
    slippers —

Sweetly he speaks whose purse has music in
    it.
Pray die, dear grandam; we will have you
    buried
All nice and decent, and we'll have a sermon
To call you pretty names, and buy some
    kerchiefs
To soak up bitter tears, and feed your tom-
    cat,
As if he never scratched us — curse upon
    him.
        (Enter six BORES.)
    All. A pleasant evening —
    Dick.   Yes a pleasant evening,
A devilish pleasant evening out of doors.
    1st Bore. What have you here to eat? I
    am not hungry,
But I might taste a pie; I am not thirsty,
But I might drink to please these honest
    fellows;
Or, as I mean to sit, I'll smoke a little.
    Dick. We're out of victual and we're out
    of wine,
There's water in the pail — smoke and be
    d——d.
    2d Bore. Lend me a book, I mean to sit a
    little,
And I am not in mood for conversation.
    Dick. Here's Worcester's Walker's John-
    son's Dictionary;
Open at Ass — a very fitting subject.
    3d Bore. I saw your very worthy grand-
    mother
A short time since; she seemed extremely
    hearty.
O what a blessing such a woman is!
In all the circle of domestic love
There is no greater —
    Dick.   No, there is no greater —
Just as you say — a most eternal blessing.
    4.h Bore. I'll take a nap — you'll wake
    me in an hour,
Or two at farthest — so I'll shut the door.
        (Goes into the bedroom.)
    Dick. And I will lock it. Sleep till bed-
    bugs wake you.
        (Locks the door.)
    5th Bore. Come boy, let's have a game or
    two of chequers
Before we try the chess, and then back-
    gammon,
Or else a little whist — just run along
And order up some claret and some oysters.
    Dick. My board is broken and my foot is
    lame.
    6th Bore. I think of making something of
    a call,
And so I'll take my coat and waistcoat off,
Wait a few hours until the rest are gone
And I will read you something I have
    written.
        (Cry of fire.)
    Five Bores. O, there's a row — good
    night — we'll call again.
        (Exeunt five BORES.)
    Dick, solus. Go, blessed boobies, and the
    devil singe you —

Sleep, snoring lubber, and the night-fiend
  gnaw you —
Another step before the door is bolted!
      (Enter TOM.)
Ah, soft Lothario, with thy lady cheek,
Didst thou exhale upon us from a dew-drop?
Or wast thou wafted on an evening zephyr?
    Tom.   I hang myself to-morrow — Julia's
  bolted!
Off in a tangent with that ugly captain!
I did not care for Julia — I was tired
Of all her tricks and fancies — but to think
Of such a rocket tied to such a stick
Would make one hang himself for human
  folly.
So once again, for universal woman!
Does the new coat sit close about the waist?
    Dick.   Ay, put a pismire's girdle on a
  porpoise,
It will sit closer than a sailor's jacket.
Now diet for a while on water-gruel,
And take a dose or two of bleaching salts,
And run a razor round the barren course,
And when you're hanged for stealing, men
  will say
He was a pale, thin pigmy, with a beard.
    Tom.   Why, man you're biting as a
  seedling radish.
Did Clara pout? nay, do not look so rosy,
Her mother told me all about your love,
And asked me of your prospects and your
  standing;
I told her — but no matter what I told her.
    Dick.   The wrinkled hag — and thou,
  infernal imp,
What didst thou say?
    Tom.   I only now remember
Some general hints about your evil habits,
Your sad propensity to gin and water,
Your singular asperity of temper —
I did not call you absolutely dirty,
But only rather slovenly and careless —
For rank, that you was like a serpent's rattle,
That makes some noise, though very near the
  tail —
That as to money, save the bills you owed,
You had but little to remind you of it.
I did not like it, but it was my duty,
And I am honest, so I tell you all.
    Dick.   Now, fellow, I will mash you to a
  pumice,
Or beat thee to a tumor —
    Tom.   Hold a moment
It was all stuff — I never saw the woman;
But since you seemed in such a frosty mood,
I fired a squib at your philosophy
And laughed to see it catch — so keep your
  beating
To make your children grow. — Now come
  along
And drown your anger in a good potation.
    Dick.   And you curry people down with
  lies,
And smooth it with a julep. But I'll go,
And leave that sleeping carrion in the bed-
  room,

Among his brother vermin, — peace be with
  him.
      (Exeunt.)

THE CANNIBAL

I HAD a strange and fearful dream,
  It lingers in my brain,
I've tried to blot its traces out,
  But I have tried in vain;
I would not for an angel's crown
  Have such a dream again.

It was a dark and stormy night,
  And I was all alone,
When suddenly upon mine eye
  A ghastly splendor shone,
And a fiery figure stalked along,
  And I heard a hollow moan.

He was a shape of giant size,
  He looked all gaunt and grim;
It seemed as if my locks and bolts
  Were but as threads to him; —
I always double lock my door,
  For I am short and slim.

My tongue it cleaved unto my jaws,
  As it were in a vice;
My heart lay cold upon my ribs,
  As any lump of ice;
My knees they rattled fearfully,
  As men do rattle dice.

He opened wide his earthquake jaws,
  And up his arm he flung;
Then I did give a feeble cry,
  And to the bed-post clung,
For he had mighty lion teeth,
  And a flaming, forked tongue.

He said he was a canibal,
  And that he walked by night,
And that he once had been a man,
  But now he was a sprite,
And that he knew how I was young,
  And came to take a bite.

And then he pinched my meagre cheek,
  And felt my shoulders spare,
And growled and grumbled over me,
  And pawed me like a bear;
Then I did think of all my sins,
  And tried to say a prayer.

He swore it was full many a day
  Since mortal flesh he saw,
And now he thought a burning coal
  Was lying in his maw;
With that he gnawed me with his teeth,
  And clutched me with his claw.

Then I did try once more to shriek,
  And sight and hearing fled,
But I could feel him munching me,
  As people munch their bread,

And poison breathing from his lips,
  Like vapors from the dead.

When he had done his meal he flung
  My carcass in a sack,
And shouldered what there was of me,
  As pedlars do their pack; —
I woke, — it was my breakfast-time,
  And I was on my back.

AN INVOCATION

(TRANSLATED FROM THE ARABIC)

"Awake! Awake!
Spirits of air!"

"WE sleep by day, and we watch by night,
And we flash on the darkness in meteor-light;
But a shade is over the mortal eye,
And it sees us not as we hurry by,
Well do we know that voice of thine,
We hear the word, and we see the sign."

    "Awake! Awake!
    Spirits of Fire,
    Come from the glow of the flames below,
    And gather around your sire."

"We come, we come as the lightening flies,
With the treasured wrath of the brooding
    skies,
When it leaps from the cloud on the murder-
    er's head,
And tears the shroud from the guilty dead,
And rips the sail from the quivering mast
As it rocks on the billow and bows in the
    blast;
We come, we come, we dare not stay
For we heard the sound that we all obey."

    "Spirits of earth, Awake! Awake!
    Your master calls — from your sunless
      halls,
    Come, ere the thunders break."

"We come, we come at the dreadful sign
From the crystal cave, and the golden mine,
Where the gathered rays of the diamond
    gleam,
And the ruby burns with its crimson beam;
Where, for long ages, our treasures we look
In the womb of the cavern, the heart of the
    rock,
We come, for we know the voice that flings
The chain that can fetter our sable wings."

    "Spirits of ocean, come around,
    For ye have heard the mystic word,
    And well ye know the sound."

"We come, we come from the gloomy wave
Where we float along by the sailor's grave,
And cling to the spars of the shattered wreck,
And build our thrones on the voiceless deck,

And where in the bright green ocean ray,
With shapes of the stormy deep we play,
We come, for we know the sounds that ride
Through the howl of the wind and the sweep
    of the tide."

THE MONKEYS

THERE is a love that lights the eye,
  And flashes on the brow,
Its music is a whispered word,
  Its seal a burning vow.

There is a love that hides his torch
  Beneath the rosy bowl;
And when the wine has passed the lip
  He warms the reveller's soul.

There is a love that only comes
  When joy and hope have flown,
And on the ruins of the past
  He builds his lonely throne.

There is a quiet sort of love
  That comes to later years;
When men have sighed away their sighs,
  And wept away their tears.

But not the love that speaks in words,
  Or in the wine-cup burns,
Nor that when memory's silent step
  To pleasure's grave returns, —

And not the love that dotards feel
  Creep through their shivering veins, —
Is like the love these sweet ones felt
  On Asia's scorching plains.

Oh could she speak — she cannot speak —
  And what have words to tell?
The trembling hand — the blushing cheek —
  He reads their language well.

The palms around their cradle rocked,
  The streams beneath it rolled;
They swept through leaves of orient die,
  They tossed on sands of gold.

The earth was green, the skies were bright,
  The air was sweet with sound,
While thousand birds with painted wings,
  Made melody around.

.   .   .   .

There are two little grassy mounds,
  And sleeping side by side,
Lie buried in the cold damp earth
  The monkey and his bride!

Oh, it was ever so with love —
  The flower that Eden gave —
That where it rose in freshest glow,
  Beneath it lay the grave!

THE DEPARTURE

She turned, and sought the rock once more,
  She heared the distant parting hail,
And sat her sadly on the shore
  To watch the lessening sail;
It was a bitter thing to start
The slumbers of the dreaming heart,
To break its yet unsevered chain,
And know it might not meet again.

She loved him from a very child,
  With all the love that children feel,
When streams that deepen as they flow,
  From nature's fountain steal;
When hopes with yet unbroken wing
Rise freshest from the dews of spring,
And thoughts that would alone be cold,
Grow warmer in their mutual fold.

Could he forget her? was there aught
  In sea or earth, in time or space?
How could he find another home
  Amidst the stranger race?
And would he look in brighter eyes
Lit by the sun of southern skies,
And smile to think his heart was free
From her who wept beyond the sea?

She did not ask to hear of him,
  But when her daily toil was done, —
She lingered by the darkening wave
  Beneath the setting sun;
They deemed her happy, for she smiled
As idly as a dreaming child,
And looked as she had never known
The sorrow that she mused alone.

Go to the cottage by the cliff,
  If you have never been before,
And kiss the little blushing girl
  That meets you at the door;
And if you wish to know the tale,
How changed the cheek that once was pale,
A rosy boy, with curling hair,
Will tell you all the story there.

THE FISH PIECES

Oft have I marked a pale, thin man —
  — I would not here reveal his name —
But I have seen him sadly turn
  From gaudy hues and gilded frame,
And stand in silence, hour by hour
Until his gazing eye was dim,
And look, and look, till fancy seemed
  To fry those very fish for him.

And sometimes he would wildly glance
  Upon the martyr's fiery bed,
And I could see that yearning thoughts
  Flashed fiercely through his aching head;
Well could I see his trembling hand
  Was carving out a fancied slice —

Well did I know his busy brain
  Thought that the broiling saint looked
    nice.

I could not bear to see him walk
  Among the fluttering summer things
That float along the silent floor,
  And spread their little painted wings.
What were to him the Sunset Scenes,
  Or soft Madonna's drooping hair?
Can ringlets bind the breaking heart?
  Can hunger feed on golden air?

I pitied him, for he was poor —
  I loved him, for he was alone —
The man who wears a threadbare coat
  Is seldom sought, and little known —
Alas! I saw his pallid cheek
  Each day grow thinner than before;
There was a funeral Friday night —
  That pallid cheek is seen no more!

THE GIPSY

Being, alas! thy boy forbids
  That I should call thee maid —
Thou seemest like the summer flower,
  The child of light and shade;
I would not have thee veil thy brow,
  Nor bind thy streaming hair, —
Soft falls the sun-beam through the trees,
  Light breathes the gentle air.

The arching forest twines its arms
  Above thy houseless head,
And clasping vines, and bending grass
  Beneath thy steps are spread.
And fruits that ask not stooping toil
  Are all around thee piled —
So Nature spreads her downy wing
  To shield her simple child.

Long ere the gilded palace shone,
  Or sprang the marble dome,
The pillars of the forest rose,
  And there was woman's home;
All that her untaught wishes asked,
  The field and mountain gave,
She only claimed from mortal hands
  A cradle and a grave.

Let luxury swathe her pallid child
  In purple and in gold,
And wrap the breast that faintly beats
  Beneath its silken fold;
Though she may wreath the languid forms
  That round her altar bow,
Thou canst not see the hidden thorns
  That rend her votary's brow.

Live as thou art — if soft and clear
  The rippling surface glide,
Ask not to feel the deeper streams
  That freeze beneath the tide;
If thought can breathe amidst the wild, —
  If passion there can burn,

Read what the light of Heaven may teach,
  And wish no more to learn.

Yes, they might train thine artless steps,
  And deck they brow with pearls,
And weave the spoils of farthest earth
  Among thy raven curls;
But they will see thee waste away,
  Nor heed thy fading bloom,
And heartless mirth, and sullen guilt
  Will trample on thy tomb.

Go slumber on the eagle's cliff
  Or in the lion's lair —
Sin has not sought the desert cave,
  Or stained the mountain air;
But turn thee from the tainted crowd,
  Thy wilds are still the same,
Nor blight thy yet unsullied heart
  With aught of earthly shame.

LADY DRINKING

The creature knoweth every shape,
  And taketh every name,
But in every form, and every hue,
  The creature is the same;
The morning drop, and the evening dram,
  And the noontide glass, he fills, —
And you see his face unceasingly,
  Like a dun, in the time of bills.

He slides into the soldier's lips
  From the mouth of a snug canteen;
The drum may beat, and the gun may flash,
  But the creature slips between;
He smooths the couch of the weary man,
  And diddles the sleeper's brain,
And with the ray of the breaking day,
  The creature is there again.

The maiden sits on her silken seat,
  And sips the cordial fair,
And the blush grows deeper on her cheek
  For the spite is lurking there;
The deacon walks to the tavern bar,
  And calls for a portion thin, —
But he slily winks to the waiting-boy,
  And he pours the creature in.

He clears the frog from the preacher's throat,
  And he helps the clerk to sing;
And whets the scythe of the mowing man,
  In the shape of a mighty sling;
He lends a tongue to the speechless one,
  And a flash to the coward's eye;
He burns in a kiss on the lady's lip,
  And melts in the lover's sigh.

The farmer fills his tumbler up
  And clasps his fingers round;
He says not a word, but he drains the cup,
  For the creature there is found.
In the morning mist, and the scorching sun,
  And the chill of the evening air;

In the crystal glass and the earthen mug,
  The creature still is there.

THE GRADUATE'S SONG

It's I that is a bachelor, though married to
    the Muse,
I talks with all the gentlefolks, and flirts with
    all the blues;
It's I that looks as knowing now as any body
    can,
For once I was a Sophomore, but now I am a
    man.

I quotes the ancient classicals, I knows the
    newest tunes,
I wears a coat that's elegant, and stripéd
    pantaloons;
It's I that has the shiny boots, and sports the
    spotted gills,
It's I that drinks the Burgundy, and never
    pays my bills.

I keeps a little puppy dog, I has a little cane,
I beaus the pretty virgins out and beaus them
    home again;
It's I that pins their handkerchiefs, it's I that
    ties their shoes,
It's I that goes a shopping for to tell them
    what to choose.

Who should it be, of all the world, who should
    it be but I,
That writes the pretty poetry what makes the
    women cry?
I sees the people stare at me, because I looks
    so fine,
I loves the fat old grocer men, what asks me
    out to dine.

I knows a little Latin stuff and half a line of
    Greek,
My barber is a Frencher man, he taught me
    how to speak;
It's I that makes the morning calls, it's I goes
    out to tea,
O dear! you never saw a man one half so cute
    as me.

MOONSHINE

"Oh leave me, leave me, foolish youth,
  And come not here again,
Thy vows are wasted on the wind,
  Thy prayers are all in vain."

"Lady, thy bird is singing sweet;
  Thou heedest not his lay,
But wouldst thou not remember him
  If he should fly away?"

"O, there is many another bird,
  That sings as sweet as he, Sir,
And they shall have his golden cage,
  And they will sing to me, Sir."

"But who shall make them come to thee,
  And who shall make them stay?
No, lady, thou must live alone,
  When he has flown away."

"O fiddle, fiddle, Florio,
  You're but an ugly fowl, Sir,
I mean to catch a nightingale,
  And do not want an owl, Sir."

"Then fare thee well, my lady love,
  Since all our ties must sever,
I go to find a maid more kind,
  Then fare thee well for ever."

"O silly, silly Florio,
  I meant no such a thing, dove;
There's not a bird, in all the world,
  So pretty as a ring-dove."

OCTOSYLLABICS

A GENTLE eve! the earth and air,
As fainting from the noontide glare,
Are stealing slowly from the light,
Beneath the raven wings of night;
Yet see beyond their half-shut fold
One long, bright lance of burning gold;
And glancing in the yellow ray,
The banners of retreating day.
I hear the trembling ripples creep
Along the bosom of the deep;
As ocean curls its silver sheet,
To kiss the zephyr's flying feet.

— Yes, all is fair, and I could deem
That truth was in the ancient's dream —
Hark! was there not a voice that came,
From yonder rolling orbs of flame,
Soft stealing with its solemn chime,
Through all the din of earth and time?

— There may be moments when the sound
We hear not, though 't is ever round —
The anthem of the ringing spheres,
Can stir the sense of mortal ears.
The infant sleeps and smiles — who knows
What music lulls his light repose?
The martyr smiles while demons drain
The life-blood from the shrinking vein,
The flame may scorch, the steel may tear,
The quivering source of life lie bare;
Why starts he from his bed of fire
As if he heard an angel's lyre?
O who can tell what heavenly strain
Sheds rapture on the couch of pain?

— And will no mermaid from her cave,
Lift her soft bosom through the wave?
Was all the wild Achaian told,
Of silken hair and scaly fold,
Of lonely wanderers to the shore
Who saw, and heard, and came no more,
An idle poet's empty tale,
To make the shepherd's cheek turn pale?

— A vanished dream! the time has been,
When spirits trod the nightly green,
When rocks, and waves, and hills, and plains,
Were vocal with aerial strains —
And are they gone who poured the breath
Of life, upon the lips of death;
Who peopled earth, and sea, and sky,
With things that were too fair to die?
All, all, are gone; creation's prime,
Unsullied by the touch of time,
The earth's first transient morning flush,
The star's first glow, the flower's first blush,
They saw; but all has past away,
All save the legend and the lay.

— And though Philosophy has rent
The gorgeous veil which fancy lent —
Though now no more its mystic shroud
Floats round us like a purple cloud —
Though the cold sages of the schools
Have swathed all earth in laws and rules,
And Nature like an athlete stands,
Bound in the web of subtle hands —
Who does not love to think of hours,
When every limb was robed in flowers?

— But now, with long and sullen sweep,
The wind is rising on the deep;
And Ocean flings his hoary locks
In ringlets on the broken rocks.
Is there no Nautilus to guide
His pearly skiff along the tide
With varnished beak and snowy sail,
To cut the wave, and court the gale?

— Not on those chill and frozen seas
Spreads he his wings before the breeze,
Where winds that howl and waves that roar
Clash onward to the frozen shore —
Go to the ice-bound Alps and seek
The myrtle on the glacier's peak,
But think not vainly here to find
The shapes that woo the spicy wind
Where one eternal summer smiles
On crystal seas and emerald isles.
Where Spring sits shuddering as she wears
The belt of buds that winter tears,
Think not that Nature binds with pearls
Her iron brow and sable curls.

— Farewell, wide Ocean — where I stand
Soon shall thy billows sweep the sand —
Where late the noiseless sea-bird crept,
Where insects shut their wings and slept,
Thy beating surge and dashing spray
Shall rend the living rocks away.

THE OLD GENTLEMAN'S STORY

"WHERE hast thou been, thou grey-beard
    Time,
  For this full many a year;
Art thou not tired, thou stiff old man,
  With running far and near?"

He leaned upon his rusty scythe,
    And shook his hour-glass sands,
And pointed to his worn-out shoes,
    And to his sun-browned hands;

"Lord bless you, master, no," said he,
    "I've been upon the go —
I've lost my reckoning — but about
    Six thousand years or so;

"And what with mowing this and that,
    And weeding here and there,
If I should tell you all I've done,
    Perhaps 't would make you stare.

"I visit cities now and then,
    And dig beneath their walls,
And owls and bats, and snakes and rats
    Are nestling in their halls.

"I saw the conqueror when he came
    Fresh from the crimsoned plain;
The rabble rout I heard them shout,
    Says I, 'I'll call again.'

"I'm something of a wag, and so
    When all had past away
I groped about among the weeds
    To where the warrior lay.

"With bony finger, in the dust,
    That crusted on the tomb,
I wrote — 'young gemman, I can write —
    THIS IS THE HERO'S DOOM.'

"They were big fellows, them that lived
    Five thousand years ago;
'T would take six dozen men like you
    To make one's little toe.

"It used to be tough mowing then;
    But now you've got so small
I only crack you up like fleas
    And never mow at all.

"But, oh, the women plague me so!
    I'm sure I cant tell how;
But they have posed me ever since
    I set to work till now.

"As fast as I can pull them down,
    So fast again they build;
As fast as I can tear away,
    So fast the place is filled.

"There's Azurina's yellow locks,
    I've worked from day to day,
With all my pains, to save my soul,
    I could not turn them gray.

"I've bent the stubborn forest oak,
    That stood against the storm,
But tried in vain, these forty years,
    To crook Flirtilla's form.

"They cheat the whale, they chouse the dead,
    They go from sea to skies,

They catch the May-dew from the cloud,
    And gouge the oyster's eyes.

"I make a bonfire now and then,
    And light it with a puff;
Old songs, old stories, old reviews,
    And all that sort of stuff.

"Poor —— goes to Helicon,
    To fill his brazen cup,
It's dreadful milk-and-water like,
    But I shall drink it up.

"Where's that there magazine, d'ye think,
    That people lately read?
I swallowed that — verse, prose, and all,
    The feathers and the lead.

"I've tried my styptics long enough —
    This scribbling is no crime,
It's nothing but a new disease —
    Incontinence of rhyme.

"Whatever food the victims take,
    They can not hold it long,
Murder and marriage, birth and death,
    All dribble out in song.

"Young man, I have some jobs to do,
    And must be going now" —
He raised his meagre hand and wrote
    A wrinkle on my brow.

"There, take my card, I always leave
    Them tokens when I call,
I've known you, master, many a year
    For all you look so small."

THE TAIL-PIECE

FOR *The Collegian*

KIND world, sweet world, on every earthly
    shore,
    From Boston's dome to China's porcelain
        tower,
We bend our knee in lowly guise once more,
    To ask a blessing on our parting hour.
Our bud was nursed in Winter's tempest
        roar,
    The dews of spring fell on the opened
        flower;
The stem is snapped, and blue-eyed Summer
        sees
Our lilac leaflets scattered to the breeze.

No more we float upon the tide of time,
    That fills the chalice of the star-girt moon;
The sober essay and the sounding rhyme
    Are as the echoes of a ceasing tune;
From neighboring village and from distant
        clime,
    From bare-walled study and from gay
        saloon,

We softly sink to dark oblivion's shade,
Unwept, unblest, unhonored, and unpaid.

The vagrant printer may resume his quill,
  To scribble school-boy on the nameless
    tomb;
The hard-eyed pedant call us, if he will,
  Precocious children, nursed to fruitless
    bloom;
The sad subscriber eye his tardy bill,
  And knit his brows in unavailing gloom —
The printer's satire and the pedant's frown,
The debtor's sigh, we swallow boldly down.

But thou, sweet maiden, as thy fingers turn
  The last poor leaf that claims thine idle
    glance,
If there was aught to feel or aught to learn
  In ode or treatise, vision, dream, or
    trance, —
If the cold dust of the neglected urn
  Has ever warmed thee, by some happy
    chance,
Should aunts look grim, or fathers shake the
  head,
Plead for the harmless ashes of the dead.

Ethereal being, thou whose melting eye
  Looks down like heaven where'er its
    glances fall,
On noiseless slipper, gliding softly by,
  So sweetly drest, so proper, and so tall,
The dew-fed offspring of the summer sky,
  Beau, critic, poet, soldier, each and all,
From the dormeuse, where thy soft limbs
    recline,
Sigh out a requiem o'er our broken shrine.

The fire is out — the incense all has fled;
  And will thy gentle heart refuse to grieve?
Forget the horrors of the cap-crowned head,
  The fatal symbol on a student's sleeve,
Think that a boy may grow if he is fed,
  And stroke us softly as we take our leave;
Say we were clever, knowing, smart, or wise,
But do say something, if you d—n our eyes.

Ye who have shrunk not, dangerous though
    it seem,
  To lay your hands on yet unlaureled brows,
If e'er we meet — and frown not if we deem
  Fame yet may smile on boyhood's burning
    vows —
Bound in the garlands that we fondly dream
  May yet be gathered from Parnassian
    boughs;
Yours be the praise, who led our doubtful
    way,
Till harmless Hatred threw his brick away.

Perchance we greet you, not as late we came,
  In meagre pamphlet, bound in flimsy fold,
But from a page that bears a prouder name,
  With silken covers and with edge of gold;
Look then in kindness on our higher claim
  And bid us welcome as ye did of old;
So may your lives in pleasure glide along,

Rich as our prose, and sweeter than our song.
Peace with you all — the summer sun will
    rise
  Not less resplendent that we are no more;
The evening stars will gird the arching skies,
  The winds will murmur, and the waters
    roar —
Our faded way is lost to mortal eyes,
  Our wave has broken on the silent shore —
One whisper rises from the weeping spray —
Farewell, dear readers — and be sure to pay.

CONFESSIONS OF A COCOANUT

FAR from these shores where sweeps the
    tempests' wing,
And winter tramples on the flowers of spring,
There rose a Palm upon the mountain's
    brow —
My infant cradle was its topmost bough.
Day smiled upon me with its eye of blue,
And Evening fed me with her fragrant dew;
The howling blast that chills your mother air,
Dies to a Zephyr ere it whispers there;
Your clouds, that frown from many a sable
    fold,
Melt into air or brighten into gold.

There had I lived, through changing sun and
    shade,
And known no grief but what myself had
    made.
How can I bear unshrinking to proclaim
The tale that scorches like the breath of
    shame?
Spare, gentle maiden, spare a wretch the
    pain
That wakes a pulse in every withered vein —
Yet to conceal is harder than to tell —
I pined for freedom — broke my stem — and
    fell. —

— Forgive my tears — I will not ask of thee
To track my wandering through the restless
    sea;
Those days have past — but still the sounds
    of fear
Ring wild and maddening on my dying ear.
When the strained ship stood tottering on the
    wave
An atom hanging o'er a boundless grave,
The tossing billow and the deafening roar
Yet thrill and echo on the silent shore. —
— And must I tell the petty griefs that wind
Their serpent coils around the prostrate
    mind;
How long, in contact with the meaner hoard,
I lay unpurchased on the huckster's board,
Watched by the knave, and stared at by the
    fool,
And eyed by children as they passed from
    school;
How ladies ogled, and how servants sighed,
With look all wistful and with mouth all
    wide —

How the thin dandy in his tailor's coat,
Felt in his pockets, guileless of a groat;
How lawyers saw me with dilated eye,
Too proud to cheapen, and too poor to buy;
How doctors blessed me, as the welcome sign
Of sickly seasons, when the doctors dine,
And fancy smiled at heaps of coming ills,
And viewed with joy my progeny of pills;
How sage old women called me worse than
      lead,
How witlings laughed and thought of ——'s
      head;
The skull so thick — the hair so sadly thin —
All hard without, but oh! how soft within!

— But all is over — every shade is past,
Here I have rolled to die in place at last.
No vulgar parent watched my opening
      bloom —
No host Plebian dared to seal my doom.
The early radiance of my native skies
Once more is kindled in thy beaming eyes.
Long — long hath ceased the wild-bird's
      melting strain —
I hear thee speak — its music breathes
      again —
My woes are ended, and my tale is o'er
Thy lip shall press me, and I ask no more.

THE GALLOWS BIRD'S LAST SONG

Good people, listen unto me,
   I'm going for to sing;
Tomorrow on the gallows tree
   I'm going for to swing;
I always was a modest man,
   They shouldn't treat me so,
To stick me on a scaffolding
   When people are below!

I can't just tell where I was born,
   And don't a great deal care —
If men get well into the world
   It's no great matter where:
And I've forgot the fellow's name,
   That took me to be bred —
I only know he pulled my ears,
   And so I broke his head.

It makes me sad to speak of them —
   Those loved and cherished ears;
They've been upon the pillory
   These many, many years:
It pained me much to part with them,
   Such *long* and faithful friends —
And so I took the Mayor's horse,
   To make myself amends.

The constables came after me,
   And took me up one day;
They tied my hands and called me names —
   But then I got away.
To say I stole — it made me feel
   Unutterable grief,

And so I robbed upon the road,
   To show I wan't a thief.

They're going to hang me for it now
   And this is all I've got
For standing like a gentleman
   The risk of being shot —
To have a fellow paw my neck,
   And fix it in a string —
And I a hearty lad — it seems
   A devilish paltry thing.

They're waiting for me to be dished,
   Like flocks of carrion crows;
The doctor wants my skeleton,
   The jailor wants my clothes;
The hangman has been practising
   How slip-knots should be tied;
The tanner made a morning call —
   I think he wants my *hide!*

They've put me in a picture book,
   The likeness isn't true —
My eyes were never goggle eyes,
   My nose is not askew —
And here's the sheriff at the door,
   I wish they'd let me be —
It may be pleasant work to them —
   It isn't fun to me!

REFLECTIONS IN A BALL ROOM

Young man — my neighbour on the right
   No doubt you think you're fine
Your coat's a very proper coat,
   Your boots and buttons shine,
And if you'd only hold your tongue
   You'd be a harmless flat,
But talking to that pretty girl!
   What would the man be at?

Young Miss — I like your curling hair,
   I love your melting eyes,
But was that last remark you made
   So very, very wise?
I know you have a feeling heart,
   But don't you think it's queer
To look so sweet and languishing
   On such a fool, my dear?

Old gentleman — I know you have
   A golden headed cane,
And what if you should take it up
   And sally out again?
The night, my friend, is very warm,
   The room is very full,
And those long stories that you tell,
   Old gentleman, are dull.

I hear the gentle waiter's step!
   I see the salver's gleam!
There is a joy in frosted cake —
   A rapture in a cream;
I go to join the gathering crowd,
   And thus I leave the hall.

O many heart is bounding high,
But mine the most of all!

THE TWO SHADOWS

It was an evening calm and fair
As ever drank the dews of June;
The living earth, the breathless air
Slept by the shining moon.

There was a rudely woven seat
That lay beneath a garden wall, —
I heard two voices low and sweet,
I saw two shadows fall.

Two shadows — side by side they were,
With but a line of light between;
If shapes more real lingered there,
Those shapes were all unseen.

The voice which seemed of deepest tone
Breathed something which I scarcely
heard;
And there was silence, save alone
One faintly whispered word.

And then the longer shadow drew
Nearer and nearer, till it came
So close, that one might think the two
Were melting to the same.

I heard a sound that lovers know —
A sound from lips that do not speak;
But oh! it leaves a deeper glow
Than words upon the cheek.

Dear maiden, hast thou ever known
That sound which sets the soul on fire?
And is it not the sweetest tone
Wrung from earth's shattered lyre?

Alas! upon my boyish brow,
Fair lips have often more than smiled;
And there is none to press it now,
I am no more a child.

Long, long the blended shadows lay
As they were in a viewless fold;
And will they never break away,
So loving, yet so cold!

They say that spirits walk the vale,
But that I do not truly know —
I wonder when I told the tale,
Why Fanny crimsoned so!

CROSSING THE FORD

Clouds, forests, hills and waters! — and
they sleep
As if a spirit pressed their pulses down, —
From the calm bosom of the waveless deep
Up to the mountain with the sunlit crown,
Still as the moss-grown cities of the dead,
Save the dull plashing of the horse's tread.

And who are they that stir the slumbering
stream?
Nay, curious reader, I can only say
That, to my eyes of ignorance, they seem
Like honest rustics on their homeward
way;
There is a village; doubtless thence they
came;
There was a christening; and they have a
name.

They are to us, like many a living form,
The image of a moment, and they pass
Like the last cloud that vanished on the
storm,
Like the last shape upon the faithless
glass;
By lake, or stream, by valley, field, or hill,
They must have lived; perchance are living
still.

DOMESTIC THOUGHTS

Nay, do not talk my worthy aunt,
Young eyes will never mind you,
A sober look before your face,
A stolen glance behind you;
Young Love will have his doublet on,
Before old care can waken,
And they who count on saintly ways,
Are apt to be mistaken.

No doubt she thinks you passing wise,
As often as you warn her,
And hides the mischief in her eyes,
Till you are round the corner;
And looks so honest, when you chance
To find us both together,
And makes such very prim remarks
About the pleasant weather!

If you had seen two quiet hands
That were together folded,
And known who stole your spectacles,
No doubt you would have scolded;
Or if you'd heard some words that passed
When you were standing near us —
I plugged your trumpet, auntie dear,
And so you could not hear us!

The dear old lady! so she shall,
Enjoy herself in trying,
To cut away poor Cupid's plumes,
And spoil his wings for flying;
But clip them very, very close,
For if you leave a feather,
One quill will write a billet-doux,
And off we go together!

THE FLIES

The flies! the flies! the whizzing flies!
Those little dragon things!
The air is Babel with their sounds
And twilight with their wings.

There's one is buzzing in my ear,
  And one above my eye —
Ah — I have got him in my hand —
  That miserable fly!

Thump! there's your gruel, honest friend —
  Smash! how's your liver now?
Aha! my fingers, worthy bugs,
  Are devils in a row.

Keep off, keep off, blue-bottle fly,
  With your asthmatic hum,
You're mighty loving with my nose,
  You would not like my thumb.

Stop, let him crawl a little way,
  There, — now if you must go
Just be so good as leave in pawn
  A dozen legs or so.

Well, really now, my pretty pet
  I fear I've hurt your head,
I'm sorry — but we all must die —
  The little whelp is dead.

Hand me the tongs — they come, they come
  Like pecks of living hail;
O Lord Monboddo, bless your soul.
  I wish I had a tail.

INFELIX SENECTUS

To see an old and gray haired man,
  It always makes me sad;
For why — I shall grow old myself
  That am so stout a lad.

What if one takes the portly turn,
  And swells, and puffs, and grows,
Who does not hate your walking whale,
  Your full blown human rose?

Alas! a little dapper man,
  May come to weigh a ton —
The pantaloons of twenty-two,
  Are tights at forty-one!

And then to think of getting thin,
  Is bad as bad can be;
Your eagle nose your salient chin,
  Are shocking things to me.

I'm not a baby or an ass,
  But yet my soul it shocks,
That time should whittle down my legs,
  And pick my golden locks.

Some decent calves are made of cork —
  They're awkward in a boot;
Some decent periwigs are bought —
  They're slow at taking root.

No — let me weep, I cannot bear
  The wasting hand of years;
O were there nothing else to shed,
  I would not grudge my tears.

SONG OF THE HENPECKED

O HER hair is as dark as the midnight wave,
  And her eye is like kindling fire,
And her voice is sweet as the spirit's voice
  That chords with the seraph's lyre.

But her nails are as sharp as a toasting fork,
  And her arms as strong as a bear's;
She pulled my hair, and she gouged my eye,
  And she kicked me down the stairs.

I've got me an eye that's made of — glass,
  And I've got me a wig that's new, —
The wig is frizzled in cork-screw curls,
  And the eye is a clouded blue.

She may shake her knuckles full in my face,
  And put the lamp to my beard,
And hold the broomstick over my head, —
  But I am not a bit afeard.

For I've bound her over to keep the peace,
  And I've bought me a crabtree cane, —
The justice will come, and the constable too,
  If she meddles with me again.

My head was a week in the linen cap.
  And my eye a month in the patch;
I never thought that the torch of love
  Would light such a brimstone match!

THE FAIRY WORLD

THERE is a world — a fairy world,
  That hath its place on common ground;
In every spot, on every soil,
  Where man himself is found.

Before our eyes, beneath our feet
  We see it, yet we coldly deem
Its scenes but rainbow tinted air,
  Its life an idle dream.

The fresh and bounding pulse that glows
  Along its yet unbroken course,
Clear as the fountain of the Spring
  From its untainted source;

And the glad freedom of the soul,
  Ere care has linked his leaden chain
From fancy's tangled path of flowers
  To drag it back again;

If this be life, and this is theirs —
  The leaping pulse, the joyous eye,
Why need they sigh that sterner cares
  Beyond their circle lie?

It hath its laws and edicts stern,
  Its well tried maxims, worn and sage,
Some from the grandam's reverend lip,
  And some from printed page.

It hath its legends and its tales,
  The records of departed time;

Its wondrous stories grave and true,
  Its rudely woven rhyme;

Its fabled heroes, crowned kings,
  Its warriors fierce, its giants tall;
Its wizards, and its charméd maid,
  She of the sandal small.

It hath its customs, gray with years,
  Saved from the crumbled spoils of yore,
When northern wanderers moored their
    barks
  Along the Saxon's shore.

It changeth not where all is changed,
  Though monarchs fall, and empires fade,
Still springs it, like the vine beneath
  The dying forest's shade.

Child of the round and rosy cheek,
  The laughing lip, the clustering hair,
Thine is the world of which we speak,
  Hope, peace, and joy are there.

THE LOST BOY

How sweet to boyhood's glowing pulse
  The sleep that languid summer yields,
In the still bosom of the wild,
  Or in the flowery fields!

So art thou slumbering, lonely boy —
  But ah! how little deemest thou
The hungry felon of the wood
  Is glaring on thee now!

He crept along the tangled glen,
  He panted up the rocky steep,
He stands and howls above thy head,
  And thou art still asleep!

No trouble mars thy peaceful dream;
  And though the arrow, winged with death,
Goes glancing near thy thoughtless heart,
  Thou heedest not its breath.

Sleep on! the danger all is past,
  The watch-dog, roused, defends thy
    breast,
And well the savage prowler knows
  He may not break thy rest!

TO THE LADY OPPOSITE

I wish the girl would move away —
  Why need she all the while
Sit beaming at her window seat
  With that eternal smile?
'Tis very strange, and very odd,
  And very like a plan,
With such a look and such an air
  And I a single man!

There sat she like a seraph chained
  In morning's earliest flame,
And there she leaned upon her hand
  When crimson sunset came,
And there she was at twilight hour —
  I saw the shutters close,
How slowly as with vain regret
  They folded up my rose!

I know her mother thinks it wrong —
  I know mama is right —
I know a matron and a maid
  Declare she is a fright —
I know what many folks would think —
  I know what some will say —
I know all this, and yet, ah yet
  I cannot keep away.

And I will sit, mysterious maid,
  And watch by morning sun,
And fondly gaze through mist and shade
  When the fair day is done,
And love the lips — the rosy lips
  That ne'er to me have spoken,
And wear the chain that silence wove
  And words have never broken.

CITY MADRIGALS

Come out ye cockney gentlemen,
  The ladies all are out,
And rustling silks and nodding plumes
  Are flashing all about,
The street is like a tulip bed,
  The clock has just struck one,
Come out ye cockney butterflies
  And flutter in the sun.

Come out ye pasteboard Romeos
  That strut before the scenes,
Come out ye pallid collegers
  That write in Magazines,
Come out ye tarnished veterans
  That always take the wall,
Ye stylish men, ye decent men,
  Ye shabby men and all!

Thou who dost shun the constable,
  And look from side to side,
Who goest not by Congress street
  Where tailors do abide,
Thou needst not fear the constable
  Thou shalt not meet the dun
No catchpole prowls to take thee here
  No tailor walks at one.

The maids of the metropolis
  Have robed their snowy arms
And Beacon street and Common street
  Have emptied all their charms —
Come out ye cockney gentlemen
  While flush the cheeks of Spring
And beauty's birds of Paradise
  Are all upon the wing!

TO MY NEIGHBOUR WHO SINGS, AND PLAYS ON THE PIANO-FORTE

Touch the notes lightly, fellow, one who
      dares
To paw so like a rampant catamount
But wrongs the gentle soul of Harmony.
Thou canst not bastinado into voice
Her light ethereal essence — she will breathe,
When fairy fingers light like falling leaves
Upon her couch of slumber, sweetest sounds;
But thou — O think of thine unwieldly hands
And use them sparely — silence is not woe.

— I would not blame thee for thy scorn of
      time
Yet for the sake of my most ancient friend
Time in the primer, I have love for him.
Some men have ears and some they say have
      none —
I do not mean the base external flaps,
For all have these, and some exceeding
      long —
But the nice inward feeling of the soul.
Well art thou garnished with those outward
      signs!
Ill art thou furnished with that inner sense!

— Kings have been soothed by music. There
      are times
When one whose hand is whiter than a pearl
Whose voice is clearer than a wild bird's trill
Has sung unto me till her tones like light
Have sunk into the stream of common
      thoughts
And made it bright as visions — but for thee
When the hoarse murmur of thy gurgling
      bass
Cracks into wild falsetto — I am wont
To say bad words that honesty forbids
And have black fancies threat'ning thee with
      ill.

— I have no hatred for thee — I am one
Who loves mankind because he is a man;
And were thy music wasted like the winds
Will all the air were echo, so that I
Were blest with deafness, I would only smile.
Or would'st thou sit upon a lonely rock
And raise thy tumult of unearthly sounds
If all the mermaids tore their ocean pearls
From their wet locks and flung them at thy
      feet,
I would not envy thee a single gem.

— And now when thou shalt see my simple
      lines
With these three poor initials at their foot
Let not thy temper like the porcupine
Start into rigid bristles — but be calm.
Remember that I love thee — O remember
That if I did address thee half unkindly
The mingled torrent of thy crash and screams
Fast then was bursting fresh upon my ear;

But now my sense is palsied — I have learned
To look upon thee as an erring man
More than a sinning, and I wish thee well.

LOVE–SONG

Hast thou a look for me, love?
   A glance is lightly given;
Though small the cost to thee, love,
   To me it may be heaven.

Hast thou a smile for me, dear?
   One smile may chain a rover;
A laughing lip, a flashing eye,
   And Love's first page turns over.

Hast thou a word for me, love?
   Why not a soul is near thee;
And there is none that will betray,
   And only one to hear thee.

Hast thou a kiss for me, dear?
   O spoil it not by keeping,
For cheeks will fade, and hearts grow cold,
   While youth and joy are sleeping.

TO FAME

They say thou hast a hundred tongues;
   My wife has only one;
If she had been equipped like thee,
   O, what should I have done!

The Echo

Nay, dearest stranger, do not shout;
My wife has worn the echo out.

TO A LADY WITH HER BACK TO ME

I know thy face is fresh and bright,
   Thou angel-moulded girl;
I caught one glimpse of purest white,
   I saw one auburn curl.

O would the whispering ripples breathe
   The thoughts that vainly strive —
She turns — she turns to look on me;
   Black! cross-eyed! seventy-five!

THE DESTROYERS

Sow thick thy flowerets, gentle Spring!
   The soil is ghastly bare,
And pour from every balmy leaf
   Thy sweetness on the air;
Ay, wrap the hills and vales in green,
   Waste all thy perfumed breath,
The mould is black with crumbling shapes,
   The winds are damp with death.

Soft as a kiss on lady's cheek,
   The ripples touch the shore;

Tomorrow, and the strangling shriek
　　Shall swell the billow's roar.
And many an eye that maiden loves,
　　The rolling wave shall close,
And lips that children weep to hear,
　　Lie sealed in long repose.

The scorching sunbeam sears the field
　　That gleamed with Autumn's gold,
And dying mothers bare their breasts
　　To babes whose lips are cold.
By night the livid Plague went by,
　　Scarce was a leaflet stirred —
Whence came that lone and smothered cry?
　　Why screams the carrion bird?

And, thou, the parent and the tomb,
　　That rocks and shrouds us all,
Whose bosom warms our growing limbs
　　And veils them when they fall, —
Beneath the bounding foot of life
　　Heaves up thy bursting soil,
And Pleasure's wreath is rank and green,
　　Gorged with thy loathsome spoil.

The eagle sits upon his cliff,
　　And watches for the dead;
The worm is coiled beneath the sod,
　　The slumberer's dreamless bed;
The shark is swimming in the wake —
　　None, none shall lose his claim;
Four hands have spread the banquet
　　board —
Earth, Ocean, Air, and Flame!

THE TOAD AND THE NIGHTINGALE

I CANNOT say if truth there be
　　In that fantastic tale
About the bargain made between
　　The toad and nightingale; —
But thou, — if thou hast ever called
　　One heavenly gift thine own, —
Hast let it go, and kept unsold
　　Thine ugliness alone.

O would the blazing chandelier,
　　That lights each hideous line,
But save its rays for eyes that beam
　　And cast its shade on thine!
O would the laboring echoes cease
　　Thine accents to repeat!
Thou wert in shadow doubly fair,
　　In silence doubly sweet!

WORDS TO WOMAN

Now, Lady fair, whoe'er ye be,
List for a little space to me;
A little space; I hold it crime
To clip the skirts of lady's time.

And who is he, saith many a dame,
That urges thus his idle claim?

Say, are the eyes his soul looks through
The true poetic pattern — blue?
And is his talk of groves and bowers?
And are his pockets filled with flowers?
And is he famous? has he been
Engraved on stone, like him of Lynn?

A fiddlestick, romantic maid,
For all your symbols of the trade;
As Heaven has made me, so am I,
And Heaven knew best the how and why;
And as for fame, my neighbors say
Some flattering things across the way,
And in the papers far and wide
I've seen my lines — but this aside.

Then, Lady, list; the swallow's wing
Is dripping with the dews of spring,
And down my alley, dark and blind,
One sprig, survivor of its kind,
Comes bristling up the stones between,
So thin, so crooked and so green,
Like the last virgin left alone
Of seven sweet daughters wooed and won.
All thoughts, all looks, all words, all eyes,
Are softening like the gentle skies;
And many a lip, that whispered 'No,'
Is wondering why it answered so;
For ice, that scorned December's noon,
Melts ere it feels the breath of June;
And Oh, when Heaven is warm above,
The heart, — that pendulum of love —
Beats faster, as if Time were seeing
Its sweet intensity of being.

Yes, spring has come — with all her train,
Green leaves, and "cuttie sarks," again,
As if to make us all believe
Earth paradise and woman Eve!

Now then beware; a playful trip,
A casual step, a careless slip,
May chance to show the sun and air,
What knights and ladies sometimes wear;
A hint must serve us for the nonce —
And "honi soit qui mal y pense."

To one whose path is bare and wild —
Who has no home, no wife, no child,
Who, if he loves, must love alone
Some dear abstraction of his own,
Some truths may find their way more free
Through the thin air of vacancy;
To see the governor and his aid,
One should not join the cavalcade.

Women from two extremes incline
Towards a faint dividing line,
From her, whom nature stamped a prude,
Up to the — , fie, I can't be rude;
The lemonade, and eau-de-vie,
That make our punch — society.

And each should play a different part,
To find an entrance to the heart;
What nature gave the one may hide,
The other steal what she denied.

Some borrowed glow, half-frozen maid,
Will mellow down thy native shade;
A rose, a ribband, and a curl
Will make one's grandam seem a girl.
But do not thou, luxuriant one,
Lay bare thy richness to the sun.
Not that my cheek is wont to burn —
I walk to stare and stare to learn;
But she, whose touch all hearts must feel,
Should wear no spur upon her heel!

Alas, that she, whom Nature made,
Whom Art has lent her liberal aid,
In spite of all her power to bless,
Should play the suicide in dress.
Thin spectres, must ye ever strive
To seem less palpably alive,
Afraid, lest rebel planes should swerve
And crack your buckram to a curve?
Hebes, who deem your fortune hard,
To buy your girdles by the yard,
Is not your suffering worse than vain,
To make the zone a martyr's chain?

Nor yet too brightly strive to blaze,
By stealing all the rainbow rays;
Your gaudy artificial fly,
Will only take the younger fry.
Who has not seen, and seeing, mourned,
And mourning, smiled, and smiling, scorned,
In wild ambition flaming down,
Some comet from a country town?
See, see her, in her motley hues —
Funereal blacks, and brimstone blues,
And lurid green, and bonfire red,
At once their varied radiance shed,
And skin-deep gold, and would-be pearls,
And Oh! those heaps of corkscrew curls!

Sylph of Farina's best Cologne!
Soft sighing from thy vapory throne,
Breathe life into me when I swoon,
Scared by the fiends that walk at noon!

Sweet statue! classic, chaste and fair,
Albeit cold and somewhat bare,
Give back the stern simplicity
That living woman gave to thee!

Spirit of change! whose Iris wing
Must shed its feathers every spring,
Smile on the barks, whose bosoms bear
All that fantastic France can spare!
And what no parent can refuse,
O give the daughters grace to use!

SENTIMENT

ALAS! that in our earliest blush
Our danger first we feel,
And tremble when the rising flush
Betrays some angel's seal!
Alas! for care and pallid wo
Sit watchers in their turn,
Where heaven's too faint and transient glow
So soon forgets to burn!

Maiden, through every change the same
Sweet semblance thou may'st wear;
Ay, scorch thy very soul with shame,
Thy brow may still be fair:
But if thy lovely cheek forget
The rose of purer years —
Say, does not memory sometimes wet
That changeless cheek with tears?

NEW YEAR'S ADDRESS

ONE year, God bless You! quoth the man of
    rhyme,
Is but a small parenthesis in time;
It chimes with others, like a mingling tone;
It hath its meaning though it stand alone.
Trace the short seasons from the vernal cloud
To where they slumber in their winter
    shroud;
Within that circle every human dream
Has flushed and faded like the planet's beam,
All thoughts, all passions that shall ever glide
Through living channels with their changeless
    tide,
Have had their being, and are dimly cast
In Memory's outline on the hueless past.
Life's kindling torch, and Death's enveloped
    urn
Receive the flame and ashes in their turn;
Love doats and sickens; Anger frets and dies
With every twinkle in the starry skies;
And, as the wild autumnal winds that bear
Earth's myriad foliage through the desert air,
Time sweeps the trophies with his shriveled
    wings,
Torn from the bosom of all breathing things.
What if the tempest strike a deeper stain
On the gray summit which it beats in vain?
What if the cataract scoop the quivering rock
A little deeper with its ceaseless shock?
What if a nation change its badge or name,
Is man, is nature, then, no more the same?
Alas, poor drawler, throw the quill away
That will be serious when it should be gay;
Wrench a tough feather from some veteran
    bird!
File into satire every iron word,
Let the rank plume, for which the vulture
    bled,
Drip scalding poison, and thou may'st be
    read;
But keep thy wisdom, all its odds and ends,
For blue-eyed misses and lymphatic friends.
Spirit of Dulness! not for me alone
Bends thy vague shadow from its leaden
    throne;
Thy sceptre darkens o'er a wider reign
Than the dull precincts of my wearied brain;
Speak, prostrate Caesar, from thy school-boy
    page
Green with the verdure of reviving age;
The robe of empire cannot purple now
The poppies shadowing thy patrician brow!
We leave the follies of the passing year
Save one too noisy for a quiet ear.

What though it flourish o'er the astonished town,
The saintly drapery of the prelate's gown;
What though, great Æolus, this gentle strain
Shall make dull music for thine idiot brain;
When the lost pilot steers the bark no more
Well may the rhymester of a day deplore
The freight of science, sinking fast from view,
Swamped in the verbiage of her precious crew.
Yet for the stranger, on whose lonely grave
No flowers familiar to his childhood wave,
In this frail record be one passing sigh
Breathed o'er the darkness where his ashes lie.
Oh if the errors could the wise beguile,
Warmed by the magic of his winning smile,
Be they forgotten, and above him bend
Truth for her champion, Virtue for her friend.
Hark! with the clarion that the storm has blown
A southern trumpet blends its angry tone;
See, with the drapery of the tattered sky,
The nameless banner of a faction fly;
Why breaks that menace on the peaceful breeze
That wafts the treasures of an hundred seas?
Why floats the shadow of that flag afar,
Whose folds are blazoned with a falling star?
Go to the chaos where creation lay
Ere night receded from the shores of day,
And ask the spirit, whose annulling glance
Checked each abortion of eternal chance,
Why Life was scattered, gathering into form,
And Beauty smothered ere her lips could warm?
Our last year's verses — with paternal care
We keep one copy for our unborn heir —
Touched but too lightly on the wasting flame
Whose distant sparkles perished as they came.
God of all judgements, how that awful word
Has thrilled and trembled where it since was heard;
Pale lips pronounced it at the morning's dawn;
Those lips were silent ere the day was gone.
As on the forest sinks the dewy cloud,
Death fell and dampened on the shivering crowd;
War's thunder threatens ere his arrows fly,
And Famine whispers from her blazing sky:
Thou hadst no herald till thy bursting waves
Swept the shrunk victims to their shallow graves,
Farewell, sweet reader; once the song I raised
The Transcript quoted and the Courier praised.
Ah, then no drudgery chained my buoyant mind,
And thou, dear idol of my love, wast kind,
Alas! these objects that around me gleam
Like the red phial, in a druggist's dream;
The bell that calls me from each nascent line,
(Three strokes, O stranger, on that bell are mine;)

And years, whose progress every bosom feels,
Must wear the axle while it rolls the wheels,
Shall plead for Freedom till this wreath of rhyme
To-morrow tosses from the locks of Time.

SIX VERSES

I LOVED her, but there came a blight,
  That seared my brain and chilled my heart;
I love her, yet I do not grieve
  That we are far apart.
And still I hope, before I die,
  To look into her clear blue eye.

I could not meet her in the place,
  Where once in better hours we met,
And look unaltered in her face,
  Fresh in its beauty yet; —
Nor speak unmoved the once loved name,
  Now burning with the brand of shame.

The livid waves are murmuring low,
  The lightning sleeps in yonder cloud;
But soon the rushing winds shall blow,
  And thunders rattle loud.
O then, upon the shivering sea,
  I would I were alone with thee!

Alone with thee — but sea and air
  Should raise around the dirge of sin,
And Memory's mocking lip lay bare
  Her poisoned pangs within;
And tardy Vengeance come at last
  Upon the billow and the blast.

Then shouldst thou see how sleepless wo
  Can scourge the lazy steps of time,
And hear, in accents calm and low,
  The tale of buried crime.
Thou, who my earliest love didst share,
  With me should die — like me despair.

Yet when the walled and tottering waves
  Hung o'er us in their arching sweep,
If I could hear one word of grief,
  For wrongs so dark and deep,
Thou fiends had in thy bosom slept,
  I could but weep as once I wept.

III. AESTRÆA: THE BALANCE OF ILLUSIONS

[THIS poem, first delivered before the Φ β K society of Yale College, August 14, 1850, was published the same year and only recently disappeared as a separate publication; but upon rearranging his poems for an early collective edition, Dr. Holmes included a group of *Pictures from Occasional Poems*, in which he placed certain excerpts from *Astræa*. These passages were retained without the grouped heading in his final Riverside edition, and are reproduced in this edition. *Astrœa*, however, has had an independent life so long that it seems best to reproduce it here, indicating the excerpts in their places.]

WHAT secret charm, long whispering in mine ear,
Allures, attracts, compels, and chains me here,
Where murmuring echoes call me to resign
Their sacred haunts to sweeter lips than mine;
Where silent pathways pierce the solemn shade,
In whose still depths my feet have never strayed;
Here, in the home where grateful children meet
And I, half alien, take the stranger's seat,
Doubting, yet hoping that the gift I bear
May keep its bloom in this unwonted air?
Hush, idle fancy, with thy needless art,
Speak from thy fountains, O my throbbing heart!

Say, shall I trust these trembling lips to tell
The fireside tale that memory knows so well?
How, in the days of Freedom's dread campaign,
A home-bred schoolboy left his village plain,
Slow faring southward, till his wearied feet
Pressed the worn threshold of this fair retreat;
How, with his comely face and gracious mien,
He joined the concourse of the classic green,
Nameless, unfriended, yet by nature blest
With the rich tokens that she loves the best;
The flowing locks, his youth's redundant crown,
Smoothed o'er a brow unfurrowed by a frown;
The untaught smile that speaks so passing plain
A world all hope, a past without a stain;
The clear-hued cheek, whose burning current glows
Crimson in action, carmine in repose;
Gifts such as purchase, with unminted gold,
Smiles from the young and blessings from the old.

Say, shall my hand with pious love restore
The faint, far pictures time beholds no more?
How the grave Senior, he whose later fame
Stamps on our laws his own undying name,
Saw from on high, with half paternal joy,
Some spark of promise in the studious boy,
And bade him enter, with benignant tone,
Those stately precincts which he called his own,
Where the fresh student and the youthful sage
Read by one taper from the common page;
How the true comrade, whose maturer date
Graced the large honors of his ancient State,

Sought his young friendship, which through every change
No time could weaken, no remove estrange;
How the great MASTER, reverend, solemn, wise,
Fixed on his face those calm, majestic eyes,
Full of grave meaning, where a child might read
The Hebraist's patience and the Pilgrim's creed,
But warm with flashes of parental fire
That drew the stripling to his second sire;
How kindness ripened, till the youth might dare
Take the low seat beside his sacred chair,
While the gray scholar, bending o'er the young,
Spelled the square types of Abraham's ancient tongue,
Or with mild rapture stooped devoutly o'er
His small coarse leaf, alive with curious lore:
Tales of grim judges, at whose awful beck
Flashed the broad blade across a royal neck,
Or learned dreams of Israel's long lost child
Found in the wanderer of the western wild.

Dear to his age were memories such as these,
Leaves of his June in life's autumnal breeze;
Such were the tales that won my boyish ear,
Told in low tones that evening loves to hear.

Thus in the scene I pass so lightly o'er,
Trod for a moment, then beheld no more,
Strange shapes and dim, unseen by other eyes,
Through the dark portals of the past arise;
I see no more the fair embracing throng,
I hear no echo to my saddened song,
No more I heed the kind or curious gaze,
The voice of blame, the rustling thrill of praise;
Alone, alone, the awful past I tread
White with the marbles of the slumbering dead;
One shadowy form my dreaming eyes behold
That leads my footsteps as it led of old,
One floating voice, amid the silence heard,
Breathes in my ear love's long unspoken word; —
These are the scenes thy youthful eyes have known;
My heart's warm pulses claim them as its own!
The sapling, compassed in thy fingers' clasp,
My arms scarce circle in their twice-told grasp,
Yet in each leaf of you o'ershadowing tree
I read a legend that was traced by thee.
Year after year the living wave has beat
These smooth-worn channels with its trampling feet,
Yet in each line that scores the grassy sod
I see the pathway where thy feet have trod.
Though from the scene that hears my faltering lay,

The few that loved thee long have passed
away,
Thy sacred presence all the landscape fills,
Its groves and plains and adamantine hills !

Ye who have known the sudden tears that
flow, —
Sad tears, yet sweet, the dews of twilight
woe, —
When, led by chance, your wandering eye has
crossed
Some poor memorial of the loved and lost,
Bear with my weakness as I look around
On the dear relics of this holy ground,
These bowery cloisters, shadowed and serene,
My dreams have pictured ere mine eyes have
seen.

And oh, forgive me, if the flower I brought
Droops in my hand beside this burning
thought;
The hopes and fears that marked this des-
tined hour,
The chill of doubt, the startled throb of power,
The flush of pride, the trembling glow of
shame,
All fade away and leave my FATHER's name !

[Here appears SPRING, ante p. 80.]

What life is this, that spreads in sudden
birth
Its plumes of light around a new-born earth ?
Is this the sun that brought the unwelcome
day,
Pallid and glimmering with his lifeless ray,
Or through the sash that bars yon narrow
cage
Slanted, intrusive, on the opened page ?
Is this soft breath the same complaining gale
That filled my slumbers with its murmuring
wail ?
Is this green mantle of elastic sod
The same brown desert with its frozen clod,
Where the last ridges of the dingy snow
Lie till the windflower blooms unstained
below ?

Thus to my heart its wonted tides return
When sullen Winter breaks his crystal urn,
And o'er the turf in wild profusion showers
Its dewy leaflets and ambrosial flowers.
In vacant rapture for a while I range
Through the wide scene of universal change,
Till, as the statue in its nerves of stone
Felt the new senses wakening one by one,
Each long closed inlet finds its destined ray
Through the dark curtain Spring has rent
away.
I crush the buds the clustering lilacs bear;
The same sweet fragrance that I loved is
there;
The same fresh hues each opening disk re-
veals;
Soft as of old each silken petal feels;
The birch's rind its flavor still retains,

Its boughs still ringing with the self-same
strains;
Above, around, rekindling Nature claims
Her glorious altars wreathed in living flames;
Undimmed, unshadowed, far as morning
shines
Feeds with fresh incense her eternal shrines.
Lost in her arms, her burning life I share,
Breathe the wild freedom of her perfumed air,
From Heaven's fair face the long-drawn
shadows roll,
And all its sunshine floods my opening soul !

[Here appears THE STUDY, ante p. 82.]

See, while I speak, my fireside joys return,
The lamp rekindles and the ashes burn,
The dream of summer fades before their ray,
As in red firelight sunshine dies away.
A two-fold picture; ere the first was gone,
The deepening outline of the next was drawn,
And wavering fancy hardly dares to choose
The first or last of her dissolving views.

No Delphic sage is wanted to divine
The shape of Truth beneath my gauzy line;
Yet there are truths, — like schoolmates,
once well known,
But half remembered, not enough to own, —
That, lost from sight in life's bewildering
train,
May be, like strangers, introduced again,
Dressed in new feathers, as from time to time
May please our friends, the milliners of
rhyme.

Trust not, it says, the momentary hue
Whose false complexion paints the present
view;
Red, yellow, violet stain the rainbow's light,
The prism dissolves, and all again is white.

[Here appears THE BELLS, ante p. 83.]

But how, alas ! among our eager race,
Shall smiling candor show her girlish face ?
What place is secret to the meddling crew,
Whose trade is settling what we all shall do ?
What verdict sacred from the busy fools,
That sell the jargon of their outlaw schools ?
What pulpit certain to be never vexed
With libels sanctioned by a holy text ?
Where, O my country, is the spot that yields
The freedom fought for on a hundred fields ?

Not one strong tyrant holds the servile
chain,
Where all may vote and each may hope to
reign;
One sturdy cord a single limb may bind,
And leave the captive only half confined,
But the free spirit finds its legs and wings
Tied with unnumbered Lilliputian strings,
Which, like the spider's undiscovered fold,
In countless meshes round the prisoner rolled,
With silken pressure that he scarce can feel,
Clamp every fibre as in bands of steel !

Hard is the task to point in civil phrase
One's own dear people's foolish works or
    ways;
Woe to the friend that marks a touchy fault,
Himself obnoxious to the world's assault!
Think what an earthquake is a nation's hiss,
That takes its circuit through a land like this;
Count with the census, would you be precise,
From sea to sea, from oranges to ice;
A thousand myriads are its virile lungs,
A thousand myriads its contralto tongues!

And oh, remember the indignant press;
Honey is bitter to its fond caress,
But the black venom that its hate lets fall
Would shame to sweetness the hyena's gall!

Briefly and gently let the task be tried
To touch some frailties on their tender side;
Not to dilate on each imagined wrong,
And spoil at once our temper and our song,
But once or twice a passing gleam to throw
On some rank failings ripe enough to show,
Patterns of others, — made of common
    stuff, —
The world will furnish parallels enough, —
Such as bewilder their contracted view,
Who make one pupil do the work of two;
Who following nature, where her tracks
    divide,
Drive all their passions on the narrower side,
And pour the phials of their virtuous wrath
On half mankind that take the wider path.

Nature is liberal to her inmost soul,
She loves alike the tropic and the pole,
The storm's wild anthem, and the sunshine's
    calm,
The arctic fungus, and the desert palm;
Loves them alike, and wills that each main-
    tain
Its destined share of her divided reign;
No creeping moss refuse her crystal gem,
No soaring pine her cloudy diadem!

Alas! her children, borrowing but in part
The flowing pulses of her generous heart,
Shame their kind mother with eternal strife
At all the crossings of their mingled life;
Each age, each people finds its ready shifts
To quarrel stoutly o'er her choicest gifts.

History can tell of early ages dim,
When man's chief glory was in strength of
    limb;
Then the best patriot gave the hardest
    knocks,
The height of virtue was to fell an ox;
Ill fared the babe of questionable mould,
Whom its stern father happened to behold;
In vain the mother with her ample vest
Hid the poor nursling on her throbbing breast;
No tears could save him from the kitten's
    fate,
To live an insult to the warlike state.

This weakness passed, and nations owned
    once more,
Man was still human, measuring five feet
    four,
The anti-cripples ceased to domineer,
And owned Napoleon worth a grenadier.

In these mild times the ancient bully's
    sport
Would lead its hero to a well known court;
Olympian athletes, though the pride of
    Greece,
Must face the Justice if they broke the peace,
And valor find some inconvenient checks,
If strolling Thesus met Policeman X.

[Here appears NON-RESISTANCE, ante p. 83.]

Yet when thy champion's stormy task is
    done,
The frigate silenced and the fortress won,
When toil-worn valor claims his laurel
    wreath,
His reeking cutlass slumbering in its sheath,
The fierce declaimer shall be heard once more,
Whose twang was smothered by the conflict's
    roar;
Heroes shall fall that strode unharmed away
Through the red heaps of many a doubtful
    day,
Hacked in his sermons, riddled in his prayers,
The broadcloth slashing what the broadsword
    spares!

Untaught by trial, ignorance might suppose
That all our fighting must be done with blows;
Alas! not so; between the lips and brain
A dread artillery masks its loaded train;
The smooth portcullis of the smiling face
Veils the grim battery with deceptive grace,
But in the flashes of its opened fire,
Truth, Honor, Justice, Peace and Love
    expire.

[Here appears THE MORAL BULLY, ante p.
84.]

If generous fortune give me leave to choose
My saucy neighbors barefoot or in shoes,
I leave the hero blustering while he dares
On platforms furnished with posterior stairs,
Till prudence drives him to his "earnest" legs
With large bequest of disappointed eggs,
And take the brawler whose unstudied dress
Becomes him better, and protects him less;
Give me the bullying of the scoundrel crew,
If swaggering virtue won't insult me too!

Come, let us breathe; a something not
    divine
Has mingled, bitter, with the flowing line.
Pause for a moment while our soul forgets
The noisy tribe in panta-loons or -lets;
Nor pass, ungrateful, by the debt we owe
To those who teach us half of all we know,
Not in rude license, or unchristian scorn,
But hoping, loving, pitying, while they warn!

Sweep out the pieces! Round a careless
 room
The feather-duster follows up the broom;
If the last target took a round of grape
To knock its beauty something out of shape,
The next asks only, if the listener please,
A schoolboy's blowpipe and a gill of peas.

This creeping object, caught upon the brink
Of an old teacup, filled with muddy ink,
Lives on a leaf that buds from time to time
In certain districts of a temperate clime.
O'er this he toils in silent corners snug,
And leaves a track behind him, like a slug;
The leaves he stains a humbler tribe devours,
Thrown off in monthly or in weekly showers;
Himself kept savage on a starving fare,
Of such exuviæ as his friends can spare.

Let the bug drop, and view him if we can
In his true aspect as a *quasi* man.
The little wretch, whose terebrating powers
Would bore a Paixhan in a dozen hours,
Is called a CRITIC by the heavy friends
That help to pay his minus dividends.

The pseudo-critic-editorial race
Owns no allegiance but the law of place;
Each to his region sticks through thick and
 thin,
Stiff as a beetle spiked upon a pin.
Plant him in Boston, and his sheet he fills
With all the slipslop of his threefold hills,
Talks as if Nature kept her choicest smiles
Within his radius of a dozen miles,
And nations waited till his next Review
Had made it plain what Providence must do.
Would you believe him, water is not damp
Except in buckets with the Hingham stamp,
And Heaven should build the walls of
 Paradise
Of Quincy granite lined with Wenham ice.

But Hudson's banks, with more congenial
 skies,
Swell the small creature to alarming size;
A gayer pattern wraps his flowery chest,
A sham more brilliant sparkles on his breast,
An eyeglass, hanging from a gilded chain,
Taps the white leg that tips his rakish cane;
Strings of new names, the glories of the age,
Hang up to dry on his exterior page,
Titanic pygmies, shining lights obscure,
His favored sheets have managed to secure,
Whose wide renown beyond their own abode
Extends for miles along the Harlaem road;
New radiance lights his patronizing smile,
New airs distinguish his patrician style,
New sounds are mingled with his fatal hiss,
Oftenest *"provincial"* and *"metropolis."*

He cry *"provincial"* with imperious brow!
The half-bred rogue, that groomed his moth-
 er's cow!
Fed on coarse tubers and Æolian beans

Till clownish manhood crept among his teens,
When, after washing and unheard of pains
To lard with phrases his refractory brains,
A third-rate college licked him to the shape,
Not of the scholar, but the scholar's ape!

God bless Manhattan! Let her fairly
 claim,
With all the honors due her ancient name,
Worth, wisdom, wealth, abounding and to
 spare,
Rags, riots, rogues, at least her honest share;
But not presume, because, by sad mischance,
The mobs of Paris wring the neck of France,
Fortune has ordered she shall turn the poise
Of thirty Empires with her Bowery boys!

The poorest hamlet on the mountain's side
Looks on her glories with a sister's pride;
When the first babes her fruitful ship-yards
 wean
Play round the breasts of Ocean's conquered
 queen,
The shout of millions, borne on every breeze,
Sweeps with EXCELSIOR o'er the enfranchised
 seas!

Yet not too rashly let her think to bind
Beneath her circlet all the nation's mind;
Our star-crowned mother, whose informing
 soul
Clings to no fragment, but pervades the
 whole,
Views with a smile the clerk of Maiden Lane,
Who takes her ventral ganglion for her brain!
No fables tell us of Minervas born
From bags of cotton or from sacks of corn;
The halls of Leyden Science used to cram,
While dulness snored in purse-proud Amster-
 dam!

But those old burghers had a foggy clime,
And better luck may come the second time;
What though some churls of doubtful sense
 declare
That poison lurks in her commercial air,
Her buds of genius dying premature,
From some malaria draining cannot cure;
Nay, that so dangerous is her golden soil,
Whate'er she borrows she contrives to spoil;
That drooping minstrels in a few brief years
Lose their sweet voice, the gift of other
 spheres;
That wafted singing from their native shore,
They touch the Battery, and are heard no
 more; —
By those twinned waves that wear the varied
 gleams
Beryl or sapphire mingles in their streams,
Till the fair sisters o'er her yellow sands,
Clasping their soft and snowy ruffled hands,
Lay on her footstool with their silver keys
Strength from the mountains, freedom from
 the seas, —

Some future day may see her rise sublime
Above her counters, — only give her time !

When our first Soldiers' swords of honor
    gild
The stately mansions that her tradesmen
    build;
When our first Statesmen take the Broadway
    track,
Our first Historians following at their back;
When our first Painters, dying, leave behind
On her proud walls the shadows of their mind;
When our first Poets flock from farthest
    scenes
To take in hand her pictured Magazines;
When our first Scholars are content to dwell
Where their own printers teach them how to
    spell;
When world-known Science crowds toward
    her gates,
Then shall the children of our hundred States
Hail her a true METROPOLIS of men,
The nation's centre. Then, and not till then !

The song is failing. Yonder clanging tower
Shakes in its cup the more than brimming
    hour;
The full-length gallery which the fates deny,
A colored Moral briefly must supply.

[Here appears THE MIND'S DIET, *ante* p.
85.]

The song is passing. Let its meaning rise
To loftier notes before its echo dies,
Nor leave, ungracious, in its parting train
A trivial flourish or discordant strain.

These lines may teach, rough-spoken
    though they be,
Thy gentle creed, divinest Charity !
Truth is at heart not always as she seems,
Judged by our sleeping or our waking dreams.

[Here appears OUR LIMITATIONS, *ante* p. 85.]

The song is hushed. Another moment parts
This breathing zone, this belt of living hearts;
Ah, think not thus the parting moment ends
The soul's embrace of new discovered friends.

Sleep on my heart, thou long expected
    hour,
Time's new-born daughter, with thine infant
    dower,
One sad, sweet look from those expiring
    charms
The clasping centuries strangle in their arms,
Dreams of old halls, and shadowy arches
    green,
And kindly faces loved as soon as seen !
Sleep, till the fires of manhood fade away,
The sprinkled locks have saddened into gray,
And age, oblivious, blends thy memories old
With hoary legends that his sire has told !

IV. THE HEART'S OWN SECRET

1855

[Written for the Boston Mercantile Library Association and delivered on 14 November 1855, this poem included the now separately printed poems "The Old Player," "The Exile's Secret," "The Banker's Secret," "The Lover's Secret," "The Statesman's Secret," "The Mother's Secret," and "The Secret of the Stars." Here we print the uncollected portions of the poem.]

[In place of the closing twenty-six lines of "The Old Player."]

I, A POOR actor, paid to please a throng, —
Painted and plumed in all the pride of song;
I, that have brought these mercenary strains
Whose every couplet clanks its golden chains;
I, self-enrolled among the shining set
That outrage virtue with their "Muse to let;"
Have I no visions, as again I rise
And read my welcome in your waiting eyes?
    Fresh from the hills that feed with icy
        springs
Rough brakes that rustle with the wild-bird's
    wings;
From solemn woodlands where in awful
    shade,
Heaped with green mounds, the forest kings
    are laid,
While round their graves the bleeding maples
    flow,
And mourning hemlocks droop in weeds of
    wo;
From groves of glossy beech the wood thrush
    fills
In the dim twilight with his rapturous trills;
From sweet still pastures, cropped by
    nodding kine,
Their noon-tide tent the century-counting
    pine;
From the brown stream along whose winding
    shore
Each sleepy inlet knows my resting oar;
From the broad meadows, where the mowers
    pass
Their scythes slow-breathing through the
    feathered grass;
From tawny rye-fields, where the cradler
    strikes
With whistling crash among the bearded
    spikes;
Fresh from such glories, how shall I forget
My summer's day-dream, now the sun is set ?
    And ah ! too well my burning cheek betrays
I too have clasped the jewelled cup of praise;
The cup, once tasted, like the reveller's
    draught,
The lip still clings to, till its dregs are quaffed.
    These reverend sires, with wrinkled front
        severe,

Fain would I win to pardon all they hear;
These dry, hot souls, inflamed by angry
    tongues,
Scorched with the furnace-blast from fiery
    lungs,
With liquid verse I long to soothe and cool,
And lead them, grateful, from its healing
    pool.
These rose-lipped daughters of the younger
    time,
Whose nicer ear is fed with daintiest rhyme,
Whose youthful eyes, half-threatening while
    they shine,
Must lend the light they cannot ask from
    mine,
Still would I please, if yet the power remain;
Say not, sweet listeners, that I long in vain!
    The Heart's own Secret! How a single
        word
Would tell our history, — and we die
    unheard!
When Love's dear witchery makes us more
    than kind;
When Friendship lifts the flood-gates of the
    mind;
When the red wine-cup brings its half-eclipse,
And the heart's night-birds flutter round the
    lips;
That single word the faithful traitors shun:
Tell follies, sins, and secrets, — all but ONE.
Behold the simple thread that intertwines
Its sober strand along my pictured lines.

[Before the concluding poem now "The
Secret of the Stars"]

Pictures enough! 'Tis time the gallery close;
The slumbering nod, the waking need repose.
Yet ere we rake the ashes on the coals,
One brighter spark shall fire these wearied
    souls.
The lonely man, whose story none could
    tell, —
The knave, who kept his secret till he fell, —
The lover's silent lip and wasting cheek, —
The brooding mother's hope that would not
    speak, —
The fevered statesman's soul-consuming
    dream, —
Enough of these; I ask a loftier theme!

[In place of the last thirty-four lines of
"The Secret of the Stars"]

Ye that proclaim the fierce destroyer's creed,
Shut your white lips and listen while I read:
"When tongues are fiery hot and hearts are
    cold,
"When faith grows weak and faction waxes
    bold,
"When the wise whisper and the fools are
    loud,
"When every brawler has his noisy crowd,
"When peaceful Abel leaves his fruits and
    grain
"To call hard names and shake his fist at
    Cain,

"When gray old Judah casts his open vote
"To sell his brother in the patch-work coat,
"Shout, Despots, shout across the shuddering
    wave!
"The Sexton stands by Freedom's open
    grave!"
Still let us hope! — What sudden mists arise
And veil the shapes that filled my outward
    eyes?
A vision floats before my dreaming soul; —
A proud fair maiden clasps a mystic scroll;
On hand is circled on a lofty spear,
One foot is planted on a pictured sphere.
"Behold!" she cries, "and tremble as ye read:
"This is the patriot's first and latest creed!
"Wo to the unborn children of the age
"That blots or rends its Heaven-emblazoned
    page!"
    Large is the scroll; its living lines how
        bright,
As the long legend flashes in the light!
O for one word! for those mysterious gleams
Cheat my strained vision, as in midnight
    dreams.
Spread the curled leaf that holds the solemn
    creed,
Now, now, if ever, is the hour to read!
The maiden smiles; a purple hem she tears
And blinds it fluttering to the lance she bears.
Borne on the quivering staff in upper air
The winds unfold it, flowing broad and fair;
See how it waves and widens! Now, behold!
Rayed like the morning! Fired with spots of
    gold!
I know the milk-white bands — the flaming
    bars —
My country's flag, with all its radiant stars!
One hue it borrows from the tropic's rose,
And one comes glistening from the polar
    snows,
Forever braided, till the crownless Queen
Sweeps with its folds the mighty world
    between!

V. NOTES AND ADDENDA

1895

Page 6. *Or gaze upon yon pillared stone.*
The tomb of the Vassal family is marked
by a freestone tablet, supported by five pil-
lars, and bearing nothing but the sculptured
reliefs of the Goblet and the Sun, — *Vas-Sol*
— which designated a powerful family, now
almost forgotten.
    The exile referred to in the next stanza
was a native of Honfleur in Normandy.
    Page 15. POETRY.
[On publishing this poem in the edition of
1836, Dr. Holmes wrote as follows in the
Preface:] The first poem in the collection
being somewhat discursive, I will point out,
in a few words, its scope and connection.
Its object is to express some general truths on
the sources and the machinery of poetry; to

sketch some changes which may be supposed to have taken place in its history, constituting four grand eras; and to point out some less obvious manifestations of the poetical principle. The stages assigned to the progress of poetry are as follows: —

I. The period of Pastoral and Descriptive Poetry; which allowed a digression upon home, and the introduction of a descriptive lyric.

II. The period of Martial Poetry. At the close of this division are some remarks on our want of a national song, and an attempt is made to enliven the poem by introducing a lyric which deals in martial images and language, although written only for an occasional purpose.

III. The Epic or Historic period of Poetry. Under this division of the subject, the supposed necessity of an American *Iliad* was naturally enough touched upon.

IV. The period of Dramatic Poetry, or that which analyzes, and traces from their origin, the passions excited by certain combinations of circumstances. As this seemed the highest reach of poetical art, so it constitutes the last of my supposed epochs.

The remarks contained in the last division relate to some of the different forms in which poetry has manifested itself, and to a pseudo-poetical race of invalids, whose melancholic notions are due, much oftener than is supposed, to the existence of pulmonary disease, frequently attributed to the morbid state of mind of which it is principally the cause. The allusions introduced at the close will carry their own explanation to all for whom they were intended. I have thus given a general analysis of a poem, which, being written for public delivery, required more variety than is commonly demanded in metrical essays.

Page 15. *Scenes of my youth.*

This poem was commenced a few months subsequently to the author's return to his native village, after an absence of nearly three years.

Page 18. *Gleams like a diamond on a dancing girl.*

A few lines, perhaps deficient in dignity, were introduced at this point, in delivering the poem, and are appended in this clandestine manner for the gratification of some of my audience.

How many a stanza, blushing like the rose,
Would turn to fustian if resolved to prose !
How many an epic, like a gilded crown,
If some bold critic dared to melt it down,
Roll in his crucible a shapeless mass,
A grain of gold-leaf to a pound of brass !
Shorn of their plumes, our moonstruck sonneteers
Would seem but jackdaws croaking to the spheres;
Our gay Lotharios, with their Byron curls,

Would pine like oysters cheated of their pearls !

Woe to the spectres of Parnassus' shade,
If truth should mingle in the masquerade.
Lo, as the songster's pale creations pass,
Off come at once the "Dearest" and "Alas !"
Crack go the lines and levers used to prop
Top-heavy thoughts, and down at once they drop.
Flowers weep for *hours; Love*, shrieking for his *dove*,
Finds not the solace that he seeks — above.
Fast in the mire, through which in happier time
He ambled dryshod on the stilts of rhyme,
The prostrate poet finds at length a tongue
To curse in prose the thankless stars he sung.

And though, perchance, the haughty muse it shames,
How deep the magic of harmonious names !
How sure the story of romance to please,
Whose rounded stanza ends with Heloise !
How rich and full our intonations ride
"On Torno's cliffs, or Pambamarca's side" !
But were her name some vulgar "proper noun,"
And Pambamarca changed to Belchertown,
She might be pilloried for her doubtful fame,
And no enthusiast would arise to blame;
And he who outraged the poetic sense,
Might find a home at Belchertown's expense !
The harmless boys, scarce knowing right from wrong
Who libel others and themselves in song,
When their first pothooks of poetic rage
Slant down the corners of an album's page,
(Where crippled couplets spread their sprawling charms,
As half-taught swimmers move their legs and arms,)
Will talk of "Hesper on the brow of eve,"
And call their cousins "lovely Genevieve;" —
While thus transformed, each dear deluded maid,
Pleased with herself in novel grace arrayed,
Smiles on the Paris who has come to crown
This newborn Helen in a gingham gown !

Page 19. *The leaflets gathered at your side.*
See THE CAMBRIDGE CHURCHYARD, page 5.
Page 20. *Swept through the world the war-song of Marseilles.*
The music and words of the Marseilles Hymn were composed in one night.
Page 20. *Our nation's anthem pipes a country dance!*
The popular air of "Yankee Doodle," like the dagger of Hudibras, serves a pacific as well as a martial purpose.
Page 21. *Thus mocked the spoilers with his school-boy scorn.*
Page 22. *On other shores, above their mouldering towns.*
Daniel Webster quoted several of the

verses which follow, in his address at the laying of the corner-stone of the addition to the Capitol at Washington, July 4, 1851.

Page 22. *Bore* Ever Ready, *faithful to the last.*

"*Semper paratus,*" — a motto of the revolutionary standards.

Page 24. *Thou calm, chaste scholar.*

Charles Chauncy Emerson; died May 9, 1836.

Page 24. *And thou, dear friend.*

James Jackson, Jr., M. D.; died March 29, 1834.

Page 28. THE STEAMBOAT.

Mr. Emerson has quoted some lines from this poem, but somewhat disguised as he recalled them. It is never safe to quote poetry without referring to the original.

Page 44. *As Wesley questioned in his youthful dream.*

Οἴη περ φύλλων γενεή, τοιήδε χαὶ ἀνδρῶν.
Iliad, VI. 146.

Wesley quotes this line in his account of his early doubts and perplexities. See Southey's *Life of Wesley,* Vol. II., p. 185.

Page 46. *It tells the turret.*

The churches referred to in the lines which follow are

1. "King's Chapel," the foundation of which was laid by Governor Shirley in 1749.

2. Brattle Street Church, consecrated in 1773. The completion of this edifice, the design of which included a spire, was prevented by the troubles of the Revolution, and its plain, square tower presented nothing more attractive than a massive simplicity. In the front of this tower, till the church was demolished in 1872, there was to be seen, half embedded in the brick-work, a cannon-ball, which was thrown from the American fortifications at Cambridge, during the bombardment of the city, then occupied by the British troops.

3. The Old South, first occupied for public worship in 1730.

4. Park Street Church, built in 1809, the tall white steeple of which is the most conspicuous of all the Boston spires.

5. Christ Church, opened for public worship in 1723, and containing a set of eight bells, long the only chime in Boston.

Page 54. *The Angel spake: This threefold hill shall be.*

The name first given by the English to Boston was TRI-MOUNTAIN. The three hills upon and around which the city is built are Beacon Hill, Fort Hill, and Copp's Hill.

In the early records of the Colony, it is mentioned, under date of May 6th, 1635, that "A BEACON is to be set on the Sentry hill, at Boston, to give notice to the country of any danger; to be guarded by one man stationed near, and fired as occasion may be." The last beacon was blown down in 1789.

The eastern side of Fort Hill was formerly "a ragged cliff, that seemed placed by nature in front of the entrance to the harbor for the purposes of defence, to which it was very soon applied, and from which it obtained its present name." Its summit is now a beautiful green enclosure.

Copp's Hill was used as a burial-ground from a very early period. The part of it employed for this purpose slopes towards the water upon the northern side. From its many interesting records of the dead I select the following, which may serve to show what kind of dust it holds.

"Here lies buried in a
Stone Grave 10 feet deep
Capt. DANIEL MALCOLM Mercht
who departed this Life
October 23d, 1769,
Aged 44 years,
a true son of Liberty,
a Friend to the Publick,
an Enemy to oppression,
and one of the foremost
in opposing the Revenue Acts
on America."

The gravestone from which I copied this inscription is bruised and splintered by the bullets of the British soldiers.

Page 79. THE PLOUGHMAN.

[The following is the Report referred to in the head-note as furnished by Dr. Holmes, in his capacity as chairman of the committe.]

The committee on the ploughing-match are fully sensible of the dignity and importance of the office entrusted to their judgment. To decide upon the comparative merits of so many excellent specimens of agricultural art is a most delicate, responsible, and honorable duty.

The plough is a very ancient implement. It is written in the English language p-l-o-u-g-h, and, by the association of free and independent spellers, p-l-o-w. It may be remarked that the same gentlemen can, by a similar process, turn their coughs into cows; which would be the cheapest mode of raising live stock, although it is to be feared that they (referring to the cows) would prove but lowbred animals. Some have derived the English word plough from the Greek *ploutos,* the wealth which comes from the former suggesting its resemblance to the latter. But such resemblances between different languages may be carried too far: as for example, if a man should trace the name of the Altamaha to the circumstance that the first settlers were all tomahawked on the margin of that river.

Time and experience have sanctioned the custom of putting only plain, practical men upon this committee. Were it not so, the most awkward blunders would be constantly occurring. The inhabitants of our cities, who visit the country during the fine season, would find themselves quite at a loss if an overstrained politeness should place them in this position. Imagine a trader, or a professional man, from the capital of the State, unexpectedly called upon to act in rural matters. Plough-shares are to him shares that pay no dividends. A coulter, he supposes, has something to do with a horse. His notions of stock were obtained in Faneuil Hall market, where the cattle looked funnily enough, to be sure, compared with the living originals. He knows, it is true, that there is a difference in cattle, and would tell you that he prefers the sirloin breed. His children are equally unenlightened; they know no more of the poultry-yard than what they have learned by having the chicken-pox, and playing on a Turkey carpet. Their small knowledge of wool-growing is lam(b)entable.

The history of one of these summer-visitors shows how imperfect is his rural education. He no sooner establishes himself in the country than he begins a series of experiments. He tries to drain a marsh, but only succeeds in draining his own pockets. He offers to pay for carting off a compost heap; but is informed that it consists of corn and potatoes in an unfinished state. He sows abundantly, but reaps little or nothing, except with the implement which he uses in shaving; a process which is frequently performed for him by other people, though he pays no barber's bill. He builds a wire-fence and paints it green, so that nobody can see it. But he forgets to order a pair of spectacles apiece for his cows, who, taking offence at something else, take his fence in addition, and make an invisible one of it sure enough. And, finally, having bought a machine to chop fodder, which chops off a good slice of his dividends, and two or three children's fingers, he concludes that, instead of cutting feed, he will cut farming; and so sells out to one of those plain, practical farmers, such as you have honored by placing them on your committee: whose pockets are not so full when he starts, but have fewer holes and not so many fingers in them.

It must have been one of these practical men whose love of his pursuits led him to send in to the committee the following lines, which it is hoped will be accepted as a grateful tribute to the noble art whose successful champions are now to be named and rewarded.

Page 99. THE TWO STREAMS.

When a little poem called *The Two Streams* was first printed, a writer in the *New York Evening Post* virtually accused the author of it of borrowing the thought from a baccalaureate sermon of President Hopkins of Williamstown, and printed a quotation from that discourse, which, as I thought, a thief or catchpoll might well consider as establishing a fair presumption that it was so borrowed. I was at the same time wholly unconscious of having met with the discourse or the sentence which the verses were most like, nor do I believe I ever had seen or heard either. Some time after this, happening to meet my eloquent cousin, Wendell Phillips, I mentioned the fact to him, and he told me that *he* had once used the special image said to be borrowed, in a discourse delivered at Williamstown. On relating this to my friend Mr. Buchanan Read, he informed me that *he* too had used the image, — perhaps referring to his poem called *The Twins*. He thought Tennyson had used it also. The parting of the streams on the Alps is poetically elaborated in a passage attributed to "M. Loisne," printed in the *Boston Evening Transcript* for Oct. 23, 1859. Captain, afterwards Sir Francis Head, speaks of the showers parting on the Cordilleras, one portion going to the Atlantic, one to the Pacific. I found the image running loose in my mind, without a halter. It suggested itself as an illustration of the will, and I worked the poem out by the aid of Mitchell's School Atlas. The spores of a great many ideas are floating about in the atmosphere. We no more know where the lichens which eat the names off from the gravestones borrowed the germs that gave them birth. The two match-boxes were just alike; but neither was a plagiarism. — *My Hunt after "the Captain,"* pp. 45, 46.

Page 110. INTERNATIONAL ODE.

This ode was sung in unison by twelve hundred children of the public schools, to the air of "God save the Queen," at the visit of the Prince of Wales to Boston, October 18, 1860.

Page 113. POEMS OF THE CLASS OF '29.

[The following is a roll-call of this celebrated class in Harvard College.]

Joseph Angier
Elbridge Gerry Austin
Reuben Bates
George Tyler Bigelow
William Brigham
John Parker Bullard
William Henry Channing
James Freeman Clarke
Edwin Conant
Frederick William Crocker
Francis Boardman Crowninshield
Edward Linzee Cunningham
Benjamin Robbins Curtis
Curtis Cutler
George Thomas Davis
Jonathan Thomas Davis
Nathaniel Foster Derby
Samuel Adams Devens
George Humphrey Devereux
Nicholas Devereux
Charles Fay
William Emerson Foster
Francis Augustus Foxcroft
Joel Giles
William Gray
Charles Lowell Hancock
Oliver Wendell Holmes
John Hubbard
Solomon Martin Jenkins

Albert Locke
Josiah Quincy Loring
Samuel May
Henry Blake McLellan
Horatio Cook Meriam
Edward Patrick Milliken
William Mixter
Isaac Edward Morse
Benjamin Peirce
George William Phillips
George Washington Richardson
Andrew Ritchie
Chandler Robbins
James Dutton Russell
Howard Sargent
Samuel Francis Smith
Edward Dexter Sohier
Charles Storer Storrow
George Augustus Taylor
John James Taylor
Francis Thomas
James Thurston
John Rogers Thurston
Samuel Ripley Townsend
Josiah Kendall Waite
Joshua Holyoke Ward
Ezra Weston
James Humphrey Wilder
Benjamin Pollard Winslow
William Young

Page 118. THE BOYS.
The members of the Harvard College class of 1829 referred to in this poem are: "Doctor," Francis Thomas; "Judge," G. T. Bigelow, Chief Justice of the Supreme Court of Massachusetts; "Speaker," Hon. Francis B. Crowninshield, Speaker of the Massachusetts House of Representatives; "Mr. Mayor," G. W. Richardson, of Worcester, Mass; "Member of Congress," Hon. George T. Davis; "Reverend," James Freeman Clarke; "boy with the grave mathematical look," Benjamin Peirce; "boy with a three-decker brain," Judge Benjamin R. Curtis, of the Supreme Court of the United States; "nice youngster of excellent pith," S. F. Smith, author of "My Country, 't is of Thee."

Page 141. *That lovely, bright-eyed boy.*
William Watson Sturgis.
Who faced the storm so long.
Francis B. Crowninshield.
Our many-featured friend.
George T. Davis.

Page 149. THE CHAMBERED NAUTILUS.
I have now and then found a naturalist who still worried over the distinction between the Pearly Nautilus and the Paper Nautilus, or Argonauta. As the stories about both are mere fables, attaching to the Physalia, or Portuguese man-of-war, as well as to these two molluscs, it seems over-nice to quarrel with the poetical handling of a fiction sufficiently justified by the name commonly applied to the ship of pearl as well as the ship of paper.

Page 151. *The close-clinging dulcamara.*

The "bitter-sweet" of New England is the *Celastrus scandens*, "bourreau des arbres" of the Canadian French.

Page 162. ODE FOR A SOCIAL MEETING.
I recollect a British criticism of the poem "with the slight alterations," in which the writer was quite indignant at the treatment my convivial song had received. No committee, he thought, would dare treat a Scotch author in that way. I could not help being reminded of Sydney Smith, and the surgical operation he proposed, in order to get a pleasantry into the head of a North Briton.

Page 192. *All armed with picks and spades.*
The captured slaves were at this time organized as pioneers.

Page 193. *Father, send on Earth again.*
[This hymn was sung to the tune of "Silent Night"]

Page 245. *This broad-browed youth.*
Benjamin Robbins Curtis.
The stripling smooth of face and slight.
George Tyler Bigelow.

NOTES

1974

Page 6. *And one amid these shades was born.*
This stanza alludes to the early death (June 1825) of Holmes's sister, Mary Holmes Parsons.

Page 8. *Or flourish the Stanhope gay.*
The allusion is apparently to the two-wheel, single-seat vehicle and not to the double Stanhope or to the four-wheel variety.

Page 10. THE DORCHESTER GIANT.
Between the seventh and eighth stanzas, the original text had three stanzas the election day topic seems to require. They read:

Hark! on the common there is a row!
  The giants are fighting there;
There are two parties in politics,
And they're having the matter out with sticks —
  What funny oaths they swear!

Now, go it my little man in green,
  You're lighter by a ton
Another slap on his knowledge-box —
There he is a slaughtered ox —
  It was rightly bravely done.

And there is my honest country friend
  Afoul of a cockney boy;
Ah, cockney! wo to your lantern jaws,
He's been through a training of clapper-claws,
  That was a knowing dig!

Page 11. TO THE PORTRAIT OF "A LADY."
This poem has been confused with Epes Sargent's "Portrait of a Lady" which appeared in *Illustrations of the Athenaeum Gallery of Paintings* (1830). Not printed until 1836, Holmes's poem might have been evoked by a portrait in any one of the annual exhibitions held by the Boston Athenaeum.

Page 11. THE COMET.

Encke's comet is probably in Holmes's mind; it was to intersect the earth's path in October 1832. Arago's Tract on the comet was translated by John Farrar, whom Holmes knew, and published in Boston that year.

Page 13. THE SEPTEMBER GALE.

The ostensible occasion for this poem was Alvin Fisher's painting "Landscape — September Gale," shown in the Fourth Annual Exhibition held by the Boston Athenaeum (1830).

Page 15. POETRY.

Charles Wentworth Upham had married Holmes's sister Ann.

Page 25. "Alaric's Dirge."

An allusion to Edward Everett's poem.

Page 29. ON LENDING A PUNCH-BOWL.

The occasion was the anniversary meeting of the Boston Society for Medical Improvement, February 13, 1847, held at the home of Dr. Edward Reynolds.

Page 32. THE ONLY DAUGHTER.

This poem was written for The Token of 1838, to accompany an engraving by J. Andrews after a painting by G. S. Newton.

Page 33. SONG.

At the dinner for Charles Dickens, Holmes sang his song to the Scotch air "Gramachree." Of the poets alluded to in the second stanza, Thomas Moore, the "Irish Harp," was still alive; the other allusions are obviously to Scott and Byron.

Page 35. NUX POSTCŒNETICA.

The occasion for this poem has not been identified; the allusion to Montgomery Place where Holmes lived after his marriage in June 1840 and to two children, one a baby, suggests an occasion late in 1843 or early in 1844; and the allusion to all the "boys" suggests a Harvard gathering other than the 1844 gathering of the class of '29 for which Holmes offered "a little original song" (Class Records, Harvard archives).

Page 37. A MODEST REQUEST.

Edward Everett was inaugurated as President of Harvard, April 30, 1846.

Page 39. Not such as May to Marlborough Chapel brings.

An allusion to the annual gathering of clergymen of various sects, Marlborough Chapel drawing reformers including Transcendental Unitarians. Holmes may have had Theodore Parker specifically in mind ("savage" scarcely describes Emerson). Parker's Marlborough Chapel lectures of 1841–1842, together with his "Levi Blodgett Letter" (1840) and his "South Boston Sermon" (1841) had been published in 1845.

Page 42. And, tossing . . . nymphs of old.

The more spirited original version of these four lines reads:

And each wild Bacchanal of old,
  Her Thyrsus lifts on high
Whilst Hebe, with her cup of gold
  Stands blushing sweetly by.

Page 48. In that stern faith my angel Mary died.

Holmes's sisters, Ann and Mary, both testified to their conversion and became members of their father's church.

Page 48. The whitened skull of old Servetus smile!

In the church quarrels of 1806–1839, Calvin's role in the death of Servetus was used by the Unitarians to discredit Calvinism; the Calvinists responded by minimizing Calvin's part in Servetus's death.

Page 49. Harriet Martineau.

Holmes is alluding to her How to Observe: Morals and Manners (Philadelphia, 1838).

Page 51. Like bright Apollo, you must take to Rhoades.

Jacob Rhoades, Boston hatter.

Page 51. Or thine, young athlete of the Louvre's hall.

The Discus-Thrower, very likely.

Page 52. Worcester's Maps.

Joseph Worcester's Elements of Geography . . . with an Atlas.

Page 52. "Who drives fat oxen."

Samuel Johnson's parody concludes "should himself be fat."

Page 55. The Priestleyan's copper and the Puseyan's zinc.

When this poem was first delivered, Edward Pusey had only just been suspended from preaching because of his revival of the pre-reformation doctrine of the Real Presence. Priestley's Birmingham Chapel (Unitarian) was burned by a mob in 1791 (as much for his political as his religious views); he had become one of the heroes of the Unitarians.

Page 55. Essays so dark Champollion might despair.

Emerson's Essays, First Series, published in 1841, are here implied to be as obscure as Egyptian hieroglyphics first deciphered (1821) by Jean François Champollion.

Page 55. Lectures that cut our dinners down to roots.

Holmes had attacked the dietary notions of the vegetarians Sylvester Graham and William Alcott in his lecture "The Natural Diet of Man" (1840–1841). In the lines which follow here Holmes is mocking mesmerism, phrenology, and, his bête-noir, homeopathy; these delusions are the subject of lectures given in the 1841–1842 season under the general title of "Scientific Mysticism."

Page 56. The marble Talfourd.

Sir Thomas Noon Talfourd, jurist and playwright, original sponsor of the international copyright law of 1842; Dickens dedicated Pickwick Papers to him.

Page 56. But lo! a PARCHMENT!

Holmes may be referring to the Webster-Ashburton Treaty, settling the Northeast boundary line, which Parliament was obliged to ratify when it was disclosed that Palmerston had known of and suppressed a map (in the British Museum) supporting the original American claims.

Pages 56–57. A GERMAN SILVER-SPOON . . . *the Philistine's Name!*
The Dial is manifestly the object of this satiric passage, with Emerson's poem *The Sphinx* referred to. In the first volume of *The Dial*, Jean Paul Richter receives more attention than he does in later volumes.

Page 58. THE MORNING VISIT.
Possibly written for the annual meeting of the Massachusetts Medical Society, May 30, 1849. Holmes is here recommending the "expectant" method as opposed to the "heroic." He had returned from Paris skeptical of untested therapy, being what was known as a "therapeutic nihilist."

Page 60. THE STETHOSCOPE SONG.
Certainly an occasional poem, and probably early; see C & T, pp. 395–396, for possibilities. In the sixth stanza, Holmes alludes to Pierre Charles Alexandre Louis, and in the fifteenth (p. 61) to Jean Baptiste Bouillaud (a specialist in cardiac diseases).

Page 61. EXTRACTS FROM A MEDICAL POEM.
For the Massachusetts Medical Society, May 31, 1843. In the first, Holmes symbolizes accumulated medical knowledge by a vast lighthouse which appears to have its base in the island of Cos, birthplace of Hippocrates. His specific allusions are to Thomas Sydenham ("The English Hippocrates"), John Hunter, and his own teacher Louis.

Page 62. A PORTRAIT.
Has always been taken to be that of James Jackson, Sr.; his nephew marked it so in his copy of Holmes's *Poems*, 1849. The tenses, however, suggest that the subject is dead; Jackson was very much alive.

Page 64. *He drowsed through Wistar . . . aloud on Good.*
Caspar Wistar, John Bell, Sir Astley Paston Cooper, John Mason Good, from whose works Holmes's Rip would learn anatomy, surgery, and materia medica.

Page 64. *Lancets and bougies.*
Holmes begins here a catalogue of the instruments and medicines used by practitioners of the "heroic" method.

Page 64. *Washes and Powders, Brimstone for the — which.*
For the "itch" is to be understood; Samuel Hahnemann's "system" attributed all disease to the itch; his therapy was based on the assumption that "like cures like"; in place of "twice," we understand "lice."

Page 65. *The gilded label said "Elixir Pro."*
Ostensibly "Elixir Proprietas," Paracelsus's life-preserving balsam.

Page 66. *Joe Van Wink — I mean Rip Jefferson.*
Joe Jefferson, the comedian, who played the part of Rip Van Winkle in the dramatization of Irving's story.

Page 66. *Read in old Cullen.*
William Cullen

Page 67. *Unload the portal system.*
Holmes taught his students to use plain language: to use, for example, "tie," not "ligate."

Page 68. *Poem.*
The dinner was given in honor of Holmes's retirement from the Harvard Medical School.

Page 69. *Landlord Porter.*
Z. B. Porter whose Cambridge Market Hotel became "Porter's Hotel" in 1868, when the landlord was Amos Pike. Emerson, Lowell, Longfellow are alluded to.

Page 71. *When he the master whom I will not name.*
Dr. Jacob Bigelow, known for his work on New England flora and for his essay on self-limiting diseases.

Page 73. *In Shirley's homespun days.*
Governor William Shirley, 1741–1756.

Page 82. *Yale's grave head.*
Abraham Pierson, first president of Yale and minister in Killingworth, Connecticut. Holmes is here suggesting that the members of the audience perhaps have a better title to this edition of Plato than he does.

Pages 82–83. *This old Decretal . . . my old* MAGNALIA.
Holmes was a lover of fine printing and engraving. In this catalogue of books, he begins with a specimen of incanabula and ends with the latest thing, Hawthorne's new book, *The Scarlet Letter* published in March 1850 and here neatly associated with Cotton Mather's *Magnalia*.

Page 85. *But cool Magendie.*
François Magendie.

Page 90. AFTER A LECTURE ON WORDSWORTH.
Eleven, and possibly all twelve, of the Lowell lectures of 1853 were closed with poems, but Holmes chose to preserve only seven of them, the five which appear here, *The Voiceless* (p. 99), and *The Living Temple* (p. 101). Newspaper reports of the lectures preserve only fragments of the poems that concluded the other (see C & T, pp. 534–537).

Page 90. *With ox-bow curve and sinuous twist.*
Holmes has described the tributaries of the Connecticut River, following them to the great curve the river makes between Northampton and Holyoke, Massachusetts.

Page 91. AFTER A LECTURE ON MOORE.
Thomas Moore had died in 1852. The lecture had been about Moore and Byron.

Page 93. *O happier Christian . . . Say not that Mercy has not one for him!*
In his lecture, Holmes had insisted that Shelley's religious views were irrelevant to the judgment of his poetry. Holmes is here recognizing with sympathy Shelley's scepicism.

Page 96. *How they cheered us, and — never mind — meant it all right.*

In his address of the night before, Holmes had offended the sensibilities of reformers. Some members of the audience had hissed.

Page 98. *"Doubt the patriot whose suggestions/Strive a nation to divide!"*

Originally, the second of these lines read: "Whisper that the props may slide" and in that form was a direct allusion to a speech by the Hon. Nathaniel P. Banks. Banks (1855) had declared that rather than see the institution of slavery perpetuated, he would be willing to "let the Union slide." See C & T, pp. 414–415, for a letter from Holmes to a correspondent of the *Exeter* (N. H.) *News-Letter* who had defended Holmes from another correspondent's attacks upon Holmes and the poem.

Page 99. THE VOICELESS.

Originally the closing poem of the eleventh Lowell Institute Lecture, on the Female Poets.

Page 101. THE LIVING TEMPLE.

Originally the closing poem of the tenth Lowell Institute Lecture, on the Religious Poets.

Page 102. A BIRTHDAY TRIBUTE TO J. F. CLARKE.

James Freeman Clarke was Holmes's rival poet in the Class of '29. Clarke's "broad church" attracted Holmes because of its tolerance and its freedom from doctrinaire views.

Page 102. THE GRAY CHIEF.

Written in honor of the fiftieth anniversary of James Jackson's taking his medical degree (see C & T, p. 312).

Page 103. IN MEMORY OF CHARLES WENTWORTH UPHAM, JR.

This young man was Holmes's nephew, hence the allusion to Mary Holmes Parsons, the young man's aunt and Sarah Wendell Holmes, his grandmother. To the Uphams are credited the young man's good looks.

Page 104. MARTHA.

Martha Mange, *æt.* 78.

Page 106. THE PARTING SONG.

Written to be sung by the Harvard alumni at the close of the triennial festival; a leaflet printing of the unsigned lyric was distributed to all the company.

Page 113. BILL AND JOE.

Written not for the Class of '29 but for the Harvard Phi Beta Kappa dinner of July 16, 1868, and repeated for the class at its meeting of January 6, 1869 (see C & T, p. 281).

Page 115. QUESTIONS AND ANSWERS.

This song too was written for a Harvard Phi Beta Kappa dinner (August 26, 1841) not for the class. Holmes sang the song himself.

Page 115. AN IMPROMPTU.

According to Holmes, at the time, this poem was the first genuine impromptu he ever wrote. It was written on the day of the class dinner, November 29, 1853, in his "crypt," as he called his office in the Harvard

Medical School, between his 11 and 1 o'clock classes.

Page 118. THE BOYS.

For additional and different identifications, see C & T, p. 285. Stanza seven alludes to Benjamin Robbins Curtis's dissenting decision in the Dred Scott case (1857) and to his resignation from the Supreme Court because of the case.

Page 120. A VOICE OF THE LOYAL NORTH.

At this class dinner, political feelings ran high, but after hearing Holmes read a letter from Isaac Morse of Louisiana, the class voted to drink a toast to their southern member and *"his* constitution."

Page 120. J. D. R.

James Dutton Russell.

Page 120. VOYAGE OF THE GOOD SHIP UNION.

With no land victories to rejoice in, Holmes is here extracting all possible comfort from the Federal naval victories of 1861: the occupation of Hatteras inlet (August 28–29), the capture of Forts Beauregard and Walker at Port Royal (November 7) and the occupation of Tybee Island (November 24). The next to the last stanza alludes to Farragut's mission to extend the blockade to the Gulf coast.

Page 121. "CHOOSE YOU THIS DAY WHOM YE WILL SERVE."

Although the members of the class of '29 were the first to hear this poem, it was not written for them. The poem was commissioned by Thomas Starr King to be read in San Francisco, February 9. King specifically asked for a poem that might rouse the indifferent Californians who seemed to think the war was none of their affair.

Page 122. F. W. C.

Frederic William Crocker had been Holmes's schoolmate at Andover as well as Harvard, hence "who loved our boyish years so well?"

Page 124. SHERMAN'S IN SAVANNAH.

If truly an impromptu, these lines must have been written on December 20 or 21, 1864.

Page 127. *Till P—— poked his head out of Holworthy Hall.*

John Popkin, Professor of Greek.

Page 128. *"By Zhorzhe!"* — *as friend Sales is accustomed to cry.*

Francis Sales.

Page 128. *Jim, — Harry, — Fred, — Isaac.*

James D. Russell, Henry B. McClellan, Frederic W. Crocker, and Isaac E. Morse.

Page 128. *Look, — there's our old Præses.*

John Thornton Kirkland or Josiah Quincy, probably the former.

Page 128. *Joe, give us a song.*

Joseph Angier, the classmate noted for his singing voice.

Page 128. *Well, one we have with us.*

An allusion to George Rapall Noyes, tutor for part of the time the class was at college, was still living in 1867 and had become a distinguished Biblical critic.

Page 128. *Non Peircius ipse enumeret quam.*

Benjamin Peirce had become a noted mathematician.

Page 132. *Since the days of the empire of Andrew the First.*

Andrew Jackson; the incumbent in 1871 was Andrew Johnson.

Page 133. J. A.

Joseph Angier.

Page 133. H. C. M. H. S. J. K. W.

Horatio Cook Merriam, Howard Sargent, Josiah Kendall Waite.

Page 134. *I have come to see George — Yes, I think there are four.*

There were five living in 1873. "Jim" is James Freeman Clarke.

Page 138. How NOT TO SETTLE IT.

At the urging of Samuel May, the class secretary, and with the help of the editor William D. Howells and the printers, Holmes got this political poem into the February *Atlantic Monthly* (see C & T, pp. 322–323 for the correspondence). Holmes was probably unaware that Rutherford B. Hayes was a cousin of Howell's wife.

Page 138. *Some works I find, — say Watts upon the Mind.*

Probably Isaac Watt's *The Improvement of the Mind*, 1741.

Page 138. *Then chill and bare as funeral-minded Blair.*

Robert Blair's *The Grave.*

Page 138. *When Curtius took the leap the gap that filled in.*

Marcus Curtius, who according to legend leapt armed and mounted into a gulf that had opened in the Forum in Rome, the seers having declared that the gap would not close until Rome's most prized possession was thrown into it.

Page 151. A PARTING HEALTH.

Read at a meeting of members of the Saturday Club and friends of Motley, August 8, 1857. It had then an additional stanza (presumably between the fifth and sixth stanzas here) alluding to Cromwell as a possible subject for the historian's future research. Motley asked to have it omitted (C & T, p. 352).

Page 152. WHAT WE ALL THINK.

In all editions of *The Autocrat*, this poem has an additional stanza after the eighth; the stanza was omitted in *Songs in Many Keys* and in all subsequent collections of the poems. The stanza reads:

That weakness smoothed the path of sin,
  In half the slips our youth has known;
And whatso'er its blame has been,
  That Mercy flowers on faults outgrown.

Page 154. LATTER-DAY WARNINGS.

The "late comet" must refer to the 1856 appearance of Encke's comet; Donati's comet not yet having appeared.

Page 155. *Rolls through the Hoosac Tunnel's bore.*

This railroad tunnel was so long in building that it became a standing joke; it was not ready for use until 1875.

Page 155. Till *then let Cumming blaze away.*

The Reverend John Cumming predicted with some frequency the end of the world.

Page 155. *Miller's Saints.*

Adventists, members of the church founded by William Miller (d. 1849), another prophet of a coming doomsday. In 1857–1858, a country-wide religious revival accompanied an economic depression. Miller's disciples had actually bought ascension robes, and after the second failure of his prophecies, they were to be bought at reduced prices.

Page 156. *those ladies twain/Who loved so well the tough old Dean.*

Stella and Vanessa and Jonathan Swift.

Page 158. One *Stradivarius.*

Holmes taught himself to play the violin; how well is doubtful.

Page 186. DOROTHY Q.

The painting is now in the Massachusetts Historical Society. For the genealogy that explains the poem, see C & T, p. 299.

Page 188. For riches . . . fly away.

Proverbs 23:5.

Page 189. AT THE PANTOMIME.

Written for the lecture "The Lyrical Passion," 1856–1857.

Page 192. "THUS SAITH THE LORD, I OFFER THEE THREE THINGS."

Written for a meeting of residents in Boston's Ward Six, August 28, 1862. The ward had not yet filled its quota of enlistments.

Page 192. NEVER OR NOW.

Written for the Phi Beta Kappa dinner, July 17, 1862, where the poem was introduced with the following lines:

Better the jagged shells their flesh should mangle, —
Better their bones from Rahab-necks should dangle,
Better the fairest flower of all our culture
Should cram the black maw of the Southern vulture
Than Cain act o'er the murder of his brother
Unum on our side — *pluribus* on the other!
Each of us owes the rest his best endeavor;
Take these few lines, we'll call them
        NOW OR NEVER

Page 193. HYMN.

This hymn was to be sung to Franz Grüber's "Holy Night." The platform for the singers collapsed before the ceremonies began.

Page 194. HYMN (*Giver of all that crowns our days*).

Written to be sung to the tune of "Old Hundred" at the exercises celebrating the passage of the Thirteenth Amendment, February 2, 1865. This hymn has been assigned to the wrong occasion from its printing in *Songs of Many Seasons* until this revised Cambridge edition.

Page 194. HYMN (*O God! in danger's darkest hour*).

Written to be sung at the Chicago Soldiers' Fair, May 31, 1865.

Page 195. UNDER THE WASHINGTON ELM, CAMBRIDGE.

On, though perhaps not for, the occasion of a mass meeting held in the Cambridge Common, April 27, 1861. The gathering was prompted by events of April 19; the Sixth Massachusetts Volunteer Regiment had been mobbed as it passed through Baltimore, the first troops under fire.

Page 195. FREEDOM, OUR QUEEN.

This poem and two others, *The Flower of Liberty* (pp. 196–197) and *Union and Liberty* (p. 198) were written at the request of George William Curtis as entries in a prize contest for a new national anthem. Ultimately no prize was awarded (see C & T, pp. 524–525 and, for sheet music, see C & T, pp. 517–518).

Page 196. ARMY HYMN.

Not written for any particular occasion, this song was at once appropriated for public performance, the Boston Latin School being the first to so use it. For the Jubilee concert, January 1, 1863, to celebrate the Emancipation Proclamation, Holmes added an extra stanza (C & T, p. 97).

Page 198. *Our floating turret tempts the main.*

Gustavus Vasa Fox carried the poem with him on his voyage to St. Petersburg; the ship was the ironclad *Miantonomah*, and there was doubt that it could make the trip safely (C & T, p. 272). The object of Fox's mission was ostensibly to congratulate Czar Alexander II on his escape from assassination.

Page 201. *If only the Jubilee.*

An allusion to the great National Peace Jubilee of 1869 held in Boston in a coliseum built for the occasion; the promoter secured Liszt and Ole Bull, and for "The Anvil Chorus," in addition to an outsize orchestra, one hundred Boston firemen with as many anvils.

Page 201. *And then the great organ!*

The great organ installed in the Boston Music Hall in 1863.

Page 201. *When we choose our Tycoon.*

The candidates were Grant, the incumbent, and Horace Greeley; the Democrats had no candidate. This confusion Holmes confounded — at least for the Japanese guests of honor — with a stanza omitted from all but the first printing:

For things are so mixed, how's a fellow to know
What party he's of, and what vote he shall throw?
White is getting so black and black's getting so white,
Republic-rat, Demi-can — can't get 'em right!

Page 204. AT A DINNER TO ADMIRAL FARRAGUT.

For variants and an additional stanza, see C & T, pp. 305–306. The dinner was given by the Dozen Club.

Page 205. *Van Tromp's proud besom fades from sight.*

Admiral Maarten Van Tromp, a hero of the first Anglo-Dutch War (1652–1654).

Page 205. *Hull, Bainbridge, Porter, — where are they?*

Isaac Hull and William Bainbridge were successively captains of the *Constitution* during the War of 1812; David Porter, Farragut's foster-father, had commanded the *Essex* in which Farragut first saw service.

Page 205. *The Sea-King of the "River Fight."*

Holmes here alludes to Farragut's defiance of orders that led to capture of New Orleans (April 1802) and, in the following line, to the capture of Mobile (August 1864).

Page 205. AT A DINNER TO GENERAL GRANT.

The date Holmes gives the poem is the date of the Union Club dinner for Grant; there is no public record of Holmes's poem or of any speeches on that occasion.

Page 205. *Bravely they fought who failed to win.*

This tactful allusion to the succession of unlucky generals from Winfield Scott to George G. Meade prepares for the late promotion of Grant (March 9, 1864).

Page 205. *Along the Tennessee.*

Grant's capture of Fort Henry, February 6, 1862.

Page 206. To H. W. LONGFELLOW.

The date is that of Longfellow's sailing; the poem was read at a dinner given for Longfellow by James T. Fields and his wife, May 23.

Page 206. *And one has shaped a breath in artless rhyme.*

See C & T, pp. 132–133, for Holmes's struggle with this line and the one that follows (the quotation is imaginary).

Page 206. To CHRISTIAN GOTTFRIED EHRENBURG.

George Bancroft had been appointed minister to Berlin in 1867. The first stanza is directed to Ehrenberg's microscopical researches on infusoria and the microscopic organisms of the sea and of rock formations. Bancroft could know of Holmes's special interest in such studies. He had told Holmes of Ehrenberg's blindness.

Page 207. A TOAST TO WILKIE COLLINS.

It is not clear from the text that Holmes knew that Collins had been named for the painter Sir David Wilkie; Sir David and the elder Collins, also a painter, were friends. He manifestly knows that Wilkie Collins's first name is William.

Page 208. FOR THE COMMEMORATION SERVICES.

Harvard's elaborate ceremony to honor the Union dead — Holmes's poem was for the after-dinner ceremonies.

Page 211. SHAKESPEARE.
Written for the Saturday Club's dinner.
Page 211. *Till these last years that make the sea so wide.*
An allusion to the pro-southern stand of England during our Civil War.
Page 214. POEM.
The monument to Fitz-Greene Halleck is in Guilford, Connecticut.
Page 214. HYMN.
Written to be sung by the audience to the tune of the Russian national air.
Page 215. HYMN.
This hymn too was to be sung by the audience.
Page 216. *With blasting breath the fierce destroyer came.*
Augustin Daly's Theatre had been destroyed by fire January 1, 1863; this poem was written for the opening of his new theatre.
Page 217. *Sontag or Nilsson, Lind or Malibran.*
Henriette Sontag (?), Christine Nilsson, Jenny Lind, and Marie Félicité Malibran. The dancer Holmes has in mind may be Fanny Elssler.
Page 217. *To see their offspring launch the great balloon.*
John Wise, sponsored by *The Daily Graphic*, was to have attempted to cross the Atlantic in a very large balloon in September 1873; a rent was discovered after the balloon had been partly inflated.
Page 217. *(Age spares the Pyramids — and Déjazet).*
Pauline Virginie Déjazet who continued to play ingenue roles even after she was sixty.
Page 217. *Zampa.*
This opera by Joseph Ferdinand Hérold.
Page 218. *As he who blinks through dull Dundreary's eyes.*
An allusion to Thomas Taylor's *Our American Cousin;* the part of Lord Dundreary was first played by E. A. Southern, October 18, 1858.
Page 218. *Shepherds . . . Macaires.*
Jack Sheppard and Richard Turpin, English criminals romanticized by Harrison Ainsworth; Robert Macaire is the titular hero of a play made famous by Fréderic Lemâitre; Holmes may have seen this sequel to *Auberge des adrets,* for it was first performed in 1834 when he was in Paris.
Page 221. *Look in* Eōthen.
An allusion to Alexander William Kinglake's account of his travels in the Near East (1844).
Page 225. *It was* PRESCOTT.
Colonel William Prescott.
Page 226. *Fly Pigot's running heroes.*
General William Howe and Captain Sir Robert Pigot led the attacks on Bunker Hill.
Page 227. *"Send for* WARREN*!"*
Major-General Joseph Warren.
Page 227. *And the rhymes used by Milton and Byron and Tupper most.*

Matin Tupper's doggerel was widely read in America.
Page 228. *Cochituate.*
The source of Boston's supply of drinking water.
Page 228. *"LUCY."*
Lucy Stimson; she had left the Holmes household when Holmes was a freshman at Harvard; Benjamin Peirce moved into her house in 1826 when he had roommate trouble.
Page 229. HYMN.
John Albion Andrew, admired Governor of Massachusetts, 1860–1866. The music was written by Howard M. Dow who directed a male chorus in the singing.
Page 230. *No truer soldier sleeps beneath/ The mound of Marathon.*
Howe fought in the war for Greek independence, 1826–1829.
Page 230. *The holier task he chose.*
Howe's work for the blind at the Perkins Institute. Holmes omits Howe's involvement with John Brown.
Page 230. JOSEPH WARREN, M. D.
This sonnet for the hero of Bunker Hill was written for a special issue of *The Boston Medical and Surgical Journal.*
Page 230. OLD CAMBRIDGE.
Written for a dinner at Memorial Hall.
Page 231. *Of Elmwood's sparkling Hippocrene.*
Alluding to Lowell's poem for the same occasion.
Page 231. *The yellow meetin' house.*
The First Church. The First Church was rebuilt in 1830.
Page 231. *Old Judge Winthrop.*
Probably James Winthrop, Judge of the Court of Common Pleas.
Page 231. *Israel Porter.*
Porter lived to be 100, dying in 1837.
Page 231. OLD MARCUS REEMIE.
Born 1809, he was Holmes's coeval.
Page 231. *The brothers Snow.*
The Snows ran a store.
Page 231. *Deacon William Brown.*
Deacon of the First Baptist Church in Cambridge.
Page 231. *Our Wendell's cure-all recipe.*
Wendell Phillips, Holmes's cousin, was opposed to the resumption of specie payment; the Act had been passed in January 1875, to take effect in January 1879.
Page 232. WELCOME TO THE NATIONS.
Written to be sung to the tune of Keller's Hymn by a chorus of 1200 voices.
Page 237. *Leonard's auction.*
Leonard & Co., auctioneers, had rooms on Bromfield Street.
Page 240. *Here sleeps my father's sire.*
Dr. David Holmes, father of Abiel Holmes.
Page 240. *But who the Youth his glistening axe that swings.*
John Holmes came to America in 1686.
Page 241. *See how the Deacon slants his listening ear!*

Deacon David Holmes.

Page 241. *Since Putnam dragged the wolf from Pomfret's den.*

Israel Putnam.

Page 242. *The Scholar Son.*

Abiel Holmes.

Page 245. KIRKLAND *alone such grace from Heaven could win.*

Beginning with John Thornton Kirkland, President of Harvard when he was an undergraduate, Holmes lists John Farrar (mathematics), Henry Ware (religion), Levi Hedge (logic), George Ticknor (modern languages), Sidney Willard (Latin), Edward Tyrell Channing (rhetoric), John Popkin (Greek), the last compared to Cromwell's generals.

Page 245. *This broad-browed youth . . . at Taney's side.*

Benjamin Robbins Curtis, member of the Supreme Court when Roger Brooke Taney was Chief Justice.

Page 245. *And he, the stripling . . . where Parsons gave the law,/And sphinx-like sat uncouth majestic Shaw.*

George Tyler Bigelow, member of the Supreme Judicial Court of Massachusetts when Theophilus Parsons (and after Parsons Lemuel Shaw) was Chief Justice.

Page 246. LANGDON *sits restless in the ancient chair.*

Samuel Langdon, President of Harvard, 1774–1780.

Page 246. *When from yon mansion.*

The house of the college steward, John Hastings, General Artemas Ward's headquarters; that is, Holmes's birthplace.

Page 246. *Winthrop, Hale, Eliot, Everett, Dexter, Tyng.*

John Winthrop, astronomer, d. 1779; John Hale, Richard R. Eliot, Oliver Everett, and Aaron Dexter all appear in the 1779 Triennial Catalogue with the asterisk signifying death. I do not find a Tyng anywhere in the catalogue.

Page 246. *And is Sir Isaac living?*

Newton died in 1727; John Flamsteed, in 1719.

Page 246. *Where WADSWORTH ruled and taught.*

Benjamin Wadsworth, president of Harvard, 1725–1737.

Page 246. URIAN OAKES.

President of Harvard, 1675–1681.

Page 247. *Where our proud Mother's martyr-roll is read.*

The list of the Union dead in Memorial Hall.

Page 247. *Through my north window.*

The window of his third-floor study, 296 Beacon Street, overlooking the Charles River.

Page 247. *At Boston's Rocher, half-way to Nahant.*

The restaurant Holmes compares to the famous *Le Rocher du Cancale* in Paris.

Page 249. ON THE THRESHOLD.

Written for *Golden Songs of Great Poets* (New York, 1877).

Page 249. TO GEORGE PEABODY.

This uncommissioned poem Holmes wrote in the expectation of being called up at the lunch given by the banker for guests to whom he had shown the Institutes named for him in Danvers and Peabody (originally South Danvers). The lunch was given in Peabody, not Danvers, on July 16, 1866.

Page 249. AT THE PAPYRUS CLUB.

A literary club meeting monthly at the Revere House.

Page 250. FOR WHITTIER'S SEVENTIETH BIRTHDAY.

Longfellow (stanzas 6 and 7) and Emerson (stanza 8) were present; Lowell (stanzas 9 and 10) was already in Spain taking up his duties as Ambassador.

Page 251. TWO SONNETS.

The original motto on the seal of Harvard College had been *Veritas*, changed early in its history to *In Christi Gloriam* and then to *Christo et Ecclesiae*, and this last motto was still on the seal, though *Veritas* was cut over the door of Memorial Hall.

Page 253. *But we've opened our door to the West through the tunnel.*

The Hoosac Tunnel was finally completed in 1875.

Page 253. *And we've cut off Fort Hill with our Amazon knife.*

Fort Hill was completely leveled by the summer of 1872.

Page 253. *You should see the new Westminster Boston has builded.*

Trinity Church, consecrated February 9, 1877.

Page 253. *You should see the great dome we have gorgeously gilded.*

The dome of the State House was gilded in 1874.

Page 254. *There were six of us then, — there are two of us now.*

Holmes and his brother John were the two survivors. See *The Opening of the Piano* (pp. 166–167) for an earlier reminiscence of the "Clementi" and his sister Mary's singing.

Page 256. *You have seen our gilt dome.*

In this stanza Holmes alludes to his naming Boston the "Hub of the Universe."

Page 256. AMERICAN ACADEMY CENTENNIAL CELEBRATION.

That is, the American Academy of Arts and Sciences, founded 1780.

Page 256. *Sire, son, and grandson.*

Holmes, his father, and his son were all members of the Academy.

Page 256. *Pale ghosts of Bowdoin, Winthrop, Willard, West.*

James Bowdoin, first president of the academy; James Winthrop, Samuel Willard. In the stanza following, Holmes refers to papers in the academy's *Memoirs* (I): Caleb Gannett's "An Historical Register of the Aurora Borealis," James Bowdoin's "Observations tending to prove . . . the Existence of an Orb which surrounds the whole visible material System," and Samuel Williams' "Account of a very uncommon Darkness in . . . New England"; the "philomath" seems to be an allusion to Willard's "Table of the Equations to equal Altitudes for the Latitude of the University of Cambridge."

Page 257. THE SCHOOL-BOY.
Holmes read this poem at the ceremonies, June 6, 1878.

Page 258. *The school-boy's chosen home.*
While attending Andover, Holmes lived with the Reverend James Murdock and his family. He describes here Murdock's wife, daughter, and Persis, the elderly relative who lived with them.

Page 259. *First boy to greet me.*
Thomas Clark.

Page 259. *Grave is the Master's look.*
John Adams, headmaster.

Page 259. *Less stern he seems.*
Jonathan Clement, Holmes is more charitable here than anywhere else to this teacher whom he hated.

Page 259. *One yet remains . . . thy memory dear.*
Samuel Horatio Stearns, the teacher who praised his verses.

Page 260. *The friend of joyous days.*
Phinehas Barnes.

Page 260. *Where are its gray-haired men.*
This passage lists the worthies of the Andover Theological Seminary: Samuel Farrar, Leonard Woods (the controversy was with Henry Ware), Moses Stuart, Ebenezer Porter (head of the Seminary), James Murdock. In 1828, Murdock was dismissed from his office as Professor of Sacred Rhetoric and Ecclesiastical History because he objected to having the second of the subjects taken out of the curriculum. (Ecclesiastical History could be and was deployed by the Unitarians against their orthodox opponents, notably Woods and Stuart.)

Page 261. *When great Eliphalet.*
Eliphalet Pearson, first principal of Andover. Holmes knew him as an acquaintance of his father's. He had once owned the gambrel-roofed house in which Holmes was born.

Page 262. *Is he not here whose breath of holy song.*
Ray Palmer, hymn-writer, author of "My faith looks up to thee."

262. *Such was the gentle friend.*
Horatio Black Hackett (d. 1875), New Testament scholar.

Page 262. *Such he whose record time's destroying march.*
Edward Robinson, Professor of Biblical Literature, first at Andover and then at Union; Holmes is alluding to Robinson's important book of 1841; *Biblical Researches in Palestine, Mount Sinai, and Arabia Petraea.*

Page 263. THE SILENT MELODY.
Written for the Harvard Phi Beta Kappa dinner, June 27, 1878.

Page 263. OUR HOME — OUR COUNTRY.
Holmes wrote this poem with the thought that he had a good many small boys in the audience. In his introductory remarks he said that the incident — of seeing the American ship from the tower of Pisa — was a real one.

Page 265. *When with warm "rebel" blood . . . Quincy's name.*
Holmes alludes to the Boston Massacre and the defense of the British soldiers at their trial by John Adams and Josiah Quincy.

Page 267. *Fair Lydia.*
Lydia Pinckham's "Vegetable Compound" was put on the market in 1875 and lavishly advertized.

Page 267. *Munchausen's fellow-countryman.*
Unable to leave the subject of homeopathy alone, Holmes links Samuel Hahnemann with the famous liar.

Page 267. *From the far isle that held Hippocrates.*
The isle of Cos. It is Galen who came from Pergamus.

Page 267. *Ye who . . . taught your rude lessons in Salerno's rhymes.*
Possibly an allusion to the rhyming Latin poem by Joannes de Meditano, *Regimen sanitatis Salerni,* allegedly written for William the Conqueror, or to the poems of Gilles de Corbeil, a teacher at Salerno.

Page 268. RHYMES OF A LIFE-TIME.
Dated August 2, 1880, when first printed.

Page 269. *The white façade that gleams across the way.*
The Parker House, on the corner of School and Tremont Streets.

Page 272. TWO POEMS TO HARRIET BEECHER STOWE.
It is not certain that Holmes read the first of these poems at the garden party given in Newtonville for Mrs. Stowe's birthday; he is known to have read the second one.

Page 274. TO JAMES RUSSELL LOWELL.
Read at the Harvard Commencement Day dinner, June 24, 1885.

Page 276. PRELUDE TO A VOLUME PRINTED IN RAISED LETTERS FOR THE BLIND.
The volume for which this poem was written was a selection from Holmes's Poems.

Page 277. AT THE UNITARIAN FESTIVAL.
The lines added to this poem in June are printed below among Additional Poems.

Page 277. POEM FOR THE TWO HUNDRED AND FIFTIETH ANNIVERSARY OF THE FOUNDING OF HARVARD COLLEGE.
Read by Holmes on the occasion, November 8, 1886.

Page 277. *Winthrop, our Winthrop.*
Robert C. Winthrop, chief marshall for the celebration of 1836.

Page 277. *Gray, Lowell, Dixwell.*

Alumni marshalls for 1836: William Gray, Robert Traill Spence Lowell, Epes Sargent Dixwell.

Page 277. *Otis.*

Harrison Gray Otis was to have presided, but the death of his wife prevented his appearance. Governor Edward Everett substituted for him.

Page 277. *But Kirkland . . . Quincy's.*

Josiah Quincy succeeded John Thornton Kirkland as president of Harvard and was in office in 1836; Holmes recalls also Quincy's father, a patriot.

Page 278. *Palfrey . . . Felix audacia.*

Holmes here catalogues the performers at the 1836 celebration: John Gorham Palfrey, Lemuel Shaw, Daniel Webster, Edward Everett, and Holmes himself who sang his own song; see page xxii above.

Page 278. *The good gray teacher.*

John Popkin.

Page 280. *So Mantua's bard.*

Virgil's lines allegedly prophetic of the birth of Christ.

Page 280. *Darwin.*

Erasmus Darwin; Holmes is quoting from *The Botanic Garden*, Part I, Canto I, lines 289–292. Darwin goes on to foretell a steam-driven flying machine.

Page 281. *O'er Stoughton's dust . . . Add Sanders, Sibley.*

Here a catalogue of Harvard's benefactors: William F. Weld, Nathan Matthews, James W. Sever, Daniel Austin, John C. Gray, David Sears, Edward B. Phillips, Abbott and James Lawrence, Augustus Hemenway, Charles Sanders, John Langdon Sibley.

Page 281. *Who writes in verse.*

See Additional Poems for the source of this quatrain.

Page 283. *As once of old from Ida's lofty height . . . Lit by the torch of Harvard's hallowed plain.*

This passage apparently offended James McCosh, president of Princeton.

Page 286. *The proud old Briton's by the western door,/And hers, the Lady of Colonial days.*

Holmes refers to the monument to Samuel Vassal who never lived in this country and that to Frances Barker Shirley, wife of Governor William Shirley.

Page 287. *Thus musing . . . a tablet fresh and fair.*

The monument for young men killed in the Civil War. In 1895, the church put up a monument to Holmes on the northern wall.

Page 288. HYMN — THE WORD OF PROMISE.

On this occasion three generations of the Holmes family were represented: at the afternoon ceremonies Holmes's son gave the address; at the evening service, a hymn by Holmes's father and this Hymn by Holmes were sung; Holmes himself "gave out" his Hymn. By these means, the long-standing breach between the "liberal" and the orthodox descendants of the original church was symbolically closed.

Page 288. ONE SHELTERING FOLD, ONE SHEPARD'S VOICE.

Holmes here neatly alludes to the first pastor of the church, Thomas Shepard.

Page 291. POEM FOR THE DEDICATION OF THE FOUNTAIN AT STRATFORD-ON-AVON.

At the ceremonies Holmes's poem was read by Sir Henry Irving.

Page 300. TO THE ELEVEN LADIES.

The eleven ladies included Sarah Orne Jewett and the painter Sarah Whitman.

Page 301. LA MAISON d'OR.

Holmes is punning on the name of his hostess Mrs. Charles Dorr (Mary Ward Dorr).

Page 307. READINGS OVER THE TEACUPS.

With *The Old Player*, these poems comprised the long poem *The Heart's Own Secret*, given for the Boston Mercantile Association, November 14, 1855. The "links" here were written for *Over the Teacups* (1891) and are then thirty-six years later than the "stories" and the "sequel." See Appendix II, pp. 417–418 for the hitherto uncollected passages from this poem.

Page 311. THE EXILE'S SECRET.

William Marsh of Apple Island, but Holmes is not following Marsh's life in its details.

Page 315. *"Not Mrs. Kemble's self."*

The actress, Fanny Kemble.

Page 315. THE STATESMAN'S SECRET.

Holmes had Daniel Webster in mind.

Page 321. AN UNPUBLISHED POEM.

See C & T, pp. 248–252 for the questions of the date and the occasion of this poem.

Page 322. *But who quotes Cuvier . . . cooks tripe.*

Holmes's audience would take in the allusions to the French naturalist Baron Cuvier and the French physician François Broussais who traced all disease to gastroenteritis.

Page 322. *Not all the schools from Berkshire to the Nile.*

The Berkshire Medical School was founded in 1837.

Page 322. *Oh! classic Broad Street.*

Holmes was attached to the Boston Dispensary, Broad Street, for a year (September 1836–1837); it was a charitable institution of which Holmes wrote a critical report.

Page 322. *Rich were the Queen of yon hepatic Isle.*

Queen Victoria.

Page 322. *Mme. Lachapelle.*

In Paris, Holmes studied with the younger Mme. Lachapelle.

Page 323. *Skull-crushing Davis — thy divine machine.*

The allusion here is possibly to David Daniel Davis; his *Principles and Practices of Midwifery* was published in 1836. He had assisted at the birth of Queen Victoria.

Page 323. *To modest Maygrier and concise Dewees.*
William Potts Dewees's *A Compendious System of Midwifery* was first published in 1824. Jacques Pierre Maygrier's work on midwifery had been translated in 1833 by A. Sidney Doane and published in New York.

Page 323. *Ask the Curator of our Museum — why.*
John Barnard Swett Jackson, zealous collector of anatomical and pathological specimens for the Society's Museum, to which Holmes contributed.

Page 323. *Unknown to fame had Morgagni sighed.*
Giovanni Battista Morgagni.

Page 323. *And Louis floated down oblivion's tide.*
Pierre Charles Alexandre Louis.

Page 323. *On "Brunner's glands."*
John Conrad Brunner had identified the duodenal glands.

Page 323. *And "Peyer" claimed no "patches" but his own . . . Had seen no Ileum since the days of Troy.*
Johann Conrad Peyer had discovered the lymphoid follicles in the ileum, hence for Holmes's medical audience the pun.

Page 326. *But thou, poor dreamer who hast vainly thought.*
The twelve lines that begin here were revised and used by Holmes in his 1844 address *Positions and Prospects of the Medical Student.* From this text, we repair here a defective couplet.

Pages 326–327. SUNG AT THE HUNT.
The company at Naushon Island on this occasion included the financier George Peabody, the New Bedford lawyer John Henry Clifford, and, I think, George Bruce Upton. The "Governor" and host is William W. Swain.

Page 327. AT DARTMOUTH.
The portions of this poem printed without substantive changes in *Sargent's New Monthly Magazine* in 1843 are noted below.

Pages 330–332. *Few are the cares . . . these at last are thine!*
Printed in 1843 with the title "The Rustic and the Millionaire. A Fragment."

Pages 332–333. *As some vast lake . . . In one dark vortex roll and disappear!*
Printed in 1843 with the title "A Fragment."

Pages 333–334. *Between two worlds . . . and thy sorrows o'er!*
Printed in 1843 with the title "An Every Day Tale." Holmes is here using his experiences at the Broad Street Dispensary, a medical charity for the poor.

Page 335. *And he whose voice these classics shades have known.*
Daniel Webster who in the famous Dartmouth College case had said of his Alma Mater: "It is a small college — but there are those who love it."

Page 336. To A. L. J.
This poem and the two that follow were written for Amelia Lee Jackson. Holmes and Miss Jackson would be married on June 15, 1840.

Page 337. A SCINTILLA.
Unsigned, these lines were printed and distributed among the flowers at the dinner party.

Page 337. *The world's great teachers quit their native Alps.*
Louis Agassiz had joined the Harvard faculty in 1848.

Page 337. A VISION OF LIFE.
Written for the Young Ladies' Institute, Pittsfield, Mass.

Page 338. WYCLIFFE.
Holmes thought he wrote this versification of Thomas Fuller's account of the dispersal of the reformer's ashes; see C & T, page 421.

Page 338. LETTER TO THE GOVERNOR.
William W. Swain and John Murray Forbes were the co-owners of Naushon Island; Swain was always referred to as the "Governor" of the island.

Page 339. *Wine is my foe.*
Holmes customarily protected himself at dinner parties by drinking quantities of strong tea.

Page 339. *What though the bitter grapes of wrath.*
Besides alluding to Mrs. Howe's *Battle Hymn of the Republic,* Holmes may have had in mind her unflattering reports of his Lowell Institute Lectures of 1853; although her reports in *The Commonwealth* were unsigned, it is likely that gossip reached him.

Page 340. *The God of Physic was the God of Song.*
Apollo as the Romans conceived him.

Page 340. *The "harp of thousand strings."*
Isaac Watts, Bk. II, Hymn 19.

Page 340. To J. R. L.
This poem and the one that follows were a surprise addition to Holmes's expected poem for the farewell dinner given to Lowell at the Revere House on the eve of his departure for Europe (see page 97 above). The last line here alludes to Paran Stevens who was the owner of the Revere House.

Page 341. FROM AN AFTER-DINNER SPEECH.
The meeting was held in Springfield, Massachusetts; the river then is the Connecticut and the mountain, Mt. Tom.

Page 341. CAMILLA.
Sarah Huyler Morewood (Mrs. John Rowland Morewood) had solicited from Holmes the two poems for St. Stephen's Parish which follow here. The incident described in this poem occurred when she called on Holmes to ask for the poems.

Page 341. TWO POEMS FOR THE FESTIVAL OF ST. STEPHEN'S PARISH.
The letters were enclosed in envelopes with their respective mottoes on the outside.

They were raffled for, with the winner having first choice of the envelopes, only one of which contained a dollar as well as a poem.

Page 342. CRIMEA.

These two stanzas are only a part of a poem used at the close of the lecture "The Americanized European" when the lecture was given in Cincinnati, September 6, 1855. No text of the whole has been located.

Page 343. INTRODUCTION.

With these lines Holmes introduced the poem printed above at pages 97–98. Which officer of the club or the committee for the occasion came in person to ask for the poem is unknown.

Page 343. *I thought of old Porteus, of Hare and of Burke.*

Holmes is alluding here to Captain John Porteus of the Edinburgh Civic Guard whose reprieve after a conviction for murder caused a riot. Scott uses the story in his *Heart of Midlothian*. William Hare and William Burke (Irish, not Scotch), were notorious "resurrectionists" who committed a series of murders to sell the bodies to an anatomist in Edinburgh. Since Holmes himself was an anatomist, the point would "tell" with his audience. With his allusion in the next line to the setting of Burns's *Tam O'Shanter*, Holmes has neatly enclosed his allusion to Burke and Hare between those to Scott and Burns.

Page 343. FOR THE HARVARD MEDICAL SCHOOL.

These verses were, I believe, written for one of the monthly levees of the Harvard Medical School. J. B. S. J. is the Professor of Morbid Anatomy, John Barnard Swett Jackson, and Henry Jacob Bigelow, the Professor of Surgery. The ninth stanza suggests a date close to 1856.

A manuscript in the Massachusetts Historical Society has notes of another song composed by Holmes for a medical school party; the notes are not sufficiently clear to allow a reconstruction.

To Holmes are attributed verses used by students as mnemonic devices. For the Cranial nerves: Olfactory, Optic, Motoroculi, Trochlear, Trigeminal, Abducent, Facial, Acoustic, Glossopharyngeal, Pneumogastric, Accessory, Hypoglossal, the rhyme goes: "On Old Monadnock's Tarry Top A Fat Ass German Picked A Hop."

For the Carpal bones: Scaphoid, Semilunar, Cuniform, Periform, Trapezium, Trapezoia, Magnum, Unciform, the rhyme goes: "Some Small-ladies Cannot P Therefore They Must Urinate."

Page 344. AT A DINNER TO AGASSIZ.

The poem seems to me to refer to Agassiz's 1859 visit to his native Switzerland, but there is no evidence of a dinner to welcome him home. Holmes did provide a poem for the 1857 birthday.

Page 344. A SONG FOR THE WIDOW.

Sung by a spontaneously gathered glee club, the audience joining in the chorus.

Page 345. SONG AT THE HUNT.

In 1857, John Murray Forbes took over the management of Naushon Island from "Governor" William W. Swain whose failing health prevented him from carrying on the job. Here the poet, rejecting youth, age, and the ladies as subjects for a toast, proposes instead the new manager. The *Eagle's Wing* is the ship that ferried guests from the mainland.

Page 345. THE HUNT.

A pencil draft of this poem has all the pronouns changed to the first person singular, but the plural is more appropriate, and the text in the MS Island Book is in the plural.

Page 346. TO JAMES JACKSON, M. D.

The occasion was Dr. Jackson's eightieth birthday, October 3, 1857.

Page 347. OUR SECOND SELVES.

This poem was written to close the lecture "Our Second Selves" (1857–1858 season). Holmes uses the third stanza in *The Autocrat.*

Page 348. ANSWER TO A TEETOTALER.

In the MS of the *Professor at the Breakfast-Table* Holmes had quoted a teetotaler's parody of Longfellow's *Catawba Wine*. These lines are Holmes's comment.

Page 348. THE EXAMINATION.

Written for a levee of the Harvard Medical School in the season of 1858–1859, probably the one in February 1859. The professors are as follows: II, Holmes himself; III, Henry Jacob Bigelow; IV, George Cheyne Shattuck and Edward Hammond Clarke; V, John Bacon; VI, John Barnard Swett Jackson; VII, David Humphrey Storer.

Page 348. PENITENTIA.

This apology was written to Grace Norton.

Page 349. TO E. AND L. A. WITH A PEAR.

To Mr. and Mrs. Louis Agassiz with a fine pear. The happy marriage of Elizabeth Cary and Agassiz was frequently noted.

Page 350. A LETTER TO ELIZA.

Holmes's MS does not identify the correspondent. Holmes did have a nephew named for him, the son of his sister Ann Upham.

Page 350. STAR-SPANGLED BANNER.

This stanza was first sung by Charlotte Varian, April 26, 1861; see C & T, pp. 519–523 for other performances. There noted is a second additional stanza credited to Holmes, but the attribution is in my opinion doubtful.

Page 350. TRUMPET SONG.

Written at the request of Francis J. Child for his *War-Songs for Freedom*, 1862. The Chorus was designed for voice and instruments and indicates first trumpet and then drum.

Page 351. WITH TWELVE AUTOGRAPHS.

Every couplet is signed in full and dated; presumably, the autographs were to be sold at the Baltimore Fair held at the Maryland Institute, April 18–30, 1864. They were

written at the request of Mrs. Charles C.
Bowen. Since the MS is preserved intact, it
is inferred that Mrs. Bowen wished to save
the poem.

Page 351. WEARY.
Written for the Brooklyn and Long Island
Fair in aid of the United States Sanitary
Commission.

Page 351. SONG OF WELCOME.
Written to be sung by a chorus of Boston
school children at the Musical Festival in
honor of Admiral Lessofsky, June 8, 1864.
The tune was the Russian National Air.
Holmes's authorship is known from his manu-
script; the song is unassigned in the program.

Page 352. *That heard the banging of the
"Lively's" canon.*
The HMS *Lively* engaged the USS *Consti-
tution;* The HMS *Shannon* captured the
USS *Chesapeake* after a battle off Boston
Light in the War of 1812.

Page 352. THE JUBILEE.
Written for the National Sailor's Fair,
Boston, November 12, 1864.

Page 352. TO JOHN PIERPONT.
Written for Pierpont's eightieth birthday.

Page 354. FOR A MONUMENT.
The monument was never erected. Holmes
has carefully avoided naming a discoverer.
The operation was performed by John
Collins Warren and the ether administered
by W. T. G. Morton. In the prolonged con-
troversy as to who was to have the credit of
discovery, Holmes's private opinion was that
the important act was that of Henry Jacob
Bigelow who publicized an account of the
first operations. It was Holmes who pro-
posed the terms "anaesthesia" and "anaes-
thetic."

Page 355. A WREATH OF FLOWERS.
The MS has no title but is signed in full
and dated March 31, 1871.

Page 356. WIND-CLOUDS AND STAR-
DRIFTS.
This title is given this unfinished poem on
the conjecture that it was written at the
same time as the blank verse poems in *The
Poet at the Breakfast-Table.*

Page 357. THE TOOTHACHE.
The manuscript is dated February 12,
1873. Possibly written for the Harvard
Dental School.

Page 358. IN T. G. A.'s ALBUM.
Thomas Gold Appleton, Longfellow's
brother-in-law.

Page 358. TELEGRAM TO THE BOHEMIAN
CLUB.
A genuine telegram in reply to one sent to
him telling him of his election to the Club.
The members of the San Francisco Club had
forgotten the time difference.

Page 358. A RHYMED RIDDLE.
Written for *Fair Words*, published in aid
of the St. Luke's Home for Convalescents,
Boston, 1876.

Page 359. "OVER THE RIVER."

Sent to the *Boston Daily Advertiser* with
a fictional letter signed "E Pluribus Unus";
the letter pretends that the poem is written
by "a young man of promise." Holmes's
authorship is certain from his letter to the
editor submitting it and asking for anony-
mous publication.

Page 359. *Talk of the rhyme of the "con-
ductair."*
Mark Twain's *Punch, brothers, punch.*

Page 360. TO J. R. N.
To James R. Nichols who had had two cop-
ies of Holmes's *Songs in Many Keys* hand-
somely bound by Francis Bedford of London,
giving one copy to Holmes. Holmes wrote
the poem in Nichol's copy.

Page 360. TO J. R. L.
When Lowell sailed on the *Parthia*, July
14, 1877, a revenue cutter and a steamship
tender accompanied the ship to the outer
light (on Light-House Island, "Little Brew-
ster") to allow Lowell's friends to say fare-
well, hence the lighthouse metaphor in the
poem.

Page 361. THE GOLDEN CALENDAR.
Written for *The Literary World* (Boston)
on the occasion of Whittier's seventieth
birthday. The poem was incorrectly printed
in the magazine.

Page 362. THE ALBUM FIEND.
Holmes apparently used this more than
once, for one of the two manuscripts has a
masculine pronoun in the first line. The
feminine fits the text better; so we use it
here. The data is from the manuscript with
the masculine pronoun.

Page 363. AT THE UNITARIAN FESTIVAL.
See p. 277 for the shorter and differing
version of this poem. See C & T, p. 408, for
the Introductory Remarks that accompanied
the reading of this version.

Page 363. RESPONSE TO A TOAST.
Oliver Wendell Holmes, Jr. had just been
appointed to the Supreme Judicial Court of
Massachusetts.

Page 364. DOROTHY QUINCY UPHAM.
Daughter of Holmes's nephew Oliver
Wendell Holmes Upham.

Page 365. TO YOUTHFUL RHYMESTERS.
Holmes uses the last quatrain in his Poem
for the 250th Anniversary of Harvard; the
whole was originally part of that poem,
sensibly deleted.

Page 365. FOR MISS HOWELLS' ALBUM.
For William D. Howells's daughter
Winifred.

Page 366. CENTENNIAL OF WASHINGTON'S
INAUGURAL.
Holmes had been asked for a sentiment to
complement the toast to the United States
given by President Benjamin Harrison at the
celebration held in the Metropolitan Opera
House.

Page 366. TO SARAH WHITMAN.
This thank-you note is dated September
17, 1891. Mrs. Whitman would shortly begin

the portrait of Holmes commissioned by the Philadelphia College of Physicians. Forgetting a sitting, Holmes sent a note:

> Some in rags
> Some in tags
> One in an Oxford gown.

Page 367. *An* error loci, *Boerhaave would say.*
Hermann Boerhaave, Dutch physician.
Page 367. *Friends of my earlier manhood.*
This line introduces Holmes's reminiscences of the Philadelphians he had known in his student days in Paris: William Wood Gerhard, George W. Norris, and Thomas Stewardson.
Gerhard had differentiated Typhoid and Typhus Fever (1837). Holmes and Stewardson had traveled together in England and Scotland in the summer of 1834. Near the end of the poem he alludes to Norris's care of his son brought wounded to Philadelphia after the Battle of Ball's Bluff.
Page 367. *When o'er our coffee, at the old "Procope."*
The Café Procope founded in 1691 has a long list of distinguished habitués.
Page 368. *When here our Aesculapian Congress met.*
The second annual meeting of the American Medical Association was held in Philadelphia, May 1848. The Philadelphian physicians Holmes names are Benjamin Rush, Caspar Wistar, William Edward Horner, Nathaniel Chapman, John Kearsley Mitchell. Francis is the New Yorker, John Wakefield Francis, who evidently coupled Holmes as poet-physician with Sir Samuel Garth whose verses, according to *DNB*, were to be read "only by men far advanced in post-prandial potations."
It was at this meeting of 1848 that Holmes dropped a bombshell in his Report of the Committee on Medical Literature.
Page 369. *An unborn Leidy.*
Joseph Leidy, anatomist and paleontologist. Holmes is bracketing Philadelphia medical history between Rush, patriot friend of Jefferson and Adams, and the recently deceased Leidy.
Page 369. To J. M. F. ON HIS EIGHTIETH BIRTHDAY.
John Murray Forbes; the first line alludes to the Naushon Island books, a manuscript collection of poems gathered by Forbes — many by his visitors to the island. Forbes had privately printed two collections from the MS books. The poem was given at the Saturday Club.
Page 370. ELLEN TERRY.
Written on the fly-leaf of a volume of Holmes's poems presented to the actress by the author.
Page 370. VERSION OF A FRAGMENT OF SAPPHO.

This translation is written in a very shaky hand and must be very late.
Page 369. THE COMBINATION.
For this poem and those that follow, there are no clear dates. The paper on which the poem is written is watermarked 1858.
Page 370. EPITAPH.
This epitaph and the one that follows were both sent by Homes to Oliver Wendell Holmes, Jr. in undated notes. The second was prompted by Holmes's objections to verses by his son.
Page 371. "*As forest-leaves the tribes of men decay.*"
This translation from the Iliad (Book VI) appears to be Holmes's own.
Page 371. LOVE.
Thomas Franklin Currier conjectured that this was written for some Harvard occasion.
Page 372. TO A BRIGHT BOY.
The MS has a note that the poem was written for Norton Johnson of Auburndale who edited a paper of his own printing.
Page 372. TO CORINNA.
Written for Corinna Haven Bishop; her husband was a master mariner, hence the allusion to the sea in the poem.
Page 381. ILLUSTRATION OF A PICTURE.
The picture was by Washington Allston, shown in the 1831 annual exhibition held in The Boston Athenaeum.
Page 382. LA GRISETTE.
A letter of 1833 from one of Holmes's friends to another reports having heard from Holmes, then in Paris, that he had been "making love to a pretty Grisette."
Page 385. TO THE PORTRAIT OF "A GENTLEMAN."
There were several portraits of gentlemen in the Fourth Exhibition of the Athenaeum Gallery, 1830.
Page 387. "THE WASP" AND "THE HORNET."
Both ships were in the War of 1812.
Page 388. THE DYING SENECA.
An "illustration" from the Fourth Exhibition of the Athenaeum Gallery; the painting was by Anthony Van Dyck.
Page 389. "PERDIDI DIEM."
This poem was written on a theme set by Abiel Holmes; the manuscript is in his hand. Holmes, finding it among his father's papers, annotated it: "Not very bright for a boy nearly 13 years old . . ."
Page 389. HASTY PUDDING.
Holmes wrote these verses into the minutes of the Hasty Pudding Club when he was the Secretary.
Page 389. SERENADE.
The attribution of this poem to Holmes rests on evidence that is not so solid as one could wish.
Page 390. To M. C. D.
Marianne Cabot Devereux of Salem, a friend of Holmes's sister Ann Holmes Upham. The "silken prize" was a pincushion;

Holmes had given Miss Devereux a "fool"; i.e., a very small ribbon purse, and received the pincushion in return. In 1829, Miss Devereux married Nathaniel Silsbee, Jr.

Page 390. *From yon high chamber.*

Holmes lived at home until his senior year when he moved into Holworthy.

Page 391. *Not "thoughts that breathe" but "many a word that burns."*

In this couplet Holmes is adapting and quoting a passage from Thomas Gray's *Progress of Poesy* III.3, lines 107–110.

Page 392. *The sober people . . . And think of dinner.*

Holmes's spot on this long Commencement Day program came at 12:52 according to a member of the audience who annotated his program.

Page 392. *Since ye are straining all your eyes to scan . . . of our outer man.*

Holmes, the shortest man in the class, was five foot four.

Page 393. *To S — L —.*

These stanzas are from an unlocated longer poem that Holmes apparently sent to some newspaper. In the poem which follows here, he identifies her as Sukey Lennox.

Page 393. RHYMED CHRONICLE.

A verse letter to Phinehas Barnes from Maine, hence the allusion to new students from Maine. The Praeses is President Josiah Quincy. Holmes alludes also to Judge Joseph Story, a founder of the Dane Law School (Harvard Law School) where Holmes was now a student.

Page 393. *The undergraduates have made/ Proposals for a monthly paper.*

The paper was *The Collegian* to which Holmes would contribute anonymously twenty-five poems.

Page 393. *Get Blackwood's Magazine.*

The issue for November 1829 (XXVI, 717) has a tale entitled "Malavolti" that answers the specifications.

Page 399. (TRANSLATED FROM THE ARABIC).

Holmes tells his friend Barnes that this is a lie.

Page 399. THE MONKEYS.

This and the three poems which follow are all "illustrations" from the Athenaeum Gallery Exhibition of 1830. With the exception of *The Fish Pieces*, the paintings can be identified from the catalogue of the exhibition. They are as follows: "The Monkeys," by George? Morland; "The Gipsy, after a French Picture," by Thomas Sully; "The Departure," by Thomas Doughty; and "Lady Drinking," by Gerard Terbourg [Terborch].

Page 404. *Perchance we greet you . . . edge of gold.*

The first two lines refer to *Illustrations of the Athenaeum Gallery,* published in July 1830 and so coincidental with the last issue of *The Collegian.* (See C & T, p. 18, for a description of this 46-page paper-bound pamphlet.)

The next two lines refer to a gift-book. Holmes appeared in two gift-books for 1831: *The Token* and *Youth's Keepsake,* both published in 1830. He had already appeared in the green silk *Offering* for 1829.

Page 404. CONFESSIONS OF A COCOANUT.

The attribution of this poem to Holmes is shaky, but Holmes had earlier practiced the art of "sinking."

Page 406. CROSSING THE FORD.

Written to accompany an engraving by J. Andrews after Alvin Fisher's "Passing the Ford."

Page 407. *O Lord Monboddo . . . had a tail.*

James Burnett, Lord Monboddo; Holmes could have found Monboddo's theory of man's descent from the orang-outang in Boswell's life of Johnson.

Page 412. *Like the red phial, in a druggist's dream.*

While he was studying medicine, Holmes worked in the pharmacy of the Massachusetts General Hospital.

Page 413. ASTRÆA.

Holmes's father went to Yale and there became a friend of the Reverend Ezra Stiles whose daughter became his first wife.

Page 413. *How the grave Senior . . . western wild.*

The first allusion is surely to James Kent of the class of 1781; the second is possibly to John Cotton Smith ('83), governor of Connecticut 1813–17; the third is Ezra Stiles.

VI. A CHRONOLOGICAL LIST OF DR. HOLMES'S POEMS

THE dates here assigned are the earliest verifiable dates; they are drawn from Holmes's dated manuscripts, from his letters, from the known occasion, or from the earliest printing. For the evidence for the dates (and also for authorship), see the Currier-Tilton *Bibliography* and my article, " 'Literary Bantlings' — Addenda to the Holmes Bibliography." Conjectured and doubtful dates are indicated by a question mark.

Titles of poems collected here for the first time are *preceded* by an asterisk. Titles supplied by me are bracketed here. Listed but not collected here are Holmes's mock poems (e.g. the verses of Gifted Hopkins in *The Guardian Angel*), fragments from newspapers and manuscript fragments; these titles are *followed* by an asterisk.

E. M. T.

1822. *July 25.* *Perdidi diem
1824. First verses. Translation from the Aeneid, Book I
1825. *[Charitable Ann]

1828.   *May 2.* *[Hasty Pudding]
        June 28. *Serenade
        *[To M. C. D. S.]
        *Burial of a Maiden at Sea
        *The Lover's Return
1829.   *April 28.* *Forgotten Ages (Harvard
            Exhibition)
        August 26. *A Poem. (Harvard Com-
            mencement)
        A Song of Other Days
1830.   *January 13.* *[Rhymed Chronicle]
        January 13. *To S — L —
        January 27. *Selections   from   the
            Newspapers
        February. *An Enigma [I]
        February. *Runaway Ballads, I, II
        February. The Toadstool
        March. *Enigma [II]
        March. The Last Prophecy of Cas-
            sandra
        March. *Romance
        March. *Scene from an Unpublished
            Play [I]
        April. *The Cannibal
        April. The Dorchester Giant
        April. To a Caged Lion
        April. To My Companions
        April. *Scene from an Unpublished
            Play [II]
        May. *An   Invocation,   Translated
            from the Arabic
        May. Reflections of a Proud Pedes-
            trian
        May. The Spectre Pig
        May 14. *The Monkeys
        May 21. To   the   Portrait   of   "A
            Gentleman"
        May 28. The Music-Grinders
        June. The Meeting of the Dryads
        June. The Mysterious Visitor
        June 15. *The Departure
        June 15. *The Fish Pieces
        June 15. *The Gipsy
        June 15. *Lady Drinking
        June 18. The Dying Seneca
        July. Evening, By a tailor
        July. *The Graduate's Song
        July. The Height of the Ridiculous
        July. *Moonshine
        July. *Octosyllabics
        July. *Old Gentleman's Story
        July. Stanzas
        July. *Scene from an Unpublished
            Play [III]
        July. *The Tail-Piece
        July 2. The September Gale
        July 3. From a Bachelor's Private
            Journal
        July 3. A Noontide Lyric
        July 9. *Confessions of a Cocoanut
        July 17. The Ballad of the Oysterman
        July 17. To a Blank Sheet of Paper
        July 30. *The Gallows Bird's Last
            Song
        August 6. *Reflections in a Ball Room
        August 7. The Treadmill Song

        August 7. *The Two Shadows
        September. *Crossing the Ford
        September 4. *Domestic Thoughts
        September 4. *The Flies
        September 4. *Infelix Senectus
        September 16. Old Ironsides
        October 1. *Song of the Henpecked
        October 1. The Star and the Water-
            Lily
        *The Fairy World
        *The Lost Boy
1831.   *March 12.* *To the Lady Opposite
        March 26. The Last Leaf
        April 7. Lines by a Clerk
        April 9. *City Madrigals
        April 23. *To My Neighbour, Who
            Sings, and Plays on the Piano-forte
        September. The Poet's Lot
        September. To an Insect
        October. *Love-Song
        October. L'Inconnue
        November. My Aunt
        November. *To Fame
        November. *To a Lady with Her Back
            to Me
        Illustration of a Picture, "A Spanish
            Girl in Reverie"
        ? To the Portrait of "A Lady"
1832.   *January.* The Dilemma
        March. *The Destroyers
        March. *[The Toad and the Nightin-
            gale]
        April. The Comet
        May. *Words to Woman
        May. *Sentiment
        July. Daily Trials, by a Sensitive
            Man
        July. Departed Days
        July. The Philosopher to his Love
        October. "The   Wasp"   and   "The
            Hornet"
        *New Year's Address
        A Portrait
1833.   *July.* *Six Verses
1836.   *February.* An Evening Thought, writ-
            ten at Sea
        March. Our Yankee Girls
        April. The Last Reader
        La Grisette
        June 20. A Roman Aqueduct
        September 1. Poetry. A Metrical Es-
            say,   included: The   Cambridge
            Churchyard
        September 8. A Song for the Centen-
            nial Celebration of Harvard College
        October 1. A Souvenir
        October 4. "Qui Vive?"
        November. The Hot Season
1837.   The Only Daughter
1838.   *February 7* (or *February 6, 1840*). *An
            Unpublished Poem
        May. The Parting Word
        ? *November 8.* The Stethoscope Song
        November. *Sung at the Hunt
1839.   *March.* The Steamboat
        July 24. *At Dartmouth

October. The Island Hunting-Song
October. *Hunting Song for 1839
November. Lexington
1840. *March 6.* *[To A. L. J.]
May 22. *[To A. L. J.]
May 30. *[To A. L. J.]
1841. *August 26.* Questions and Answers
1842. *February 1.* Song Written for the Dinner Given to Charles Dickens by the Young Men of Boston
November 9. Song for a Temperance Dinner
1843. *May 31.* Extracts from a Medical Poem, included: The Stability of Science, A Sentiment, A Portrait (Dr. James Jackson)
August 24. An After-Dinner Poem
1844. *August 23.* Lines Recited at the Berkshire Jubilee, Pittsfield
August 29. Verses for After-Dinner
1845. *December 22.* The Pilgrim's Vision
1846. *April 30.* A Modest Request
August 27. A Sentiment, Phi Beta Kappa dinner, Harvard
October 14. A Rhymed Lesson
1847. *February 13.* On Lending a Punch-Bowl
1848. *November.* Nux Postcœnatica
1849. *May 30.* The Morning Visit
June 20. *A Scintilla
September 27. *A Vision of Life
October 4. The Ploughman
November 7? *Wycliffe
1850. *August 14.* Astræa: The Balance of Illusions, included: The Bells, The Mind's Diet, the Moral Bully, Non-Resistance, Our Limitations, Spring, The Study
September. *Letter to the Governor
September 9. A Poem: Dedication of the Pittsfield Cemetery
November 19. *[Pleasure Remembered]
1851. *January 2.* A Song of "Twenty-Nine"
September 10. To Governor Swain
1852. To an English Friend
1853. *March 26.* After a Lecture on Moore
March 29. [After a Lecture on Scott]*
April 1. [After a Lecture on Coleridge]*
April 8. After a Lecture on Keats
April 12. After a Lecture on Shelley
April 15. After a Lecture on Wordsworth
April 22. The Living Temple
April 26. The Voiceless
April 29. At the Close of a Course of Lectures
May 5. Poem for the Meeting of the American Medical Association
November 29. An Impromptu
1854. *January 1.* *To Julia Ward Howe
September 13. The New Eden
November 23. The Old Man Dreams
December 1. The Hudson
1855. *May 1.* A Sentiment (American Medical Association)

May 9. *[Letter to the Connecticut State Medical Society]
May 29. Farewell to J. R. Lowell
May 29. *[To J. R. L. "Hosea Biglow's folks is gone"]
May 29. *[To J. R. L. from Homer Wilbur]
June 27. *[From an After-Dinner Speech]
August 9. *[Camilla]
August 9. *[Two Poems for the Festival of St. Stephen's Parish: I. A Dollar's Worth, and II. Faith]
September 7. *[Crimea]
November 14. *[The Heart's Own Secret, additional lines], included: The Old Player, The Banker's Secret, The Exile's Secret, The Lover's Secret, The Mother's Secret, The Secret of the Stars, The Statesman's Secret
December 22. Semi-Centennial Celebration of the New England Society, New York
Agnes
1856. *January 10.* Remember — Forget
January 18. Birthday of Daniel Webster
January 25. *[Introduction] For the Meeting of the Burns Club
February 22. Ode for Washington's Birthday
November 6. Our Indian Summer
At the Pantomime (revised version of 1874)
1857. *?February.* *For the Harvard Medical School
?May 28. *At a Dinner to Agassiz
July 16. Meeting of the Alumni of Harvard College
July 16. The Parting Song, Festival of the Alumni
July 30. *A Song for the Widow
August 8. A Parting Health, to J. L. Motley
September 21. *Song at the Hunt
September 23. *[The Hunt, Naushon, 1857]
September 25. Sun and Shadow
October 3. *[To James Jackson M. D.]
November. Latter-Day Warnings
December. Ode for a Social Meeting
December. Prologue
December 12. *Our Second Selves
Album Verses
1858. *January 14.* Mare Rubrum
January 18. *Variations on an Aria
February. The Chambered Nautilus
April. What We All Think
May. The Last Blossom
May 18. A Good Time Going!
May 26. The Two Armies
June. Spring Has Come
June 1. *Adieux à la Vie (translation)
July. *Les Bohémiens (translation)
August. Musa

Contentment
September. The Deacon's Masterpiece.
September 22. The Last Look
October. Parson Turell's Legacy
November. Old Man of the Sea
Æstivation
Avis
1859. *January.* De Sauty, An Electro-Chemical Eclogue
January 6. The Boys
January 17. The Opening of the Piano
January. *[Answer to a Teetotaler]
January 25. For the Burns Centennial Celebration
?February. *[The Examination]
February 22. At a Birthday Festival
March. The Promise
April. The Crooked Footpath
May 25. The Gray Chief
July. Robinson of Leyden
July. The Two Streams
August. St. Anthony the Reformer
August 29. At a Meeting of Friends
September. Midsummer
October. Iris, Her Book
October. Under the Violets
November. Hymn of Trust
November 14. Boston Common: Three Pictures
December. A Sun-Day Hymn
1860. *January 5.* Lines
February 27. *Penitentia
April 4. A Birthday Tribute to J. F. Clarke
April 15. In Memory of Charles Wentworth Upham, Junior
June 16. For the Meeting of the National Sanitary Association
July 19. [Toast to Lemuel Shaw]*
August. *[To E. and L. A. with a Pear]
October 18. International Ode
? *[A Letter to Eliza]
1861. *January 3.* A Voice of the Loyal North
January 7. Martha
March 25. Brother Jonathan's Lament for Sister Caroline
April 27. Under the Washington Elm
April 29. *The Star-Spangled Banner
May 1. Prologue to *Songs in Many Keys*
May 21. Army Hymn
August. Parting Hymn
September 14. The Sweet Little Man
September 25. Vive la France !
November. The Flower of Liberty
December. Union and Liberty
Freedom, Our Queen
1862. *January 23.* J. D. R. 1862
January 23. Voyage of the Good Ship Union
April 18. To My Readers
July 17. Never or Now
August 12. To Canaan

August 28. "Thus Saith the Lord, I Offer Thee Three Things"
November 10. *Trumpet Song
December 4. Choose You This Day Whom Ye Will Serve
1863. *November 3.* An Impromptu, at the Walcher Dinner upon the Completion of the Great Organ for Boston Music Hall in 1863.
1864. *January 7.* F. W. C.
January 7. The Last Charge
January 26. *[With Twelve Autographs]
February 17. *Weary
April 23. Shakespeare Tercentennial Celebration
May 25. In Memory of John and Robert Ware
June 7. Hymn Written for the Great Central Fair in Philadelphia
June 8. *Song of Welcome to the Russian Fleet
July 21. *An Old Graduate's Verses
November. *Prelude, Naushon
November 5. Bryant's Seventieth Birthday
November 10. A Sea Dialogue
November 12. *The Jubilee
December 7. God Save the Flag !
1865. *January 5.* Our Oldest Friend
January 5. Sherman's in Savannah
January 30. Edward Everett
February 4. Hymn after the Passage of the Thirteenth Amendment
March 25. A Farewell to Agassiz
April 6. *To John Pierpont
May 30. Hymn for the Fair at Chicago
June 1. For the Services in Memory of Abraham Lincoln
July 6. At a Dinner to Admiral Farragut
July 20. No Time Like the Old Time
July 21. For the Commemoration Services, Cambridge
July 31. At a Dinner to General Grant
One Country
1866. *January 4.* My Annual
February 22. *To the Harvard Association of New York City
May 4. *[For a Monument (Ether monument, Boston)]
August 17. America to Russia (August 5 according to the Russian calendar)
1867. *January 10.* All Here
February 27. *[For Longfellow's Birthday]
July. Another's ! by Gifted Hopkins*
July. She moves in splendor, by Gifted Hopkins*
July 18. Chanson without Music
September. The Triumph of Song, by Gifted Hopkins*

O Daughter of the Spicéd South, by
    Gifted Hopkins*
Oh Would, oh would that thou were
    here, by Gifted Hopkins*

1868.   *January 9.* Once More
    May 27. To H. W. Longfellow
    July 16. Bill and Joe
    August 21. At the Banquet to the
      Chinese Embassy
    November 5. To Christian Gottfried
      Ehrenberg

1869.   *January 6.* Hymn for the Class-
      Meeting
    January 6. The Old Cruiser
    June 15. A Hymn of Peace
    July 8. Poem at the Dedication of the
      Halleck Monument
    July 19. To George Peabody
    September 14. Humboldt's Birthday

1870.   *January.* Nearing the Snow-Line
    January 6. Even-Song
    May 25. Rip Van Winkle, M. D.
    October 6. Hymn for the Celebration
      at the Laying of the Corner-Stone
      of Harvard Memorial Hall, Cam-
      bridge
    October 14. *[On Receiving a Stolen
      Apple]

1871.   *January.* Dorothy Q.: A Family Por-
      trait
    January 5. The Smiling Listener
    March 31. *[A Wreath of Flowers]
    December 9. At the Banquet to the
      Grand Duke Alexis
    December 9. Welcome to the Grand
      Duke Alexis

1872.   *January.* Homesick in Heaven
    January. The Organ-Blower
    January 4. Our Sweet Singer, J. A.
    February. Fantasia
    March. Aunt Tabitha
    May. Wind-Clouds and Star-Drifts
      [I]
    June. Wind-Clouds *etc.* [II]
    July. Wind-Clouds *etc.* [III]
    August. Wind-Clouds *etc.* [IV]
    August 2. At the Banquet to the
      Japanese Embassy
    September. Wind-Clouds *etc.* [V]
    October. Wind-Clouds *etc.* [VI]
    November. Wind-Clouds *etc.* [VII]
    November 13. After the Fire
    December. Epilogue to the Breakfast-
      Table Series
    ? *Catullus: De Arrio, lxxxii
    ? *[The Reluctant Minstrel]
    ? *[Wind-Clouds and Star-Drifts]
    January 9. H. C. M., H. S., J. K. W.
    January 9. What I Have Come For
    February 12. *[The Toothache]
    April 16. For the Centennial Dinner
      of the Proprietors of Boston Pier,
      or the Long Wharf
    June 19. *[Charade]
    June 25. The Fountain of Youth
    June 26. A Poem Served to Order

    December 3. Address for the Opening
      of the Fifth Avenue Theatre
    December 16. A Ballad of the Boston
      Tea-Party

1874.   *January.* Old-Year Song
    January 8. Our Banker
    February 16. A Toast to Wilkie Col-
      lins
    February 22. *[In T. G. A.'s Album]
    February 28. *[Telegram to the Bo-
      hemian Club]
    April 29. Hymn at the Funeral Serv-
      ices of Charles Sumner
    June 23. Hymn for the Dedication of
      Memorial Hall at Cambridge
    October 7. Opening the Window
    October 7. Programme, for SONGS OF
      MANY SEASONS
    December 15. At the "Atlantic" Din-
      ner

1875.   *January 7.* For Class Meeting
    May 13. Grandmother's Story of
      Bunker-Hill Battle
    June 17. Joseph Warren, M. D.
    July 3. Old Cambridge
    October 7. Hymn for the Inauguration
      of the Statue of Governor Andrew
    October 18. "Lucy:" for her Golden
      Wedding
    November 11. The Song of the Sheet*

1876.   *January.* A Familiar Letter
    January 6. "Ad Amicos"
    January 26. *[Charade]
    February 8. A Memorial Tribute . . .
      In Memory of Dr. Samuel G. Howe
    February 14. *A Rhymed Riddle
    May 8. Unsatisfied
    May 11. How the Old Horse Won the
      Bet
    May 15. * "Over the River," A New
      Version
    June 9. *My Excuse for Not Writing
    June 26. An Appeal for "The Old
      South"
    July 4. Welcome to the Nations
    September 22. *To J. R. N.

1877.   *January 4.* How Not to Settle It
    February 21. The First Fan
    June 27. To Rutherford Birchard
      Hayes
    July 4. A Family Record
    July 4. The Ship of State
    July 14. *To J. R. L.
    ?October. On the Threshold
    November 28. My Aviary
    December 17. For Whittier's Seven-
      tieth Birthday
    December 17. *The Golden Calendar,
      To J. G. W.

1878.   *January 10.* The Last Survivor
    February 21. Two Sonnets: Harvard
    June 6. The School-Boy
    June 27. The Silent Melody

1879.   *January 8.* *[May it Please your
      Honors' Worships.]

January 9. The Archbishop and Gil Blas
May 3. In Response
May 27. For the Moore Centennial Celebration
June 14. Welcome to the Chicago Commercial Club
June 25. Vestigia Quinque Retrorsum
December 3. The Iron Gate

1880. *January.* The Coming Era
January 8. The Shadows
April 4. To James Freeman Clarke
April 6. *The Album Fiend
May 26. American Academy Centennial Celebration
June 30. Harvard
August. At the Papyrus Club
October 21. Benjamin Peirce
December 28. Our Home — Our Country

1881. *January 5.* Boston to Florence
June 8. Poem at the Centennial Anniversary Dinner of the Massachusetts Medical Society
June 30. Post-Prandial
August 2. Rhymes of a Life-Time
September 27. On the Death of President Garfield
November 29. The Golden Flower

1882. *January 5.* In the Twilight
February 21. *Alma Mater
March 8. At the Unitarian Festival (12 lines)
May 31. Youth
June. Our Dead Singer
June 1. *At the Unitarian Festival (24 additional lines)
June 14. At the Summit (Harriet Beecher Stowe)
June 14. The World's Homage
December 6. The Flâneur: During the Transit of Venus
? Fear Not the Fires*
? Your proof is what?*

1883. *January 4.* A Loving-Cup Song
January 30. *[Response to a Toast]
April 12. Poem read at the Dinner given to the Author by the Medical Profession of the City of New York
June 7. *[Dorothy Quincy Upham]
September. King's Chapel

1884. *January.* At the Saturday Club
January 10. The Girdle of Friendship
February. Cacoethes Scribendi
July 24. Ave, Prelude to *Illustrated Poems*

1885. *January 8.* The Lyre of Anacreon
May 6. A Welcome to Dr. Benjamin Apthrop Gould
June 15. Prelude to a Volume Printed in Raised Letters for the Blind
June 15. *To J. R. L. Homeward Bound
June 24. To James Russell Lowell

June 25. To the Poets Who Only Read and Listen
November 23. *To Mark Twain on His Fiftieth Birthday.
December 12. To Frederick Henry Hedge, at a Dinner Given him on his Eightieth Birthday

1886. *January 7.* The Old Tune
February 12. Hymn — The Word of Promise
November 8. *[To Youthful Rhymesters] A deletion from Poem for the Two Hundred and Fiftieth Anniversary of the Founding of Harvard College
December 15. Hymn for the Two Hundredth Anniversary of King's Chapel

1887. *January 6.* The Broken Circle
April 24. *[For Miss Howells' Album]
June 7. Hymn read at the Dedication of the Oliver Wendell Holmes Hospital at Hudson, Wisconsin.
September 17. Hail, Columbia!
October 17. Poem for the Dedication of the Fountain at Stratford-on-Avon
December 17. To John Greenleaf Whittier on His Eightieth Birthday

1888. *January 5.* The Angel-Thief
March 1. At My Fireside
August. La Maison d'Or
October 21. *To the Reverend S. F. Smith, D. D.
November 28. For the Dedication of the New City Library, Boston.
? How blithely wakes the morning beam!*

1889. *January 10.* After the Curfew
February 22. To James Russell Lowell, at the Dinner Given in His Honor at the Tavern Club, on His Seventieth Birthday
April 30. *[Centennial of Washington's Inaugural]
October 2. To the Eleven Ladies Who Presented Me with a Silver Loving Cup

1890. *February 7.* The Rose and the Fern
March. "And have I coined my soul in words for naught," by a tyro*
March. The Peau de Chagrin of State Street
May. I Like You and I Love You
July 15. Tartarus
July. Too Young for Love
August. The Broomstick Train; or, The Return of the Witches
October. At the Turn of the Road
October. "My beloved, to you," by a tyro*
October. "My house is on fire!," by a tyro*
November. Invita Minerva
December. But One Talent

1891. *April 12.* For the Window in St.
        Margaret's
        September 17. *[To Sarah Whitman]
        October. James Russell Lowell: 1819–
        1891
        To My Old Readers
1892. *January ?* *[To Sarah Whitman]
        April 18. *The Living Dynamo
        April 30. *Poem on the Occasion of
        the Presentation of My Portrait to
        the Philadelphia College of Physi-
        cians
        September 7. In Memory of John
        Greenleaf Whittier
1893. *February 23.* To the Teachers of
        America
        February 25. *To J. M. F. on His
        Eightieth Birthday
        May 31. Hymn written for the

        Twenty-fifth Anniversary of the
        Reorganization of the Boston
        Young Men's Christian Union
        November 21. Francis Parkman
1894. *January 17.* *To Ellen Terry
        ? *Version of a Fragment of Sappho
Undated.   *[The Combination]
            *[Epitaph]
            *[Epitaph]
            *[Illusion]
            *[In the Dead Season. Cam-
            bridge.]
            *[Love]
            *[The Poet Grows Old]
            *[To an Autograph Collector]
            *[To a Bright Boy]
            *[To Corinna]

INDEX OF FIRST LINES
INDEX OF TITLES

INDEX OF FIRST LINES

INDEX OF TITLES